INTERPRETING CENSORSHIP IN CANADA
Edited by Klaus Petersen and Allan C. Hutchinson

It has been part of the liberal tradition to decry censorship in all its forms, and to dissociate censorship from democratic forms of government. The twenty-three contributors to this book view censorship pragmatically. They aim to treat it as a constituent feature of any system of social control or practice. By capturing and analysing the social, political, cultural, and economic components of restriction of freedom of expression and access to information, they go beyond the merely ideological pro- and anti-censorship arguments, exposing the extent of censorship in Canada today, exploring its structures, and showing what it reveals about our political culture.

Because censorship manifests itself in so many ways, the diversity of approach in this book contributes to the authors' purpose, which is to enhance our awareness not only of the practice of censorship, but also of how censorship discourse as an expression of thoughts, values, and social behaviour changes over time.

Despite their different approaches, the contributors to this volume agree in their perception of censorship as a value-driven instrument of power. Socially organized activity cannot occur without censorship, and the questions probed in this study concern forms of censorship, the implementation of censorship, and the interests served.

KLAUS PETERSEN is a professor in the Department of Germanic Studies at the University of British Columbia.

ALLAN C. HUTCHINSON is a professor at Osgoode Hall Law School, York University.

KLAUS PETERSEN AND
ALLAN C. HUTCHINSON, EDITORS

Interpreting Censorship in Canada

UNIVERSITY OF TORONTO PRESS
Toronto Buffalo London

© University of Toronto Press Incorporated 1999
Toronto Buffalo London
Printed in Canada

ISBN 0-8020-4164-7 (cloth)
ISBN 0-8020-8026-X (paper)

∞

Printed on acid-free paper

Canadian Cataloguing in Publication Data

Main entry under title:

Interpreting censorship in Canada

Includes bibliographical references and index.
ISBN 0-8020-4164-7 (bound)   ISBN 0-8020-8026-X (pbk.)

1. Censorship – Canada.   2. Censorship.   I. Petersen, Klaus, 1937–   .
II. Hutchinson, Alan C.

Z658.C3I57 1999   363.3'1'0971   C99-930695-2

University of Toronto Press acknowledges the support of the Canada Council and the
Ontario Arts Council for our publishing program.

Contents

Preface

In recent years, Canadians have experienced a host of controversies and bitter conflicts that put in question both the consensus over their basic social values and the very core of what they liked to perceive as the 'Canadian identity.' Examples are the struggle of women and minority groups for recognition and freedom from discrimination and harassment; emotional parliamentary debates over Bills C-54 (pornography, 1987), C-128 (child pornography, 1993), and C-41 (anti-hate law, June 1995); ongoing debate in legal circles over the limits of legislation affecting free speech; protests over the influence of fundamentalist religious values on the government's agenda; the battle by schools to preserve the professional integrity of teachers and librarians in the face of increasing pressures to comply with conflicting ideologies and cultural interests; the difficulties for universities created by the introduction of speech codes; irritation among artists over cultural ownership in a multicultural society; passionate calls for a restriction of press reports on crime and violence; and efforts to regulate computer networks. All these controversies and conflicts have to do with the question of free expression and censorship. In any of them, a solution would require a consensus on how to balance free speech against other social values.

In terms of comparative statistics, Canada certainly does not rank among the more repressive countries. In its *World Report 1991*, the Article 19 International Center on Censorship, for instance, expressed relatively few concerns over restraints of free speech for Canadians.[1] Yet a closer look from within shows that also in this country all public media – be it public speaking, political brochures, books and magazines, the press, films, videos and video games, computer networks, radio and TV broadcasting, the press, theatres, libraries, or schools – function in the shadows of censorship. Government and public institutions, for all kinds of reasons, impose (and threaten to impose) restrictions on the production and distribution of material considered objectionable. Restraints result from laws and by-laws, from the regulatory and supervisory authority of government agencies and public institutions, from corporate power, and from socially structured proscriptions.

The press, radio, and television have regularly commented on bureaucratic interference, repressive legislation, major court rulings on the freedom of speech, and judicial bans of court reporting. Alliances like the Canadian Civil Liberties Association, the Toronto Arts Group for Human Rights, and the Canadian Committee Against Customs Censorship, as well as professional organizations like the Writers Union of Canada, P.E.N. Canada, the Canadian Booksellers Association, and the Canadian Library Association, have made great efforts to raise the public's awareness of incidents of censorship.

The yearly 'Freedom to Read Week,' promoted by the Book and Periodical Development Council (BPDC) is an example. To provide documentation, the BPDC has distributed since 1984 kits with lists of banned material, newspaper articles, intellectual-freedom statements, reports on legislative initiatives, and so on. A 1982 'discussion guide' of the Canadian Library Association, entitled 'Not in Our Schools?!!!' and a 1990 *International Freedom Handbook* compiled for the Ontario Library Association serve the same purpose.[2]

While these publications have brought many recent instances of censorship to the public's attention, they provide neither an exhaustive analysis of particular cases nor an extensive assessment of censorship in any given area of public speech. The reason is not only their pedagogical, if not polemical, intention, but also the fact that they depend for the recording of incidents almost entirely on press reports. The basis of this information is often fragmentary, and ignorance remains about the conclusion of a case whenever it is not followed up in the newspapers. A richer and more reliable source are the collections of court decisions like the *Dominion Law Reports* (D.L.R.) and the *Reports of the Supreme Court of Canada* (S.C.R.). But even here, not more than a slice of the picture is glimpsed since these collections gather only censorship cases that have come before the courts, and only the higher-level courts at that. Film censorship is the one area that allows for a more comprehensive assessment because the provincial censor or classification boards either publish annual reports or give out statistics and information about the classification process upon request. These reports usually include also information about the number of impounded films and about criminal charges laid against theatre owners and distributors.

Scholarly research has directed considerable attention to the subject of censorship in recent years, most notably in the United States. The vast majority of studies focus either on one of the so-called 'injurious' forms of expression (pornography, defamation, hate propaganda, and the like), or a particular medium (such as the press, television, film, books, libraries, and schools) of a specific country. In addition, there are bibliographies,[3] national and international surveys,[4] some comparative studies,[5] theoretical works,[6] and analyses of specific cases.[7] As to Canadian academic research on censorship issues, the scarcity of documented incidents and of reliable statistics may explain why it has limited itself to a relatively small number of facets of 'state censorship.' Since the proclamation in 1982 of the Canadian Charter of Rights and Freedoms, the greater quantity of this scholarship has investigated the Charter's impact on the statutory regimes of indecency, sedition, racist incitement, defamation, pornography, and hate propaganda. Most of it includes a discussion of such censorship-related issues as media access to court proceedings, commercial speech, access to information, privacy rights, and the elusive task of defining the obscene.[8] This jurisprudence and criticism provides considerable clarification of restraints in the area of governmental and judicial control because drawing the borderlines between public and private powers and rights implicitly determines the legal framework of censorship.

Yet the analysis of censorship in legal scholarship is usually based on a too narrow perception of censorship as a power monopoly of the state and as an 'exception' to freedoms guaranteed under the Charter. This perception discourages inquiry into the much more frequent forms of 'constituent censorship' that develop within the authority structures of the media, of corporations, bureaucracies, schools, universities, churches, and the body politic.

In relation to the Canadian media, there is hardly any work that offers a comprehensive study of censorship. Film censorship is fairly well covered – at least until 1981.[9] The suppression of books has been the object of some academic research, but only in connection with schools and libraries.[10] In terms of non-fiction, hate literature has been the object of critical research also.[11] As part of larger legal studies on freedom of information, there has been some investigation on restrictions of the press and of broadcasting.[12] There are also historical studies of censorship focusing on specific periods or past suppression of certain political or religious ideas.[13] A short article by Leonard Connolly in the 1994 edition of the *Encyclopedia of Post-Colonial Literatures in English* offers a very brief history of literary censorship in Canada. Restraints on other media like the visual and performing arts,[14] publishing (particularly children's literature), politically subversive brochures, advertisements, pornographic magazines, videotapes, and computer networks have been discussed only in the context of a large number of scattered legal papers on aspects of the Charter, the War Measures Act, the Food and Drugs Act, the Customs Act, the Young Offenders Act, various statutes of the Criminal Code, and provincial legislation and municipal by-laws.

The purpose of the present volume is not just to fill certain gaps, however. Considered as a whole, the above mentioned body of information and analysis illustrates more than anything that the whole concept and practice of censorship is an essentially contested one. Not only is there controversy over its extent and excesses, there is considerable disagreement as to what counts as censorship. In particular, it is hotly debated whether all constraints on persons' freedom of expression amount to censorship or whether censorship is confined to those restrictions that are imposed by state institutions. In a world in which the sources, speed, and amount of expression proliferate at a bewildering pace, the very suggestion that expression can, let alone should, be unconstrained is open to challenge: the form of expression affects its substance. What is treated as a constraint by some is more an exercise of choice by others. And while the term 'censorship' suggests an antagonism of constraint and freedom, there is a growing opinion today that the two may be related in a free and democratic society.

In such an intellectual and social climate, there is a pressing need to reconsider and re-evaluate the whole debate over and around censorship. The authors of this book see censorship in an expansive way that treats it as a constituent feature of any system of social control or practice. Thus, it is essential that the investigation of censorship take into account its varied political, social, economic, and psychological contexts. Taboos, prejudices, and fears are at the root of many initiatives to restrict freedom of expression and information. In the political arena, the consideration of political power and public policy can help to explain the censorial processes and practices of governments. Many instruments of censorship are moulded by the particular forms of production and distribution and by the potential influence of various media. The clarification of ideological dispositions and tendencies can shed light on the religious and social values that pressure groups seek to protect or suppress by means of censorship. More than anything, it is the profit principle that can explain the range and the limits of the production and distribution of knowledge and information today.

The multifaceted nature of censorship is behind the interdisciplinary design of this book. It contains nineteen chapters which were written by twenty-three specialists from thirteen disciplines at nine Canadian universities. Considered as a group of scholars, only a few of the contributors rank among the known experts on censorship. This may seem unusual, but it is the result of a conscious decision. With such a divisive and controversial issue, we wanted to avoid both the activists and those who are known to have already made up their minds (and possibly lost their intellectual curiosity) about this topic. Further, we did not simply invite individuals to contribute any essays which would fit under the project's title. Instead, we first designed the conceptual framework and the structure of the book and then invited scholars who, on the basis of their previous research, appeared to be eminently capable both of contributing original empirical work within the Canadian context and of breaking new theoretical ground for the issue of censorship.

The interdisciplinary model underlying their contributions does not merely assume that full knowledge of censorship will be achieved by putting together the sum of the partial knowledge delivered by each of them. To be sure, at one level, this study aims to expose the extent of censorship in Canada today, to explore its nature, and to find out what its exercise may tell us about our political culture. It also wants to contribute to the understanding of censorship as a multifaceted and highly controversial concept of social control. At the same time, however, interdisciplinarity is understood here to follow a model of investigation that allows individual contributors to invoke and deploy different categories and definitions as determined by the perspectives and methodologies of their individual disciplines. The goal is not to arrive at a programmatic conclusion. Instead, we want to enhance the awareness that not only the practice of censorship but also the discourse about it is an immediate expression of changes in thoughts, values, and social behaviour over time.

The decision to allow for this plurality of views and approaches resulted in a selection of specific topics at the expense of general coverage. This will explain the gaps in the volume. We carefully considered giving Quebec and its controversial language policy special consideration but decided against it. A discussion of censorship in regard to this province's distinct cultural and historical context would require much more than could possibly be accomplished in a short essay. This does not mean, of course, that most of what is said in the following chapters does not apply as much to Quebec as it does to the other Canadian provinces.

Malcolm Dean's book *Censored! Only in Canada* covers the history of film censorship in Canada until 1980. This is why we did not commission another piece on the same topic for our book. To bring Dean's research up to date and to provide at least an insight into the censorship scheme of provincial film-censor boards and its legal foundations, we include, in an appendix, an excerpt from a 1983 decision of the Ontario High Court of Justice in which the censorship practice of the Ontario Film Censor Board was successfully challenged as an infringement of freedom of speech.

Despite the apparent fluidity and indetermination, the contributors to this volume agree in their perception of censorship as a value-driven instrument of power used by an authority to control, restrict, or otherwise interfere with the form or content of expression or the free flow of information. It is not their intention to deride this control as such. Socially organized activity cannot occur without censorship and the question therefore is not 'censorship or free speech' but censorship in what form, by whom, and in whose interest? In a liberal democracy and a multicultural society such as ours, this perception of the political nature of censorship is one of the prerequisites for the solution of its inherent conflicts.

We thank the Hampton Foundation and the Office of the Dean of Arts at the University of British Columbia for their generous support of this project, as well as Simon Archer for his research assistance.

KLAUS PETERSEN
ALLAN HUTCHINSON

NOTES

1 See *Information Freedom and Censorship: World Report 1991* (Chicago: Library Association Publishing Association 1991), 80–7.
2 Judith Dick, *Not in our Schools?!!! School Book Censorship in Canada: A Discussion Guide* (Ottawa: Canadian Library Association 1982); and Diane Granfield, ed., *Intellectual Freedom Handbook* (Toronto: Ontario Library Association 1990). See also Peter Birdsall and Delores Broten, *Mind War: Book Censorship in English Canada* (Victoria: CANLIT 1978). In Jude Johnston and Joyce Mason, eds., *Issues of Censorship* (Toronto: A Space 1985), fifteen Canadian artists and writers articulate a variety of critical views of censorship.
3 James R. Bennet, *Control of Information in the United States. An Annotated Bibliography* (Westport, Conn.: Meckler 1987); Frank Hoffmann, *Intellectual Freedom and Censorship. An Annotated Bibliography* (New York: Scarecrow 1989).
4 Leon Hurwitz, *Historical Dictionary of Censorship in the United States* (Westport, Conn.: Greenwood Press 1985); Jonathon Green, *The Encyclopedia of Censorship* (New York: Facts on File 1990).
5 David Tribe, *Questions of Censorship* (London: Allen and Unwin 1993); Ilan Peleg, ed., *Patterns of Censorship around the World* (Boulder, Colo.: Westview Press 1993).
6 Jay E. Daily, 'Censorship, Contemporary and Controversial Aspects of,' in Allen Kent and Harold Lancour, ed., *Encyclopedia of Library and Information Science*, vol. 4 (New York: Marcel Dekker 1970), 338–81; Sue Curry Jansen, *Censorship: The Knot That Binds Power and Knowledge* (New York: Oxford University Press 1988).
7 See, for example, William J. Westherby, *Salman Rushdie: Sentenced to Death* (New York: Carroll and Graf 1990); Odile Krakovitch, *Hugo Censuré: La Liberté au*

Theatre au XIXe Siècle (Paris: Calmann-Levy 1985); Earl R. Hutchison, *Tropic of Cancer on Trial: A Case History of Censorship* (New York: Grove Press 1968); Bob Reitman, *Freedom on Trial: The Incredible Ordeal of Ralph Ginzburg* (San Diego, Calif.: Publishers Export 1966).

8 See, for instance, David Schneiderman, ed., *Freedom of Expression and the Charter* (Calgary: Thomson Professional Publishing Canada 1991).

9 See the chapter on Canada in Neville March Hunnings, *Film Censors and the Law* (London: George Allen and Unwin 1967), 248–78; and Malcolm Dean, *Censored! Only in Canada: The History of Film Censorship – the Scandal off the Screen* (Toronto: Virgo Press 1981).

10 David Booth, *Censorship Goes to School* (Markham, Ont.: Pembroke Publishers 1992); Lois Bewley, 'Censorship and Librarians,' *Canadian Library Journal* 40, no. 6 (1983), 353–7; Alvin M. Schrader and Keith Walker, 'Censorship Iceberg: Results of an Alberta Public Library Survey,' *Canadian Library Journal* 43, no. 2 (1986), 91–5; Alvin M. Schrader, Margaret Herring, and Catriona de Scossa, 'The Censorship Phenomenon in College and Research Libraries: An Investigation of the Canadian Prairie Provinces 1980–1985,' *College and Research Libraries* (July 1989), 420–32; Alvin M. Schrader, 'A Study of Community Censorship Pressures on Canadian Public Libraries,' *Canadian Library Journal* 49, no. 1 (1992), 29–38.

11 Steve Mertl, *Keegstra: The Trial, the Issues, the Consequences* (Saskatoon: Western Producer Prairie Books 1985); Lorraine Eisenstat Weinrib, 'Hate Promotion in a Free and Democratic Society,' *McGill Law Journal*, 36 (1991), 1416–49; Richard Moon, 'Drawing Lines in a Culture of Prejudice: R. v. Keegstra and the Restriction of Hate Propaganda,' *U.B.C. Law Review*, 26 (1992), 99–143; and 'The Zundel Appeal: A Criminal Reports Forum,' *Criminal Reports*, 56 (1987), 77–96.

12 See, for instance, Gordon Stuart Adam, *Journalism, Communication and the Law* (Scarborough, Ont.: Prentice-Hall of Canada 1976); and Kathleen E. Mahoney and Sheilah L. Martin, *Broadcasting and the Canadian Charter of Rights and Freedoms: Justifications for Restricting Freedom of Expression*, Government of Canada, Task Force on Broadcasting Policy, vol. 32, 1985.

13 See, for instance, Gregory S. Kealey, 'State Repression of Labour and the Left in Canada 1914–20: The Impact of the First World War,' *Canadian Historical Review*, 73, no. 3 (1992) 281–314; Werner Bausenhart, 'The Ontario German Language Press and Its Suppression by Order-in-Council in 1918,' *Canadian Ethnic Studies* 4, no. 1 (1972), 35–48; and Gary Botting, *Fundamental Freedoms and Jehovah's Witnesses* (Calgary: University of Calgary Press 1993).

14 There is an entry on censorship in Eugene Benson and L.W. Conolly, eds., *Oxford Companion to Canadian Theatre* (Toronto: Oxford University Press 1989), 81–4, with a brief historical overview of theatre censorship in Canada.

CENSORSHIP IN CANADA

1

Censorship! Or Is It?

KLAUS PETERSEN

The extant critical literature on speech restraints shows striking differences in the interpretation of the term 'censorship.' Those who investigate a particular form of restraint or a specific case usually have little difficulty in using the term. There is easy agreement, for instance, that the seizure of magazines by police, the banning of a film by a public authority, or the pseudo-conviction of the British author Salman Rushdie by Iranian religious fanatics are all manifestations of censorship. But whenever the attempt is made to use a term that includes all forms of speech restraint, the various approaches yield different results. In many cases the definition is simply tailored to the particular scope of a study.[1]

Entries in reference books show that their authors used different organizing principles in order to arrive at a workable definition. A common method is to look for sources and targets. In the *International Encyclopedia of the Social Sciences*, for instance, both public and private forms of censorship are grouped into four categories: political censorship, religious censorship, censorship of obscenity, and censorship affecting academic freedom.[2] Another common method is based on the distinction between the various agents of censorship. The 1985 edition of *Collier's Encyclopedia*, for example, states: 'The three principle forms in which censorship has been exercised within historic time may be distinguished as church censorship, state censorship, and private censorship.'[3] *The Encyclopedia Americana*, which distinguishes between 'preventive censorship' and 'systemic limitations,' describes the first as 'a system under which official censors must give permission before communications of a specific type can lawfully be made.' The second notion (systemic limitations) is divided into 'judicial control of censorship,' which would cover any restriction on free expression subject to judicial enforcement or limitation, and 'extra-judicial censorship,' which would include restraints enforced by government agencies and private organizations as well as self-censorship.[4]

While such entries in most cases acknowledge the increasing importance of non-governmental censorship, they still put the greater emphasis on official restrictions. The *New Encyclopedia Britannica* (1990), for example, says about censorship: 'It occurs in all manifestations of authority to some degree, but in modern times it has been of special importance in its relation to government and the rule of law.'[5] This observation is clearly contradicted in the most recent edition of the *International Encyclopedia of Communications* by the statement that 'official or government censorship makes up only a small part of the actual censoring activity in any society.'[6]

In more substantial analytical studies, the long-standing preoccupation with infringements by governments and government agents again results in narrow perceptions of the term. For the legal scholar Ilan Peleg, censorship simply is 'the systematic control of the content of communication by a government through various means.'[7] For the historian H.C. Gardiner, an essential element in the concept of censorship is that 'control is exercised by an authority that has legitimate power to enforce the restrictions that may be imposed.'[8] Similarly, the lawyer Harriet Pilpel sees such limitation primarily in government injunctions against speech and the subsequent imposition of punishment by the courts.[9] At the other end of the spectrum are scholars like the communications specialist Sue Curry Jansen, who sees the potential for censorship in any process of human communication. Jansen believes that 'censorial authority may be secured by social customs; by the practices of political, economic, religious, educational, or cultural institutions; by established semantic conventions; or by prevailing rules of reason.'[10]

Does censorship, as defined by Jansen, include any processing of information, such as book-selection policies of public libraries, school-board decisions on school curriculum, or a university professor's choice of textbooks for his courses? Do theatre, film, and book reviews in newspapers, the hiring and firing of staff in the mass-media industries, or copyright laws qualify? What, if any, are the differences between censorship, control, manipulation, inhibition, persuasion, and misinformation? The extant body of research shows that legal critics, anthropologists, psychologists, linguists, sociologists, and political scientists answer these questions quite differently. And considered as a whole, their critical work on the topic not only illustrates the multiplicity of applicable approaches but also helps us with understanding the multilayered, multifaceted, and everchanging nature of censorship.

Viewed from the perspective of political liberal theory, censorship is a state limitation of the freedom of expression and of the free access to information.

Under a totalitarian system of government, restraints may include the submission of materials to prior scrutiny; the prohibition of further reproduction, publication, and circulation of material; and the regime's unlimited control over official information. The theory of this monolithic and leaden type of repression is, of course, much simpler and its practice more straightforward than the diverse modes of censoring public speech and publication in liberal democracies. In the latter, the intentions, instruments, and practices of censorship involve an intricate and always controversial balance between the power of government to enforce speech-related prohibitions, on the one hand, and procedural safeguards against the abuse of governmental authority, on the other. What distinguishes the practice of censorship in liberal democracies from that in totalitarian systems is that the former does not allow official restrictions without due process of law.

In Article 19(2) of the International Covenant on Civil and Political Rights, the definition of individual freedom of expression includes a person's 'freedom to seek, receive and impart information and ideas of all kinds, regardless of frontiers, either orally, in writing or in print, in the form of art, or through any other media of his choice.'[11] Such a guarantee is offered by most democratic constitutions. The American First Amendment, for example, states: 'Congress shall make no law ... abridging the freedom of speech or of the press.'[12] The German Grundgesetz (Basic Law) stipulates in its Article 5: 'There shall be no censorship.'[13] But, since the freedom to express oneself may conflict with the welfare of society or with guaranteed individual rights, the judiciaries in both countries eventually saw fit to interpret the key concepts ('freedom' and 'censorship') in a way that would allow for exceptions.[14] The Canadian Charter of Rights and Freedoms is more direct in that it subjects its guarantees expressly 'to such reasonable limits prescribed by law as can be demonstrably justified in a free and democratic society.'[15] Under certain circumstances, therefore, in Canada censorship may be considered an accepted part of government or of the requirements of social living.

Thus, contrary to solemn declarations on human rights by national regimes and international organizations, restraints on the freedom of speech are not always illegitimate even in liberal democracies. There is in fact no country in the world that grants its citizens an absolute right to say or publish anything under any circumstances. To begin with, whole groups of the population – usually the young, prison inmates, the mentally ill, the military, and public servants – are denied an unrestricted freedom of expression. As for the rest, limitations of this freedom are legally employed by most states as an exceptional measure to safeguard national security, to protect religious and minority groups, to safeguard public order and the rule of law, to strengthen public health and welfare, to uphold public morals, to guard the welfare of the young, and to secure individual physical and social integrity. If a form of expression jeopardizes these interests it may be deemed to be irresponsibly in error. As a rule, limitations to the freedom of speech are therefore understood to be a means of protecting society against such allegedly harmful expression. For example, explaining the purpose of legitimate censorship, a 1947 report of the American Commission on Freedom of the Press speaks of 'legal corrections of misused liberty of expression' and sees such misuse where 'an utterance or publication invades in a serious, overt, and demonstrable manner personal rights or vital social interests.'[16] Almost fifty years later, on 26 April 1994, a German Supreme Court decision held that freedom of expression does not extend to the right to lie as a deliberate instrument of policy.

Accordingly, liberal democracies have limited freedom of expression to varying degrees. This can be discerned from a significant number of statutes prohibiting crimes and offences such as treason, sedition, high treason, blasphemous and defamatory libel, the disruption of religious worship, hate propaganda, the spreading of false news, public mischief, literature on illicit drug use, obscenity, and indecency. Legislatures, governments, government agencies, and the courts derive legitimate powers of censorship from such legal provisions. The defamation of legislatures and the courts may result in contempt proceedings under common law.

The primary concern of liberal theory, therefore, is state censorship as it issues from all three powers of government. Such censorship takes the form of repressive legislation passed by legislatures, administrative and regulative intervention by governments and government agencies, and punishment by the courts for proscribed forms of expression and conduct. The legislative power to enact restrictions has been sanctioned in principle by the courts, which have ruled that certain forms of speech do not qualify as 'expression' as perceived by the fathers of the constitution (United States), that certain types of restrictions fall within permissible exceptions (Canada), or that certain restraints do not qualify as 'censorship' in the legal sense of the term (Germany).

In addition to criminal statutes that in a general way forbid these kinds of expression, there are laws such as Canada's War Measures Act (now replaced by the less sweeping Emergency Act) and the Official Secrets Act that entitle governments to introduce additional restrictions in times of civil unrest or to hold back information from the public under certain circumstances. Furthermore, each of the modern mass media (press, film, videotapes, radio, television, computer networks, telephone, and advertising) is subject to restrictions that vary with its specific mode of production and distribution and with its degree of influence. Of these, film-censorship laws often take the form of prior restraint.

Moreover, provincial and municipal regulations and by-laws can also severely restrict performances, exhibitions, demonstrations, public speaking, and the display of texts and pictures on billboards. Some of the laws that are meant to protect the rights of particular persons or groups may even result in the censorship of others. The statutes on criminal libel, for instance, the purpose of which is to protect the reputation of the individual, limit the freedom of speech of those who defame. In Canada, the Young Offenders Act limits the freedom of the press and the right of the public to know whenever reporters are prevented from divulging the names of offenders under a certain age. The copyright law and hate-law provisions have the same effect.

Police, customs officers, the Post Office, censor boards, and public prosecutors are the most visible agents of government censorship. For example, under certain circumstances, the police may ban demonstrations, disperse public gatherings, or arrest people on picket lines; customs officers may seize films, videos, books, and magazines at the border if their content is prohibited by law; the Post Office may refuse to forward obscene material; censor boards may ban or cut obscene films; and prosecutors may decide to indict individuals for speech offences. Censorship is routinely undertaken by government officials under executive privilege. An immigration officer, for instance, may refuse to grant a visa to individuals who intend to give public lectures on a controversial topic. Especially pervasive is government censorship resulting from the licensing power of municipal bodies, and the financial control and day-to-day administrative powers of various ministries and government departments which oversee and regulate important public venues of communication and distribution of knowledge, such as broadcasting, schools, universities, and public libraries. State bureaucracies also exercise considerable control over access to official news and information.

Judicial censorship can result from public prosecution, the autonomous decision of a judge, or the judicial accommodation of competing private claims. In the first case, censorship involves the punishment of expressions of opinion whose content or form is forbidden by law. In the second case, a judge would act on his own initiative and ban the reporting of specific details of a trial or charge someone with contempt of court. The third case would include litigation. Here, interested parties would compete for the power to censor; individuals, companies, or organizations would defend their freedom of speech against governmental infringements or seek an injunction to silence others. But in all cases judicial censorship is bound by existing laws and the principle of due process. The judiciary, therefore, may be a source of censorship but it may also serve as bulwark against it. In countries like Canada and the United States, most if not all of the restrictive statutes and regulations have been challenged in court.

It is difficult to determine the success of those who enforce or advocate state censorship. It may well be that restrictions or the threat of punishment for certain types of expression have contributed to internal stability, national security, some individual's physical and social integrity, or the protection of minority groups from discrimination. Much more doubtful is the success of attempts to control public morals. The threat of punishment may have a chilling effect resulting in self-censorship, but its extent is again difficult to measure. Those who are targeted by censorship, such as writers, publishers, printers, book dealers, theatre managers, impresarios, librarians, teachers, artists, and gallery owners, have a much clearer picture of the damage that a particular act of censorship – the banning of a film, the seizure of books or magazines, an indictment, or the enforced cancellation of an art exhibition – can cause all those involved in producing, distributing, and exhibiting materials. Apart from the frustration of being inhibited in their work, such people may incur significant material losses. It is no coincidence that the protest against state censorship usually originates from these circles.

Since Samuel LaSelva will discuss the liberal model of constitutional freedom of expression and censorship in greater detail in chapter 3 of this volume, it is sufficient in this overview to draw attention to the two concepts of liberty which political philosophers like Isaiah Berlin and Charles Taylor have described as 'negative' and 'positive.'[17] Adherents to the negative theory in its crudest form see freedom as the absence of external legal obstacles. By invoking traditional rationales for free speech (the democratic form of government, human self-realization, the pursuit of truth), they try to determine how legal formalities, conditions, restrictions, and penalties stack up against constitutionally guaranteed rights and freedoms. This approach allows liberals to highlight flaws in the legislation and jurisprudence relating to free expression, to expose the improper delegation or exercise of censoring authority, or to identify the procedural safeguards against the imposition of undue restrictions.

Those who lean towards a 'positive' theory of freedom, on the other hand, identify liberty not only with individual independence but also with collective self-government and thus are inclined to seek a balance between claims to freedom of expression and competing social values and individual and minority rights (equality, privacy, commerce, freedom from discrimination). Their perception of censorship as a political issue permits an understanding of infringements as either the result of social conflicts or the instrument with which to solve these conflicts.[18] For those who believe in this 'positive' theory of freedom, exceptions to freedom of expression are not inconsistent with the premises of a liberal democracy. While allowing that the hate-speech and obscenity provisions of the Criminal Code do limit freedom of expression, they would argue, for example, that both hate speech and pornography may have a silencing impact on the members of particular groups and so are themselves like acts of censorship.

Profound changes in the character of contemporary discourse/knowledge production make it more difficult to understand censorship simply within the paradigm of unjustified state interference with individual liberty. The political plurality of liberal democracies, the dynamics of profit-driven free-market economies, the shifting social arrangements of modern societies, and the development and expansion of new communication technologies have all changed or expanded the direction and the form of censorship in important ways. While the conventional institutions and the rules of state-sponsored restrictions mentioned above are still in place and effective, it is important to realize that infringements on the freedom of expression as experienced within corporations, in the media, in public institutions of learning, in private organizations, and in any other of society's channels of communication do not always originate from government agencies or the courts – in fact, there are good reasons to believe that the most widespread practices of censorship today are non-governmental.[19]

In order to understand the structure of censorship we must discontinue treating it as a technical issue of legal doctrine and instead isolate and disentangle the elements of its social figurations whenever state- or non-state actors are seen as having the power to control contributions to public discourse. In this wider social and political context we may still understand censorship in pejorative terms as an act of interference whenever we find two conflicting preferences and the enforcement of one over the other. Censorship, from this perspective, takes place whenever someone wants to say, write, publish, distribute, or exhibit anything (or inform herself about it) and is prevented by someone else from doing so.

Thus, censorship arises from relations of influence and control between participants, as indicated in this definition: *censorship is a value-driven instrument of power used by an authority to control, restrict, or otherwise interfere with the form or content of expression or the free flow of information.* It is best defined with respect to relative and shifting power relations. Censoring power takes the form of force, or the threat of force, of punishment, material loss, curtailment of influence, or the promise of rewards. It may also result from an administrative act that is ignorant of or indifferent to the preferences of those who are affected by it.

The linking of censorship with manifestations of power seems at first to serve only to complicate the issue because power is such a complex and multilayered concept. As John Kenneth Galbraith wrote in his study *The Anatomy of Power*:

Unmentioned in nearly all references to [power] is the highly interesting question as to how the will is imposed, how the acquiescence of others is achieved. Is it the threat of physical punishment, the promise of pecuniary reward, the exercise of persuasion, or some other, deeper force that causes the person or persons subject to the exercise of power to abandon their own preferences and to accept those of others? In any meaningful reference to power this should be known. And one should also know the sources of power – what it is that differentiates those who exercise it from those who are subject to the authority of others.[20]

If we apply these questions to censorship – its participants, its purposes, and its degree of enforcement – the concept becomes so diverse and pervasive that one's first reaction is to wonder where to draw the line.

Nevertheless, it is impossible to ignore the relationship between censorship and power because the exercise of the former is always determined by authority structures. It is in the nature of any form of social organization that individuals and groups find themselves in a network of ever shifting positions of domination and subordination. All communication and all efforts to control it, be it in the media, corporations, bureaucracies, schools, universities, churches, or the body politic, are implicitly and explicitly affected by such authority structures. David Tribe is right, therefore, in saying that 'the history of censorship is part of the history of society. For it is related to the ideological and practical needs of communities, or – as some would say – of their rulers, constricting and relaxing as social pressures wax and wane ... Its operation is as varied as social anthropology itself.'[21] What Tribe describes as 'pressures' is another word for power. Any history of censorship, including that provided by Tribe himself, will show that the exercise of censorship always did and always does tell the story of someone (an individual, a group, an organization, the state, or the church) who imposes or threatens to impose his or its will on others.

In his account of power, Galbraith distinguishes between three instruments: 'condign,' 'compensatory,' and 'conditioned.' He defines the first as power that 'wins submission by the ability to impose an alternative to the preferences of the individual or group that is sufficiently unpleasant or painful so that these preferences are abandoned.' Compensatory power, in contrast, 'wins submission by the offer of affirmative reward – by the giving of something of value to the individual so submitting.' Finally, conditioned power 'is exercised by changing belief.' This form of power, which, according to Galbraith, is essential to the functioning of the modern economy and body politic, is acquired by 'persuasion, education, or the social commitment to what seems natural, proper, or right.'[22] Compliance here is not usually recognized as a form of submission.

In my effort to explore the nature of censorship, Galbraith's description of the three types of instruments of power will help to define its parameters. We certainly can speak of 'condign' instruments of censorship. Most of us abstain from using speech in public that is prohibited by law lest we suffer punishment. Members of professional organizations and employees of public institutions submit to codes of conduct that forbid the use of certain forms of speech. Those who belong to political parties or private organizations and groups will refrain from public expression of any dissident views they may hold, since this could provoke punishment such as a reprimand or even expulsion. Commercial establishments require silence in the interest of profits; public speakers may avoid addressing controversial issues for fear of verbal rebuke; and we all are familiar with the fear of speaking openly when faced with the moral condemnation by other individuals or the community. Likewise, the term 'compensatory instrument of censorship' can be helpful when describing censorious activity. In all the social settings described, it 'pays' to conform. Not to say or write what one would like to may be considered worthy of approval or the benefits of membership and belonging, of employment, promotion, and monetary reward.

Condign censorship is usually visible. When applied by the state (legislative, administrative, and judicial censorship), it may effect the largest number of people. It is supposed to be objective, democratic, and just. Within public institutions such as libraries, schools, and universities, it is also supposed to follow mandated regulations and guidelines which represent agreed-on interests. This is not the case in private organizations, commercial establishments, or the private sphere, where condign censorship is exercised by decidedly partisan, profit-driven, or personal concerns.

While individuals may initiate and exercise censorship, it is through organizations that the highest degree of censorship power is generated. Organizations have the structure to make their members submit to common objectives (security, success, profit, performance, education), and as a consequence they have the means to restrict their freedom of expression. This is particularly true of the state, with its powerful legislative, administrative, and judicial instruments, and for large corporations, including the media, with their centralized control systems. Organizations also have greater access to compensatory power. Much weaker is the ability of organizations (other than the state) to exercise censorship beyond their membership.

Private-interest groups tend to succeed with external censorship if they gain representation in legislatures, in government agencies (censor boards), or in administrative bodies of public institutions (school boards, sexual-harassment committees, and so on). Pressure tactics such as challenges to textbook selections and to book acquisitions by school libraries may also lead to success. When it is argued that restrictions are intended for the public good, or at least reflect the interests or perceptions of a larger group of people, their chances of success will increase. The claim that censorship is sought to protect the rights of underprivileged sections of the population has been particularly effective. Public criticism and abuse are also known to have sufficient condign power to censor the individual who does not readily submit to codes of speech and behaviour. But, in the main, private-interest groups must rely on education and persuasion in their efforts to impose their values and beliefs on others.

What I have said about condign and compensatory censorship so far relates only to the abridgment of free expression. There is, however, a second type of censorship and that is interference with the free flow of information. The former type of censorship is directed against the freedom to speak, write, act, or distribute information; the latter is directed against a right, the right to know. The first is intrusive and coercive; the second is neither. Most organizations are engaged in controlling information in order to pursue more effectively their particular objectives. This may include attempts to suppress the dissemination of allegedly harmful speech, to cover up mistakes, and to conceal true intentions. While such intentions are rarely articulated, each organization (governments, the courts, libraries, schools, corporations, private associations) has its own set of 'official' grounds for justifying its powers of processing and selecting information: security, the rule of law, order, morality, professional ethics, good education, affirmative action, and so on. Almost all the information that we receive has been selected and processed. Whether this selection process constitutes censorship is determined not only by the good intentions of those who carry it out but also by the effect it has on others. Depending on the participants' place in power relationships, they may experience this activity either as a form of choice or as one of restraint.

Libraries and their book-selection practices are a case in point. Their purchasing and removal policies as much as limited funds routinely require choices that eliminate certain books, journals, newspapers, and so on from circulation. This affects different categories of people in different ways. One group are the authors and publishers, whose access to readership and whose profits are curtailed; another group consists of users who are prevented from obtaining the material of their choice. Librarians like to claim that selection does not amount to censorship. Henry Reichman, who argues that point in typical fashion for the American Association of School Administrators and the American Library Association, maintains: 'Clearly articulated and professionally formulated selection policies and procedures differ fundamentally from the mode of operation of the censor.'[23] His description of the required judgments as 'intelligent,' 'appropriate,' 'necessary,' and 'reasonable' (selection), on the one hand, or 'personal,' 'biased,' and 'improper' (censorship), on the other, is typical of the semantic strategy of a group's claim to professionalism. This line of argument is understandable but it addresses only half the issue. Whether the librarian's choices are 'biased' and 'personal' or 'reasonable' and 'appropriate' by the standards of existing policies makes no difference in terms of the limiting effect his or her actions may have on others.

The same applies to schools. It is hardly likely that anyone would argue in principle against the government's role in overseeing public education. But, as Mark G. Yudof points out: 'If government is to educate children, to operate public schools, and to select teachers, books and courses, a basic decision has been made about the communication of skills, attitudes, values, and beliefs, between generations. Education and indoctrination, information and values, cannot be neatly disentangled.'[24] We generally accept that school professionals are regularly involved in editorial decisions over the content and materials for programs and courses. But all this again requires choice and selection with the possible consequence of censorship. While 'authors, editors, and publishers have no constitutional right to have their books purchased by the state for dissemination in public schools,' as Yudof argues,[25] their access is nonetheless limited. And to the degree that we consider minors unable to make the right choices, we select information in their (presumed) interest, even in cases where they articulate dissenting preferences.

Furthermore, in their role as social institutions, schools and universities exercise censorship of expression under the guise of rules of conduct – and such restrictions are also increasingly applied to teachers and professors.

In his provocative essay 'There's No Such Thing as Free Speech, and It's a Good Thing Too,' Stanley Fish argues that 'free speech' is never 'independent of a community context informed by interest,' and that any expression implies both the affirmation of values and the negation of 'alternatively possible articulation.'[26] Viewed from this perspective, censorship could be seen as just another form of expression. This notion is not very helpful, however. If we want to determine when and how we practise or suffer restraints, it is essential that we define boundaries lest the term 'censorship' become meaningless. For that reason I would distinguish between expressions whose implied limiting power is incidental and expressions whose primary purpose or major consequence consists of the limiting of someone's freedom of speech. It is only the second category that deserves to be called censorship.

Much more useful is Fish's argument that little is gained if we see the issue of free speech and censorship from the point of view of general principle: 'The question of whether or not to regulate will always be a local one, and we can not rely on abstractions that are either empty of content or filled with the content of some partisan agenda to generate a "principled" answer. Instead we must consider in every case what is at stake and what are the risks and gains of alternate courses of action.'[27] Indeed, the analysis of a particular case can be complex. As a participant in ever shifting power relationships, a perpetrator in one set of circumstances may well become a casualty in another. An act of censorship may effect a single person, a group, or a whole population, it may be temporary or limited to a particular location, and it may be based on existing procedures or in violation of them.

In general terms, Fish's emphasis on interested speech is also well taken: liberals will argue that censorship always discriminates; social activists may point out that it leaves space for others, that it is stopping some from drowning out others. But, in either case, I would argue that censorship is always a means of protecting certain values and suppressing others. Its urgency and extent are related to the conflict over these values in a given society, and this makes censorship a key index of influential trends, prejudices, anxieties, taboos and moral sensibilities in a political culture.

In liberal democracies like Canada, the suppression of objectionable ideas or of their presentation has undergone a noticeable change of direction in recent years. Traditionally, restrictions were directed at ideas and activities considered injurious to broadly defined communal values, customs and traditions like 'law and order,' 'good morals,' and 'true religion.' What motivates proponents of censorship today are usually much more specific rights and interests. With the exception of pornography and obscenity, which may still provoke morally motivated restraints with relatively broad support, it is values like privacy, equality, and commerce that have moved into the centre of conflicts about this issue.[28] People are less intent on controlling blasphemy, obscenity, and sedition than defamation, sexism, racism, and violence.

Values are also at the root of the resistance to censorship. While power per se may not be a proper subject for indignation, censorship easily provokes the charge of being improper, illegitimate, unconstitutional, or morally wrong. Liberals like to argue that its immediate effect is that it takes away, that it limits a right or a freedom. In their eyes it ranks among the negative measures of social control – even if it is justified by one noble end or another.

Nevertheless, the resistance to restrictions is usually as fraught with hypocrisy as are many of its justifications. We forget too easily that every form of social organization requires a certain number of negative devices. We often ignore also how easily we fall into the role of the censor when our own (legitimate) interests are at stake. Organizations for the defence of civil liberties, for instance, tend to rally behind statements like 'books, newspapers, and magazines are the instruments of freedom.'[29] This may be so under certain circumstances, but one look at the propaganda material of totalitarian ideologies and regimes tells a different tale. Writers and publishers who exercise censorship whenever they invoke their copyright should pause before demanding the abolition of censorship 'in all forms.'[30] And yes, 'books are pure expression,'[31] but they are also a commodity and as such are subject to trade and tariff regulations. The dividing line between protected and proscribed expression is always the product of an accommodation of competing claims.

In a book on authority, Richard Sennet made the point that domination 'is a necessary disease the social organism suffers. It is built into the chain of command. The chain of command is an architecture of power which inherently does injury to the needs and desires of some at the will of others.'[32] The perception of censorship as an instrument of power fits well into Sennet's description of social relationships and their coercive aspects. Keith Spicer, for instance, a well-known expert on journalism and broadcasting in Canada, once defined censorship quite simply as 'one authority deciding what will enter the minds of weaker others.'[33] However, it is important to understand that the relationship of domination and submission need not always be forced upon us. In censorship research remarkably little has been said about situations where we enter into power relationships, not only for certain advantages they may offer us, but also with full knowledge and agreement that by doing so we forego some of our rights and freedoms. On a larger scale, some restrictions may be considered part of the social contract. In joining a limited-purpose organization we give up, to an extent, our freedom of speaking publicly in ways that are contrary to its purpose. In fact, any membership in a group implies voluntary curbs on individual choice. Such curbs may be the result of tacit agreement, they may be negotiated and concluded deliberately, or they may be part of statutory membership obligations.

Within the framework of constitutionally mandated exceptions and rules of due process, the limitation of people's freedom of expression and of their right to access of information through legislative restrictions, government powers, and judicial decisions is not necessarily illegitimate. Without the partial surrender of the right to educate our children, schools could not function. The teacher's authority is inevitably endowed with some censoring power to choose materials and methods. He or she cannot be expected to give equal consideration to all texts when compiling the literature for his or her classes. As was stated earlier, budgetary restraints and limited space result inevitably in a degree of censorship in libraries, and so do purchasing policies and legal requirements. Professionals like doctors, university professors, judges, or lawyers must submit to rules of conduct to safeguard their clientele from verbal abuse or violation of privacy. It would be absurd to insist that publishers invest an equal amount of money in every manuscript submitted. Under a democratic form of government, the media are entitled to ask employees to follow particular ideo-logical orientations or profit interests. A Catholic newspaper can hardly be expected to offer unbiased coverage of religious events.

The problem lies elsewhere. Since censorship is hardly ever recognized or defined positively, those who have the power to use it find it relatively easy to extend its limits, to conceal its application, or to enforce it under a different name. This is what makes censorship often so insidious. Government will rarely content itself with limited powers and roles, and its power advantage enables it to introduce regulations, codes, and standards in such a way that infringements on free expression and information will occur in a much more subtle – but not less effective – form than through bans or confiscation. Withholding information from people is undemocratic in that it jeopardizes their right to exercise control over their own fate. Special-interest groups may capture the censoring power of an authority. The power of money is a perennial hazard to free expression. The political, moral, and social norms that determine proscribed expressions are often so vague that lawmakers, public servants, and the judiciary are given con-siderable scope for subjective judgments. Agents of censorship such as parlia-ments, government agencies, courts, libraries, schools, and the media industries are run by people who are as prone to ideological preconceptions and prejudices as anyone else. Their explanatory powers help to conceal the true nature of restrictions. We find it much easier to justify the practice of censorship by call-ing it by a more palatable name, like the enforcement of a rule of 'conduct,' like 'education,' 'standards,' 'selection,' 'empowerment,' or 'correctness.'

A sober look at today's systems of discourse and knowledge production should make us realize that both the concentration of communicative power and the sheer scale of the flow of information make the distinction between selec-tion and censorship increasingly difficult. 'Mediated' expression has become inescapable and the goal, therefore, must be not to abolish control and selection but, first, to expose their interests and consequences, and, second, to democra-tize the process so that a diversity of expression and information is ensured.

NOTES

1 In a book on library and school censorship published jointly by the American Library Association and the American Association of School Administrators, for instance, we read: 'Put briefly, censorship is the removal, suppression, or restricted circulation of literary, artistic, or educational materials – of images, ideas, and

information – on the grounds that these are morally or otherwise objectionable in light of standards applied by the censor.' See Henry Reichmann, ed., *Censorship and Selection: Issues and Answers for Schools* (n.p., 1993).

2 Henry J. Abraham, 'Censorship,' in David L. Sills, ed., *International Encyclopedia of the Social Sciences,* vol. 2 (n.p.: Macmillan and the Free Press 1968), 356. The special mention of one particular target of censorship (academic freedom) is as unusual as it is arbitrary.

3 Russel Kirk, 'Censorship,' in *Collier's Encyclopedia,* vol. 5 (New York 1985), 630.

4 Louis Lusky, 'Censorship,' in *The Encyclopedia Americana. International Edition,* vol. 6 (Danbury, Conn.: 1990), 161–6.

5 *The New Encyclopedia Britannica,* 15th ed., vol. 3 (Chicago: 1990), 21.

6 Sue Curry Jansen, 'Non-Government Censorship,' in *International Encyclopedia of Communication,* vol. 1 (New York: Oxford 1989), 249.

7 Ilan Peleg, ed., *Patterns of Censorship around the World* (Boulder, Colo.: 1993), 4.

8 H.C. Gardiner, 'Censorship,' in *New Catholic Encyclopedia,* vol. 3 (New York: 1967), 391.

9 Harriet F. Pilpel, 'Freedom of the Press – American Style,' in *The First Freedom Today* (Chicago: American Library Association 1984), 43.

10 Sue Curry Jansen, 'Non-Government Censorship,' in *International Encyclopedia of Communications,* vol. 1 (New York: 1989), 250.

11 General Assembly Resolution 2200A of 16 December 1966, *Human Rights. A Compilation of International Instruments,* vol. 1 (New York: 1993), 28.

12 *American Bill of Rights, being Amendments I to X, XIII to XV, XIX, XXIV and XXVI to the Constitution.*

13 *Grundgesetz für die Bundesrepublik Deutschland,* Article 5.

14 For comments, see Thomas I. Emerson, 'Freedom of Expression,' in Robert B. Downs and Ralph E. McCoy, eds., *The First Freedom Today: Critical Issues Relating to Censorship and to Intellectual Freedom* (Chicago: 1984), 36–8; Thomas I. Emerson, 'Statement on the First Amendment,' *The First Freedom Today,* 38–43; and Bernd Rieder, *Die Zensurbegriffe des Art. 118 Abs. 2 der Weimarer Reichsverfassung und des Art. 5 Abs. I Satz 3 des Bonner Grundgesetzes* (Berlin: 1970).

15 *Canadian Charter of Rights and Freedoms,* pt. I of the *Constitution Act, 1982,* being Sched.B. of the *Canada Act 1982,* 1982 (Engl.) c. 11.

16 'A Free and Responsible Press,' quoted from Walter Tarnopolsky et al., *Newspapers and the Law* (Ottawa: Canadian Government Publishing Centre 1981), 8.

17 Isaiah Berlin, *Four Essays on Liberty* (London: Oxford University Press 1969), 8–72; and Charles Taylor, 'What's Wrong with Negative Liberty,' in Taylor, *Philosophy and the Human Sciences* (Cambridge, U.K.: 1985), 211–29.

18 See, for instance, David Schneiderman, ed., *Freedom of Expression and the Charter* (Calgary: Thomson Professional Publishing Canada 1991); and Kathleen

Mahoney, 'Obscenity and Public Policy: Conflicting Values – Conflicting Statutes,' *Saskatchewan Law Review*, 50 (1985–6), 75–109.

19 I disagree with Thelma McCormack, who writes as follows about non-governmental censorship: 'There are other forms of censorship – organizational, economic, and self-censorship – but state censorship has the most serious consequences for our cultural institutions and our climate of opinion.' See Thelma McCormack, 'If Pornography Is the Theory, Is Inequality the Practice?' *Philosophy of the Social Sciences*, 23, no. 3 (1993), 299.

20 J.K. Galbraith, *The Anatomy of Power* (Boston: Houghton Mifflin 1983), 3.

21 David Tribe, *Questions of Censorship*, 47.

22 Galbraith, *The Anatomy of Power*, 4–6.

23 Henry Reichman, *Censorship and Selection: Issues and Answers for Schools* (Chicago: 1993), 6.

24 Mark G. Yudof, 'The State As Editor or Censor: Book Selection in the Public Schools,' in *The First Freedom Today*, 58.

25 Ibid., 60–1.

26 Stanley Fish, *There's No Such Thing As Free Speech, and It's a Good Thing Too* (New York: 1994), 103, 108.

27 Stanley Fish, *There's No Such Thing*, 111.

28 See David Schneiderman, 'Freedom of Expression and the Charter: Being Large and Liberal,' in Schneiderman, *Freedom of Expression and the Charter*, xxix–xli.

29 'Statement of the basic tenets of the Committee for Freedom of Expression of the Book and Periodical Council' (Toronto), *Freedom to Read Week Kit* (Toronto: 1990).

30 See Carey McWilliams, in *Censorship: For and Against*, 63.

31 Charles Rembar, in *Censorship: For and Against*, 203.

32 Richard Sennet, *Authority* (New York: Knopf 1980), 189.

33 Keith Spicer, 'Laurence Beats Censors' Wrath,' *The Province*, 11 January 1987.

2

Chameleon on a Changing Background: The Politics of Censorship in Canada

REG WHITAKER

Censorship has existed, does exist, and undoubtedly will continue to exist in Canada. The politics of censorship – the political framework in which censorship and its objects are defined and within which censorship operates – have, however, changed dramatically over the years, and with these changes, censorship itself has changed. How censorship is viewed, how it is understood in relation to the different elements of Canadian society, how what at one moment may seem a comforting security against threats can become at another moment itself a threat, are all political questions to which the answers change as the way in which people understand the political sphere changes.

Censorship is inherently political in at least two senses, if we understand politics to be about the exercise and impact of power. First, censorship has most often been associated with the direct exercise of state coercion. Even though private censorship represents an important part of contemporary censorship, it is at least indirectly dependent upon a state legal framework that supports the exercise of private censorship. The ability to set the rules of publicly acceptable discourse, of who can speak and what can be said, and thus to consign some to silence while giving voice to others, is obviously an important attribute of sovereignty, a prerogative that the modern nation-state jealously guards always at the formal level, even when the actual practice of state censorship may have fallen into relative disuse. In recent times, the power to invoke the legitimate and ultimately coercive sanction of state support on behalf of 'special interest' censorship has itself become a public good contested by various groups to enhance their status and symbolic power vis-à-vis other groups. The prize is the identification of the group with the state itself as the political expression of the society or community.

This leads to a second, distinct, sense in which censorship is inherently political: its exercise simultaneously legitimizes and delegitimizes different groups in society and thus reinforces or changes power relationships. Censorship of gay and lesbian art, for instance, simultaneously delegitimizes 'deviant' sexualities, while legitimizing dominant sexualities. Hate-literature censorship reinforces the illegitimacy of Holocaust deniers and validates the experience of Holocaust survivors and their descendants.

Recent censorship battles around pornography have been variously viewed by protagonists with quite different perspectives as either a defence of Christian family values against permissive assaults on the moral fabric of society; or a defence of women and children against violent, degrading, and sexist male aggression. That both moral conservatives and (some) feminists should apparently find themselves on the same side alerts us to an underlying problem. The politics of censorship is less about concrete results (who gets what in terms of redistribution of economic resources) than about the redistribution of symbolic resources. Legitimation/delegitimation is not directly about gaining/losing economic rewards or maintaining economic privilege (although it may well have an indirect influence); culture wars may reflect structures of privilege/resentment but they are not fought on this terrain but rather on the terrain of discourse, symbol, image. For those to whom politics is mainly or exclusively about economics, censorship battles appear trivial, irrelevant, or diversionary. To the participants, however, they are powerful and engaging struggles over values, with high stakes in terms of cultural security/insecurity, of personal and collective social worth.

Looked at over a relatively long period (the twentieth century), Canadian censorship practices would appear to have undergone a profound shift. From a strong state-centred practice evident certainly in two world wars but also in everyday peacetime censorship of print and film media, and of works of art, all done in the name of the 'community,' there has been a move to a more decentralized societal-centred practice in which contending groups in society invoke state support for censoring the expressions of other groups' tastes and moral standards. This shift, I would argue, parallels a shift in the discursive structure of Canadian politics, specifically the decline of the political narratives (liberalism, conservatism, social democracy) that once described and explained political life to Canadians. These narratives, although competitive with one another, were also complementary, tending to work together as part of a system, in their ensemble describing a relatively stable notion of political community for which the state stood in as effective guarantor and protector. The decay of these narratives, accelerating in the last decade of the twentieth century, has not led to the rise of effective new narratives to replace the old, or at least not to a new ensemble that describes a working societal consensus. Instead we see fragmentary narratives that often play directly against one another (neo-liberalism, minoritarian identity politics, majoritarian populism) and a consequent collapse of the overarching paradigm of the state/community. In this more divisive context, censorship has by no means vanished from the political stage, but it has changed its social role. Instead of posing as a tool, or weapon, in defence of the community/state against threats to its integrity, it now assumes the less ambiguous but more contentious guise of a weapon to be deployed in social and political struggle for symbolic mastery within society.

We should be clear about what is meant by political narratives. Canadian society has seen many grand stories that explain the world to individuals and situate them within the world – in Louis Althusser's terms, that interpellate individuals.[1] Some of these have been sweeping in scope, especially religions, belief systems that not only situate individuals in relation to the secular community but in relation to the universe and the meaning and destiny of life. These we may term metanarratives.

Political narratives are less comprehensive in intention, purporting to explain only one aspect of community, the organization and exercise of political power. They might be termed qualified metanarratives in the technical sense that citizens in democracies must be mobilized to vote and participate in ways that make the institutions operate relatively systematically. The political world must be simplified into collective choices, and these choices take on certain comprehensive qualities. They become, in effect, all-purpose explanations of political phenomena for people, most of whom are generally too busy with other matters to be immersed in politics. Unusually, in this instance, they are required, as nonspecialists, to exercise sovereign choices in the specialized political realm. People are not generally asked to make authoritative decisions by collective choice in, say, medical treatment. Hence there are no popular narratives regarding different health-care approaches to guide citizens: specialists are consulted who have their own bodies of knowledge, but this knowledge is not put into play as a competing popular explanation structuring collective choice by patients.[2] With regard to politics, matters are rather different, hence the need for comprehensive, all-purpose explanations widely accessible and persuasive to large numbers of people. These same narratives, moreover, play an important role for political practitioners as well, helping to organize their activities by describing and identifying friends and foes, and by offering standards, 'principles,' for judging their own and others' performance, along with criteria for designing public policy. Hence the requirement that political narratives make comprehensive sense of political matters.

Political narratives are not, however, metanarratives in the deeper sense that they explain the wider, non-political world, at least in anything more than cursory, ultimately unsatisfactory ways. Political narratives thus typically refer to or invoke true metanarratives as authority for their specifically political explanations. Religion, or religiously derived stances on moral issues, has often been a stand-in for the missing metaphysics of political narratives. Liberal and conservative political stories have often derived their vigour from religious values external to the political sphere – and indeed may strive for greater authenticity and weight by invoking non-political moral authority on their partisan behalf. In Canada, even the history of the social-democratic narrative is deeply implicated in a particular version of religious truth: the Social Gospel, and other political movements, such as the now defunct Social Credit or Reform in the 1990s, have also had close ties to Christian, most often evangelical, teachings. It is noteworthy that Canadians have generally looked askance at true political metanarratives that hold pretensions as secular religions. Communism and fascism were both viewed as 'totalitarian' ideologies better understood as external threats than as metanarratives that could sink deep roots in Canada itself.

I have made a point of the limited scope of Canadian political narratives because the relative externality of metaphysics and morality to the political sphere goes some distance towards explaining the apparently apolitical, and certainly non-partisan, nature of much censorship in earlier decades. When artistic or commercial expression was interfered with in the name of the protection of morals or public decency, this cause was rarely invoked as a specific part of a particular political narrative. Both liberalism and conservatism tended to accept the existence of an overarching Christian moral framework and the duty of the secular arm to protect a Christian society against offences to the public morals. Although liberals tended to emphasize, rhetorically at least, the liberties of the individual and the hard-fought establishment of rights and freedoms, including freedom of expression, it cannot be said that the political expression of liberalism in the form of successive Liberal governments showed any less zeal than less vocally liberal governments in enforcing state censorship over morals, especially sexuality. The infamous censorship exercised by the Customs Department, for instance, reached its moralistic apogee under Liberal governments in the late 1940s and early 1950s.

It is true that Christianity in Canada never spoke with one voice and that, in the nineteenth and even well into the twentieth century, differences between Catholic and Protestant often overshadowed even the cleavage between English- and French- speaking Canadians. The political narratives that guided Canadian politics were not entirely innocent of this division – the conservative or Tory narrative was seemingly most friendly to mainstream Protestantism; liberalism, somewhat oddly but for historical, if not to say opportunistic, reasons, seemed more welcoming to Catholicism; while social democracy traded on connections with the Methodist and United Church traditions and Social Credit/Reform with evangelical Protestantism. Yet there have been few occasions in the twentieth century when a particular God or particular church was mobilized as a political partisan.[3] But, if this meant that Canadian political life tended to avoid some of the excesses of self-advertising religiosity evident in American political narratives, it did not signify that religious values were absent from Canadian public life, merely that they were widely accepted as transcending political partisanship. In practice, this could mean a Canadian enthusiasm for censorship that easily rivalled its American neighbour, albeit on a more non-partisan basis.

Just as religion represented a sacred (if contested and sectarian) body of beliefs and values that stood above the partisan struggles of politics, so nationalism represented another set of powerful symbols and discursive signs that the more lowly political narratives might try to invoke and press into service on their behalf. Certainly the Tory narrative in English Canada once worked very hard at trying to associate the symbols of crown and empire, of all things British, with its own political project. In this endeavour, it had on its side history and the ethnic politics of the last century and the iconographic figure of Sir John A. Macdonald ('A British subject I was born, a British subject I shall die'). Though it could not match Toryism in the ostentatious proliferation of Union Jacks, liberalism had its own, more autonomous Canadian nationalism to invoke, as it did with increasing confidence through the twentieth century, as large-scale non-British immigration undermined the salience of British (Anglo-Saxon) symbols in an increasingly multicultural and multiethnic Canada.

Nationalism in Canada was always a double-edged sword, given the huge differences between English and French Canada, differences that provoked radically divergent and often conflictual responses to nationalist symbols. Prior to the Quiet Revolution in Quebec in the 1960s, when the divisiveness of previous efforts at nationalist symbolism was recognized and a new, anodyne bilingual, bicultural gospel of 'National Unity' was proclaimed, nationalism was invoked strongly in the leading political narratives of English Canada. But it was invoked in ways that were most often analogous to the political uses of religion: transcendent values that all Canadians could agree upon, even if their specific political application might be subject to partisan debate. Thus, the censorship exercised in two world wars, in the first instance by a Conservative followed by a Conservative-Liberal Union government, and in the second by a Liberal government that eschewed non-partisan alliances, was the subject of surprisingly little partisan criticism or complaint. And, as recently as 1970, when a Liberal government led by a prime minister with credentials as a civil libertarian instituted censorship of the press under the authority of the War Measures Act – invoked under the putative threat of an 'apprehended insurrection' – there was little criticism and no effective challenge from other mainstream political quarters, at that time at least.

Perhaps the most important point to be derived from this cursory study of the earlier era of political narratives is that partisan stories about politics tended to fall short of the gates of the 'community' and the 'nation.' The deepest values of the community, religious and national, were generally beyond the reach of political particularity. Being above mere politics, their defence against threats from within and without was generally non-controversial. Hence federal and provincial regimes of all partisan stripes practised censorship, and political oppositions rarely focused their criticism on this aspect of public policy. Criticism was generally left to dissenting elements of civil society and to opinion in the media that occasionally gave voice to such dissenters. The targets of censorship were perceived threats to the society and/or the state, the latter seen as a concrete embodiment of the society and its apparatus of authority (the 'crown'), especially when defence of Canada from external military threats, or from internal threats of subversion, were involved. Expressions that questioned, undermined, or attempted to bring into disrepute the institutions and values of the society/state were, in effect, outside the pale. Whether they were to be silenced through censorship might be a matter of partisan dispute, but usually about means, not ends. That is to say, prudential calculations might be made as to whether censorship in a specific instance might only draw more attention to the offending opinion or expression, or whether it might have the unintended effect of threatening less offensive opinions or expressions. But these political debates would generally fall short of questioning the legitimacy of censorship itself as an appropriate and normal exercise of sovereign authority.

The history of film censorship offers useful lessons. As the most popular new medium of mass culture early in the century, the cinema quickly inspired provincial censorship actions across Canada. For the first few decades, the objects of the censors' disapproval tended to fall into two broad categories: depictions of behaviour on screen that undermined public morals (usually but not always in terms of sexuality), and the expression of anti-patriotic themes that were believed to subvert the nation and/or the state. In short, the state was censoring the cinema with two threatened objects in mind: the 'society' as a moral community that regulated private behaviour under religious sanctions that transcended mere politics; and the state itself. The latter, however, was understood not as a particular partisan regime but as the stand-in for and the protector of the society. Thus, occasional efforts by provincial censors to cut newsreel references judged politically embarrassing to governing parties might themselves become the object of partisan controversy. The defence of the state against 'subversion' by foreign enemies or by domestic forces judged outside the pale of legitimacy was, on the other hand, relatively uncontroversial, as witnessed by the cutting of scenes judged too pro-German prior to or during the Second

World War. In the 1920s, even American patriotic symbols were cut from films, since these might be considered damaging to pro-British Canadian nationalist sentiments. Similarly, sporadic efforts were made by provincial film-censor boards to cut 'communistic' or pro-Soviet scenes from films in the Cold War era.[4] Instances of censorship of National Film Board (NFB) documentaries tended to follow political lines: a 'pro-Soviet' film during the war (when the USSR was an ally); a 'left-wing' interpretation of Balkan conflicts; and a film shot on location with the communist forces during the late stages of the Chinese civil war, before the NFB as an institution fell victim to an anti-communist purge.[5]

A similar pattern emerges with regard to the use of customs controls as a mechanism for print censorship. The power to ban books was vested in the minister of national revenue by a clause that allowed the prohibition of entry into Canada of 'books, printed matter, drawings, paintings, prints, photographs or any representations of any kind of a treasonable or seditious nature, or of any immoral or indecent character.' In the 1930s, although no official list of banned publications was made public, the 'vast majority' of books and magazines seized were reported to be classified as of 'indecent character' rather than as seditious. During the war, sedition rose sharply as preferred criteria. In the early Cold War era, anti-communism was a continuing factor, with books by Trotsky, Stalin, and even the British Labourite Ramsay MacDonald falling under suspicion, along with more numerous specimens of apolitical indecency like Norman Mailer. In 1954 a Customs official was quoted as dismissing a contemporary scare over 'subversive' literature in public libraries by pointing out that 'seditious books couldn't get to the libraries when they are already screened at the border.' As late as 1955, a controversy surrounded the seizure of copies of *The Atom Spy Hoax*, by a left-wing American journalist, which questioned the Canadian government's handling of the Gouzenko spy affair in 1945–6. Yet, with the waning of early Cold War hysteria by the 1960s, Customs' concern over sedition against the state declined dramatically as fears over threats to public morals once again rose.[6]

The political narratives of the past tended to take community for granted, as a consensual notion that stood outside partisan politics. By extension, the state, as the concrete embodiment of community, also stood to an extent beyond partisan politics as well. Hence the protection of the state, although not the defence of a particular party government, partook of the aura of 'community.' During two world wars, censorship was exercised extensively on all forms of communication, both public and private. Much of this was justified in terms of military security, but it typically went well beyond protecting information that might be of technical assistance to the enemy, to encompass censorship of material considered 'demoralizing' to the war effort or subversive of the values the state was defending.[7] Critics tended to become themselves the target of state suspicion, and criticism of censorship was itself censored.[8]

The various narratives, despite their apparently competitive nature, in effect collaborated with one another in a complementary defence of the existing order. For example, during the Cold War era, social democracy was both to a limited extent a target of 'Red scare' propaganda and, significantly, a key element in the anti-communist consensus that extended across the 'legitimate' political spectrum. Shared conceptions of community and of the limits of legitimate dissent circumscribed the area within which competing political narratives could contest the allegiance of Canadians, and within which censorship would be viewed as partisan misuse of office and unacceptable illiberality. When a Social Credit government in Alberta in 1937 introduced legislation openly designed to censor and control a press that was hostile to that government in the interest of disseminating information favourable to Social Credit, the lieutenant governor reserved consent and the federal government referred the proposed legislation to the Supreme Court of Canada, where it was declared *ultra vires*.[9] Indeed, the very existence of a competitive political system and a free press was proof of the superiority of the Canadian political system to the totalitarian enemies that threatened it from outside – and from subversive groups allied to these enemies who threatened it from within, whose views had to be contained by less than liberal means where necessary, including censorship. By contrast with the Alberta Press Act, the Quebec government in the same year passed the notorious 'Padlock Law' that made it an offence to 'propagate communism or bolshevism' by any means in a 'house' in the province (which could be then closed by the province), or to publish or distribute any literature propagating or 'tending to propagate' communism (undefined in the legislation). 'Communists' were beyond the pale: the law was not referred by the federal government to the Supreme Court, nor was federal disallowance contemplated. The Padlock Law remained on the books and was actively utilized by the Quebec government for twenty years before a private challenge to the highest court finally led to a ruling of unconstitutionality in 1957 (on grounds of jurisdiction).[10]

Another example of the power of exclusion: there was never really a 'free' debate in the late 1940s about Canadian participation in the Marshall Plan and in the North Atlantic Treaty Organization (NATO) because dissenting views were prevented from gaining widespread dissemination and dissenters were removed from positions that provided them public podiums, not least in the social-democratic party in Canadian legislatures and in the trade-union movement, where purges were voluntarily carried out against opponents of the Marshall Plan and NATO.[11]

The decay of grand narratives has been a widely noted phenomenon throughout Western societies. The relative decline of the power and influence of the great institutions of civil society, be it established churches, trade unions, or political parties, shadow or reflect the weakening of traditional intellectual and moral certitudes that has been described as a crisis of authority or a crisis of legitimacy. The state in democratic societies, with its inbuilt expectations of public accountability, has particularly suffered a loss of public esteem and a rise of distrust towards its role. While the private sector might appear to have benefited in the short term from this shrinkage of expectations around the public sector, corporations too have not escaped the generalized suspicion of large institutions and their increasingly shop-worn ideological justifications and rationales. Various explanations have been put forward, from the alienation of modern society to economic globalization and the penetration of global communications and global commercial culture into national and local particularities. There is no space here to consider these arguments, but, whatever the explanation, the impact on previously dominant political narratives has been devastating: the great 'isms' of Western political life have fallen into discredit and disarray. The effects have been most dramatic on the left, where greater weight had always been placed on ideology, but political narratives of the centre and right have not been immune to a decay that is no less ruinous for being less visible.

If there has been a generalized legitimacy crisis in Western democracies, Canada has found itself on the cutting edge, with the effects already more apparent there than in most other Western countries. Canada has been particularly exposed because the Canadian state has been under severe pressure, from both within and without, for an extended period of time. Global market forces have eroded the capacity of the Canadian national state to act effectively as an economic manager, while the rise of the Quebec sovereignty movement has brought the political legitimacy of the state and the constitution into question. The implicit social contract that underlay post-war relations among government, business, and labour has broken down with the assault on the welfare state and the triumph of an anti-statist, neo-liberal model of fiscal and monetary policy. While this has happened elsewhere, it has coincided in Canada with a persistent questioning of the fundamental political basis of the state, embodied in two Quebec referenda seeking secession in fifteen years, with another on the horizon. A populist and egalitarian attack on the older elite-driven structures of governance (in which the older political narratives were deeply implicated) has eroded the trust and deference that underpinned the political process. The legitimacy crisis in Canada is thus compounded, with the different elements playing against one another in unpredictable ways.

It is no surprise to note the rapid decay of the older political narratives. Liberalism, conservatism, and social democracy have all atrophied and/or undergone transformations that leave their narrative structures unrecognizable. Conservatism, once imbued with 'Tory' notions of tradition, organic hierarchy, deference to the crown, and continuity with Britain, has been transformed into an American-style doctrine of militant free enterprise that seeks the destruction of crown institutions as impediments to the triumph of market forces. Social democracy has failed to propose viable alternatives to the new neo-liberal discourse and is reduced to a rearguard defence of fraying social programs. Liberalism, once a narrative that intricately linked capitalism with social reform through cautious administrative redistribution and Keynesian stabilization, has abandoned the latter at all but the rhetorical level. None of the old narratives has been able to respond effectively to the challenges to national legitimacy.[12]

With the decline and crisis of these narratives, what has taken their place? The discourse of neo-liberalism seems triumphant throughout the Western world, but it is not really a replacement for a political narrative, being mainly an economic model that fails to address deep needs for political expression and communitarian identity. At best, it must be dressed up in borrowed clothes that lend a popular legitimacy that hardly arises from the technocratic discourse itself. In Canada, two new narrative streams have begun to reshape political space. One is the politics of identity, a phenomenon dialectically related to the crisis and decline of the national state. Identity politics is, in Manuel Castells's words, 'the process of construction of meaning on the basis of a cultural attribute, or related set of cultural attributes, that is/are given priority over other sources of meaning.'[13] For Canada, the critical point is that identities are subnational and refocus attention and loyalties away from the national state towards attributes that emphasize differences,[14] rather than universality, among the constituent elements of the political order. The most salient attributes of identity politics have been culture, language, ethnicity, gender, and sexual orientation – with the first two being especially powerful in Canada. The most spectacular case of identity politics is the Quebec sovereignty movement, which seeks fulfilment in secession from the Canadian political community altogether. Sovereignist parties have rewritten the scripts of Quebec/Canadian politics, first at the provincial level beginning in the 1970s and then at the federal level in the 1990s.

Although generally stopping short of secession, aboriginal demands for self-government and recognition as a 'third order' of government (after the federal and provincial levels) are founded firmly on the idea of cultural self-determination. Gender and race/ethnicity have also come to play leading roles in defining the political agenda. The constitutional politics that has achieved such prominence in the past two decades (itself an indication of drastically changing parameters of political space) has focused not only on questions of accommodation/separation of Quebec but on aboriginal claims and on equity and recognition demands around gender, ethnicity, and culture: adversarial litigation around the equality sections of the Charter of Rights has paralleled debates over the constitutional extension of these rights. First bilingualism and then multiculturalism and (multiethnic) immigration have generated deep and often divisive political controversy.

The second new political narrative generated by the contemporary crisis   has been what I call the 'new populism.' While some have spoken of a neo-conservative discourse that emerged in the 1980s, combining so-called moral majoritarianism, the conservatism of the Christian Right, and 'family values' with anti-statism and economic laissez-faire, this American-style description misses much of the Canadian reality. Here, the impact of the Quebec sovereignty movement on the rest of the country, through two Quebec referenda and three rounds of attempted constitutional reform within a decade and a half, cannot be discounted. English-Canadian impatience with 'special treatment' of Quebec and demands for recognition of the equality of the provinces have developed in tandem with a strong populist backlash against the elite-accommodation model of federalism that had previously dominated. These sentiments have combined with a reaction to the liberal welfare state, with its mushrooming deficits, rising tax burden, and redistributionist politics, especially since it appeared to favour 'special treatment for special interests.' The new populism integrates neo-liberal economic policies with anti-welfare-state social conservatism (the market will provide a 'fairer' system of redistribution than the politically biased welfare state); it also seeks to democratize the political system to allow the majority to take control back from the minorities and special interests. This new political narrative has made some inroads across the political spectrum, but it has found its most focused image in the Reform Party, which in a short period of time has displaced the older conservative narrative and its increasingly incoherent political expression in the Conservative party.

The new populism is indeed new, even though it incorporates older elements in its discourse. Above all, it is in a dialectical relationship with identity politics, being in some measure a reaction to gains (modest though they may be) made by groups seeking recognition and benefits via the liberal welfare state. Similarly, identity politics sharpens group consciousness and feeds politicization as these gains (seen as rights and entitlements) are rolled back in the downsizing of the state. Just as the older, now eclipsed, narratives played together systematically, so too identity politics and the new populism operate together in an antagonistic/complementary way, competing with one another yet at the same time drawing both energy and self-definition from the very existence and threat of their antagonist. This process was highlighted dramatically in the 1997 federal election when the Reform Party targeted 'Quebec politicians' as the enemies of national unity, while the Bloc Québécois pointed to Reform's anti-Québec stance to rally Québecers back to the sovereignist cause.

There is one dramatic difference between the old and new dialectic of political narratives, with serious consequences for the role of censorship in Canadian society. The old narrative system presupposed, as I have suggested, a consensual notion of community that transcended politics. The state had a double identity, both as the government, which was under partisan control, and as the embodiment of community, which was beyond partisanship. The new narrative system tends to weaken consensual identification with the community, because it is the very boundaries of the community itself, the terms of citizenship, that are the subject of political controversy. The state loses yet more obviously: generalized distrust of the state comes from all sides. The populists see the state as a blockage to private-sector economic growth and as the mechanism for redistributing resources away from the taxpaying majority and into the hands of the special interests. Identity-politics advocates, on the other hand, increasingly see the state as attacking their rights and their social programs as a direct result of neo-liberal restructuring and white-male backlash against groups seeking equity.

The community and especially the state are now much more politically contested concepts than at any time in the past. I argued earlier that censorship was exercised within the framework of a widespread, although never complete, acceptance of the uncontested nature of these concepts. Thus, censorship in defence of public morals and censorship in defence of the state both presupposed and benefited from a popular and elite consensus that such interference in freedom of expression was not normally motivated by partisan considerations seeking to empower one political narrative over another. This is no longer the case. In an altered political landscape, censorship is no longer rationalized in apolitical terms, but rather in specific and pointed political terms. Although it could well be argued that, in the past, the apolitical aura surrounding censorship was a sham that concealed eminently political exclusions from the pale of legitimacy, today there is little sham, little concealment, little mystification. Instead, partisans of different political narratives demand censorship for the avowed purpose of publicly delegitimizing their opponents. 'Culture' is a contested terrain, intimately and intricately bound up with the borders of community; the state is more and more seen, not as an entity above the partisan fray, but as an armoury to be raided for weapons (one of which is censorship) in the struggle for power and status among contending groups in society.

The first casualty of the new order is the capacity of the state to defend itself through censorship. The last time the Canadian state made any concerted effort to utilize censorship against alleged threats of subversion or treason was in October 1970, during the Front de libération du Québec hostage crisis. Under the authority of the War Measures Act, newspapers and radio and television stations were told what they could not report about the crisis. Although this policy received surprisingly little criticism at the time, thus conforming to earlier wartime censorship experience, there was later a relatively strong reaction to what was seen as an excess of state authoritarianism without substantive justification, even by many who had supported the government during the crisis. The War Measures Act was later repealed by a successor government and replaced by an Emergencies Act that makes no mention of censorship powers – unlike the War Measures Act, which explicitly granted powers over 'censorship and the control and suppression of publications, writings, maps, plans, photographs, communications and means of communication'[15] – and even states explicitly that 'fundamental rights' are not to be overridden even in a national emergency.[16] During the Gulf War, there was no effort to censor news. It would seem that, in the current age of demands for transparency and accountability of governments to taxpayers, overt censorship by the state against perceived threats to its integrity will likely be met by deep suspicion. The Access to Information Act to a degree shifts the onus towards citizens' right to government information. As the Somalia affair shows, government departments may well play fast and loose with the letter of this legislation; cynical information management to protect the public image of government is the contemporary defence mechanism of choice. But the days of direct intervention in the civil society to protect the state through overt censorship now appear numbered.

This hardly means, however, that censorship is in decline, merely that it has shifted away from the state as initiator to the state as facilitator of censorship demands posed by groups in civil society. This phenomenon was first manifested with the demands for legislation censoring or suppressing 'hate propaganda' targeted against particular religious and ethnic groups. Such demands, especially centring around revivals of anti-Semitism in the wake of the Holocaust, were first heard in the early 1950s and rose in volume in the 1960s. But it was only in 1970 that the first anti-hate criminal laws were enacted in Canada. Since then, various Criminal Code amendments have been enacted to control the advocacy or promotion of genocide or the wilful promotion of hatred against an 'identifiable group' ('distinguishable by colour, race, religion or ethnic origin'). In addition, another section of the Criminal Code that prohibits wilful spreading of false news has been activated against those promoting Holocaust denial.[17] Moreover, a legal framework has also grown up to encourage civil tort action against those defaming identifiable groups. The well-known cases of Ernst Zundel, the neo-Nazi Toronto publisher, Jim Keegstra, the Alberta schoolteacher, and Malcolm Ross, a teacher in New Brunswick, have all involved the teaching or spreading of Holocaust denial and anti-Semitic incitement.

Anti-Semitism has by no means been the only tripwire. Other racial, religious, and cultural groups have launched censorship campaigns, some successful, many unsuccessful, against public communications perceived to be threatening or demeaning. Examples include the failed campaign by some Canadian Muslims to ban Salman Rushdie's *Satanic Verses*, a campaign that tried to enlist the state via its customs controls and also to encourage/intimidate private booksellers from stocking the title (the latter tactic achieved some limited and localized success but failed overall); the protest by black activists against the Royal Ontario Museum's *Heart of Africa* exhibit which did not bring about the closure of the show but did succeed in driving the curator out of a teaching career and eventually out of Canada altogether; and the campaign against the revival of the musical *Showboat*.

In the changed context of censorship, it is local municipal governments or even police forces that are more likely to take censorship initiatives than the national or provincial states. Quasi-governmental public-sector bodies may find themselves even more vulnerable to the pressures of particular groups to intervene. Universities and colleges have initiated speech codes regulating forms of expression impinging on group identities. In Ontario, the former New Democratic Party government introduced so-called 'Zero Tolerance' guidelines to regulate speech at Ontario colleges and universities that extended even into private conversations overheard by a third party and relayed at second hand. Resistance from universities on the grounds of jurisdictional autonomy kept these regulations off university campuses, but they remain applicable to community colleges. It might be noted that the speech codes voluntarily enacted by universities usually carry disciplinary action for violations. Serious issues have been raised about academic freedom in this context of group-sponsored censorship and enforced so-called 'political correctness.'[18]

Anti-pornography campaigns by feminists, launched on a variety of fronts, have met with some successes, including a crucial court decision (*Butler*) which will be examined shortly. These campaigns have been significantly different from the censorship of morally offensive material in the past. Pornography is no longer considered as offending a consensual moral code, understood and tacitly agreed upon by most members of the community. To anti-pornography feminists, what is offensive about pornography is its demeaning portrayal of women (and children) as objectified targets of male aggression. The struggle to control pornography is seen as part of a more broadly based attack on patriarchal structures of domination and thus part of a confrontation with rather than a defence of existing moral codes.[19]

The apparent dovetailing of anti-pornography feminism with moral conservative 'family values' campaigns on the political right has occasioned much discussion and debate.[20] Lise Gotell has argued that underlying 'panics' over pornography, both in the past and in the present, is a desire for moral regulation of what is seen as 'out of control' sexual behaviour. 'Anti-pornography feminist discourse, the moral-conservative discourse of the New Right, and the increased political support for anti-pornography regulation,' she writes, 'all share the same tendency towards reactionary foundationalism. Reactionary foundationalism is at heart a form of discursive strategy in which "Truth" trumps politics and one with a broad appeal in these times of post-modern anxiety.'[21]

While it is important to stress underlying continuities, discontinuities are also significant. New Right moral conservatism couches its arguments in favour of censorship rather differently than in the past. Instead of simply defending a consensual moral community from immorality and corruption, today's populist conservatives are just as apt to invoke metaphors of struggles for cultural and political hegemony in an admittedly divided community. Censorship campaigns against expressions of gay, lesbian, and bisexual sexualities, for instance, now must contend with the new reality that these 'deviant' forms of behaviour are no longer illegal, that indeed, people of non-heterosexual orientation may even be relatively aggressive equity-seekers empowered by Charter rights and by a public climate warmer and more encouraging than ever before (even capitalism has discovered the profits to be gained by cultivating the 'gay market'). 'Family values' anti-gay campaigns are thus guided now by a more explicit model of social conflict; rather than the society versus anti-social deviants, it is more a question of 'us' (white, heterosexual, Christian middle-class taxpayers) reasserting 'our' privileged place in the hierarchy of social merit. Indeed, the desperation that drives such campaigns often seems fuelled by a sense of resentment over loss of status and an anger that 'they' are apparently winning and that 'their' gains must be rolled back before it is too late. Moreover, these same advocates of censoring expressions of gay and lesbian sexuality may themselves be subject to counter-campaigns of censorship for depicting gays and lesbians in hateful or demeaning ways.

In such a context of social/cultural conflict, governments find it difficult to steer a legislative course on censorship that can draw on anything like a social consensus. This is well illustrated in the cases of bills C-114 and C-54 in 1986–7, failed attempts at legislative definition and regulation of obscenity. Until the 1980s, reflecting the consensual basis described above, pornography law had effectively been made by the executive and judicial branches. In the changed circumstances of the 1980s, the issue had become deeply politicized and the Conservative government of Brian Mulroney attempted to take political advantage of this. A government with a neo-conservative agenda making electoral gestures towards issues like law and order and zero tolerance of drug abuse appeared to see legislated censorship of pornography as a promising policy gambit. Not only did censorship appeal to the family values moral-conservative constituency, an important presence in the government's parliamentary caucus, but the emergence of anti-pornography feminism offered the opportunity of gaining legitimacy from a quite different direction. At the same time, a new social-scientific discourse was emerging that purported to offer empirical evidence of the linkage between consumption of pornography and acts of sexual violence, thus adding the support of politically neutral 'science' to forces of both right and left behind a new censorship initiative. The government first appointed a committee (the Fraser committee) to look into the question, which argued in its 1985 report that while 'very reluctantly' it had to concede that it could not causally link pornography with 'violent crime, sexual abuse of children, or in the disintegration of communities and societies,'[22] it nonetheless could find other compelling grounds, especially 'equality,' for the regulation of pornography:

[Our] emphasis on equality will ... require a shift from the traditional focus on immorality as a basis of criminal prohibitions ... [to] a theory that views pornography as an assault on human rights ... Our recommendations are to create offences not on concepts of sexual immorality but rather on the offences to equality, dignity, and physical integrity which we believe are involved in pornography ... In the same way that freedom of expression may not extend to statements wilfully promoting hatred, or be outbalanced by the need to protect the equality rights of others, so the same conclusions can be reached in the case of certain forms of pornographic representation ... In our opinion the most hateful forms of pornography are subversive of policies and values favouring equality.[23]

The Fraser committee proposed to decriminalize depictions of non-violent sexual activity, reflecting a lessened concern about moral corruption, while at the same time stepping up criminal sanctions against child pornography and depictions or descriptions of violent abusive sexual activity. In short, the committee moved towards the new anti-pornography feminist discourse while failing to endorse strongly either New Right arguments or the new social-scientific discourse.

When the Conservative government brought down its first legislative attempt (Bill C-114) a year later, it abandoned most of the Fraser committee's recommendations in a sharp shift to the right. All types of pornography, including depiction of all forms of sexual activity, violent or consensual, mainstream or deviant, were to be criminalized. Evangelical conservatives applauded, as did some women's groups. But civil-libertarian protests were heated, and these groups were joined by a number of leading feminist organizations. Without a consensus, and with opposition as passionate as support, the bill died on the government's order paper. The following year another bill (C-54) was introduced, with a few changes from its predecessor, including an attempt to introduce a distinction between erotica and pornography. This version won back support from some feminist groups, but opposition remained strong and by the end of the year the government's drive to push through C-54 had declined to the point where this version, too, died. With this, the Conservatives lost all enthusiasm and made no more legislative attempts at moral regulation of the society through censorship in their second term, from 1988 to 1993. As two close analysts of this debate, Robert Campbell and Leslie Pal, conclude:

The hard reality was that Canadians were, and are, fundamentally divided on this issue. Moral and sexual issues divide people on ideological, religious and cultural grounds. The Conservative government proposed to deal with pornography in a way that coherently reflected a particular moral approach. The existing legal regime with regard to pornography was perhaps sloppy, unpredictable, uncertain, and incoherent. In a sense, this reflected the fundamental divisions in Canadian society. In its attempt to impose order on the Criminal Code, the Conservative government gave concrete expression to these social and ideological divisions and opened itself up to widespread criticism and ridicule ... Principles were articulated equally effectively by well-organised and active interest groups: civil libertarians, librarians, artists, gays, and socialist feminists on the one side and church groups, police and customs officials, and radical feminists on the other. Most governments simply lack the authority to act in a situation like this, or are unwilling to pay the political costs that would inevitably result from pursuing one position over another.[24]

With the failure of legislation, attention turned once again to the executive and judicial branches. Customs censorship continued in an apparently capricious and arbitrary manner, as with the well-publicized case of the Little Sister's lesbian bookshop, constantly harassed by Customs seizures of books, a case that finally led to a 1996 court decision that ruled Customs action in this case was contrary to the Charter of Rights (but did not rule that Customs censorship of books is itself unconstitutional). Most important of all was a land-mark decision by the Supreme Court of Canada (*R. v. Butler*, 1992) that ruled that the obscenity section of the Criminal Code was justified under section 1 of the Charter as a 'reasonable limit.' *Butler* reflected arguments put before the court by LEAF (Women's Legal Education and Action Fund) and was hailed by American anti-pornography feminist Catharine MacKinnon. Yet, while reflect-ing feminist arguments about harm to women and children, *Butler* appears to have reinforced censorship of unconventional or alternative sexualities even as it has contributed to liberalization of 'straight' or mainstream sexuality; indeed, in the wake of *Butler*, it would appear that the main targets of censorship drives have been gay and lesbian materials.[25]

Butler cannot be seen as a definitive decision in that controversy and conflict will certainly continue. It could hardly be otherwise when censorship so obvi-ously targets particular groups in a society where group identity, its expression and recognition, is central to political meaning. The legislative branch having failed to act, the executive and judicial branches will continue to offer contested terrain over which censorship battles will rage, without the kind of consensus once offered by a notion of shared community with the state as its embodiment. Of course, that notion of consensus was always misleading, masking exclusions and marginalizations. At least it can be said that the contemporary debate takes fewer hostages to hypocrisy, although the resulting strains on the body politic are intense.

Censorship, like the chameleon, has undergone a significant change in appearance with the change in its context. It is still the same beast, despite appearances. Legitimacy and illegitimacy are still the objects: censorship, by authoritatively drawing the boundary between voice and silence, effectively draws the boundary between the legitimate and the illegitimate. In liberal-democratic societies, the process of authoritative silencing is fraught with the gravest of difficulties, at both the practical and theoretical levels. Paradoxically, the very insecurities that are endemic to a 'free' society reinforce and impart urgency to the demands that a 'line must be drawn.' With the decline in the con-sensus over community, and the decline of the state as an autonomous actor on behalf of the community, the political decisions over drawing the line have shifted to a more open struggle within civil society. The state as facilitator in censorship battles located within the society finds itself in a less comfortable, more politicized role than when it acted on behalf of what was taken for a con-sensus in the society. Censorship is still, however, an essential attribute of sov-ereignty. In liberal-democratic societies like Canada, the contemporary legitimacy crisis simply makes the exercise of censorship more controversial than ever before. The chameleon remains.

NOTES

1 Louis Althusser, *Lenin and Philosophy and Other Essays* (London: New Left Books 1971), 162–3.

2 I do not wish to imply that there are no medical narratives, or medical 'models,' that play important parts in structuring acceptable medical practice and health-care systems, merely that these do not work in the same populist way as political narratives because they do not need to. Instead, they work within a more specialized terrain of the production and definition of scientific knowledge and discourses concerning technological and pharmacological diffusion. The 'professionalisation' of medicine was accomplished precisely to insulate the standards of the 'profession' from the political sphere as much as possible.

3 Perhaps the nearest example would be Premier Maurice Duplessis's Union Nationale regime in Quebec in the 1930s to the 1950s, but here the close connection between church and party might better be understood in the context of Quebec nationalism in the era prior to the Quiet Revolution and the secularization of that nationalism. The example of the Social Credit premiers of Alberta, 'Bible Bill' Aberhart and the Reverend Ernest Manning, might seem to offer an English-Canadian variant of religion infusing a political narrative, but it is interesting to note that on the matter of provincial film censorship, in which Social Credit played an active role, the actual record of the Aberhart and Manning governments differed little from that of the Saskatchewan film-censor board under social-democratic political auspices from 1944 to 1964. The defence of Christian public morals was in effect a cause that stood above specific political narratives, projects, or parties.

4 Malcolm Dean, *Censored: Only in Canada: The History of Film Censorship – the Scandal off the Screen* (Toronto: Virgo Press 1981), is the source for provincial film censorship.

5 Gary Evans, *John Grierson and the National Film Board: The Politics of Wartime Propaganda* (Toronto: University of Toronto Press 1984), and *In the National Interest: A Chronicle of the National Film Board of Canada from 1949 to 1989* (Toronto: University of Toronto Press 1991); Reg Whitaker and Gary Marcuse, *Cold War Canada: The Making of a National Insecurity State, 1945–1957* (Toronto: University of Toronto Press 1994), 227–60.

6 Peter Birdsall and Delores Broten, *Mind War: Book Censorship in English Canada* (Victoria: CANLIT 1978), 3–14.

7 On censorship in the First World War, see Jeffrey Keshen, *Propaganda and Censorship during Canada's Great War* (Edmonton: University of Alberta Press 1996). On the period of the Second World War, see Pierre-André Comeau, Claude Beauregard, and Edwidge Munn, *La démocratie en veilleuse: rapport sure le censure, récit de l'organisation, des activités et de la démobilisation de la censure pendant le*

guerre de 1939–1945 (Montréal: Québec/Amérique 1995); Gillis Purcell, *Wartime Press Censorship in Canada* (MA thesis, University of Toronto 1946).

8 Reg Whitaker, 'Official Repression of Communism during World War II,' *Labour/ le Travail* 17 (spring 1986), 139–41, 160–2; Ramsay Cook, 'Canadian Freedom in Wartime' (MA thesis, Queen's University 1955), and 'Canadian Freedom in Wartime,' in W.H. Heick and Roger Graham, eds., *His Own Man: Essays in Honour of A.R.M. Lower* (Montreal: McGill-Queen's University Press 1974), 37–53.

9 G. Stuart Adam, 'The Sovereignty of the Publicity System: the Case of the Alberta Press Act,' in Adam, ed., *Journalism, Communication and the Law* (Scarborough: Prentice-Hall Canada 1976), 154–72.

10 Lucie Lorin, 'Communisme et liberté d'expression au Québec: la "Loi du Cadenas" 1937–1957,' in Robert Comeau and Bernard Dionne, *Le Droit de se taire: histoire des communistes au Québec de la première mondiale à la révolution tranquille* (Outremont, Que.: VLB 1989), 112–33. Of course, the contrasting treatment of the Alberta and Quebec acts by the federal government cannot be separated from power politics: Quebec was much more important to Ottawa in terms of votes than Alberta.

11 See Whitaker and Marcuse, *Cold War Canada,* 266–72, 310–63 on the role of 'Cold War social democracy' and the trade-union movement in Canadian politics during this era.

12 I have sketched out this crisis of political narratives at greater length in 'Canadian Politics at the End of the Millennium: Old Dreams, New Nightmares,' in David Taras and Beverly Rasporich, eds., *A Passion for Identity: An Introduction to Canadian Studies* (Toronto: Nelson 1997), 119–37.

13 Manuel Castells, *The Information Age: Economy, Society and Culture*, vol. 2: *The Power of Identity* (Oxford, U.K.: Blackwell 1997), 6.

14 By speaking of difference in opposition to universality, I am not supporting the controversial insistence of some liberal analysts that there is an implicit *intention* to divide in identity politics. Indeed, the politics of difference may often reflect a desire for equity, and thus a fuller sharing in the wider community, rather than for separatism, but it is premised upon the *recognition of difference*. See Charles Taylor, *Multiculturalism and the Politics of Recognition* (Princeton: Princeton University Press 1992).

15 RSC 1970, c. W-2, s. 3 (10 (a).

16 35-36-37 Elizabeth II, c. 29. The preamble states that 'the Governor in Council, in taking such special temporary measures, would be subject to the Canadian Charter of Rights and Freedoms and the Canadian Bill of Rights and must have regard to the International Covenant on Civil and Political Rights, particularly with respect to those fundamental rights that are not to be limited or abridged even in a national emergency.'

17 Edwin W. Webking, *Freedom of Expression: Hate Literature* (Calgary: Alberta Civil Liberties Research Centre 1995), especially 1–13.

18 See John Fekete, *Moral Panic: Biopolitics Rising* (Montreal: Robert Davies Publishing 1994); Peter C. Emberley, *Zero Tolerance: Hot Button Politics in Canada's Universities* (Toronto: Penguin 1996).

19 For a measured explication of feminist anti-pornography, see Dany Lacombe, *Blue Politics: Pornography and the Law* (Toronto: University of Toronto Press 1994), and her earlier *Ideology and Public Policy: The case against Pornography* (Toronto: Garamond Press 1988). The same arguments are viewed through a less sympathetic lens in Brenda Cossman, Shannon Bell, Lise Gotell, and Becki L. Ross, *Bad Attitude/s on Trial: Pornography, Feminism, and the Butler Decision* (Toronto: University of Toronto Press 1997).

20 Varda Burstyn, ed., *Women against Censorship* (Vancouver: Douglas and McIntyre 1985).

21 'Shaping *Butler:* The New Politics of Anti-pornography,' in Cossman et al., *Bad Attitude/s*, 100. See also the introduction to the same volume by Brenda Cossman and Shannon Bell, 3–47.

22 Special Committee on Pornography and Prostitution, *Report* (Ottawa: Government of Canada 1985), 49 (hereinafter referred to as the Fraser committee).

23 Fraser committee, 267.

24 'Sexual Politics: Pornography Policy in Canada,' in Robert A. Campbell and Leslie A. Pal, *The Real Worlds of Canadian Politics: Cases in Process and Policy* (Peterborough, Ont.: Broadview Press 1989), 151.

25 This is the argument of Cossman et al., *Bad Attitude/s*.

3

Pluralism and Hate: Freedom, Censorship, and the Canadian Identity

SAMUEL V. LaSELVA

The traditional arguments against censorship and for free expression are well known.[1] Frederick Schauer's *Free Speech: A Philosophical Inquiry* considers five key arguments: (1) the argument from truth; (2) the argument from democracy; (3) free speech and the good life; (4) individuality and free speech; and (5) the inutility of suppression.[2] The first and fifth arguments received early and classic expression in Milton's *Areopagitica* and Locke's *A Letter Concerning Toleration*. For Milton and Locke, censorship not only was an impediment to the discovery of truth, but its very practice was incoherent since (as Locke held) coercion cannot produce sincere belief.[3] The third and fourth arguments were famously discussed in *On Liberty*, where John Stuart Mill argued that censorship denies individual autonomy and undermines social progress. The second argument – which connects free expression with democratic government and regards censorship as an infringement of the rights of citizenship – is one of the key contributions of American political theory and has been vigorously defended in *Free Speech and Its Relation to Self-Government* by Alexander Meiklejohn.[4] Taken together, these five arguments appear to exhaust the subject of censorship by demonstrating its inutility and by justifying a comprehensive principle of free-expression based on such values as truth, democracy, individuality, and social progress.

But the issue of censorship is not disposed of so easily. There exists almost universal agreement that the right to free expression can be limited if its exercise causes serious harm to others. By appealing to this consideration, radical feminists argue for censorship without denying the importance of free expression. Pornography, they insist, should not be conflated with erotica: erotica expresses mutuality and respect; pornography demeans and harms women. If this is so, then pornography falls outside the protection of the free-expression principle and comes within the purview of the censor. In a famous decision,

Regina v. *Butler*, the Supreme Court of Canada accepted the substance, if not the form, of the radical feminist argument. The court held that material that exploited sex in a degrading or dehumanizing manner fails the community-standards test, not because it offends against morals, but because it is perceived by public opinion to be harmful to society, particularly to women.[5] Moreover, the Court went on to say that the message of obscenity is analogous to hate propaganda.[6] By so doing, the court linked the *Butler* case with its earlier *Keegstra* decision, in which it held that the criminalization of hate propaganda was a valid restriction of free expression in a free and democratic society. In both decisions, the court acknowledged the importance of free expression but justified censorship.

Keegstra and *Butler* are controversial decisions. To many Canadians, they appear well intentioned but ultimately futile because legal sanctions are an inadequate method for solving deep-rooted social problems such as hate propaganda and pornography. To many American commentators, these Canadian decisions seem altogether wrongheaded. The United States Supreme Court has refused to restrict hate speech, in part because of its belief that in an open society 'debate on public issues should be uninhibited, robust, and wide-open.'[7] If American experience is taken to be the last word on free expression, the Canadian hate-speech decisions are not only futile; they are also incompatible with the existence of a free and democratic society. However, *Keegstra* and *Butler* raise questions that cannot be settled by appealing to the lessons of American constitutional law. Canada is different from the United States, partly because its pluralism is unlike the American variety. Canadian pluralism, I shall suggest, not only requires a distinctive understanding of free expression but also reopens the issue of censorship.

A False Start: American Doctrine in the Supreme Court of Canada

Canadians are not always fully aware of the differences between their own society and the American model. Such a lack of awareness sometimes results from the fact that Canadians and Americans subscribe to a number of important general values such as democracy, federalism, and individual rights. Moreover, the American achievement in some areas of constitutional government is so impressive that Canadians cannot ignore it, and are sometimes hesitant to depart from it. Free expression is one such area. In *Keegstra*, a majority of the judges did depart from the American model, but only after attempting to show that American case law could be used to support the restriction of hate speech. The dissenting judges, in an opinion written by Justice Beverley McLachlin, responded by insisting that the majority had misunderstood American doctrine, and they concluded that 'if the guarantee of free expression is to be meaningful, it must protect expression which challenges even the very basic conceptions of our society.'[8] The dispute about American case law is significant, because it demonstrates the pervasive influence of the American model and the corresponding failure of Canadian judges to come to terms with American exceptionalism.

At the centre of the dispute was the United States Supreme Court decision of *Beauharnais* v. *Illinois*, decided in 1952. In that case, a sharply divided court upheld the constitutionality of a state law that, among other things, forbade, 'any person ... to publish, present, or exhibit in any public place ... any lithograph, moving picture, play, drama or sketch which ... exposes the citizens of any race, colour, creed or religion to contempt, derision, or obloquy.'[9] The majority decision, written by Justice Felix Frankfurter, sided with the advocates of the group-libel legislation. Frankfurter held that group libel fell outside the protection of the First Amendment and that the legislature could take reasonable measures to mitigate racial conflict. In disposing of the case, he drew in part on the 1942 decision of *Chaplinksy* v. *New Hampshire*, in which the Supreme Court put forward a two-level speech theory and decided that certain 'fighting words' were not protected by the First Amendment. If, as *Chaplinsky* held, there are words 'which by the very utterance inflict injury or tend to incite an immediate breach of the peace,' and if such words are not protected by the constitution, then it is reasonable to conclude, as did Frankfurter in *Beauharnais*, that group defamation or hate speech is not protected.[10]

For the judges of the Supreme Court of Canada, the significance of *Beauharnais* turned not on its content so much as on whether it was still valid law in the United States. Writing for the majority, Chief Justice Brian Dickson noted that American constitutional law was essential for the disposition of *Keegstra*, in part because those who attacked the validity of Canadian hate-propaganda legislation drew heavily on First Amendment jurisprudence. Moreover, he agreed that 'the practical and theoretical experience of the USA is immense, and should not be overlooked by Canadian courts.' But, although he found American free-speech jurisprudence useful, he was dubious as to its applicability to hate propaganda in Canada. It is at this point that his argument becomes difficult to follow and, according to his critics, both confused and erroneous. For, after noting (plausibly) that 'our Charter is different' from the United States Bill of Rights, he went on to add (implausibly) that it is 'not entirely clear that *Beauharnais* must conflict with existing First Amendment doctrine.'[11]

The response to Chief Justice Dickson's understanding of American First Amendment jurisprudence has been anything but favourable. Not only was his interpretation repudiated by a number of Canadian Supreme Court judges, but academic commentary borders on derision. In reply to Dickson, one constitutional lawyer flatly stated that '*Beauharnais* is no longer good American law.'[12] To be sure, the United States Supreme Court has never explicitly overruled *Beauharnais*, but the tenor of modern First Amendment jurisprudence is strongly against it. The 1978 case of *Collin* v. *Smith*, decided by the Seventh Circuit Court of Appeals, is also relevant. The case concerned a proposed march by a Nazi group in a predominantly Jewish village that contained a significant number of Holocaust survivors. The citizens opposed to the march invoked *Beauharnais*, but the Court of Appeals decided against them and the Supreme Court allowed the decision to stand. Though hate speech was repugnant to Americans, the First Amendment protected even such speech. 'If these civil rights are to remain vital for all,' the Court of Appeals held, 'they must protect not only those society deems acceptable, but also those whose ideas it quite justifiably rejects and despises.'[13] The implication for Canada, according to the critics, is not merely that Chief Justice Dickson misunderstood First Amendment jurisprudence, but also that the decision in *Keegstra* to uphold hate-speech legislation is inconsistent with a genuine commitment to free expression.

The criticism can be stated more bluntly: *Keegstra* significantly erodes free expression because it conflicts with First Amendment jurisprudence. But, when the criticism is so stated, it becomes problematic. A key difficulty is that it reifies and universalizes First Amendment jurisprudence. The point is not simply that Canada is different from the United States and possesses a distinctive constitutional culture; Chief Justice Dickson recognized as much, even if many of the critics of *Keegstra* have not. Rather, the focus needs to be shifted to the universalistic claims of those who appeal to the lessons of American constitutional experience. Far from providing eternal truths, modern First Amendment jurisprudence is highly particularistic. Not only does it presuppose a distinctive moral vision that is difficult to universalize, but it has been responsive to political circumstances that are not easily generalized.

Such a conclusion challenges the standard view of free speech in the United States. According to it, modern First Amendment jurisprudence presupposes no moral vision at all but simply enables individuals (and, ultimately, the nation as a whole) to make informed choices between competing goods. In political philosophy, the most sophisticated defence of this position is John Rawls's *A Theory of Justice*. According to Rawls, democratic government should be neutral between conceptions of the good so that individuals can advocate and choose the plan of life best suited to them. Only in this way does government respect individual choice and human dignity.[14] What is significant about Rawls's theory, however, is that its crucial claims about neutrality are difficult to sustain. In an influential critique Michael Sandel has arrived at just such a conclusion. After noting the parallels between Rawls's theory and First Amendment jurisprudence, he suggests that the 'case for protecting speech by bracketing moral judgements is not neutral at all, but presupposes a controversial theory of personhood and speech.' A theory that protects hate speech or violent pornography, he says, fails to respect persons as members of particular communities and does not acknowledge the injury that speech can inflict independent of the physical harm it may cause. Moreover, protecting speech by insisting that local communities bracket moral judgment, he adds, carries costs for self-government by preventing political communities from acting democratically to realize the good of respect for persons as 'situated selves.' The procedural republic envisioned by modern First Amendment jurisprudence, he concludes, 'tolerates speech more by respecting it less, by failing to take seriously its power to inflict injury on its own.'[15]

Sandel's basic point is that modern First Amendment jurisprudence presupposes the moral and political philosophy of the procedural republic, which exalts individual autonomy at the expense of community membership and discounts the personal and social harms that flow from the exercise of detached freedoms. Sandel's argument highlights the moral particularities of First Amendment jurisprudence, yet it does so in a way that is too dismissive of American constitutional experience. Rather than confining himself to the position that the procedural republic is logically incoherent and morally self-destructive, Sandel makes clear that his larger purpose is to urge Americans to recover the civic virtues of the early republic. The difficulty with his argument is not simply that its prescriptions for change may be unrealistic, in that the civic virtues of the early republic were part of a form of life that is no longer available to Americans. An even more serious difficulty is that he regards modern constitutional developments as pathological and seems unable to recognize that, whatever their shortcomings, they are responsive to the conditions of American social and political life.

Modern First Amendment jurisprudence is particularistic but not pathological. In a study of hate speech in the United States, Samuel Walker has arrived at just such a conclusion. Like Sandel, Walker acknowledges that United States constitutional law, as interpreted by the courts, permits fewer restrictions on speech now than it did at the end of the eighteenth century or even after the Second World War. With *Chaplinsky* and *Beauharnais* as solid precedents, the law on hate speech might have developed differently and the Nazis group might have been denied the right to march in Skokie. But between *Beauharnais* and Skokie, there occurred the civil rights movement, which powerfully shaped First Amendment jurisprudence and provided important lessons for minorities and disadvantaged groups. 'The "lessons" of the civil rights movement,' Walker writes, 'were that the interests of racial minorities and powerless groups were best protected through the broadest, most content-neutral protection of speech.'[16] According to a report by Human Rights Watch, which Walker cites, 'the United States stands virtually alone in having no valid statutes penalising expression that is offensive or insulting on such grounds as race, religion, or ethnicity.' On the issue of hate legislation, the report suggested, the world could be divided into 'the United States and the rest.'[17] First Amendment jurisprudence is unique rather than pathological, and its uniqueness is a function of American exceptionalism and the civil rights movement. As a result, it is of limited value not only to those who support the *Keegstra* decision but also to those who criticize it. With respect to free expression and censorship in Canada, the use of First Amendment jurisprudence obscures rather than illuminates the central issues.

Pluralism and Expression: The Case of Canada

If the United States is unique because of its unqualified rejection of hate-propaganda legislation, Canada is unique because of its enthusiastic endorsement. 'Canada,' writes Joseph Magnet, 'has more hate propaganda legislation than any other country in the world.' For Magnet, Canada's position is a matter for regret, because anti-hate legislation 'has no discernible benefits' and a large number of social costs.[18] Moreover, Canada's reliance on such legislation is often regarded as non-rational or even irrational. One critic has suggested that Canada's acceptance of anti-hate legislation derives from the fact that 'Canadian legal culture is more natural-law oriented than is the highly positivistic, post-Realist US legal system.' The same critic speculates that Canada has more speech taboos than the United States, and that its anti-hate legislation is a misguided attempt to 'repress troubling thoughts bubbling up from society's collective identity.'[19] Such explanations are unsatisfactory. They not only neglect crucial features of Canadian society such as its distinctive brand of pluralism; they also obscure the relationships between pluralism, free expression, and censorship.

That pluralism can provide an argument for censorship is well known, even if it is not well understood. In *Keegstra*, both the majority decision and the dissenting opinion focused on it. Chief Justice Dickson not only relied on sections 15 (equality) and 27 (multiculturalism) of the Canadian Charter of Rights and Freedoms to support his decision, but he also insisted that 'multiculturalism cannot be preserved let alone enhanced if free rein is given to the promotion of hatred against identifiable cultural groups.'[20] If Canada is a multicultural society, Dickson reasoned, the protection of its multiculturalism justifies censorship in some cases. Justice MaLachlin also acknowledged the importance of multiculturalism, yet she denied that it justified a regime of censorship. Using section 27 to restrict free speech, she said, 'is subject to the objection that it would leave unprotected a large area of arguably legitimate social and political debate.'[21] Not only do different people have different ideas about what undermines multiculturalism, but the guarantee of free expression, she insisted, must protect even statements that challenge multiculturalism and other basic values. In *Keegstra*, the majority and the minority arrived at opposing conclusions, but they agreed on a conceptual issue. For them, the key question raised by Canadian multiculturalism was whether or not an appeal to pluralism could sustain a case for censorship.

While the question addressed by the judges is important, it is not the most basic question. Pluralism does not simply raise the question of censorship; it also raises a logically prior question about the justification of free expression. The most famous justifications of free expression, as we have seen, are the arguments from truth, from democracy, from individuality, from the good life, and from the inutility of suppression. But none of these justifications captures the essence of pluralism and its distinctive justification of free expression. In some countries, the pluralistic justification is irrelevant or comparatively unimportant, because the public culture is assimilationalist and the public morality is shaped by a strong commitment to uniform citizenship based on undifferentiated rights. The United States once was and still may be an example of such a country.[22] In any case, Canada is unlike the United States, because its commitment to pluralism has a strong historical basis as well as a deep moral foundation. 'Canada, with its policy of "multiculturalism within a bilingual framework" and its recognition of Aboriginal rights to self-government,' writes Will Kymlicka, 'is one of the few countries which has officially recognized and endorsed both polyethnicity and multinationality.'[23] There are, of course, strong opponents of pluralism and multiculturalism, and one critic has gone so far as to speak of Canada's 'mosaic madness.' But even the critics of Canadian multiculturalism are more often concerned with controlling its negative effects than with imposing social uniformity.[24]

Recognizing pluralism has implications for the way in which groups are incorporated into Canadian society. As Canada's prime minister, Pierre Trudeau was an enthusiastic supporter of multiculturalism. 'A vigorous policy of multiculturalism,' he said, was the foundation of society characterized by 'fair play to all.'[25] Trudeau also insisted, before and after he became prime minister, that Canadian pluralism represented a distinctive kind of society. Nothing, he said, 'could be more absurd than the concept of an "all-Canadian" boy or girl.'[26] Moreover, he called on French and English to create a truly pluralistic country. French and English are equal, he insisted, because each 'has the power to break the country.' But if they collaborate, 'Canada could become the envied seat of a form of federalism that belongs to tomorrow's world.'[27] In Canada, pluralism includes federalism as well as multiculturalism. As a result, Canada has not only rejected the idea of a melting pot, which requires immigrants and other groups to embrace a monolithic national identity. It has also refused to accept the idea of cultural solitudes – a system that segregates groups, minimizes contact between them, and denies the existence of basic common values. Put another way, Canadian pluralism neither assimilates groups nor hives them off.

Recognizing pluralism also has implications for the free-speech principle. If a country is composed of groups that are distinctive but that interact and share some common values, free expression acquires a function that is not adequately captured by the classical justifications. 'Much public expression,' writes Joseph Raz, 'portrays and expresses aspects of styles or forms of life.' This fact, he goes on to say, 'is often either overlooked or taken for granted.'[28] To overlook it, however, is to obscure a key function of free expression in a pluralistic society such as Canada. A group with a distinctive way of life uses public expression in at least two ways. First, public expression validates for the group's members the way of life they have adopted and reaffirms the group's continuing commitment to its distinctive identity. Second, those outside the group are made aware that their society has members who differ from themselves in significant respects. Not only does public expression enhance the group's dignity and sense of self worth, but the absence of public validation can make the group suspect and unattractive. As a result, the expression of group differences cannot be confined to the private realm or otherwise concealed from public view. In Canada, groups with different ways of life increasingly seek public recognition, and the challenge is both to acknowledge distinct identities and to reconcile divergent aspirations.

If pluralism has distinctive implications for free expression, the character and force of the pluralistic justification need to be recognized.[29] Not only is its character such that it cannot be subsumed under the classic justifications, but it adds a crucial dimension that the older justifications neglect.[30] The pluralistic justification is unlike the argument from truth because its purpose is to represent and portray a way of life, rather than to make truth-claims on its behalf or to test it in the free market of ideas. The pluralist and democratic justifications should also be distinguished. Under the democratic justification as it has been traditionally understood, free speech is essential because the people are sovereign and government is the servant of the people. The pluralistic argument recognizes that government is the servant of the people, but (unlike the democratic justification) it does not conceptualize the people as a monolithic unity and does not rely on the principle of unrestricted majority rule. The most significant parallels are between the pluralistic justification and the argument from individuality. The latter regards free expression as inseparable from personal autonomy and individual dignity, and values diversity for its social as well as its personal benefits. The pluralistic justification, however, shifts attention to the group, thereby transforming an old argument into a new rationale for free expression.

In *Keegstra*, the Supreme Court did not explore the connections between pluralism and free expression. Instead, it focused on the implications of pluralism for censorship. It assumed that the arguments for free expression were well known. It also assumed that the only task that remained was to determine the justified limitations on free expression. For the judges, the question was whether multiculturalism could provide grounds for limiting free expression, in particular hate speech. The judges divided on the issue, with both the majority and the minority citing First Amendment jurisprudence to buttress their opinions. But American judicial precedents should be used with caution. It is not simply that they lack authoritative force in Canada. Even more important, their persuasive value is limited. Canada is a different kind of society, and its pluralism is unlike the American variety. Consequently, Canadian pluralism contributes a new rationale for free expression that is neglected by the classic arguments and is not easily reconciled with First Amendment jurisprudence. By so doing, it also reopens the issue of censorship in a pluralistic society.

From Tolerance to Censorship

Censorship is not a new issue. Discussion of it raises difficult questions about the rights and duties of the citizen and about the limits of tolerance. For many, the solutions provided by First Amendment jurisprudence settle those questions. In an innovative discussion of hate speech in the United States, Lee Bollinger has noted that First Amendment jurisprudence bristles with paradoxes. America, he believes, overprotects speech: hate speech is in itself unworthy of protection 'and might very well be legally prohibited for entirely proper reasons.' But it does not follow, he continues, that 'a choice to tolerate such speech [is] irrational or unwise.'[31] Americans tolerate the intolerable, and they are wise to do so. For Bollinger, the wisdom of such a paradoxical policy does not derive from the value of free speech so much as from the evils of intolerance and the dangers inherent in persecution. The danger is that suppression of hate speech will create an intolerant society in which the enormous benefits of tolerance are lost. The overprotection of speech, Bollinger writes, is part of a 'self-protecting political strategy, a response to a perceived reality of ever-threatening intolerance and prejudice by the politically powerful against the politically weak.'[32] Arguments for the overprotection of speech have also found favour in Canada. 'Supporters of our anti-hate law,' writes Alan Borovoy, '[must] face an issue that has too often been neglected: the virtual impossibility of formulating a prohibition ... [that will not catch] in the same net a lot of speech which it would be clearly unconscionable for a democratic society to suppress.'[33]

Such arguments are unquestionably important, but they do not settle the issue of hate propaganda. Part of the response to them is that tolerance is not unlimited, under either the classical arguments or First Amendment jurisprudence. As to the classical arguments, Karl Popper called for recognition of the paradox of tolerance. 'If we extend unlimited tolerance even to those who are intolerant,' he wrote, 'then the tolerant will be destroyed, and tolerance with them.'[34] Even John Locke said that there were limits to toleration.[35] As to First Amendment jurisprudence, the judges who ruled in favour of the neo-Nazis in Skokie acknowledged that there were circumstances under which the march could be justifiably prohibited. Bollinger himself has arrived at much the same conclusion. Besides recognizing that intolerance is sometimes justified, he supports tolerance by appealing to a presumption in its favor. 'The free speech principle,' he writes, 'requires us to begin with a *strong presumption* in favour of toleration, which can be overcome only after it is determined that the society has little or nothing to gain [by the exercise of tolerance].'[36] Unlike an absolute rule, a presumption can be rebutted or defeated. Moreover, although Bollinger believes that the presumption of tolerance was not rebutted in Skokie, his argument suggests that the neo-Nazi march could have been suppressed if (as a matter of fact) the costs and harms of the march had been great enough.

Tolerance and censorship, then, are ordinarily linked to the calculation of harm. There is, however, a famous argument for tolerance that appears to settle the censorship issue, and it does so in a way that avoids difficult questions about harm. Alan Borovoy, who has been already quoted, makes such an argument. For if, as he contends, it is impossible to formulate rules restricting hate propaganda that do not also outlaw legitimate speech, then censorship turns out to be an impractical and unattainable option in a free and democratic society. The argument about 'the inutility of suppression' is not itself unambiguous, however. In its broadest versions, it amounts to a general theory about the incompetence of government. 'Freedom of speech,' writes Schauer, 'is based in large part on a distrust of ... government to make the necessary distinctions, ... an appreciation of the fallibility of political leaders, and a somewhat deeper distrust of governmental power in a more general sense.'[37] But if the argument is so stated, virtually all government action is suspect and it becomes difficult to see why the regulation of speech should be no more objectionable than, say, economic transactions. To avoid this difficulty the argument is often formulated more narrowly. In its narrower versions, it is commonly known as 'the slippery slope' argument or as the 'where do draw the line?' argument.

Although distinguishable, these arguments possess a common core.[38] In both cases, the appeal is to the existence of linguistically imprecise boundaries, and the concern is that complex empirical facts can produce an erosion of seemingly fixed legal categories. 'If you censor this, then you will have to censor that.' Hence, nothing should be censored. Taxation could easily be substituted for censorship, in which case the argument becomes: 'Do not tax, because if you tax this, then you will have to tax that.' The response to both arguments is the same. The business of government, as Bentham said, is regulation, and the danger of over-regulation is real enough. Yet, even if it is granted that over-regulation is more likely and more detrimental in the area of speech than in other areas, it does not follow that the solution is to prohibit regulation altogether. In fact, judges in Canada and the United States have seldom arrived at such conclusion. It is far more usual for them to insist, as they do in the United States, that government regulation in sensitive areas such as speech should be subject to strict scrutiny; or, as in Canada, that such regulation must satisfy the Charter's reasonable-limits clause. In a constitutional democracy, 'the slippery slope' leads neither to arbitrary power nor to inaction but to the development of stringent (if not always adequate) legal and political safeguards.

Even so, censorship is not a measure undertaken lightly. Its justification requires (among other things) not only that it should be efficacious, but also that it should prevent significant harm. In a stimulating discussion of *Keegstra* L.W. Sumner focuses on the issue of harm and complexities raised by it. 'For years,' he writes, 'I accepted the civil-libertarian case against the criminalization of hate propaganda ... Now ... I want to explain why I have come to change my mind.'[39] The civil-libertarian case, according to Sumner, is based not on considerations of abstract right but on the pragmatic conviction that the social costs of attempting to control hate propaganda are higher than the costs of leaving it unhindered. Moreover, Sumner notes that the calculation of harm was also a key issue in *Keegstra*, with the majority and minority disagreeing only about the results of the calculation. A common assumption of civil libertarians is that hatemongers represent only a small minority of Canadians and should be simply ignored. 'Keegstra,' writes Alan Borovoy, 'should have been allowed to wallow in the obscurity he so richly deserves.'[40] But Sumner no longer shares this assumption. 'I have ... come to be more impressed,' he writes, 'by the depth and tenacity of the intolerance towards racial and ethnic minorities by ... many ordinary Canadians.' When this factor is combined with 'the corrosive effects of racism on those who are its actual victims, then ... there is no convincing case against some form of criminal legislation governing hate propaganda.' Civil libertarians believe otherwise, but Sumner thinks that they have little evidence to support their position and he finds '[their] tone of absolute conviction ... hardest to understand.'[41]

Sumner's account of the harm caused by hate propaganda is thoughtful but incomplete. Missing from it is recognition that harm is a moral category and acknowledgement of the connection between harm and pluralism. Both points are often overlooked. Harm is frequently depicted as a neutral criterion for determining when law should be used to control conduct. Thus, those who argue against the legal enforcement of morality couple their opposition with the claim that law should be used only to prevent harm-to-others. But 'harm to others' is not a morally neutral category, in part because it depends on the distribution of rights and duties within the legal system, which in turn depends on morality. For example, theft clearly falls under the harm-to-others principle, but theft depends on the existence of property rights and such rights are not morally neutral. 'The criminal law,' writes Neil MacCormick, 'in so far as it is concerned with fending off harmful behaviour is *necessarily* geared to protection of what are legitimate interests *according to a certain dominant political morality.*'[42]

As for pluralism, it is connected to harm in at least two ways. First, a society that is pluralistic will have a different conception of harm than one that is not. Thus, a society that endorses multiculturalism brings into existence categories of harm and offensiveness that are not universally recognized. Second, a pluralist society not only recognizes distinctive kinds of harm but is itself a source of them. 'One of the difficulties in making multiculturalism politically acceptable,' writes Jospeh Raz, 'stems from the enmity between members of different cultural groups.'[43] Such enmity is not simply due to ignorance but is endemic to multiculturalism and other forms of value pluralism. By insisting that there is no single scale of value and that different forms of life are worthwhile, multiculturalism requires people to choose between rival values and commitments, and thereby to value what they choose and to disapprove of those who choose differently. Of course, people can step back from their choices and appreciate the values in other ways of life. Even so, a multicultural society creates, according to Raz, 'an inescapable tension between acceptance and rivalry between competing valuable ways of life, which forever threatens to destabilise.'[44]

In a famous book, John Stuart Mill insisted that representative government 'was next to impossible' in a country made up of nationalities that spoke different languages, because in such a country 'mutual antipathies are generally much stronger than jealousy of the government.'[45] In the case of Canada, an opinion similar to Mill's was vividly expressed by André Siegfried. Canada, he said, was a precarious creation because it was characterized, not by unity of purpose, but by 'impassioned rivalries' and by 'an immemorial struggle.' For Siegfried, French and English were 'like brothers that hate each other ... [and] have to dwell under one roof.'[46] Like Mill before him, Siegfried provided an assessment that is too one-sided to be taken as representing the whole truth. For, although Canadians have unquestionably experienced impassioned rivalries and mutual antipathies, they also celebrate the cooperative virtues, share a common identity, and have sought to create a community of belonging that includes all citizens. But the very one-sidedness of Siegfried's assessments helps to illustrate that the benefits of Canadian pluralism cannot be taken for granted. Because this is so, Canadians cannot take discussion of censorship for granted either, or assume that pluralism always provides arguments against censorship.

Conclusion

A recent study has noted that 74 per cent of ordinary Canadians believe in laws prohibiting speech and writing that promotes hatred towards a particular group, and that 'the reaction of [Canadian] elites is just as lopsided in support of anti-hate legislation as that of ordinary citizens.'[47] When judged from the standpoint of First Amendment jurisprudence, such findings are distressing because they appear to suggest that Canadians are less committed than Americans to civil liberties. Canadian civil libertarians often arrive at just such a conclusion and believe that the Canadian Charter of Rights and Freedoms should be used to strike down anti-hate legislation rather than to support it. Whatever the merits of such a position, its crucial limitation is that it takes Canada for granted and assimilates it to the American model. But Canada is different from the United States, in part because it celebrates both multicultural citizenship and multinational federalism. As a result Canadian pluralism not only differs from the American variety, but it also has distinctive implications for free speech and censorship. Canadians do not value free speech less than Americans. Rather, they value it differently. One difference is that pluralism provides a powerful justification for free speech that is unlike the rationales celebrated by First Amendment jurisprudence, and is even unlike the classical defences of free speech found in the writings of Milton, Locke, and Mill. However, pluralism also has implications for the concept of harm, and in this way it yields a distinctive argument for censorship.[48] In the United States, free speech often tests the limits of liberal tolerance. In Canada, it just as often requires an understanding of the nature and boundaries of pluralist tolerance.

In *Keegstra*, a majority of the judges upheld Canada's anti-hate legislation. *Butler* extended the ambit of harm to include certain forms of pornography because of 'the threat to equality resulting from the exposure to audiences of certain types of violent and degrading material.'[49] American feminist lawyers like Catharine MacKinnon have applauded *Butler* and argued that it provides a model for the United States to follow.[50] But, to many American civil libertarians, both *Keegstra* and *Butler* seem confused and wrongheaded. Thus, Ronald

Dworkin has not only argued that there is a right to pornography; he has also insisted that feminists like MacKinnon mix together different types of harm and fail to demonstrate that 'exposure to pornography ... causes more actual incidents of assault.'[51] Yet the issue of pornography and hate literature are more complex than the debate between MacKinnon and Dworkin makes them appear. Ultimately, they raise questions about public morality, and there is good reason to believe that countries with different public moralities will disagree about such fundamental issues as pornography, hate literature, and censorship.

NOTES

1 I am grateful to Allan Hutchinson and Klaus Petersen for their helpful comments on a draft of this essay.
2 Frederick Schauer, *Free Speech: A Philosophical Inquiry* (Cambridge, U.K.: Cambridge University Press 1982), 3–86.
3 John Locke, *A Letter concerning Toleration* (Indianapolis, Ind.: Hackett Publishing 1983), 46. See also Jeremy Waldron, 'Locke: Toleration and the Rationality of Persecution,' in Susan Mendus, ed., *Justifying Toleration* (Cambridge, U.K.: Cambridge University Press 1988), 79–86.
4 Alexander Meikeljohn, *Political Freedom* (New York: Oxford University Press 1965), 8–28. This volume contains Meiklejohn's most important writings on free speech.
5 *Regina v. Butler.* Canadian Criminal Cases (3d) 70 (1992), 146.
6 *Regina v. Butler*, 162.
7 See, for example, the discussion by Harry Kalven, *The Negro and the First Amendment* (Chicago: University of Chicago Press 1966), 64.
8 *Regina v. Keegstra.* Canadian Rights Reporter (2d) 3 (1990), 296.
9 *Beauharnais* is discussed, for example, by Kalven, *The Negro and the First* Amendment, 22.
10 See Samuel Walker, *Hate Speech* (Lincoln: University of Nebraska Press 1994), 65.
11 *Regina v. Keegstra*, 223.
12 James Weinstein, 'An American's View of the Canadian Hate Speech Decisions,' in W.J. Waluchow, ed., *Free Expression* (Oxford, U.K.: Clarendon Press 1994), 179.
13 Walker, *Hate Speech*, 126.
14 John Rawls, *A Theory of Justice* (Cambridge, Mass.: Harvard University Press 1971), 243–50.
15 M.J. Sandel, *Democracy's Discontent* (Cambridge, Mass.: Harvard University Press 1996), 89. See also his 'The Procedural Republic and the Unencumbered Self,' *Political Theory* 12 (1984), 81–96.

16 Walker, *Hate Speech*, 126.
17 Cited in Walker, *Hate Speech*, 4.
18 Joseph Magnet, 'Hate Propaganda in Canada,' in W.J. Waluchow, ed., *Free Expression* 229, 244.
19 Weinstein, 'An American's View,' 219–20.
20 *Regina* v. *Keegstra*, 236.
21 *Regina* v. *Keegstra*, 291–2.
22 See, for example, Nathan Glazer, *Ethnic Dilemmas 1964–1982* (Cambridge, Mass.: Harvard University Press 1983), 209–29, 254–73.
23 Will Kymlicka, *Multicultural Citizenship* (Oxford, U.K.: Clarendon Press 1995), 22.
24 Reginald W. Bibby, *Mosaic Madness* (Toronto: Stoddart 1990), 3, 180, 207.
25 Pierre Trudeau, 'Statement on Multiculturalism,' in H.D. Forbes, ed., *Canadian Political Thought* (Toronto: Oxford University Press 1985), 350.
26 Pierre Elliot Trudeau, *Conversation with Canadians* (Toronto: University of Toronto Press 1972), 33.
27 Pierre Elliott Trudeau, *Federalism and the French Canadians* (Toronto: Macmillan 1968), 31, 178–9.
28 Joseph Raz, 'Free Expression and Personal Identification,' in Waluchow, ed., *Free Expression*, 9–10. See also James W. Nickel, 'Freedom of Expression in a Pluralistic Society,' *Law and Philosophy* 7 (1988–9), 281–93.
29 My discussion of the force and character of the pluralistic justification in this section of the chapter should be read together with my analysis (below) of the connection between pluralism and censorship.
30 Compare Schauer, *Free Speech*, 15–72.
31 Lee C. Bollinger, *The Tolerant Society* (New York: Oxford University Press 1986), 9.
32 Bollinger, *The Tolerant Society*, 99.
33 A. Alan Borovoy, 'How Not to Fight Racial Hatred,' in David Schneiderman, ed., *Freedom of Expression and the Charter* (Calgary: Thomson Professional Publishing 1991), 243.
34 K.R. Popper, *The Open Society and Its Enemies*, vol. 1. (London: Routledge and Kegan Paul 1969), 265. See also Rawls, *A Theory of Justice*, 216–21.
35 Locke, *A Letter concerning Toleration*, 49–50.
36 Bollinger, *The Tolerant Society* 197. Emphasis added.
37 Schauer, *Free Speech*, 86.
38 Frederick Schauer, 'Slippery Slopes,' *Harvard Law Review* 99, nos. 1–2 (1985), 380.
39 L.W. Sumner, 'Hate Propaganda and Charter Rights,' in Waluchow, ed., *Free Expression*, 154.

40 Borovoy, 'How Not to Fight Racial Hatred,' 247.
41 Sumner, 'Hate Propaganda and Charter Rights,' 170, 171, 174. See also Allan C. Hutchinson, *Waiting for Coraf: A Critique of Law and Rights* (Toronto: University of Toronto Press 1995), 89–102, 213–20.
42 Neil MacCormick, *Legal Right and Social Democracy* (Oxford, U.K.: Clarendon Press 1986), 30.
43 Joseph Raz, *Ethics in the Public Domain* (Oxford, U.K.: Clarendon Press 1994), 163.
44 Ibid., 165.
45 John Stuart Mill, *Utilitarianism, Liberty, Representative Government* (repr. London: J.M. Dent 1962), 361.
46 André Siegfried, *The Race Question in Canada* (Toronto: McClelland and Stewart 1966), 14, 85. See also *Report of the Special Committee on Hate Propaganda in Canada* (Ottawa: Queen's Printer 1966), 25, 33. And Charles Taylor, *Multiculturalism and 'The Politics of Recognition'* (Princeton, N.J.: Princeton University Press 1992, 64–8. Taylor suggests (at 64): 'Multinational societies can break up because of a lack of (perceived) recognition of the equal worth of one group by another. This is at present ... the case in Canada.'
47 Paul M. Sniderman, Joseph F. Fletcher, Peter H. Russell, and Philip E. Tetlock, *The Clash of Rights* (New Haven, Conn.: Yale University Press 1996), 64.
48 I should emphasize that my objective in this paper is not to articulate standards capable of settling concrete cases in law. Instead, I treat pluralism, free expression, and censorship as philosophical topics, and I use legal cases to explore moral and philosophical issues within a Canadian context.
49 *Regina* v. *Butler*, 159.
50 Catharine A. MacKinnon, *Only Words* (Cambridge, Mass.: Harvard University Press 1993), 93–104.
51 Ronald Dworkin, *Freedom's Law* (Cambridge, Mass.: Harvard University Press 1996), 219. See also his *A Matter of Principle* (Cambridge, Mass.: Harvard University Press 1985), 351–72.

4

Judging Speech: An Inquiry into the Supreme Court's Theory of Signification

MARIANA VALVERDE[1]

The texts that make up Canada's obscenity law can be analysed with a view to understanding how courts govern the production and distribution of images and words by giving certain moral standards the force of law. Though this type of analysis is one of the tasks of this chapter, it is hardly original since critical legal scholars and gay/lesbian activists both in Canada and elsewhere have critiqued the 'modernization' of obscenity law in the same manner, showing that despite some changes in the justifications used to legitimate obscenity law, moralism has by no means been eliminated. Given the existence of this critique, I have chosen to take the analysis of obscenity law beyond accusations of moralism by asking a new question: how do the court's ideas of morality, sex, and the body relate to its implicit and explicit theories of language and meaning?

The question of meaning is an important one because the systems of censorship that are documented in this book are not simply power machines: they are also, as Michel Foucault would say, truth machines. Truth machines have their rules not only for deciding between true and false speech but also, and more fundamentally, for deciding what is to be counted as speech in the first place. The theories that underlie the process of 'judging speech' (in both senses of that phrase) are therefore of more than purely academic or theoretical interest.

As Stanley Fish among others has pointed out,[2] legal institutions tend to assume a particular philosophy of language, a particular view of the way in which words relate to things. Most judicial speech presupposes that meanings are inherent in words, and that although true meanings are sometimes difficult to discern or somewhat fuzzy, nevertheless they are *there*, in words themselves. This presupposition is flatly contradicted by contemporary studies of the workings of language and culture, not to mention by post-Wittgenstein philosophies of language, which start from the insight that meaning is not only shaped but even created in social interaction.

A second and related assumption about language made by law as an institution is that texts and/or speech are ontologically distinct from 'actions.' 'Freedom of speech' provisions apply precisely only to that which the courts have previously classified as speech, while homicide laws apply to actual conduct, not to murder mysteries. Of course, the courts have recognized that it is not easy to draw the line between speech and action in a number of situations, from libel and defamation law to hate crimes. But by continuing to talk about 'a line,' the suggestion is that despite the existence of a grey area or penumbra, there are two ontologically distinct realms, speech and action. Thus, the speech/action opposition is not a binary one, since a grey or in-between area is recognized, but it is nevertheless regarded as an opposition. The Supreme Court agonized at length about 'drawing the line' between speech and action in the 1990 *Keegstra* decision upholding hate-speech laws. But it was only in the 1992 *Butler* decision that the court produced a truly dizzying *reversal* of the opposition between speech and action that is embedded in the Criminal Code as a whole, and in law in general. In *Butler*, the court decided that a large cultural realm (pornographic videos and magazines) should be judged not for its meaning but from the point of view of its social effectivity, particularly its potential to cause harm. Many feminist and race-critical legal scholars have praised this approach, since they have themselves argued, from a different standpoint, that free-speech provisions are a liberal cover for the continuation of systemic racism and sexism.

Throughout the long battles between pro- and anti-censorship activists and scholars, neither side appears to have noticed that the back-and-forth slippage between speech and action that marks the *Butler* decision has, paradoxically, led to a situation in which certain bodily actions – appearing before the law as potentially indecent *conduct*[3] – have come to be governed through the *Butler* decision, whose explicit purpose is to govern the availability of *representations*, not bodies. Sexual conduct (or for that matter non-sexual conduct, such as women taking off their shirts in hot weather)[4] has come to be governed through the law on obscene representations, as if bodies were nothing but discourses – as if, in other words, Canadian courts had decided to agree with Jacques Derrida that 'there is nothing outside the text.'

The way in which judicial bodies switch from the classical theory of language, in which words have inherent meanings, to a postmodern theory in which the meaning not only of particular obscene publications but even of the very term 'obscenity' is to be derived from examining social effects (what literary theorists would call the 'performativity' of the word) may appear as unique, as a contradiction caused by the judges' poor understanding of the philosophy of language. But, although judges are undoubtedly naive about language, there are more systematic reasons for the existence of the complicated dialectic of social reality and discourse, conduct and expression, that can be observed in judicial rulings on obscenity and indecency. The other two binary oppositions examined in this chapter – judicial subjectivity versus community objectivity, and moralism versus the test of harm – turn out to deconstruct themselves in the very texts that set them up in a process similar to the way in which the speech/action, discourse/body binary is simultaneously upheld and undermined.

The fact that three different judicial dilemmas take the form of a binary opposition that is simultaneously upheld and undermined raises a more general methodological point. Many social-legal scholars believe that deconstruction consists of playing with language without engaging in any critical study of the way in which law and other social systems reproduce systematic power relations. To refute this belief, this chapter shows that the deconstructive method is in fact well suited to the task of demonstrating that the production of legal speech helps to reproduce and justify all the systematic power structures that underlie liberal mass democracies.[5] The way in which existing social relations of power are taken up, reproduced, and given a new lease on life in legal texts can be analysed through the traditional methods of critical legal studies, such as the Marxist critiques used by Canadian legal scholars to debunk the ideology of 'rights.'[6] These methods are certainly relevant to obscenity law: they have been used to good effect by Brenda Cossman and her co-authors to demonstrate that bourgeois ideologies of morality are central to the *Butler* decision despite that text's claims to be effecting a post-moralistic move towards a harm-based approach.[7] My own analysis, although politically sympathetic to the work of Cossman et al., nevertheless uses the methods of deconstruction rather than those of the critique of ideology, partly because they happen to suit the particular subject at hand and partly because I would like to persuade progressive socio-legal scholars (particularly in Canada) that deconstruction is not the politically suspect, nihilistic methodology that many people imagine it to be. I do not want to engage in a theoretical debate here, since I think it is more persuasive to let the detailed arguments of the chapter serve as a concrete demonstration of the political uses of deconstruction, but it may be useful to say a few words to dispel a couple of mistaken assumptions about deconstruction that are often made by progressive scholars.

Many people now use 'deconstruction' as a fancy word for critique, for instance, by saying that 'we must deconstruct heterosexism.' This usage, popular among students, is quite incorrect, for several reasons. First, one can deconstruct only culturally constructed *oppositions*, not single terms – much less material institutions, which can be taken apart only with a great deal of work that goes far beyond the discursive. Second, as a method, critique tends to presuppose that even though the discourses being analysed may be ideological

covers for certain interests, the critique itself lies beyond ideology.[8] The deconstructive move, by contrast, is not one performed by the critic from a standpoint
somewhere above and beyond power and ideology. Deconstruction is an imma-
nent analysis that simply exposes the text's own contradictions. If the text does
not deconstruct itself, in other words, the critic has no business imposing deconstructive methods on it. The heart of my argument will therefore be the demonstration of how judicial texts *themselves* deconstruct the very oppositions that
they set up.

The first opposition that deconstructs itself – speech versus action – can be
seen in a comparison of the 1990 *Keegstra* Supreme Court decision with the
1992 *Butler* decision. We will see here that, while Keegstra's anti-Semitic dia-
tribes are located firmly in the realm of speech – with the Supreme Court split
on the question of whether prohibiting such speech is justified – the pornographic materials seized from Butler's Winnipeg shop, though said to contain
'meaning,' are nevertheless not granted recognition as speech. Pornography
appears to be located in some kind of limbo between speech and action,
between expression and sexual conduct, between the mind and the body.

The second section will consider the binary opposition drawn by Canada's
Supreme Court since at least 1980 between the subjective moralism of old-fashioned obscenity law and the enlightened, modern, objective standards gathered
under the rubric of 'community standards of tolerance.' We will see that the ridicule heaped by the higher judges on moralistic lower-court judges, a ridicule
obviously intended to align the Supreme Court with enlightenment and cultural
pluralism, is rather a smokescreen, since the much-touted community turns out
to be unable to speak for itself, either directly or through experts. The 'community' turns out to be but a phantasm in the minds of the very judges whose personal views were supposedly deemed irrelevant.

Finally, the *Butler* court's addition to the repertoire of judicial tools to defend
obscenity law will be considered. Without directly attacking their own previous
creation – community standards of tolerance – the *Butler* court puts forward a
new test of obscenity: the test of 'harm' or, more precisely, 'risk of harm.' The
court constructs a binary opposition between the English Victorian criterion of
'corruption of morals' and the modern, Canadian, objective standards implied
by the fashionable catchphrase 'risk of harm.' But, as we shall see, the court
fatally undermines its own actuarialism by deploying moral criteria to define
'harm.'

It would be easy to read the court's self-deconstruction as an effect of the
judges' disavowal of their own personal moralism. But I think it would be profitable to look a little deeper and consider whether the court's deconstruction of
its own move towards objective, post-moralistic standards is perhaps a *neces-*

sary move rooted not in personal biographies but in the court's need to legiti-mize its own meaning-production. The court's major problem in obscenity law is that, unlike most of the Criminal Code, obscenity provisions attempt to gov-ern representations rather than conduct. If it is often difficult for the criminal law as a whole to discern the intent of an accused in a particular situation, it is even more difficult to ascertain the 'real meaning' of an image or a text, as obscenity trials have traditionally demonstrated. And, if judging speech is diffi-cult in the case of a book by a known author, it is even more difficult in the case of a text (a film, for instance) whose authorship may be fragmented or anony-mous, such that one cannot easily talk about authorial intent, and whose distri-bution and hence its meaning-in-use[9] is unpredictable. There are, therefore, genuine difficulties facing the justices. But these are rarely discussed openly and explicitly – perhaps because, if the Supreme Court were to admit that the meaning of pornography is not 'in' the picture itself but is rather created in the interaction between a specific consumer and an object that is always ambigu-ous, multi-authored, polyvalent, and many-layered, it might occur to somebody outside the bench to apply this same insight to judicial texts. In other words: if the justices admitted all of the difficulties involved in the rather impossible project of refining obscenity law, the court's own speech would suddenly be at risk of becoming contextual, ambiguous, and polyvalent. And since the court's greatest (and always unspoken) fear is that some day there may no longer be a Supreme Court with the power to assume a regulative function vis-à-vis other speech, the spectre of undecidability[10] that haunts the Supreme Court's pro-nouncements on obscenity cannot even be named, much less addressed.

Judicial Speech and 'Discounted' Speech: From *Keegstra* to *Butler*

The *Keegstra* decision employs judicial speech to classify hierarchically other types of speech as more or less worthy of the very title of 'speech.' Upholding the hate-speech section of the Criminal Code, Chief Justice Brian Dickson made an argument to the effect that curtailing the rights of those 'few' individu-als who produce 'hate propaganda' is not an infringement of expression that can be justified as valid in a free and democratic society, given the 'pressing and substantial' concern that Parliament has shown to defend the rights of 'various cultural groups.'[11] In an argument whose unusual length is more an indication of the author's defensiveness than of the strength of his logic, Dickson writes that speech is not significantly impaired through the hate-speech provision, and he gives two main reasons for this. First, there are only 'a few individuals' con-cerned, and their right to expression is more than outweighed by the rights of racial and religious minorities to be free from harassment and from 'humiliation and degradation.'[12] Second, only statements that can be shown to flow from a 'wilful promotion of hatred' are subject to criminal prosecution: hence, the law is not overly broad because it applies only to cases of virulent, demonstrable 'hatred.' Throughout his argument, Dickson is obviously at pains to mollify civil-libertarian opinion, while at the same time expressing views on the rights of minorities that are very much in keeping with the general trend of Supreme Court decisions on equality rights in the late 1980s.

Dickson's detailed defence of hate-speech law, then, makes hate into a key criterion separating merely offensive from criminal speech; but, while discoursing on hate, Dickson does not define the crucial operative term 'propaganda.'[13] 'Hate propaganda' is in Dickson's text defined negatively only: it is the outer boundary, perhaps even the opposite, of speech: 'Indeed, one may quite plausibly contend that it is through rejecting hate propaganda that the state can best encourage the protection of values central to freedom of expression, while simultaneously demonstrating dislike for the vision forwarded by hate-mongers.'[14]

Hatemongers (whose specific characteristics are never spelled out) are thus constructed as outside the state, through a circular argument. First, racist statements are constructed as less than speech, for instance, in Dickson's taken-for-granted statement about 'the discounted value of the expression at issue';[15] this is then used to discount those few individuals from whose mouths such statements are supposed to issue naturally. Dickson saved the hate-speech law: but he also saved the liberal assumption dear to the Canadian ruling class that racism is not a systemic feature of Canadian society but is rather the deliberate work of a few deviant individuals producing 'hate' propaganda.

The eloquent civil-libertarian dissent written by Justice Beverley MacLachlin agrees wholeheartedly with Dickson's majority on the question of the nature of racism. Hate propaganda – which she also declines to define – does not constitute a sufficient danger to the Canadian polity to warrant criminal prosecution, she argues, a position that has the effect of trivializing racism and other forms of prejudice and hate.[16]

Two years later, in *Butler*, the three Supreme Court justices who had eloquently defended the right to expression of 'hate-mongers' changed sides. The decision (unanimous on all but minor points) was in fact written by Justice John Sopinka, one of the dissenters in *Keegstra*. In sharp contrast to Dickson's defensiveness in *Keegstra*, Sopinka does not feel obliged seriously to consider civil-libertarian arguments for 'sexual speech.' He takes it for granted that pornography is even lower than the 'discounted speech' of anti-Semites: it is non-speech, or at best quasi-speech. This exclusion of pornography from the field of expression is not done directly: indeed, Sopinka even chastises an overtly moralistic lower-court judge who believes that pornography has no meaning at all. Lower-court judges may consider smut to be a dangerous thing with no expressive content: but at the more enlightened, better-educated level of the Supreme Court, the judicial exclusion of 'porn' from speech is *performed* rather than defended. The classification of pornography on the side of the body and sex rather than on the side of words and meaning is effectively performed through the court's constant slippage from representation to (sexual) reality.

A key passage in which this slippage from representation to conduct is enacted occurs in Justice Bertha Wilson's interpretation, in the 1985 *Towne Cinema* decision, of the notoriously ambiguous words of the obscenity provision, 'undue exploitation of sex.'

As I see it, the essential difficulty with the definition of obscenity is that 'undueness' must presumably be assessed in relation to consequences. It is implicit in the definition that at some point the exploitation of sex becomes harmful to the public or at least the public believes that to be so. It is therefore necessary for the protection of the public to put limits on the degree of exploitation, and, through the application of the community standard test, the public is made the arbiter of what is harmful to it and what is not. The problem is that we know so little of the consequences that we are seeking to avoid. Do obscene movies spawn immoral conduct? Do they degrade women? Do they promote violence? The most that can be said, I think, is that the public has concluded that exposure to such material which degrades the human dimensions of life to a *subhuman or merely physical* dimension and thereby contributes to a process of moral desensitisation must be harmful in some way. It must be therefore be controlled when it gets out of hand, when it becomes 'undue.'[17]

This passage makes the questionable assumption that women are degraded by pornographic images themselves, not by men who might or might not have been affected by what they see – an interesting inversion of the 'reasonable' common-sense view of the relation between discourse and reality. Further eroding any possibility of effecting a distinction between fantasy images and real-life sex, Wilson makes the additional (and related) assumption that sexual representations 'degrade' humanity because they reduce life to the 'subhuman or merely physical dimension' – a Christian view of sexuality that, if a lower-court judge were to utter it, might well be denounced by the Supreme Court as moralistic and insufficiently modern. Wilson's transparently Christian views are reauthorized by Sopinka in *Butler*, since he approvingly cites the whole passage reproduced above.

The *Butler* court's well-known elaboration of a new standard for obscenity, then, depends on the prior and largely implicit construction of a hybrid object hovering somewhere between representation and conduct, between the signifier and the signified. On the one hand, pornography must be expression, since it carries meaning; but, on the other hand, pornography is discussed as it if were life, a form of life threatening to degrade us if it is allowed to 'get out of hand.' Rather than being positioned along with hate propaganda as a distasteful relative of other, 'higher' forms of speech, this hybrid entity is placed on the outer boundary of the uniquely human realm of speech. We do not know exactly where 'subhuman' sexuality is located; but it is clearly close to, if not fully within, the realm of instinct and lust that Western culture has traditionally labelled as 'animal' (that is, as subhuman). This positioning of sexual representation outside (human) expression, authorized by the prior (Christian) assumption that 'merely physical' sex is subhuman until redeemed by higher values, is not one that can be directly challenged by lawyers and other readers of judicial texts since it is never explicitly articulated and defended. Rather, it is a construction that has already taken place before the 'judging speech' begins.

The *Butler* court indirectly acknowledges that obscenity law, specifically the 1985 *Towne Cinema* decision, had not served to put an end to the public controversies about the arbitrary character of obscenity-law enforcement. Making a fresh attempt to re-legitimize both the obscenity statute and the Supreme Court's own speech, Sopinka and his colleagues took a phrase that had already appeared in previous decisions and erected it into a new test of obscenity: degradation and dehumanization.[18] This phrase is given particular powers by being classified as the criterion that distinguishes legal from illegal pornography, as follows. First, all pornography is explicitly sexual. (Violent movies, therefore, are not pornographic unless they are also sexual.) Then, all pornography that is violent – by which it is unclear if they mean pornography that merely depicts violence or pornography that glorifies violence – is illegal; and pornography involving children is always illegal. Within the rather large category of materials that are not violent and do not involve children, the category that is most likely to be in dispute, we are told that the court is issuing a new ruling that only pornography portraying people being treated in a 'degrading and dehumanizing' manner is potentially obscene.

The phrase 'degrading and dehumanizing,' deeply rooted in Western culture's mythic binary opposition between the animal realm of necessity and instinct and the human realm of freedom and love, is absolutely crucial to the workings of censorship in this country. How can the vague and subjective words 'degrading' and 'dehumanizing' be given some semblance of objectivity and legitimacy? Sopinka never defines the terms, but he explains them by saying that 'among other things, degrading or dehumanizing materials place women (and sometimes men) in positions of subordination, servile submission, or humiliation.' This new string of terms has the effect of aligning the court slightly more with feminism than with Christianity, since the feminist argument about pornography has been that certain sexual representations are dehumanizing not because they are sexual but because they promote 'subordination.' But while performing a certain political move – an acknowledgement of feminism – the court's words provide no semantic clarification whatsoever, since what is or is not humiliation or subordination is as much a matter of opinion as what is degradation. S/M sexual practices, for instance, are regarded by many as inherently degrading because they appear to involve 'servile submission'; but the people who engage in these practices argue that it is the so-called 'bottom' who controls the activity and defines the limits, so that there is in fact no domination but simply a cathartic re-enactment or even a parody of domination. S/M practitioners feel that they are practising sexual liberation, not sexual submission, and that there is no reason why, in an officially multicultural society such as Canada, they should not aspire to the status of being one minority among many, on a par with constitutionally protected religious minorities whose practices around gender might strike other Canadians as involving servile submission.

Sopinka is clearly aware that the meaning of terms like 'degrading' is not uncontroversial. Without naming S/M, he provides a rebuttal of the S/M community's argument that whatever consenting adults choose to do is not degrading to them: 'consent cannot save materials that otherwise contain degrading or dehumanizing scenes.'[19] As we shall see in the concluding section, it is highly significant that Sopinka acknowledges only implicitly that there are sexual minorities in Canada. If he were to acknowledge and debate with such minorities, this would undermine the sociologically naive notion of *national* community standards, a notion dear to the heart of Supreme Court justices (or at least to the heart of the anglophone judges). By refusing to acknowledge directly the S/M community, Sopinka rejects the field of popular democratic struggles, positioning himself, along with his colleague Wilson, in a meta-realm above and beyond the people: the supreme realm of a sovereign law that rules rather than responds to popular opinion and popular practices.[20]

The workings of this meta-realm can be observed only indirectly. One of its curious features is that all the meaning-producing power that has been taken out of pornographic or erotic representations seems to have been transfused into the court's own speech. The court's powers of speech transcend the usual limitations of earthly institutions: while other institutions are generally limited to governing either words or actions, judicial speech declares itself authorized to judge other people's speech *and actions* at the same time and through the same act of judgment. Because violence is bad and sexual humiliation is bad, therefore pornography is bad, the court reasons, as if the ethical judgment made about conduct necessarily transferred to the always unstable and – in the case of much if not all pornography – always ambiguous signifier.

Wilson (in *Towne Cinema*) and Sopinka (in *Butler*) are not alone in writing as if images or words had the power to leap out of pages and hit women, and as if judges had the magical power to adjudicate questions of conduct and questions of meaning in a single decision. In *Keegstra*, Dickson had already drawn a questionable parallel between, on the one hand, the criminalization of hate speech, and, on the other, the drinking and driving provisions criminalizing an act which merely poses a *risk* of harm, an activity that is only *potentially* harmful.[21] An analogy – indeed, an identity – is created between the physical effects of drunk driving on traffic and the presumed effects of hate propaganda and pornography on the minds of particular individuals. Therefore, the slippage from judging meanings to judging conduct is rooted not so much in a sloppy theory of language and culture as in a not-at-all mistaken theory of the nature of judicial speech.

Yet, despite the move to judging pornography through its effects, as if obscenity law were on a par with gun control, today's Supreme Court justices do not take the old Victorian approach of classifying pornography as a bad thing. The justices we have are, after all, not Victorians: for instance, they have heard of erotica. Erotic *art*, as distinguished from pornography, is grudgingly said to be potentially expressive. Exploring the features of erotic art would endanger the court's fundamental project of judging pornography by its presumed real effects, however. Therefore, the brief paragraph on 'the defence of artistic merit' – which is a reverse-onus provision and thus does not entitle the defendant to the presumption of innocence – avoids discussing the ontological status of pornography. It simply states that a film or text could be shown to be exempt from prosecution if an obscene part 'does not merely represent "dirt for dirt's sake" but has a legitimate role when measured by the internal necessities of the work itself.'[22]

By saying that erotic art's specific difference is that it is *not* dirt for dirt's sake, the court is saying that pornography as a whole *is* dirt for dirt's sake. Although some 'dirt for dirt's sake' is now to be allowed because we want to be a post-moralistic, enlightened nation-state and not a narrowly puritanical one, nevertheless, the best that can be said about erotic art is that the 'dirt' of which it is composed serves a higher aesthetic or cultural purpose and is therefore redeemed. The defence of artistic merit does acknowledge that erotic art – which is to be sharply but mysteriously distinguished from pornography – might possibly convey some meaning. Yet, since this defence is a reverse-onus provision, artists are forced to pay legal counsel to prove that their work is the exception that proves the general rule that sexual speech is 'merely physical.'

Not being content to turn speech into a form of 'physical' action, the Supreme Court has recently decided that an activity that most people would regard as more physical than a picture, namely the form of stripping known as lap-dancing, is to be regulated not through nuisance laws but rather through the text of the *Butler* decision. Lap-dancing poses a risk of harm and is therefore 'indecent' according to *Butler*, although of course *Butler* says nothing about the indecency or otherwise of actual individual bodies, confining itself merely to the textual category of 'obscenity.'[23] It is as if strippers' bodies have become a representation of obscene representations, a second-order, hyper-discursive entity. Even the non-erotic and non-commercial bodily conduct of a woman who claimed the right to take her shirt off in hot weather came to be governed through the *Butler* text on texts. Two Ontario Court of Appeal judges felt that breasts were not necessarily sexual, and were therefore not indecent, at least not in the particular context of the accused; while the third judge stated that whether or not the act of taking off one's shirt is sexual or not is irrelevant, because the only valid test of community standards of tolerance is 'risk of harm,' and since no harm was likely to follow from the shirt removal, the woman ought to be acquitted.[24] So while, under *Butler*, some words might have become governable under action categories such as 'harm,' a few years later bodies have become governable under the explicitly discursive category of 'obscenity.' Deconstructionist legal critics could not have said it better.

The Dialectic of Judicial Subjectivity and Community Objectivity: The Community-tolerance Test

How can a thoroughly modern, culturally pluralistic, post-moralistic Supreme Court justify the existence of obscenity law? Given the notoriously arbitrary decisions of Canada Customs officials regarding prohibited importations (see the essay by Bruce Ryder in this volume), the court has found it necessary to save the honour and legitimacy of law in general by modernizing and 'objectivizing' obscenity law. This modernization has been effected in two stages.

The first modernization was effected in the 1962 *Brodie* (*Lady Chatterley's Lover*) case and reaffirmed and elaborated in the 1985 *Towne Cinema* decision. Taking sides with the more enlightened courts of Australia and New Zealand and against 'old-fashioned' British law, the Canadian Supreme Court decided that the test of obscenity was not what judges found personally objectionable but rather whatever exceeded the *community*'s standard of tolerance. In *Towne Cinema*, Chief Justice Dickson rebuked a lower-court judge for having used 'his own subjective standards of taste' rather than 'community standards.'[25] Addressing the difficult (and never yet solved) question of how a judge is sup-

posed to enforce the vaguely worded obscenity statute without recourse to his/
her own opinions, Dickson stated that evidence about the content of community
standards, from such experts as members of provincial film-censor boards or
from other sources, should not only be allowed but even required. Madam Justice Wilson joined Dickson in chastizing the hapless trial judge: 'It is clear from
the trial judge's reasons that he saw his role not as applying the community
standard but as raising the standard if he personally thought it was too low.'[26]
But, having climbed on the pedestal of democracy to criticize the moralism of
the lower-court judge, she then undermines democracy by disagreeing with
Dickson about the way in which standards are to be determined: 'Evidence of
the community's standard of tolerance may well be useful and indeed desirable
in many cases. None the less, I do not consider that there must be evidence,
expert or otherwise, which the trier of fact accepts before a particular publication can be determined to violate the community standard. *It is the opinion
of the trier of fact on the community standard of tolerance with which we are
concerned.*'[27]

We can see here that the opposition between subjective moralism and the
supposedly objective test of 'community tolerance' is thoroughly deconstructed by the same people who claim to be upholding it. The same Supreme
Court justice who ridicules the trial judge for his efforts to raise the community's moral tone then goes on to say that the judge is the sole authority on the
content of community standards. It is interesting that Wilson, who impressed
feminists around the world by ruling (in *Lavallee*) that courts ought to hear
from expert witnesses in the matter of 'battered women's syndrome,' feels that
while sexist judges need expert help to understand battered women, they need
no help whatsoever in understanding the equally complex workings of sexual
representations.

Since *Towne Cinema*, although expert evidence has sometimes been used, as
suggested by Dickson, it has never been clear what exactly counts as evidence
or what weight it should have. Sociologists and art critics are sometimes used as
expert witnesses in obscenity cases, but, as Becki Ross's account of her own
experience as an expert indicates, the courts do not necessarily recognize
'expertise' in these matters.[28] Public-opinion polls regarding the acceptability
of certain images or texts would be the obvious technique to introduce evidence
regarding the views of the community: but the defendants in obscenity cases are
rarely in a position to commission such polls, and Statistics Canada, which regularly produces polls on most subjects of legal relevance, has always stayed
away from questions of sexual morals. In any case, as it will become clear in the
following section on 'risk of harm,' the courts seem peculiarly resistant to relying on the technology of public-opinion research, perhaps because of their

vested interest in sharply limiting the power and authority of non-legal 'experts,' not only in the area of obscenity law but in other areas, for instance, in litigation on equality rights.[29]

The determination of obscenity is made even more complicated by the fact that the standard to be used is not the standard we all have for what we would tolerate in our presence but rather the standard we have *for others*. If community opinion is difficult to measure, it is even more difficult to measure community tolerance: any public-opinion poll that wanted to be legally relevant would have to undertake the tricky task of asking Canadians what standard they would use to govern what some generalized Other can consume. It would nevertheless be possible, if the judicial will existed, to carry out some kind of research to shed some light on what the 'community' thinks about the availability of pornographic and erotic materials. Such research would be an obvious tool to use in building the edifice of a modern, 'objective,' enlightened, Canadian law. But Supreme Court judges, much as they despise judicial subjectivism in the lower courts, are unwilling to endorse, in their rules of evidence, the sorts of techniques of knowledge production generally used to produce 'objective' standards.

In fact, the cure prescribed by the Supreme Court for judicial moralism and subjectivism turns out to be the illness itself. In a textbook case of an opposition that deconstructs itself, Justice Wilson admits (in *Towne Cinema*) that 'the community standards test itself, however, necessarily contains an element of subjectivity ... I believe this is so because what Canadians would consider to be acceptable for other Canadians is likely to depend heavily on which other Canadians they have in mind.'[30] This makes sense at the level of the 'reasonable man': if a magazine is made available only in a gay bookstore that is not at street level but up several flights of stairs, its impact is different than if it is given out free in schoolyards. Most members of the community would agree with this. The logic of law, however, cannot tolerate social differentiation and such a feat of contextual thinking, at least where obscenity is concerned.[31] Therefore, Wilson, having introduced the possibility of contextual moral standards, immediately recoils from it, going on to state that 'segregating the community into different groups for purposes of ascertaining the standard of tolerance' is simply unacceptable. Pluralism, which is usually regarded as a positive social feature in Canadian official discourse, is here described as 'segregation' – in a clever allusion that has the effect of stigmatizing what would in another context be a self-satisfied recognition of diversity. Why is Wilson, who is unusually well informed about issues of diversity and the law, be pushed to label contextual moral standards as a form of 'segregation'? It is because recognizing pluralism would lead the courts to using a fully contextual analysis rather than the 'inherent meaning' analysis favoured by the Supreme Court, which would in turn mean that, God forbid, there would be no longer be one 'national community standard.'

The attempt to identify the community with the boundaries of the nation-state is a peculiar one, given that today's discourse tends to deploy 'community' to validate local and ethnic ties *as against* the increasingly tenuous links of national citizenship.[32] But the Supreme Court, one of the few federal institutions that has neither been gutted nor had its authority devolved to the provinces and/or the private sector, has a deeply vested interest in identifying the 'community' with the nation-state, not so much to validate the community as to validate the increasingly tenuous Canadian federal state.

National interests, however, can be identified and defended through different technologies. Lacking the will to scientific 'objective' knowledge, and lacking also the political will to acknowledge the sexual and cultural pluralism of Canadian society, both the *Towne Cinema* court and the *Butler* court end up rejecting their own democratic aspirations, invoking instead a nineteenth-century notion of 'the moral consensus of the nation.' The phrase 'moral consensus' is actually used in Wilson's judgment in *Towne Cinema;*[33] and, since Wilson stated there that no expert evidence need be introduced to ascertain the precise content of this moral consensus, one is left with the impression that she is a firm believer in the long-discredited and potentially authoritarian Rousseauian notion of a 'general will': a transcendental moral consensus that is more fundamental than and independent of the vulgar empiricist 'will of all' measured by elections and public-opinion polls.

The community-tolerance test, therefore, far from shifting power from the judge to the community, has the effect of crowning judges as philosopher-kings. The standards are said to be those of the community, but courts – which means judges, since obscenity cases are not tried by juries – are the only ones empowered to decide what the community feels, in the same way that Emile Durkheim empowered the sociologist and Plato empowered the philosopher-king. The structural contradiction between the claim to judicial sovereignty and the simultaneous acknowledgement that the people (or more accurately, the community[34]) is sovereign causes the court's theory of meaning to self-destruct. It is not the court's own opinion of morality that is now being used, we are told, but rather the court's authoritative insight into the 'moral consensus' of the nation-state. The 'community standard of tolerance' developed to transcend judicial subjective moralism thus ends up giving judicial subjectivism a new authority by clothing it in the mantle of popular sovereignty.

'Risk' and 'Harm': The Perils of Pseudo-Actuarialism

Judge Sopinka's decision in *Butler* begins with a lengthy and (for the Supreme Court) unusually polemical binary opposition between the moralistic, British, God-made obscenity law embodied in the *Hicklin* test and the contemporary, post-moralistic, Canadian, community-made standards of current obscenity law. Developing the views on obscenity and harm articulated in 1985 by Wilson in *Towne Cinema*, Sopinka states that the Canadian Supreme Court justices no longer see themselves as the protectors of the morals of the people (a role authorized by the *Hicklin* test). Without acknowledging sexual pluralism as a valid form of social diversity, Sopinka nevertheless indirectly acknowledges that the moral authority of courts to save the public from being morally corrupted has been successfully contested in contemporary Canadian society, and that there is in any case little consensus about what is or is not offensive or immoral.

Despite the efforts of the *Towne Cinema* court to relegitimize obscenity law by deploying the ambiguous phrase 'community standards of tolerance,' throughout the 1980s there continued to be much public dispute about judicial and extra-judicial decisions on obscenity. Even such organs of the establishment as the Toronto *Globe and Mail* ridiculed the censorship decisions of Canada Customs officials, and the gay/lesbian community obtained a degree of public support for its claim that the obscenity law was being enforced in a discriminatory fashion. The *Butler* court was thus forced, in its landmark 1992 decision, to make yet another attempt to relegitimize obscenity by introducing a new test: the test of 'harm.' This was presented as simply a refinement or an operationalization of 'community standards,' hence creating a line of continuity between old and new obscenity law. The continuity is more wishful than real, however: the harm test undermines the very idea of community standards to the extent that harm is deployed as an objective category that is precisely the opposite of opinion. Sopinka sometimes says that the community's opinion is the only arbiter of what is obscene, but at other times he states that judicial determination of risk of harm is the only criterion. To cut through this Gordian knot, Sopinka quotes an earlier statement by Chief Justice Dickson to the effect that, when the two norms clash, judicial opinion (not surprisingly) takes precedence over popular opinion: 'Even if certain sex-related materials were found to be within the standard of tolerance of the community, it would still be necessary to ensure that they were not "undue" in some other sense, for example in the sense that they portray persons in a degrading manner.'[35] This puts the community in its place, well below that of the judge. And least one judge since *Butler* – Judge Coulter Osborne, of the Ontario Court of Appeal – has proceeded to use the

Butler test of 'risk of harm' as a *substitute* for the community-standards test, a move that reiterates the dismissal of popular practices of tolerance: 'It follows from *Butler* that in applying the community standard of tolerance test, the court must consider what harm will accrue from exposure to the allegedly obscene act or material ... Tolerance cannot be assessed independently of harm.'[36]

All assessments of risk are machines for governing deviance in particular ways, and the judicial test of risk of harm is no exception. The *Butler* court states that all sexually explicit material 'which subjects people to treatment that is degrading or dehumanizing'[37] is pornographic but not necessarily obscene. The trigger that results in such material becoming obscene and hence subject to criminal prosecution is whether the degrading or dehumanizing material poses a risk of harm: 'explicit sex [*sic*: explicit porn] which is degrading or dehumanizing may be undue,' that is, legally obscene, 'if the risk of harm is substantial.'[38]

This argument is congruent with Catharine MacKinnon's argument on the question of pornography. It may well be that, as the feminist lawyers in LEAF claimed, the Supreme court was receptive to the arguments made by MacKinnon et al. in the brief presented by the Women's Legal Education and Action Fund (LEAF).[39] But few feminist commentators have analysed the text of *Butler* closely enough to discover that women are never regarded by the Supreme Court as the main victims of pornography. Rather, it is *society* – or, occasionally, the abstract values of equality and dignity – that are the victims, with women in a subsidiary, metonymic role. 'Harm in this context,' Sopinka writes, 'means that it predisposes persons to act in an antisocial manner ... Antisocial conduct for this purpose is conduct which society formally recognises as incompatible with its proper functioning.'[40]

Sopinka, then, has been sufficiently enlightened by feminism to agree that violence against women is a social problem and that male batterers are socially deviant. But, like Dickson's language in *Keegstra* regarding hate propaganda, Sopinka's strikingly functionalist language of anti-social conduct seeks to incorporate the feminist insight about gender difference and the gendered nature of power into a liberal framework in which violence against women is said to be the conduct of a few deviants – and therefore *not* a systemic feature of 'society.' From the court's point of view, it does not essentially matter that it is women who are demeaned by pornography, since women's feelings are of no more relevance than the opinions of the 'community.' What matters is the judge's opinion about the way in which some representations do or do not cause harm to society, regardless of who is portrayed as being submissive or harmed in the representation in question. Obscenity is for the court an offence against the society and against the state, even if it is women who are harmed.

Sopinka goes on: 'Harm in this context means that it predisposes persons to act in an antisocial manner, as, for example, the physical or mental mistreatment of women by men, or, what is perhaps debatable, the reverse. Antisocial conduct for this purpose is conduct which society formally recognises as incompatible with its proper functioning.'[41] The syntactic awkwardness of the phrase 'or, what is perhaps debatable, the reverse' is not due to Sopinka's bad style but rather to the extremely awkward effort simultaneously to acknowledge feminist critiques of male violence *and* to 'de-gender' violence by briefly evoking the counter-factual spectre of women battering men.

It thus follows that, for the courts, lesbian and gay male pornography is just as obscene as heterosexual pornography. The fact that there is no subordination of women as a group, or indeed of any other group, being effected in either lesbian or gay male pornography is of no relevance. Indeed, there is nothing in Sopinka's words to prevent the 'moral majority' from arguing that feminism, especially lesbian feminism, is even more anti-social and hence potentially harmful than male violence. The post-*Butler* practice of targeting gay and lesbian materials for prosecution is thus not a 'perversion' of *Butler*'s 'true' meaning but rather an authorized extension of the *Butler* project simultaneously to name and undermine feminism.[42]

The American legal feminist Ann Scales, in an article that praises the Canadian Supreme Court for fulfilling the wildest dreams of American feminists, grandly states that 'obscenity law in Canada is now about gender equality.' But she has a footnote immediately after the term 'gender equality' admitting that 'nowhere does the *Butler* court cite the gender equality provisions of the *Charter*.'[43] The court agrees with MacKinnon that words can wound and can therefore be subject to criminal prosecution, but it does so for reasons that directly contradict feminism's emphasis on gender as a fundamental structural distinction. Feminism's starting point is precisely the insight that society/humanity has been defined from a masculine perspective, and that the experiences of women are not adequately contained in gender-neutral accounts of 'society.' But the court, judging feminism as well as obscenity, crowns itself as the sole authority on harm and rejects the notion that the standpoint of women should be used to decide questions of sexual representation.

That the text of *Butler* manages the remarkable feat of using feminist-sounding language to undermine feminism's basic insights on gender power is not simply this author's interpretation: it was also the view held by the judge in the famous post-*Butler* case involving the home-made lesbian S/M publication *Bad Attitude*. In a Toronto provincial court in 1993, Judge Claude Paris found a particular fantasy narrative in the magazine obscene according to *Butler*, saying that gender ought to be irrelevant in the determination of risk of harm in obscenity cases. His statement thus implicitly asserts that neither sex nor harm is fundamentally gendered.[44] The view that the risk of harm posed by pornography is so detached from gender structures that it can attach itself to lesbian situations (or even, 'what is debatable,' to female violence against men) demonstrates that the phrase 'risk of harm,' however feminist-sounding, does not have the same meaning for the Supreme Court as it does for feminists.

Whether 'harm' is interpreted as harm to a homogeneous 'society,' to the moral consensus of the nation, or to women's specific gender interests, the harm of pornography is not presented as a matter of scientific fact. Sopinka puts the 'reasonable man,' or perhaps more accurately, the judge's own internalized image of the reasonable man, in the position of naming and evaluating harm: 'While the accuracy of this perception [about harm] is not susceptible to exact proof, there is a substantial body of opinion that holds that the portrayal of persons being subjected to degrading or dehumanizing sexual treatment results in harm, particularly to women and therefore [sic] to society as a whole ... It would be reasonable to conclude that there is an appreciable *risk* of harm to society in the portrayal of such material.'[45]

The term 'risk,' therefore, does not operate as an actuarial category: there are no probability calculations measuring the likelihood that men who read pornography will comit violent acts. Risk – as we might suspect from the telling word 'reasonable' – operates here as a synonym for the old social and legal category of 'dangerousness.'[46] That is why the adjudication of risk potential is not a matter for forensic experts but rather for the courts. The courts have always made rulings on what and who is sufficiently dangerous to require a breach of normal civil liberties, and so judges have no trouble ascribing to themselves the power to decide unilaterally which representations pose a 'risk' of 'harm' without relying either on feminist scholarship on violence against women or on probabilistic calculations of forensic risk.

'Risk of harm' is a wonderfully useful phrase precisely because it can act as a switch-point among several unrelated social forces: the movement against violence against women, the criminological project to replace moralistic judgments of individuals by probabilistic calculations regarding populations, and the old legal concern to establish 'dangerousness.' Through its close connection with the phrase 'degradation or dehumanization,' which acts in turn as a switch-point between feminist insights on objectification and Christian philosophies of the flesh, 'risk-of-harm' acts to update and yet preserve obscenity law. The risk of harm test makes Canadian law modern, objective, and sensitive to the women's movement – while simultaneously preserving the old notion of a non-gendered 'general will' or national moral consensus that is imperfectly reflected in public opinion but is somehow discernible by judges, at least Supreme Court judges. Far from replacing moralism, then, the actuarial language of risk of harm manages – in what one might describe as a typically Canadian fashion – to effect a compromise that will please as many diverse interests as possible without ever actually engaging in, or even revealing, the conflicts and contradictions that constitute civil society and fragment the state.

Conclusion: Theorizing, Meaning, or the Legal Emperor's New Clothes

The basic move unifying the Supreme Court's decisions in *Towne Cinema*, *Keegstra*, and *Butler* is the project to redefine a certain domain of expression as not-quite-expression, such that it becomes governable through tests normally applied to action. Risk of harm has become the most successful of these. The risk-of-harm test suggests that what Dickson labelled as 'discounted' forms of speech, especially pornography, are to be judged not by their meaning but by their effect. And yet the move to replace subjective moralism by objective standards of harm undermines itself, since, as demonstrated in the analysis of the 'degrading and dehumanizing' test, the *content* of 'harm' turns out to be determined in at least a large part through the inescapably moral view that the problem with pornography is that presents a 'merely physical' view of life.

What about the Supreme Court's own speech? How does the court generate and judge its own speech? Is there any effort to establish the potential or actual harm caused by judicial speech on the gay/lesbian community, on the work of avant-garde artists, or on the lives of strippers? Of course not, responds the law, offended by the very idea of such a question being asked. The law is a text concerned with being right, not an action to be empirically evaluated according to its effects. The Supreme Court's conduct and speech presupposes but simultaneously conceals the belief that, while some speech should be governed according to the 'harm' criterion (in turn given a moral content), its own speech is not subject to any such evaluation, whether by empirical/actuarial experts, feminists, people involved in the production of erotic art and in the sex trade, or professional ethicists. The law's text wishes to be self-referential, self-contained, transparent, and univocal.

While never admitting that the Supreme Court's speech could ever be subject to the test of 'risk of harm,' the court undermines its own epistemological sovereignty in several places. The text of *Butler* bears many traces of the pitched battles fought inside and outside Parliament regarding the updating of obscenity law, the issue of violence against women, and the question of how to effect and justify moral regulation in a pluralistic society. As is traditional, the text of *Butler* does not directly name any of these battles – there is no mention whatever, for instance, of the very public campaign by gay activists to call attention to the censorship practices of various official bodies.

The reasons for this taken-for-granted tradition of social vagueness in judicial writing lie, it seems to me, in the fundamental mechanisms of judicial-truth machines. In an era in which the neoliberal emphasis on self-governance and choice has become the hegemonic politic, internationally as well as nationally, bodies claiming supra-popular sovereignty are forced to create rhetorical techniques to remove their own authority from the field of struggle and place it on a higher realm above the fray. The undemocratically chosen judges of the court, therefore, cannot name conflicts in civil society specifically, any more than the Queen or the Vatican can directly name particular local social movements. Such naming would acknowledge pluralism and unwittingly initiate a dialogue that can never take place if the sovereigns are to remain sovereigns and not just important citizens. It makes sense, therefore, that the United States Supreme Court's texts are less euphemistic and more directly political than the Canadian ones, for the Canadian court lacks even the tokenistic democracy of having Supreme Court appointments ratified by an elected body. Canadian judges can more freely engage in what one might call the euphemistic imperative of sovereign speech.

The action of the Supreme Court's own speech – its political effectivity, its actual or potential social harm – cannot, therefore, be directly acknowledged. The court has to hold on to the nineteenth-century view that legal meaning is found in texts themselves, even though this theory, apart from having been thoroughly discredited by philosophy at least since Ludwig Wittgenstein, is also in sharp contradiction to the theory that the court actually uses to evaluate other forms of speech. When judging obscenity and indecency cases, the court quite happily joins forces with postmodernism, in arguments that assume that it does not really matter if something is an actual body or a video, a thing or a text, since words can become things that wound and actual breasts can become instances of obscene expression. But its own speech is quietly removed from its social context and its social effectivity. The court is thus caught up in an irresolvable contradiction – what Derrida would call 'an aporia' – for it needs to uphold a theory of meaning that has been rejected not only by philosophers and social scientists but even by the justices themselves in their work of judging.

The postmodern deconstruction of the speech/action binary that the Supreme Court has produced in its judging work, therefore, is not reflexively applied to the court's own expression.[47] For, if such an eventuality were to be even contemplated, the bodies of the legal sovereigns would suddenly lose their clothes. And such an act of indecency would put the whole state at risk of harm.

NOTES

1 I am grateful to Alan Hunt, Peter Fitzpatrick, and Philip Stenning for their encouragement and their insightful comments on an earlier draft of this chapter, and to Bruce Ryder for emergency support and legal education.
2 Stanley Fish, *There's No Such Thing as Free Speech* (New York: Oxford University Press 1994); Stanley Fish, *Doing What Comes Naturally: Change, Rhetoric, and the Practice of Theory* (Durham, N.C.: Duke University Press 1989).
3 'Lap dancing ruled indecent by Supreme Court,' *Toronto Star*, 13 March 1997, 1.
4 Ontario Court of Appeal, *R. v. Jacobs*, 9 December 1996, unreported.
5 A pioneering example of the use of deconstructive methods to promote the general aims of critical legal studies is Peter Fitzpatrick's *The Mythology of Modern Law* (London: Routledge 1992).
6 Allan Hutchinson, *Waiting for Coraf: A Critique of Law and Rights* (Toronto: University of Toronto Press 1995); Michael Mandel, *The Charter of Rights and the Legalization of Politics in Canada* (Toronto: Wall and Thompson 1989).
7 B. Cossman, S. Bell, L. Gotell, and B. Ross, *Bad Attitude/s on Trial: Pornography, Feminism, and the Butler Decision* (Toronto: University of Toronto Press 1997).
8 For a critique of 'critique' that takes a Foucaultian rather than a deconstructive line of argument, see Nikolas Rose, 'Beyond the Public/Private Division: Law, Power and the Family,' in Fitzpatrick and A. Hunt, eds., *Critical Legal Studies* (Oxford, U.K.: Basil Blackwell 1987).
9 In semiotics, the term 'meaning-in-use' is deployed to stress that words or statements do not have a single fixed meaning but rather have different meanings depending on who uses them and in what specific context.
10 For Derrida, meaning can never be definitively fixed but is rather subject to an endless process of deferral (J. Derrida, 'Differance,' in *Margins of Philosophy* [Chicago: University of Chicago Press 1982].) Law's attempt to fix the meanings of terms and of actions, therefore, necessarily relies on setting arbitrary origins and end points (as will be shown in this chapter in relation to law's theory of what is speech). Law's view of meaning is not merely incorrect, however, in Derrida's view: it is also implicated in a foundational act of violence that sets up law as the ultimate, ungrounded authority. See Derrida, 'Force of Law: The Mystical Foundations of Authority,' in D. Cornell et al., eds., *Deconstruction and the Possibility of Justice* (New York: Routledge 1992).
11 Dickson CJC in *Keegstra* 1990, 61 C.C.C. (3d), 3.
12 Dickson, in ibid., 36.
13 Dickson borrows the term 'hate propaganda' from a 1966 blue-ribbon committee

that released a report on hate propaganda in Canada, which he quotes at some length. It was this report that led to the 1970 Criminal Code amendment criminalizing 'the wilful promotion of hatred.'

14 Dickson in *Keegstra*, 50.

15 Dickson in *Keegstra*, 65.

16 M. Matsuda et al., *Words That Wound: Critical Race Theory, Assaultive Speech, and the First Amendment* (Boulder, Colo.: Westview Press 1993).

17 Wilson in *Towne Cinema*, quoted by Sopinka in *Butler*, 148.

18 In *Keegstra*, Dickson had discussed the 'degradation and humiliation' caused by hate propaganda, while a Judge Borins, in *R. v. Rankine Co.*, used the phrase 'degrade and dehumanize' to refer to pornography films. The latter phrase is quoted by Sopinka in *Butler*, at 146. Dickson's phrase in *Keegstra* is not used, perhaps because Sopinka was on that occasion on the other side, but Sopinka does reference Dickson's judgment in *Towne Cinema*, which also used the words 'degrading' and 'dehumanizing' (Sopinka in *Butler*, 147).

19 Ibid., 146–7.

20 For my thoughts on the sovereignty of the Supreme Court's speech, I am indebted to Peter Goodrich, *Languages of Law* (London: Weidenfeld and Nicolson 1990).

21 Dickson in *Keegstra*, 59.

22 *Butler*, 149.

23 *R. v. Mara*; 1997 S.C.J. No. 29. The brief oral judgment issued by the court on March 12 is not yet available in written form, but it was widely reported in the newspapers on 13 March 1997.

24 *R. v. Jacob*, Ontario Court of Appeal, 9 December 1996, unreported.

25 *Towne Cinema v. The Queen*, Supreme Court of Canada, 1980, 18 C.C.C. (3d), 194.

26 Wilson in *Towne Cinema*, 195.

27 Wilson, in *Towne Cinema*, 211.

28 Becki Ross, in B. Cossman et al., *Bad Attitude/s*.

29 M. Valverde, 'Social Facticity and the Law: A Social Expert Witness' Eyewitness Account of Law,' *Social and Legal Studies* 5, no. 2 (June 1996), 201–17.

30 Wilson in *Towne Cinema*, 214.

31 The law of indecency appears to have become a repository for all of the contextual and sociological thinking that has been expelled from obscenity law. Ontario Court of Appeal Judge Karen Weiler has gone so far as to say that the test of indecency is so fully contextual that national community standards are not relevant to its determination, for indecency depends on the particular intentions and effects of the specific situation. (*R. v. Jacob*, Ontario Court of Appeal, 9 December 1996, unreported).

32 N. Lacey and L. Zedner, 'Discourses of Community in Criminal Justice,' *Journal of Law and Society* 22, no. 3 (September 1995), 301–25.

33 Wilson, in *Towne Cinema*, 215.

34 A political-theory treatise could be written on the ways in which the 'community standards' test presupposes and empowers a theory of Canadian sovereignty that effects a compromise between the populism of U.S. jurisprudence and the British alignment of the courts with monarchical-type sovereignty. The community is not 'the people' of U.S. law, since it does not represent itself; but it has a more democratic flavour than the Law Lords.

35 Dickson, quoted by Sopinka in Butler, 148.

36 Osborne, J.A., in *R. v. Jacob*, Ontario Court of Appeal, 9 December 1996, unreported, pp. 22–3.

37 *Butler*, 150.

38 *Butler*, 151.

39 That the LEAF brief was primarily written not by Canadian lawyers but by MacKinnon was a well-kept secret at the time, since anti-censorship activists would have used this information to discredit LEAF's intervention, but subsequently this has become widely known. For an insider's account of LEAF's involvement in the *Butler* case, see Karen Busby, 'Litigating Equality and Sexual Representation,' *Canadian Journal of Law and Society* 9, no. 1 (spring 1994), 165–92. A critical account is found in L. Gotell, 'Litigating Feminist Truth,' *Social and Legal Studies* 4, no. 1 (1995).

40 *Butler*, 150–1.

41 Sopinka in ibid.

42 See Jeffrey Toobin, 'Annals of Law: X-rated,' in *The New Yorker* (3 October 1994), 70–8, for documentation on how Toronto porn stores were being told to govern themselves according to *Butler*. (This article also interviews Andrea Dworkin, who distances herself from *Butler*, and Catharine MacKinnon, who praises the court's judgment).

43 Ann Scales, 'Avoiding Constitutional Depression: Bad Attitudes and the Fate of *Butler*,' in *Canadian J. of Women and the Law*, vol. 7 (1994), 358.

44 B. Cossman et al., *Bad Attitude/s*.

45 Sopinka in *Butler*, 146, 147. Emphases added.

46 For an argument about the ways in which the supposedly scientific measurement of 'risk' is often but a euphemism for the old notion of 'dangerousness,' see M. Douglas, *Risk and Blame* (London: Routledge 1993).

47 Judith Butler's recent analysis of the U.S. Supreme Court's ruling on cross-burning as permissible speech analyses the harm caused by judicial speech. She points out that the debates about campus free speech and race and gender harassment that have plagued progressives in the United States tend to create the illusion that the

main forms of harm and violence occur within civil society, hence taking attention away from the continuing coercion and violence emanating from the state, including the speech of the Supreme Court. See J. Butler, 'Burning Acts – Injurious Speech,' in A. Parker and E.K. Sedwick, eds., *Performativity and Performance* (New York: Routledge 1995).

5

Beyond Censorship: An Essay on Free Speech and Law

JOEL BAKAN

If earlier periods in Canada's communications history were marked by attention to the issues of national unity and broad public access, the current era will likely be remembered for its deep concern about censorship. The key issues in today's discussions and debates about broadcasting, newspapers, universities, the arts, and other communications channels relate to censorship. And there tends to be wide agreement that censorship is bad. To call someone a 'censor' is itself censorious – it condemns what that person is doing. It leaves little room for argument. Like the labels 'sexist' or 'racist,' 'censor' suggests something undesirable in the person or action it describes. The censor is a person or institution that is too weak, corrupt, or authoritarian to tolerate a robust diversity of ideas. Suppression of ideas, truths, and other forms of knowledge is not something enlightened people want to embrace or condone. Censorship, in short, is widely viewed in North America today as an evil force and a major threat to free speech.

Most roads in debates about censorship lead to law. Censorship usually involves a legal prohibition on speech, or a legal authorization to some official to prohibit speech.[1] Criticism of censorship often is articulated in the legal language of free-speech rights. The obvious essay on law and censorship would describe the rules and grants of authority that explicitly restrict or prohibit speech, organize and categorize them, and discuss whether their infringements of free speech are justified. I intend to do something else. I critique, rather than rely upon, the conception of law embedded in the concept of censorship. Today in North America, it is private power, not public legal restrictions on speech, that may pose the greatest threat to free speech. Law creates private power by protecting, among other things, property and contract rights and conferring corporate status on business enterprises. Private power, in turn, enables those who have it to propagate their messages and close off avenues for others to do so.

Law's role in constituting power relations, including those of communications, lies beyond the conception of law that dominates censorship discourse. Important relationships between law and communications thus remain unexplored within the censorship paradigm. In short, free speech, which I understand to signify an egalitarian, pluralist, and democratic conception of communications,[2] is poorly served by the focus on censorship that dominates the concerns of its advocates.

The first section of this essay examines the theory of law underlying censorship discourse and argues that it follows the contours of liberal legality. In the second section, I discuss how law shapes the social relations of communications, even where it does not take the form of direct restrictions, and I illustrate my points by analysing two case studies: schools and streets. The final section draws on these examples to argue that an exclusive focus on censorship in analyses of communications and knowledge-production can actually serve to undermine free speech.

Censorship's Theory of Law

Law is understood in censorship and anti-censorship discourse as explicit, direct, and promulgated by government and state agencies. It takes the form of rules that restrict speech (for example, criminal restrictions on obscenity or hate literature;[3] regulatory restrictions on advertising;[4] provincial licensing and zoning regimes that limit clubs and cabarets to certain kinds of entertainment;[5] judicially imposed injunctions on particular broadcasts or other communications,[6] or grants of authority to officials to restrict speech (for example, provincial regulation of cinemas, which includes certain standards relating to sex and violence, rating systems, and boards to apply the standards; decisions by city councils as to whether and where a protest march can occur; or Canada Customs agents' discretion to admit or not admit certain materials).[7] Broader definitions of censorship include private restrictions as well as governmental and state ones. Klaus Petersen, in this volume, defines censorship as 'a value-driven instrument of power used by an authority to control, restrict or otherwise interfere with the form or content of expression or the free flow of information,' a definition sufficiently broad to include private actors. 'There are,' according to Petersen, 'good reasons to believe that the most widespread practices of censorship today are non-governmental,' in the sense that they originate within corporations, the media, and private organizations.[8]

Whether censorship is construed narrowly to include only governmental and state actors, or more broadly to include private actors as well, the concept contemplates only *discrete* limitations and restrictions on communications, ones that are imposed by one actor on another. Arguably, that is censorship's defining feature: it contemplates, as Petersen notes, an authority's 'single or repeated act[s] of limitation.' Corporate control of communications, as a general phenomenon, is therefore not censorship, in his view, though 'an analysis of each individual case'[9] may reveal that particular corporate acts are acts of censorship. Petersen readily admits that drawing the line at discrete restrictions does not capture every process of knowledge suppression, but, he reasons, 'it is essential that we define boundaries, lest the term "censorship" become meaningless.'[10]

I want to argue that, in drawing the boundary at discrete restrictions, censorship discourse manifests a liberal theory of law. 'Legal rules and reports of cases [are taken] as the universe'[11] and the 'far-flung ramifications of legal ordering' are not investigated.[12] I have used the term 'atomism' to describe this aspect of liberal legalism: 'atomism represents rights as belonging to individuals (or groups), with other individuals (or groups) and institutions or state agencies having corresponding duties. It constructs social conflict in dyadic terms, as an accumulation of discrete clashes between rights-bearers and duty-holders, each clash potentially resolved by adjusting the relationship between the two disputants. Power relations and social conditions beyond the rights/duty dyad are irrelevant; disputes are considered and resolved outside the multilayered and complex social relations in which they arise.'[13]

The emphasis on discrete acts of repression in censorship discourse leaves out questions about how law creates conditions – structures and institutions – that differentially empower various speakers and messages. Questions are generally not raised about how law indirectly contributes to the domination of some ideas and the suppression of others through its constitution of the conditions under which knowledge is produced. The presumption of censorship discourse is that people *have* freedom of expression which is then taken away by some legal rule or act – by an act of censorship. The possibility that power relations of communications and knowledge production – ones that are sustained by law – systematically suppress the speech of some groups while facilitating that of others, and therefore that freedom of expression is already seriously encumbered for these groups before an explicit legal restriction is applied, is not integral to the analysis.

Beyond Direct Restrictions

Laws that affect communications indirectly are ones that grant some people power to propagate their ideas or to restrict the speech of others. Their purpose is not to restrict or propagate speech, but they sustain social and economic relations that have that effect. Laws that sustain private power – in particular the laws of property, contract, and corporations – fall into this category. With respect to property law, a web of common law and statutory rights entitle owners to determine which and on what terms people can enter and remain on their property and thus to control who can say what on their property. The full coercive power of the state will be brought to bear on those who refuse to comply with the dictates of property owners. They will be arrested, charged, and punished under the law of trespass. Having a property right thus means having power over others, including the power to control their speech. In this regard, Peter Hogg states: 'With respect to private property, the general rule (of both the common law and civil law) is that the owner has the power to determine who uses the property and for what purpose. This means that the owner has the power to determine the extent if at all that the property can be used as the location of signs, placards, pickets, speeches or other kinds of expression. This rule of proprietary power obviously affects the kind and amount of expression in our society.'[14] Property rights enable their owners to propagate speech, as well as restrict it, a point of particular relevance if the property they own is a newspaper, broadcasting facility, or publishing house.

Turning to contract law, freedom of contract, its fundamental principle, holds that private actors are free, within the constraints of legislative rules and some common-law exceptions, to enter agreements to exchange their property with whomever they wish and on whatever terms they wish, so long as certain formal requirements are met. So, for example, under the law of contract a newspaper or broadcaster can determine to whom it sells advertising space and from whom it buys material. Next there is the law of corporations, a set of legal rights and procedures that enhance the private power conferred on enterprises by property and contract law. Under corporate law, managers and directors are required to make only those decisions that can be linked to firms,' and thus investors,' interests. A newspaper or private broadcaster's primary responsibility is to its shareholders, not to provide access to different groups or serve other public interests.

To be sure, the rights and powers conferred on enterprises by property, contract, and corporate laws are regulated by governments and legislatures in ways that are designed to advance public goals. The Broadcasting Act, consumer-protection laws relating to advertising, and restrictions on concentration of ownership in the newspaper industry are examples of such legislation in the area of communications. Yet the extent to which regulatory law significantly limits the exercise of economic power in the public interest is debatable. Much clearer is the fact that regulatory regimes created over the last century are being dismantled by governments in Canada and elsewhere, and as legislative regulation of the market is rolled back – or redesigned to give greater scope to market relations – the power conferred on actors by the laws of property, contract, and corporations becomes greater. Through deregulation, corporations, whose primary purpose is to make money for investors, become less encumbered by public laws in exercising their rights of property and contract. To similar effect, privatization extends the reach of private legal ordering by shifting ownership and responsibilities for service-provision from public to private bodies.

The fear of direct legal regulation of speech that drives anti-censorship positions tends to obscure the widening influence of corporate power on communications that is resulting from deregulation and privatization. This is not to suggest that concerns about censorship are always misplaced. My point is that censorship discourse monopolizes, and sometimes distorts, debates about knowledge and communications. Arguments about the media, education, public order, hate literature, or pornography too quickly become debates about censorship, obscuring important issues and analyses that lie outside that concept's scope. In an effort to be suggestive rather than exhaustive, I want to illustrate my point by examining two domains of knowledge production – schools and streets.

Schools

Schools[15] are important sites of knowledge production in society. In schools children and young adults are required by law to be exposed to curricula designed by the state.[16] Direct legal restrictions on curriculum content – censorship – are surely an important concern in relation to schools. In several jurisdictions of the United States, for example, teaching about lesbians and gay men in a positive way is explicitly forbidden. There are three categories of such laws.[17] The first bans all discussion of homosexuality within the school curriculum (examples of this can be found in a New York City school-district resolution). A second category of laws prohibits advocating that homosexuality is acceptable (Utah and Arizona have such bans). The third category is more a form of required propagation – teachers must teach that homosexuality is unacceptable. In Alabama and Texas, for example, legislation requires curricula on sex education to emphasize 'in a factual manner and from a public health perspective, that homosexuality is not a lifestyle acceptable to the general public and that homosexual conduct is a criminal offense.'[18] These laws are largely the result of an organized lobby effort by conservative and far-right religious organizations.

Without wanting to downplay the importance of concerns about such restrictions, I want to argue that law's impact on curriculum extends beyond the imposition of direct restrictions. How production of the curriculum is organized – who controls it and what interests are served by the process – necessarily has an impact on its content. School law, as it currently exists in most North American jurisdictions, is an elaborate system of rules and standards that establishes public and democratic control over curriculum and other educational matters. Elected governments, legislatures, and school boards run schools and create curricula through legislation, regulations, and by-laws, the overall purpose of which is to advance the public good and ensure equal access for students. No doubt much is lost in the translation from theory to practice. Public education has many flaws – the possibility of restrictions on gay and lesbian curriculum content is one. But public education, even at its worst, answers to democratic and egalitarian ideals that provide at least some bases for accountability and progress. The school curriculum must be justified against standards that reflect these ideals, and there are avenues of participation for members of the public to debate and shape what schools are doing.[19]

The ideals and standards of public education are, however, threatened by increasing involvement of business in schools, a form of privatization. Governments are reducing funding for education, thereby causing schools to rely more and more heavily on corporate subsidies and sponsorships and to accept a corporate role in curriculum development.[20] Consequently, there is, according to education critic Michael Apple, 'growing pressure to make the perceived needs of business and industry into the primary goals of the school.'[21] 'To be successful,' states David Kearns, former U.S. deputy secretary of education and former chief executive officer of Xerox, 'the new agenda for school reform must be driven by competition and market discipline, unfamiliar ground for educators. Business will have to set the new agenda.'[22] Ontario's premier Mike Harris agrees. Through Bill 160, his government seeks to centralize control over education so as to impose 'changes that investors look for.'[23]

When business sets the school agenda, it does so in accordance with its own interests. Business corporations become involved in education to make money for their investors and to foster societal conditions that facilitate making money. Corporate sponsorships in schools are a form of 'strategic philanthropy,' which 'ties giving to tangible financial results'[24] and, more generally, aims to instil corporate values in children. Serving the needs of students, teachers, parents, or the general public is not within a corporation's mandate, unless doing so can be justified as good for business. Though there may be some overlap of interests between the former groups and business, and to this extent some benefits may flow to these groups from the involvement of business in education, for business, the bottom line is the bottom line. The logic of corporate law and practice ensure that the interests of shareholders and the firm in general are paramount over those of other groups. The various goals for business in getting involved in schools follow from this logic. 'The first,' according to Maude Barlowe and Heather-Jane Robertson, 'is to secure the ideological allegiance of young people to a free-market world view on the environment, corporate rights and the role of government. The second is to gain market access to the hearts and minds of young consumers and to lucrative contracts in the education industry. The third is to transform schools into training centres producing a workforce suited to the needs of trans-national corporations.'[25] A fourth purpose, not noted by the authors in this passage, is to profit from the provision of education services.

Different techniques are used by businesses to realize these goals. First, corporations target schools for advertising campaigns. Under one scenario, advertisements are brought directly into the classroom through teaching kits and other kinds of materials.[26] These involve both promotion of products (a school program on nutrition sponsored by McDonald's uses a Big Mac to illustrate the four food groups)[27] and corporate public relations (Proctor and Gamble's classroom Decision Earth program states that 'clear cutting removes all trees ... to create new habitats for wildlife. P&G uses this economically and environmentally sound method because it most closely mimics nature's own processes. Clear cutting also opens the floor to sunshine, thus stimulating growth and providing food for animals).[28]

Another scenario is represented by Whittle Productions' Channel One, a broadcast program designed exclusively to reach students in middle and secondary schools with advertisements. The company produces original programming with ten minutes of news and two minutes of advertising. Schools contract for a three-year period agree to let 90 per cent of their students watch the program daily in exchange for a satellite dish, two VCRs, televisions for each classroom, and wiring-and-maintenance facilities. Despite the fact some states have barred Channel One from classrooms, it is a highly profitable operation that claims to reach 40 per cent of all middle and high school students in the United States. Proponents of Channel One point to the free equipment and exposure to news students get, and claim that the advertising has no effect on students (a curious argument given the hundreds of thousands of dollars companies pay for advertising spots on the channel). Studies demonstrate, however, that exposure to the show increases students' product evaluations and desires to buy the advertised products, as well as fostering consumer-related attitudes of materialism, results that may be partly explained by the 'implicit endorsement of these products by the schools, that is, by permitting them to be advertised in school.'[29]

Though corporate-prepared materials may sometimes have educational value, they are inevitably oriented in ways that reflect the perspectives of the corporations that produce them. Self-interest, the driving force behind corporate involvement in schools, is what motivates corporations to provide schools with curriculum materials. As Ed Swanson of Modern Talking Pictures (an educational marketing company) states: 'If there's a cardinal rule in preparing sponsored material it is that it must serve the needs of the communicator first.'[30] Another educational marketing executive, Joseph Fenton of Donnelley Marketing, makes the point this way: 'The kids we're reaching are consumers in training. You want to reach consumers at their most formative point.'[31] Through the advertising embedded in such materials, corporations are able to create new markets for their products, improve their public image, and instil in children the general values and perspectives of corporate capitalism. The interests of students, their parents, and society as a whole in educating children and young adults are, at best, of ancillary importance.

A second trend in the privatization of schools is the creation of for-profit schools. Buoyed by his considerable success with Channel One, Chris Whittle proposed creating for-profit schools, which he (and many others) believe could outperform public schools at less cost. Under the label of the Edison Project, Whittle claimed that he could charge no more than the public school system spent on each student, provide scholarships to 20 per cent of students, and still yield a profit. This highlights a significant trend in the United States towards turning the provision of education from kindergarten through grade twelve into a profit-driven business.[32] Though private schooling is not a new phenomenon, if, as Whittle and others wish, for-profit corporations come to bear the primary responsibility for educating large numbers of school-age children, that would represent a major shift. Whether or not this occurs largely depends on legislatures' and governments' willingness to adopt some form of voucher system – an idea first proposed by Milton Friedman and currently being pushed by business and the right[33] – under which governments would transfer directly to parents the amount it costs to educate a child in the form of a voucher that can be used to pay the child's tuition at a school, whether public or private, of the parents' choice. With such a scheme in place, for-profit schools would compete with public schools for state-subsidized consumers of education. The Milwaukee school system is currently running a pilot project on vouchers, and intense lobbying to implement the idea continues across the United States. Voucher systems would, according to one commentator, likely exacerbate socio-economic segregation of students – causing 'greater inequality and the further deterioration of a common educational experience as social goals of schooling are sacrificed to consumer sovereignty.' Such systems could also increase government spending on education by as much as 25 per cent because of the need for an elaborate infrastructure for record-keeping, monitoring, accreditation, transportation, information systems, and dispute resolution.[34]

For-profit corporations are also getting into the business of running and managing public schools. Following Whittle's trail is again instructive since it is here that the Edison project ended up. Though the project never established its own private schools (mainly because voucher systems have not yet been created on a large scale), it has been hired to manage existing public schools. Whittle is not alone in this. In 1993 Education Alternatives Inc. (EAI), a publicly traded company, signed a five-year $180-million contract to run nine public schools in Baltimore. Two years ago it contracted with the city of Hartford, Connecticut, to run its entire school system, one that comprises 32 schools with 24,000 students and costs $171 million a year to run. EAI's pitch to school boards and investors is summed up by the company's chair, John Golle: 'We figure we can reduce operating and administrative costs by 25% and put 20% back in the classroom. The other five % will be our profit.' Perhaps not surprisingly, EAI failed in these lofty objectives – both Baltimore and Hartford ended up cancelling their deals with the company. Trading in EAI shares was suspended for a time, and the shares dropped tenfold in value from the time it had first made the deal in Baltimore.[35]

What does all of this have to do with law and censorship? As I argued above, privatization is a legal process involving the transfer of control over an institution, or parts of it, from government to a private, usually for-profit, enterprise. When corporations create curricula, or own schools or run them, they are controlling areas of the education system that were previously controlled by public authorities. This represents a shift in the legal regimes governing these activities. Corporations are legally obliged to advance the interests of their shareholders; public authorities are legally obliged to advance the public interest. Democracy in corporations is limited to shareholders' rights to vote; democracy in public institutions – such as legislatures and school boards – involves participation and voting by all members of the public. This shift in legal regulation is bound to affect the nature of curricula and education more generally. Corporate decisions about who and what are given voice – and, correspondingly, who and what are silenced – will be driven by concerns about profit and shareholders' interests. The theory of law in censorship discourse cannot contemplate the indirect effects of such shifts in legal regulation. Though censorship in schools is important, it is only part of the story about law, schools, and knowledge production.

The Street

The 'street'[36] occupies a central place in the democratic imagination. It is a public urban space, a place where people meet and congregate, where they rally, protest, march, picket, shout through megaphones, convey various forms of information, and simply enjoy their 'freedom just to be, to have a place in public.'[37] The 'ideal of a truly public place' and the 'heterogeneity of open democracy'[38] are embodied in the street. The idea of freedom of speech draws much of its evocative power from the street, for example, through images of protesters in Tiananmen Square, soapbox orators at Speaker's Corner in London's Hyde Park, and civil-rights and labour marches. The street plays an important role in Canadian freedom-of-expression law. In *Saumur* v. *City of Quebec* (1953),[39] a pre-Charter case, the Supreme Court of Canada struck down a by-law which gave the chief of police power to determine whether pamphleteering in city streets would be permitted. The plurality of judges held that the law violated the constitution's implicit protection of free speech. More recently, the Supreme Court of Canada held that the Charter protects people's right to freedom of expression on publicly owned property, at least where the exercise of that right is consistent with the uses of the property.[40] Handing out leaflets in a government-owned airport terminal and postering on public utility poles were each held by the court to be protected by freedom of expression.[41]

Public property, such as the street, is the only place where individuals who do not own or have access to the various forms of private property used to produce knowledge – broadcast facilities, newspapers, advertising firms, and so on – can reach an audience with their messages, a point acknowledged by the Supreme Court of Canada:

If members of the public had no right whatsoever to distribute leaflets or engage in other expressive activity on government-owned property (except with permission), then there would be little if any opportunity to exercise their rights of freedom of expression. Only those with enough wealth to own land, or mass media facilities (whose ownership is largely concentrated), would be able to engage in free expression ... The ... eminent goals [of protecting freedom of expression] would be frustrated if for practical purposes, only the favoured few have any avenue to communicate with the public.[42]

Similar concerns are found throughout United States jurisprudence on free speech and the street. Taken for granted in the expression of such concerns, and in the felt need of courts to protect speech on public property, is the fact that people have no free-speech rights on private property.

Emerging United States jurisprudence on the street and free speech focuses on the right of individuals to use the streets to survive, marking a shift from its earlier emphasis on rights to engage in political marches, rallies, leafleting, or speech-making. Whether panhandling is protected by the First Amendment from restrictions imposed by city by-laws and ordinances or state legislation has become a major free-speech issue in the 1990s. The American Civil Liberties

Union and a number of commentators argue that it is so protected.[43] The argument has been successful in some courts. Two courts in California, for example, have enjoined enforcement of anti-begging laws, and a court in New York has done the same.[44] The argument for protecting panhandling is that it is a form of political speech and thus entitled to the highest level of protection offered by First Amendment law: a panhandler's solicitation of money is construed as unintentionally conveying political messages – that poverty exists, and that it leads to substantial hardship and suffering. Anti-panhandling advocates dispute whether these, or any, political messages are conveyed and suggest that at best panhandling is a form of commercial speech and therefore deserving of only minimal constitutional protection.[45]

Canadian and United States jurisprudence on free speech and public property emphasizes the kinds of concerns captured by censorship discourse – namely, laws that directly restrict people's speech on the street – and debate focuses on whether such restrictions are justified. The cases discussed above fall within this framework. The street is taken as a given, a pre-political surface, and questions are raised about how law acts upon it.[46] I want to argue, again, that we should go a step farther and ask how law contributes to the creation and destruction of the street itself: what is law's role in constituting the social and geographic relations that are the street? How, through these processes, does it affect the realization of free-speech values? The street is not just a physical road – it is a set of social and legal relations. Whether it exists as a place of social interaction and what form it takes depend on the combined operation of law relating to private property, public ownership, and zoning. When space is legally ordered through private-property relations, free speech is not legally protected. Public ownership of property is necessary for constitutional protection of free speech. How the law divides up public and private property thus has profound implications for the protection of speech.

Privatization of public space – represented by shifts from public to private control and ownership of space – is a significant trend in both residential and urban planning and zoning. On the residential side, gated neighbourhoods, walled off from surrounding areas and regulated through networks of covenants relating to use and services, are now home to as many as four million people in the United States.[47] They represent, in the words of one study, 'a trend away from increased governmental control over land use and governmental provision of services and toward an increased reliance on privately created controls and privately supplied services.' Such neighbourhoods, the study adds, 'provide a new and more potent way to exclude unwanted persons and uses from the company of those rich enough to afford the increased control and privacy supplied in such developments.'[48]

Gated neighbourhoods are, perhaps, best understood as just an extension of the privatizing logic of residential zoning, a far more pervasive practice. How places are designed by law, in terms of permitted uses and aesthetics, propagates a strong sense of who and what is acceptable in that place.[49] Zoning of certain neighbourhoods that excludes all but single-family dwellings creates what are, in effect, private enclaves. Publicly owned streets occupy a small proportion of the total property in such areas, and various forms of regulation (such as anti-noise by-laws) ensure that the roads in these neighbourhoods are not meant to be used as streets, in the sense of places of public interaction.[50] Single-dwelling zoning requirements are intended to create neighbourhoods that signify and enforce a pastoral setting and middle-class values of domesticity and private property. Private home, yard, and garden define the ethos of the neighbourhood and mark it as a place of retreat from the public world of the street.

Privatization of space is a trend in urban as well as residential zoning and planning. Today, zoning law, in terms of what it permits as much as what it requires, is facilitating a trend in North American cities towards abandoning the streets altogether. As one commentator notes:

Canada's sidewalks are changing; they are moving indoors into private property. During the last several decades, Canadians have witnessed the erosion of traditional streets where public life transpired. The automobile, the skyscraper, the dispersed residential suburb, and the shopping mall have contributed to the demise of a pedestrian oriented, outdoor street life in our city cores ... Much of the country's civic life now occurs indoors on privately owned, publicly used, pedestrian places in the form of above-ground 'skywalks' between buildings, ground level office and retail complexes, atriums and shopping malls, and below ground shop lined tunnels.[51]

The movement of social life and interaction from public outdoor spaces to privately controlled indoor spaces is a major phenomenon in large North American cities.[52] In Toronto's downtown core, ten kilometres of tunnels connect 1100 shops and services, 63 buildings, 19 shopping malls, 5 subway stations, 4 hotels, the stock exchange, and city hall. Thirty-six principal corporations own the various buildings that comprise the underground network. The tunnels are used by approximately 100,000 pedestrians each day. Similar tunnel systems exist in Vancouver and Montreal. In Calgary and Edmonton, elevated and enclosed walkways are used instead of tunnels. More than eighty other North American cities have similar enclosed pedestrian systems, and they are a major phenomenon in Europe and Asia as well.

Tunnels and skywalks are usually privately owned. They are like malls in this

regard, places designed and used for public interaction but governed and controlled by private owners, generally large corporations, who have complete
authority to determine who can say what on their premises. Political demonstrations and speech, especially of groups – such as labour or poor people – that
challenge corporate-consumerist ideology, are highly unlikely in these places.
Demonstrators, along with panhandlers and homeless people (to return to some
issues discussed above), are simply thrown out by the private security forces
employed by the owners. 'The proprietors must maintain an atmosphere conducive to business, which necessitates prohibiting those members of the public
and activities they perceive as detracting from this objective.'[53] Even without
the actual use of coercive force, malls, tunnel systems, and elevated walkways
are hostile places for people who do not fit neatly into the image of middle-class
consumer. On city streets, there is an expectation of a heterogeneous mixing of
people. The environment created by mall owners and their tenants is substantially different. Here the middle-class consumer is made to feel welcome, while
others are decidedly unwelcome. The presence of security guards and surveillance equipment, as well as design and decoration (fountains, atriums, and so
on), are all subtly and not-so-subtly suggestive of a place where poor people,
political people – people who are there for reasons other than joining in the public rite of consumption – are not welcome.[54]

Moving indoors is not the only mode of privatizing space. The Urban Enterprise Zone (UEZ) is another phenomenon of relatively recent origin that may
pose a threat to free-speech values. Unlike malls, tunnels, and skywalks, it does
not necessarily involve shifts in the physical dimensions of public space but
rather the imposition on existing spaces of new legal and economic relations.
Such zones began in the United States in the mid-1980s – as of 1991 thirty-
seven states and the District of Columbia had legislation allowing for UEZs.
They 'seek to revitalize ... [a] state's most distressed communities' by attracting
major corporations to an area through 'sales tax exemption and reductions, corporate business tax credits, and unemployment insurance tax exemptions.'[55] It is
questionable whether and to what extent UEZs revitalize neighbourhoods,[56] but
even if there are some such benefits it is important to consider the wider effects
of building a neighbourhood around the needs of one or more corporations.
Marilyn Rubin and Edward Trawinski, supporters of UEZs, note that UEZs foster 'a change in the attitude of local government,' a 'cooperative attitude' that
lets 'the corporations know that government at all levels is willing to provide an
environment hospitable to the needs of its businesses.'[57] The effect of the UEZ
is, in short, to place considerable pressure on governmental officials to regulate
in ways conducive to the major corporations involved. Where conflicts arise
between the use of streets as places of social interaction and political speech

and the interests of the corporations, there is a real risk the latter will prevail over the former.

The Politics of Censorship

The concept of censorship captures only one of many different types of legal process that repress speech. That is the point I have illustrated by examining schools and streets. Ending the essay here, I would conclude that the problem with the concept of censorship is primarily an analytical one – it obscures important avenues of inquiry into law's relationship to speech. Furthermore, I suggest that the dominance of the concept of censorship can actually serve to undermine free speech. Within its terms, a direct restriction on speech – anyone's speech and any kind of speech – is necessarily a blow to free speech: censorship is always presumptively wrong because it always denies free speech. It might be justifiable, but only if necessary to avoid serious harm. To be against censorship one must elevate concerns about speech, as a form of behaviour, over questions of substance – who is speaking, what are they saying, and in what context of power relations? The only relevant moment and event is that of the direct legal restriction on speech. Power imbalances in the abilities of different groups and individuals to speak and be heard, themselves products of histories of legal and social relations, are ignored. As is true of other kinds of formalism, anti-censorship positions can contradict the very values underlying them.

Once we consider that people's power to propagate speech and restrict the speech of others is unequal – a result of legal and social relations – it becomes possible (albeit counterintuitive) to imagine that direct restrictions on one person's speech could advance the freedom of speech of another. Legislative restrictions can be an equalizing corrective to unequal power relations of communications. An example illustrates the point: 'If, in a roomful of people, some have access to a public address system, and the rest have just their unamplified voices, the latter will be drowned out. Their right to freedom of expression will be empty, its exercise entirely ineffective. A rule forbidding use of amplification devices would limit the power of microphone holders to get their points across, but it might enhance the capacity of the unamplified to express their views.'[58] Limits on election-campaign advertising spending, Canadian content and alternative-viewpoint requirements in broadcasting regulation, and restrictions on concentration in the newspaper industry – all of which have been challenged as violations of free speech – can be understood in this way. In short, creating a public domain of freedom of expression may require restricting the free-speech rights of private actors.

Schools and streets again illustrate the point. A state legislature could, for example, prohibit the use of Whittle's Channel One in public schools, as the legislatures of California and New York have done. This is an explicit restriction on speech, but its purpose can ultimately be justified in terms of free-speech values – namely, as protecting the curriculum from the narrowing influences of advertising. One might similarly propose restrictions in relation to other types of corporate influences on the curriculum such as the corporate-prepared packages discussed above. Supporting such measures is difficult if one holds a general anti-censorship position with its presumption against any restrictions on speech. With respect to zoning, legislation could be used to impose obligations on property owners (such as the corporations that own malls or tunnel systems) to respect the free-speech rights of people on their property. In 1986, a task force appointed by the attorney general of Ontario recommended amendments to Ontario's Trespass to Property Act that would do this.[59] The bill that incorporated these amendments never passed, partly because of effective lobbying by the shopping-mall industry and small business.[60] Such legislation, however, might itself be seen as restricting the free speech of property owners – by compelling them to use their property to support certain messages.[61] A general anti-censorship position, with presumption against all government restrictions and compulsions of speech, might clash with a desire to support such legislation.[62]

Herein lies the paradox of the recent ascendancy of concerns about censorship: censorship talk focuses on the need to protect the rights and powers of private actors to communicate free of governmental interference at precisely the historical moment when the increasing power of private actors – corporations that are driven by profit and are accountable only to their shareholders – is threatening free and open communications. Within the free speech or anti-censorship paradigm the presumed evil is restricting someone's, *anyone's*, speech. Drawing distinctions among groups occupying different positions in social and power relations is against the rules. This in-built universalism, typical of liberal discourses, commits one to attacking all restrictions and supporting all speech, regardless of the consequences for free speech itself.

Conclusion

I have argued that the concept of censorship has a narrow conception of the relationship among law, communications, and knowledge production. Law is implicated not only in directly restricting speech – the exclusive emphasis of censorship discourse – but also in constituting unequal social relations and conditions of speech. Censorship discourse is thus both under-inclusive – leaving out those legal mechanisms that contribute to the restriction of speech; and over-inclusive – bringing in all direct restrictions on speech, even those that aim to equalize social relations of speech. The solution is not to broaden the concept of censorship. Nor do I think that concept should be abandoned. It is useful for drawing our attention to discrete legal restrictions on speech. But it must be put into some context. Its monopoly on the politics of communications must be challenged. Regardless of what area of communications and knowledge is our analytical or political concern – and I concede my examples of schools and streets are but two of many – we must consider how the social relations of knowledge and communications, and the legal relations that sustain them, shape conditions that allow some to speak and silence others. The concept of censorship illserves the ideal of free speech to the extent that it impedes such consideration.

NOTES

1 I use the terms 'law' and 'legal' in a non-technical sense to convey the formal rules, principles, and standards of institutions. Legislative enactments, governmental regulations, municipal by-laws, judicially created common law, and rules and decisions of government commissions are certainly species of 'law,' but so too, at least for purposes of this discussion, are the rules and regulations of major public institutions – universities, schools, hospitals – and large private corporations. Also, when I speak of restrictions I mean 'control, restrict, or otherwise interfere with' speech: see Klaus Petersen, 'Censorship! Or Is It?' in this volume. This definition includes exercises of authority that require speech, as well as those that prohibit it. In this light, note that the Supreme Court of Canada has held that compelled speech violates freedom of expression as much as restrictions on speech: *Slaight Communications Inc.* v. *Davidson*, [1989] 1 SCR 1038.
2 For a fuller account of my understanding of these values, see Joel Bakan, *Just Words: Constitutional Rights and Social Wrongs* (Toronto: University of Toronto Press 1997), 9–11.
3 See, for example, *R* v. *Keegstra*, [1990] 3 SCR 697; *Ross* v. *New Brunswick School District No. 15*, [1996] 1 SCR 825.
4 See, for example, *Ford* v. *Quebec (Attorney-General)*, [1988] 2 SCR 712; *Irwin Toy Ltd.* v. *Attorney-General of Quebec*, [1989] 1 SCR 927; *Rocket and Royal College of Dental Surgeons (Re)*, [1990] 2 SCR 232.
5 See, for example, *Rio Hotel* v. *New Brunswick*, [1987] 2 SCR 59.
6 *Dagenais* v. *CBC*, [1994] 3 SCR 835.
7 *Little Sisters Book and Art Emporium* v. *Canada*, [1996] BCJ No. 7 (BCSC).

8 Klaus Petersen, 'Censorship! Or Is It?' 9.

9 Ibid., 4.

10 Ibid., 13.

11 Peter Fitzpatrick, *The Mythology of Modern Law* (London: Routledge 1992), 3.

12 Alan Hunt, *Explorations in Law and Society: Toward a Constitutive Theory of Law* (New York: Routledge 1993), 16.

13 Bakan, *Just Words*, 48.

14 Peter Hogg, *Constitutional Law of Canada*, 3rd ed. (Toronto: Carswell 1992), 979.

15 I focus on schools, not education in general. The issues of privatization and corporate involvement in universities is a large one, and there is no question that while these trends are still nascent in schools, they are a runaway train in post-secondary education. See, for discussion of this point, Bill Readings, *The University in Ruins* (Cambridge, Mass.: Harvard University Press 1996), and Howard Buchbinder and Janice Newson, 'Corporate-university Linkages in Canada: Transforming a Public Institution,' *Higher Education* 20 (1990), 355–79.

16 Not surprisingly, curriculum content is a site of ideological conflict. As one commentator says of the school curriculum: 'The decision to define some groups' knowledge as the most legitimate, as official knowledge, while other groups' knowledge hardly sees the light of day, says something extremely important about who has power in society ... What counts as knowledge, the ways in which it is organised, who is empowered to teach it, what counts as an appropriate display of having learned it and, just as critically, who is allowed to ask and answer all these questions are part and parcel of how dominance and subordination are reproduced and altered in this society.' Michael W. Apple, 'The Politics of Official Knowledge: Does a National Curriculum Make Sense?' *Discourse* 14 (1993), 1–16 at 1.

17 See Nancy Tenney, 'The Constitutional Imperative of Reality in Public School Curricula: Untruths about Homosexuality As a Violation of the First Amendment,' *Brooklyn Law Review* 60 (1995), 1599–1651, for detailed discussion of these categories and for examples.

18 *Ala. Code* s. 16–40A–2 (Supp. 1992); *Texas Health & Safety Code Ann. s. 15–716* (as cited in Tenney 1995).

19 The public outrage at Ontario's Bill 160 – a piece of legislation that would take control of education away from local school boards and consolidate it in the Ministry of Education – was based partly on the bill's removal of such avenues of participation.

20 The Ontario government indicated that it would cut close to one billion dollars out of the public school system.

21 Apple, 'The Politics of Official Knowledge,' 4–5.

22 Cited in David Shenk, 'Tomorrow's Classroom Today,' *Spy Magazine* (July/August 1994), 22.

23 Mike Harris, 'This system is broken: Mike Harris battles Ontario's status quo' [interview], *Maclean's Magazine*, 10 November 1997.

24 Nicole Harris, 'Things go better with Coke's money,' *Business Week*, 15 September 1997, 36. According to the author: '"Strategic philanthropy" [is] rapidly changing the face of corporate charity in the US. Funds disbursed to non-profit organisations by companies' marketing departments have soared more than ten-fold since 1986, to 2.5 billion last year.'

25 Maude Barlow and Heather-Jane Robertson, *Class Warfare: The Assault on Canada's Schools* (Toronto: Key-Porter Books 1994), 79.

26 For discussion of other examples of corporate-sponsored materials, as well as other methods of corporate involvement – such as sponsorships and direct-targeting of students in advertizing campaigns – see Barlowe and Robertson, *Class Warfare*; Consumers Union, *Captive Kids: A Report on Commercial Pressures on Kids at School* (Yonkers, New York: Consumer Education Services 1995); E.J Gong, Jr., 'Lessons laced with ads used in more classrooms: corporate sponsored teaching aids pitch more products to students,' *Seattle Times*, 1 April 1996; David Shenk, 'Tomorrow's Classroom Today.'

27 Barlowe and Robertson, *Class Warfare*, 84.

28 Shenk, 'Tomorrow's Classroom Today.'

29 Bradley S. Greenberg and Jeffrey E. Brand, 'Television News and Advertising in Schools: The "Channel One" Controversy,' *Journal of Communication* 43 (1993), 143–51. Rod MacDonald, president of the Youth News Network, a Canadian version of Channel One (though not nearly as successful as Channel One), implicitly supports this idea in noting that the value to advertisers of the network is that it gives them an opportunity to get around the fact that 'they can't get their messages across at all to students who zap away from advertisers at home' (cited in Barlowe and Robertson, *Class Warfare*, 157). When teachers require them to watch advertisements, in other words, the problem of ignoring advertisements at home is solved. 'When you have a captive audience,' explains Don Baird, president of School Properties USA, 'the message you give them can be [heard] for the next ten years in a positive environment. It's not a ten second thing.' Cited in Shenk, 'Tomorrow's Classroom Today.'

30 Shenk, ibid.

31 Ibid.

32 Peter Schrag, '"F" is for fizzle: The faltering school privatisation movement,' *American Prospect*, no. 26 (May-June 1996), 67–71.

33 The activities of think-tanks like the Reason Foundation – which receives 78 per cent of its close to $4-million budget from 26 private foundations and 62 corporations – are devoted to privatizing education.

34 Henry M. Levin, 'Educational Vouchers: Effectiveness, Choice, and Costs,' paper

presented at Annual Meeting of the American Economics Association, New Orleans, 4 January 1997. The author is David Jacks, professor of higher education and economics, Stanford University.

35 A description of the EAI story can be found in Schrag, '"F" is for fizzle.'

36 A term I use to include not only streets but also public places that may not literally be streets, such as plazas, town squares, and parks, where there is a tradition of public speech.

37 Jeffrey Hopkins, 'Excavating Toronto's Underground Streets: In search of Equitable Rights, Rules and Revenue,' in John Caulfield and Linda Peake, eds., *City Lives and City Forms* (Toronto: University of Toronto Press 1996), 70.

38 David Harvey, 'Social Postmodernism and the City,' *International Journal of Urban and Regional Research* 16, no. 588–601 (1992), 591 (as cited in Hopkins, 'Excavating Toronto's Underground Streets').

39 [1953] 2 SCR. 299.

40 This is a summary of a set of doctrines established by the court in *Committee for the Commonwealth of Canada* v. *Canada*, [1991] 1 SCR 139 and *Peterborough* v. *Ramsden*, [1993] 2 SCR 1084.

41 These were the issues in *Committee for the Commonwealth of Canada*, and *Peterborough* v. *Ramsden* respectively. One can legitimately wonder how far Canadian courts will go in protecting free speech when it comes to political demonstrations in the streets. In *Cheema* v. *Ross* (1991) 82 DLR. (4th) 213, the British Columbia Court of Appeal held that there was no infringement of freedom of speech when a police officer enforced a municipal noise by-law to prevent a member of the Communist Party of Canada from using a loudspeaker – and this despite the fact that equally loud public-address systems used by other groups at the rally were not found to offend the by-law. On 25 November 1997 I personally observed a severe and heavy-handed crackdown on peaceful protesters at the Asian-Pacific Economic Conference (APEC) on the University of British Columbia campus. Overall, the police managed to ensure that the world leaders participating in the conference were insulated from even knowing there were protests taking place. Students were prohibited from getting anywhere near the site of the meeting. When they peacefully protested this by walking up to the police line holding them back, they were pepper-sprayed, handcuffed, roughed up, and detained for twenty-four hours. Some students were detained, or threatened with detention, for refusing to take down signs put up along the motorcade route, and asked to undertake to refrain from all further protest (with no apparent time limit) as a condition of release. The events made a mockery of whatever constitutional rights to protest in public places exist.

42 *Committee for the Commonwealth*, 198, *per* L'Heureux-Dube J. (cited with approval by the court in *Peterborough*).

43 Helen Hershkoff and Adam S. Cohen, 'Begging to Differ: The First Amendment and the Right to Beg,' *Harvard Law Review* 104 (1991), 896; Nancy A. Millich, 'Compassion Fatigue and the First Amendment: Are the Homeless Constitutional Castaways,' *U.C. Davis Law Review* 27 (1994), 255. I am in general agreement with Allan Hutchinson's critique of Hershkoff and Cohen, and the approach it represents, in his *Waiting for Coraf: A Critique of Law and Rights* (Toronto: University of Toronto Press 1995), 95–101.

44 *Berkeley Community Health Project* v. *City of Berkeley*, No. C 95–0665 CW, 1995 WL 293899 (N.D. Cal 1991) (rev'd and remanded, 38 F.3d 1514 (9th Cir. 1994); *Blair* v. *Shanahan*, 775 F. Supp. 1315 (N.D. Cal. 1991); *Loper* v. *New York City Police Dept.*, 999 F.2d 699 (2d Cir, 1993).

45 Robert Ellickson, 'Controlling Chronic Misconduct in City Spaces: Of Panhandlers, Skid rows, and Public-Space Zoning,' *Yale Law Journal* 105 (1996), 1165–1248 at 1230.

46 Other examples of direct restrictions in the context of zoning and planning are easy to imagine. Restrictions on, to take two examples from very different contexts, architectural design (Comment, 'Zoning Law: Architectural Appearance Ordinances and the First Amendment,' *Marquette Law Review* 76 [1993], 439) or the sale of sexual services (*Prostitution Reference Case*, [1990] 1 SCR 1123) can be construed as directly restricting free speech. Noise control or littering by-laws may be similarly construed if they are enforced in ways that effectively restrict speech. See *Peterborough* v. *Ramsden*, *Commonwealth for the Committee of Canada*, *Irwin Toy Inc.* v. *Quebec*.

47 Mary Massaron Ross, Larry Smith, and Robert Pritt, 'The Zoning Process: Private Land-Use Controls and Gated Communities: The Impact of Private Property Rights Legislation, and Other Recent Developments in the Law,' *Urban Lawyer* 28 (1996), 801–17. See also Edward Blakely and Mary Snyder, *Fortress America: Gated and Walled Communities in the United States* (Cambridge, Mass.: Lincoln Institute of Land Policy 1995).

48 Ibid., 802–3. Gated neighbourhoods have an analogue in company towns – towns where employees of a company reside and that are owned by the company.

49 Zoning law is where this happens. Through it, local governments regulate the nature and uses of private property and thus help shape the spaces and places of social life. The following provision (from British Columbia's *Municipal Act* RS Chap 323, 45 Eliz. 2, s. 903[1]) is typical of legislation throughout North America: 'A local government may, by by-law, do one or more of the following: ... regulate within a zone the use of land, buildings and structures, the density of the use of land, buildings and structures, the siting, size and dimensions of buildings and structures, and uses that are permitted on the land, and the location of uses on the land and within buildings and structures; regulate the shape, dimensions and area,

including the establishment of minimum and maximum sizes, of all parcels of land
that may be created by subdivision ...'

50 Martha Lees, 'Preserving Property Values? Preserving Proper Homes? Preserving
Privilege: The pre-Euclid Debate over Zoning for Exclusively Private Residential
Areas, 1916–1926,' *University of Pittsburgh Law Review* 56 (1994), 367–440 at
370.

51 Jeffrey Hopkins, 'Excavating Toronto's Underground Streets,' 63.

52 The following statistics are found in ibid.

53 Ibid., 70–1.

54 See Margaret Crawford, 'The World in a Shopping Mall,' in Michael Sorkin, ed.,
Variations on a Theme Park (New York: Noonday Press 1992), 27, and Mike Davis,
'Fortress Los Angeles: The Militarization of Urban Space,' in Sorkin, ed., *Varia-
tions on a Theme Park*, 169.

55 Marilyn Rubin and Edward Trawinski, 'New Jersey's Urban Enterprise Zones: A
Program That Works,' *Urban Lawyer* 23, (1991), 461–71 at 461–3.

56 Scott A. Tschirgi, 'Aiming the Tax Code at Distressed Areas: An Examination and
Analysis of Current Enterprise Zone Proposals,' *Florida Law Review* 43 (1991),
991–1040, 1028–35.

57 Rubin and Trawinski, 'New Jersey's Urban Enterprise Zones,' 470–1.

58 Bakan, *Just Words*, 72.

59 R. Anand, *Task Force on the Law concerning Trespass to Publicly-used Property As
It Affects Youth and Minorities* (Toronto: Ministry of Attorney General's Office
1987).

60 Hopkins, 'Excavating Toronto's Underground Streets,' 75.

61 Legislation requiring broadcasters or newspaper owners to allow different groups to
use their property for speech are generally thought to limit the owners' free-speech
rights and it is likely that similar logic would apply to mall owners required by legislation to permit speech.

62 Bakan, *Just Words*, 72.

6

The Censorship of Commercial Speech, with Special Reference to Tobacco Product Advertising[1]

WILLIAM LEISS

The government of Canada's nearly decade-long attempt to ban tobacco advertising and restrict tobacco marketing has been one of the most prominent censorship issues in the recent past. The original attempt, in the 1988 Tobacco Products Control Act (hereafter TPCA), was struck down by the Supreme Court in 1995 (although the ban had been in effect throughout that period); the new ban, in the more simply titled Tobacco Act of 1997, was in the courts before the ink was dry on the legislation and certainly also will wind its way to the Supreme Court.

Advertising is known in legal terms as 'commercial expression' or 'commercial speech,' and in order to understand what is happening with tobacco marketing, we must first situate it within this broader category, which is where this paper begins. Traditionally, courts have afforded commercial speech a lesser degree of protection than, say, political speech, and so the key question here is: What principles govern the legitimate legal scope of control over commercial speech? The censorship of commercial speech is official control over the circulation of objectionable material. In our society such controls are, for example, designed to protect the public from misleading advertising, child pornography, or inducements to behaviour that might be injurious to health (misuse of therapeutic drugs). Seeking to restrict or ban tobacco advertising is warranted by a health-protection objective; but the most important point is that, in this case as in some others, restriction on commercial speech is intrinsically related to an attempt to control the use of a commercial product or activity itself, by subjecting some (but not necessarily all) of the aspects of its production, distribution, and consumer use to the purview of criminal law.[2]

If some restrictions on commercial speech are generally regarded as legitimate, why did the TPCA fail? The answer, according to the majority opinion of the Supreme Court, is that the government provided insufficient justification for the *scope* of the restriction on speech that was mandated in the act. As will be shown in this chapter's first section, the opinions supporting the court's majority decision regarded the government's defence of the act before the courts as poorly presented and argued, so much so as to invite thinly veiled rebukes from some justices. The government clearly had these judicial opinions in mind when it drafted the new Tobacco Act, although no one knows for sure if it will fare better than its predecessor did against legal challenge.

But legal arguments are only part of the story. What is the substantial *social interest* in restricting commercial speech for tobacco products? Tobacco manufacturers strenuously deny that there is any 'intent' in tobacco advertising either to persuade non-smokers in general to take up smoking or, especially, to persuade young persons to start smoking for the first time in their lives. Addressing these contentions becomes the cornerstone of any attempt to provide a broad, 'social' justification (rather than a purely constitutional one) for the restriction of commercial speech in this case. Hence, I devote the second section of this chapter to the demonstration that, first, all advertising is inherently an exercise in persuasive communication, and second, that this persuasive intent cannot be limited so as to avoid the two unintended persuasive acts noted above. This reasoning provides another substantial justification for the control over 'tobacco speech.' I conclude that restricting commercial speech about tobacco is also eminently reasonable from the standpoint of good public policy, and that it is only the scope of the restriction on tobacco advertising – that is, whether all such expression, or only some of it, should be censored – and not its justification in principle that is now at issue in our society.

Judged according to the social interest in restricting speech about tobacco, however, the Tobacco Act, like its ill-fated predecessor, fails ultimately in its purposes because it operates within too narrow a domain. The flaw is that governments in Canada and elsewhere do not seem able to construct a reasoned, overall conception of appropriate social-control measures for an entire class of substances to which tobacco – more particularly, its component nicotine – belongs. For want of a better term I call them 'psychoactive substances'; the class includes tobacco, alcohol, narcotics, cannabis, 'recreational drugs,' and some prescription drugs. The final section of this chapter is devoted to providing a matrix of the various modes of legal and social control over access to psychoactive substances in Canada, so that we can see the tobacco and health-protection issue – and its relation to controls over the marketing of tobacco products – in its proper context, which is rarely done. I argue for a balanced approach to this entire set of controlled substances, and for the need to construct a rationale for the controls over each in relation to specific social concerns.

What follows from this context-setting is a case for tight controls over some forms of commercial expression about tobacco products (direct retailing, marketing, and advertising) and for looser control over others (for example, sponsorships and other forms of indirect marketing). In this way we could achieve an enhanced level of social-control objectives while avoiding both expensive and protracted litigation and also the legitimate concerns about the total suppression of commercial speech for a product that still enjoys consumer support in a significant fraction of the population.

Commercial Speech and the Legal Test of Restrictions on Tobacco Speech

The dramatic tests of restrictions on speech often occur in our courts, and tobacco is no exception to this rule. Canada has had a bruising contest of this sort already, and there will be more to come here, as well as in the United States. However, as I shall try to show, the framing of these issues in terms of constitutionally protected rights of expression has not been, at least so far, entirely satisfactory. For, when the varieties of opinion in the collected ruminations of our judges are looked at as a whole, they do not appear to give us firm guidance in the matter: two of the most important Supreme Court decisions on controls over advertising to date have both been decided by a single vote, with the justices splitting many different ways in offering their reasons for one side or another; and in the tobacco case (referred to hereafter as *RJR-MacDonald*), there were also two different judgments from senior justices at the Quebec Court of Appeal.[3] Since these are well-considered opinions it is only fair for us to review them. But the quite unsettled state of judicial opinion also justifies us in looking beyond it to a broader context, namely, the nature of the social interest in controlling psychoactive substances.

Constitutional protection of speech as an element in individual liberty has a long history in U.S. jurisprudence, but it was only in the mid-1970s that 'commercial speech' was recognized explicitly as enjoying the protection of the First Amendment. The recent trend, in which commercial speech first came to be considered as entitled to judicial protection at all, albeit some lesser degree of protection as compared with 'political speech,' appears to be headed towards reducing any significant difference in the level of judicial protection being afforded to them.[4] This does also seem to be the path followed by the Supreme Court of Canada in the much shorter comparable history here, that is, the protection of expression under the Canadian Charter of Rights and Freedoms (Part I of the Constitution Act, 1982, section 2[b]). The ambiguities apparent in the U.S. legal tradition already have cropped up in Canada: commercial speech is sometimes said to lie at some distance from the 'core' of the guarantee of freedom of expression (what we can call 'political speech' is the core) and therefore is entitled to some lesser degree of protection than is the core.[5] But, as we shall see, this is an extremely loose characterization, which means that the operational applications – whether or not certain types of restrictions are lawful – have a highly arbitrary nature.

Section 1 of the Charter requires that any particular limitations on expression imposed by governments be 'reasonable' and 'demonstrably justified in a free and democratic society.' This means that the burden of argument for justifying any such limitations rests with the government. In the *Oakes* case (1986) the court devised a set of tests to ascertain whether those conditions have been met; in general, the application of those tests does not appear to depend strongly on what type of speech is at stake. These tests fall into two groups, two general principles and three subsidiary ones. The two general principles are, first, there must be a high level of importance attached to the objectives of any law which seeks to override the Charter protection of expression, and second, the means chosen to achieve the law's objectives must be 'proportional' to the expected outcome of the legislation. The three subsidiary tests are all designed to provide a basis for a judgment on proportionality.

Three matters are considered in determining proportionality: the measures chosen must be rationally connected to the objective; they must impair the guaranteed right or freedom as little as reasonably possible (minimal impairment); and there must be overall proportionality between the deleterious effects of the measures and the salutary effects of the law.[6] The three tests of proportionality are the operational mechanisms for the legitimate restrictions on expression. I will return to them later.

In the brief period of Charter litigation before the TPCA and its ban on advertising reached the Supreme Court, an earlier and most directly relevant decision was rendered in the case known as *Irwin Toy* (1988), where a narrow majority upheld Quebec's law prohibiting television advertisements directed at children under thirteen. One basis of the majority's reasoning was its acceptance of evidence from social-science literature that children under the age of thirteen could be regarded as being incapable of critically evaluating the manipulative intent of advertising. As David Schneiderman has observed, where the 'legislative objective is to prevent harm to identifiable groups,' the court will frame its pragmatic reasoning on proportionality more generously (that is, in deferring to the legislative intent); thus, the ban on advertising to children survived the 'attenuated *Oakes* test applied in *Irwin Toy*.'[7] The TPCA drafters attempted to follow this reasoning explicitly; section 3 read in part: 'The purpose of this Act is ... to protect young persons and others, to the extent that is reasonable in a free and democratic society, from inducements to use tobacco products and consequent dependence on them.'[8] In order to see why the legal tradition so far does not give us much useful guidance in the matter of controlling speech about tobacco, we need to understand why what was lawful in *Irwin Toy* was not so in *RJR-MacDonald*.

The TPCA's purpose was straightforward, namely, to safeguard the health of the Canadian public in part through a complete denial of the right to commercial speech on behalf of tobacco.[9] The implicit logic of section 3 was likewise transparent and may be 'unpacked' as follows:

- Protection of health is an acknowledged function of government;
- tobacco use is a significant and well-demonstrated threat to health;
- all and any advertising and promotion of tobacco constitutes an inducement to the use of tobacco products; and
- therefore, such inducements ought to be prohibited.

But what kind of statements are these intended to be? More to the point, should they be considered separately, one by one, or as a composite? Finally, what kinds of statements are they *required* by the Supreme Court to be, if they are to support adequately a restriction on speech? A good deal of confusion resides here.

The last set of questions has been decisive for the legal test of restricted speech. For the proportionality test evolved quickly after *Oakes* into a form where some kind of 'demonstration' would be required as to whether or not the type of restriction passed the hurdle of the three tests. This turns out to be an opening wedge for the broad utilization of social-science research in Charter litigation.[10] For example, take the 'rational connection' test. Considering the logic of the TPCA's section 3, is there a rational connection between the means chosen (the advertising ban) and the objective sought (protection of health)? One can assemble a host of studies from the social-science literature that are at least *pertinent* to the attempt to answer this question, and the government did so in its legal defence of the act. But do those studies *establish* such a rational connection? Is this different from making a *plausible* case for believing that there is such a connection? In short, what is the kind of 'proof' needed in order to pass the test?

A brief review of the TPCA's passage through three levels of judicial review will show how murky an area this is. *RJR-MacDonald* was first heard by a single judge (without jury) of the Quebec Superior Court, Mr Justice Jean-Jude Chabot. The federal government filed two kinds of evidence in defence of the act, namely, scientific descriptions by medical experts of the health hazards associated with tobacco use, and evidence about the nature of marketing, including expert analysis of internal tobacco-company marketing studies which had been obtained under disclosure. The expert medical reports were comprehensive and were supported by the filing of massive documentary material, including every one of the U.S. Surgeon General's elaborate reports on smoking. But Justice Chabot simply refused to examine the medical evidence in court, saying in effect that it was irrelevant to the case! This was so astonishing that, when the government appealed Justice Chabot's decision that the act was unconstitutional, it took the unusual step of refiling the entire body of its evidence with the Court of Appeal.

The Court of Appeal reversed Justice Chabot's decision by a 2–1 vote on all grounds. Writing for the majority, Mr Justice Louis LeBel commented dryly:

With respect ... the conclusions of the judge below [Chabot] do not take into account the evolution in the Supreme Court's application of this framework [*Oakes*] to constitutional cases since 1986. There is also a misunderstanding as to the nature of the evidence required to justify governmental or Parliamentary action, particularly with regard to economic and social policy. Interpreted literally, mechanically, without subtlety, the *Oakes* test and the burden of proof thus imposed on the government would more often than not deny Parliament the capacity to legislate.[11]

These comments go to the heart of the matter regarding the relation in Canada between judicial opinion and 'political opinion,' as exercised through Parliament, on matters such as restrictions on expression. For the question as to what exactly has to be demonstrated, both as to form and content, to pass the three-part *Oakes* test admits of neither a straightforward nor a settled answer. The result – as is shown in the discussions about the government's second try to control advertising speech (the 1997 Tobacco Act) – is to leave legal specialists still guessing, fully ten years after this all started to unfold, as to whether particular strategies chosen by Parliament will find favour with the Supreme Court's majority.[12]

The dissenting opinion at the Appeal Court by Justice André Brossard set up the main argument which the majority would use at the Supreme Court, namely, that the TPCA's advertising ban did not meet the minimal-impairment test of *Oakes*.[13] Specifically, Justice Brossard mentioned the possibility that, if the ban were restricted to certain types of advertising, as defined by its content – in particular, 'lifestyle' advertising – there would be no problem in meeting that test. Writing for the majority, Supreme Court Justice Beverley McLachlin said:

While one may conclude as a matter of reason and logic that lifestyle advertising is designed to increase consumption, there is no indication that purely informational or brand preference advertising would have this effect. The government had before it a variety of less intrusive measures when it enacted the total ban on advertising, including: a partial ban which would allow information and brand preference advertising; a ban on lifestyle advertising only; measures such as those in Quebec's Consumer Protection Act to prohibit advertising aimed at children and adolescents; and labelling requirements only ... In my view, any of these alternatives would be a reasonable impairment of the right to free expression, given the important objective and the legislative context.

The justices' annoyance is reflected in a statement that appears a few paragraphs farther on: 'Not only did the government present no evidence justifying its choice of a total ban, *it also presented no argument before us on the point.*'[14]

The last point is the critical one, and it is important to address it, since the new legislation has followed faithfully the court's direction, distinguishing between and defining three types of advertising (brand-preference, informational, and lifestyle) and specifically permitting the first two while banning the third.[15] Yet the government's bizarre failure, in defending its ill-fated TPCA, to argue that the scope of the act's broad ban on advertising was the minimum necessary impairment of expression required to achieve its health-protection objective will continue to have consequences under the new legislation.[16] First, regulators will find that trying to keep separate the three types of advertising is easier said than done, and that the creative minds that flourish at the ad agencies will get huge enjoyment out of testing these distinctions. The record to date of our rather indifferent attempts to oversee the content of alcohol advertising, particularly its lifestyle aspects, does not inspire confidence. Just about the only way of effectively controlling advertising content is to require regulatory pre-approval of ad content and design, the way it has been done in the case of prescription-drug advertising, but this approach is not used in the new Tobacco Act. Second, lawyers for the tobacco industry already have staked out the position that the section 22 definitions of the three types represent a back-door route to another broad ban: 'You may not [ss. 22 and 27] advertise a tobacco product except as permitted. What is permitted is what is called brand preference advertising and informational advertising. The evidence will show when this matter, as it will, comes to court, that no ad can be drafted which would fit within what is supposedly permitted without taking a serious risk of going to prison.'[17] While this may just be the usual lawyer's bluster, it also may be that some justices eventually will agree and strike down the new tobacco legislation.

More important, the government could have advanced decent arguments on behalf of the broad ban in the TPCA, using expert witnesses, to seek to persuade the court that the very nature of image-based advertising would make the threefold distinction virtually inoperable in practice. The demonstration of these practical difficulties would at least have tempered the court's annoyance, and may even have persuaded *one* additional justice to switch sides, thus changing the outcome. This weakness in the presentation of the government's defence of the TPCA was evident from the beginning, at the trial phase. Instead, the government concentrated its energies on assembling an overwhelming body of evidence on health risks, when anyone could have predicted that – as indeed happened – at the two senior levels of review none of the justices would evince any doubt about the nature of the health risks associated with tobacco use. The dissenting opinion from the Supreme Court, written by Justice Gerard LaForest, shows that these justices were willing to overlook the government's failure even to argue the minimal-impairment point largely because, for them, the self-evident importance of the health-protection objective overrode the need for any other justification for the restriction on speech represented in the TPCA's broad ban on advertising.

The Supreme Court's majority opinion suggests that an impairment of tobacco speech that had been crafted along the lines of *Irwin Toy* – prohibiting all promotion directed at children and adolescents – would have survived the *Oakes* test. It suggests also that an entirely different strategy, namely, a partial ban discriminating among three types of advertising, also would survive the test, and indeed this approach has been adopted in the new Tobacco Act. But what we lack, after the protracted litigation on the TPCA, is a critical examination of whether either or both of those alternative strategies are plausible means to the attainment of the health-protection objective. Nor do we have a reasoned defence of the other approach, namely, the TPCA's broader ban. Such a possible line of reasoning was indicated earlier, in reference to section 3 of the TPCA: If *any* type of advertising could be reasonably construed as an inducement to use (as it can), and if prohibiting all inducements to use of tobacco is a reasonable health-protection measure (as it is), then it can be argued that a ban on all advertising is not an unreasonable impairment of speech. However, it is not up to the courts to provide such arguments, and those who were responsible for providing them (the federal authorities) failed to do so.

Where does all this leave us with respect to the legal reasoning on restricting speech on tobacco? Not very far ahead, I believe, because of two different types of failure to date. The first is the government's, as just indicated. The second is that of the courts. The main problem here is the essential vagueness of judicial opinion on just where commercial speech sits with regard to the constitutional protection of expression in general. If political-type speech is at the core of this protected domain, and commercial speech is not a part of that core yet still somewhere in that domain, just where is it? Here is what Justice McLachlin, writing for the majority that struck down the TPCA, tells us: 'Commercial speech, while arguably less important than some forms of speech, nevertheless should not be lightly dismissed.'[18] With due respect to the learned justice, what is that supposed to mean? On the basis of the jurisprudence to date, it seems to mean that any senior justice will decide, depending on the particular case, circumstances, and arguments before the bench, whether to apply the *Oakes* tests strictly or loosely, and it will be virtually impossible for the rest of us to predict the outcome. The idea that one can distinguish sensibly between the 'core' and 'non-core' types of protected speech has never been well developed and, I suspect, ultimately cannot be defended; in short, the idea offers no guidance as to where commercial speech differs from other speech so far as its entitlement to constitutional protection is concerned.

Nevertheless, Canadian courts now appear to take it for granted that commercial speech is entitled to constitutional protection of some sort even though, so far as I know, no senior justice has ever devoted a decent argument to the basic point. There is at least a case to be made which denies this, and it has been reiterated recently, although the weight of opinion among legal scholars seems to be on the other side.[19] What the record of Canadian jurisprudence to date at the senior levels – applying the *Oakes* test to advertising in *Irwin Toy* and *RJR-MacDonald* – appears to show is that there is a preponderance of opinion in setting a relatively high hurdle for justification of the *degree* of impairment of speech, for commercial speech as for any other, specifically in requiring strong arguments where any broad impairment is contemplated. (With respect to the other two tests, rational connection and the balance between the benefits and costs of impairment, there appears to be more leeway afforded by the courts on the nature and type of evidence and argument required to sustain an impairment.)

And yet one wonders if the justices appreciate how difficult it is for any strategy for partial impairment of commercial speech to succeed in its objective of health protection. A look at how image-based advertising works may shed some light on those difficulties. This will lead us into our final section, where social control over tobacco use is examined in relation to our interest in controlling use of an entire set of related psychoactive substances. The point in doing this is to try to show two things: first, that control over commercial speech is only an aspect of the attempt to control the use of a substance; and second, that at least some of our difficulties, both legal and social, with respect to how to control tobacco use (including commercial speech about tobacco) lie in our society's inability to devise a rational set of social controls for the entire set of related psychoactive substances.

Advertising as Persuasive Communication

Advertising is a special type of social communication, namely, persuasive communication or, more precisely, 'a persuasive form of marketing communications
designed to stimulate positive response (usually purchase) by a defined target
market.'[20] Its specific purpose is to encourage consumers to purchase and use
the brands of goods or services offered for sale by the firm that pays for those
campaigns: 'The different promotion methods can all be seen as different forms
of communication. But good marketers don't want to just "communicate." They
want to communicate information which will lead target customers to choose
their product. Therefore, they are interested in (1) reinforcing behaviour, or (2)
actually changing the attitudes and behaviour of the firm's target market.'[21] To
enhance the persuasive effect of their messages, modern advertisers have
always filled their campaign strategy and materials with references relating to
what is happening in the surrounding social world. These references carry
meanings that 'spill over' the limited confines of the product message and inter-
sect with the larger processes of changing attitude and behaviour formation in
society. I call this the 'generation of surplus meanings,' and what I mean is
explained more fully later. First, I wish to list the main features of advertising
considered as a powerful form of persuasive communication:[22]

- *Advertising is about the linkages between people and products.* The main
  function of advertising is to communicate powerful images of the relations
  among people in acts of using products.
- *Advertising is a special form of persuasive communications*, that is, communications that are intended to stimulate us to think or do something.
- *There is little 'hard' information in national consumer-product advertising.*
  Rather, we find primarily an elaborate exercise in the construction of meaning by advertisers, through the association of images uniting persons, products, and settings.[23] Ad creators *encode* sets of meanings in their designs, and
  consumers *decode* these meanings. But there is not, and there cannot be, any
  control over the decoding process, so consumers can 'play' with the meanings encoded in ads. This device of using association to create meaning out of
  images permits a high degree of ambiguity in the message itself. Thus, the
  full range of meanings which all consumers – whether they are in the
  intended target market for the product or not – can extract from these images
  cannot be controlled at the source (that is, by the ad creator).
- *Advertisers use their predominant position in all media channels to transmit
  powerful images of lifestyle change.* By means of sophisticated design strategies, for about seventy-five years advertisers have been promoting not just

products and brands but also changes in the attitude and behaviour patterns of individuals in different societies.

- *Advertising is a multifaceted promotional method for bringing a firm's messages about its products to public attention.* Advertising is an integral part of what is called the 'marketing mix,' which is the total promotional effort made by a firm on behalf of its products.

Viewed in terms of communicative strategy, modern advertisements constitute inducements, communicated through powerful positive imagery, to participate in the activities that are represented, either explicitly or implicitly, in the advertising design. Advertisements are inducements to attitude and behaviour change in the broadest sense, incorporating both explicit and implicit suggestions to persons for participating in the activities that are shown in advertising imagery.

Surplus Meaning

Meaning or significance stands for everything about ad content that may resonate within the mind of a consumer when he or she experiences that content. Surplus meaning is the entire set of potential meanings in acts of social communication (such as advertisements), as decoded by audiences, as well as the effects of the decoding process on attitude and behaviour formation among members of audiences; such effects are over and above the literal statement of the message that is contained in the surface level of representation in every such act, for example, an advertisement. In advertisements this literal statement of the surface text is what may be called its 'universal message,' which is, I think it is safe to say, what every viewer of ads takes for granted on the basis of common sense: 'This ad is an inducement for me to try (or to continue to use) this product.' Surplus meaning may be generated both in encoding and in decoding activities.

Any component of ad design potentially may give rise to the generation of surplus meaning in the sense defined above. If the product package is shown, that may elicit memories of experiences related to the product (for example, if one's mother or father habitually used it, or a good friend now uses it, and this memory calls up positive feelings of close interpersonal relations). If any kind of background setting appears, that may generate significant meanings of widely varying kinds for different viewers. And if any representation of the human person appears, that may cause a resonance for an individual for one or more of the countless social experiences in his or her life. As indicated earlier, the ad creators will try to channel these meaning-generations along certain preferred lines (as tested with focus groups and so on), but they certainly cannot control all of them.

It is evident to most people, I believe, that *every* type of advertisement must be regarded as a general inducement to consume the product. (I doubt whether there is any firm which spends its revenues on advertising and which doubts the common-sense truth of this proposition.) And, if any such ad is seen or heard by any person who does not at that time consume such a product, or (if doing so) does have a resolve to discontinue that practice, then by the same token such an ad also is an inducement for that person either (a) to change her or his attitude towards the social activity of consuming such a product, or (b) to change her or his behaviour, that is, to begin using such a product (or suspend a resolve to discontinue doing so).

A Note on Brands and Target Audiences

Brand Preference

In cases where product advertising has been controversial for a long time (alcohol and tobacco products are good examples), the most common defence of that advertising is that it is intended to influence only brand choice among consumers who already use the product. In particular, it is claimed, those advertisements are not attempting to increase the amounts consumed; are not directed at those who do not use the products; and especially are not targeted at young people, who are commonly thought to be highly impressionable.[24]

But surely the inducement to try a brand that one is not now using, or alternatively not to do so (that is, to remain loyal), both of which are also and necessarily inducements not to cease the activity of using the product, cannot possibly be separated from the inducement to the activity itself: presumably one does not select a brand just to admire the package but rather to use the contents. And this type of inducement is precisely what the broad prohibition on advertising in the Tobacco Products Control Act was intended to forestall. Thus, it seems to me that the defence that only brand choice among confirmed users is at stake is simply not relevant to the purposes of a ban on advertising.

One simply cannot promote a product array (collection of brands) in today's marketplace without linking the brand images either to (a) some type of 'setting' – which may escape the prohibition on lifestyle advertising – or (b) more abstract visual images, for example, playing with colours, that allow the free play of mental association.[25] In other words, *any* successful brand-preference advertising for tobacco products that will be done, as permitted under the Tobacco Act, will certainly be an inducement to attitude or behaviour formation and *ipso facto* an inducement to use.

Target Audiences

It has also been claimed that the target audience for tobacco-product advertising is the proportion of the population as a whole that still uses those products (that is, already committed users). But it should be apparent from the foregoing discussion, and indeed from common-sense reflection, that neither product manufacturers themselves nor their advertising agencies can control completely the composition of the audience who will be addressed by their messages. Thus, to the extent that any tobacco-product promotional activities contain inducements to the activity of using the product (and I have shown above that they do contain such inducements), the messages generated by those activities must be presumed also to reach those persons who do not now use these products, as well as those who do use them but are attempting to stop doing so. In general, all promotional messages that are available to the general public must be presumed to be addressed to the entire audience of actual and potential users of the products so promoted.

With respect to the target audience (young persons) who are thought to be especially at risk from persuasive communications of all types, there is an unfortunate irony in the brand-choice defence that has been mounted in the case of tobacco-product advertising. What the brand-choice defence says, in effect, is that the entire marketing effort is being directed at accentuating brand images. But among all current marketing strategies it is precisely the generation of strong brand images per se that is most attractive to young persons![26] This appears to be grounded in, among other things, the need for identity for these age groups. Everyone has seen the proliferation of highly visible brand images of all types on clothing worn by young people in recent years. The general fixation by many young persons today on strong brand images raises concerns about the stated strategy of tobacco-product manufacturers to concentrate their marketing efforts on accentuating their own set of brand images.

Tobacco as a Psychoactive Substance: Controlling the Speech or the Product?

I have argued that the Canadian legal tradition to date is not of much help in staking out a firm position on limiting commercial speech about tobacco. As seen by the Supreme Court's majority judgment in *RJR-MacDonald*, the federal government inexplicably failed to make any argument at all to justify its choice of a scope for its ban on tobacco advertising in the TPCA – inexplicable, because such an argument could have been made, and of course should have been made. But in addition, the collective wisdom of the courts to date has not been especially clear or consistent as to how much protection will be afforded to commercial speech in specific cases, and why. This is a shame, because from the standpoint of public policy, the situation indeed should be quite clear, as mentioned earlier, when it is put into the following four-step series of propositions:

- Protection of health is an acknowledged function of government;
- tobacco use is a significant and well-documented threat to health;
- any and all advertising and promotion of tobacco constitutes an inducement to the use of tobacco products; and,
- therefore, such inducements ought to be prohibited.

Then why do we appear to be forever spinning our wheels on this issue? Perhaps one answer is that we insist on separating weighty issues of social policy that ought to be considered together. Tobacco control is a prime example, and we are unlikely to arrive at a better consensus in this area until we change our approach to it.[27] The basic problem is that for at least twenty years we have misclassified tobacco use as a social-policy issue, treating tobacco as if it were just a slightly hazardous but otherwise ordinary consumer product, such as a household cleaner, which should carry a warning sign and be kept out of the reach of young children, rather than as what it is in fact: a highly addictive drug whose easy availability is anomalous in relation to the way we treat all similar substances. The truth of the matter is that tobacco products are 'in pith and substance' (as the courts like to say) drug-delivery devices.[28] So far as the main use pattern is concerned, that is, smoking, why else would people deliberately draw toxic gases into their lungs, produced by the combustion of tobacco, marijuana, and hashish, opium, or anything else of this nature, if it were not to achieve the drug 'hit'?

The drug in question (nicotine) has remarkable properties and a versatile set of effects as a psychoactive substance, and one of the great ironies associated with this issue is that it was the tobacco industry that first discovered through rigorous scientific research on receptors in the brain how tobacco achieved its many different effects on mood and behaviour.[29] The issue of whether tobacco should be considered an addictive substance was settled in the affirmative in Canada from a public-policy perspective almost ten years ago, when an expert panel selected by the Royal Society of Canada issued its report, *Tobacco, Nicotine and Addiction*; since that time similar conclusions have been affirmed by the United States Institute of Medicine and published research results supporting this view have been proliferating.[30] Addiction is functionally equivalent to dependence, which is the term more commonly used these days, perhaps because 'addiction' had acquired some irrelevant moral baggage and stigma;

nicotine, cocaine, heroin, and alcohol all meet the medical criteria established for dependence. Given the seriousness of this health issue, the continuing and contemptible obfuscation on this point by the tobacco industry's public-relations spokespersons and lawyers in Canada and elsewhere is a scandal.[31]

At first glance we appear to confuse the public-policy issues even further when we lump tobacco with these other dependence-creating substances, because, of course, the record of unenlightened action in this broader domain in North America is appalling. Nowhere is this truer than in the notorious 'war on drugs' in the United States, where the clearly evident net cost to both society and individuals is so huge that persisting along this route defies reason.[32] But the fundamental wrong in all this is the criminalizing of all aspects of the production, distribution, and personal use of certain arbitrarily chosen types of dependence-creating substances, and of course Canada shares this stupidity with the United States and other nations.[33] The remedy is to create some form of largely decriminalized social-control framework for a whole set of medically recognized psychoactive substances, including nicotine. But, apart from the work of the LeDain Commission on the Non-medical Use of Drugs in the 1970s, whose progressive recommendations were ignored, Canadian public policy appears utterly unwilling to countenance even a reasoned discussion of this need.[34]

The relevance of drug policy to the censorship of speech about tobacco is, quite simply, that control over speech is a necessary but strictly subordinate element in a larger social-control framework for psychoactive substances. This has never been clearly recognized in our increasingly excited debates over tobacco use, and it is past time to place it at the centre of the discussion. With respect to psychoactive substances, controls over marketing and promotion are only one element (not the most important one) among others, namely, controls over some key aspects of production, distribution, possession, and individual use. An array of relevant substances and of the applicable control measures now in place is shown in Table 1.[35]

There are three pieces of relevant legislation in Canada and as of 1997 two of them are new. We have already discussed some aspects of the Tobacco Act; also in 1997 the old Narcotic Control Act was replaced by a new law entitled the Controlled Drug and Substance Act.[36] When we align tobacco alongside the other known dependence-creating substances in the context of applicable legislation, a huge number of anomalies leap off the page. I shall comment here only on those directly relevant to the social control over tobacco use.

Again, the main theme is to see control over speech as an integral aspect of an appropriate level of control over product use for a specific set of substances. In this context a number of general points can be made:

Table 1
Control of Commercial Speech as a Part of Product Control (Prepared by Tony Fleming)

Applicable legislation	Tobacco TA[6]	Alcohol Provincial	Schedule I substance[1] CDSA[7]	Schedule II substance[2] CDSA	Schedule III substance[3] CDSA	Schedule IV substance; prescription drugs[4] CDSA or F&DA[8]	Hospital drugs[5] F&DA
1. Criminal law							
(a) possession		some[9]	X[10]	X[11]	X[12]	X[13]	some
(b) seek or obtain			X[14]	X[15]	X[16]	X[17]	
(c) trafficking/sale	some[18]	X[19]	X[20]	X[21]	X[22]	X[23]	
(d) import/export		X[24]	X[25]	X[26]	X[27]	X[28]	
(e) produce	X[29]		X[30]	X[31]	X[32]	X[33]	some[34]
(f) punishment							
i, possession			s. 4 (3)[35]	s. 4(4,5)[36]	s. 4(6)[37]		
ii, seek/obtain			s. 4 (7)[38]	s. 4 (7)[39]	s. 4 (7)[40]	s. 4 (7)[41]	
iii, traffic	X[42]		s. 5 (3)[43]	s. 5 (4)[44]	s. 5 (3)[45]	s. 5 (3)[46]	
iv, export/import			s. 6 (3)[47]	s. 6 (3)[48]	s. 6 (3)[49]	s. 6 (3)[50]	
v, produce	X[51]		s. 7 (2)[52]	s. 7 (2)[53]	s. 7 (2)[54]	s. 7 (2)[55]	
vi, advertise	X[56]						
2. Control over distribution							
(a) strict			criminal	criminal	criminal		X[57]
(b) licensed		X				X[58]	X[59]
(c) regulation	age[60]	age					

Table 1 (*Continued*)

	Tobacco	Alcohol	Schedule I substance[1]	Schedule II substance[2]	Schedule III substance[3]	Schedule IV substance; prescription drugs[4]	Hospital drugs[5]
3. Control on use							
(a) individual	X	intox.[61]				X[62]	
(b) profession						doctor[63]	doctor[64]
4. Taxation	X	X					
5. Controls on marketing	X[65]	X[66]				X	X
6. Controls on advertising:							
(a) by media		Code				X[67]	X[68]
(b) all	X[69]						

1 Heroin, cocaine, opiates, and morphine are included in this category.
2 Cannabis, excluding non-viable seeds and stalks (hemp).
3 Amphetamines, LSD, hallucinogenic mushrooms, and mescaline are included in this category.
4 Schedule IV narcotics can be obtained by prescription in certain situations. Only those drugs listed in Schedule IV are considered narcotics. The over 600 prescription drugs listed in Schedule F of the Food and Drug Regulation are not considered narcotics and are not regulated as such.
5 These are drugs such as radiopharmaceuticals and biologics (vaccines).
6 Tobacco Act S.C. 1997. c. 13, proclaimed in force on 25 April 1997. The Hazardous Products Act, R.S.C. 1985. c. H-3, defines tobacco as a 'restricted' product in a schedule to the act. Products included within his schedule include matches, carriages, and strollers for infants. However, sections 3 and 12 of the act expressly exempt tobacco from the application of the act.
7 Controlled Drug and Substances Act, proclaimed in force 14 May 1997.
8 Food and Drug Act, R.S.C. 1985, c. F-27.
9 Minors are prohibited from possessing alcohol.

Table 1 (*Continued*)

10 S. 4 (4)
11 S. 4 (4)
12 S. 4 (4)
13 It is not illegal to possess Schedule IV to VI substances under the CDSA, or to possess drugs.
14 S.4 (2)
15 S. 4 (2)
16 S. 4 (2)
17 Section 4 (2) (a) allows an individual to seek an authorization to obtain a controlled substance only if they disclose the particulars of each substance for which they are seeking an authorization and disclose the particulars of all previous authorizations within the preceding 30 days.
18 Sales to person under 18 prohibited (s. 8, Tobacco Act). Sales in quantities less than 20 cigarettes prohibited (s. 10).
19 Sale of alcohol is prohibited unless done under authority of a permit.
20 S. 5 (1)
21 S. 5 (1)
22 S. 5 (1)
23 Possession for the purpose of trafficking is illegal; therefore, Schedule IV substances may be possessed for personal use only (s. 5(2)). Prescription drugs may be sold only by an individual licensed to prescribe (c.01.041 FDA Reg.).
24 Only a provincial government or the federal government may import alcohol (s. 3 Importation of Intoxicating Liquors Act, R.S.C. 1985,c. I-3.
25 S. 6 (1)
26 S. 6 (1)
27 S. 6 (1)
28 Schedule V and VI substances are also included. There may be exemptions available under the regulations (s. 6(2)). For prescription drugs, an importer must have a licence to sell in order to import (c.01.045 Food and Drug Reg.).
29 All tobacco products must be manufactured in conformity with the regulations (s. 5 Tobacco Act). Manufacturers must provide information about the product and its emissions to the government (s. 6 Tobacco Act).
30 S. 7 (1)
31 S. 7 (1)
32 S. 7 (1)
33 Exemptions may be available in the regulations (s. 7 (2)). A licence is required to manufacture prescription drugs (g.02.001 FDA Reg.).
34 A licence is required to manufacture Schedule C or D drugs (S.12 FDA).
35 Maximum sentence is 7 years for indictable offences and 6 months and $1,000 for summary offences. Where both indictable and summary offences are available the crown has the option of proceeding at trial either by indictable offence or by summary offence. The difference is determined by which penalty the crown will seek to obtain.
36 Where less than 1 kg of cannabis (Schedule. VIII) is involved, it is a summary offence punishable by 6 months and $1,000. Where greater than 1 kg is involved, the maximum penalty 5 years less a day for indictable and 6 months and $1,000 for summary offences.
37 The maximum penalty is 3 years for indictable and 6 months and $1,000 for summary.

Table 1 (*Continued*)

38 The maximum penalty is 7 years for indictable and 6 months and $1,000 for summary.

39 The maximum penalty is 5 years less a day for indictable and 6 months and $1,000 for summary.

40 The maximum penalty is 3 years for indictable and 6 months and $1,000 for summary.

41 The maximum penalty is 18 months for indictable and 6 months and $1,000 for summary.

42 Violation of sections 8, 9, 11 or 12 (sale to young people and method of sales) is a summary offence, punishable by $3,000 for a first offence and $50,000 for subsequent convictions (s. 45 Tobacco Act).

43 The maximum penalty is life in prison.

44 The maximum penalty is life in prison, unless the amount involved is less than 3 kg (Schedule. VII), in which case the penalty is 5 years less a day under an indictable conviction.

45 The maximum penalty is 10 years for indictable and 18 months for summary.

46 The maximum penalty is 3 years for indictable and 1 year for summary.

47 The maximum penalty is life in prison.

48 The maximum penalty is life in prison.

49 The maximum penalty is 10 years for indictable and 18 months for summary.

50 The maximum penalty is 3 years for indictable and 1 year for summary. For Schedule VI substances, the penalties are the same as for Schedule III substances. For Schedule V substances, the penalties are the same as for Schedule IV substances.

51 Manufacturing a tobacco product that does not conform to the regulations (s. 5) is punishable by a maximum fine of $100,000 and 1 year in prison on summary conviction and $300,000 and 2 years in prison on indictable conviction (s. 43 Tobacco Act).

52 The maximum penalty is life in prison.

53 The maximum penalty is life in prison, except for offences involving marihuana, which is punishable by 7 years.

54 The maximum penalty is 10 years for indictable and 18 months for summary.

55 The maximum penalty is 3 years for indictable and 1 year for summary.

56 Promotion of a tobacco product in violation of the act or regulations (s. 19) is punishable by a maximum fine of $100,000 and 1 year in prison on summary conviction and $300,000 and 2 years in prison on indictable conviction (s. 43 Tobacco Act). Violation of the labelling requirements set out in s. 15 by a retailer is punishable by $50,000 on summary conviction; manufacturers are liable for fines up to $300,000 and 2 years in prison (s. 46 Tobacco Act). Persons violating the advertising provisions (ss. 13, 20, 21, 22, 23, and 27) may receive a maximum fine of $300,000 on summary conviction (s. 47 Tobacco Act).

57 A licence is required under the FDA Reg.

58 Part G, Div.4 of the FDA Reg. describes the restrictions.

59 Part C Div. 3 and 4 of the FDA Reg. describes the restrictions.

60 Sales to persons under 18 are prohibited (s. 8 Tobacco Act).

61 Public intoxication and driving under the influence are prohibited.

62 S. 4 (2) (a) CDSA restricts the ability of persons to obtain certain prescription drugs.

63 FDA Reg. sets out licensing requirements for 'practitioners' in Part G, Division 4.

64 FDA Reg. sets out licensing requirements for 'practitioners' in Part G, Division 4, and for hospitals in Division 5.

Table 1 (*Concluded*)

65 Labels on tobacco products must contain the information required by the regulation s. 15 Tobacco Act). The use of product-brand elements in event sponsorship are restricted (s. 24, 25). The use of product-brand elements on non-tobacco products is restricted where the product is associated with young people or a prescribed lifestyle, i.e., an adventurous or glamorous activity (s. 26, 27). Offering any inducements for the purchase of a tobacco product is also prohibited (s. 29).

66 The use of commonly known alcohol names such as 'rye whiskey' is restricted to products which meet content and alcohol by volume requirements pre-scribed in the FDA Reg. (Part B, Division 2).

67 Prescription drugs may be advertised to the public only by reference to name, price, and quantity (c.01.044 FDA Reg.).

68 S. 3 of the FDA prohibits any advertisement for any drug that claims to be a 'treatment, preventative or cure' for any conditions listed in Schedule A, which includes cancer, alcoholism, and heart disease. Any sale of any product so advertised is similarly prohibited.

69 Section 18 of the Tobacco Act defines 'promotion' very broadly to include any representation about a product, by any means. Section 19 prohibits all pro-motions, except in accordance with the act and reg. s. 21 prohibits the use of any real or fictitious character or person in advertisements. Section 22 restricts ads to media not targeted to young people and prohibits 'lifestyle' ads which associate tobacco with a desirable activity. Sections 24 and 25 limit the use of brand elements at sponsorship events.

- There should be no criminalizing of possession for personal use of any dependence-creating substance, and of course this includes tobacco.[37] All of these substances provide important benefits to a segment of the population that should not be denied reasonable access to safe supplies of all of them.
- Society has a legitimate interest in controlling – but not denying completely – access by individuals to dependence-creating substances, especially young persons.[38] The available modes of appropriate social control are many and include, but are not limited to: licensing and inspecting production facilities; licensing and regulating distribution facilities; restricting distribution to licensed medical professionals; taxation; limiting amounts available to individuals and specifying age of access; regulating all aspects of promotion and advertising associated with the substances in question.
- An enlightened society has a duty to devise and provide adequate services to assist individuals who are addicted to such substances, by such means as: ensuring the availability of non-contaminated supplies; creating innovative programs for reduction and cessation of use; and providing pertinent information.[39]
- In all cases the chosen modes of control should be the minimum needed to limit the harm done to individuals by the abuse (but not the use) of dependence-creating substances, so far as possible, without unduly interfering with the rights of adult individuals to use and even abuse such substances so long as no evident harm is done to others.
- Society has a legitimate interest in taking special precautions about controlling – or even seeking to deny – access to all such substances by young persons; and
- Finally, there are two main unsettled points. With respect to tobacco, what are the anomalies in our approach to it as a member of this set of substances that ought to be corrected? And, in view of society's clearly legitimate interest in controlling all aspects of product availability and use with respect to this set of substances, what is society's legitimate interest in controlling inducements to their use directed at individuals – in general, and specifically in relation to tobacco?

In my view we can answer these questions sensibly and reasonably only if they are set within the context that has been outlined above.

The chief anomaly to date with respect to tobacco – considered as a full member of this substance set – is that there has been a clearly inadequate level of control over access to tobacco products. Federal government policy in Canada since the time of the TPCA's crafting in the late 1980s has exacerbated this anomaly by seeking to institute a broad ban on promotional activity for products that continue to be available in tens of thousands of retail outlets every-where. This silliness may be explained, but not excused, by the evident unwillingness of politicians to reduce sharply the nice profit margins on these products enjoyed for so long by so many voters. This anomaly simply must be addressed, and the logical place to start is to restrict the distribution of tobacco products to a much smaller number of licensed outlets on some version of the traditional Canadian model of alcohol retailing. This much is obvious. More controversial would be any proposal to adopt for tobacco the long-standing alcohol-control model in the areas of (a) simple possession by underage persons and (b) any product consumption in public places (outside licensed establish-ments). I do not wish to make any such proposal here, but merely to raise the issue as worthy of discussion.

Finally, where does control over any 'inducements to use' – the nub of the controversy over commercial speech here – fit within the broad model of soci-ety's legitimate interest in superintending drug dependence? When the issue is put into this context the answer seems to be crystal clear, so long as one is will-ing to acknowledge at least the plausibility of the following assertions:

- Some or many (but not all) individual users have acknowledged difficulties with managing well their consumption of dependence-creating substances, in terms of its impact on achieving their own life-goals;
- Individuals can easily gain access to all the information they need, relative to personal choices about using dependence-creating substances, from sources other than the manufacturers and distributors of those substance who stand to profit by these activities; and
- Inducements to use of any kind on behalf of these substances by commercial entities undermine society's legitimate interest in limiting – and indeed, perhaps, actively discouraging (although not prohibiting) – the extent of personal use of these substances.

It follows from these assertions that society has a clear right to ban all such inducements as a public-policy measure.[40]

Once this right is recognized and affirmed, as it should be in Canadian soci-ety, then the implementation of specific control measures for each type of sub-stance can be tempered with a good dose of common sense and a due regard for historical and cultural traditions. In the case of tobacco, I believe that it was unwise for the federal government, in drafting the Tobacco Act, to follow the Supreme Court's ill-considered *obiter dicta* on the reasonableness and practi-cality of differentiating between brand-preference and 'informational' advertis-ing, on the one hand, and lifestyle advertising, on the other.[41] *Direct* marketing of any kind to consumers by commercial entities for a known dependence-creating substance is contrary to legitimate social policy and may reasonably be banned. However, the commercial firms that provide these drugs should not be made pariahs in their own land. This applies to tobacco companies as well as to the established pharmaceutical manufacturers which one day, when enlightened policy finally prevails, will produce under regulatory supervision safe supplies of heroin, cocaine, opium, LSD, and other now-criminalized substances to consumers in socially approved distribution modes. All of them ought to be allowed to undertake controlled indirect marketing and promotion on behalf of their brands and products.

Indirect marketing – for example, marketing to health professionals who act as intermediaries for consumers – has long been permitted in the case of prescription drugs under a regulatory pre-approval mechanism. Governments will be appalled at the suggestion that they might do this for tobacco products or even (*horribile dictu*) for now-criminalized drugs! But this is only because they have the silly notion that one day no one will want to use any of these substances, an apparently compelling fantasy but a fantasy nonetheless. Other forms of indirect marketing such as sponsorships of cultural and sporting events, where company names and logos are featured, certainly could be tolerated so long as a pre-approval mechanism were in place to prevent abuse of the no-inducement rule. In this way governments could (as they should) simultaneously give explicit recognition to the legitimacy of limited personal use of these substances, the legitimacy of the interests of the commercial firms which are allowed to manufacture and distribute them, and the legitimacy of their own measures designed to exercise some reasonable control over all of this. If this were to happen, we might be able to end the ultimately futile haggles over the scope of commercial speech for tobacco, because finally we would have been able to put that relatively minor concern in its proper context. It is an unfortunate fact that, in realigning entrenched social policy, there will always be some losers as well as winners. The change in direction recommended above would, alas, mean rather less work for lawyers.

NOTES

1 Research on this subject was supported first by a Social Sciences and Humanities Research Council (SSHRC) strategic grant and by contract research with Health Canada, and more recently through the eco-research chair in environmental policy at Queen's University, supported by the Tri-Council Secretariat (National Science and Engineering Research Council, Medical Research Council, SSHRC) and

Imperial Oil. The author is grateful for the friendship of two colleagues who are important figures in the long struggle over legal control of tobacco products: Fernand Turcotte, Faculty of Medicine, Université Laval, and Neil Collishaw, formerly of Health Canada and now with the World Health Organization in Geneva.

2 A reader of this chapter asked why control over advertising should be regarded as 'censorship.' According to the standard dictionary definitions, censorship has two main characteristics: first, there is control over the circulation of 'objectionable' material in society, and second, this control is exercised by officials – in a modern state, officials operating under the provisions of legislation. Restricting or banning tobacco advertising by governments represents a partial or complete ban on certain types of expression in the marketplace of ideas, namely, speech about tobacco products. These bans are overseen by government officials. An example of a partial ban is the censorship of prescription-drug advertising, wherein the content of such ads (which is controlled according to certain rules) must be reviewed and approved in advance of publication by Health Canada officials. Censorship of commercial speech is, therefore, the subset of the more general field of commercial regulation that deals with all forms of expression about products and services.

3 *Irwin Toy* was 3-2 at the Supreme Court, with one opinion each for the majority and the minority (I have not examined the Appeal Court decision); *RJR-MacDonald* was 2-1 at the Appeal Court – with one opinion on each side – and 5-4 at the Supreme Court, where there were four important and different opinions. In total, therefore, there have been at least eight substantial opinions for these two cases.

4 Martin H. Redish, 'Tobacco Advertising and the First Amendment,' *Iowa Law Review*, 81, no. 3 (March 1996), 589–639, sections I and II. See also David A. Strauss, 'Constitutional Protection for Commercial Speech: Some Lessons from the American Experience,' *Canadian Business Law Journal*, 17, no. 1 (1990), 45–54.

5 Cf. David Schneiderman, 'A Comment on *RJR-MacDonald* v. *Canada (A.G.)*,' *UBC Law Review*, 30, no. 1 (1996), 165–80 at 171. I have relied heavily on this excellent article in what follows.

6 Supreme Court of Canada, *RJR-MacDonald* v. *Canada (A.G.)*, 21 Sept. 1995, opinion of Justice McLachlin, SCR ¶130.

7 Schneiderman, *A Comment* on *RJR-MacDonald* v. *Canada*, 173–5.

8 *Tobacco Products Control Act*, S.C. 1988, c. 20, s. 3.

9 The TPCA was challenged on a host of constitutional grounds. In the discussion that follows I limit myself exclusively to the freedom-of-expression issues.

10 John Kiedrowski and Kernaghan Webb, 'Second Guessing the Law-Makers: Social Science Research in Charter Litigation,' *Canadian Public Policy* 19, no. 4 (1993), 379–97.

11 Court of Appeal, Reasons of LeBel, J.A., *Attorney General of Canada* v. *RJR MacDonald Inc.*, 15 Jan. 1993, 36–7.

12 Senate of Canada, Proceedings of the Standing Committee on Legal and Constitutional Affairs, Evidence (Bill C-71), 20 March and 1 April 1997.

13 Justice Brossard also raised another issue which became important to the Supreme Court's majority, namely, the government's refusal (invoking confidentiality) to supply a document relevant to the case, a study apparently on the comparative merits of a partial versus a total ban. This refusal clearly annoyed the justices: see *RJR-MacDonald* v. *Canada*, ¶166.

14 Ibid., ¶¶163–9; the first quotation is at ¶164, the second at ¶167 (emphasis added). Justice McLachlin made the minimal-impairment test the key hurdle for the legislation and subordinated the third test (proportionality) to the former (¶175): 'A finding that the law impairs the right more than required contradicts the assertion that the infringement is proportionate.' In general, even the majority found no problem with the rational-connection test, joining the Appeal Court in criticizing Justice Chabot's ridiculously loose reasoning on this point. With reference to Justice McLachlin's characterization of the TPCA as instituting a 'total ban on advertising,' it should be noted that in his dissenting opinion Justice LaForest called it a partial ban. For example, point-of-sale publicity was not prohibited.

15 *Tobacco Act*, S.C. 1997, c. 13, s. 22.

16 It may be objected that this is clearly apparent only with the benefit of hindsight, and that the government lawyers could not have predicted that this point would be crucial in the court's reasons for judgment. I do not agree: it seems to me that *any* type of broad ban on expression so offends the Charter protections that some argument to defend it as the minimum (necessary) impairment is an unavoidable necessity. Moreover, a *plausible* argument in its defence (not a 'proof,' for there is no such thing) in the tobacco case is quite easy to construct.

17 Statement by Colin Irving, legal counsel for RJR-MacDonald, Senate of Canada, Poceedings of the Standing Committee on Legal and Constitutional Affairs, 1 April 1997, issue no. 52:28.

18 RJR-MacDonald ¶170.

19 The case is made by Allan C. Hutchinson, 'Money Talk: Against Constitutionalizing (Commercial) Speech,' *Canadian Business Law Journal*, 17, no. 1 (1990), 1–34. For the other side, see Robert J. Sharpe's comment, ibid., 35–44; Sharpe, 'Commercial Expression and the Charter,' *University of Toronto Law Journal*, 37 (1987), 229–59; and Stefan Braun, 'Should Commercial Speech be Accorded Prima Facie Constitutional Recognition under the Canadian Charter of Rights and Freedoms?' *Ottawa Law Review*, 18 (1986), 37–53.

20 K. J. Tuckwell, *Canadian Advertising in Action* (Scarborough, Ont.: Prentice-Hall 1988), 3.

21 E.J. McCarthy et al., *Essentials of Marketing*, 2nd cdn. ed. (Homewood, Ill.: Irwin 1988), ch. 15, passim (italics in original).

22 See the full discussion in W. Leiss, S. Kline, and S. Jhally, *Social Communication in Advertising*, 2nd ed. (Toronto: Nelson 1990); R. Marchand, *Advertising the American Dream* (Berkeley: University of California Press 1985); and S. Ewen, *All Consuming Images* (New York: Basic Books 1988).

23 In *RJR-MacDonald* the Supreme Court's majority suggested that 'informational' advertising should not be impaired although lifestyle advertising could be, and in drafting the new Tobacco Act the government followed this guidance, defining it as information about 'the product and its characteristics.' It is amusing to contemplate just what kind of ad content the justices had in mind here, especially since the tobacco industry keeps the nature of the non-tobacco additives in its products a trade secret.

24 This canard is recycled endlessly by tobacco industry public-relations personnel. A recent statement is from Robert Parker of the Canadian Tobacco Manufacturers Council: 'The one thing that advertising does not do is persuade people to start smoking.' (Senate of Canada, Poceedings of the Standing Committee on Legal and Constitutional Affairs, Evidence (Bill C-71), 1 April 1997, 62.) One wonders whether this statement would surmount the hurdle of proof demanded by the tobacco industry in court actions for the opposite proposition, namely, 'proof' that tobacco advertising causes consumption. Would this industry also say that its advertising makes it easier for smokers to quit (as most report they wish to do), which is also a health-protection objective?

25 S. 22 of the *Tobacco Act* defines lifestyle advertising as 'advertising that associates a product with, or evokes a positive or negative emotion about or image of, a way of life or an aspect of living such as glamour, recreation, excitement, vitality, risk or daring.' As someone who admires the creativity of ad designers, I am looking forward to seeing the many ways in which they will seek to communicate their messages while avoiding these prohibitions. One of the most inspired and effective ad campaigns of the last decade, created on behalf of the U.K. cigarette brand 'Silk Cut,' has already shown exactly how to do this!

26 See, for example, two articles by Jo Marney in *Marketing* (15 Nov. 1982 and 27 June 1983), reporting on studies carried out by the Child Research Services Division of the McCollum Spielman agency.

27 See, further, W. Leiss, 'Tobacco Control Policy in Canada: Shadow-Boxing with Risk,' *Policy Options*, 18, no. 5 (June 1997), 3–6.

28 There is a new concern about the easy availability of nicotine-maintenance devices used for smoking-cessation programs: K.E. Warner, J. Slade, and D.T. Sweanor, 'The Emerging Market for Long-term Nicotine Maintenance,' *Journal of the American Medical Association*, 278 (1997), 1088–92.

29 Stanton A. Glantz et al., *The Cigarette Papers* (Berkeley: University of California Press 1996), ch. 3; Richard Kluger, *Ashes to Ashes* (New York: Knopf 1996), 741–7.

30 *Tobacco, Nicotine and Addiction* (Ottawa: Royal Society of Canada 1989); B.S.
Lynch and R.J. Bonnie, eds., *Growing up Tobacco Free* (Washington, D.C.:
National Academy Press 1994), ch. 2, 'The Nature of Nicotine Addiction,' 27–68;
Nature, 382, no. 6586 (4 July 1996), 255–7.

31 See the recent obfuscations by the same Parker: Senate of Canada, Proceedings of
the Standing Committee on Legal and Constitutional Affairs, Evidence (Bill C–71),
1 April 1977, 107ff.

32 'The War on Drugs Is lost,' *National Review*, 12 (Feb. 1996), 35–48. I am indebted
to Barry Beyerstein of Simon Fraser University for supplying this and other materials used in this section.

33 See, generally, P. Hadaway, B.L. Beyerstein, and J.V.M. Youdale, 'Canadian Drug
Policies: Irrational, Futile and Unjust,' *Journal of Drug Issues*, 21, no. 1 (1991),
183–97. Barry Beyerstin, Bruce Alexander, Patricia Hadaway, and their colleagues
have published many excellent articles and books on this subject.

34 As noted below, the criminal-law power should be retained largely with respect to
only two aspects of these matters: first, regulating the supply of the drugs in question – specifically, regulating their safety and quality – to protect health; second,
controlling the provision of psychoactive substances to persons under the age of
legal majority. The retention of the criminal-law power for these aspects would be
the basis of federal authority in this area. Other controls on the retailing of psychoactive substances, for example, would lie within provincial jurisdiction, on the
model of alcohol retailing.

35 I received capable assistance in the preparation of Table 1 for this paper from Tony
Fleming, an MA at Queen's University Law School. And I am very grateful for
helpful comments made on an earlier draft of this paper by David Schneiderman,
Centre for Constitutional Studies, University of Alberta.

36 This is itself an obfuscatory enactment, mainly because it provides no explicit
rationale for its existence, simply defining a controlled substance as one that is
listed in any of the schedules to the act! And, of course, it solves none of the
known problems associated with criminalizing certain substances.

37 In view of this paper's length I am not going to argue this point here, and in any
case it has been argued well by others. On tobacco in this context, see P. Hadaway,
B. Beyerstein, and M. Kimball, 'Addiction as an Adaptive Response: Is Smoking a
Functional Behaviour?' *Journal of Drug Issues*, 16, no. 3 (1986), 371–90; P. Hadaway and B. Beyerstein, 'Then They Came for the Smokers but I Didn't Speak up
Because I wasn't a Smoker: Legislation and Tobacco Use,' *Canadian Psychology*
28, no. 3 (1987), 259–65.

38 Again, I cannot make adequately the case for these propositions here, so they will
have to subsist as *obiter dicta*. Beyerstein and others note that the original criminalizing of the possession of substances such as heroin and opium in North America

was strongly motivated at the time by racist ideologies. Obviously, being opposed to criminalization does not mean being against the creation of other, largely non-criminal social strategies for controlling access to psychoactive substances.

39 One of the saddest aspects of our society's perverted, pseudo-moralistic approach to the use of psychoactive substances is that we take no responsibility for cases of death and illness caused by the provision of unsafe supplies illegally to users who have no other means of obtaining these drugs. This is a mark of shame for a society that likes to imagine itself as 'the best in the world.'

40 I believe that the perspective advanced in this essay, seeing all advertising as inherently an inducement to use, would provide a plausible rationale for legal control over all tobacco advertising that might well satisfy the *Oakes* test for a majority of judicial authorities.

41 As mentioned earlier, the federal government has only itself to blame for being hurled into this pit by the courts.

7

Undercover Censorship: Exploring the History of the Regulation of Publications in Canada[1]

BRUCE RYDER

The history of the censorship of publications in Canada is, for the most part, a hidden history. Apart from relatively rare criminal prosecutions, and in contrast to the regulation of film, video, radio, and television by provincial and federal administrative bodies, there has been little in the way of visible, public regulation of publications. In addition, there has been very little scholarly exploration of the regulation of publications in Canada.[2] One could be forgiven for forming the mistaken impression that censorship of publications has been an exceptional event in this country.

One aim of this chapter is to begin the process of shedding some light on a few of the institutional mechanisms through which censorship of publications has been carried out in Canadian history. Another is to argue that the topic of censorship is best conceptualized broadly, as the exercise of power in relation to the creation or dissemination of knowledge. Censorship, in this approach, is not necessarily a political evil, so much as it is an inevitable feature of social organization. The exercise of power over publications should neither be condemned out of hand by cries of 'Censorship!' nor removed from public scrutiny by denials of censorship that rely upon narrow understandings of the term. Instead, we should evaluate the exercise of power in relation to publications by asking who is exercising power, over what expressive materials, according to what criteria and procedures, for what purposes, and in whose interests.

In popular usage, the word censorship is frequently used to express a conclusion regarding the legitimate uses of power. It is reserved for exercises of power in relation to knowledge that are considered illegitimate or unacceptable. Good exercises of power – editorial decisions made in compiling this volume, for example – are rarely considered censorship. It follows that censorship has no fixed meaning; rather, its meanings are as abundant as political theories regarding the nature of power and its legitimate uses. The only constant in popular usage is that censorship is always a dirty word. Censorship is bad. It is something other people do.

The meaning we each attach to censorship is thus determined by a set of prior normative assumptions about the legitimate uses of power. Hence, the difficulty of reaching a consensus in particular cases. Nevertheless, we should be able to agree on the breadth of our field of inquiry. If, for example, we restrict our analyses to state repression of expression through the use or threatened use of criminal sanctions, we distort and artificially restrict discussions of creators' freedom of expression and the public's access to representations. We need to think more broadly about how the production and dissemination of knowledge is organized in society.[3] For this reason, following Sue Curry Jansen, we understand censorship here as the deployment of power to shape the creation and dissemination of knowledge. By exploring its mechanisms and effects, we are exploring the nexus between power and knowledge.[4]

Measured by the actual or threatened deprivation of physical liberty, criminal prosecution does represent one of the most serious kinds of state censorship. It is also a high-visibility form of censorship that attracts public attention and generates controversy. It can be an effective means of regulating publications when there is a strong consensus among the judiciary and others in positions of power condemning the expressive materials at issue, as was the case with communist expression in the interwar years and as is the case with child pornography in the 1990s.

More commonly there exists no political or juridical consensus about which publications are undesirable and whether criminal prosecutions are an appropriate means of regulation. The language adopted in criminal legislation is often sufficiently open-ended to accommodate a wide range of meanings. A superficial reading of legal texts can yield the illusion of social consensus that the criminal justice system cannot deliver in practice. In these circumstances, criminal prosecutions become a highly ineffective way of pursuing censorship objectives.

The shifting and indeterminate character of legal categories of regulation has consistently hampered attempts at criminalizing the sale or distribution of publications. Precisely because criminal prosecution takes place in an open forum, where a defence is mounted and serious public debate and interest in the targeted materials is generated, its potential excesses will frequently be constrained in a democratic society. The political pressures towards suppression will not necessarily yield in the face of this obstacle, however; they may achieve greater success through less visible, less accountable means of accomplishing censorship objectives. When this occurs, the denial of censorship becomes a common and self-serving refrain of authorities exercising power over knowledge, a denial that is facilitated by narrow definitions of censorship that focus on actual or threatened state deprivations of the physical liberty of authors, publishers, distributors, or retailers. In liberal democracies the apparent promotion of intellectual self-determination is a necessity and the practices of censorship are thus in need of disguise. We need not be party to such dissembling in our own analyses.

When we focus on the questions of who is exercising power in relation to knowledge, with what qualifications, over what expressive material, according to what criteria and procedures, for what purposes, and in whose interests, the problems with how the regulation of publications has been carried out in Canada become apparent. Power over publications has been exercised by persons with questionable authority, training, or expertise, according to procedures that are largely hidden and unaccountable, by deploying criteria that are vague and indeterminate if specified at all, usually for the purpose of forestalling perceived challenges to the existing moral or political order. Ironically, these weaknesses are largely a product of the difficulties in liberal-democratic theory and practice of regulating the content of publications openly. Where political pressure is exerted towards suppression, concerns about censorship and a lack of consensus about its appropriate mechanisms and forms have led the state away from criminalization and towards less visible, less accountable forms of regulation. The result is that too many Canadians have been either uninformed or complacent: so long as the exercise of power over publications has been invisible, there has been nothing to worry about.

To illustrate these points, I will conduct a brief review, drawn primarily from public archival sources, of the origins, features, and practices of three institutions that have exercised significant power over the distribution of publications in Canada. I will examine Canada Customs' still-existing powers to prohibit the entry of imported publications; the Alberta Advisory Board on Objectionable Publications' exercise of power over the distribution of magazines for two decades beginning in 1954; and the Ontario attorney general's Obscene Literature Committee's exercise of power over allegedly obscene publications in the 1960s.

Canada Customs Prohibitions of Imported Publications

I do not like to admit that we are running a censorship board of any kind. I prefer to speak of it as an unpleasant duty of classification under the tariff.[5]

David Sim, deputy minister of customs and excise, Department of National Revenue, 1953

On 26 January 1923 the commissioner of customs and excise issued circular 244–C to Customs collectors. Under the heading 'Prohibited Books and Publications,' it read as follows: 'The importation of the following book or publication is prohibited under Item 1201, Schedule 'C' and Section 11 of the Customs Tariff, *1907*, viz: *Ulysses*, by James Joyce, Published for the Egoist Press, London, by John Rodker, Paris, 1922. Seizures of this book by officers of Customs and Excise are to be reported to the Department on Form K-9 in the usual course.'[6] And so it was that a book now recognized as one of the masterpieces of twentieth-century literature came to be banned in Canada. At the time there was no legal right to appeal a Customs ruling to a court. Once a book was added to the list of prohibited publications, it stayed there until Customs officials changed their minds, often decades later. In 1949 journalist Blair Fraser reminded David Sim, the deputy minister of customs and excise, that *Ulysses* was still banned in Canada. Sim took the book with him on vacation and decided that it was no longer obscene.[7] And thus the ban on *Ulysses* came to be lifted in the fall of 1949 as quietly and as fortuitously as it had been imposed, with no fanfare, indeed no public announcement.

A similar story could be told for thousands of other books and periodicals banned by Canada Customs. A great deal of censorship of books and periodicals has been and still is carried out through relatively invisible and unaccountable administrative decision making by officials in the Department of National Revenue.

The current source of the power accorded to Customs officers to prohibit the importation of publications is the Customs Tariff.[8] Tariff item 9899.00.00 lists prohibited goods that can be seized at the border. It reads as follows:

Books, printed paper, drawings, paintings, prints, photographs or representations of any kind that

(a) are deemed to be obscene under subsection 163(8) of the Criminal Code;
(b) constitute hate propaganda within the meaning of subsection 320(8) of the Criminal Code;
(c) are of a treasonable character within the meaning of section 46 of the Criminal Code; or
(d) are of a seditious character within the meaning of sections 59 and 60 of the Criminal Code.

It is one of the many tasks of Customs officials at border points and international mail depots to determine the correct tariff classification of all goods entering the country. Section 58 of the Customs Act[9] empowers an officer, defined simply as a person employed in the administration of the act, to determine the tariff classification of all imported goods, including whether publications should be classified as prohibited under Tariff item 9899.00.00. The statute makes no attempt to ensure that the designated officers have any relevant training or opportunity to develop expertise. The same is true of the officers empowered to render decisions on requests for redetermination, namely, 'Tariff and Values Administrators' at the first level of internal review (sections 59 and 60) and the deputy minister of national revenue at the second level (section 63). Whether these decision makers will have any training, experience, or expertise relevant to drawing the line between legal and illegal forms of expression is a matter the statute leaves to chance. Apart from the right to appeal the deputy minister's redetermination to court (sections 67 and 71), no special procedures are established by the act for determining whether publications should be classed as prohibited. The legislative policy of the Canadian government appears to be that such determinations are to be treated as raising legal issues no different in difficulty or importance than those raised by the determination of the correct tariff on other goods. The elementary point that other tariff classifications have nothing to do with freedom of expression appears to have been overlooked in the drafting of the legislation.

One of the reasons for this is that the origins of Tariff item 9899.00.00 can be traced back prior to Confederation. The 1847 Customs Act of the province of Canada prohibited the importation of 'books and drawings of an immoral or indecent character.'[10] In 1859 'paintings and prints' were added to the prohibition.[11] This prohibition was reproduced in identical terms by legislation passed in the first session of Parliament in 1867.[12] The following year Parliament added 'printed papers' and 'photographs' to the kinds of materials prohibited, and added treason and sedition to the grounds for prohibition.[13] The prohibition remained in place in this form until 1985, when the Federal Court of Appeal struck down the words 'immoral or indecent' on the ground that they constituted an overly vague restriction on freedom of expression as guaranteed by the Charter of Rights and Freedoms.[14] Within three weeks Parliament had passed an amendment to fill the gap and fully restore Customs' censorship powers at the border; the vague prohibition on the immoral and indecent was replaced with a supposedly clear prohibition on the obscene. In addition, Parliament added a long-overdue prohibition on hate propaganda to what is now Tariff item 9899.00.00.[15]

Until 1958 there was no right to appeal the ban of a publication to a court. Prior to that time, an importer dissatisfied with the Department of National Revenue's determination could appeal to the Tariff Board. The Tariff Board did not hear an appeal of a banned book decision until 1958 when an appeal was launched by Dell Publishing, the publisher of the paperback edition of the best-seller *Peyton Place*, banned by Customs in 1956. A majority of the Tariff Board found that the book had been improperly classified as immoral or indecent because 'the sexual episodes are made to appear decidedly unattractive in themselves or swiftly to give rise to remorse or retribution' and therefore the book would have the effect of inhibiting 'impure thoughts' rather than inducing them.[16]

The majority were clearly not comfortable in their first and, as it turned out, last engagement with the role of censor of imported publications. They hastened to add in a postscript to their decision that they did not consider either themselves or Customs officers 'qualified to make the kind of decision involved in classifying books' under the Tariff Code. 'Such decisions,' they suggested, 'should be made by courts with appropriate jurisdiction in criminal matters.'[17] While this wise advice was later implemented as departmental policy from 1962 to 1967, unfortunately it was not heeded by Parliament. After the *Peyton Place* ruling, Parliament passed an amendment relieving the Tariff Board, but not Customs officers, of the task of passing judgment on prohibited publications.[18] Henceforth, an importer could appeal a decision of the deputy minister to the courts.

The historical record of Customs prohibitions is difficult to compile, given that most decisions were made by individual officials without a public hearing or a public announcement. Official memoranda were issued to Customs collectors from the 1880s to the late 1950s instructing officials to detain particular titles at the border.[19] Beginning in 1895 and until 1958, Customs maintained a consolidated list of book and magazine titles prohibited by these memoranda. It should be emphasized that the publications banned by official memoranda that appear on the consolidated lists represent only the tip of the iceberg. The lists were not intended to be exhaustive; officials were free to prohibit other titles at the border without specific instructions from Ottawa.

The first list of prohibited publications, forwarded to collectors in 1895, was a modest one. It listed 47 newspapers and periodicals, all published in the United States.[20] From these beginnings, the consolidated list of prohibited publications grew steadily over time. In 1899, 55 titles were on the list; in 1909, 64; by 1914, the list had grown to 100 titles composed of books and periodicals deemed to be immoral or indecent.[21] During and following the First World War, socialist and communist literature was added to the list. The number of morally and politically unacceptable publications banned by official memoranda continued to grow during the 1920s and the 1930s. Self-congratulatory annual accounts of the department's book-banning accomplishments appeared in the

National Revenue Review, published from 1933 to 1939. These articles were printed under titles such as 'Stemming the Tide of Obscene Publications,' 'Checking a Putrid Flood,' and 'Keeping Out a Flood of Obscene Publications' that clearly revealed the department's attitude to its censorship powers. For example, after noting that 43 books and 24 periodicals were banned by official memoranda in 1933, the department praised itself for the 'considerable degree of success' that its 'constant efforts' and 'vigilance' had secured in intercepting 'large quantities' of indecent and immoral publications.[22] By 1946, the consolidated list of prohibited publications had swollen to 632 titles, of which 262 were periodicals and 370 books.[23] The department's attempt to respond to the growth of the paperback book trade is evident in the 1952 edition of the list: of the 660 publications prohibited, 574 were books.[24] In the six years from 1952 to 1957, another 503 book titles were prohibited.[25]

According to Deputy Minister Sim, the reason for distributing a list of prohibited publications to Customs officers was that the classification of books 'must be a matter of opinion. If no direction were given on this matter from headquarters it seems clear that the administration of the item would vary with the foibles, predilections or prejudices of our various collectors and appraising officers across the country.'[26] In 1958 the consolidated list of prohibited publications was disbanded. The memorandum sent to collectors advised that 'the elimination of the listing does not mean that sanction is given for the unrestricted entry of goods but rather emphasises the necessity for vigilance upon the part of all examining officers.'[27] Guidance on doubtful publications was to be obtained by forwarding them to headquarters for a ruling.

The minister of national revenue responsible for this change, George Nowlan, objected to Customs officials playing the role of judge and jury in relation to publications.[28] He called it a 'difficult and nasty task' and stated that officials of the department 'are much better qualified to deal with increasing the seasonal tariff on cabbages and cucumbers than to pass moral judgement on literature coming into the country.'[29] Nowlan instructed departmental officials to stop banning books at the border in 1962 unless they had been previously determined to be obscene by a Canadian court.[30] This policy was short-lived. By 1967, concerns about radical political literature and pornography had put Customs back in the business of exercising its own judgment on the legality of imported publications.[31]

While the targets of Customs censorship have shifted dramatically over the decades, the basic problems in its administration of the regime of censorship at the borders have remained constant. One problem has been a general lack of accountability. For example, the policy of successive governments was to keep the consolidated list of prohibited publications secret. In response to requests by

Members of Parliament to take the public into the department's confidence, successive ministers of national revenue refused on the ground that to reveal the titles of banned books would give them free advertising.[32] As Blair Fraser put it, 'the policy of the Canadian Government is that Canadians are not allowed to know which books they are not allowed to read.'[33]

Problems of accountability were exacerbated by the failure of Customs to provide a hearing to publishers, importers, or authors or to issue adequate reasons for its decisions, problems that continue to this day. In a comparative study of censorship published in 1928, Morris L. Ernst and William Seagle noted with frustration that the Canadian government 'refused to indicate' the grounds for banning particular publications and 'in many instances has been unwilling to indicate the part of the writing which was objectionable.'[34] Similarly, in 1946, the American writer James T. Farrell, whose novel *Bernard Clare* had been banned that year,[35] published an article in the *Canadian Forum* pointing out that nobody

had taken the trouble to send me any specific information concerning the precise reasons for this act of censorship ... The silence of Canadian officials, their refusal to answer questions, to meet argument and protests, their refusal even to specify precisely what chapters Mr. Sim considers indecent – all this constitutes a forecast. It reveals the attitude of Canadian officials on books and on the question of the artist's right to freedom of expression. If they will ban my book without a hearing, if they will uphold officials who ban Balzac, Trotsky, Joyce, Lawrence and others, they will be likely to ban still further books.[36]

Given the lack of accountability for their decisions, it is no surprise that Customs officials over the years have demonstrated a capacity for extremely elastic interpretations of their powers to prohibit publications.[37] The notion that the exercise of power by the Customs department has been supervised by legal norms has proven to be a formal mirage rather than a practical reality. A few examples will suffice to illustrate this point. In 1899 buttons saying 'Victory to the Boers' were prohibited on the ground that they were 'clearly of a seditious character in Canada.'[38] The forty-seven American periodicals on the 1895 list of prohibited publications, such as *The American Farmer* and *The Home and Fireside*, were banned on the ground that they contained advertisements of an 'objectionable character.'[39] Atheist publications, such as *The Truth Seeker*,[40] and socialist periodicals, such as *Mother Earth*[41] and *The New Masses*,[42] were banned for many years. In 1939 the news magazine *Ken* was banned for printing a cartoon making fun of King George VI's suggested visit to the World's Fair. As the editors of *Canadian Forum* commented, 'the sight of this, apparently, would have loosened the imperial bonds unduly.'[43] In the House of Commons, the minister of national revenue said that the cartoon was 'offensive' and was considered to come 'within the terms of the provisions of the Customs Tariff relating to such publications.'[44]

It is remarkable that Customs censorship practices managed to escape any sustained examination in a public forum until 1994. In that year, their deficiencies were finally lifted from over a century of administrative darkness and exposed to the glare of a two-month court proceeding in a constitutional challenge launched by Little Sisters Book and Art Emporium, a Vancouver bookstore specializing in gay and lesbian literature.[45] In his ruling,[46] Justice Kenneth Smith found that since its inception in 1983, Little Sisters has suffered at the hands of Customs;[47] that gay and lesbian bookstores and publications are particularly vulnerable to the 'arbitrary consequences' of Customs censorship, far out of proportion to their relative share of imported material;[48] that 'there are many examples of inconsistencies in Customs' treatment of publications';[49] that delays of months or even years in making determinations are not uncommon;[50] that a great many 'qualitatively questionable' determinations are made, including the detention of a 'disturbing amount of homosexual art and literature that is arguably not obscene';[51] that Customs continued to ban any depiction of anal penetration until the eve of the trial in 1994 despite the lack of legal authority to do so and despite the advice tendered by Department of Justice lawyers in 1992 that Customs was acting illegally;[52] that there is no mechanism in Customs' procedures for receiving evidence of a book's merits and thus many books are ruled obscene without adequate evidence;[53] that Customs officers are inadequately trained, many receiving only a few hours of instruction on obscenity law;[54] that Customs officers 'do not have sufficient time available to consistently do a proper job' and thus take 'short cuts' by 'such expedients as thumbing through books';[55] and that few initial determinations of obscenity are appealed, and, of the few that are, few succeed.[56] In conclusion, Justice Smith wrote with some understatement, there are 'grave systemic problems in the customs administration.'[57]

The evidence in the Little Sisters case confirmed James Farrell's observation a half-century earlier that 'what often gives Canadian censorship a bad name is on-the-spot censorship by local customs officials who sometimes feel that riding their own prejudices is interpreting the law.'[58] Unfortunately, Justice Smith left intact Customs' legal powers of censorship, arguing that the problems he identified were a result of faulty administration, rather than any flaw inherent in the legislation. But it is the Customs Act itself that places the task of adjudicating the bounds of constitutionally protected expression in the hands of individual Customs officials. Asking inadequately trained and unqualified officers, without the benefit of even a rudimentary hearing, to determine on a routine basis whether publications fall within current definitions of child pornography, treason, sedition, obscenity, or hate propaganda places everyone, including those officers, in an absurd situation. So long as Tariff item 9899.00.00 is enforced through the procedures set out in the Customs Act, the systemic problems identified in the Little Sisters case, endemic throughout Canadian history, are likely to persist.[59]

Alberta Advisory Board on Objectionable Publications, 1954–73

We are really an anti-censorship group. The distributors are just as anxious as we are to provide children with decent reading material.[60]

Anna P. Maure, chair, Advisory Board on Objectionable Publications, 1958

The Alberta board, and the Ontario committee described in the next section, were both products of the diminishing ability of Customs to exercise control over print publications in the 1950s. The mass production and distribution of cheap publications – comic books, paperback novels, magazines – was a new phenomenon facing Canadians in the years following the Second World War. The growth in cross-border trade soon overwhelmed Customs' ability to screen out all allegedly 'immoral' or 'indecent' publications, and, in any case, many foreign publications now had separate print runs in Canada. The heightened accessibility of popular literature to youth and the 'lower classes' spawned a great deal of activism on the part of parent-teacher associations, home and school associations, religious organizations, women's groups, and other civic organizations in the late 1940s through to the mid-1950s.[61] This wave of activism led by middle-class women centred on protecting youth from corrupting social influences. It produced an amendment to the obscenity provision of the Criminal Code in 1949 that added a prohibition on crime comics[62] and led to the establishment of a special Senate committee in 1952 to make a thorough investigation of the problem of 'salacious and indecent literature.' In its 1953 report, the committee noted that Canada had been 'flooded ... from one ocean to the other' with 'the soft-covered book, selling at a small price; numerous periodicals and magazines; and a more recently threatened immense influx of the digest types of sex literature.' In the recent past, roughly '200 book stores could be policed by the available force without difficulty.' With the advent of 'modern mass production and distribution, with at least 9,000 outlets in Canada,' the challenge of policing the distribution of literature was more formidable.[63] The Senate committee provided a forum for the expression of Canadians' concerns, described the extent of the problem, and expressed the need for more effective regulation, but it did not come up with any new proposals for accomplishing this goal.

In 1954 public pressure seeking effective action continued in Alberta. After convening a public meeting attended by the distributors and members of organizations such as the Catholic Women's League, the farm women's unions, and the University Women's Club, the Alberta government established the Advisory Board on Objectionable Publications. Its terms of reference were 'to study and investigate the question of crime and other objectionable comics and salacious magazines and to recommend effective action to prevent their sale and distribution in the province.'[64]

The 'effective action' adopted by the board, with the approval of the government, was the establishment of a working arrangement with the wholesale distributors of magazines whereby the distributors agreed to refrain from distributing titles to retailers in the province if the board had deemed them objectionable. From the establishment of the board until the late 1960s, the four news distributors who held a virtual monopoly over magazine distribution in the province invariably followed the board's recommendations. The board maintained a list of objectionable publications that it forwarded to the distributors. The tacit agreement with the distributors was that the attorney general would not institute or encourage obscenity prosecutions in return for their adherence to the board's recommendations.[65] The advantages of this system of regulation were described succinctly by the original chair of the board, Anna P. Maure: 'By working through them you cut off the dispersal of magazines at the source and avoid undesirable pressure groups, or publicity as public censors.'[66]

At first, the board was composed of citizens who were active at the initial meeting or who were known to be interested in the issues. Over the years, the board consisted of six or seven members selected on the basis of education and community standing and reflecting as well a concern about gender and regional balance. Most had university degrees and extensive involvement in voluntary community associations. Professional expertise appeared to play a secondary role in the selection of members; they were housewives, librarians, teachers, businessmen, accountants, and lawyers.

The board made an effort to screen all magazines distributed in the province. If board members were unanimously of the view that a magazine was objectionable, it would be added to the withdrawn list and the distributors would be notified accordingly. All subsequent editions of a magazine would then be withdrawn from circulation in Alberta. The board had a policy of entertaining a request for reconsideration made by one of the distributors if at least six months had passed since a magazine was added to the list. The board would then consider whether or not the content of the magazine had changed sufficiently to warrant 'reinstatement.' The board's decisions and its list of objectionable publications were sent to the distributors and to the police, but otherwise kept secret. The policy agreed upon between the board and the wholesale distributors was that the list of withdrawn publications would not under any circumstances be released to the public.[67]

The words used in the board's terms of reference – 'objectionable' and 'salacious' – had no legal meaning. In the board's practice, these terms embraced a far broader range of publications than criminal prohibitions on obscene publications. Board members acknowledged that criminal prosecutions of many of the publications they deemed objectionable would have been unsuccessful. This would have been true, for example, of *Rolling Stone*, banned for six months from October 1969 to April 1970.[68] It would also have been true, at least by the mid-1960s, of nudist magazines such as *Sunshine and Health*, 'girlie' magazines like *Dude* or *Escapade*,[69] crime magazines like *Real Crime Detective*, tabloids such as *Hush*, *Flash*, or *Justice Weekly*, men's magazines like *Man's Daring Action*, and romance or confession magazines such as *Confidential Confessions*, all of which were still on the board's list of objectionable publications in 1972.[70]

The stated goal of the board's efforts was to restrict the availability of publications that would be harmful to the proper moral development of children and adolescents.[71] Board members paid lip service to the notion that they should not be restricting adults' right to decide for themselves what they should or should not read. However, they did not seem troubled by the fact that their recommendations had this effect for magazine readers in Alberta. They gave no consideration to ways to prevent exposure of publications to youth while maintaining adults' freedom to read. Thus, their efforts had much in common with other post-war efforts that, as Mary Louise Adams has argued, employed 'youth' as 'a rhetorical trope in attempts to maintain dominant sexual and moral standards.'[72]

The board chose not to regulate newspapers or books. Readers of these materials were considered less open to corrupting moral influences. The attorney general's office was of the opinion that 'it would be an impossible task' for the board to review the thousands of novels sold in stores and on newsstands.[73] Nor did the board pursue the suppression of comics, even though they had generated much of the public concern that had led to the board's creation in 1954. Instead, the board restricted itself to publicizing the moral failings of comics. In 1956 the government printed and distributed 40,000 copies of a pamphlet prepared by the board entitled 'What's wrong with comic books?'[74]

The board thus restricted its advisory role to magazines. By 1959, 118 magazines had been withdrawn from sale.[75] By the end of 1964, the board reported that there were 168 magazines on its list and 'the problem as it pertains to magazines, tabloids and comic books is now reasonably well controlled.'[76] By the end of its operations, the board's recommendations had led to the withdrawal of more than 260 magazines from Alberta at one time or another; of these, 228 remained on the 1972 list of objectionable publications.[77] About two-thirds of these were men's magazines of the 'girlie' or action type. Several dozen detective or true-crime magazines were banned, along with a dozen romance or confession magazines and a handful of scandal-sheet tabloids.

The board's members never formulated explicit criteria for assessing whether or not publications were objectionable. Yet the criteria they applied can be pieced together from the board's minutes and from the brief reasons they gave to distributors for their decisions. Descriptions or depictions of sex were a primary target. Any form of 'perverted sex' was objectionable. While the term was not defined, it embraced at a minimum homosexuality, masochism, sadism, and cannibalism. Concern about 'perversions' became especially pronounced and focused on homosexuality in the 1960s. In 1963 the board passed a resolution that any publication containing 'one or more articles predominantly dealing with perversion be classified as objectionable.'[78] As the chair explained to a new appointee to the board in 1969, 'if the magazine illustrates lesbianism etc., it is practically automatically suggested for withdrawal.'[79] Apart from 'perversions,' the board also found objectionable 'unhealthy concepts of sex,' which included 'immoral sex,' 'dirty sex,' 'illicit sex,' 'unnatural sex,' 'excessive sex,' and 'sex orgies.' There is no indication in the records that members of the board considered there to be such a thing as a healthy sexual representation. *Playboy* was ruled unobjectionable, but only on the ground that its price placed it beyond the reach of most adolescents.[80] The board found 'excessive' or 'detailed accounts of brutality' to be objectionable, whether or not they were associated with sex. Gruesome illustrations, horror, and descriptions of 'dope addiction' also justified withdrawal. Detective magazines were objectionable if they held the police or other authorities in disrepute, glorified crime, or overplayed sex.[81]

A striking and consistent omission from the board's discussions was any consideration of the artistic or literary merits of the publications it recommended for withdrawal. At the time, debates were raging in Canada and elsewhere about whether and where to draw the line between 'literature' and 'filth,' or 'art' and 'obscenity.' As Ian Hunter et al. have argued, these debates were generated by a 'mutation of the cultural field': sexual writings that had previously circulated as a distinct genre within a restricted private sphere were now appearing in popular forms of literature receiving mass distribution. Hence, 'the characteristic dilemma and preoccupation of twentieth century obscenity law: how to distinguish between art and pornography when these appear together inside main-stream educative culture?'[82]

Obscenity law in Canada, especially for the twenty-year period beginning in the late 1940s, became the site of a contest between an older regime of regulation 'based on the policing of a social pathology' and an emergent 'regime of regulation organised around an aesthetic norm.'[83] The former approach, dominant since the late nineteenth century, took as its standard the test of obscenity set out in *R.* v. *Hicklin*: whether the material in question had 'the tendency to deprave and corrupt those whose minds are open to such immoral influences.'[84] It measured obscenity by the potential impact of material on groups that were considered vulnerable to moral corruption, such as youth. The fact that a publication had artistic, literary, or scientific merit was irrelevant. Therefore, the opinions of experts on such matters were of no concern. Nor did it matter that only a small part of a publication posed a risk of moral corruption. Any moral danger branded the publication as a whole obscene.

The aesthetic approach, by contrast, placed publications with artistic or literary merit beyond the reach of obscenity law. It followed that expert assessments of the aesthetic merits of a publication had to play a significant role in determining legality. And the publication as a whole had to be assessed, not just isolated passages. The new regime of aesthetic regulation increasingly challenged and ultimately replaced the *Hicklin* approach in the 1960s. The turning point was the 1962 ruling of the Supreme Court of Canada in *R.* v. *Brodie*.[85] Of the seven members of the court who directly addressed the issue, five said that *Hicklin* was no longer the law in light of the new definition of obscenity added to the Criminal Code in 1959.[86] In freeing *Lady Chatterley's Lover* for circulation in Canada, the principal majority judgment of Justice Wilfred Judson adopted the norms of aesthetic regulation. He put at the centre of his analysis the idea that 'the serious-minded author must have freedom in the production of a work of genuine artistic and literary merit.'[87]

The Alberta board's debates and practices were unaffected by this shift in regulatory norms. Its approach throughout its operations fell squarely within the *Hicklin* tradition of suppressing publications that posed a risk of moral corruption. The board's existence thus enabled Alberta news-stands to be regulated according to a defunct juridical paradigm into the 1970s. The growing gap between the board's practices and the legally triumphant aesthetic mode of regulation was largely responsible for the breakdown in the board's relationship with distributors in the late 1960s and early 1970s.[88] The board disbanded in the summer of 1973 before being officially dissolved in November 1976.[89]

In justifying their role during the board's tenure, members took for granted that censorship was to be avoided but argued that their work was consistent with that goal. They repeatedly emphasized that they had no legal powers, that they acted in an advisory capacity only, and that they had no binding authority to prevent the sale of publications they found objectionable. Only by bringing obscenity prosecutions pursuant to the Criminal Code could coercive power be brought to bear and thus censorship accomplished.

Yet, as we have seen, the board's agreement with the distributors enabled it to exercise considerable power over the popular forms of reading material available to Albertans. The compliance of distributors did have the consequence of obviating the need for censorship through criminal prosecutions. However, to describe this approach as 'voluntary anti-censorship,' as the board did, was to look at its effects solely from the perspective of the parties to the working agreement, namely, the government and the distributors. They participated in the agreement because both had something to gain from the lifting of the burdens, uncertainties, and embarrassments that accompanied criminal prosecutions of allegedly obscene publications.

However, from the point of view of writers, publishers, or readers, the board's 'anti-censorship' working arrangement facilitated a substantially heightened degree of censorship of which the public was at best dimly aware. Far from being 'voluntary,' the restrictions on Albertans' access to magazines were imposed upon them without their knowledge. In part because it craftily sidestepped public controversy, the board's approach proved to be far more effective than a campaign of criminal prosecution ever could have been in restricting distribution of, and therefore access to, what it considered morally objectionable reading material.

The work of the Alberta Board on Objectionable Publications was itself an objectionable exercise of power over popular forms of periodical literature given that it was carried out in secret, with no accountability to anyone other than the distributors, according to criteria that explicitly ignored from the beginning evolving legal standards of obscenity, and through appointees with no apparent qualifications for the task. The irony of the story is that the obvious deficiencies of this form of censorship were rationalized and made possible by the claim that the board's work had nothing to do with censorship in the first place.

Ontario Attorney General's Obscene Literature Committee, 1960–72

... anything approaching Government censorship of reading material must be avoided at all costs.[90]

W.B. Common, deputy attorney general, chair, Obscene Literature Committee, 1960

Nobody can argue there is censorship in Ontario, it doesn't exist.[91]

Robert B. Porter, member of the Obscene Literature Committee's advisory panel, 1963

The Ontario Obscene Literature Committee was a product of political forces similar to those that produced the Alberta board. Despite a regular flow of correspondence seeking action against allegedly immoral publications in the 1930s, 1940s, and 1950s, the Ontario attorney general's office was extremely reluctant to initiate criminal prosecutions. Lawyers in the department appeared to share a desire to suppress the forms of literature targeted by the reformers; however, they were of the view that prosecutions were not an effective or legitimate way of achieving this goal. This was their view even after a 1949 Criminal Code amendment[92] which removed one obstacle to obtaining convictions by eliminating the need for the crown to prove that distributors had knowledge of the obscene contents of publications.[93] In their letters replying to complaints and petitions, they repeatedly offered three practical reasons for their reluctance to prosecute.

First, they pointed out that the only predictable result of an obscenity prosecution was to increase the circulation of the book or magazine at issue. The contents of a publication and its merits would be debated in open court and reported in detail by an attentive press. The resulting publicity meant that obscenity prosecutions tended to enhance rather than diminish the circulation of the targeted publications, especially if the prosecution ended with an acquittal, as it did more often than not. A good example was the unsuccessful prosecution in Brantford in 1949 of the American News Company for distributing Irving Shulman's novel *The Amboy Dukes*.[94] The same phenomenon recurred in the years ahead when books such as Grace Metalious's *Peyton Place*,[95] D.H. Lawrence's *Lady Chatterley's Lover*,[96] and John Cleland's *Fanny Hill*[97] enjoyed remarkable sales after public legal proceedings were initiated.

Secondly, the crown's track record with respect to obscenity prosecutions was not good and it was difficult to predict whether prosecutions in the future would be successful. The legal standard of obscenity prior to the 1959 Criminal Code amendment – whether the material in question had 'the tendency to deprave and corrupt those whose minds are open to such immoral influences'[98] – had become a battleground between radically different interpretations and social theories, a troubling state of affairs for any criminal prohibition. Despite the moral certainties of the activists seeking an aggressive approach to prosecution, there was no social or juridical consensus on the meaning of obscenity after the late 1940s. Hence the frustrated lament of the deputy attorney general who had approved the laying of the unsuccessful obscenity charge in *The Amboy Dukes* case: 'if that particular book is not obscene, I give up.'[99]

Finally, the publications most often targeted by activists in the 1950s were relatively disposable forms of literature – comics, periodicals, or paperback books with a short shelf life. An obscenity prosecution had to be brought against a particular publication. A successful prosecution would thus have no direct effect on the availability of new editions of comics or magazines or the hundreds of new paperback titles that would have since appeared. The attorney general and crown lawyers were unwilling to undertake the kind of sustained campaign of prosecutions necessary to combat this situation.

In the mid-1950s, groups frustrated by the inaction of the attorney general's department heightened the political pressure. Their stated goal was the protection of youth from the corrupting influences of salacious literature. In November 1955 the Catholic Women's League launched a 'Decency Crusade': its members combed news-stands and stores in Ontario seeking to persuade retailers to remove from sale any titles appearing on the National Organization for Decent Literature's list of 300 objectionable publications.[100] In February 1956 letters flooded into the attorney general's office urging the continuation through legal means of the campaign against objectionable comic books and obscene literature.[101] Later that month, Attorney General Kelso Roberts met with the representatives of seventeen civic and religious organizations. They presented him with a brief requesting that he establish a 'review board which could advise him regarding the presence and sale of obscene publications in this province.'[102] Roberts delivered a lengthy speech in the legislature a few days later, reviewing these events and the law and promising to 'make great strides in closing the gap in this troublesome and moral-upsetting problem.'[103]

The attorney general's response was in fact cautious and measured. In June 1956 he invited eight members of the public to join him on a committee, later to be named the Obscene Literature Committee, to continue the 'study of the problems of salacious literature already instituted' by the department.[104] Representation on the committee was divided by gender and political perspective. The four women on the committee had been active in the recent campaigns against indecent literature. Evelyn Markle, for example, was the president of the Toronto archdiocesan council of the Catholic Women's League that had spearheaded the 1955 'Decency Crusade.' The four men on the committee had different kinds of expertise; one was a businessman, and the other three were journalists. Most prominent among them, and most influential on the committee, was Arnold Edinborough, then editor of the Kingston *Whig-Standard*. Deputy Minister W.B. Common served as chair of the committee, and his liberal attitudes towards expressive freedom shaped the committee's activities. The men were by profession inclined to be suspicious of the kinds of moral activism favoured by the 'ladies' on the 'distaff side' of the committee.

The committee, and the attorney general's office, was in no great hurry to complete its study of the problem of salacious literature. A report was commissioned from Johann Mohr, then a doctoral candidate at the School of Social Work at the University of Toronto. Mohr's report, delivered in 1958, found that 'there is no major concern in regard to obscene and indecent literature in the Province of Ontario at the present time.' Nevertheless, he recommended that 'preventive action' be taken to avoid any deterioration of the situation that might lead to a renewal of 'emotionally laden public reaction.'[105] He favoured the establishment of an advisory committee to examine any publications identified by public complaints and to make recommendations on withdrawal to the distributors. This 'administrative procedure of preventive justice,' he argued, would have the advantage of eliminating 'coercion' and 'unwanted publicity.'[106]

The Periodical Distributors of Canada (PDC) had already indicated its desire to have an advisory body put in place that would remove the need for criminal prosecutions. A combination of developments had put the distributors in a difficult position. Since 1949, they had been vulnerable to obscenity convictions regardless of whether they had knowledge of the contents of a publication.[107] They were businessmen who valued their standing in their communities and churches and thus wanted to avoid being branded as the peddlers of smut. Yet they claimed it was physically impossible to review all of the publications they handled, a task for which, in any case, they said they were not 'culturally equipped.'[108] Moreover, Customs censorship could no longer be counted upon to assist them; now that Customs was less effective, the distributors found themselves 'in worse jeopardy' of criminal prosecution.[109] The distributors had been withdrawing publications 'behind the scenes' on the advice of local groups, but trying to do so effectively at the community level was too difficult; they needed 'a little guide and help' from the attorney general.[110]

After much agonizing about the details, an advisory panel was finally appointed in May 1960. Its four members were carefully selected by Common and Edinborough. They were all men selected on the basis of their professional expertise. David Coon, a lawyer, would serve as chair. The other members were Robert Porter, a librarian; Berners Jackson, a professor of English literature; and Johann Mohr, the sociologist who had prepared the 1958 report. In a press release, Attorney General Roberts announced that his 'panel of experts' would determine whether material forwarded by the public fell within the meaning of obscenity in the Criminal Code. If so, the members of the PDC would withdraw these publications from sale. 'Such procedure,' he advised, 'is not intended in any way to be censorship. The panel of experts exists merely to help the public clarify its own opinion on what is objectionable material.'[111]

In contrast to the Alberta board, which worked to define a category of 'objectionable' publications, the Ontario advisory panel stated that its role was to make recommendations on whether publications submitted to it were likely to be found obscene by a court if subjected to a criminal prosecution. It relied on court decisions to provide guidance. It therefore had a legal point of reference which the Alberta board lacked. But the law of obscenity was in a state of flux in 1960; the 1959 amendment had signalled a new but uncertain change of direction. The new criminal standard for obscenity was 'the undue exploitation of sex' as a dominant characteristic of a work. This formulation explicitly left behind the view, common until the 1950s, that any sexual representation, whether in words or pictures, was likely to deprave or corrupt and was therefore obscene. The question after the 1959 amendments was to determine the point at which the exploitation of sexual themes became 'undue' and 'dominant.'

The advisory panel used this opportunity to usher in a new era of aesthetic, educative regulation of sexual representations. Its members did not develop explicit criteria to guide their assessments of publications; however, they were clearly of the view that, if a book had literary value, it should not be recommended for withdrawal. The panel ruled that Henry Miller's novels *Tropic of Cancer* and *Tropic of Capricorn* were 'serious and significant literary works that would be inoffensive to the vast majority of enlightened readers in Ontario.'[112] Similarly, *Lady Chatterley's Lover*, taken as a whole, was not obscene.[113] Nor was the panel willing to recommend the withdrawal of *Fanny Hill*,[114] William Burrough's *Naked Lunch*,[115] or any other serious work written by a recognized author.

The second regulatory innovation introduced by the panel was to divide clearly the field of sexual representations into the normal and the perverse for the purposes of defining 'undue exploitation.' Sexual representations that appealed to normal persons, or would help create normal persons – that is, heterosexuals with conventional sexual tastes – were not deemed obscene. This included depictions of female nudity or descriptions of heterosexual sex. As far as nudist and 'girlie' magazines were concerned, the panel simply suggested that retailers be advised to keep them out of the reach of children.[116] 'I see nothing wrong with bare bosoms,' David Coon said, 'and I readily admit I'm a fan of Playboy magazine. It's all a matter of tasteful presentation.'[117]

On the other hand, books or magazines that depicted sexual perversions or deviations were obscene. From the panel's point of view, the problem with the police in the early 1960s was that they considered 'bondage photos' or 'lesbianism' to be 'rather silly' and unworthy of action, while they took too much action against 'straight sex.' The advisory panel's view was that publications with 'numerous descriptions of the normal sexual act' were not half as dangerous as ones featuring 'lesbianism, homosexuality and masochism, brutality and sadism.'[118] The law, in the panel's approach, was enlisted to serve a normalizing educative role in relation to sexuality. Thus, a pocketbook entitled *Male Bride* was withdrawn because it featured a story of a homosexual man that ended with him falling happily into the arms of his lover.[119]

By conceiving of the task as one requiring interdisciplinary professional expertise, the attorney general's department was able to deflect political responsibility to the panel while also marginalizing the 'distaff' point of view that had led to the formation of the original committee in 1956. The attorney general congratulated the advisory panel on the 'exceedingly objective manner' in which it had handled the issue while steering clear of 'the fields of controversy where so often it ends.'[120]

In the first four years of its operations, the panel recommended that 112 particular issues of periodicals and 97 pocketbooks be withdrawn from circulation.[121] If the publications were distributed by a member of the PDC, they were invariably withdrawn from circulation not just in Ontario but across the country.[122] If they were distributed by independent operators who were not members of the PDC, prosecution would follow the advisory panel's recommendation. The result was that the panel 'forced the really lurid stuff off the normal bookstands into a small area' where it was handled by 'disreputable dealers' or 'fringe operations.'[123] By the late 1960s, there were very few complaints by members of the public or referrals from police forces, and thus the work of the committee gradually declined in volume until it ended entirely in the early 1970s. The committee was disbanded by the attorney general in 1972.[124]

Like most people exercising power over publications, members of the advisory panel spent a great deal of time convincing themselves and others that they were not involved in censorship. By keeping things quiet, and providing an outlet for public complaints, they hoped to 'keep the vigilante groups from getting books banned.'[125] Meanwhile, few Canadians realized that their choices of reading material were restricted by a group of four men in Toronto operating in response to local complaints.

The advisory panel pursued a hidden, quiet, unaccountable form of decision making, all in the service of a supposedly enlightened mode of regulation premised on aesthetic, educative, and normalizing criteria that finessed the waning forces of conservative moral regulation just prior to the dawning of a new wave of feminist activism. By suggesting that legal consequences should attach to its division of the field of sexual representations into the normal and the perverse, the panel legitimized the mass circulation of heterosexual representations, at the same time as it insisted on more focused efforts being directed at the marginalization and suppression of representations of gay, lesbian, and other minority sexualities. The panel thus helped set the stage for the obscenity battles of the decades ahead.

NOTES

1 I would like to express my thanks to the Social Sciences and Humanities Research Council of Canada for its financial support of research at the National Archives of Canada (NAC) and to Andrew Gibbs (Osgoode Hall Law School, Class of '98), Jamie Todd (Osgoode Hall Law School, Class of '97), and Patrick Nugent (Faculty of Law, University of Alberta, Class of '97) for their able research assistance.

2 A useful survey of the law can be found in Brenda Cossman, *Censorship and the Arts: Law, Controversy, Debate, Facts* (Toronto: Ontario Association of Art Galleries 1995). A valuable digest of newspaper stories on book censorship can be found in Peter Birdsall and Delores Broten, *Mind War: Book Censorship in English Canada* (Victoria: CANLIT 1978).

3 Works that approach issues of free speech and censorship from this broader perspective include Joel Bakan, *Just Words: Constitutional Rights and Social Wrongs* (Toronto: University of Toronto Press 1997), ch. 4; Stanley Fish, *There's No Such Thing as Free Speech ... and It's a Good Thing Too* (Oxford: Oxford University Press 1994), ch. 8; Allan C. Hutchinson, *Waiting for Coraf: A Critique of Law and Rights* (Toronto: University of Toronto Press 1995), ch. 7; Ian Hunter, David Saunders, and Dugald Williamson, *On Pornography: Literature, Sexuality and Obscenity Law* (New York: St Martin's Press 1993); and Sue Curry Jansen, *Censorship: The Knot That Binds Power and Knowledge* (Oxford: Oxford University Press 1993).

4 Sue Curry Jansen, *Censorship*.

5 *Proceedings of the Special Committee on Sale and Distribution of Salacious and Indecent Literature* (Ottawa: Queen's Printer 1953) at 186.

6 NAC, RG 16, #1057.

7 Blair Fraser, 'Our Hush-Hush Censorship: How Books Are Banned,' *Maclean's Magazine*, 15 Dec. 1949, 24–5, 44.

8 S.C. 1997, c. 36, s. 136.

9 R.S.C. 1985 (2nd Supp.), c. 1, as amended by S.C. 1997, c. 36, ss. 166–72.

10 'An Act for repealing and consolidating the present Duties of Customs in this Province,' *Province of Canada Statutes*, 1847, 10 and 11 Vict., c. 31 at 1427.

11 'An Act respecting Duties of Customs,' *Consolidated Statutes of Canada*, 1859, 22 Vict., c. 17, Schedule A at 261.

12 *An Act Imposing Duties of Customs*, S.C. 1867, 31 Vict., c. 7, Schedule E.

13 *An Act Imposing Duties of Customs*, S.C. 1868, 31 Vict., c. 44, Schedule E.

14 *Luscher* v. *Deputy Minister Revenue Canada*, [1985] 1 F.C. 85 (C.A.).

15 *An Act to amend the Customs Tariff*, S.C. 1985, c. 12.

16 *Dell Publishing Co. Inc.* v. *Deputy Minister of National Revenue for Customs and Excise*, (1958) 2 T.B.R. 154, 155.

17 NAC, RG 79, vol. 276, file 471. This comment, contained in the decision released by the Tariff Board, was omitted from the reported version of the decision in *Dell Publishing*.

18 S.C. 1958, c. 26, s. 3.

19 The official memoranda can be found in NAC, RG 16, Series A-3, vols. 849–50 (for the period 1876–86), volumes 871–87 (1893–1919), vol. 1057 (1919–24), and volume 888 (1925–7). The official memoranda from 1928–47 can be found in the Metro Toronto Reference Library, Special Collections.

20 NAC, RG 16, Series A-3, vol. 871.

21 These three lists can be found in NAC, RG 16, Series A-3, volumes 874, 876, and 877 respectively.

22 (1933) 6(4) N.R. Rev. 4. The other annual reports can be found at (1934) 7(4) National Revenue Review 6–7; (1935) 8(4) N.R. Rev. 4–5; (1936) 9(4) N.R. Rev. 3–4; (1937) 10(5) N.R. Rev. 3; (1938) 11(5) N.R. Rev. 3–4; (1939) 12(6) N.R. Rev. 4–5.

23 NAC, RG 16, Series A-3, vol. 1062.

24 Parliament of Canada, Sessional Paper no. 187, 12 May 1952, NAC, reel T-357.

25 Mimeographed Lists of Books Prohibited in 1952–1961, Library of Parliament, Ottawa.

26 Testimony of David Sim before the Special Committee on Sale and Distribution of Salacious and Indecent Literature. See the committee's *Proceedings* at 181.

27 Memorandum G-1, 22 Oct. 1958, Archives of Ontario (AO), RG 4–32, 1964, file 1911. The change in policy is discussed in Arnold Edinborough, 'Censorship,' *Saturday Night*, May 1964, 12.

28 See Peter Newman, 'The Books Canada Bans,' *Maclean's*, 3 June 1961, 67; Robert Weaver, 'Lady Chatterley and All That,' *Tamarack Review* 21 (1961), 49.

29 *House of Commons Debates*, 27 Aug. 1958, 4177.

30 *House of Commons Debates*, 7 Nov. 1963, 4485; 'No barrier to bringing back filthy books,' *Globe and Mail*, 7 Nov. 1963, 1; William French, 'Who killed censorship?' *Globe and Mail*, *Globe Magazine*, 9 Oct. 1965, 6.

31 See William French, 'Books and bookmen,' *Globe and Mail*, *Globe Magazine*, 29 April 1967, 18; George Bain, 'My secret life,' *Globe and Mail*, 3 May 1967, 6. The minister denied that there had been any change in policy: *House of Commons Debates*, 3 May 1967, 63.

32 *House of Commons Debates*, 12 March 1935, 1652–3; 14 April 1947, 1998; 23 April 1947, 2329; 11 Feb. 1948, 1103; 20 Feb. 1948, 1437; 29 Sept. 1949, 357; 24 Nov. 1949, 2206–7; 6 Dec. 1949, 2812–7; 28 Feb. 1957, 1727.

33 Fraser, 'Our Hush-Hush Censorship' at 24.

34 Morris L. Ernst and William Seagle, *To the Pure: A Study of Obscenity and the Censor* (New York: Viking 1928), 297.

35 Memorandum Series D-3, 2nd revision, no. 32, 31 May 1946.

36 James T. Farrell, 'Canada Bans Another Book,' *Canadian Forum*, Nov. 1946, 176 at 178; James T. Farrell, *The Dominion of Canada vs. 'Bernard Clare'* (New York: Vanguard 1947). For a full account of this episode, see Joseph Griffin, 'James T. Farrell vs. The Dominion of Canada: A Case of Censorship,' *Dalhousie Review*, 68 (1988), 163. Another book of Farrell's, *Gas-House McGinty*, had been banned in 1945 without his knowledge. Memorandum Series D-3, 2nd revision, no. 15, 25 June 1945.

37 The erratic nature of Customs censorship was the focus of critiques by journalists: see Hector Charlesworth, 'The Customs Department's Book Censorship,' *Saturday Night*, 19 April 1924, 5; J. Ross McLean, 'Bad Books in Canada,' *Saturday Night*, 6 April 1935, 10; editorial, *Canadian Forum*, June 1939, 72; Blair Fraser, 'Our Hush-Hush Censorship.'

38 Memorandum no. 1076B, 27 Dec. 1899, NAC, RG 16, Series A-3, vol. 874.

39 Memorandum no. 749B, 23 March 1895, NAC, RG 16, Series A-3, vol. 871.

40 *Truth Seeker* first appeared on the consolidated list of prohibited publications in 1899 (NAC, RG 16, Series A-3, vol. 874) and stayed there until at least 1946 (NAC, RG 16, Series A-3, vol. 1062).

41 Copies en route to subscribers in Saskatchewan were detained in 1910. See *Mother Earth*, 5, no. 9 (Nov. 1910), 276. The magazine was later banned by official memorandum in 1916 (Memorandum no. 2023–B, 13 July 1916, NAC, RG 16, Series A-3, vol. 879). It remained on the consolidated list of prohibited publications until at least 1946 (NAC, RG 16, Series A-3, vol. 1062).

42 Banned by Circular 575–C, 4 March 1927. The magazine was released by Memorandum Series D, no. 3, supplement no. 39, 11 Feb. 1936, and then banned again by Memorandum Series D, no. 3 (revised), Supplement no. 12, 30 Sept. 1939.

43 *Canadian Forum*, 19 (June 1939), 72.

44 *House of Commons Debates*, 29 May 1939, 4652.

45 A full account of the proceedings can be found in Janine Fuller and Stuart Blackley, *Restricted Entry: Censorship on Trial*, 2nd ed. (Vancouver: Press Gang 1996). For an excellent analysis of the broader legal and political context in which the *Little Sisters* case has arisen, see Brenda Cossman, Shannon Bell, Lise Gotell, and Becki L. Ross, *Bad Attitude/s on Trial: Pornography, Feminism, and the Butler Decision* (Toronto: University of Toronto Press 1997).

46 *Little Sisters Book and Art Emporium* v. *Canada (Minister of Justice)*, (1996) 131
   D.L.R. (4th) 486 (B.C.S.C.)., affirmed (1998) 160 D.L.R. (4th) 385 (B.C.C.A.).
47 Ibid., paras. 95–100 at 514–16.
48 Ibid., paras. 105 and 251 at 517 and 553.
49 Ibid., para. 109 at 518.
50 Ibid., paras. 112–13 at 519.
51 Ibid., paras. 115 and 252 at 519 and 554.
52 Ibid., para. 267 at 557.
53 Ibid., para. 116 at 519.
54 Ibid., paras. 38–41 and 116 at 501–2 and 519.
55 Ibid., paras. 81 and 113–15 at 511 and 519.
56 Ibid., para. 82 at 512.
57 Ibid., para. 250 at 553.
58 'Canada Bans Another Book' at 178.
59 This is an abbreviated version of the discussion in Brenda Cossman and Bruce
   Ryder, 'Customs Censorship and the Charter: The *Little Sisters* Case,' *Constitutional Forum*, 7, no. 4 (1996), 103.
60 Quoted in 'Censorship in Alberta,' *Calgary Albertan*, 4 June 1958.
61 Mary Louise Adams, 'Youth, Corruptibility, and English-Canadian Postwar
   Campaigns Against Indecency, 1948–1955,' *Journal of the History of Sexuality*, 6
   (1995), 89.
62 S.C. 1949, c. 13. The crime-comics campaign and its social determinants are discussed in Mary Louise Adams, *ibid.*; Augustine Brannigan, 'Delinquency, Comics
   and Legislative Reactions: An Analysis of Obscenity Law Reform in Post-War
   Canada and Victoria,' *Australian Canadian Studies – A Multi-Disciplinary Review*,
   3 (1985), 53; Augustine Brannigan, 'Mystification of the Innocents: Crime Comics
   and Delinquency in Canada 1931–1949,' *Criminal Justice History*, 7 (1986), 111;
   Janice Dickin McGinnis, 'Bogeymen and the Law: Crime Comics and Pornography,' *Ottawa Law Review*, 20 (1988), 3.
63 'Report of the Special Committee appointed to examine into the Sale and Distribution of Salacious and Indecent Literature,' 29 April 1953, *Senate Journals*, 1953,
   386 at 387.
64 Order-in-council 1801/54, passed pursuant to the *Cultural Development Act*, S.A.
   1946, c. 9. In 1958 the terms of reference were widened to include 'tabloids':
   Order-in-Council 1776/58.
65 Thomas Jackson to Donald Steele, 1 April 1963; Donald Steele to the deputy attorney general, 19 April 1963 ('it would be a complete breech [*sic*] of faith by your
   department if you were to institute action relative to any magazine which the Board
   has held to be unobjectionable'). Provincial Archives of Alberta (PAA), 92.197,
   box 1, file 9.

66 Anna P. Maure to R.C. Primeau, 9 Nov. 1959, PAA, 92.197, box 1, Secretary's Files, 1959.

67 Anna P. Maure to Douglas Peck, 14 Nov. 1959, PAA, 92.197, box 1, Secretary's Files, 1959.

68 Aleta Vikse, chair, to Mr Smith, 27 Oct. 1969 (informing him that *Rolling Stone* was withdrawn), PAA, 92.197, box 2, file 6; Jann Wenner to Aleta Vikse, 27 Jan. 1970 (sending 'best wishes for your enlightenment' from *Rolling Stone*), PAA, 92.197, box 2, file 2; minutes of the meeting of the Advisory Board on Objectionable Publications, 24 April 1970 (reinstating *Rolling Stone*), PAA, 79.254.

69 1962 issues of *Dude* and *Escapade* were found to be not obscene by the Supreme Court of Canada in *R. v. Dominion News & Gifts (1962) Ltd.*, [1964] S.C.R. 251.

70 'List of Magazines Suggested for Withdrawal by the Advisory Board on Objectionable Publications as of October, 1972,' PAA, 79.254, file 'Feb.1971–Dec. 1972.'

71 T. Jackson, 'Recommendations to the Advisory Board on Objectionable Publications,' 3 July 1962, PAA, 92.197, box 2, file 4.

72 Adams, 'Youth, Corruptibility' at 90. See also Mary Louise Adams, *The Trouble with Normal* (Toronto: University of Toronto Press 1997).

73 John Hart, solicitor, attorney general's Department, to B. Skagen, 9 March 1955, PAA, 92.197, box 1, file 3.

74 The answers to the question posed in the title of the pamphlet were: comics glorify crime, present immoral concepts of sex and marriage, foster prejudicial attitudes, portray violence and horror, are inartistic, and are detrimental to the development of good reading skills. A copy of the pamphlet can be found in AO, RG4–32, 1964, file 1911.

75 Anna P. Maure, chair, to O.L. Boucher, 19 Nov. 1959, PAA, 92.197, box 1, Secretary's Files, 1959.

76 Donald Steele, chair, 'Report to the Provincial Secretary on the Activities and Operations of the Advisory Board on Objectionable Publications,' 24 Feb. 1965, PAA, 92.197, box 2, file 1.

77 'List of Magazines suggested for withdrawal.'

78 Minutes of the Advisory Board on Objectionable Publications, 14 June 1963, PAA, 92.197, box 2, file 1.

79 Aleta Vikse, chair, to Doug Crowe, 22 Oct. 1969, PAA, 92.197, box 2, file 6.

80 T. Jackson to S.L. Melton, 15 June 1962, PAA, 92.197, box 1, file 4.

81 Minutes of the board meeting of 29 Sept. 1961, PAA, 92.197, box 1, file 4.

82 Williamson, *On Pornography* at 138.

83 Ibid. (describing similar debates in Great Britain).

84 *R. v. Hicklin*, (1868) L.R. 3 Q.B 360, 371.

85 [1962] S.C.R. 681.

86 Obscene publications were defined as ones in which 'a dominant characteristic' was the 'undue exploitation of sex.' S.C. 1959, c. 41, s.11.

87 [1962] S.C.R. at 705.

88 Joseph Busheikin, vice-president, United News, to Aleta Viske, chair, 4 July 1969 (suggesting that the board's standards had not evolved to keep 'pace with changes in society'), PAA, 92.197, box 2, file 6; Aleta Vikse to A. Holowach, provincial secretary, 28 Sept. 1970 (noting that some distributors were refusing to cooperate with the board's recommendations), PAA, 92.197, box 2, file 2.

89 Order-in-council 1194/76.

90 Report prepared by W.B. Common on the meeting of the Obscene Literature Committee, 12 Feb. 1960, AO, RG4–32, 1964, file 1911.

91 'Proceedings of the Obscene Literature Committee,' 8 Oct. 1963, 15, AO, RG4–2, file 227.5.

92 S.C. 1949, c. 13.

93 The need to prove knowledge of the obscene nature of a publication had prevented the crown from obtaining convictions in a number of prosecutions in Ontario. See, for example, *R.* v. *Britnell*, (1912) 4 D.L.R. 56 (Ont. C.A.), and trial proceedings in AO, RG 4–32, 1911, file 530 (Albert Britnell acquitted of obscenity charges on the ground that it was not proven that he had knowledge of the contents of two novels, Hubert Wales's *The Yoke* and Elinor Glyn's *Three Weeks*); *R.* v. *American News Co. Ltd.*, (1941) 76 C.C.C. 151 (Ont. Co. Ct.) (charge of obscenity dismissed on the ground that the accused company had no knowledge of the contents of the 9 Dec. 1940 edition of *Life* magazine); *R.* v. *National News Co.*, unreported judgment of the Carleton County Court, Judge A.G. McDougall, 25 July 1949, AO RG 4–32, 1948, file 787 (charge of obscenity dismissed on the ground that there was no evidence that the accused company had any knowledge of the contents of the nudist magazine *Sunbathing and Health*).

94 *R.* v. *American News Co.*, Brant County Court, 23 Nov. 1949, unreported. See 'McAree classes "Dukes" as "a literary work,"' *Globe and Mail*, 23 Nov. 1949 at 8; 'Judge finds no proof "Amboy Dukes" obscene,' *Toronto Telegram*, 24 Nov. 1949 at 3.

95 A 2–1 majority of the Tariff Board held that *Peyton Place* was not obscene in *Dell Publishing*.

96 A 5–4 majority of the Supreme Court of Canada held that *Lady Chatterley's Lover* was not obscene in *R.* v. *Brodie*.

97 A 3–2 majority of the Ontario Court of Appeal held that *Fanny Hill* was not obscene in *R.* v. *Coles Co.*, (1965) 49 D.L.R. (2d) 34.

98 The 'deprave and corrupt' test originated in *R.* v. *Hicklin*, (1868) L.R. 3 Q.B. 360, 371. The Ontario Court of Appeal endorsed this test as late as 1957: see *R.* v. *American News Co.*, [1957] O.R. 145 (C.A.) (upholding a conviction of the defendant company for distributing the pocketbook novel *Episode* by Peter Denzer).

99 Letter from C.R. Magone, deputy attorney general, to Mr Justice Gerald Fauteux of the Supreme Court of Canada, 25 Nov. 1949. Mr Justice Fauteux in his reply of 2 Dec. 1949 noted that the book was 'given a nice publicity, and the whole affair may illustrate the difficulties of those entrusted with the enforcement of our laws.' AO, RG 4–32, 1949, file 270.

100 AO, RG 4–2, file 92.2. See 'CWL group asks booksellers not to display "objectionable" pocket books,' *Quill & Quire*, Nov. 1955, 11; '1,000 Women on prowl for blacklisted books,' *Toronto Star*, 15 Nov. 1955 at 16; 'Mixed reception for Book crusade,' *Toronto Telegram*, 15 Nov. 1955 at 1.

101 AO, RG 4–2, files 91.8 and 92.1.

102 Brief dated 24 Feb. 1956, AO, RG 4–2, file 91.7.

103 *Ontario Legislative Debates*, 29 Feb. 1956, 638.

104 Kelso Roberts to committee members, 18 June 1956, RG 4–2, file 91.6.

105 J.W. Mohr, *Report on a Study of Obscene and Indecent Literature* (1958) at 48, AO, RG 4–2, file 122.2.

106 Ibid. at 69.

107 The distributors' concerns were fuelled by two successful obscenity prosecutions in Ottawa. In the first, *R. v. National News Co. Ltd.*, [1953] O.R. 533 (C.A.), the distributor was fined a total of $1,100 dollars for distributing four paperbacks and seven 'girlie' magazines. The novels were Tereska Torres's *Women's Barracks*, Erskine Caldwell's *Tragic Ground* and *Journeyman*, and Mae West's *Diamond Lil*. The magazines were *Paris Models*, *Peep Show*, *Gala*, *Eyeful*, *Titter*, *Wink*, and *Beauty Parade*. In the second, *R. v. American News Co. Ltd.*, [1957] O.R. 145 (C.A.), the distributor was fined $5,000 for distributing Peter Denzer's paperback novel *Episode*.

108 These views were expressed in briefs submitted to the attorney general's office in 1954 and 1957. See AO, RG 4–32, 1954, file 26, and RG 4–2, box 92, file 105.5 respectively.

109 See the 'Proceedings of the Obscene Literature Committee,' 17 Nov. 1958, at 74 and 77. AO, RG 4–2, file 134.11.

110 Ibid. at 37, 38, and 65.

111 Press release on indecent literature, 18 May 1960, AO, RG 4–2, box 210, file 210.6.

112 David A. Coon to Peter Martin, president of Martin, Gordon Publishing, 16 March 1964, AO, RG 4–32, 1964, file 662.

113 David A. Coon to chief of police, Metropolitan Toronto, 20 June 1960, AO, RG 4–32, 1964, file 1740.

114 'Advisers on obscene literature say Fanny Hill may stay on sale,' *Globe and Mail*, 27 Nov. 1963.

115 David A. Coon to W.B. Common, 1 March 1963, AO RG 4–32, 1964, file 1890.

116 '4-man panel views each nude on merits,' *Globe and Mail*, 4 Jan. 1961 at 5;
'Don't ban it!,' *Toronto Telegram*, 14 Nov. 1963; David A. Coon to Fred M. Cass,
11 March 1963, AO, RG 4–2, box 210, file 210.6.

117 Quoted in 'He's paid to read dirty books,' *Toronto Telegram*, 1 Nov. 1962, 7.

118 David A. Coon, 'Proceedings of the Obscene Literature Committee,' 30 Jan. 1961,
20, AO, RG 4–2, file 158.2.

119 Roy Shields, 'Fanny Hill,' *Canadian Weekly*, 11 April 1964, 18.

120 Fred Cass to David Coon, 19 March 1963, and Fred Cass to Robert Porter, 9 Oct.
1963, AO, RG 4–2, box 210, file 210.6.

121 The advisory panel filed regular reports with deputy minister Common which list
the publications recommended for withdrawal. See AO, RG 4–32, 1964, file 1890,
and RG 4–2, file 227.5

122 'He's paid to read dirty books,' 7.

123 'Proceedings of the Obscene Literature Committee,' 8 Oct. 1963, at 30 and 52.
AO, RG 4–2, file 227.5.

124 AO, RG 4–2, box 545, file 545.2.

125 Shields, 'Fanny Hill' at 18, quoting David Coon.

8

Censorship in Schools: Orthodoxy, Diversity, and Cultural Coherence[1]

SHAHEEN SHARIFF and
MICHAEL MANLEY-CASIMIR

Three children's books, *Asha's Mums, Belinda's Bouquet,* and *One Dad, Two Dads, Brown Dad, Blue Dads* recently sparked a heated debate in British Columbia. Headlines in the *Vancouver Sun* tell the story: 'Ban urged on teaching about homosexuality';[2] 'Trustees decided gay issue was not for classroom;'[3] 'Surrey school trustees ban three books about same-sex families';[4] 'Clark, Ramsey deplore Surrey's ban on books about same-sex families;' 'Clark says ban is outrageous';[5] and 'Librarians urge Surrey school board not to ban books.'[6]

Since March 1997, when the British Columbia Teachers Federation (BCTF) formed a panel to eliminate homophobia within the public school system, debate has swirled around the issue of whether same-sex families should be included in classroom discussions of family groupings. Despite support from the Ministry of Education, the BCTF, and the British Columbia School Trustees Association for use of the above-mentioned books in the curriculum, the Surrey school board banned them both from the classroom and from school libraries. It's move was endorsed by the British Columbia Confederation of Parent Advisory Councils (BCCPAC). At its annual conference held at the end of April 1997, the BCCPAC passed a resolution recommending exclusion of curriculum materials dealing with same-sex couples on the basis that 'when homosexuality is taught, it becomes an avenue of advocacy for homosexuals and thus teaches that homosexuality is acceptable as a healthy lifestyle.'[7] Taken at face value, this debate involves homophobia and homosexuality. A closer look reveals far deeper roots.

At the heart of this and any other controversy involving censorship in the school setting are questions of norms and values. Who has the ultimate responsibility to decide what is taught in public schools? Who has the final say – the government, school boards, or parents? What is the character and nature of censorship in schools?

This chapter confronts such issues by characterizing the nature and extent of external censorship pressures on the school as a cultural institution; by reviewing instances of censorship in Canada, with examples including formal legal challenges to school-curricula materials and library books as well as incidents involving political pressure on school boards to effect particular curricular inclusions or exclusions; and by examining the process of self-censorship through which classroom teachers attempt to avoid controversial issues in teaching. The chapter concludes by discussing the policy implications and cultural connections of such censorship in terms of the development of a curriculum of conformity and orthodoxy, and the implications of such a curriculum for the civic order in a constitutional democracy.

The School as a Cultural Institution

Censorship in a school setting essentially involves the intersection of cultural institutions, namely, law, education, and the public school curriculum, and the inherently normative character of such institutions. The claim that law and education are fundamentally cultural institutions rests on the recognition that they have similar and complementary functions in society. Each in different ways is concerned with fundamental values, their transmission and preservation; each must adapt to and accommodate shifts in values and the reflection of these values in policy and practice; each is inherently normative, that is, concerned with individual and collective aspirations, personal behaviour and community mores, social ideals, and prized beliefs of the culture.

One of the basic functions of the public school is to educate children to become socially responsible adults who will maintain and pass on established cultural norms, thereby preserving the normative order of society. The normative order here means the collection of norms or expectations concerning what people should do that exists as ideas in the minds of the members of society.[8] In this sense, the public school becomes a 'servant of society' because, to accomplish its purpose, it must meet social expectations. Consequently, the school curriculum necessarily takes on a central, culturally grounded role; it becomes the vehicle through which cultural values are conveyed to the next generation.

As society diversifies, the cultural function of the curriculum becomes increasingly complicated. Disagreements arise as to whose values represent the 'canons of truthfulness.'[9] Disputes centre on which cultural values society should endorse as legitimate and truthful. Controversies are fuelled by individuals and groups who have conflicting perceptions of what values the school is mandated to teach, what materials it is to use, and who should decide what is taught. These controversies are often turbulent and the school finds itself all too frequently in the 'crucible of conflict.' Censorship arises from this conflict. Specifically, it arises from formal legal challenges, from political pressures on school boards, and from self-censorship by classroom teachers, school principals, and librarians.

Considerations of the notion of censorship inevitably involve the idea of power.[10] Censorship occurs when bureaucrats, administrators, educators, and politicians abuse their power, or are influenced by others who use that power for their own interests. In the school context, it involves the power exerted by one group to decide what the children of others will learn. School authorities can be coerced into teaching values endorsed by those who wield the most power.

The question then arises whether all those with the discretion and authority to determine what is to be taught in schools are censors. Ultimately, somebody has to make selection decisions which are inevitably discretionary and involve value judgments. In a U.S. survey conducted by the National Council of Teachers of English, one school librarian differentiated her responsibility to select library books from that of parents seeking the removal of books from the library in these terms: 'When I look at my choices, I concentrate on the ones I mean to include in the library; when I look at the other person's stack, I focus on the books he or she wants to keep out of the library. I select; they censor. Our criteria blend: the books I reject are ones I don't think the children are ready for; the ones they censor are books they don't think their children are ready for.'[11] This passage demonstrates the very fine line – and intrinsically problematic distinction – between censorship and selection, often one of perception about what books have educational and social value. And, since perceptions of values differ and often reflect passionately held ideological positions, conflict inevitably ensues.

The Social and Statutory Context: Conformity, Deference, and Dissent

The selection and approval of curriculum materials – what is to be taught through the formal curricula of public schools – together with the mobilization of opposition to some of these materials occurs in both a socio-political and a statutory context. The character of that context, in some senses, describes the play of the tensions and conflicts that occur between conformity and orthodoxy, majority control and minority resistance; and, furthermore, it suggests the conflict resolution required in each case, whether relatively informal or through formal adjudication.

One particularly illuminating and powerful analysis is provided by Stephen Arons in *Compelling Belief*.[12] Arons discusses school censorship in terms of a curriculum of conformity and orthodoxy in the United States and argues that American courts have largely ruled in favour of school boards, thereby demonstrating a deference to the political process. He describes the stance taken by American courts as 'the inability of the law to incorporate the reality of family life and conflicts into its decisions because it would threaten prevailing ideologies or instructional institutions.'[13] I his view, the law's 'one-eyed' perception of the war over orthodoxy has enhanced conflict in society rather than promoted cohesion.

Such deference has, in the assessment of two prominent American commentators, characterized the Canadian tradition even more intensely than it has in the United States. A decade and a half ago, Edgar Friedenberg argued that Canadians, despite their multicultural heritage, exhibit a pervasive pattern of deference to authority.[14] Lipset attributed much of Canada's evident deference to traditional authority to the political evolution of Canadian institutions, which, in contrast to the revolutionary experience of the United States, had been framed by a counter-revolutionary history. This history, in Lipset's view, has led to an acceptance of elitism, traditional authority, established cultural values, 'law-abidingness,' and political deference.[15] Such observations probably capture only part of the socio-political reality of a society, yet they seem to ring true, at least in anglophone Canada. As a result, there may well be more willingness here than Arons documents in the United States to defer to the judgment of those statutorily empowered to make curricula selection and approval decisions.

The Canadian constitution[16] confers upon the provinces the responsibility to legislate in matters of education. Provincial legislation delegates broad discretionary powers to school boards and their employees – school superintendents, principals, and teachers. Furthermore, guidelines handed down by provincial ministries of education often impose a degree of conformity and orthodoxy in the name of democratic responsiveness. The relevant statutes and regulations across Canada disclose that the lieutenant-governor-in-council, the minister of education, and local school boards have the primary jurisdiction to determine what will, or will not, be included in the curriculum. Provincial school statutes and regulations authorize the organization and administration of schools and the implementation of educational programs.

In a culturally pluralistic society, educational decisions about what students are taught and what they learn – the curriculum – shape the character of that particular society. As Fred Inglis notes, 'a curriculum is no less than the knowledge system of a society, and therefore not only an ontology, but also the metaphysics and ideology which that society has agreed to recognise as legitimate and truthful; it sets the canons of truthfulness.'[17] The curriculum represents a way of perceiving the world, depending upon where one lives in Canada. Thus, the knowledge system of an elementary school in Prince Edward Island may differ considerably from the knowledge system of an elementary school in

Richmond, British Columbia; similarly, such perceptions may differ widely between schools and students in Quebec and those in Nunavut.

Needless to say, curriculum decisions may differ depending upon which political party is in government. Educational policies espoused by the Reform Party may well differ greatly from those of the New Democratic Party or the Bloc Québécois. Each political party brings its own set of values to the table, and these values in turn affect legislation and policies and may provoke disputes and consequent censorship. Furthermore, political parties are influenced by private-interest groups and by parents who exert subtle control or overt influence through political pressure.

Case Studies of Censorship Events

In 1995 Mary Jean Herzog conducted a study of school censorship in the rural hills of Appalachia in the United States.[18] She categorized school censorship in terms of the nature of censorship events, the objects of censorship, the initiators of censorship, and the motivation of the protesters.

The nature of school censorship centres around community values, school location, cultural influences, religious beliefs, and public controversies. Arons describes such events as involving 'corrosive, irreconcilable and proliferating conflict between government and family.'[19]

The objects of censorship include curriculum materials, school texts, school-library books involving cultural literacy, scary stories, fantasy, folktales, violence, occult, witchcraft, taboo words, secular humanism, sexuality, creationism versus evolution, and political correctness.

The initiators of censorship primarily consist of those who seek to maintain a curriculum of orthodoxy and conformity. This generally involves the far-right censorship network. At the other end of the spectrum, censorship is increasingly initiated by liberals and those farther to the left. The initiators of censorship include parents and/or special interest groups (individual/family values), teachers, administrators, librarians, authors, and politicians (as agents of the state). The result is conflict between family values and school or governmental authorities.

Arons defines the motivation of the protesters as 'a general struggle for meaning ... one between the forces of private dissent and the agents of public orthodoxy.'[20] Those who challenge school curriculum are often motivated by one or many of the following:

- religious and moral differences;
- fundamentalist parental overprotection or modern liberal values;

- politics, authoritarianism, and a dessire to protect administrative jobs;
- fear of psychological manipulation;
- different interpretations of the purpose of education;
- fear of change; and
- words and meanings taken out of context.

Herzog's classification provides a useful perspective for discussing cases of censorship in schools.

The results of a Canadian survey conducted by the Book and Periodical Council (1991) disclosed that many school-censorship events and challenges to school curriculum occur without public knowledge, which makes their frequency difficult to determine. Knowledgeable commentators agree that the majority of censorship cases in Canada rarely reach the courts.[21] According to Earl and Margaret Hurlbert, moreover, few Canadian legal cases have addressed specific school-censorship events.[22] Few pre-Charter cases dealt with freedom of expression in the school context: an exception is the 1968 case of *R.* v. *Burko*, which involved university students who returned to their old high school to distribute controversial literature in the school halls; they were found guilty of trespass.[23]

Early Charter cases involving school board decisions indicate that initially the judiciary stepped cautiously. Judges expressed the view that courts are not mandated to concern themselves with the implementation of rights in the school context. For instance, in *Mahe et al* v. *Province of Alberta*,[24] Judge Charles E. Purvis wrote: 'The courts have attempted to provide guidance in interpreting the Charter, but must not interfere by decreeing methods or becoming involved in ongoing supervision or administration. It should restrict its function to recognising and declaring a denial of rights created or recognized by the Charter.' Justice Bertha Wilson, on the other hand, in reviewing cases in light of section 15 of the Charter, concluded: 'It is hoped that subsection 15(1), together with section 1, will go some way toward preventing the bench from largely delegating its review responsibilities to the parent or state agency, as has traditionally been the case.'[25]

The Legal Cases

While the Supreme Court of Canada has yet to address censorship issues in the school context, some cases have come before lower courts and tribunals. A particularly strong example is that of *Serup* v. *Prince George School District*.[26]

Julia Serup regularly attended the library of the Prince George senior secondary school with one purpose in mind. She wanted to review the books available to students to ensure they contained 'suitable' material. She particularly did not want her son exposed to any books that would adversely affect his (or her own) moral standards. On one visit to the library, Serup reviewed a book entitled *Boys and Sex*. She challenged the book and a by-law of the school district and obtained the striking of a committee to review the book. Her efforts were successful. In April 1984 the book was removed from the school library.

In June 1984 Serup challenged a book entitled *Girls and Sex*. As a result of her second attempt at censorship, the school principal refused her access to the school library on the grounds that her presence would disrupt or negatively affect the pupils. The school superintendent did, however, send her a letter allowing her access to the library on the provision of four days' notice to the principal or his delegate; such access was to be outside school hours at a time convenient to Serup and to the principal or his delegate; access would be limited to once in each term; Serup would not be allowed to remove books from the school library and she would be expected to use the services of the public library system in Prince George. She challenged the school board on the ground that her rights under section 2 of the Charter had been infringed.

The British Columbia Supreme Court ruled that there was no infringement under section 2 and, even if there had been, such infringement would have been justifiable as reasonable under section 1. Justice Cyril Landers noted that the primary objective of the school was to educate its students with minimal disruption. Harm from disruption would far outweigh Serup's Charter rights. To support his argument, Landers discussed public expectation on this issue. He reasoned as follows (at 761–2):

Even though I have found that there has been no infringement of Mrs. Serup's rights under section 2, I feel constrained to express my opinion that even if there had been a violation of section 2, in the case at bar, the limitations are reasonable and demonstrably justified in a free and democratic society. The general public would not wish to see any discordant events or disruption with the main objectives of their schools and that is tuition [sic: teaching] ... Persons or organisations might take advantage of such an institution as a forum for dissemination of ideas of any kind or for the purpose of censoring or prohibiting the dissemination of education by educators with whom they may disagree. The harm of such occurrences would far outweigh the alleged infringement of Mrs. Serup's desire to determine the suitability of books in the school library, and thereafter express her opinion on them.

Serup's motivations were not addressed by the court. She obviously felt compelled to protect not only her son, but all the students at Prince George secondary school. In her opinion, books dealing with sexuality such as *Boys and Sex* and *Girls and Sex* would have a negative impact on the students' moral values. She clearly felt threatened by society's changing norms and believed that sexuality is a private matter for discussion at home. According to Serup, schools should not expose students to books on sex (regardless of whether they are of high school age). The court's decision in this case supports Arons's contention that judges often fail to understand the realities of conflicts between school and family values.[27] By shifting the focus to the disruption of teaching, the court managed to avoid addressing the whole complex issue of whether the school or the parents are ultimately responsible for deciding what information should be accessible to children, and what they should not read.

Diversity and Challenges to Tradition: Questions of Religion and Compulsory Attendance

Majoritarian decisions about what students learn in the public schools have the effect of imposing a state-sanctioned orthodoxy upon the students who attend these schools (as well as their families). Such an orthodoxy invites challenge by minority groups who feel coerced and forced to conform to the dominant majoritarian view. Challenges also arise when, as has occurred in Canada, the society itself changes, becoming increasingly heterogeneous and multicultural. Diversity has provoked an array of challenges to traditional school practices. Gregory Dickinson and William Dolmage highlight some recent Ontario Charter cases to illustrate how the policy commitment to multiculturalism has raised serious questions of educational purpose in Canadian society.[28] The common element in these cases is that 'they all involved challenges (by parents or parent groups) to educational regulations or policies resting on traditional assumptions about the nature and purpose of schooling, especially in the context of religion.'[29] Here we sketch four cases to illustrate these challenges.

The first case, *Zylberberg et al v. Sudbury Board of Education*,[30] involved a challenge to section 28(1) of Regulation 262 under the Education Act, requiring public schools to begin and end the day with a reading of the Lord's Prayer and a passage from the Bible. Non-Christian and atheist parents claimed that their children's rights under section 2(a) of the Charter were being infringed. The Sudbury school board agreed that section 28(1) was an infringement but used section 1 of the Charter to argue that the infringement was minor, since the purpose of the legislation was to promote moral values which justified the infringement. The Ontario Court of Appeal ruled that the law did not meet the proportionality test in *Oakes*;[31] that it was more than a minor infringement on the rights of the non-Christian children; and that, rather than being useful, the exemption clause stigmatized the students as non-conformist. As a result, Regulation 262 was amended to allow opening and closing exercises involving assembly readings that do not promote any particular religion. Here, the Ontario court took a more liberal construction of discrimination under the Charter, and the result has been a shift away from religious orthodoxy in the public schools.

The plaintiffs in *Canadian Civil Liberties Association* v. *Ontario (Minister of Education) (C.C.L.A.)*[32] requested the complete removal of religious exercises from the curriculum of Ontario public schools. They charged that section 28(4) of Regulation 262, which made two one-half-hour periods of religious education per week compulsory for all students, was coercive. The school board, relying on section 1 as a defence, again defended the limit on the pupils' freedom under section 2(a) of the Charter by contending that religious classes were necessary to teach moral values. The Ontario Court of Appeal found that section 28(4) clearly violated the Charter and failed the *Oakes* test. Moreover, it held that, since curriculum falls under government responsibility, section 24(1) of the Charter was relevant. The court ordered that the school board amend its regulations to remove the compulsory religious-education curriculum. As a result, the Ministry of Education ordered all public schools to become secular by ceasing all indoctrinal teachings and providing a curriculum that did not promote any one religion. Both *Zylberberg* and *C.C.L.A.* are examples of successful legal challenges to counter religious orthodoxy. Not all such challenges, however, have been successful.

The applicants in *Adler* v. *Ontario (Minister of Education (Adler)*[33] challenged the Ontario government's refusal to provide funding for private religious schools as a violation of section 2(a) of the Charter. They also raised the equal-benefits clause in section 15 of the Charter, arguing that parents who wished to send their children to public school gained the benefit of a free public education. The plaintiffs argued that: they could not send their children to the public schools or separate schools for reasons of conscience, primarily because the moral values taught at those schools were different from those they wished their children to espouse; the compulsory-attendance laws required them to send their children to public schools; and the conflict between their beliefs and the compulsory-attendance requirement put them in a compromising position vis-à-vis the majority. Hence, they were required to conform to the majoritarian orthodoxy.

The Ontario Court of Appeal held that these parents were free to send their children to public schools if they wished; compulsory-attendance laws contain an exemption clause permitting home or private schooling. Moreover, the parents' decision to send their children to private schools was a result of their own personal choice and had nothing to do with government action. The Ontario government is not required to fund private schools; to do so, a political rather than a legal decision would be required. In other words, the court refused to deal with the issue, leaving it to government discretion.

The removal of religious content from public schools also resulted in court action. *Bal* v. *Ontario*[34] involved a claim that the trilogy of *Zylberberg*, *Adler*, and *C.C.L.A.* had resulted in amendments to school regulations which removed the board's discretion to allow for alternative minority-religious schools. Payment of tuition was also raised as an issue. The plaintiffs argued that parents who were unable to afford a private school education were compelled to send their children to public schools which promoted values of secular humanism. This conflicted with the values they taught at home. Not surprisingly, the court adopted the line of reasoning used in Adler. Dickinson and Dolmage note that 'while the state cannot deny or limit the citizen's exercise of religious freedom, it is not required to support the exercise of that freedom through public funding or religious schools either inside or outside of the public school system.'[35]

The court also observed that public schools do not promote secular humanism but are religiously neutral. According to the court, minority students who attended a public school would not be coerced into adopting religious views incompatible with those they learned at home. In conclusion, the court held that the applicants' freedom of expression had not been denied. They were free to believe in whatever they wished as long as the public school was not used to promote those values.

Arons discusses the issue of home schooling in the United States and demonstrates how little support there was, at that time, for families who made the choice to educate their children at home. He argues that their decisions are perceived as a threat to the existing school system. Furthermore, the educational bureaucracy, with support from the courts, works to make such families feel threatened and isolated. According to Arons, 'the family that chooses to teach its children at home is a kind of social mutant.'[36] He suggests that, even when compulsory-attendance laws provide exemptions allowing for home schooling, the program of study is always subject to approval by the local superintendent, and it is the content of the program of study that becomes contentious or a source of conflict between parents and the school.

Compulsory-attendance cases in Canada have often focused on conflicts of values between minority religious groups opposed to the majoritarian ideology of public education. Two examples illustrate the point. A 1957 case, *Perepolkin* v. *British Columbia (Superintendent of Child Welfare)*, involved legislation applying to Doukhobor children. The Doukhobor community in British Columbia wanted to educate its children at home. The court held that the provisions for compulsory-school attendance were *intra vires* the provincial legislation and did not unduly interfere with religious freedom, thus forcing the children to attend the public school.[37]

The Canadian judiciary's stance regarding compulsory-attendance laws was further demonstrated in the landmark Alberta case *R*. v. *Jones* (1983–6). The Supreme Court of Canada's judgment in this case, involving a clergyman who educated his three children and others in the basement of his church, said that the mandatory-attendance provisions of the School Act did not deprive parents of their right to educate their children as they see fit and thus did not offend the principle of fundamental justice.[38] Equally, the court held that these provisions did not offend a person's freedom of conscience and religion.[39] The Provincial Court had acquitted the accused clergymen of truancy charges when the prosecution could not present sufficient evidence to show that his children were receiving insufficient instruction; the Alberta Court of Appeal had reversed the judgment and convicted him; now the Supreme Court of Canada dismissed his appeal.[40]

While censorship involves the deliberate attempt to intervene by removing from schools those aspects of curriculum or teaching that offend the complaining parties, the imposition of a state-approved orthodoxy is seen by minority groups as equally distasteful, requiring a degree of conformity inimical to basic values and freedoms. Such challenges have, as illustrated, often reached formal adjudication but many challenges are brought, fought, and resolved at the community level. It is to these instances of censorship that we now turn.

Non-Legal Challenges by Parents

The majority of censorship cases in Canada rarely reach the courts. Complaints by parents most often involve religious, or moral concerns grounded in cultural, religious, or individual beliefs and value systems. Surprisingly, parents have challenged many award-winning books. While Margaret Laurence's highly acclaimed novel *The Diviners* won the governor general's award for fiction, in February 1976 it was removed from the Grade 13 required reading list by the principal of Lakefield High School in Peterborough, Ontario (Laurence's own community). This action was taken as a result of complaints by parents about the perceived immorality of five pages in the book containing passages dealing with sex. A twelve-member review committee decided to keep the book despite a 4300-name petition requesting its removal. This controversy polarized Peterborough. Interestingly, despite the protest against the book, all the school board members who voted in favour of retaining it were re-elected the following year. Moreover, those candidates who opposed the novel were not elected as school trustees. The message conveyed by the community of Peterborough indicated support for high-quality literature notwithstanding concerns regarding perceived moral damage to students who read such books.

The *Diviners* was also the subject of a challenge in Winnipeg in 1978. Dan Duggan, a local pastor, wanted it removed from the grade 12 curriculum at Grant Park High School because of the same five pages dealing with sex. The media got wind of the challenge and reported the incident. The *Winnipeg Tribune* interviewed the pastor and Jeff Dorman, head of Kelvin High School's English department.[41] The pastor felt that his complaint was needed to alert parents to the importance of monitoring what their children were being taught in school. Dorman said that, although he did not use the book in his course, he saw no reason why it should not be used. 'There is no question that Margaret Laurence is one of the outstanding figures in Canadian literature.'[42]

Judith Dick discusses Canadian school-censorship controversies in her book *Not in Our Schools?!!!* At the end of each section describing a particular censorship incident she asks some thought-provoking questions. With respect to the Grant Park case, she asks us to consider the following:

• Do books that contain references to sexuality belong on the Grade 12 curriculum if they meet educational objectives? On the Grade 9 curriculum?
• The pastor cited snippets from the book to support his viewpoint; however, he admitted that he had not read the book thoroughly. Is it important to read sections of the book in the context of the whole in order to judge morality?
• Is it significant that the pastor was not a member of the community to whom he was addressing his complaints?

With these questions Dick focuses attention on important issues. Passages contained in books must be read within the context of the whole if the proper meaning is to be conveyed. Words and phrases, particularly those involving sex, profanity, or moral issues, can be misconstrued if taken at random and read out of context. Furthermore, by complaining about what was being taught outside his local community, the pastor in the Grant Park case attempted to impose his own clearly orthodox views on morality. While his fears were real, Dick questions whether he was justified in imposing his beliefs on those who did not share his views. Moreover, students in a Grade 12 classroom are arguably mature enough to comprehend references to sex in their proper context. Thus, selection or censorship of reading material for school children should take into account their age level and maturity – a fundamental educational consideration.

One of the most consistently challenged books in Canadian schools over the last fifteen years is J.D. Salinger's *Catcher in the Rye*. While parents have objected to foul language in the book, it has been removed in very few cases. Students themselves have stood up and argued for the retention of the book. It was, however, taken off reading lists for high schools in two Ontario counties, Kent and Norfolk, in 1981. The school board in Etobicoke, Ontario, also requested its banning in 1982. When quotes from the book were circulated to parents in Huron County, the Writers Union considered circulating another extract from the book, one that shed light on Salinger's real message. The quotes circulated by the parents read as follows:[44]

Page 22: 'He started clearing his Goddam fingernails with the end of a match'; Page 32: 'Jane said he was supposed to be a playwright or some Goddam thing'; Page 192: 'What the hellya doing?'

The section selected for circulation by the Writers Union read as follows:

Page 173: 'Anyway, I keep picturing all these little kids playing some game in this big field of rye and all. Thousands of little kids, and nobody's around – nobody big. I mean – except me. And I'm standing on the edge of some crazy cliff. What I have to do, I have to catch everybody if they start to go over the cliff – I mean if they're running and they don't look where they're going I have to come out from somewhere and catch them. That's all I'd do all day. I'd be the catcher in the rye and all, I know it's crazy, but that's the only thing I'd really like to be.'

According to June Callwood,[45] the Writers Union legal consultant vetoed its suggestion because she felt that the union would be no smarter than the censors if it also resorted to circulating snippets from the book out of context.

Another award-winning novel subjected to censorship in schools is W.D. Valgardson's *Gentle Sinners*. According to J. O'Connor a group of parents in Fort Garry, Manitoba (going by the name of Parents for Quality Education), objected to the book on the grounds that it depicted women as sexual objects and old people as useless. The parent group felt that negative family values were being conveyed to the children. Valgardson challenged the request for the book's withdrawal and the Fort Garry school board supported him. *Gentle Sinners* survived the challenge and was reinstated in the curriculum. Valgardson argued that the parents had misunderstood his intent, which had been to draw attention to the way in which society perceives women and old people. In other words, his goal was to raise awareness of the realities faced by women and old people, thereby hoping to change the way society treats them.[46]

Dick notes that, while pressure groups may succeed in the banning or removal of certain books from schools, counteracting pressure groups have formed and have often been successful.[47] She cites, for example, the Society for Freedom of Choice in Huron County. This group was successful in having John Steinbeck's *Of Mice and Men* and Salinger's *Catcher in the Rye* reinstated. Though it failed to have *The Diviners* returned to the high school reading list, it made a point of asking board members to read the book in its entirety rather than relying on the snippets presented by pro-banning groups.

Our discussion of books challenged over family values would not be complete without returning to the controversy in British Columbia surrounding the three books cited at the outset of this chapter, namely, *Asha's Mums*, *Belinda's Bouquet*, and *One Dad, Two Dads, Brown Dad, Blue Dads*. In this case, the minister of education, Paul Ramsey, described the banning of the book, as 'very wrong-headed.'[48] His comments were supported by Premier Glen Clark:

It's outrageous in 1997 for school boards to be engaging in this kind of activity. Surely we have learned from the past that burning books is no solution, that education is part of the solution and I would have hoped that school boards, of all people, would know that education is a key part of dealing with these questions and you don't deal with them by destroying books, you deal with them by talking to people and discussing these issues openly and honestly. I think it's a sad comment on the Surrey School board.[49]

Nevertheless, as noted, the Surrey school board ban obtained the support of the Confederation of Parent Advisory Councils. Two resolutions were passed at the confederation's annual general meeting held on 26 and 27 April 1997. The first, put forward by some of the Surrey parents, recommended that anti-harassment policies, rather than school curriculum, should be used to protect homosexual students from discrimination. This resolution passed by a 204–93 margin. The second, more controversial resolution recommended exclusion of curriculum material dealing with same-sex couples, as well as materials prepared by gay and lesbian advocacy groups.[50] This resolution scraped through by a small margin of 165–158. The council also issued a statement saying it does not support promotional material of any kind in school, 'whether from political parties, product marketing firms or special interest groups.'[51]

The Surrey case graphically illustrates the conflict at work when one group of parents seeks to impose its will and values on others. The Surrey school board, supported by BCCPAC, endorsed the views of a particular group of parents who felt that their family values would be threatened if their children were exposed to any discussion of homosexuality as an acceptable way of life. The initiators of censorship action in this case were members of non-profit society which called itself the Citizens Research Institute. This organization circulated a declaration of family rights forbidding student involvement in any school program which 'discusses or portrays the lifestyle of gays, lesbians, bisexual and/ or transgendered individuals as one which is normal, acceptable or must be tolerated.'[52] The declaration included a threat of legal action against any teachers or administrators who attempted to discuss this type of lifestyle in the public schools.

More important, Robert Pickering, then chair of the Surrey school board which banned the three books, was a director of the Citizens Research Institute. Consequently, his election to the school board put him in a powerful position to censor school curriculum and thereby impose the values of the Citizens Research Institute on the public schools. Despite a legal opinion obtained by the Ministry of Education, confirming that threats contained in the institute's declaration had no force and effect, teachers who lived in communities that by and large supported the declaration no doubt felt threatened. Any teacher would certainly think twice about introducing discussions on same-sex families in their classrooms. Hence the declaration had far-reaching effects by enabling the majority to use censorship as a way of enforcing a curriculum of orthodoxy and of pressuring teachers to engage in self-censorhip in order to avoid being singled out in a highly sensitive controversy.

While Robert Pickering maintained there was no conflict of interest between his position on the Surrey school board and his membership in the Citizens Research Institute, Surrey teachers participated in public protests against the ban and have more recently commenced a legal action against the Surrey school board in the Supreme Court of British Columbia. Furthermore, they have filed three grievances against the Surrey school board, claiming that the ban has created an environment that discriminates against gay and lesbian teachers. According to the president of the teachers association, one grievance was based on the fact that the collective agreements state that teachers are to be provided with a workplace free of discrimination, which is defined as 'any action which is based upon a person's race, colour, creed, age, sex or sexual orientation.'[53] The teachers association has also pressed the government to approve the books, thereby overturning the Surrey school board ban.

In the meantime, the *Vancouver Sun* reported that the Surrey school board fax machine was used to fax invitations to all schools for a Vancouver conference organized by the Citizens Research Institute.[54] One parent and conference organizer, Charlotte Snow, is quoted as fully supporting the ban despite the fact that she has not read the books: 'I don't have to see them ... It's their objectives and goals I am opposed to.'[55] According to Snow, one book on the resource list from the Gay and Lesbian Educators of British Columbia contained graphic sexual descriptions. She is quoted as saying 'I have the right to protect my children.'[56]

At the other end of the spectrum, about forty parents and students have formed a group called Heterosexuals Exposing Paranoia to support the books. As one student notes: 'Everybody should be educated ... They are trying to ignore the whole thing, but it will make people more homophobic.'[57] The student's comments raise important questions. Will the issue go away if the books are banned? Should controversial content be ignored, or should it be discussed with the children in such a way as to educate them and raise awareness of the issues involved? As society diversifies, these questions will not disappear; on the contrary, they will rather multiply and become more frequent.

In 1993 a school play, written by an Abbottsford high school teenager named Katherine Lanteigne, attracted much media attention. The play was entitled *If Men Had Periods* and, as its title suggests, involved teenage sexuality. Lanteigne had entered it in a competition in the hope of qualifying for a $1,000 scholarship. The Abbotsford school board banned the play because it contained sexually explicit and foul language. Lanteigne appealed the school board's decision and the *Vancouver Sun* conducted a survey of its readers requesting the public's views on the banning.[58] Finally the CBC became involved and offered Katherine $1,000 to allow an airing of the play on CBC television. Of the readers surveyed by the *Sun*, 50 per cent felt that the author would probably not have won the scholarship because the play was in bad taste, but they disagreed with the ban. According to *Sun* readers, the banning resulted in much undeserved publicity and $1,000 for the author. This entirely defeated the school board's desire and intention to make the play go away!

Sometimes parents and community members, regardless of religious or racial background, fear the influence of witchcraft and the occult. One controversial incident occurred in Manning, Alberta, in September 1991, on the first day of school. In an unprecedented action, parents stormed the principal's office and took him hostage! Their motivation? They opposed the *Impressions* series selected for use by the Alberta government as class readers at the elementary school level.[59] What did the *Impressions* series include that caused such a volatile reaction? According to one of the main authors, David Booth, the series was created by 'first gathering high-quality works of children's literature to include in a reading series.'[60] The authors focused on critically renowned, award-winning children's authors and illustrators. They attempted to balance the needs of various communities and to avoid stereotyping and racist content. The protestors, for their part, were concerned about fairy tales and stories that, in their view, included witchcraft and violence.

Children's stories have traditionally often referred to witches and goblins. One story included in the *Impressions* series was entitled *Inside My Feet* written by Richard Kennedy, it involved magic boots that kidnap a child's parents and take them to a giant. The child then fools the boots into leading him to the giant. According to Booth, well-known children's authors like Jim Trelease and Jane Yolen have endorsed the story and showered it with praise. Yet it evoked highly passionate and negative feelings not only in Alberta but also in many areas of the United States. Booth attributes this to the work of highly organized religious groups in the United States which filter their ideas across the border to Canada, such as Phyllis Schafley's Eagle Forum, Jerry Falwell's Moral Majority, The Pro Family Forum, and Mel and Norma Gablers' Educational Research Analysts of Longview, Texas. These groups, like the recently formed Citizen's Research Foundation in Surrey, British Columbia, aim to ensure that schools teach their values rather than those of others. Such groups can have a substantial impact in convincing parents that their children's values (and thus their own) are in danger of being obliterated.

Bruno Bettelheim, the well-known child psychologist and author, maintained that fairy tales containing good and evil are crucial to children's moral development. Hence, if all evil is censored our children will grow up in a moral vacuum.[61] How will they develop moral standards to help them make ethical decisions as adults? Censorship often works as a self-fulfilling prophecy. It may result in children 'growing up amidst a rubble of collapsed cultural meanings and dysfunctional social values'[62] if controversial subjects are banned from classrooms and realistic adaptations are not made by schools to keep up with the changing needs of society. Furthermore, controversy can fuel healthy educational debates if all points of view are allowed expression.

Shakespeare's plays have also been banned from school libraries for their inclusion of the supernatural. Plays such as *Hamlet, Macbeth, The Tempest*, and *A Midsummer Night's Dream* have been removed at the request of Christian or Jewish groups.[63] The game *Dungeons and Dragons*, which can become an obsession for pre-adolescents, has also sometimes been censored. One teacher organized a pre-teen club to supervise the game. A parent complained because she feared that the club was a cult, and the principal requested that the teacher discontinue the club activities. Parents can also censor from political motives. A Toronto parent requested the removal of a Chinese magazine, the *Peking Review*, on the ground that it was propaganda. The magazine was moved to a part of the school library accessible only to teachers.

Canadian legislation with respect to freedom of expression provides school boards with broad discretionary powers. A study of challenges to books in Manitoba's public and school libraries by D.R. Jenkinson, disclosed that one-half of the complaints about books in schools/school libraries come from within the institution itself.[64] In other words, much of the time, principals, teachers, secretaries, clerks, and other school employees take it upon themselves to question materials; in effect they engage in self-censorship. The BPC quotes from the study as follows:

- Principal in a rural K-12: 'I have on a number of occasions destroyed books I felt did not reflect the community's, nor my own, personal taste and values.'
- Library technician – rural 7–9 school: 'I have to admit to trying to be selective in what is acquired for this library. I am not anxious to "rock the boat." With school enrolment down, job security is a priority.'
- Library Clerk – rural 9–12 school: 'So as to keep the parents from getting nasty, I try to choose books which I feel will be of interest to the students but will keep the parents happy.'
- Librarian – in Ontario – Said she greatly admired Kevin Major's work but said the following about his first award winning novel *Hold Fast*: 'But of course I don't have it in the school library; I know my principal wouldn't stand for it.'
- In a small Nova Scotia community, a newly appointed school principal came across *Hold Fast* in the school library which had been established and maintained by parent volunteers. He blocked out the words he regarded as offensive and returned the book to the shelf without consulting parents or staff.
- A woman principal in a Toronto collegiate refused to re-order a prose collection *Man and His World* because she felt it was sexist.[65]

In British Columbia, a North Vancouver teacher asked the Ministry of Education to remove *Catcher in the Rye* and *Let's Visit Russia*.[66] Dick also notes that a textbook introduced by the New Democratic Party government in Manitoba, entitled *Co-operative Outlooks*, was challenged by a former economic development minister who referred to the text as socialist junk. As a result, teachers in Manitoba did not use it and it was eventually sold at discount to an institution in Saskatchewan.[67]

Educators who self-censor fear controversy which may cost them their jobs, and thus they make every effort not to deviate from the norm. Many adopt conformist attitudes to please the majority. What a teacher does and says both inside and outside the classroom can affect his or her career. In Canada, local community values can play a large role in determining a teacher's actions not only within the classroom but also in their private lives.

Policy Implications and Cultural Connections

Over the last ten to fifteen years, Canadian society has changed substantially. British Columbia alone has made room for thousands of immigrants from Hong Kong and the Pacific Rim. This has had an effect not only on the province's economy but also on its demographics and urban growth. Municipalities such as Richmond, Surrey, Coquitlam, Port Moody, and even Maple Ridge have expanded from sleepy suburbs into large urban centres. Schools are bursting at the seams, and portables are required in many areas to accommodate children moving into the new areas. The provincial government has had to fund construction of many new schools amidst competition among municipalities.

As school boards struggle to deal with available space, curriculum adjustments are also required to accommodate an increased number of non-English speaking Canadians. Some schools consist primarily of students for whom English is a second language, increasing the demand for ESL teachers. In response to an increased demand for change in language-education policy, the Ministry of Education recently completed new curriculum guides for French 5–12, and Punjabi 5–12. New provincial curricula for those grades in Chinese, Japanese, Spanish, and German will be available in September 1997.

All this is bound to have an effect on Canadian families who have lived in Canada for many generations, particularly those who espouse primarily Christian traditions and values. New immigrants bring with them different values, habits, and perceptions. Should they abandon these and adopt those traditionally taught in Canadian schools? To what extent must the curriculum be adapted to the needs of every child who enters the school system? Once again we arrive at the question of 'whose values?' – a question that is inherently contestable and contested.

Furthermore, as the number of single-parent families and homosexual couples increase, there is a greater acceptance of liberal values by some members in society – values like respect for privacy, equality, tolerance of diversity, open-mindedness. This shift can result in polarization and cultural conflict. Those who would rather cling to traditional roles and values begin to feel uncomfortable; they fear losing control and worry about their children being exposed to and adopting values that differ substantially from their own. The fast-moving pace of technology – computers, the Internet, and television – enhances their anxiety.

As individuals feel threatened and confused by exposure to new lifestyles, cultures, and technologies, they use censorship to preserve the values they grew up with. They try to return to a system of known values, and the most logical place to retrieve the stability of known values is the school system, where they themselves learned some of their values. Thus, the school system becomes a scapegoat if it is perceived to be abdicating its responsibilities, namely, those of passing down traditional values.[68]

The case studies discussed in this chapter demonstrate the difficulties involved in maintaining cohesion in a diverse society. The teaching of norms and values that meet with the approval of all members of society is difficult, if not impossible. Politicians and educators involved in selecting school curriculum and library/classroom materials have the authority to 'select' what will be taught in schools. The selection of appropriate materials and resources is defensible when the dominant considerations are educational – that is, concerned with the development of the child's intellectual abilities. Selection becomes censorship when political pressures are applied by educational officials or by community groups comprising the majority or a vocal minority with the goal of eliminating the curriculum perspectives they oppose. Censorship of this type narrows the curriculum, removes diversity, and can, if accommodated, result in a curriculum of conformity and orthodoxy. Non-legal case studies demonstrate that self-censorship is a common occurrence within educational institutions. Teachers, principals, and school librarians sometimes find it simpler to work within a curriculum of conformity and orthodoxy than to speak up in support of controversial materials and so jeopardize their employment.

What are the implications of such a curriculum for the civic order in a democracy? A crucial question in Canada is whether the civic order can survive if the system of compulsory public education is not restructured at a time of significant cultural tensions and political factionalism. Many forces influence the nature and extent of censorship in Canadian schools. If we are to find solutions to school conflict arising from censorship, we must first determine the necessary preconditions to civic coherence. Canada prides itself on being a multicultural country. Uncritical endorsement of multiculturalism may, however, mask the tensions created by such a policy, which, in an extreme form, affirms diversity at the expense of civic cohesion. Such tension provokes the question: What is, or can be, 'common' about a civic order that apparently prizes diversity over coherence? As David Carr argues: 'Coherence seems to be a need imposed on us whether we seek it or not. Things need to make sense. We feel the lack of sense when it goes missing. The unity of self, not as an underlying identity but as a life that hangs together, is not a pre-given condition but an achievement. We keep at it. What we are doing is telling and re-telling, to ourselves and to others, the story of what we are about and what we are.[69]

The case studies discussed in this chapter indicate that censorship often occurs ostensibly to uphold family values. *Serup* is one illustration of this point. Other cases have demonstrated, however, that censorship sometimes occurs at the expense of parental or individual family values, freedom of conscience and belief, and religious rights. The case studies also suggest that, when those doing the selecting are coerced or feel pressured to censor in order to avoid controversy, it is ultimately Canadian society that pays the price. It becomes largely a question of who establishes legitimacy in the decision-making process. If teachers cannot comfortably express their views without the threat of losing their jobs, they cannot discharge their responsibilities in a professional manner. If children are sheltered from changing values and controversial subjects, they may be unable to function in modern society as adults. When freedom of expression is stifled, so is creativity.

In June 1989 the Language Study Centre of the Toronto Board of Education put together a teacher's guide entitled *Bias, Controversy and Censorship in Language Arts/English*.[70] It provides a comprehensive analysis of the issues and recommends how teachers can deal with these issues without sweeping them under the rug. Dick[71] and Booth[72] also agree that controversial issues must be faced and discussed rather than hidden away. How long can children be protected from exposure to diversity? In fact, more often than not, banning controversies attracts attention to the offending material and more people read the books out of curiosity.

As we pointed out earlier, the selection of curriculum materials and content is necessary to provide a quality educational experience. Somebody has to make these selection decisions. Typically, the legitimacy of the process rests with a broadly based consultative curriculum committee, established under the aegis of the provincial Ministry of Education and including in its membership representatives from many constituencies: ministry officials, teachers, parents, subject experts, *inter alia*. Such a process usually yields a curriculum acceptable to the mainstream culture. Herein lies the seeds of controversy. As Canadian society continues to diversify, school teachers and administrators are required to use the curriculum to maintain cohesion and avoid conflict. At the same time they attempt to instil in Canadian children moral values, including integrity, compassion, tolerance, and respect for diversity in a complex society.

The case studies also demonstrate that, when teachers, parents and students have organized and supported censored books and material, they have been successful. It is encouraging to see the British Columbia Ministry of Education show support for the books banned in the Surrey controversy. By introducing new second-language education policies and supporting the BCTF in its decision to reduce homophobia in the schools, the government is at least addressing the issues. It is also encouraging to see teachers and students organize in support of freedom of speech in response to the Surrey controversy. Case studies have shown similar success when students and teachers supported the literary content of books such as *Catcher in the Rye* and *The Diviners*. The Toronto Board of Education teacher's guide *Bias, Controversy and Censorship*[73] is also a step in the right direction.

Furthermore, if the civic order is to be maintained in a diverse society – if the tension between the demand for civic coherence and the imperative of social diversity is to be reconciled, school boards must implement well-thought-out, educationally defensible, and balanced policies which address controversial issues. Dick, Booth, Reichman, and the Toronto Board of Education, all make recommendations for clearly defined written policies which can be implemented by schools to ensure that good literature and positive values are preserved and supported and that diverse value systems are respected, understood, and accepted.[74] They recommend that books should not be removed when offensive words are taken out of context or simply because they are challenged. Committees consisting of teachers, parents, and administrators can be formed to review selected and challenged materials. Controversial issues should be discussed and debated with the students, and appeal procedures should be clear and set out in writing.

Educators should attempt to increase awareness of the advantages of diversity to society as a whole and learn from each others' differences. Political or hate propaganda can be countered with two or three books providing different perspectives on the same subject, as well as consistent and accurate historical information. Issues dealing with homosexuality, family values, race, and stereotyping can also be discussed if well-balanced points of view are provided. Children cannot gain an all-round education if they are exposed only to narrowly constructed perspectives. They will be unable to function in today's diverse society if they are ill-equipped to deal with issues such as homosexuality, racism, and sexism. While the deliberate and thoughtful selection of curriculum materials related to the age and developmental level of the child is an essential condition of education practice, censorship of controversial materials is a form of educational malpractice because it fundamentally undermines the essence of education – the development of the autonomous, critical capacity of each and every student.

NOTES

1 An earlier version of this paper was presented on 13 June at the 1997 Learned
   Societies Meetings at Memorial University, Newfoundland, under the aegis of
   the Canadian Society for the Study of Education. We wish to acknowledge the
   comments of Stuart M. Piddocke, Monica Escudero, and Klaus Petersen on this
   version.
2 S. Bell, *Vancouver Sun*, 28 April 1997, B1.
3 Ibid., B6.
4 P. Fong and K. Bolan, *Vancouver Sun*, 25 April 1997, B1.
5 K. Bolan, *Vancouver Sun*, 26 April 1997, A1, A20.

6 K. Bolan, *Vancouver Sun*, 24 April 1997, B1, B5.

7 Bell, 'Ban urged on teaching about homosexuality,' *Vancouver Sun*, 28 April 1997, B1.

8 S. Piddocke, 'Social Sanctions,' *Anthropologica* 10, no. 2 (1968), 261–85.

9 F. Inglis, *The Management of Ignorance* (Oxford, U.K.: Blackwell 1985), 22–3.

10 K. Petersen, 'Censorship! Or is it?' in this volume.

11 James E. Davis, ed., *Dealing With Censorship* (Urbana, Ill.: National Council of Teachers of English 1979).

12 S. Arons, *Compelling Belief* (Amherst: University of Massachusetts Press 1986).

13 Ibid., vii.

14 E.Z. Friedenberg, *Deference to Authority: The Case of Canada* (White Plains, N.Y.: Sharpe 1980).

15 S.M. Lipset, *Revolution and Counterrevolution: Change and Persistence in Social Structures* (New York: Basic Books 1968).

16 Canadian Charter of Rights and Freedoms, Part I of the Constitution Act, 1982, being Schedule B to the Canada Act 1982 (U.K.) 1982.

17 Inglis, *The Management of Ignorance*, 22–3.

18 M.J.R. Herzog, 'School Censorship Experiences of Teachers in Southern Appalachia,' *International Journal of Qualitative Studies in Education*, 8, no. 2 (April–June 1995), 137–48.

19 Arons, *Compelling Belief*, viii.

20 Ibid., vii.

21 J. Dick, *Not in Our Schools?!!!* (Ottawa: Canadian Library Association 1982), and d. Booth, *Censorship Goes to School* (Markham, Ont.: Pembroke Publishers 1992).

22 E.L. Hurlbert and M.A. Hurlbert, 'Student's Rights,' in *School Law under the Charter of Rights and Freedoms*, 2nd ed. (Calgary: University of Calgary Press 1992), 43–93.

23 *R.* v. *Burko* (1968), 3 D.L.R. (3d) 330 (Ont.Mg.Ct.) 324. See also *Nova Scotia Board of Censors et al* v. *McNeil* [1978] 2 S.C.R. 662; 84 D.L.R. (3d) 1, 44 C.C.C. (2d) 316. The court in this case refused to deal directly with freedom of expression.

24 [1985] 64 Alberta Reports 535 at 55–6 (Alberta QB); (1990), 106 N.R. 321 (S.C.C.).

25 J. Wilson, 'Children and Equality Rights,' in A.Y. Bayesfsky and M. Ebert, eds., *Equality Rights and the Canadian Charter of Rights and Freedoms* (Toronto: Carswell 1985), 322.

26 (1987) 39 D.L.R. (4th) 754, (1987) 14 B.C.L.R. (2d) 393, (1987) 33 C.R.R. 162.

27 Arons, *Compelling Belief*, 1986.

28 G.M. Dickinson and R.W. Dolmage, 'Education, Law and Multiculturalism: A Trio Becomes a Quintet,' in William Foster, ed., *Education in Transition: Legal Issues in*

a Changing School Setting (Chateauguay, Que.: Lisbro 1995), 79–109. See also Dickinson and Dolmage, 'Education, Religion, and the Courts in Ontario,' *Canadian Journal of Education*, 21, no. 4 (fall 1996), 363–83.

29 Ibid., 7.
30 [1988] 29 O.A.C. 23 (C.A.).
31 *R.* v. *Oakes* 26 D.L.R. (4th) 200.
32 (1990), 71 O.R. (2d) 341 (C.A.).
33 (1992), 9. O.R. (3d) 676 (Div Ct.) aff. (1994) 19 O.R. (3d) 1 (C.A.) [1996] S.C.J. No. 110 139.
34 (1995), 21 O.R. (3d) 681 (Gen. Div.).
35 Dickinson and Dolmage, *Education in Transition*, 101.
36 Arons, *Compelling Belief*, 1986, 92.
37 (1957) 23 W.R.R. 592; 27 C.R. 95, 120 C.C.C. 67, 11 D.L.R. (2d) 417 (B.C.C.A.).
38 (1986) Alta. L.R. (2d) 97 at 125.
39 Ibid. at 123.
40 Ibid., 97–129.
41 J. Drabble, 'Pastor Protests "Immoral" Book,' *Winnipeg Tribune*, 3 Feb. 1978, 3.
42 Ibid.
43 Dick, *Not in Our Schools?!!!* 3.
44 J. Callwood, 'Reason Not Passion,' in *Books in Canada* (Ottawa: Canadian Library Association 1979), 42–3.
45 Ibid.
46 J. O'Connor, 'Author fires back at critics: obviously struck home,' *Winnipeg Sun*, 6 April 1990.
47 Dick, *Not in Our Schools?!!!*, 43.
48 Bolan, 'Clark, Ramsay deplore Surrey's Ban.'
49 Ibid., A1, A20.
50 Bell, 'Ban urged on teaching about homosexuality.'
51 Ibid.
52 K. Bolan, 'Surrey school chair linked to anti-gay group,' *Vancouver Sun*, 6 May 1997, A1, A8.
53 K. Bolan, 'Teachers in Surrey fight gay book ban,' *Vancouver Sun*, 9 May 1997, B1, B4.
54 Ibid., B1, B4.
55 Ibid., B4.
56 Ibid.
57 Ibid.
58 K. Lanteigne, 'Excerpts from the play If Men Had Periods,' *Vancouver Sun*, 1 May 1993.

59 J. Booth, D. Booth, Phenix, and L. Swartz, *Impressions: Teacher Anthology Four* (Toronto: Holt, Rinehart and Winston 1986).

60 Booth, *Censorship Goes to School*, 59.

61 B. Bettelheim, *The Uses of Enchantment: The Meaning and Importance of Fairy Tales* (New York: Vintage Books 1989).

62 Arons, *Compelling Belief*, viii.

63 M. Leiren-Young, 'I am a Jew–Shakespeare and his censors,' *Vancouver Sun*, 7 Sept. 1996, A19.

64 D.R. Jenkinson, 'The Censorship Iceberg: The Results of a Survey of Challenges in School and Public Libraries,' *School Libraries in Canada*, 6 (fall 1996), 19–22, 24–30.

65 Book and Periodical Council, Freedom to Read Week, 15–22 February, *Challenged Book List* (Toronto: 1991), 14, 15.

66 Dick, *Not in Our Schools?!!!* 16.

67 Ibid.

68 Arons, *Compelling Belief*, x–xi.

69 D. Carr, *Time, Narrative and History* (Bloomington, Ind.: Indiana University Press 1986).

70 Toronto Board of Education, Language Study Centre, *Bias, Controversy and Censorship in Language Arts/English: A Teacher's Guide*, rev. ed. (1989).

71 Dick, *Not in Our Schools?!!!*, 63.

72 Booth, *Censorship Goes to School*, 13.

73 Toronto Board of Education, *Bias, Controversy and Censorship.*

74 Dick, *Not in Our Schools?!!!*, 69–71; Booth, *Censorship Goes to School*, 79–83; H. Reichman, *Censorship and Selection: Issues and Answers for Schools* (Arlington, Va.: American Library Association, Chicago, and London/American Association of School Administrators 1993) 62–5; Toronto Board of Education, *Bias, Controversy and Censorship*, 27–50.

9

Walking the Tightrope: Management of Censorship Attempts in Canadian Libraries

ANN CURRY

Being confronted by someone clutching a book or gesturing towards a computer screen while angrily announcing 'Look what I found in this library!' is a familiar though dreaded part of the current Canadian library scene. Those voicing their concerns may be parents concerned about books about witches in a school library, students upset by Holocaust revisionist materials in a university library, or adults disturbed by what they can find through a public library Internet computer program. Regardless of the complainant, librarians find the management of these concerns extremely stressful, partly because the information being protested against is often associated with sex, religion, or race and therefore often has a volatile emotional base, and partly because librarians are trained to meet customer needs. Censorship attempts occur when the needs of an individual customer or small group clash with what the librarian perceives to be the overall needs of the population served. This chapter will examine how different perceptions of the purposes of libraries lead to censorship challenges, the subject and technology areas in which challenges have occurred, and the ways in which librarians are managing those challenges.

The Purpose of Libraries

Censorship affects the various types of libraries – school, university, public, and special – in different ways because these libraries have different purposes and clientele. The primary purpose of a school library is to support the curriculum: teachers and parents assume that students can find resources there which will help them complete class projects.[1] In some cases, however, the library also contains materials either in book or electronic format which the teacher-librarian hopes will expand a child's horizons and/or improve reading ability. Challenges to the library collection usually come from these areas, the fiction books or the Internet sites which are not directly related to the curriculum but serve to supplement it.

Like school libraries, university and college libraries exist to support student course work, but they carry the added responsibility of supporting the research interests of faculty members.[2] From the small number of complaints that these libraries receive, it is evident that society allows the university much leeway with its collection, possibly because users are assumed to be educated adults, not vulnerable members of society who might be 'unduly' influenced by unconventional ideas. As well, the place in the university of open debate, which requires knowledge of the various sides of an issue, is still acknowledged, despite the more restrained atmosphere engendered by 'political correctness.'

The question of censorship within special (company, government) libraries rarely arises since these collections are narrowly focused and serve a limited clientele.[3] Disagreements about the actual purpose of the library can still arise, however. For example, a dispute arose in the mid-1980s when an Alberta deputy minister ordered a department librarian to remove from her library several documents which were critical of Conservative Party policies. The librarian maintained that the special library should contain pertinent information (both pro and con) about government initiatives so that both department employees and Opposition members could be better informed. The deputy minister disagreed, saying that the library collection should not contain material 'harmful' to the government in power because this would be self-defeating. The librarian temporarily removed the material but returned it after several Conservative members said that they needed to understand clearly Opposition arguments when preparing position papers.

The confusion about library purpose and clientele affects public libraries more than any other library type. In the broadest interpretation of purpose, public libraries exist to serve all members of the community by making available a wide range of materials and providing the best representations of all points of view.[4] For some, however, the purpose of public libraries is much more narrow: the improvement of society through education. These citizens envisage public libraries as promotional vehicles for the eradication of societal evils such as racism, overt sexuality, and violence. If the library serves this role, the collection should not contain any materials that portray these evils in a positive light, or indeed, any light at all. This constitutes censorship in the eyes of many librarians and library customers.

Another role often expected of public libraries is that of a bastion of democracy, but just what democratic values they are upholding is often unclear. If democracy is interpreted to mean strictly the rule of the majority, then librarians should shape their collections to represent just the views of the majority – the platform of the provincial or municipal party in power or the values of the dominant community group. On the other hand, libraries' democratic role can be interpreted as service to all individuals in the community, even to those individuals or minority groups whose political, religious, or sexual views the majority finds offensive. According to this view, all those whose taxes support libraries should be able to find information relevant to their needs in the library, whether those needs pertain to information about socialism, sexual education, or witchcraft. For some, a key aspect of democracy involves the right of individuals or groups to move within society without suffering offence. Those who support this view contend that the psychological harm individuals suffer from being exposed to offensive racial, sexual, or religious library material is unacceptable in a democratic society concerned with the well-being of its citizens. Others, however, maintain that free speech combined with access to controversial materials, no matter how offensive to some, is an essential bulwark of democracy and far more important than the right not to be offended. The possibility of a person being offended by materials in the library is part of the price of democracy, and paying that price ensures the health of democracy rather than its demise.

The essential question about the purpose of public libraries revolves around what should be in the 'commons,' the public realm that evolved from the community-owned property in the centre of medieval villages where livestock was grazed and sheltered and where the village square developed. In Garret Hardin's 1968 article 'The Tragedy of the Commons,' the author expands this idea of the commons to encompass the greater realm of all public space and public institutions. He discusses the tendency for people to assume that decisions reached individually will be the best decisions for the commons. In other words, we assume that by pursuing our own best interest, the interests of society are best served. In refuting this, Hardin states that this freedom to demand actions meeting one's own needs 'brings ruin to all.'[5] Public libraries are part of the modern 'commons,' and so Hardin's views are applicable to library purpose as it relates to censorship. Those who seek to censor library collections to conform with their personal moral, religious, or political views do not view public libraries as truly part of the commons. They do not see that the strength of libraries depends on an inclusive view of community where everyone is represented and where all views are sheltered, not just those of the most vocal or those in power.

Library Associations

Most professional library associations endorse documents that strongly support intellectual freedom as part of the purpose of libraries. The Canadian

Library Association (CLA) Bill of Rights states that 'libraries have a basic responsibility for the development and maintenance of intellectual freedom.' The bill further states that 'it is the responsibility of libraries to guarantee and facilitate access to all expressions of knowledge and intellectual activity, including those which some elements of society may consider to be unconventional, unpopular, or unacceptable.' This contention that libraries have a fundamental anti-censorship role to play appears in similar statements from Canada's provincial associations, the American Library Association (ALA), and the [British] Library Association. The ALA has always been a leader in this area – its frequently updated four-hundred-page *Intellectual Freedom Manual* gives detailed policies about intellectual-freedom and how to manage censorship challenges in all types of libraries. The management section includes chapters titled 'Before the Censor Comes: Essential Preparations,' 'Procedures for Handling Complaints,' 'The Censor: Motives and Tactics,' and 'Pressure Groups: Politics, Religion, and Censorship in Libraries.' The ALA clearly views censorship as an area of conflict for librarians and recommends education and vigilance as essential tools for dealing with challenges.

The Canadian Library Association has not prepared a manual about censorship, but the similarities in CLA and ALA intellectual-freedom philosophies allow Canadian librarians to adapt most American policies for use in individual libraries. The most frequently adapted policies relate to meeting-room access, complaint procedures, children's material, audiovisual material, and electronic resources. Always underpinning these policies, however, is the aforementioned Bill of Rights, which Canadian librarians value strongly. Crystallizing the professional viewpoint on difficult censorship issues, this 'ready-made' statement is frequently used by librarians in the heat of a challenge, when the time to research and formulate such statements is scarce. The ability to attribute intellectual-freedom philosophies to a national body is especially valuable, since groups or individuals wanting to censor library materials are more likely to respect a nationally approved statement than a locally produced document which can be misinterpreted and labelled as the librarian's personal opinion. Librarians who receive challenges may also contact the CLA headquarters in Ottawa for support. They frequently ask the association's executive director and/or the chairperson of the intellectual-freedom committee to give advice or lend support when they receive demands to remove material from their collections.

Sex

Materials dealing with sexuality-oriented materials are the most challenged items in Canadian public libraries, according to studies by the author[6] and Alvin

M. Schrader.[7] Sexually oriented materials are also frequently challenged in school libraries.[8] Complaints about this material in public libraries are usually based on the customer's perception that the material is 'improper' and that public money should not be spent on such 'trash.' Those wishing to have the materials removed often fear that the material may be read by 'vulnerable' people who may engage in the sexual acts described. An interesting sideline to this type of challenge is that the customer sometimes accuses the librarian of engaging in the acts portrayed in the material or, at the very least, of approving of them. This springs from the notion that librarians must approve of all the information in their libraries, or else why would they order the materials? Sexual materials often targeted are those explaining heterosexual or homosexual acts, for example, *The Joy of Sex* and the *The Joy of Gay Sex*, with those having photographs and illustrations targeted most often. Customers often contend that they do not want these types of materials in *their* library, giving the impression of ownership and care. This feeling of connection is useful for fund-raising efforts, but it is hard to dispel temporarily when complaints are received. The issue of children's access to materials containing sexual references is often the most contentious, for some parents wish to protect their children from such information. That other parents might want their children to have access to sexual materials is unthinkable to the complainers, and, in the end, irrelevant.

The 1997 case of the book *Women on Top: How Real Life Has Changed Women's Sexual Fantasies* illustrates the current confusion in Canada about what is obscene, who can remove materials from libraries, and what should be on public-library shelves. Acting on an anonymous tip voiced during a radio phone-in show, Winnipeg police told the Winnipeg public-library staff that they could be charged with distributing obscene materials (under section 163 of the Canadian Criminal Code) if they did not remove the book from the collection. The police based their action on advice from the Manitoba attorney general's office, but after the threat of removal was issued, a second crown lawyer disputed the likely illegality of the material. The 1991 book is based on interviews with women who describe in detail their sexual fantasies: it had circulated over 300 times in the Winnipeg library without complaint. In defence of the library, library spokesperson Heather Graham said 'society has a great mixture of interesting types of people with a variety of philosophies. So it's our intent to build a collection that's very broad-based.'[9] After some confusion, the police withdrew their threat to remove the book. The information about the possible obscene nature of the material had already been circulated to all British Columbia Royal Canadian Mounted Police detachments. Consequently, the RCMP in three B.C. communities attempted to remove the book from their community libraries. In two cases, the public libraries did not own the material, but in the Merritt library the librarian refused to surrender the book until the RCMP produced a court order. Alice Dalton, chief librarian of the Thompson-Nicola regional district, was 'appalled' at the RCMP's actions, and Ken Dolder, lawyer for the district's libraries, was concerned that 'someone decides in their personal opinion that the book is obscene and then promotes their own view without any determination from the courts.'[10]

In another 1997 case, the sexual content complained about was far less explicit, but just as incendiary. Responding to complaints from a small group of parents, the Surrey school board banned three picture books from school libraries and classes. The three books, Asha's Mums, One Dad, Two Dads, Brown Dads, Blue Dads, and Belinda's Bouquet, all portray same-sex parents. Sybil Harrison of the British Columbia Library Association spoke against the ban: 'We strongly believe in the importance of having a wide range of books available for children. There are probably lots of same sex parents and families and they need information and stories that represent their point of view and existence.'[11] The executive director of the CLA, Karen Adams, also issued a statement: 'There's always going to be someone offended by books in every library.'[12] Despite these objections, the school board voted to ban the books, a decision that is currently being appealed by a Surrey kindergarten teacher. Her appeal to the British Columbia Supreme Court is supported by a $40,000 donation by the B.C. Teachers Federation[13] and by affidavits from well-known children's writers Robert Munsch and Dennis Lee. According to Lee's affidavit, the challenged books 'situate stories, feelings and fun with words within the context of a family configuration which most children do not know firsthand – that of same-sex parents. In the process they are bound to reduce the tendency to mockery and cruelty with which many children greet things they are unfamiliar with.'[14]

Books about or containing allusions to homosexuality have been extensively targeted in North American libraries in the 1990s. In fact, two books about same-sex parents – Daddy's Roommate and Heather Has Two Mommies – have been the most challenged books in U.S. public and school libraries during this decade (Canada does not collect national data in this area). Some parents feel that their public or school library is promoting homosexuality by stocking these books, rather than (as the librarians maintain) just representing a reality in society and a wide range of ideas. That public and school libraries promote all the ideas contained within their collections cannot be possible: many fiction and non-fiction books contain descriptions of a murder – which the library does not condone or promote!

Librarians use a variety of skills to manage censorship challenges, particularly when the complaints concern sexually oriented materials. Studies have shown that having a board-approved collection policy in place long before the

challenge is received is the best management technique.[15] These policies usually echo the intellectual-freedom philosophy of the CLA in stating that the
library acquires a wide variety of materials, including those 'which some elements of society may consider to be unconventional, unpopular, or unacceptable.' Also included are statements that assert that the public library will not act
in loco parentis – if parents are concerned, they should accompany their child to
the library. A statement about how the library selects material is sometimes
included in the policy. Although the statement may list specific review sources,
its primary purpose is to explain the difference between selection and censorship according to professional library practice. Lester Asheim has perhaps
stated it best:

Selection begins with a presumption in favor of liberty of thought: censorship with a presumption in favor of thought control. Selection's approach to the book is positive, seeking its values in the book as a book and in the book as a whole. Censorship's approach is
negative, seeking for vulnerable characteristics wherever they can be found – anywhere
within the book or even outside it. Selection seeks to protect the right of the reader to
read; censorship seeks to protect – not the right – but the reader himself from the fancied
affects of his reading. The selector has faith in the intelligence of the reader: the censor
has faith only in his own.[16]

The Question of 'Promotion'

What constitutes 'promotion' of an idea often underlies disagreements about
what should be in library collections, and so it is no surprise that censorship
challenges often include the charge that a library is promoting an idea. This
problem of interpretation of 'promotion' has affected public libraries in Britain
as they struggle with section 28 of the Local Government Act of 1988. The act
states that a local government shall not (a) intentionally promote homosexuality
or publish material with the intention of promoting homosexuality; (b) promote
the teaching in any school of the acceptability of homosexuality as a pretended
family relationship. Although the British Library Association tried to clarify
that public-library collections could not be targeted by this legislation, the
House of Commons refused to include such clarification. In response, and with
the advice of many library solicitors, public libraries have tended to minimize
the exposure of any material dealing with homosexuality. These measures
include moving certain books so that they are in a secluded corner, withdrawing
any booklists prepared on this subject, and/or being much more selective about
the acquisition of such materials.[17] Although Canadian librarians are not operating under such legislation, the charge that they are promoting a particular sub-

ject or viewpoint by having material on the library shelves often surfaces. For example, charges of 'promotion' were part of the protests when books on the revisionist view of the Holocaust were 'found' at the Edmonton Public Library,[18] when the book *No Place for Me* about a white witch was found in a school-library collection,[19] and when the three same-sex parents books noted above were challenged.[20]

Community Values

One of the most problematic concepts in the censorship debate is 'community values.' The term has posed problems in the Canadian court system when judges have referred to community values when determining whether or not an item is obscene.[21] The use of the term in a more colloquial sense also causes problems when citizens or library board members press for the public or school-library collections to be reflective of community values. Who is 'the community?' In many cases, those who advocate for 'community values' believe that all 'right-thinking' people hold values similar to their own and they underplay the tensions that exist within communities. They emphasize the difference between communities, not within the communities themselves. Those who champion community values as a primary library-selection criterion also ignore the idea of dominance – the fact that the most confident and vocal members of the community may be espousing their ideas (which are then taken as the norm) while the silent or less assertive members' views are seldom taken into account. Two recent cases illustrate the difficulties of relying on community-values judgments. In 1995 the book *Lethal Marriage* was challenged in Ontario on the basis that it betrayed the values of the communities in which the Homolka/Bernardo murders occurred, in addition to causing distress to the victims' families. This book describes the trials of Karla Homolka and Paul Bernardo for the sexual torture and murder of two teenage girls, including details from the videotapes of the murders shown at Bernardo's trial. The mothers of both murdered girls protested the inclusion of the book in their local libraries. The St Catharines Library removed the book from circulation because it was 'an extremely sensitive local issue,' but the Burlington Library retained its copies.[22] In noting the local nature of the issue, the St Catharines Library acquisitions manager referred to the extreme pain that the community had suffered, pain that she felt the book exacerbated. In the second case, arising in 1992, a group of citizens in Sechelt, British Columbia, protested against the inclusion of the book *Maxine's Tree* in the school library because of its anti-clearcut logging theme. The protesters felt that the book did not reflect the community values of their community, which was highly dependent on the logging industry.[23]

The Impact of Budget Cuts

Many librarians fear that shrinking budgets in all types of libraries will accomplish what the censor could not. Intellectual freedom is best promoted when libraries can provide a wide range of materials, but this is only possible when money is available to add materials that introduce new ideas, present new interpretations of existing ideas, and replace stolen or damaged items. When faced with drastically reduced budgets, collection managers may not be able to add new materials, or they may be forced to order only those materials that are mainstream and will circulate very highly. The books, videos, and music materials that are at the edges of the spectrum because they focus on avant-garde or minority viewpoints may be eliminated in the selection process because the non-controversial best-sellers consume the scarce budget dollars. Insufficient funding makes more difficult the purchase of materials for racial minorities and gay/lesbian communities. The purchase of replacement copies is often curtailed, prompting librarians to avoid purchase of books on sexuality or witchcraft which are often stolen by the curious too shy to check them out or by the offended who feel that 'unauthorized withdrawal' is a moral act. No library can purchase all materials published, but the drastic reductions in acquisitions money faced by many Canadian libraries mean that a limited collection lacking even one item reflecting a minority point of view is the result. These 'safe' collections do not reflect the diversity of opinion about a subject, only the opinions of the mainstream.

To supplement shrinking budgets, public libraries are increasingly reliant on corporate sponsorship. These gifts must be negotiated carefully, however, to ensure that the intellectual freedom of the library is not compromised. Libraries have accepted money for putting company names and/or logos on such library property as library cards, overdue slips, and book bags. Donations have been acknowledged by naming special rooms, separate collections, book-stack shelving units, and entire buildings after corporations.[24] The problem with sponsorship, however, is that this 'labelling' may lead citizens to believe that the advertised company is exerting undue influence over the library, that this public acknowledgement of money donated discredits the library's supposed neutrality. In the author's study of censorship in Canadian public libraries, she found that almost 50 per cent (14 of 30) of directors of large urban public libraries thought that sponsorship posed a real threat to the intellectual-freedom philosophy promoted by their libraries.[25] They believed that sponsorship could undermine public-library principles because the donated funds were really part of a business venture pursued with expectation of return, an objective at odds with the impartiality encouraged in both the building environs and the collection.

Even the Canadian directors who supported sponsorship did so because they believed it to be essential for the library's survival, rather than a desirable thing. They felt that careful management of the terms of sponsorship agreements could contain any moves by a corporate body to extend its influence. Most directors in the study differentiated between sponsorship of events and sponsorship of the collection. They felt that a company donation towards programming within the library was most desirable, while company funding of actual library resources was to be avoided since this carried the greatest potential for intellectual-freedom problems. Directors told anecdotes about legal firms, insurance associations, and large corporations under threat by environmental groups giving money for resources and then attempting to shape the collections to reflect better the organization's goals.

Shrinking budgets for education have also meant that school libraries have suffered in terms of resources and staffing. When hard choices must be made between funding the school sports team and funding the school library, it appears that the library is sometimes neglected. In many school districts in Canada, the position of teacher-librarian has disappeared – the libraries are staffed with parent volunteers or library technicians. Shaping a vibrant, well-rounded collection for students requires a thorough knowledge of library processes, including the new resources available for purchase. Integrating the library's resources into the classroom through liaison with the teachers requires expertise not usually held by technicians or volunteers. The net affect of these poorly resourced, under-staffed school libraries is that a wide range of information is not presented to students through the library and, through neglect, many key sources, some of which may be controversial, are not available to students.

Truth and Untruth

The area of truth/untruth is one that poses many problems for librarians, particularly in public and academic libraries. Many public-library directors believe that material which many people consider to be untrue should be included in library collections: they maintain that library customers have a responsibility to form their own opinions about the quality of the facts presented.[26] But some librarians differentiate between two kinds of untruth – one of which is unacceptable. The acceptable untruth is often associated with 'fads' such as special diets, homeopathic medicine, and theories about unidentified flying objects, areas that will not cause deep-seated offence or physical or psychological harm. Unacceptable untruth is associated with theories in the historical or scientific fields of history and race theory, with the revisionist claims about the Jewish Holocaust being a primary example. This issue continues to surface in society in general and with regard to library collections.[27] Although 80 per cent of the public-library directors in the author's study maintained that material that was critical of the generally accepted information about the Jewish Holocaust was appropriate for a public-library collection, 80 per cent of those in agreement wanted special conditions attached to management of this difficult material.[28] The most common condition was that the material itself be identified as revisionist. This condition is unusual for library collections, for material is usually tagged with subject headings which identify the subject or content, not the point of view, for example, liberal, conservative, communist. Other conditions set by directors were that this material should be purchased only in small quantities and only by very large libraries, and that the authors must be 'respectable.' Canadian librarians clearly feel that this material is one of the most problematic areas they manage and carries the greatest potential for censorship calls by the community.

Meeting Rooms and Display Spaces

Canadian librarians must manage not only complaints about materials in the collection but also complaints about other library services such as program rooms and community art-gallery space. These areas are highly visible and therefore more prone to protests. Although some community members might tolerate views offensive to them within books sitting quietly on a library shelf, having those views presented verbally in a program room or displayed visually in an art-gallery painting is an affront they will not permit. An example of this occurred in Saskatoon in 1990. The public library's book and periodical collection contained much information on AIDS and safe sexual practices, but when a community-health organization planned to show an AIDS information film in the library program room several residents objected. They tried to disrupt the film presentation and threatened the chief librarian; the library board strongly supported the film showing, which eventually proceeded. To counter protesters' complaints, both the chief librarian and the board chairperson cited the CLA Bill of Rights regarding censorship and the Saskatoon Library's policy on booking meeting rooms which was based on that policy.

More recently, race-relations activists and the B'Nai Brith objected in November 1996 to the Greater Victoria Public Library renting space to the Canadian Free Speech League for a two-hour seminar. The league maintained that it is a law-abiding group concerned only with promoting freedom of expression, but objectors accused the group of promoting views that incite hatred against minority groups. They wanted the league banned from library premises. Alan Dutton of the Canadian Anti-Racism Education and Research

Society said that 'I think the municipality and the City of Victoria have to understand the importance of not providing access to groups that have contributed to the disunity of this country by promoting views that are racist, that oppose immigration and multiculturalism.'[29] Victoria city council further complicated the situation on 14 November by passing a motion which restricted rental of its own facilities to groups deemed not to be 'hate' related. This motion, however, did not influence the Victoria board, which, advised by Chief Librarian Sandra Anderson, voted to continue renting meeting-room space to groups, even if controversial, as long as they were law-abiding. In their decision, the board members noted that they were upholding the principles articulated by the CLA and that they felt their library had a basic responsibility to develop and maintain intellectual freedom.[30]

In a similar situation, Alan Dutton protested against a meeting of the Canadian Free Speech League held on 11 May 1997 at the West Vancouver Memorial Public Library program room, which the league had rented for the purpose. During this meeting Doug Collins, controversial columnist for the *North Shore News*, presented his views about free speech in general and freedom of the press in particular. The topic was of interest to those who both agreed and disagreed with Collins's views, for he was soon to appear before the British Columbia Human Rights Tribunal to respond to complaints brought forward by Michael Elterman, chair of the Canadian Jewish Congress, Pacific Division. Elterman's complaints centred on one of Collins's columns in which he called the movie *Schindler's List* 'Hollywood Propaganda.'[31] The meeting was held as scheduled, with chief librarian Jack Mounce citing library policies and defending the use of the library meeting room by groups wanting to discuss community issues, even those offensive to some citizens.

As evident in these examples, formulating a policy for meeting-room use and obtaining library-board support of that policy before complaints arise is judicious management practice. In a study of censorship concerns affecting thirty of Canada's largest public libraries, 87 per cent of the libraries had written policies regarding meeting-room use. The directors of these libraries said that some groups required special attention because their bookings engendered complaints and because protests during their programs might cause noise and commotion, disrupting the normal operations of the library and possibly endangering customers.[32] Directors singled out groups that were right-wing, religious, political, and 'hard-selling' commercial as those whose bookings they would monitor closely. The advice on program rooms and art galleries most commonly given by directors in the study was to put a disclaimer on all contracts and advertising saying that use of space by an organization did not mean that the library endorsed the organization's views. In summary, city of Victoria library director

Anderson appears to have represented the outlook of most Canadian library directors when she strongly supported the right of controversial groups to use library meeting rooms. In her view, the events held in the rooms were just another form of information, 'live action rather than print,' and really just an extension of the book collection.

The Internet

The Internet is exciting and desirable new territory for libraries, but one that also brings the censorship challenges that often accompany new technologies.[33] Librarians in all types of libraries have welcomed this resource, which allows patrons access to information that decreased budgets cannot provide. Instead of purchasing expensive or esoteric documents which might be seldom used, librarians can provide access to these works through the Internet. Government reports that might take months to arrive are now available on the net as soon as published. As well, information that might never appear in paper form is now available through websites. Librarians are providing advice and guidance on Internet searching both to those with home-computer access and to those without. What a boon for all libraries, especially those isolated from major centres! But with this wealth of information from websites around the world has come calls for censorship, particularly in school and public libraries. Although the books and journals in a library often contain similar information to that presented on the Internet, 'projecting' that information on the computer screen makes it far more visible than opening a book with the same information in a secluded library carrel. As other students in a school library or other customers in a public library walk past, they may be confronted by images or text which they do not wish to see. This far more public viewing of information makes those concerned about the vulnerable in society much more aware of what others (particularly children) are reading. Those who wish to limit access to this new resource fear as well the allure of the searching process itself: it appears to be far more exciting to spend hours searching for sexual graphics with complicated Internet codes than to look up Dewey call numbers in a library catalogue.

The disorganized nature of the Internet world is both its charm and its flaw. The Internet has been described as all the books in the Library of Congress being dumped on the floor, with no order. The keyword indexing of most search engines leads to wonderfully serendipitous results when one keys in selections – if you want information on coke you will get the drug, the drink, and the distilled product of coal.[34] If you want information on cancer, you will get thousands of 'hits' on everything from the zodiac sign to totally unsubstantiated miracle cures. If asked, librarians may be able to direct users to recommended sites with reliable information, but many users choose to search the net themselves, stumbling upon sources that they find objectionable or perhaps searching the 'universe' for thrilling new sources of sexual titillation. For many small public libraries that offer a limited range of controversial material, gaining access to this greater universe has been a shock, particularly for the customers.

Some public-library customers have pressured librarians to prevent both inadvertent and deliberate access to controversial material on the Internet. These customers have suggested various methods of restricting Internet access, particularly for children. These methods include installing 'blinders' around computer screens so passers-by cannot see the screen, requiring children to have written parental permission to use the Internet, denying library Internet access to children under sixteen, and installing filtering software programs such as Surfwatch and NetNanny on their terminals.

The efficacy of filtering programs and whether or not their installation on public-library terminals constitutes censorship engendered heated debate throughout 1997. Even the Internet itself has been used as a forum for discussions about filtering software: lengthy arguments have appeared on computer-discussion groups such as the Canadian intellectual-freedom list IFreedom and the American listservs Publib and Alaoif. The official stance of the ALA and CLA is that librarians should avoid filtering because it limits access to information and censors certain types of information deemed unsuitable by a small group of customers. For example, Surfwatch in its own website notes that its product blocks any website or webpage which predominantly contains links to material that is sexually explicit, contains violence or hate speech, or information about drugs, alcohol, or gambling. Blocking this information, however, means that much good information is also blocked, since keyword searching is used to eliminate sites. For example, all websites containing the word 'breast' may be blocked, thereby denying the customer access not only to sexually explicit sites but also to all sites about breast cancer. Sites with the word 'sex' in the title are usually blocked as well, thereby denying customers information about sex education. Strange blocking also occurs. For example, a site on 'Mars Exploration' was blocked because the word 'sex' appears in the phrase. How have Canadian libraries handled calls for Internet filters? Most have resisted filter installation by insisting that, as with other material in the library, parents are responsible for supervising the material their child selects. As well, librarians have wanted to avoid the legal liability that would come with advertising that a computer was 'guaranteed' not to deliver any information which might offend. Although some parents might be comforted by such a claim, librarians know that the vast array of websites, the unreliability of filters, and the superb searching skills of many library customers make such guarantees worthless.

Conclusion

Canadian librarians draw on a wide range of management skills when confronted with censorship challenges. Their ability to negotiate with concerned customers, members of their governing bodies, and sometimes the press requires expertise not unlike that of a tightrope walker. Librarians must balance the competing interests of various constituents while adhering to the basic purposes of their libraries and the tenets of intellectual freedom as set out by the CLA. This challenge is further complicated by the nature of most censorship confrontations: the subjects being discussed – sex, religion, race – are ones encumbered with deep personal emotion. It is essential that librarians persevere in walking the tightrope so that Canadian libraries continue to provide a forum for the expression of competing ideas.

Freedom of expression is the very foundation of political life; without it, there is no choice of liberal or conservative philosophy, of right or left. The instincts for freedom and individual responsibility are the keystones to social organization and to democratic government. In the last resort, it is not the force of law but only the force of free intelligence that can save a people from its own folly.[35]

NOTES

1 Kathleen W. Craver, 'Challenges,' in *School Library Media Centers in the 21st Century: Changes and Challenges* (Westport, Conn.: Greenwood Press 1994), 141–50.

2 Richard M. Dougherty and Ann P. Doughtery, 'The Academic Library: A Time of Crisis, Change and Opportunity,' *Journal of Academic Librarianship*, 18 (January 1993), 346.

3 Ellis Mount, 'The Nature of Special Libraries and Information Centers,' in *Special Libraries and Information Centers*, 3rd ed. (Washington, D.C.: Special Libraries Association 1995), 2–13.

4 Miriam Braverman, 'From Adam Smith to Ronald Reagan: Public Libraries as a Public Good,' *Library Journal*, 107 (February 1982), 397–401; Verna L. Pungitore, 'Mission of Public Libraries,' in *Public Librarianship: An Issues-Oriented Approach*. (New York: Greenwood 1994), 27–41.

5 Garrett Hardin, 'The Tragedy of the Commons,' *Science*, 162 (13 December 1968), 1244.

6 Ann Curry, *The Limits of Tolerance: Censorship and Intellectual Freedom in Public Libraries* (Lanham, Md.: Scarecrow Press 1997), 134.

7 Alvin M. Schrader, *Fear of Words: Censorship and the Public Libraries of Canada* (Ottawa: Canadian Library Association 1995), 114.

8 David Jenkinson, 'Censorship Iceberg: Results of a Survey of Challenges in Public and School Libraries,' *Canadian Library Journal*, 43 (February 1986), 7–21.

9 Jill Mahoney, 'Book not obscene after all, police decide,' *Globe and Mail*, 27 May 1997.

10 Maria Jimenez, 'RCMP Raids Libraries for Sex Bestseller,' *The Vancouver Sun* 17 May 1997.

11 'Groups to argue against books ban,' *Vancouver Sun*, 24 April 1997.

12 Ibid.

13 Catherine Porter, 'BCTF gives $40,000 to fight book ban Case,' *Vancouver Sun*, 10 November 1997.

14 Kim Bolan, 'Authors join surrey books fray,' *Vancouver Sun*, 3 Oct. 1997.

15 Dianne McAfee Hopkins, *Factors Influencing the Outcome of Challenges to Materials in Secondary School Libraries* (Washington, D.C.: Department of Education, Office of Educational Research and Improvement, Library Programs 1991), 5–13. See also Alvin M. Schrader, *Fear of Words*, 40; Ann Curry, *Limits of Tolerance*, 121.

16 Lester Asheim, 'Not Censorship but Selection,' *Wilson Library Bulletin*, 28 (September 1953), 67.

17 Curry, *The Limits of Tolerance*, 78.

18 Wojciech Buczynski, 'EPL should have no neo-Nazi books,' *Edmonton Journal*, 10 June 1988.

19 'The attempted banning of *No Place for Me*, *Globe and Mail*, 17 Feb. 1995.

20 Kim Bolan, 'Authors join Surrey.'

21 Cynthia A. MacDougall, 'The Community Standards Test of Obscenity,' *University of Toronto Faculty of Law Review*, 42 (1984), 79–83.

22 'Book fictitious, pornographic, Mahaffy says,' *[Kitchener] Record*, 27 Oct. 1995; 'Bernardo case book pulled from library,' *[Kitchener] Record*, 28 Oct. 1995.

23 'Loggers protest book,' *Globe and Mail*, 21 Feb. 1992.

24 Doug Saunders, 'Corporate identity to cover library: budget slashing prompts move,' *Globe and Mail*, 23 Oct. 1996; Madge Aalto, 'Green Light for Logos,' *Quill and Quire*, 62 (October 1996), 13.

25 Curry, *The Limits of Tolerance*, 174.

26 Ibid., 104.

27 'How free will speech be in B.C?' *Vancouver Sun*, 10 May 1997; 'RCMP shred book,' *Calgary Sun*, 24 Jan. 1995.

28 Curry, *The Limits of Tolerance*, 107.

29 'Free speech isn't just for the politically correct,' editorial, *Victoria Times Colonist*, 30 Oct. 1996.

30 Denīse Helm, 'Library open to all groups," *Victoria Times Colonist*, 27 Nov. 1996.
31 Douglas Todd, 'Use of library for Collins' rally sparks outcry,' *Vancouver Sun*, 10 May 1997.
32 Curry, *The Limits of Tolerance*, 156.
33 Anthony Keller, 'Patrolling the Internet,' *Globe and Mail*, 2 Dec. 1996.
34 Peter Wilson, 'Taming the wild web,' *Vancouver Sun*, 9 March 1996.
35 Alvin M. Schrader, *Fear of Words*, 122.

10

The Ethos of Censorship in English-Canadian Literature: An Ontopornosophical Approach[1]

LORRAINE WEIR

One has to be completely taken in by this internal ruse of confession in order to attribute a fundamental role to censorship, to taboos regarding speaking and thinking; one has to have an inverted image of power in order to believe that all these voices which have spoken so long in our civilisation – repeating the formidable injunction to tell what one is and what one does, what one recollects and what one has forgotten, what one is thinking and what one thinks [s]he is not thinking – are speaking to us of freedom.

Michel Foucault, *The History of Sexuality*, 60

In your Word all is uttered at one and the same time, yet eternally. If it were not so, your Word would be subject to time and change, and therefore would be neither truly eternal nor truly immortal.

St Augustine, *Confessions*, XI:7 (259)

I begin with a caveat. The multidisciplinary approach used here is grounded in disciplines ranging from rhetoric and the history of literary criticism to Canadian social and literary history and from contemporary theory to recent Canadian case law. Since there is no one language or lexicon available for the performance of this task, there is no obvious vehicle of access for the reader whose point of departure is other. But one must start somewhere and so I reach for the tools of one of my own trades, poststructuralist theory, in the knowledge that the history of hermeneutics and of Canadian literary realism are fundamental to my argument but may not be fundamental to the reader's location. I have attempted to supply contexts, partly through ample endnotes, but these may well be superfluous for some readers while minimalist for others. Yet the work requires this mode of multidisciplinary synthesis for, as I argue here, censorship is so deeply implicated in English-Canadian literary history that one needs a variety of nets to keep 'it' from slipping through and retaining its canonic – and hegemonic – status of invisibility. My argument is simple, its defence rather complex.

To inquire into censorship and English-Canadian literature is to inquire into the discursive production of the Canadian literary institution, into the formation of reviewing practices and their complex relations to the professoriate, and into the construction of 'community.' To the extent that these various nodes in the ever-shifting networks of meaning-production called 'literature' are embedded in the ancient art of interpretation known as hermeneutics, they were also caught up in nineteenth- and early-twentieth-century Canada in social-purity discourse and so-called 'muscular Christianity.'[2]

Purification through literature and, more specifically, through the teaching of English assumed the status of a pedagogical as well as a moral program of social transformation thought to be necessary in an age of emergent social and economic mobility. Young ladies and gentlemen in the making required not only a firm grasp of the King's English (a class marker as decisive as other forms of 'good manners') but also a clear understanding of those codes of decorum thought to be instilled by literature, particularly fiction.

Enter literary 'realism' and traditional hermeneutics onto the stage of Canadian gentrification, aided and abetted by university English departments possessed of an Arnoldian fervour to convert and ennoble the masses through a liberal application of grammar, rhetoric, and good example.[3] This 'moral obligation' to the community coincided by the late 1960s with the entry of courses devoted entirely to Canadian literature into the university curriculum[4] and the reinforcing of the status of Canadian literature as a mirror of the 'real world' of Canadian experience in contrast to the world of culture and tradition represented by Chaucer, Shakespeare, Milton, et al. During the mid-1960s Northrop Frye, one of the great champions of the constitution of Canadian literature as an academic subject, was to maintain that the opportunity to study our own literature is essential to the formation of the 'Canadian imagination' and to Canada as a nation.[5] Thus, whereas in the same period in the United States and Britain, literary 'realism' signified representation of 'ordinary,' sometimes gritty details of 'ordinary' lives, rendered in terms recognizable to 'ordinary' readers, in Canada 'realism' took on the code of civility and the mission of decorum propounded by its advocates. To risk otherwise was to court censorship and/or possible oblivion.

In this context, traditional hermeneutics (as opposed to its ostensibly secularized transformation, so-called 'practical criticism'[6]) became an invaluable ally, for its theological foundations legitimized its deployment as interpretive strategy within a moral agenda of social purification, and thus of making 'real' only those elements that could be accommodated, whether in the classroom or in literary reviews, to inscribing the 'normal' as 'truth.' Civility became the limit of realism and the hallmark of the interpretative technology which produced it.

Civility is sacramental in this tradition of text- and reader-production. What is produced undergoes transubstantiation: the text becomes the world/the world is the text. Canon-formation operates on the basis of a slightly aestheticized moral agenda, selecting as defining cases of what 'is' only those texts that enable its proclamation. Whereas international realism (for lack of a better term) frequently operated a socially transformative agenda at the level of more or less Marxist critique, English-Canadian realism typically opted for a sanitized 'reality,' preferring 'region' to revolution, 'man' and 'the land' to sweat and blood. It is, in other words, the business of traditional hermeneutics to evaluate, to produce a canon whose constituents exemplify in their 'canonicity' precisely the canon-generative strategies that enabled their selection. In Canada, hermeneutics conjoined with realism has for more than a century occupied the position of 'common sense.'

How can we think the critical tradition that constituted and has endeavoured to sustain this hermeneutic/'realist' formation? How can we think the impact of hermeneutic ideology upon a legal system whose practitioners have little sense of the history of interpretive moves which they use so frequently as to render the very rhetoric of meaning-production invisible in the service of its 'contents'? How, in a literary-juridical context, can we express social consensus or the mind of the 'reasonable man' but by operating the very hermeneutic technology which vests those constructs with a seemingly unassailable authenticity? Among many possible cases, take three – *Butler*, *Scythes*, *Little Sister's*[7] – as examples of some of the operations of traditional hermeneutics in the courtroom.

In *Butler*, the first constitutional challenge to the 1959 obscenity law, the Supreme Court attempted to define more clearly the concept of 'community' and, in particular, 'what the community would tolerate others being exposed to on the basis of the degree of harm that may flow' (*Butler*, 454) from 'exposure' to representations of sex classified in this case as pornographic. The court's concern here is that 'harm in this context predisposes persons to act in an anti-social manner' (454), and that 'harm' is occasioned by exposure to the 'portrayal' of 'explicit sex which is degrading or dehumanising' (454). 'Exposure to images,' the court asserts, 'bears a causal relationship to changes in attitudes and beliefs' (455), presumably resulting in 'anti-social' attitudes. Analysing section 163 of the Criminal Code (on obscenity) in his minority judgment, Justice Charles Gonthier identifies *representation* as crucial for certain types of 'scenes might be perhaps be legal if done between consenting adults, but they become obscene when they are represented' (513). That is, what is 'usually hidden behind a veil of modesty and privacy' (513) becomes obscene when it is *represented.* 'After all, it is the element of representation that gives this material its power of suggestion' (517), not surprisingly given that 'representation here is understood in the sense of public suggestion' (511). What is 'suggested' is 'the content of the representation' (511).

Whereas *Butler* is concerned with generic pornography, *Scythes* is focused on *Bad Attitude*, a lesbian erotic magazine, copies of which had been seized by the police from the Glad Day Bookshop in Toronto in April 1992. Here, as Brenda Cossman has argued, the problem for the court is that 'the *representation* of gay and lesbian sexuality ... is degrading and dehumanizing,' although the court asserts that 'sexual orientation is not relevant in determining community standards.'[8] Nonetheless, referencing *Butler*, Justice Claude Paris of the Ontario Court of Justice (Provincial Division) convicted the owners of the bookshop of obscenity, ruling that the public needs to be protected from lesbian erotica which would 'predispose individuals to anti-social behaviour' (*Scythes* 1993, 3), presumably of a lesbian sort.

In *Little Sister's*, the familiar concerns with community standards and harm are revisited, this time with the addition of an exegesis of the 'internal necessities' or artistic merit test. The occasion was the challenge to prior restraint mounted by the Little Sister's Bookstore of Vancouver after more than a decade of experiencing detention by Canada Customs of shipments of gay and lesbian books and magazines. Among many witnesses with literary expertise, novelist Nino Ricci had a significant impact on Justice Kenneth Smith, whose judgment records Ricci's concerns when evaluating a text for artistic merit: 'structure and plot development; internal consistency and credibility; new and complex use of language; complexity in the psychology of the characters, in the development of situations, and in the examination of themes; intent of the author ... and social and historical context of the work' (Smith quoting Ricci's testimony, *Little Sister's*, 226).

In grafting Ricci's classically hermeneutic criteria onto the theory of representation advanced in *Butler* and *Scythes*, *Little Sister's* not only reinforced the dominance of the hermeneutic/realist formation triumphant in the very invisibility of its hegemony, but also reasserted a causal connection between text and world such that the 'contents' of the text become the 'contents' of quotidian 'reality.' Justice Smith was, however, prepared to assert the necessity of this operation in the context of the 'need for self-affirmation and empowerment through expression' which he takes to be a 'dominant theme prevalent in homosexual art and literature' (229). But what remains unchallenged here is the sacramental conjunction of word and world such that 'representation' effects the transformation of one into the other. It is a conjunction which is among the hallmarks of American feminist legal theorist Catharine MacKinnon's intervention in *Butler* via LEAF (Women's Legal Education Action Fund) and crucial to the articulation of a feminist anti-pornography position in Canadian law.

MacKinnon's version of speech-act theory employs a familiar strategy: the word *is* the world, word *is* act. In *Only Words* MacKinnon argues that 'speech that is sex has a different relation to reality than speech that is not sex has'. Since 'pornography does what it says,' 'to express eroticism is to engage in eroticism, meaning to perform a sex act.'[9] Thus 'speech that is sex' *is* sex; word *is* act in the world: what is expressed/represented *is* reality in the world. The gap between modern hermeneutics and post-structuralist theory over the past thirty years is seldom clearer than in MacKinnon's kernel axioms whose unimpeded progress in Canada bears witness to the close fit between her theory of pornography and the prevailing ideology of sacramental hermeneutics in the production of 'literature' in Canada. The imbrication of discursive formations here is complex, ranging, as noted above, from the Arnoldian foundations of traditional English departments to the construction of realism as a transparent agent of civility to the deployment in Canadian literary criticism of a hermeneutics of speculary containment. It is this moment of epistemic crisis which MacKinnon figures, with such dire consequences.

Yet in the 1990s there has been a shift in Canadian writing – whether literary or theoretical or both – and sometimes even in pedagogical styles in English departments, and issues of realist control have begun radically to transform. *Butler, Scythes,* and *Little Sister's* also record that complexity of epistemic rupture. But the *judgments* in these cases fail to reflect that rupture, taking refuge instead in what is not only a more conservative position in Canadian social thought but also a much more traditional position in the history of meaning-production around texts constituted as 'literary.' In the course of what Jonathan Dollimore has referred to as 'transgressive reinscription,'[10] we need briefly to revisit St Augustine and some aspects of the history of hermeneutics before considering censorship in English-Canadian literature in more detail.

So, to begin again. The production of 'realism' as a narrative and epistemic strategy is an aspect of an evangelical call to representation based in part on a theological assumption of the redemptive relation of Christ as Word (logos) to the world. Through received interpretations, the believer encounters the Gospel as a move on the journey toward redemption. For St Augustine, God's words are signs that do not deceive though post-lapsarian human intelligence may be flawed in its understanding of their complexities. Translation may be necessary, its type or primary figure in this tradition being Christ himself as shape-shifter between divine and human realms. Christ enters human history as language, the Virgin Mary's words of acceptance – *'Fiat,'* 'Let it be' (Luke 1:38) – at the moment of the 'annunciation' being traditionally construed as the moment of translation when 'the Word was made flesh.' It is this event that is commemorated and, in Roman Catholic practice, reproduced at the moment of transsubstantiation in the Mass, which is to say that the transformation of the substances of bread and wine into the body and blood of Christ (the sacrament of the Eucharist) marks the ultimate proclamation of word as act as 'truth.' Within the Catholic tradition, this is, so to speak, as 'real' as it gets, a sacramental act of translation.

But the problem of reading God's book remains, whether the Bible as text or the world as terrestrial expression of sacred inscription wherein humankind might read God's message. Both are imbricated in the production of Christian hermeneutics as a technology of meaning-production grounded in God's word sounding in a mutable text, post-Babel and subject to textual 'corruption' whether in the form of flawed translations or textual inconsistencies or of the layers of interpretations that precede any new intervention and that must also be elucidated in the contextualization of that intervention. Traditional hermeneutics sought to operate a systematic interpretive technology designed to 'restore' the text to its 'original' (divine) version and to mediate the text's journey into the world by elucidating and proclaiming the text's 'truth.' In other words, hermeneutics operated as a truth-production apparatus and was institutionalized as such in both ecclesiastical and secular contexts, including pedagogy and jurisprudence.

To sketch in the history of Christian hermeneutics from the early medieval period to the Enlightenment, tracing its interfaces with the development of a system of jurisprudence grounded in precedent and other interpretive techniques borrowed from hermeneutics, would require far more space than I have here. Suffice it to say that the post-Reformation development of a Protestant hermeneutics that emphasized clarity, simplicity, and accessibility as exegetical goals was also constituted as a 'return' to the basics, to a 'common-sense' approach to the text which easily transmuted itself into a conviction of the *literality* of the sacred text. God's eminent reasonableness accounted for the transparency of the text such that the faithful, with a little help from hermeneutics, could themselves (that is, without the intervention of the clergy) see the truth of the text.

The history of British jurisprudence from the Enlightenment on reflects a secularized version of this 'common-sense' foundation of interpretation, grafted onto an empiricist ideology. This conjunction has enabled the proliferation of legal precedents (and indeed the system of precedent itself) based on ideologically – and methodologically-bound – adherence to a construction of reasonableness, transparency of meaning, and a speculary relation of language to world such that what is produced in one medium will translate and thus replicate in another. Thus, the assumption that the law will change the world is an aspect of the hermeneutic and theological assumption – indeed, conviction – that the text, God's book, will change the world. Further, the conjunction of word and world is foundational to the movement of human and individual history towards 'redemption' as the fulfilment of God's promise to the "chosen" people.' Consider hermeneutic redemption as the after-life of safe texts.

What happens when literary realism meets this conjunction of ontology and theology, or what Jacques Derrida refers to as 'ontotheology,'[11] through the interpretive operations of hermeneutics? 'Truth' is produced and the speculary relation of text to world is collapsed in a redemptive act of translation   such that one becomes the other, one's 'Truth' becomes the other's 'meaning.' The 'world' comes to be configured as a realist text. The text is always already the world but replicates it so that the textual 'frame' bounds the image of the world and sharpens the focus, delineating the specificity of the image and producing what Derrida calls 'the truth in painting,' the 'moment' when possession of the image hovers at the edge of vanishing, dispossession. This is the moment of interpellation when realist ideology is briefly glimpsed *as* transparency, the sacramental moment when 'word' becomes 'flesh' translated abruptly into bodies, words, things.[12]

We might call this the ontopornosophical moment when realism, truth, text, world, language, body escape the orderly clutches of the hermeneutic machine and – stripped of its requisite operations of context, intention, linguistic specificity, figurative language, diction, genre, period, and so on – the 'text' is without 'meaning' and the 'reader' as sovereign Subject deconstructed. This is the moment of hermeneutic angst which *Butler* registers. Here, as the word made flesh goes wildly wrong in what is thereby constituted as 'pornography,' the hermeneutic enterprise needs to be reconstituted and reaffirmed such that its operations will be performed only upon safe texts, harm-less texts, texts that *as* texts pre-exist readers. Drawn deeply into hermeneutic-repetition compulsion, into this desperate ideology of foundationalist normativity, *Butler* can only *exclude* those texts that endanger its normative, hegemonic technologies of meaning-production. The very transparency that hermeneutics claims has 'itself' become transparent lest the whole rhetoric of jurisprudence become untenable and the 'process through which judges give meaning to ... ambiguous concepts ... [be seen as] an ideological one,' as 'just words.'[13]

To give an account of censorship in English-Canadian literature is to enquire into a politics of exclusion so pervasive as to be virtually invisible. Dominant formations of the literary canon have largely been produced in the academy by professors whose reviewing practices and textbook orders typically coincide to produce both literary reputations and sales. The combination of the marginal economy of Canadian publishing, with its typically small print runs and government subsidies, together with the relatively small size of the Canadian book-buying public, has produced a climate in which non-'mainstream' concerns have been difficult to address – or, more often, simply not addressed at all. The rapid transformation in publishing and teaching patterns since the late 1980s highlights this situation in retrospect. Happily, in the late 1990s it is not uncommon for Canadian university English departments to offer Canadian and post-colonial courses which include materials by writers located outside the anglo-heteronormative community. Similarly, some would argue that 'theory' is now included in many curricula and that undergraduates are more likely than a decade ago to encounter a problematizing of the traditional pedagogy of 'practical criticism' or applied hermeneutics. But, if the beginning of modern theory is Ferdinand de Saussure's critique of the rhetorical commonplace associating the words *Arbor* and *Equos* with drawings of a tree and a horse, it is still not difficult to find undergraduates – and sometimes colleagues – who, unconsciously living a sacramental hermeneutics, find it exceedingly painful to grasp Saussure's point about the *arbitrariness* of these conventions.[14] Those students are in good company, however, for *Butler* and *Little Sister's*, among many other legal as well as literary examples, share the same problem, reading texts referentially, imagining actions deposited in the seams of language. Perhaps the call to censorship always as an aspect of its 'formative power'[15] bears an element of hermeneutic angst at the margins of the 'real.'

Historically, in English-Canadian literary criticism, such angst has often been configured in terms of 'civility' as a mode of resistance to violations of what Derrida terms 'le propre' – the proper, propriety, decorum, civilization.[16] The late-nineteenth-century economy of 'light, soap, and water' finds its corollary in Matthew Arnold's commitment to redemption through English studies as the long arm of moral reform reached out to assail those afflicted with bad grammar and bad habits. As Gary Kinsman has shown in terms of a purity reformer like William Lund Clark, sex education for young boys exuded a similar ethos. They were to avoid 'degrading influences, wrong thought and wrong pictures, and the company of "immorally clothed young women." [Clark] recommended that they drink neither tea nor coffee and refrain from dancing, and that they seek improved ventilation and take frequent baths. Through these means they could produce a strong character and a pure self.'[17]

Literary hygiene made similar demands. The critic's role was that of teacher, interpreter, arbiter of good taste, and custodian of 'the health and purity which have distinguished Canadian prose and verse in the past,' as Ray Palmer Baker put it in 1920.[18] For Charles Mair in 1875, the critic was guardian of the 'new Dominion' which 'stands, like a youth upon the threshold of his life, clear-eyed, clear-headed, muscular and strong, though in need of guidance.'[19] In giving his allegiance to 'what is actually being lived among us,' W.A. Fraser wrote that the critic supports and maintains 'Truth.' In an article published in 1899 in the *Canadian Magazine*, Fraser maintained that 'above all else we must have Truth. We are strong, rugged people. Our country is great in its God-given strength – its masculine beauty. Canada is one of Mother Earth's bravest, sturdiest sons. Even our climate is boisterous and strength-producing. Strength begets Truth, and Truth makes Strength God-like.'[20]

Along the road to godliness, the critic will discover what Archibald Mac-Mechan termed the 'Decency Principle,' according to which the majority of fiction-readers 'ranks itself decisively on the side of the angels,'[21] a position from which the critic might be able to adjudicate – favourably – the text's adherence to codes of plausibility, authenticity, sincerity, and vitality, and even wholesomeness and virility. As W.J. Keith writes in 1985 of Stephen Leacock, 'What comes off the page is a man talking.'[22] 'Precise, decorous, civilized, touched with wit,' says Munro Beattie (without a trace of irony) in 1965 of Eli Mandel.[23]

What price wholesomeness? What I have elsewhere referred to as the 'discourse of civility' operates as a strategy of containment in literary histories of English-Canadian literature, just as it does in social-purity discourse in general during this period. However, this rhetoric persisted in Canadian literary criticism long after its transmutation in other domains, lingering into the 1980s in, to take one example, a journal as influential as *Canadian Literature*. Founded by George Woodcock in 1959, *Canadian Literature* remains one of the leading journals in the field – some would argue, the pre-eminent journal with a well-established international as well as national circulation. Stalwartly rejecting the 'Mandarin' stance of the academic critic,[24] Woodcock insisted that despite his journal's connection to the University of British Columbia, it would serve the interests of 'real people,' both writers and readers (64[1975]4). Amplifying this commitment, Woodcock's successor, W.H. New, has reasserted the value of literature as a 'radical force ... in reclaiming the existence of commonsense community values' and of a 'style of life [which] depends on circumstances, moral understandings, custom, ceremony and other non-exclusive claims upon a complex heritage' (87[1980]4).

The populist-anarchist rhetoric of Woodcock's editorials becomes a more explicitly liberal-communitarian rhetoric under New. Whereas Woodcock inveighs against 'specialization' (11[1962]4) with its 'mind-made palaces' (1[1959]5), favouring the vitality of the 'public critic' (49[1971]5), New champions 'public values,' 'the persistence of human aspiration,' and a 'passion for moral conscience and the possibility of individual choice,' for, New writes, 'to be a people ... is to be an embodiment of shared values' (104[1985]5). However, as Nikolas Rose has observed of the shifting political allegiances associated with this term, 'community' can take on an exclusionary character perpetuating those discursive formations of 'civility' noted above. As Rose puts it, 'liberalism began to govern by making people free yet inextricably linking them to civility.'[25]

I take the editorial traditions of Canadian Literature during its first three decades as representative of a complex of discursive strategies invoked in the process of 'normalizing the subject.'[26] Through the formation of a distinctively Canadian set of variations on literary 'realism' in which, as Lawrence Mathews has maintained, 'so much of what realism normally includes has been edited out,'[27] it has been possible for the dominant critical tradition to ensure that texts become canonic on the basis of the possibility of their being inscribed within the moral values of the 'commonsense community.' Thus, the formation of what came to be known as 'List B' at the 1978 Calgary Conference on the Canadian Novel, a self-conscious exercise in canon production generated on the basis of a mail ballot sent by Malcolm Ross, editor of McClelland and Stewart's New Canadian Library, to a select group of Canadian academics and writers who had been invited to attend the event. In his letter accompanying the ballot, Ross indicated that he hoped the conference would 'propose a list of significant Canadian novels that can serve as a guide to those interested in the masterworks of our literary tradition.'[28] The resulting list of ten novels comprises one example of modernist disjunction – Sheila Watson's The Double Hook – and nine examples of texts typically construed in terms of hermeneutic strategies of 'reality'-construction: Margaret Laurence's The Stone Angel and The Diviners, Robertson Davies's Fifth Business, Sinclair Ross's As for Me and My House, Ernest Buckler's The Mountain and the Valley, Gabrielle Roy's The Tin Flute, Mordecai Richler's The Apprenticeship of Duddy Kravitz, Hugh MacLennan's The Watch That Ends the Night, and W.O. Mitchell's Who Has Seen the Wind.

Crucial to the delineation of its opposite, this is the paradigm of the 'normal': the use of selection strategies that produce the desired 'community' to be canvassed; the production of 'results' from a 'democratic' ballot sent to a pre-selected electorate; the emphasis on the classroom-utility value of texts that will be conducive to the re/production of authority and moral order; the interfacing of student expectations with faculty ease in the generation of pleasant class discussions redolent of harmonious relations. Ideology as performative.

It is not surprising, then, that three texts from List B have been constituted as occasions of censorship, for the same logic that attests to distinction may attest equally to what the *Butler* lexicon terms 'degradation.' Thus, *The Diviners* has been one of the most controversial novels ever taught in Canadian high schools. From 1978 on it was removed from schools in Huron Country, Orangeville, and Lakefield, Ontario, and Kings County, Nova Scotia, among others. It has been challenged in many school districts, and in several cases reinstated after examination by board committees. In 1985 the Peterborough County Board of Education (which operates schools in Lakefield, Ontario, where Margaret Laurence lived until her death) was challenged by a municipal councillor to ban *The Diviners*, *A Jest of God*, and *The Stone Angel*. A board committee set up to review the books rejected the challenge.[29] 'Sexual episodes' and 'profane words' (including the line 'Now I'm crying, for God's sake,' from *The Diviners*) were the problem in Peterborough.[30] Pentecostal minister Sam Black displayed copies of *The Diviners* with 'four-letter words and sex scenes highlighted in yellow.' He 'invited people to sign a petition in the lobby of his Peterborough church "in defence of decency." "I think these passages were written to arouse people," he said, quickly adding he wasn't aroused himself.'[31] As recently as March 1994, the same novel was again targeted by a parents' group in the Ottawa area that wished to have *The Diviners* removed from local high schools.

Beyond the paradigm of List B but consistent with its principles, Alice Munro's *Lives of Girls and Women* was also removed from the Peterborough high school curriculum in 1978, again as a result of parental wrath. The Catholic Women's League in the town of Kingsbridge, Huron County, was concerned about 'gutter talk and blasphemy' as well as sexual references in Munro's and Laurence's books.[32] They were successful in having *Lives of Girls and Women* and *The Diviners* banned from local school curricula. Further attempts to have Munro's book removed from high school curricula took place in 1982 in Toronto at Malvern Collegiate and in 1984 in Etobicoke where a trustee of the local Board of Education described the book as 'porn, pure and simple.'[33] Other examples of bannings include the 1987 campaign by Parents for Quality Curriculum in Victoria County, Ont., against *The Diviners*, *A Jest of God*, and *The Stone Angel* as well as John Newlove's anthology, *Canadian Poetry – The Modern Era*, and Al Purdy's *Selected Poems*. As in the 1994 attempt to suppress another poetry anthology in Sechelt, British Columbia, the concern appears to have been 'anti-establishment attitudes'[34] disseminated through poems, a concern as well with the children's book *Maxine's Tree* by Diane Leger. In February 1992 an official of the International Woodworkers of America asked that Leger's book be withdrawn from circulation in primary-school libraries in Sechelt because *Maxine's Tree* '"indoctrinates" children into an anti-logging or extremist viewpoint.'[35] The school board rejected this request.

Parents for Quality Curriculum was again involved in an attempt to ban a book on the basis of 'explicit sexual references, violence, negative relationships and attitude toward organized religion.'[36] Their target was W.D. Valgardson's *Gentle Sinners*, and although they did not succeed in 1989, their luck changed in 1991 when the Victoria County school board agreed to review the matter and the teacher in question decided not to use Valgardson's book again.

Not sex but 'vulgarity' was the concern voiced by certain Ontario parents about Mordecai Richler's *The Apprenticeship of Duddy Kravitz*, which was unsuccessfully challenged in 1982 in Etobicoke and 1990 in Essex County.[37] Like Canada Customs' penchant for detaining texts on the basis of their titles (*The Sexual Politics of Meat*, a feminist-vegetarian text, being one outstanding example of this practice),[38] the school board in Abbotsford, British Columbia, successfully censored student Katherine Lanteigne's play, *If Men Had Periods*. The school board prevented Lanteigne from entering her play in a regional drama competition.[39] The regional library board in the same area was also involved in March 1995 in a successful attempt to remove a gay and lesbian newspaper, *XTRA!West*, from among the free publications available at the library entrance. When lawyers advised that banning only this publication might cause problems with the Charter, the board banned an additional thirty to forty publications.[40] When these publications were reinstated, *XTRA!West* was placed out of children's sight.[41] Most recently the Surrey school board has been involved in the banning from the primary-school curriculum of three books (*Belinda's Bouquet, Asha's Mums*, and *One Dad, Two Dads, Brown Dad, Blue Dad*) depicting gay and lesbian families.[42]

This is precisely the point where *Butler* intersects with *Little Sister's*, where the banning of books already in circulation intersects with Canada Customs' tactics of suppression at the border. Central to the *Little Sister's* case has been the selective detention of books, magazines, and newspapers thought to have gay and/or lesbian content and ordered by the Little Sister's Bookstore in Vancouver. Thus, in one of the most well-publicized incidents associated with the trial, Celia Duthie of the mainstream Duthie's bookstore chain in Vancouver successfully imported copies of books which, when ordered by Little Sister's, had already been detained by Customs. That the bookstore's lawyer, Joe Arvay, had been requested by the crown lawyers to provide copies of these books adds to the irony of Duthie's strategem.[43]

Similarly selective practices were at work in the detention of the Kiss and Tell Collective's book *Drawing the Line*, published by Press Gang in Vancouver but distributed by Inland Book Company of East Haven, Connecticut. When the photographic installation documented in this volume began to attract attention in American magazines like *Deneuve* and *Libido*, *Drawing the Line* was seized on a return journey to Canada, en route to Edmonton.[44] Persimmon Blackbridge describes the 1991 exhibition:

The photos are arranged on the gallery walls, starting with relatively non-controversial photographs with no nudity or explicit sex, and with photos which are deliberately constructed to cover a range of problematic and controversial issues. Viewers are invited to express their opinion of the various photographs, to 'draw the line' as regards their personal limits. Women viewers write their reactions directly on the walls around the photographs ... The gallery walls are soon scrawled over with writing. The pictures float in a sea of text, no longer functioning as separate sexual images, but set literally within the context of debates, discussions, and disagreements about sexual representation.[45]

Evidently, the problem for Canada Customs was that the photographs were 'of' two women, Blackbridge and Lizard Jones.

When representation fails to function as a device for the normalizing of the subject, both representation and subject disappear. In the case of Jane Rule, this has meant the 1990 detention by Canada Customs of *The Young in One Another's Arms*, in 1993 of *Contract with the World*, and in the same year of Donna Deitch's film *Desert Hearts*, a cinematic version of Rule's novel, *Desert of the Heart*. As Janine Fuller and Stuart Blackley note in *Restricted Entry*, this 1985 film 'circulated freely in Canadian movie houses and video stores for years before being detained by Customs en route to Little Sister's in 1993.'[46]

For Timothy Findley, disappearance took the form of a classic example of what I have referred to as translation. Findley writes: 'In Sarnia, a 17-year-old schoolgirl attempted to have my novel, *The Wars*, removed from her curriculum because – and I quote – it advocates homosexuality. When she was asked why she thought this, she gave as her reason a scene in which a man is gang-raped. Advocates homosexuality. An interesting interpretation of rape.'[47] The novel and the teacher survived, Findley comments, though both were damaged in the process. It is an experience that will be familiar to many teachers working with Findley's novel.

Translatio: borne across. As Mary Douglas puts it in *Purity and Danger*, 'uncleanness or dirt is that which must not be included if a pattern is to be maintained.'[48] Once the mess of interpretive confusion has been cleared away, the pattern will be obvious, for 'those species are unclean which are imperfect members of their class, or whose class itself confounds the general scheme of the world.'[49] The 'community' resists the shifting of its values. The young reader in Sarnia resists the shifting of her world map. Her misprision enables the retention of her world: homosexuality is rape, rape is violation, homosexuality is violation in need of 'advocacy'; heterosexuality (that which is violated) is not in need of advocacy (since it speaks everywhere, always).

Lise Gotell writes with reference to Canadian obscenity law: 'implicit ... is the assumption that the depiction of sexual practices that lie outside of majoritarian norms constitutes a threat to the community itself.'[50] What is dangerous in the case of Findley's novel, therefore, is the representation of rape *among men* just as what is dangerous in the Kiss and Tell Collective's exhibition is sex *between women*. Since what cannot be spoken is same-sex love (which is gently suggested several times elsewhere in *The Wars*), it must be spoken instead as rape lest heteronormative innocence be transgressed. What cannot be spoken is the 'Truth' of representation when that 'Truth' sets a male character in the raped position reserved for a female.[51] Thus, the *representation* of rape is translated into the *event* of homosexuality such that a book must be banned in order to restore 'community' consensus, not to mention 'hygiene.'

In the context of the courts, a more complex hermeneutics must be invoked but the results in cases like *Butler* and *Little Sister's* as well as *Scythes* reinforce this notion of consensual reality. Given that the hermeneutic technology for the construction of 'community standards' by the courts lines up quite precisely with that for the construction of literary meaning and value within the realist tradition in Canada, it is not surprising that the courts succeed in making them corroborate each other. If the construction of homosexuality and lesbianism by the courts can be read as a subset of legal constructions of heterosexuality gone 'wrong,'[52] as it were, into pornography and obscenity, then we may construe the hermeneutics of the heterotext as fundamental to its othering. Thus, arguments about pornography are always already arguments about realism, the transparent case of all representation in this normative system. Without realist configurations of representation and without community training in their 'commonsense' production, pornography could not be seen to function. Without the logothetic economy[53] of word made flesh, representation could not function as event. Without the construction of speech acts as (sacramental) events, pornography could not be construed as performative.[54] Without the faith community trained in their reception, speech acts could not achieve event consensus. Without the assumption of stable meaning, text and context, 'common-sense' hermeneutics – whether in the 'community' or in the courts – would, as Derrida has argued, shatter into iteration.[55]

Truth-conditional discourse requires presence,' a transcendental signified, in order to produce the 'truth' of word and flesh. And the 'truth' of the body that is never in question is the 'truth' of its reproductive heteronormativity to which the courts endlessly confess. Foucault has written of confession 'as one of the main rituals we rely on for the production of truth' in Western societies. Confession requires interpretation; confession 'could only reach completion in the one who assimilated and recorded it,' who verified and deciphered it, who constituted 'a discourse of truth on the basis of its decipherment.'[56] Confession brings with it 'penance' which is 'harm,' a way of measuring whether there has been enough disgust or degradation. 'Disgust signals the need to undertake further labors of purification,' writes William Ian Miller.[57] Purification is the revenge of the bourgeois subject upon 'dirt.'

Consider the experience of an expert witness like Becki Ross at the *Bad Attitude (Scythes)* trial:

Try as I could, I was unable to argue for the specificity of lesbian s/m fantasy, and at the same time underscore the *fluidity* of sexual desire, and be understood ... I learned that developing subtle distinctions and negotiating fine points of interpretation are skills that must be abandoned in the courtroom ... When I responded to the Crown's questions by underlining the import of nuance and diversity, my answers were often demeaned ... Judge Paris warned me that my attitude was corroding my credibility and the helpfulness of my testimony ... He disciplined me several times over the course of my testimony much as a dominatrix would punish her 'prey.' When I string these occasions of punishment and humiliation together, I find ineluctable, ironic confirmation of the trial itself as ritualized s/m theatre.[58]

My own experience as an expert witness for the plaintiffs at the Little Sister's trial was focused differently and certainly less painfully. After I read aloud a passage describing water sports (sex play involving urine) from Jack Hart's book, *My Biggest O* (1993), crown counsel Hans Van Iperen's face assumed an expression of fastidious disgust. Did I not, Van Iperen inquired in an apparently empathetic manner, did I not find the thought of urine on a man's face disgusting? Such conspiratorial gestures of disgust invite reciprocity. And how could one not reciprocate for to disagree would be to be identified with that which occasioned disgust in the first place. This is civility in action, one of the most powerful forms of censorship in bourgeois daily life. To disagree is to mark the boundary of one's own exclusion from community consensus about what, as P. Stallybrass and A. White argue, community has 'marked out as low – as dirty, repulsive, noisy, contaminating ... [The] very act of exclusion ... [is] constitutive of ... [bourgeois] identity.'[59] A positive response would have purified disgust and legitimized the crown's position. My negative response nonetheless served to reinforce Van Iperen's position and he turned away, making a throwaway gesture of disgust: a moment's victory in the form of silent propriety.

In seeking to embody community standards, Van Iperen needed to encode the 'truth' of his point, as Brenda Cossman has argued, in tolerance however graciously dismissive his enactment of it. Thus, the 'obviousness of this distinction [between presence and absence of urine, in Van Iperen's example] is underscored by the fact that no expert evidence is required to establish it. The line between good sex and bad sex is an 'instinctive' matter – a matter of common sense for a judge who will, presumably, simply recognise it when he sees it.'[60] So the situation is inverted and finessed, a subtle courtroom demonstration of the sheer bad manners of water sports anywhere, let alone among men.

On the surface, an inconsequential moment. Perhaps similarly inconsequential was Van Iperen's deference to Jane Rule during her testimony as expert witness at the same trial. As she does in her essays, Rule evoked a liberal-humanist context in her statement, in many ways meeting the court on its own ideological ground. She spoke of genre distinctions, evaluation of works of art, artistic purpose and merit; about the moral status of certain texts and about narratives that 'over and over again ... deal with circumstances that lesbians actually go through.'[61] Rule concluded her statement with a powerful expression of 'community' and identity which left many in the courtroom deeply moved: 'Of course we have writers who are writing erotica, and so we should. I celebrate that. But we are not a community churning out sex tracts. We are a community speaking with our passion and our humanity in a world that is so homophobic that it sees us as nothing but sexual creatures instead of good Canadian citizens, fine artists, and brave people trying to make Canada a better place for everybody to speak freely and honestly about who they are.'[62]

In speaking the language and using the hermeneutic technology of community consensus and liberal values, Rule inadvertently positioned herself in the place of exclusion delineated for her as an exhibit, as witness to the detention of her own work. She was, in other words, made to speak herself as pornography within the frame of a hegemonic discourse which had already constituted her work as such.

My sentence echoes Catharine MacKinnon's in *Only Words*: 'When words of sexual abuse are in our mouths, that is pornography, and we become pornography because that is what pornography is.'[63] The representation is the event. The event is the representation. One witnesses in word and flesh, in flesh as word. MacKinnon renders visible that moment of transparency when Augustinian hermeneutics serves its sacramental purpose and transcendence is effected and revealed. Like Augustine, MacKinnon renders this process doctrinal (doxa) through, with, because of, and co-created with the faith community for which, from which, and of which she speaks. The sacramental moment is thereby transiently constitutive of the transcendence that it voices.

What is transcended is sex. Brenda Cossman frames the argument in terms of the 'internal necessities' and 'artistic defence' tests as presented in *Butler*. A binary opposition between 'good sex' and 'bad sex' is set up such that one is what the other is not, just as Nino Ricci's and Jane Rule's similar invocations of hermeneutic criteria set up an opposition between the court's understanding of what Ricci is and what Rule is not.[64] The representation of the 'merely physical' is 'subhuman' and must be harmful.[65] As Cossman demonstrates, the subhuman world of '"dirt for dirt's sake"'[66] has been associated by the courts with heterosex gone 'bad' – that is, pornographic – and with homosex and lesbosex in general. According to the terms of mind-body dualism, where 'bad sex' emphasizes the 'merely physical,' 'good sex' emphasizes the mind. 'In this opposition, the body, the physical, the sensual, are seen as base, as bad, in need of control and, ultimately, transcendence.'[67] The only sex that can be the subject of art is 'sex that transcends its physical nature by appealing to the intellect, the emotions, the soul.'[68]

If the ultimate appeal of hermeneutics is to transcendence, its ultimate vehicle – beyond the vast armamentarium of exegetical procedures – is faith. Faith in God the word, in scriptures and church as the loci of the gospel, and, paradoxically, faith that renders hermeneutics superfluous[69] and without which hermeneutics operates as a meaning-generating technology *sans* revelation. For hermeneutics does not *account* for mystery but, rather, traces its architectonics in language. It is faith that constitutes the lived experience of the scriptures as community and that, by the time of Luther and his heritage in the work of Freidrich Schleiermacher and Wilhelm Dilthey, constitutes community as the location and agent of consensual hermeneutics.[70] In other words, faith as ideology renders the technology of meaning-production which serves it transparent to itself. Consciousness of the technology of interpretation is subsumed as those kinds of meaning produced by this technology come to seem synonymous with 'meaning' itself. As 'common sense,' hermeneutics is, within its own terms, simply what is obvious when interpretation is required. Hermeneutics then seems to be 'the only game in town.'[71] Its operations have become the defining constituents of meaning such that other 'games' are unavailable, even unimaginable. Paul de Man figures this faith-proclamation as 'resistance to theory.'[72] Here we can see it also as a profound reinscription of the 'hermeneutic circle'[73] bounding the normalized subject or, in terms of

Brenda Cossman's argument, constituting 'good sex' as the circumference of meaning and/as the 'real.'

Schleiermacher writes of literary meaning-production: 'When I have exhausted the meaning of every part of the text, there is nothing left to be understood.'[74] Thus, hermeneutics reaches its destination. On the other side, the place of 'nothing,' there *is* only transcendence. What is produced out of this 'nothing,' what has been produced in the courts and in the literary academy in Canada, is censorship.

NOTES

1 This paper is for Jane Rule and Helen Sonthoff, whose world and whose kindness twenty-five years ago enabled me to begin to imagine mine, and for Sarah Rauch in the daily negotiation of a place called home.
2 On social-purity discourse in Canada, see Mariana Valverde, *The Age of Light, Soap, and Water: Moral Reform in English Canada, 1885–1925* (Toronto: McClelland and Stewart 1991); Gary Kinsman, *The Regulation of Desire: Homo and Hetero Sexualities*, rev. ed. (Montreal: Black Rose 1996), ch. 6; Carolyn Strange, *Toronto's Girl Problem: The Perils and Pleasures of the City, 1880–1930* (Toronto: University of Toronto Press 1995).
3 On the 'rise of English studies,' see Terry Eagleton, *Literary Theory: An Introduction* (Oxford, U.K.: Basil Blackwell 1983), ch. 1; Chris Baldick, *The Social Mission of English Criticism, 1848–1932* (Oxford, U.K.: Oxford University Press 1983); Gerald Graff, *Professing Literature: An Institutional History* (Chicago: University of Chicago Press 1987); Nan Johnson, *Nineteenth-Century Rhetoric in North America* (Carbondale: Southern Illinois University Press 1991); Heather Murray, *Working in English: History, Institution, Resources* (Toronto: University of Toronto Press 1996).
4 Margery Fee has identified the first Canadian literature course taught in a Canadian post-secondary institution as a 1907 summer course at Macdonald Institute, an affiliate of the Ontario Agricultural College. Scattered courses through the 1940s and 1950s included Canadian literary texts and were offered at such institutions as McMaster University, the University of New Brunswick, the University of Saskatchewan, and the University of Alberta. See M. Fee, 'Canadian Literature and English Studies in the Canadian University,' *ECW*, 48 (1992–3), 22–3.
5 See Northrop Frye's 'Conclusion' to the *Literary History of Canada* (1st ed. 1965), reprinted in *The Bush Garden: Essays on the Canadian Imagination* (Toronto: Anansi 1971). See also Frye, *The Educated Imagination* (Massey Lectures, second series, Toronto: CBC 1963).

6 See Ivor A. Richards, *Practical Criticism: A Study of Literary Judgment* (1929; rept. N.Y.: Harcourt, Brace & World 1964).

7 These cases are referenced as: *R. v. Butler* (1992) 1 S.C.R. 452; *R. v. Scythes* (1993) (Ont. Ct., Prov. Div.) Paris J.; *Little Sister's Book and Art Emporium* v. *Canada (Minister of Justice)* (19 Jan. 1996). Doc. Vancouver A901450 (B.C.S.C.).

8 Brenda Cossman, 'Feminist Fashion or Morality in Drag? The Sexual Subtext of the *Butler* Decision,' in Brenda Cossman, Shannon Bell, Lise Gotell, Becki L. Ross, *Bad Attitude/s on Trial: Pornography, Feminism, and the Butler* Decision (Toronto: University of Toronto Press 1997), 135. The influence of Cossman's brilliant analysis will be evident throughout my analysis.

9 Catharine A. MacKinnon, *Only Words* (Cambridge, Mass.: Harvard University Press 1993), 61, 40, 33. MacKinnon helped to write the LEAF factum submitted in *Butler* and remains a major influence on Canadian anti-pornography feminists. For an analysis of LEAF's intervention in *Butler*, see Lise Gotell, 'Shaping *Butler*: The New Politics of Anti-Pornography,' in Cossman et al., *Bad Attitude/s*, 48–106. On MacKinnon and speech-act theory, see Judith Butler, *Excitable Speech: A Politics of the Performative* (N.Y.: Routledge 1997). My thanks to Jodey Castricano for the latter reference and for a careful critique of the first draft of this paper.

10 Jonathan Dollimore, *Sexual Dissidence: Augustine to Wilde, Freud to Foucault* (Oxford, U.K.: Clarendon Press 1991), 33.

11 Jacques Derrida, 'Differance,' in *Margins of Philosophy*, trans. Alan Bass (Chicago: University of Chicago Press 1982), 1–27. Derrida's term 'ontotheology' denotes the collapse of theology into ontology. 'Pornosophy' is Shannon Bell's coinage in 'On ne peut pas voir l'image [The image cannot be seen],' in Cossman et al., *Bad Attitude/s* 199–242.

12 Jacques Derrida, *The Truth in Painting*, trans. Geoff Bennington and Ian McLeod (Chicago: University of Chicago Press 1987). On interpellation, see Louis Althusser, 'Ideology and Ideological State Apparatuses,' in *Lenin and Philosophy and Other Essays*, trans. Ben Brewster (New York: New Left Books 1971).

13 Joel Bakan, *Just Words: Constitutional Rights and Wrongs* (Toronto: University of Toronto Press 1997), 112. See also Dany Lacombe, *Blue Politics: Pornography and the Law in the Age of Feminism* (Toronto: University of Toronto Press 1994), 95 and passim.

14 Ferdinand de Saussure, *Course in General Linguistics*, in Charles Bally and Albert Sechehaye with Albert Riedlinger, eds., trans. Roy Harris (London: Duckworth 1983), 65, 77–8.

15 Judith Butler, *Excitable Speech*, 144.

16 See Derrida, 'Differance,' and *Of Grammatology*, trans. Gayatri Chakravorty Spivak (Baltimore, Md.: Johns Hopkins University Press 1974), pt. I.

17 Kinsman, *The Regulation of Desire*, 119.

18 Ray Palmer Baker, *History of English-Canadian Literature to the Confederation* (1920; repr. N.Y.: Russell and Russell 1968), 188. For a detailed discussion of Canadian literary histories, see Lorraine Weir, 'The Discourse of "Civility": Strategies of Containment in Literary Histories of English Canadian Literature,' in *Problems of Literary Reception/Problemes de reception litteraire*, E.D. Blodgett & A.G. Purdy, eds. (Edmonton: Research Institute for Comparative Literature 1988), 24–39.

19 Charles Mair, 'The New Canada,' *Canadian Monthly*, 8 (August 1875), repr. in Carl Ballstadt, *The Search for English-Canadian Literature* (Toronto: University of Toronto Press 1975), 151.

20 Ballstadt, *The Search for English-Canadian Literature*, 157.

21 Archibald MacMechan, *Head-Waters of Canadian Literature* (Toronto: McClelland and Stewart 1924), 208.

22 William J. Keith, *Canadian Literature in English* (London: Longman 1985), 25.

23 Munro Beattie, 'Poetry 1920–1935,' in Carl F. Klinck et al., eds., *Literary History of Canada*, 2nd ed. (Toronto: University of Toronto Press 1977), vol. 2, 306.

24 From an editorial by George Woodcock in *Canadian Literature*, 49 (1971) 5. Subsequent references to this journal appear in parentheses after the quotation. For a detailed discussion of *Canadian Literature*, see Lorraine Weir, '"Maps and Tales": The Progress of *Canadian Literature*, 1959–87,' in *Questions of Funding, Publishing and Distribution/Questions d'edition et de diffusion*, I.S. MacLaren and C. Potvin, eds., (Edmonton: Research Institute for Comparative Literature 1989), 141–59.

25 Nikolas Rose, 'Governing Liberty,' 17 Sept. 1997 lecture, Green College, University of British Columbia.

26 See Lorraine Weir, 'Normalizing the Subject: Linda Hutcheon and the English-Canadian Postmodern,' in Robert Lecker, ed., *Canadian Canons: Essays in Literary Value* (Toronto: University of Toronto Press 1991), 180–95.

27 Lawrence Mathews, 'Calgary, Canonization, and Class: Deciphering List B,' in Lecker, *Canadian Canons*, 158.

28 Malcolm Ross, 'Letter with the Ballot,' in Charles R. Steele, ed., *Taking Stock: The Calgary Conference on the Canadian Novel* (Downsview, Ont.: ECW Press 1982), 158.

29 'Challenged Books List' (Toronto: Book and Periodical Council 1994), 4.

30 Brenda Cossman, *Censorship and the Arts: Law, Controversy, Debate, Facts* (Toronto: Ontario Association of Art Galleries 1995), 101.

31 John Goddard, 'Morality and Margaret Laurence,' repr. in *Index on Censorship*, 4/8 (1975), 3.

32 *Vancouver Sun*, 23 May 1978.

33 'Challenged Books List,' (1994), 5.

34 'A Chronicle of Freedom of Expression in Canada,' pt. 1 (1914–94), 5. At http://insight.mcmaster.ca/org/etc/pages/chronicle.

35 'Challenged Books List,' (1994), 4.

36 Ibid., 7.

37 Ibid., 6.

38 'A Chronicle of Freedom of Expression in Canada,' 5.

39 Cossman, *Censorship and the Arts*, 142.

40 Ibid., 146.

41 'A Chronicle of Freedom of Expression in Canada,' pt. 2 (1995–present), 1.

42 *GALE Force: Newsletter of the Gay and Lesbian Educators of B.C.*, 7:6 (June 1997).

43 Janine Fuller and Stuart Blackley, *Restricted Entry: Censorship on Trial*, Nancy Pollak, ed. (Vancouver: Press Gang 1995), 30–1.

44 Ibid., 72.

45 Ibid., 71–2.

46 Ibid., 76.

47 Timothy Findley, 'The enemies of expression surround us,' *Vancouver Sun*, 11 July 1992.

48 Mary Douglas, *Purity and Danger: An Analysis of the Concepts of Pollution and Taboo* (1966; repr. London: Routledge 1984), 41.

49 Ibid., 56.

50 Gotell, in Cossman et al., *Bad Attitude/s*, 84.

51 Cf. Cossman on 'heteroswitching,' ibid., 135–8. My debt to Eve Kosofsky Sedgwick, *Epistemology of the Closet* (Berkeley: University of California Press 1990), pervades this section of the chapter.

52 See Cossman in *Bad Attitude/s*, 134.

53 Roland Barthes's term 'logothesis' signifies language-making. See Barthes, *Sade/Fourier/Loyola*, trans. Richard Miller (N.Y.: Hill and Wang 1976), 3. Barthes's comments on Sade are apropos: 'The legal condemnation of Sade is ... based on a certain system of literature, and this system is that of realism: it postulates that literature "represents," "figures," "imitates"; that the conformity of this imitation is what is being offered for judgment ...; lastly, that to imitate is to persuade, to seduce: a schoolroom viewpoint with which, however, an entire society, and its institutions, agrees' (ibid., 37).

54 On pornography as performative, see J. Butler, *Excitable Speech*, 68–9. My argument here is indebted also to Mark Cousins and Parveen Adams, who note that 'what is always being represented, over and over again [in MacKinnon's *Only Words*], is the moment of the collapse of representation and event into each other, the moment that creates and re-creates the world of the text.' See Cousins and Adams, 'The Truth on Assault,' *October*, 71 (winter 1995), 100.

55 See Jacques Derrida, 'Signature Event Context,' in *Margins of Philosophy*, 307–30.

56 Michel Foucault, *The History of Sexuality*, trans. Robert Hurley (N.Y.: Pantheon 1978), 66–7.

57 William Ian Miller, *The Anatomy of Disgust* (Cambridge, Mass.: Harvard University Press 1997), 204.

58 Becki L. Ross, '"It's Merely Designed for Sexual Arousal": Interrogating the Indefensibility of Lesbian Smut,' in Cossman et al., *Bad Attitude/s*, 174.

59 P. Stallybrass and A. White, *The Politics of Transgression* (1986), quoted in Laura Kipnis, '(Male) Desire and (Female) Disgust: Reading *Hustler*,' in *Cultural Studies*, Lawrence Grossberg, Cary Nelson, and Paula A. Treichler, eds. (N.Y.: Routledge 1992), 377.

60 Cossman in *Bad Attitude/s*, 110.

61 Jane Rule, 'Detained at Customs' (Vancouver: Lazara Press 1995), 12. See also Jane Rule, *A Hot-Eyed Moderate* (Toronto: Lester and Orpen Dennys 1986).

62 Rule, 'Detained at Customs,' 18–19.

63 MacKinnon, *Only Words*, 66.

64 Cossman in *Bad Attitude/s*, 111.

65 Ibid., 112.

66 *Brodie* (1962), 181, quoted in Cossman in *Bad Attitude/s*, 113.

67 Cossman in *Bad Attitude/s*, 112.

68 Ibid., 114.

69 Cf. St Augustine, *On Christian Doctrine*, trans. D.W. Robertson (N.Y.: Macmillan 1958), XXXIX:43 (p.32).

70 See Friedrich D.E. Schleiermacher, selected from the *Compendium of 1819* in Kurt Mueller-Vollmer, ed., *The Hermeneutics Reader* (N.Y.: Continuum 1989), 72–97; Wilhelm Dilthey, 'The Development of Hermeneutics,' in *Wilhelm Dilthey: Selected Writings*, H.P. Rickman, ed. and trans. (Cambridge, U.K.: Cambridge University Press 1976), 246–63.

71 Stanley Fish's phrase: *Is There a Text in This Class? The Authority of Interpretive Communities* (Cambridge, Mass.: Harvard University Press 1980), 355.

72 Paul de Man, *The Resistance to Theory* (Minneapolis: University of Minnesota Press 1986), 3–20.

73 The 'hermeneutic circle': 'The whole of a work must be understood from individual words and their combination but full understanding of an individual part presupposes understanding of the whole' (Dilthey, *Selected Writings*, 259).

74 Schleiermacher in Mueller-Vollmer, *The Hermeneutics Reader*, 94.

11

'Pornography Disguised as Art': Some Recent Episodes concerning Censorship and the Visual Arts in Canada

SCOTT WATSON

One could argue that there is no such thing as censorship of the visual arts in Canada. Other media have been and are subject to regulation and institutional censoring bodies. But legislation has never been directed solely at the visual arts or artistic matters per se. A notable exception is video art. Even in this case, however, video works have fallen into the hands of state censors only if their special status as art works has been refused and they have been classified as film.[1]

Visual arts are, however, especially vulnerable to laws that criminalize obscenity and pornography. Those laws recognize redeeming artistic merit as a defence, but that concept (as arts groups themselves recognized) is ill-defined and offers weak protection against a charge of obscenity. Furthermore, though obscenity laws take special care to exempt the arts, this exemption is highly problematic and can be, in effect, a legal instrument for defining a work of art or threaten it as such. The result is that, while there is supposedly nothing specific in our laws that regulates artistic production or exhibition, art works do get censored, artists vilified, and exhibitions closed.

Proponents of obscenity laws reassure the arts community that their productions are not the objects intended to be regulated. But, in the highly publicized case of Toronto artist Eli Langer, new codes against child pornography were used, at various stages, to charge a gallery director, an artist, and, finally, the latter's paintings.[2] Throughout his defence of his paintings Langer argued that his paintings were conceived to abhor, not celebrate, abuse of children. However, as in so many cases where public protest and the law battle art, works of art made in a spirit of protest and criticism can become identified with the problem they represent. This vexing confusion in which representation becomes identified with action is at the root of the contemporary manifestations of a desire to censor the visual arts.

The 'redeeming' status of art is an artefact from previous eras when the establishment of high culture on European models was an essential part of nation building. Such times, during which a consensus of educated and powerful people would agree that millions of tax dollars must go into mounting productions of *Swan Lake* for the sake of the nation, will probably never return. In Canada, state support for the arts has been a post-Second World War phenomenon. It was partly a reaction against Nazi philistinism. Nazi persecution of modern and avant-garde art gave contemporary art considerable moral capital for decades after the war. There was also a belief, backed by sociology, that the arts improved life.[3] There are many indications that this widespread belief is now evaporating. The Reform Party, for example, advocates no state support for the arts and the abolition of agencies like the Canada Council. Recent controversies involving Canadian art galleries and what they exhibit also indicate that the old humanist arguments that used to buttress art when it was called obscure, boring, or pornographic have lost their power.

The idea that art improves or edifies is an ashen spectre. As a living concept, it has been expiring in the academy under the general critique of humanism called postmodernism for the past thirty years or so. Concurrently, a new politics of the right advocates the abolition of all state funding for social-engineering programs, among which it includes state support for the arts. On the street, politicians began to rediscover that the world of art offered examples of absurd, elite uses of tax money about the same time that activists discovered the politics of representation. The Canada Council, for example, is attacked not only by politicians of the right because it has funded gay theatre groups, but also by minorities who have charged that the council discriminates against non-Eurocentric forms and idioms. This is the context in which one considers the question of censorship in the visual arts in Canada today.

Few would disagree with the observation that the limits of permissible expression, especially in questions about and representations of sex, are wider or 'freer' than they were in the 1950s or 1960s. But there has been a recent upsurge in censorious activity. New laws, important court decisions, and a politicization of the idea that artistic expression ought to have legal limits all have contributed to the new climate. Meanwhile, the character of obscenity itself has changed considerably over the last forty years. For a long time, the focus of obscenity scandals was the depiction of nudity and 'fornication.' One should not belittle the very real and traumatic experiences of individuals in the arts who were charged in those days, but educated opinion tended to be on their side. Being charged with obscenity in the arts meant that you were in the company of D.H. Lawrence, James Joyce, and Henry Miller. Today, however, educated opinion is divided about the nature and effect of pornography and there is little aura of bohemian heroism attached to being charged with producing child pornography.

The pornography laws of Canada and the *Butler* decision that upheld and clarified them are not intended to regulate artistic production in Canada. The idea of legislating codes for creative expression is probably anathema to most Canadians. Yet *Butler* is about art. The desire to regulate and modify artist production and distribution is embedded in Canada's pornography laws.

Brenda Cossman argues that the *Butler* decision relies on a wholly negative theory of sex and that it perpetuates a fundamentally inhumane and unscientific view of the subject.[4] A less dramatic, but still important point, is that *Butler* depends on an unsubstantiated 'positive' theory of art. When Mr Justice John Sopinka wrote the majority decision he defined the 'artistic defence' in these terms: 'The portrayal of sex must then be viewed in context to determine whether it is the dominant theme of the work as a whole. Put another way, is undue exploitation of sex the main object of the work or is this portrayal of sex essential to a wider artistic, literary or other similar purpose?' As Cossman points out, the basic assumption is that sex has no meaning and is therefore a negative phenomenon. There is also an assumption regarding artistic purpose. Justice Sopinka assumes that artistic purpose is readily distinguishable from pornographic intent. But the history of art and literature of many cultures contain works that are about the primacy of sexuality in human affairs and that are solely concerned with this topic. Pornography is part of art history and has even become an academic subject. For many scholars involved in retrieving the histories of sexual minorities, pornography has become a key tool in mapping such histories. Legislation restricting visual representation is, in effect, legislation that restricts freedom of artistic expression.

One could choose from a number of recent 'scandals' to make the point that, while anxiety about contemporary art is easily turned into a kind of comic political theatre, other factors give Canadian art/censorship controversies their particular character. One need only look to the United States to see the templates for the arguments and strategies deployed by extreme right-wing groups whose goal is to eliminate the National Endowment for the Arts. Slower to take hold and by and large without the full-blown blood-curdling rhetoric characteristic of attacks on arts funding in the United States, the Canadian phenomenon nonetheless reflects the Americanization of cultural discourse in Canada. While the Canadian controversies demonstrate the scope and power of pro-censorship forces, they equally show us that Canadian institutions are ill prepared for the confrontation.

Telling art galleries what they can and cannot exhibit has become a much more open, media-friendly practice in recent years. A call to censor is made in

the name of one or more publics, who are not only unencumbered by old defer-
ences to high culture but also hostile to it. These new censoring, or would-be
censoring, publics have a potential influence on institutions that is out of proportion to their numbers. Institutions that once relied heavily on state subsidies
are now dependent on private money that can be made nervous by pressure
groups. Because there is no due process involved when a group mounts a campaign against a gallery, it is difficult to quantify the effects. But it is elementary
to assume that galleries that have endured one pressure campaign will not wish
to endure another. There are several examples to draw from. Each is telling in
its own way of the larger issues at play.

In 1995 the Vancouver Art Gallery included several contemporary works in
its collection in an installation of the Goya series *The Disasters of War.* Goya's
etchings are an excoriating critique of man's inhumanity to man. Among the
works included with the Goya prints were Andreas Serrano's *Piss Pope I* and
Piss Pope II. Part of a series of large photographic prints that involve icons and
bodily fluids, the *Piss Popes* depict a plastic bust of the pope in a brilliant
orange-yellow atmosphere that seems like an artificially heightened sunset.
Only the gallery label by the work identifies the orange-yellow medium as
urine.

The label is a text fraught with some anxiety. In an attempt to foresee and
forestall a negative reaction to the work, the text admits and then tries to disperse the iconoclastic power of the work:

The pair of works can be read as an irreverent attack on the church, specifically Roman
Catholicism. They can be considered, however, as more complex, poetic meditations on
the relationship between the individual and the church, between religion and spirituality.
In a tactile sense, what is more private than bodily fluids? The rituals of Catholicism are
rooted in this visceral material. Think of the Eucharist – the faithful devouring the body
and blood of Christ – the ecstasy of the martyr – traditional representations of the Cruci-
fixion – which both attract and repel through their contradictory beauty.[5]

This earnest but inattentive language, one can see in retrospect, actually provided the basis for the organized reaction against the work. What the label does
not tell the gallery goer is that the *Piss Popes* are among the series of works Serrano produced using religious icons in 1987–8 and that *Piss Christ* from this
same series is an object of considerable notoriety in the United States. In 1989
Senator Alfonse D'Amato tore up a Serrano catalogue on the Senate floor.
Thirty-five senators then signed a declaration denouncing Serrano's work as
'shocking, abhorrent and completely undeserving of any recognition whatsoever.'[6] Along with the work of Robert Mapplethorpe and others, the example of

Serrano's 'piss works' became the prime documents in a movement first to censor, then to cut, and ultimately to abolish the National Endowment for the Arts in the United States. No one in the Canadian gallery world would not know of these events, but the Vancouver Art Gallery, ideologically committed to exploring the relationship between art and society, chose not to refer to the controversy in its commentary on the work.

Canada's art vigilantes, however, know who Andreas Serrano and Alfonse D'Amato are and they took the permission implicit in the exhibition label to read the work as an attack on the Roman Catholic Church. To the great surprise of the art gallery, many responded to the perplexing question, 'Is the head of Pope John Paul II polluted by its drowning in piss or enriched by its submersion in the glow of a golden liquid?' by choosing the first option.

The *Piss Popes* were notorious works when the Vancouver Art Gallery bought them in 1989. The curatorial justification recommending purchase did not touch on this, but it did promote the notion that Serrano's work is transgressive: 'Serrano creates a startling subjective aura around his figures by violating them.'[7] Shortly after the purchase was approved, a member of the acquisition committee, Toni Onley, resigned. The public attack he subsequently launched on the gallery was mainly focused on the gallery's priority in acquiring photographic and conceptual art of which the Serranos were examples. In singling out the Serranos, Onley implied that these works were a kind of 'hate art,' a term that gained wider currency when the controversy finally erupted full-scale in 1995. Onley claimed that 'if it [the *Piss Popes*] had been anti-Semitic we would not have considered it. If it had been anti-Islam the curators would not have dared to bring it forward for purchase.'[8]

Positioning the work as 'hate art' is meant to discredit not just the art and artist but society's attempts to combat discrimination of minorities through human rights codes by suggesting that there is something conspiratorial about laws that protect minority interests and the liberal intelligentsia that espouse them. Despite Onley's campaign, the gallery exhibited the Serrano works without incident on two separate occasions before concerted efforts to have the gallery remove the works from its collection began in 1995.

The *Piss Pope* photographs are actually considerably more abstract than the titles might indicate. The vessel, for example, is not depicted. So the viewer of the photograph cannot tell that the plastic bust is immersed in anything. The pictures do not, despite the impression given in some press accounts, depict an act of urination. It is important to pause for a minute on what the *Piss Popes* look like. For the controversy that ensued is about another, imaginary work constructed by groups calling for the work to be censored. This imaginary work looks rather different than the actual art work. In a call for censorship by a Vancouver columnist for *The Province*, Susan Martinuk, Serrrano's works became pictures of 'a urine-soaked Pope.'[9] Martinuk's readers are left to picture a representation of the pope himself, soaked in urine, not a plastic bust that, strictly speaking, cannot be penetrated by liquid or 'soaked.' Later Martinuk asks her readers to 'consider the facts. The pieces are larger-than-life photographs of a bust of the Pope floating in the artist's urine.' And later still she adds: 'A bust of the world's foremost religious figure photographed as it drowns in urine.' These descriptions imply a narrative element that the photographs in fact lack. But such an element easily comes forward when, spurred by the title, members of the audience discover the nature of the amber medium and its source.

The idea that the pope, or plastic bust of the pope, is 'drowning' comes from the exhibition label in the gallery. Nuance, innuendo, and the literal reading of similes and metaphors are the tactical weapons of censorship advocates, whose readings of the works of art they would like to remove from gallery walls are usually so partial that they constitute the construction of altogether new works that differs considerably from the ones in question. These 'fictional' works become the lightning rods for the indignation of a public that has, in many cases, never seen the 'real' works. Paradoxically, in the case of the Vancouver Art Gallery and the Serrano photographs, the gallery supplied some of the language that would be used against it.

Martinuk, who still writes for *The Province*, asked for censorship of more than Serrano. Her article refers to other works in the exhibition that she considers part of the problem. The *Piss Popes*, she writes, 'are hung alongside a series of sketches [*sic*] that satirise the oppressive role of the Catholic Church following the Napoleonic wars.' These works, which, according to Martinuk, promote hatred against the church, are, of course, not by Andreas Serrano but by Francisco Goya. Anyone reading the article will conclude either that Martinuk has mistakenly thought that the pictures of the disasters of war are Serranos or that she has never heard of Goya and does not realize she is calling for the censorship of canonical work. Martinuk's call to censor the work of Francisco Goya in *The Province* might be an unwitting one, but it is based on the right-wing reading of the curatorial concept. Thaddeus Pruss, writing in *British Columbia Report,* is offended by Serrano's work, but he is much more offended by the context in which it has been placed. By placing the Serranos with the Goyas the gallery has implicated 'the Pope in monstrosities of war and mass suffering' and 'resorted to the art of making the present Pontiff guilty by association with the evils portrayed by Goya.'[10] As Pruss points out, not without some justification, the exhibition label for the *Piss Popes* practically asks the viewer to read the works as an attack on the church. The president of the Catholic Civil Rights League, Thomas Langan, also charged that the Vancouver Art Gallery, by showing the two artists together, was attaching the crimes of the Inquisition to Pope John Paul II. 'What is the gallery trying to say by linking the present Holy Father with Goya's protests? What does it mean? Does it mean the Vancouver Art Gallery is saying the present Pope is the biggest hypocrite in the world when he issues encyclicals on the splendour of truth?'[11]

To this sort of criticism the gallery had thin rejoinders. In fact, the gallery itself had supplied the terms of the right-wing critique in the first place. When opposition to Serrano's work took the form not only of demonstrations but of a letter-writing campaign to the gallery, then director Brooks Joyner responded with a letter of his own that emphasized the connections to be made between Serrano's work and, placed 'in a contemporary context,'[12] Goya's *The Disasters of War*. This invited the reading of Goya's critique of the Inquisition as a critique of the current pope. The gallery played the elitist card, declaring that 'the gallery and its programmes may be in advance of general public taste.' This stance, as expected, was greeted with some derision.

In the end, the anti-Serrano lobbyists succeeded in persuading one sponsor, the Bank of Montreal, to withdraw support from the gallery. The local diocese of the Catholic Church also ended all gallery tours for its students. Officials at the gallery shrug these off as minor, repairable consequences. But, if resistance to organized calls to censor lead to alienation of sponsors and community groups, it is not hard to see how difficult a series of such campaigns might prove to be for an institution like the Vancouver Art Gallery.

One could speculate that, had the gallery offered no interpretation of Serrano's work, not used his work to place Goya 'in contemporary context,' or explained itself in different terms, the furore may not have arisen. But it could not have known any of this beforehand. What it faced was a call to censor it could not possibly have obeyed (although I doubt that Vancouver Art Gallery visitors will see the Serranos again for quite some time). Once the pro-censorship forces mobilized there could be no dialogue. Nor did the gallery seem willing to fight it out within the intellectual framework established by the controversy. As a result, it is not clear what would have happened if the gallery created its own anti-censorship coalition. Such a coalition could have challenged the special-interest groups and their accusation that the gallery was guilty of a hate crime.

This is but one example of a symptom of something at work in the larger society. Art galleries can no longer count on a general acceptance of their expertise. Despite the fact that we are so often said to live in a culture that is more and more bombarded by images, we are not becoming more image literate. Works of art that have aroused controversy are read partially and literally. As a result, an altogether fictional work is often the object of a public debate about censorship. While institutions are alarmed by what appears to be a new vigilantism at their gates, they would do well to consider in what ways their own programs to translate complex issues into populist entertainment invite activist responses.

Joanne Lamoureux's analysis of the controversy that followed the exhibition of Jana Sterbak's *Vanitas: Flesh Dress for an Albino Anorexic* (1987) at the National Gallery of Canada in 1991 asks us to consider the seriousness of the negative response to the work.[13] In other words, she asks us to consider that the controversy illuminated the work in a way the gallery could not foresee, because, she implies, the institutional agenda itself tries to contain and forestall meaning in the works of art it displays. Institutions court wider and wider audiences but do not really expect these audiences to bring new insights to their exhibitions. A curatorial culture steeped in critical theory, which everywhere proclaims the efficacy of art works to change social consciousness, is paradoxically in a state of perpetual astonishment when people react to the social agenda they have been encouraged to read in works of contemporary art.

Sterbak's 'Vanitas' or 'meat-dress' is a sculpture that must be reconstituted every time it is exhibited. It is a dress made from flank steak that is displayed on a hanger suspended in the gallery. As the exhibition progresses the meat will dry out. In 1991 Sterbak was given a retrospective by the National Gallery of Canada and the meat-dress was included in the exhibition.

At the time the National Gallery had already endured a year-long controversy over its purchase of Barnett Newman's *Voice of Fire* for $1.8 million (Canadian).[14] That controversy had been generated by Felix Holtmann, chair of the standing committee on culture during the last years of the Mulroney government. The media responded to Holtmann's ability to throw mud at the cultural elite and the controversy over *Voice of Fire* became a national spectacle. The media also found in Holtmann, who once complained that by playing Mozart and Beethoven the CBC promoted 'foreign' music, a figure of fun and ridicule. Holtmann's business was hog farming, and so there quickly developed a narrative of old-stock types like the hillbilly pig farmer versus the effete snob.

The outrage over *Voice of Fire* touched on dimensions ranging from a revival of populist sentiment against egghead art to the concern of cultural nationalists that thought too much money was being spent on American art. The controversy over Sterbak's meat-dress briefly changed the character of the populist attack on high art and Canada's National Gallery. As Lamoureux observes, instead of the usual battle between populist 'common-sense' and the expertise of cultural mandarins, the meat-dress allowed Felix Holtmann to display his expertise, which is the world of meat production and marketing. When Holtmann said that Sterbak's meat-dress belonged in the butcher's store, he spoke from his authority as an expert in meat. When Sterbak refuted her critics by saying that the problem was not scarcity of meat but a scarcity of solutions to the problem of poverty, she spoke as a non-expert on economics and food production. In this way an odd balance was struck.

Lamoureux mined the controversy to disclose a relationship between the display and retailing of meat, especially in department stores, and Sterbak's work, which is about the display of the female body and, in a way, is also a critique of the boutique/department store aesthetics of today's museums. Holtmann was provoked by what he saw as the violation of the sanctity of food in its use in a museum display where it would never be used by being eaten, but 'wasted.' His negative reaction highlights atavistic relationships between food, animal sacrifice, and religion, associations that are arguably meant to be evoked by the artist herself. As Lamoureux's investigation demonstrated, these associations themselves have a history that imbricates department store displays of food and clothes with museum displays of art. She cites, for example, a novel by Emile Zola, *Le Ventre de Paris*, in which the protagonist, Claude Lantier – better known as the tragically failed artist in Zola's *The Masterpiece* – designs and executes a display of meat for a shop window, declaring it to be his artistic masterpiece. By excavating the history of food display as art (other examples would include Dutch still life and works by Andy Warhol and Claes Oldenberg), Lamoureux discovers a site where notions of religious sacrifice and the life of the commodity intermingle. Or, as she puts it, the controversy over Sterbak's meat-dress is a place where Bataille and Benjamin meet. In this case she is able to argue that the public scandal over the meat-dress, while played out in the media for its grotesque and carnival aspects, is actually the reverberation of the more distressing aspects of the art work's 'message' in a social sphere. Furthermore, this is amplified by the museum's inability to handle controversy.

Religious conservatives are almost always to be found behind calls for censorship of art works that touch on religion or sexuality. It is fairly evident that many of the controversies are directed at works that contain representations of homosexuality or that in any way offend religious sensibilities. But little attention has been given to the way censorship battles serve as an economic indicator. Nor has there been much analysis of the ways in which the resurgence of prohibitionist movements of all kinds, from anti-smoking to anti-pornography, might relate to a shift in Canada's class dynamic.

We might begin such an investigation by noting that the attacks on galleries and museums have an aspect of class conflict to them. The province of an educated elite, museums are attacked for spending public money in a time when social services are being cut and unemployment is high. This is a subtext of all these controversies and was central to the meat-dress incident.

Other recent controversies point to another, but related, social indicator.

There is an accelerating breakdown in the separation between private and public spheres. This is the theme of any writing on the phenomenon of celebrity in the twentieth century. It is also partly a political phenomenon. For example, the gay and lesbian civil-rights movement depends not just on the increased visibility of our numbers but also on a certain relinquishment of what was once private to a public forum. More than a few of Canada's censorship debates take place in the context of this forum in that they are animated by a minority resistance to the gay and lesbian civil-rights movement. While an interrogation of the social meaning of privacy is integral to a liberationist movement, like the one for gay rights, it is also an instrument used on the other end of the political spectrum. Deployed by prohibitionists and conservative religious groups, it amounts to a demand that the private sphere be obliterated altogether.

The demands of a coalition of journalists and fundamentalist Christians which fomented a controversy in Winnipeg beginning in the fall of 1996, illustrate how some interest groups can initiate a furore over art and define its terms. These demands amounted to a wish to exert a censoring control not just over what is published and exhibited but also over extracurricular activities by employees of arts organizations.

In the summer of 1995, Meeka Walsh, editor of *Border Crossings,* a Winnipeg-based magazine of the visual arts, was invited by the Tom of Finland Foundation to sit on an international jury for its Annual Emerging Erotic Art Contest. The Tom of Finland Foundation is a Los Angeles-based organization mandated to promote the legacy of Tom of Finland and to encourage gay erotic art. As its letterhead declares, 'If sex is important, erotic art is important.'[15] Walsh suggested to the foundation that she be joined in Winnipeg by Wayne Baerwaldt, curator of the Plug-In Gallery. In February 1996 Baerwaldt received a binder with photocopies of the entries from the foundation along with forms to assign each submission a rating from one to ten. Shortly thereafter, Walsh and Baerwaldt met and ranked the images. The process took about two hours and was conducted in the evening at a coffee house. The return of the binder and the rankings concluded the jury process. There was no fee for sitting on the jury.

The winning picture, *Cocksuckers for Christ*, was published in the spring 1996 issue of *The Tom of Finland Foundation Dispatch*.[16] The drawing depicts a priest giving a blow job to Jesus. The summer issue printed the picture again with a page of excerpts from letters by foundation members. Eight of thirteen responses were negative. The drawing managed to offend a considerable number of people who otherwise subscribed to and supported an organization devoted to the promotion of gay erotic art. But the negative letters to the *Dispatch* focus not on how the drawing offends the letter-writer but on how it might offend others and stir up homophobia. These letter-writers turned out to be prescient, if timid.

On 25 September 1996 a Winnipeg radio talk show brought the contest 'to light,' and the controversy began.[17] By mid-October a loosely connected coalition of fundamentalist Christians, right-wing journalists, and Reform Party activists had organized a campaign to force the province to demand that Walsh and Baerwaldt be dismissed from their positions. The province had the power to achieve this, argued the coalition, by withholding grants from the Manitoba Arts Council which both Plug-In and *Border Crossings* regularly receive.

The two journalists who led the coalition to remove Walsh and Baerwaldt from their jobs were Michael Coren of the *Financial Post* and Naomi Lakritz of the *Winnipeg Sun*. Lakritz's biweekly column is called, in this case chillingly, 'Straight Talk.'[18] Both columnists advance the argument that the winning drawing would constitute a 'hate crime' if a religion other than Christianity had been involved. As Lakritz puts it, 'It's only because of the new multiculturalism's peculiar intolerance of everything Christian that Walsh and Baerwaldt can get away with elevating the profane to the sacred.' Michel Coren claims that the picture 'is as hateful as the rantings of a Holocaust denier or the screams of a Klansman.'

In language that can only be called ugly and inflammatory, Lakritz characterizes Walsh and Baerwaldt as 'parasitic poseurs,' 'lampreys,' 'perennial leeches,' 'pretentious hypocrites,' and 'welfare cases.' (In a subsequent letter to the *Winnipeg Sun*, Thomas Langan, president of the Catholic Civil Rights League, thanked Lakritz 'for her thoughtful words.')[19] Coren calls them 'grant-assisted Canadians.' Neither Walsh nor Baerwaldt exhibited or published the drawing, nor were their organizations involved in the erotic drawing contest, but both journalists argue that they were asked to be judges because of the credibility they have gained from their association with Plug-In and *Border Crossings*. Thus, argues Coren, 'the first task is to remove all public funding from the pair and let them survive, or not, in the arts world ... The second task is to ask ourselves whether *Border Crossings* and the Plug-In Gallery should be funded in any way with public money ... The ultimate step is to consider censorship of all forms of pornography disguised as art.' Lakritz wants an end to public funding of Plug-In, *Border Crossings*, and 'their ilk.'

Organization of a public protest fell to Myrna Howard, the wife of a Salvation Army chaplain. In early October, Howard sent a letter 'to all concerned Christians,' urging them to write Harold Gilleshammer, minister of Culture, heritage, and recreation, demanding the removal of Walsh and Baerwaldt from their positions.[20] By mid-December, Howard was able to take 1500 letters to the Manitoba legislature. The province's Tory government, however, reacted cautiously but firmly in rejecting the drive to oust Walsh and Baerwaldt and to cut funding for their organizations. Gilleshammer pointed out that the drawing was not exhibited or published by the organizations and that 'no taxpayer's money was involved whatsoever.'[21] Earlier, Michelle Bailey, a government press secretary, had declared what ought to have been obvious: 'The minister has nothing to do with this ... When they judged the contest it was separate from groups which are funded by the province.' But, she added, 'it would have been different if the picture appeared in the gallery or the magazine. We can't dictate what these people do on their own time.' How would it have been different? The press secretary's statement was a way of sending a signal that, yes, the picture was deplorable and the minister would like to act but could not. Premier Gary Filmon publicly called the drawing 'offensive.'[22] Needless to say, the government's response did not satisfy. Lakritz used her 'Straight Talk' column to lash out at the premier, demanding that he cut funding to Plug-In and *Border Crossings* immediately.

Howard had weakened her credibility considerably with an ill-chosen analogy in her initial, rallying letter when she wrote, 'I believe that they [Walsh and Baerwaldt] are as dangerous and hateful to Christians as Jim Keegstra is to the Jewish people.' And then, she exhorted, 'Just as Christ overturned the tables of the moneychangers in the temple, so must we follow His example, and take action.' Walsh is of Jewish ancestry.

Because Walsh and Baerwaldt did not do anything other than agree to look at and evaluate a drawing, which in theory they also could have deplored, and because no public money was used in facilitating their 'action,' their opponents had no case. Even so, the situation portrayed by the vigilantes was the incendiary notion that Walsh and Baerwaldt received government money in order to view works like *Cocksuckers for Christ*. At first Walsh and Baerwaldt found the situation grotesque but manageable. But on 26 October, both the offices of *Border Crossings* and Wayne Baerwaldt's house were broken into. There have been death threats among the steady stream of abusive calls. The situation had and has the potential to produce violence.

The entire episode leaves us with a few questions. What did the press secretary mean when she said that things would have been different if Walsh and Baerwaldt had shown, published, or in any way involved their organizations in the dissemination of *Cocksuckers for Christ*? Did she imply that, under certain circumstances, the government's arms-length relation to the Manitoba Arts Council, which awards cultural grants, would be breached? And is it material like *Cocksuckers for Christ* that would occasion such a breach? I think she did and it is the formulation of this possibility that is the success of the anti-Wash/ Baerwaldt campaign.

Another question concerns the overarching themes and narratives at work in the campaign for censorship. Not content merely to condemn the drawing on its own terms, the leaders of the pro-censorship forces in this case insist that Christians are persecuted in the present social context, be it by 'multiculturalism' or the arts in general. The implication is that 'hate laws' are made in the interests of others, non-Christians certainly, because while Walsh and Baerwaldt go unpunished, others, like Jim Keegstra, are called to account when it is a question of characterizing non-Christians. According to Lakritz, our society has 'banned' Jesus while it 'hypes tolerance of every heritage but its own.' In this odd universe, tolerance of 'others' is itself a form of intolerance of Christians.

The drawing is, in the first place, most offensive to people who find representations of homosexuality offensive. If Naomi Lakritz, Michael Coren, Myrna Howard, and their supporters were not homophobic, the drawing would not have brought them to the pitch of anger that it did. I am assuming that, unless they found it on a website or through a copy of *The Tom of Finland Foundation Dispatch*, which is distributed only to subscribers, none of these three or the 1500 letter-writers has ever seen *Cocksuckers for Christ*. Lakritz describes the drawing as 'a painting [sic] of a priest performing an indecent act on Jesus.' Michael Coren is coy: 'Rather than describe the prize-winning entry in detail and cause offence to many people, let me merely say the work consists of a graphic depiction of a priest having oral sex with Jesus Christ.' Two paragraphs later, Coren declares: 'Nor is the figure in the picture merely of Christ, but of Christ crucified ... The picture implies that it is permissible to take perverse sexual advantage of a bound figure. The awarding of a prize to such a picture legitimises the very picture and the very action.' In other words, for Coren, a representation condones what it represents. In some way a representation is the equivalent of the action it represents, and representations, like actions, invite moral judgment. But words are representations too. 'Indecent act' and 'perverse,' used to describe oral sex between two men, represent homophobia. This is more important than what is actually in the picture. Contrary to Coren, the Christ figure in the drawing is not on the cross but sitting, with one hand holding a book and the other resting on the priest's shoulder. Coren has invented a drawing to describe to his readers. In a way, Michael Coren is the artist who produced *Cocksuckers for Christ*.

It is a striking pattern in the increasing skirmishes between anti-arts-funding groups, which include Christian Heritage and the Reform Party, that the picture in question need never be seen, descriptions being much more able to carry layers of information and to connote stock narratives in the far-right mythology of how the world works. Situations like the controversy in Winnipeg over *Cocksuckers for Christ* beg the question whether censorship is really the issue, even as it is so forcefully called for. Because the drawing was never shown, no exhibition of it could be 'censored.' The issue was public funding for the arts. The ammunition was homophobia, fear of religious and ethnic diversity, and exasperation with the rights of 'individuals.'

When the story broke, Walsh's first press response to the *Winnipeg Sun* was to argue against the homophobic characterization of *Cocksuckers for Christ*. She is quoted as saying, 'It can be seen as an act of love ... It's an image depicting oral sex – it's not violent ... not pornography.' But accepting a challenge over interpretation and categorization leaves the debate incomplete. If we have to insist an image is not pornographic, what are we saying about pornography?

Certainly naming it pornography or art is, on first examination, important. Coren denounces 'pornography disguised as art.' Groups going after art and artists first try to deny artistic identity, as if it were axiomatic that a representation that is not art ought to be more subject to censorship than one that is.

With few exceptions, those of us who work in art institutions respond to accusations of pornography with a kind of well-intended condescension. Surely Walsh does not really mean that a drawing called *Cocksuckers for Christ* is not pornographic. Rather, she is signalling that she has conceded, in advance, that pornography is problematic, and that erotic social commentary should be exempt from the category, should be 'not pornography.' When she asserts that the drawing is not violent she is already thinking through Canada's pornography laws and the *Butler* decision to uphold them. I think that we must ask again what the attack on pornography is about in the first place. Or whose pornography? If we accept the dictionary definition of pornography as representations of sexual acts intended to arouse desire, then whose desire is aroused by an image of a priest with his mouth on Christ's penis? Michael Coren's? Naomi Lakritz's? In fact, the drawing is pornographic because it incites their disgust at the desires of others. It is at this level that we must understand the new attacks on the visual arts. It has to do with social movements that tap into deep urges for a society without change. So far, when the art/pornography/censorship debate reaches a political forum, the terms follow, but do not challenge, the basic underlying assumptions that the debate has been founded on.

The Winnipeg controversy indicates that the debate about pornography is also about the withering away of the individual. The drive to silence and punish Baerwaldt and Walsh was on the surface about the pornographic drawing they adjudicated. But as the dispute forced more and more people to speak at increasing levels of political responsibility up to and including the premier of Manitoba, the issue became one of individual rights and privacy which were only vaguely and tentatively defended by the representatives of the state.

Of graver interest are cases where institutions themselves have acted to censor. Perhaps the most disturbing recent case of institutional censorship of art occurred at the University of Saskatchewan in late 1993 when a student's work was removed from the student exhibition, 'Staging Identities,' at the university's Snelgrove Gallery.[23] The issue of personal privacy was paramount in this case, as it was in Winnipeg, but in Saskatoon many of the terms of the debate were reversed and inverted.

Christopher Lefler had applied to graduate school and been accepted with a proposal to continue to develop his work as a gay activist. As an activist he had, in 1992, helped organize a ceremony for civic arts bodies to mark that year's Day Without Art, an annual international event staged to raise awareness about AIDS. The guest speaker was Sylvia Fedoruk, then lieutenant governor of Saskatchewan. On Valentine's Day of the following year Lefler wrote Fedoruk a long letter, in different 'voices,' which describes his experience of homophobia and recent events in Saskatchewan and in the nation, such as the banning of a play about a gay football hero at a Swift Current High School or then Justice Minister Kim Campbell's back-pedalling on her promise to see sexual orientation included in the Canadian Human Rights Act. The letter-writer claims that it is known that Fedoruk is a lesbian. It asks her to 'come out,' claiming, in essence, that she supports the status quo of institutionalized homophobia by her silence on this issue.

Amazingly enough, the lieutenant governor replied to this letter. Headed 'Personal and Confidential,' Fedoruk's letter explains the limits of the office of lieutenant governor. She cannot introduce topics into the public debate. 'Indeed, I am probably more constrained in this regard than any other citizen of Saskatchewan. I therefore find your criticism and quite cruel accusations to be hurtful and unfair.' If Lefler's letter is unsettlingly personal, partly whispered, partly shouted, Fedoruk's letter responds in kind with an inappropriate tone of grievance. Interestingly, her letter rejects Lefler's 'unwarranted assumptions' but does not say which ones.

The letters, in binders bearing the university seal, constituted Lefler's art work in the Snelgrove Gallery. Soon after the exhibition opened, Lefler's work was removed from the gallery on the instruction of Patrick Browne, vice-president (academic) who had been called to the scene by Doris Hassel, acting head of the Department of Art and Art History. Lefler received notice of the removal from Elizabeth Mackenzie, the Snelgrove's curator and the person responsible for the contents of exhibitions. Mackenzie explained that legal advice was being obtained by Doris Hassel and herself regarding Lefler's right to represent the identity of others in his art work and the rights of such individuals to prevent such disclosures. Lefler responded in writing, demanding an explanation and accusing Hassel of censorship. Asking for an answer in writing, he also stated that all further correspondence would be part of the art work and could be included in the exhibition.

But Doris Hassel was not in charge of the operation of censoring and threatening Christopher Lefler. For this occasion her authority was dissolved, albeit at her own initiative, as was the gallery curator's. Instead of answering Lefler, she gave his letter to Patrick Browne. Browne had already written Lefler in extraordinarily bullying terms.

In his first letter, Browne wrote Lefler that, after meeting with the head of the Department of Art and Art History, the dean of arts and science and the dean of graduate studies and research were 'unanimously of the view that this material is neither appropriate nor acceptable for inclusion in any exhibition of student art at this University.' The letter continues that, 'in addition to being offensive and reprehensible,' 'advice from our solicitor indicates that this "work" is potentially libellous and publication or exhibition of it in a public place might cause the University to be legally liable to a suit.' One has difficulty imagining a scenario in which the lieutenant governor would sue either Lefler or the university where she had once been chancellor.

Of interest here are the terms 'offensive' and 'reprehensible.' Browne claims that these qualities of the work are sufficient to warrant suppressing it and it is the legal opinion that is extra or 'in addition.' But surely Browne means the opposite of what he is saying or he would never have sought legal opinion. In fact, it is the legal opinion that renders Browne's claim that the work is offensive and reprehensible unnecessary and excessive. Browne concludes his letter: 'I am very concerned about the ethical questions your behaviour in connection with this incident raises. It is behaviour that is not consistent with that which is expected of students of this University. I am therefore considering what additional disciplinary action may be appropriate in your case.'

While Browne's rage is directed wholly at Lefler, his object is censure, censor, and possibly discipline. But the force and excessiveness of his reaction derives from his revulsion at the alleged sexual orientation of Lieutenant Governor Fedoruk. Considering that the 'work' is both the two letters and the act of making them public, what exactly is 'offensive' and 'reprehensible?' Presumably it is the act of naming Fedoruk a lesbian. But this cannot be an offensive or reprehensible act unless being a lesbian is in itself offensive and reprehensible. The words 'offensive' and 'reprehensible' then attach to Fedoruk's lesbianism. So, while Lefler will be the focus of attack, he is not by any means the sole source of revulsion. Similarly, when Mackenzie informed Lefler that a legal opinion was being sought on whether Lefler could disclose Fedoruk's lesbian identity and if she had recourse to prevent him, the presumption is that this identity is hidden, secret, shameful. There would be no ruckus had Lefler claimed that Fedoruk was straight. The irony is that none of these people was really trying to protect Fedoruk at all. Their reactions revealed instead that they too knew the rumours and believed them to be true. That Browne could so easily circumvent due process with vague threats and allusions to legal opinions he has never produced is surprising. But we should not underestimate the shattering power that disgust over other people's sexual appetites can exert.

After he had written his first letter to Lefler, Browne received Lefler's letter to Hassell. It enraged him even more. He wrote another letter to Lefler, specifically responding to Lefler's promise to include all correspondence in the exhibit. Reiterating his distaste for Lefler's work, Browne makes it even clearer that it is the letters, and the matters in them, that disgust him. 'Not only is material of this nature offensive, it does not constitute art in any sense of the word, and is not suitable for exhibition. You are hereby forbidden to submit any further material to this exhibition. Failure to comply with this directive will result in your immediate suspension from the University and could lead to your expulsion.' He concludes by again suggesting that he is 'considering what appropriate disciplinary action the University may take in relation to this incident.' Browne does not specify what is offensive about 'material of this nature,' nor does he specify the crime and its punishment.

Lefler disobeyed Browne's 'directive.' He placed in the Snelgrove Gallery two Xerox posters. One was a picture of himself, the other of Fedoruk, and over these were written names of famous gays and lesbians of history. Browne made good on his threat and Lefler was barred from the grounds of the University of Saskatchewan, finally being expelled in May 1994.

On the day of his expulsion hearing, Lefler learned that he had been awarded $10,000 from the Saskatchewan Arts Board. His proposal was to continue to work on the issues of 'outing' and homophobia. Lefler's expulsion and his grant became an issue on local hot-line radio and within days Conservative MLAs were calling for the rescinding of Lefler's grant in the legislature. At first, the minister responsible for the Arts Board, Carol Carson, upheld the principal of arm's length adjudication, but then within days, citing 'legal implications,' she asked the Arts Board to cancel the grant. For the first time in its forty-year history, the Arts Board rescinded a grant, claiming that after 'a careful review of The Privacy Act of Saskatchewan, the board had reasonable grounds for believing Mr Lefler's work may be unlawful.' Jim Russell, a Saskatoon lawyer, points out that the parties that have sought to silence and discipline Lefler – that is, the university, the government, and the Arts Board – have 'despite requests for further elaboration' not offered any explanation or authority for 'the proposition that drawing attention to the sexual orientation of a prominent public figure poses a legal risk.'[24]

Lefler's position, or more to the point, the idea of questioning what had happened to him and by what authority, did not gain much support in the academic world of the University of Saskatchewan or among Saskatchewan gay activists. Perhaps for them the controversy was clouded by the issue of whether a person should be 'outed' against his or her wishes. Arts groups were, however, very concerned, especially at the precedent-setting political interference in the grant process. This might have given a green light to those who think they can agitate on a case-by-case basis to affect the decisions of arts boards even if they cannot succeed in instituting a process of 'community' accountability that is to their liking.

The Winnipeg controversy and the Lefler case make an interesting pair. In Saskatoon, a staggering display of power was displayed in order to protect an individual's privacy, whereas in Winnipeg a grass-roots movement, to which the government was forced to speak, wished to eliminate privacy. Both situations derived much of their high emotion from a homophobia that is obviously still potent enough in our society to mobilize and consolidate all sorts of irrational causes. Among those causes we could list the movement to abolish public funding for the artists, the movement to discourage ethnic and religious diversity, and the movement to regulate sexual representations. All of these movements, in turn, thrive in a culture that increasingly colonizes the remains of individuality with the imperatives of the marketplace.

NOTES

1 The Government of Ontario introduced Bill 82 on 28 May 1984, passing it into law in February 1985. The bill amends the Ontario Theatre Act, expanding the powers of the film censor to include all exhibition spaces for film and video. Subsequently, Ontario arts activists organized Six Days of Resistance in which art galleries and artist-run centres screened material without submitting it first to the censor. Only one screening was 'censored,' but not by the Theatre Board. A planned screening at the National Film Theatre of Louis Malle's film *Pretty Baby*, which was banned in Ontario, was cancelled by Queen's University, on whose property the theatre is located. No group was charged for disobeying Bill 82 as a result of the Six Days. See Kerri Kwinter, 'Ontario Open Screenings: Six Days of Resistance against the Censor Board, April 21–7, 1985,' *Issues of Censorship* (Toronto: A Space 1985). Although Bill 82 was not repealed, film-maker John Greyson claims that a victory of sort was won and that today groups do not submit videos to the Ontario Censor Board. There have been no prosecutions. See John Greyson, 'Preface: Don't Cry for Me, Project P,' in *Suggestive Poses: Artists and Critics Respond to Censorship* (Toronto: Toronto Photographer's Workshop and the River Bank Press 1997).

2 Toronto artist Eli Langer was the first artist to be charged under Canada's child pornography laws. Charges against the artist and Mercer Union were eventually
   dropped. Yet a trial ensued as the crown sought permission to destroy Langer's
   seized paintings under forfeiture law. In order for the crown's application to succeed, it had to convince the court that Langer's paintings were child pornography,
   not art. The crown lost the case. See 'Prosecutor drops porn charges against artist,'
   Globe and Mail, 25 February 1994. See also Robin Metcalfe, 'The Warders of
   Memory,' in *Suggestive Poses*, 29–41.

3 The idea that art has a beneficial effect on the individual, the family, and the community was popularized among an educated middle class in Canada in the years
   following the last war. In this context there was of course a clear distinction to be
   drawn between art and pornography. See my 'Art in the Fifties: Design, Leisure and
   Painting in the Age of Anxiety,' in *Vancouver: Art and Artists, 1931–1983*, (Vancouver: Vancouver Art Gallery 1983).

4 Brenda Cossman, 'Feminist Fashion or Morality in Drag? The Sexual Subtext of
   the *Butler* Decision,' in *Bad Attitude/s on Trial: Pornography, Feminism, and the
   Butler Decision* (Toronto: University of Toronto Press 1997).

5 The label copy and other documents relating to the Vancouver Art Gallery exhibition 'Francisco Goya: The Disasters of War,' 18 February–22 October 1995' are
   from Vancouver Art Gallery files. The curator was Andrew Hunter.

6 William H. Honan, 'Serrano defends photo of cross in urine,' *Globe and Mail*, 19
   August 1989.

7 From the curatorial justification presented to the Vancouver Art Gallery acquisitions committee. Written by Gary Dufour and dated April 1989.

8 Cited by Jerry Collins, 'Mixing metaphors in the toilet,' *British Columbia Report*, 4
   September 1995.

9 Susan Martinuk, '"Artistic Freedom" no excuse for Urine art,' *The Province*, 6
   November 1995.

10 Thaddeus W. Pruss, 'If this is acceptable, then anything goes,' *British Columbia
    Report*, 4 September 1995.

11 Cited in ibid.

12 The letter Vancouver Art Gallery Director J. Brooks Joyner sent to all those who
    wrote protesting the *Piss Popes* was published in *British Columbia Report*, 4 Sep-
    tember 1995.

13 Johanne Lamoureux, 'A Lesson in Vanity: Jana Sterbak's Flesh Dress' and 'Lesson
    From a Flesh Dress: Food and Fabric in Zola's Art of Display.' Unpublished papers
    presented at the Vancouver Art Gallery, 1996.

14 See Bruce Barber, Serge Guilbaut, and John O'Brian, eds., *Voices of Fire: Art,
    Rage, Power and The State* (Toronto: University of Toronto Press 1996).

15 Letters from the Tom of Finland Foundation and other material about this contro-
    versy are from the files of Meeka Walsh.

16 '"Cocksucker" Controversy,' *The Tom of Finland Foundation Dispatch*, summer 1996.

17 The radio station CJOB contacted Meeka Walsh and asked if she would appear on a talk show about issues raised in a letter it had received from the Reform Party of Canada concerning her involvement in the Tom of Finland Erotic Art Contest.

18 Michael Coren, 'Prize-winning porn disguised as art,' *Toronto Sun*, 22 January 1997. The same article appeared as 'Consider censorship of all forms of pornography disguised as art,' in the *Financial Post*, 22 January 1997. See also Naomi Lakritz, 'Christians bashing is hate crime,' the *Winnipeg Sun*, 26 September 1996, and 'Parasitic poseurs violate decency,' ibid. 14 December 1996.

19 *Winnipeg Sun*, 28 September 1996.

20 Myrna Howard, 'To all concerned Christians,' 2 October 1966. No letterhead.

21 Kevin Conner, 'Churches go on offensive,' *Winnipeg Sun*, 5 October 1996.

22 Nadia Moharib, 'Letters lash artists,' *Winnipeg Sun*, 14 December 1996.

23 The correspondence referred to in this section was provided to me by the artist.

24 Jim Russell, 'A Gaze Blank and Pitiless as the Sun,' *Fuse*, vol. 18, no. 2.

12

Canada, Censorship, and the Internet[1]

DONALD F. THEALL

Writing about Canada, censorship, and the Internet (Net) must be a forward-looking, futuristic activity, since there has been little discussion of problems of content on the Internet. If Keith Spicer, the former chair of the Canadian Radio-television and Telecommunications Commission (CRTC) and currently the policy director of the Canadian Library Association, had been correct in February 1996 when he declared at a conference in Toronto that 'there is no question of censoring the Internet in Canada,' this chapter would never need to have been written. At the time, Spicer was echoing the former MIT professor and Information Highway guru, Nicholas Negroponte, who in an address at the same conference had said that it is impossible to censor the vast flow of data on the Net.[2]

This chapter opens with an overview of the Internet's beginnings and with an analysis of the first major incident in Canada to raise the question of control of the flow of content on the Internet – the trial of Karla Homolka. It will then examine some implications of the establishment of the Information Highway Advisory Council (IHAC), including a discussion of its name, and of the first major Canadian Federal Court decision concerning the Internet.

Canadian issues cannot be examined apart from a thorough understanding of the structure and organization of the Internet, and of how its global, transnational nature means that legislative, legal, and diplomatic activity throughout the world – particularly the United States – affecting the Internet will have a major impact in Canada. This will assist in understanding the tremendous difficulties in the way of control and regulation because of the multi-technological complexity of the Internet, and the potential effects that has on freedom of expression and communication. Since a recent U.S. Supreme Court case exemplified those complexities and their consequences for the regulation of information on the Internet, and since Mr Justice John Sopinka of the Supreme Court of Canada has emphasized the importance of 'the American Experience,' the prob-

242 Donald F. Theall

lem of understanding the Internet and its possible legal and diplomatic implications will be developed in relation to the debate concerning the U.S. Communication Decency Act (CDA) and the U.S. Supreme Court's decision as to its constitutionality.[3]

Subsequent to that U.S. Supreme Court decision (*Reno* v. *ACLU*), both government and industry have developed blocking/filtering software as the preferred solution – which will shift responsibility for control of content to individuals and to the private sector. The dangers implicit in control of content by the private sector and/or individual self-censorship will be explored here, together with the practicality of achieving the goal of protecting children from offensive material while not limiting the freedom of adult expression. Filtering will be examined in light of the technical feasibility of controlling the Net. In conclusion, the challenges posed by this unique new medley of technologies for preserving freedom and maximizing the value of the Internet will be assessed.

A complex series of fundamental questions arise from this massive change in the international availability and flow of information. How will it transform our way of life, our fundamental institutions and our values? How far should a society go to protect collectively the presumed innocence of its children? How does such a technology raise pressing new issues about the freedom of adult expression and communication? How open and accessible should research and the institutions that sustain and promote research be?

To begin to understand the scope of the problem, it is important to understand how the Internet – frequently misleadingly referred to as the Information Highway or Superhighway (a term supposedly coined around 1980 by the current vice-president of the United States, Al Gore) – came to be, how its creators conceived it and intended it to operate, and how it subsequently developed in its early stages.

Beginnings

The history of the 'Information Superhighway,' which began as the U.S. military's ArpaNet and later developed into a loosely linked association of university researchers, government agencies, and computer hardware, software, and service providers, reaches back to the 1970s and 1980s. What came to be dubbed the Internet, however, was of limited interest until the massive entry of commercial players in the 1990s, which resulted from the Net's new capacity to carry multimedia messages emulating the advertising capabilities of TV and the flexibility of VCRs.[4] The very newness of the Internet as a massive social concern (Canada's IHAC only having reported to the government in 1996) means that any exploration of the possibility or advisability of regulating the Net must consider what is being done in other jurisdictions and project what might happen in the future, particularly since the Net's designers deliberately created a communication system which operates so randomly that it cannot be shut down – messages will be transmitted even if many of its nodes (the various computers it connects) are blocked or damaged by sabotage, attack, or covert operations.

At its very inception, the Net's designers assured that messages transmitted through it would reach their destination. To achieve this end the Net had a somewhat 'chaotic' structure. Messages flowing across it are broken up into small packets of information (portions of the original message) which take different routes to reach their destination. It is a rhizomic network, not a unidirectional highway. If a packet can not be successfully routed through one set of nodes, it is rerouted through another so that it will ultimately reach its destination. For the purposes of this examination of censorship and control, it is neither necessary nor feasible to go into further technical detail.[5]

Some of the multitude of possibilities offered to users of the Internet for communicating or transferring information include: person-to-person electronic mail, commonly known as 'e-mail'; moderated or unmoderated discussion and newsgroups whose members communicate to the entire group by e-mail; online interactive chat groups similar sometimes to a conversation and at other times to a public debate; facilities for posting and transferring files (FTP or File Transfer Protocol), and reading or viewing (by Gopher) files of printed or kinoaudiovisual material; and the World Wide Web, which permits the display and online manipulation of all varieties of material, often interactively, thus providing for online galleries of images, online radio and TV broadcasts, online library catalogs, and online libraries.

Such a complex new technology will require radically different approaches to the regulation of its content. Substantial difficulties to any form of governmental control arise from several factors: the Internet's international nature; ARPA's having designed a highly decentralized, sabotage-proof communication system; the freewheeling way the Net developed for over a decade before the current commercial and wide public use of it; its extensive use for correspondence; and the possibilities it has offered and continues to offer as an open forum for interactive discussion on any subject. It is possible that this technology will even require a reconsideration of existing laws governing the regulation of content – issues such as hate propaganda and obscenity.

This has created a complex series of tensions between those alarmed, on the one hand, at the possible loss of a unique international opportunity for freedom of expression and communication, for a free exchange of creative discovery in the arts and other areas of cultural production, and for freedom in research and the dissemination of ideas; and, on the other hand, those who have been persuaded that the Net is a major means for hawking pornography, terrorism, drug culture, and racial hatred, thus endangering society and especially the children who use it. While it is generally conceded that the Net is not primarily or even largely concerned with such negative activities, there continue to be expressions of panic about its harmful nature. Meanwhile, the birth and development of the Internet in the research and artistic communities without any form of government intervention has spawned among many of its users a deep concern about all expressions of moral panic that might lead to a radical transformation of the Net and a restriction of its value.

The Homolka-Bernardo Case

Only in 1993 did the control of content on the global computer network become a major concern to the broad Canadian public. In that year the judge presiding over the trial of Karla Homolka (charged with her husband, Paul Bernardo, with the murder of two teenaged girls in St Catherines, Ontario) placed a publication ban on the proceedings. For the first time in Canadian judicial history, a massive transnational challenge was presented to the Canadian judiciary's authority to control the publication of information during a trial. Websites and online discussions and newsgroups in the United States and elsewhere (as well as other U.S. and international media) published details of the trial which then, through the Internet, easily found their way back into Canada, undermining the court order limiting what the press could publish about the trial. (This was dramatized by the police seizure of an issue of the U.S. computer magazine *Wired* which discussed the case.) In spite of the court order, Canadians who wanted banned information could easily access a number of websites in the United States which provided information (and misinformation) about the trial. They could also participate in discussions through those Usenet newsgroups (online discussions via e-mail) specifically dedicated to the Bernardo-Homolka case.

Apart from posing the problem of whether, given the new potentialities of 'cyberspace,' the judiciary could uphold bans against publication, there was further fallout from the Bernardo-Homolka case when McGill University,[6] followed by a number of other universities, immediately asserted the responsibility of the university under law to control the reception of content within its own constituency because of its liability as an Internet service provider (ISP). This led to other universities, such as Waterloo, not only restricting the Bernardo-Homolka material to Internet users in the university (professors, students and other members of the university community) but extending these restrictions by removing access to various Usenet newsgroups which the administrators felt might be in violation of Canadian laws regarding obscenity and hate literature.

While initially this may have seemed appropriate, Canadian Supreme Court Justice Sopinka, a relatively conservative jurist on issues of obscenity and hate propaganda, observed in a public address at the University of Waterloo that the banning of electronic bulletin boards to university staff and students had created a 'tremendous amount of controversy in the academic world' for 'the hallmark of learning is free, uninhibited and robust debate. Censorship is the antithesis of this process.'[7] Exploring the question as to whether such administrative decisions might be 'subject to scrutiny under the *Charter*,' he noted that the precedent in *McKinney* v. *University of Guelph* (1990) left open the possibility that 'if governing bodies engage in acts of censorship, they run the risk of [those decisions] being classed as government action and subject to the control of the *Charter*.'[8] In this regard it is pertinent to observe that in the United States the First Amendment has been applied to state universities.

Canada and the Information Highway

The Bernardo-Homolka case and the creation of IHAC focused public, and particularly media, attention on the problem of controlling the Internet. Intense media coverage in Canada and the United States immediately triggered a growing concern with the Internet's purported dangers: permitting children to access information about explosives, terrorism, drugs, and all modes of sexual activity; providing a forum for indecent and offensive speech, including 'hate speech'; giving various predators, especially pedophiles, opportunities to stalk children; and enabling various pornographers and rapists to threaten or harass women. Subsequently, there has been substantial debate regarding these supposed dangers and the extent to which the Net has increased them. It has been widely accepted in Canada that the Internet should be subject to those laws governing hate literature, child pornography, and obscenity and that ISPs may well have some liability with respect to the materials they transmit. As well as being prosecuted for crimes, ISPs might be sued for defamation (such suits have succeeded in other jurisdictions, such as Australia) or for assisting in violations of copyright.

When the Homolka ruling occurred, the government of Canada was a long way from having a policy regarding the potentialities and problems of the newly developing global network, particularly the control of content. Shortly after, IHAC was established with the then recently retired principal of McGill University, David Johnston, as its chair. Primarily charged to examine the commercial and social development of the Information Highway, IHAC, as will become apparent later, nevertheless had to consider the question of control of content.[9] But there were problems in readily following the U.S. lead, as the government of Canada did when it adopted the buzz phrase "Information Highway," popular with industry and the media. By uncritically accepting the analogy between the Internet and a highway, and by extending the analogy to broadcasting and cable-casting, IHAC has potentially distorted the understanding of the technologies involved. For example, if ISPs are viewed as cable distributors, this is very different from considering them as operating like a common carrier, such as the telegraph or the telephone.

The Case of Vancouver Freenet

The power of this analogy was graphically illustrated in 1996 by one of Canada's earliest judicial definitions and precedents concerning the Internet. The decision, which broadly addressed the question of the Net's structure, arose from an action against the federal government by the Vancouver Freenet (a community-based internet service). This case specifically involved questions of control of content, since the Ministry of Revenue was denying charitable tax status to the Freenet on the basis that 'it did not exercise sufficient control over how the facility was used so as to ensure its use was consistent with a charitable purpose.'[10] In delivering judgment in *Vancouver Regional FreeNet Assn.* v. *Canada (Minister of National Revenue* — M.N.R.), Justice James Hugessen specifically used the analogy between the Net and a highway. He began by noting that, since the Income Tax Act does not define 'charitable' or 'charity,' it is necessary to go back to 'an obscure and not always consistent corner of the law of England, the starting point of which is the Charitable Uses Act, 1601.' The preface to that act speaks of 'the repair of bridges, ports, havens, causeways, churches, seabanks and highways.'

Justice Hugessen, with apparent realization of the ironies involved, adopted the phrase 'Information Highway' to suggest that the Freenet as an ISP is part of a major instrument of communication in the 1990s. He justified his opinion by suggesting that the Net is just like the highways, causeways, and bridges in 1600 and that, as with those public ways, the traffic flowing along it should be free of restriction – that is, there should be no control of content except where that content is violating a specific law: ' A real highway or bridge in the time of the first Elizabeth ... might be used by persons going to market as well as to church or school. It might also be used by highwaymen or by absconding debtors. The nature of the traffic, however, did not serve to dilute or diminish the great public good provided by the facility itself.'[11]

While this decision is directed specifically towards the problem of tax status, it also stands for the proposition that there should not be any censorship of or prior restraint to the flow of information across the Internet. While the analogy implicit in the phrase 'Information Highway' is useful in emphasizing the latitude that must be permitted to services which provide connectivity to the Internet, and while Justice Hugessen's decision quite rightly implies a strong burden of justification against prohibiting or controlling any free flow of information across the Internet, neither the analogy nor Hugessen's use of it fully takes into account the complex role that the Internet and freely available access services such as the Vancouver Freenet provide. Later, in decisions by two U.S. courts, a more complex analysis of the Internet reveals the immense legal problems involved in its regulation and control, particularly with respect to 'indecent' and 'offensive' content.

The Internet as Chameleon

To write about the problems that the Internet poses for any form of regulation, it is necessary to cope with its chameleon-like nature. The Internet fits the description given the modernist novel by Malcolm Lowry, author of *Under the Volcano*. Such novels, Lowry wrote, 'can be regarded as a kind of symphony, or in another way a kind of opera – or even a horse opera. It is hot music, a poem, a song, a tragedy, a comedy, a farce and so forth. It is superficial, profound, entertaining and boring, according to taste. It is a prophecy, a political warning, a cryptogram, a preposterous movie, and a writing on the wall. It can even be regarded as a sort of machine: it works too, believe me.'[12]

For the media analyst, the Net is just as complex and enigmatic. It is a kind of postal service or town hall meeting – or even an electronic Hyde Park. It is a newspaper, a bookstore, a library, a museum, a cable service, and so on. An encyclopedic learning machine, it is superficial, profound, entertaining, and boring. It is disc player, TV, movie theatre and videotext (writing on a screen). It is powerful, all-pervasive, and threatening. It is a machine that subsumes and may annihilate all electronic media!

One problematic aspect of the coming-of-age of the Internet as a global, and very likely *the* future global communication network, arises from the way that various electronic technologies have moved beyond media to become what can only be described as a pan-medium, super-medium, or hyper-medium.[13] Another is how these technologies have impinged upon a privileged notion of speech by creating the possibility for integrated, interactive communication utilizing still and moving images, sound, gesture, rhythm, speech, and a wide range of print and calligraphy to produce kinoaudiovisual messages. Such theoretical constructs as the French philosopher Jacques Derrida's concept of 'grammatology,' Walter Ong's positing of an extended or secondary 'orality,' or Canada's Marshall McLuhan view of 'intrasensory tactility' can be regarded as conceptual correlates anticipating the contemporary mode of kinoaudiovisual communication. This feature of the Net challenges those historical approaches to modes of communication that have granted a unique, privileged status to speech and print in contradistinction to other modes – whether visual, gestural, or kinesthetic or the extensions of these through electromechanical and electrochemical means. Therefore, the first problem that legislatures and courts will have to face in their approach to the Internet is to understand the genuine complexity of this new medley of technologies and to anticipate how decisions and policies concerning its potential benefits and dangers could affect its future value to society.

As early as 1982, in his future-oriented magnum opus, *Technologies of Freedom*, Ithiel de Sola Pool, a MIT political scientist specializing in communication policy, explained how the evolving computer and telecommunication technologies would create a crisis in communication policy. He noted that 'each new advance in the technology of communications disturbs a status quo. It meets resistance from those whose dominance it threatens, but if useful, it begins to be adopted.' Since this technology is new and still in a state of development, 'technical laymen, such as judges, perceive ... [it] ... in that early, clumsy form, which then becomes their image of its nature, possibilities, and use. This perception is an incubus on later understanding.'[14] Governments, legislators, and regulatory agencies confronting the problems raised by the new technology tend to follow the historic pattern by creating analogies to earlier technologies. Early attempts at understanding the telegraph were devised on analogy with the railroads, just as the telephone was initially viewed as an extension of the telegraph. The early treatment of cable television as if it were broadcasting has illustrated how such analogies eventually are misleading and create confused and often conflicting policies which are inappropriate for the more complex and convergent modes of communication that emerge as the technologies mature. De Sola Pool concludes his analysis by confronting the situation of the convergence of media, prophetically forecasting: 'Historically, the various media that are now converging have been differently organized and differently treated under the law. The outcome to be feared is that communications in the future may be unnecessarily regulated under the unfree tradition of law that has been applied so far to the electronic media.'[15]

Moving beyond Media

The current controversy surrounding the freedom of communication on the Net is specifically directed at how much regulation, if any, is feasible. The quest for analogies has been a predominant feature of the ensuing debate, a quest frustrated by the multiplicity of genres and types of activity that the Net seems to embrace, ranging from chats about sports and fashion to advanced scientific and technological research material, avant-garde art, and complex intellectual and political controversy. Understanding these technologies and critiquing and correcting the problem that convergence presents with respect to the use of analogies need to be supplemented by another perspective. As communication moves beyond media and thus beyond the word, the question arises as to whether the privileging of speech (and of writing) in discussions of censorship or laws controlling content is tenable in a situation where we have what some have described as a 'secondary orality' but which might be more precisely be described as an all-encompassing mode of expression embracing the verbal, vocal, visual, gestural, and kinesthetic in an integrated whole.[16]

Recent discussions have suggested that interdiscursive dialogue and innovative cultural productions have always played a role in the exploratory transformation of language and of other modes of communication. This implies that an openness of communication has an ecological role to play in the development of modes of expression which will permit interdiscursive exchange between individuals and between groups whose interests, backgrounds, and sociocultural formations may differ.

If this is valid, as I have demonstrated elsewhere, it must have profound implications for the suggestion that images – still, moving, or multimedia – ought to be controlled more rigorously than words.[17] Our received wisdom privileges speech and writing over other modes and media of communication, just as the American constitution does. But, given such an approach, what sense is to be made of the Canadian Charter of Rights and Freedoms, which speaks of 'freedom of expression, including freedom of the press and other media of communication,' in contradistinction to the United States Bill of Rights, which, for historical reasons, only guarantees 'freedom of speech' and 'freedom of the press'?

Is it not possible that a document drafted in the 1980s by the government of Pierre Trudeau, an admirer of Marshall McLuhan, was intended to broaden our legal comprehension of communication and hence to extend the guarantee of freedom beyond what was granted in the U.S. constitution? While current jurisprudence has been quite conservative in applying the 'reasonableness' clause of section 1 to section 2 of the Charter of Rights and Freedoms, it seems quite likely that in the 1980s a greater breadth was intended. Regardless of how we might argue with respect to the intention of sections 1 and 2 of the Charter, the very existence of claims concerning the exploratory and developmental nature of new technological modes of production, reproduction, and dissemination of communication and expression will become increasingly complicated by the integrated nature of the Internet.

The Communication Decency Act

The problem has not yet been as dramatically confronted in Canada as it has been in the United States. In 1966 the U.S. Supreme Court upheld the judgment of a Federal District court in *ACLU* v. *Reno* that the Communication Decency Act was unconstitutional. This ground-breaking case, which has generated major judicial precedents in the United States concerning Internet censorship, should be of continuing interest to those making policy and legislation with respect to the regulation of Net content in Canada and elsewhere.

The background to the case was the decision of the Clinton-Gore administration to push through Congress the Telecommunications Act of 1996, legislation the entire Telecommunication Industry (phone companies, cable companies, and satellite companies as well as the computer industry) wanted. In the late stages of debate on this bill, exploiting the urgency of the White House to have it approved, a group of conservative senators – encouraged by fundamentalist religious organizations, coalitions supporting family values, conservative feminists, anti-abortionists, and other right-of-centre groups – sponsored the CDA, an amendment directed at banning 'indecent' and 'patently offensive' material from the Net by criminalizing it. This amendment, along with the Telecommunications Act of which it was a part, was passed by Congress and signed into law by President Clinton. The Legislation made it illegal to transmit any indecent or obscene material or any 'patently offensive' expression, 'knowing that the recipient of the communication is under 18 years of age.'[18] Conviction would have resulted in the imposition of either a fine or up to two years' imprisonment. The first of the act's provisions added the category 'indecent' to current statutes, thus supplementing existing obscenity laws; the second coined a term for an entirely new category, 'patently offensive.'

Led by the American Civil Liberties Union (ACLU) and the American Library Association (ALA), a group of forty-five corporate and individual plaintiffs challenged the constitutionality of various provisions within the act by applying for an injunction on the ground that these provisions violated the first and fifth amendments of the U.S. constitution (that is, the amendments guaranteeing freedom of speech and the press and due process under law, respectively).[19] What is important for Canadians about the two levels of adjudication in *ACLU* v. *Reno* (apart from the transnational nature of the Internet) is that the case brought together such a large, diverse group of plaintiffs who were knowledgeable concerning the Internet, its design, its use, and its implications for human development. The findings of fact in the initial judgment by the District Court in Philadelphia provides a copious outline of the current state of the art in computerized telecommunications, an outline that identifies the dangers and difficulties of controlling content on the Net. 'It is no exaggeration,' the 'Findings of Fact' declare, 'to conclude that the content of the Internet is as diverse as human thought.'[20] The very nature of the medium permits a situation where a 'content provider' is not a traditional speaker but may actually be a medley of speakers. Since the listeners and speakers who constitute this 'medley' can easily change roles through the Net's interactivity, 'content providers' have little or no editorial control for 'in the argot of the medium the receiver can and does become the content provider and vice-versa' (#80). The justices conclude that 'the Internet is therefore a unique and wholly new medium of worldwide communication' (#81).

All parties to the action in the District Court agreed that the Net contains sexually explicit material, but the court also found that, contrary to the implications of some news media and activist groups, 'there is no evidence that sexually-oriented material is the primary type of content on this new medium' (#83). Much of the sexually explicit material involves material of considerable value and benefit to society – sometimes artistic, sometimes medical and sometimes sound social advice (for example, information concerning the prevention of AIDS, advice to teens about the dangers of drugs or about their concerns over sexuality). The court also noted in its findings that 'even the government witness, Agent Howard Schmidt, Director of the Air Force Office of Special Investigations, testified, "the odds are slim" that a user would come across a sexually explicit site by accident.'

The complexities of the case resulted in all three justices writing separate opinions, even though their judgment that the act was unconstitutional was unanimous. Their opinions raise a number of crucial points:

- 'Those responsible for minors [should] undertake the primary obligation to prevent their exposure to such materials.'
- Four characteristics of the Internet are of 'transcendent importance.' First, the Internet presents low barriers to entry. Second, these barriers to entry are identical for both speakers and listeners. Third, as a result of these low barriers, astoundingly diverse content is available. Fourth, the Internet provides significant access to all who wish to speak in the medium and even creates a relative parity among speakers.
- 'Since much of the communication on the Internet is participatory, i.e., is a form of dialogue, a decrease in the number of speakers, speech, fora, and permissible topics will diminish the worldwide dialogue that is the strength and signal achievement of the medium.'
- The benefit of Internet communication is that so much speech occurs and that speech is easily available to the participants.

- 'The Internet is a far more speech-enhancing medium than print, the village green, or the mails ... Some of the dialogue on the Internet surely tests the limits of conventional discourse. Speech on the Internet can be unfiltered, unpolished, and unconventional, even emotionally charged, sexually explicit, and vulgar – in a word, "indecent" in many communities. But we should expect such speech to occur in a medium in which citizens from all walks of life have a voice. We should also protect the autonomy that such a medium confers to ordinary people as well as media magnates.'
- The Internet raises in an entirely new way the problem as to what community standards the Internet is to be judged by.

Although the U.S. First Amendment and the Canadian Charter approach 'freedom of expression and communication' differently, the nature of the Net raises issues that will ultimately affect both countries. Leaving aside for the moment points 1 to 5, let us first explore point 6, the problem of community standards, a concept currently interpreted differently in Canadian and U.S. law. In *ACLU* v. *Reno* both U.S. courts posed, by implication, a central question: in a free and democratic society, what cost in suppressing communication is reasonable to protect children from 'dangerous' information? Such an inquiry must extend beyond the purview of the CDA hearings, eventually necessitating more adequate definitions of obscenity and child pornography and reopening the problem of the criminalization of possession of child pornography. All the justices in the District and Supreme Court further noted, that the Internet will require new ways of legally delineating community standards since what might well be denominated 'a global metropolis' now exists through the Net.[21]

The Problem of Community Standards

While the U.S. Supreme Court has defined a community standard to be a local community standard, the Canadian Supreme Court as recently as *Regina* v. *Butler* (1992) reiterated the approach taken in *Towne Cinema Theatres Ltd.* v. *The Queen* (1985), namely that there is a national community standard in Canada which is not the standard existing in specific communities. In 1992 Justice Sopinka observed: 'The community standards test has been the subject of extensive judicial analysis. It is the standards of the community as a whole which must be considered and not the standards of a small segment of that community such as the university community where a film was shown ... or a city where a picture was exposed ... The standard to be applied is a national one.'[22] In elaborating on the nature of the community-standard test, Justice Sopinka went on to observe that the court in its earlier decision 'reviewed the case law and found: The cases all emphasize that it is a standard of tolerance, not taste, that is relevant. What matters is not what Canadians think is right for themselves to see. What matters is what Canadians would not abide other Canadians seeing because it would be beyond the contemporary Canadian standard of tolerance to allow them to see it.'[23]

Chief Justice Brian Dickson's position in the 1985 case of *Towne Cinema* suggests that the rule in questions of content is not taste, but tolerance, amplified by the principle that Canadians embrace the view that, with respect to content, the law is not what Canadians think is all right for themselves to read or see but what others should think and see – the paternalistic 'do what I say not what I do.' Since 1985, the term 'zero tolerance' has become all-pervasive with respect to disapproved behaviour – ranging from smoking to child abuse and including pornography and other illegal or offensive content. However, this aspect of the community-standard test will have to confront the challenge the Net presents for the definition and delimitation of a community, a factor concealed by the rhetoric that the Net as a 'global village' is a global community. In reality, the Internet is a global megalopolis encompassing multitudes of cultural difference.

There are further complications. When it is said that community standards must be national, this does not mean the standards of a small segment of that community such as the university community where a film was shown (*R. v. Goldberg*, [1971] 3 O.R. 323 [C.A.]) or a city where a picture was exposed (*R. v. Kiverago* (1973), 11 C.C.C. [2d] 463 [Ont. C.A.]). If this really is the situation, then the complex multiculturalism that has developed in Canada over the last few decades presents a formidable problem to discovering and articulating a community standard which is not a lowest common denominator of a multiplicity of different groups of individuals. Second, if one accepts the fact that different provinces and regions of the country are distinct, then it must be recognized that there are historic differences in Canada which the concept of a single nationwide community standard obviates. Third, specialist communities such as universities, research institutes, research libraries, and hospitals have always in practice had a latitude concerning obscenity, indecency, or patently offensive materials which has partly been sustained by the various 'redeeming value' clauses of the obscenity and child pornography sections of the Criminal Code. With the emergence of the Net, which is, among other things, a research library, the common room of a series of global research institutes, the conference room for professional consultations, and a multitude of global university classrooms, the 'redeeming value' clauses do not necessarily avoid the strong likelihood of the *Butler*-defined community standard creating a chilling effect that will ultimately result in de facto prior restraint. This would be especially true if boards and senior administrators were to take steps to protect themselves and their institutions from possible liability.[24]

The problem is even more severe. A distinction is sometimes made between first-class and second-class speech: first-class speech includes recognized literary and art work, professional writings, and the like; second-class speech include newly emerging artistic activity, everyday cultural production, and the banter – sometimes indecent and patently offensive – of the interchange in heated discussions.[25] Since it is difficult to anticipate an individual jurisdiction's or court's approach to what might be obscene or even as to what might constitute child pornography, the expression and communication of many individuals is silenced through fear of possible prosecution. The result will be to reduce sharply freedom of speech and expression. On the Net, the restraints are imposed not only by the fears of the users but also by the fears of ISPs, BBSs (owners of computer bulletin boards or newsgroups), and institutions, such as libraries and universities. This type of prior restraint is especially threatening with respect to ongoing creativity within the arts and cultural production – which, as noted above, may well have a specific ecological role in the exploratory transformation of language and communication – or to academic research that probes into problematic areas of human behaviour.

In the opinions rendered by U.S. courts in *Reno* v. *ACLU*, the tensions that arise from the Net's instantaneity and shrinking of space are clearly identified. Both U.S. courts found the 'community standards' test to be problematic when applied to the Net, since there are inevitably conflicts between local standards and national standards. As Justice Stevens notes in the majority decision:

The 'community standards' criterion as applied to the Internet means that any communication available to a nation-wide audience will be judged by the standards of the community most likely to be offended by the message ... The regulated subject matter includes any of the seven 'dirty words' used in the Pacifica monologue, the use of which the Government's expert acknowledged could constitute a felony ... It may also extend to discussions about prison rape or safe sexual practices, artistic images that include nude subjects, and arguably the card catalogue of the Carnegie Library.

If attempts to regulate Net content within the United States could produce such conflict about community standards, what would be the result if an international agreement could be made, as the Canadian government desires? Or returning to *Regina* v. *Butler*, what constitutes the whole community on the Internet?

IHAC's Recommendations on Illegal and Offensive Content

Approaching the problem of control and regulation of content, IHAC commissioned a report from Industry Canada on 'Illegal and Offensive Content on the Information Highway.'[26] After receiving this copious and thorough report, IHAC made only a few fairly general recommendations concerning the control of content. These recommendations would apply existing laws to the Internet, although they clearly recognize the problem of differing international community standards and the need to clarify the differences between the treatment of private and public communication on the Net. In summary, IHAC's final recommendations indicate that the government should fine-tune existing laws controlling content; encourage the holding of inter-jurisdictional international meetings to discuss the control of content; clarify ambiguous legal definitions for owners of Internet services; urge ISP's to create voluntary codes of ethics and adopt modes of dispute resolution; and provide research-and-development funding to develop filtering and other control mechanisms for individual use in homes and to aid the police in improving enforcement.[27] IHAC, possibly disregarding the complexity of the new technology, also recommended assigning regulation of cultural content on the Internet to the CRTC, arguing that it constituted an extension of broadcasting and cable communication.

The major problems in IHAC's report result from the commission's being misled by the implications of the Information Highway analogy and from its failure to draw sufficient distinctions about the unique features of the Net. IHAC does not confront the deliberately 'anarchic' or 'chaotic' features which characterized the Net from its inception by ARPA. Provided with a broader understanding of the problems, the U.S. District Court did so by citing and endorsing the testimony of an expert witness for the plaintiffs: 'What achieved success was the very chaos that the Internet is. The strength of the Internet is that chaos.' On this point, Justice Dalzell's commented: 'Just as the strength of the Internet is chaos, so the strength of our liberty depends upon the chaos and cacophony of the unfettered speech the First Amendment protects.' By the mid-1990s the purposefully 'chaotic,' random structure of the Net was well recognized. Equally well recognized was its unique nature. The U.S. Supreme Court not only concurred with, but strengthened, the District Court's stress on this uniqueness.

Justice John Paul Stevens of the Supreme Court, endorsing Judge Dalzell's comment in his decision for the lower court, takes note of the 'participatory, dialogic and overwhelmingly inclusive nature of the discourse which takes place on the Internet. While dialogue on the Internet frequently tests the limits of conventional interchange, the Internet is a far more speech-enhancing medium than print, the village green, or the mails.' Recognizing the autonomy and empowerment that the Internet represents to a wide range of people, Justice Stevens also agreed with Judge Dalzell's observation that 'any content based regulation of the Internet, no matter how benign the purpose, could burn the global village to roast the pig'; Stevens himself noted that 'in *Sable* ... we remarked that the speech restriction at issue there amounted to "burn[ing] the house to roast the pig." The CDA, casting a far darker shadow over free speech, threatens to torch a large segment of the Internet community.' This very feature of the Internet has led a concerned group of Canadian lawyers to organize LOGIC (Legal Group for the Internet in Canada), whose co-founder and chair has emphasized that 'due to the nature of the Internet, including its history, culture, amorphousness, and universality, it is quite impossible to effectively regulate ... [for] The very essence of the Internet is anarchy, a diametrical opposite of authority.' He further alleges that IHAC's report fails because it shows a confused understanding of the nature of the Internet.[28]

Industry Canada's Study on Content-Related Liability

In 1996, apparently in response to one of IHAC's recommendations, the government through Industry Canada commissioned an *Internet Content-Related Liability Study.*[29] Four lawyers were appointed and directed to produce a report on the potential legal liabilities of ISPs in providing access to the Internet. In developing this study they were specifically prohibited 'from elaborating policy options or formulating recommendations for legislative amendment' and from examining 'whether Internet activities should be regulated under telecommunications or broadcasting legislation.'[30] Their mandate permitted wide consultation with those involved with the Net, especially the commercial and industrial players. In the final report the authors noted that their study 'appears to be the first of its kind in the world on the specific legal issues of liability for content circulating on the Internet.'[31]

This report reviews the possible problems of liability in the provision of Internet access, focusing on four areas: the Criminal Code (obscenity, child pornography, and hate propaganda); trademark infringements; civil liability; and copyright infringement. The report's general conclusion observes that 'the Internet revolution poses various challenges in applying, enforcing and abiding by existing laws,' but, if amendments to those laws are necessary, they should be made *de minimis* and in as technologically neutral as possible, always keeping in mind the balancing of the 'interests of users, publishers and disseminators on the one hand and those of authors on the other, while preserving freedom of expression and only imposing limits on such freedom as is necessary in a free and democratic society.'[32]

While carrying out its analysis of possible applications of specific laws to the provision of access to the Internet, this Industry Canada report once again does not examine its nature, its accompanying technologies, or the radical differences between it and preceding technologies. Consequently, the exercise has created as many problems as it solves, for it pressures the ISPs without reviewing the adequacy or inadequacies of the laws involved or discussing the issue of laws in the context of the Internet's uniqueness. The report actually contributes to the rush to equate an ISP with a publisher or distributor – the effect being to impose a massive prior restraint on use of the Net before any judicial review is undertaken by the Canadian courts.

Although the terms establishing this study excluded any consideration of the CRTC's role in regulating the Net, it seems clear that the CRTC could regulate Canadian-based activity under the Broadcasting and Telecommunications acts.[33] This is an important issue that must be faced, particularly with reference to questions of the wisdom and practicality of such regulation when applied to content on the Net, in contradistinction to content in other modes of telecommunication or broadcasting. The attendant question, which has not yet been confronted since the Canadian government is still trying to pursue the censorship problem primarily under existing legal and legislative structures, is whether the unique nature of the Net, given its complex assemblage of multiple modes of communication, permits it to be treated adequately and successfully simply as a broadcast or a telecommunication transmission.

International Initiatives by the Government of Canada

Subsequent to the IHAC report and initiatives of the Clinton-Gore administration in the United States, the government of Canada has exhibited considerable interest in promoting international discussions leading to control of content on the Net. Most recently (summer 1997), Lloyd Axworthy, minister of External Affairs – citing the usual concerns about terrorism, drugs, obscenity, and child pornography – has stressed the need for a global policy on content. The real question that arises, as broached earlier, is what problems would arise in the attempt to articulate such a policy. For example, if there were an international policy and an electronic edition of Salman Rushdie's *Satanic Verses*[34] was made available on the Internet, Canada would certainly have to consider Iran's request to ban it, because under Iranian law the novel is a criminal activity and hate speech; but Canada would ultimately have to reject the Iranian position, since banning it would violate sections 1 and 2 of the Charter. And, while Canada might enjoy the support of the United States, the United Kingdom, and much of the Commonwealth and Europe, in upholding Rushdie's freedom of expression, would Iraq, or China, or India agree? A multitude of such problems could be cited which are quite predictable considering the differing international interpretations of and attitudes towards section 19 of the United Nations Charter of Rights, which guarantees freedom of speech and expression.

To put these questions in a more immediate context, could Canada even work out a compromise with the United States on such issues? At the moment, there is a standard of tolerance in the United States concerning hate propaganda which does not necessarily apply in Canada. For example, U.S. websites have been willing and legally able to provide neo-Nazi material banned in Germany and Canada. When Germany, pursuant to its laws banning neo-Nazi activity, blocked Internet sites within Germany from accessing a bulletin board in Denmark which carried neo-Nazi material, this Danish site was immediately echoed by three major U.S. universities – MIT, Stanford, and the University of California – all of which were of vital importance to international-research networks. Consequently, to ban the offensive material, Germany had to decide whether or not to prevent their research institutes and universities from contacting these sister institutions in the United States. And even if a ban were to have been effected, would it have been possible totally to control all possibilities for the dissemination of the offensive information? With vastly differing standards of what ought or ought not to constitute protected speech and expression, is a sensible, workable international agreement feasible, and even if it were, would it be desirable?

One further international question with respect to content on the Internet concerns the languages that are to be used on this technology. France has already attempted to apply laws regarding language to the Internet, and the Quebec Federation of Labour has already asserted the need to extend Quebec's language laws to the Internet.

Would it be acceptable for a country to block material that was not in an official language? This is apparently what France wished to do in bringing an American university's French branch to court for using English on the Internet. The complexities of the problems posed by such a procedure and the attaining of a broad international agreement will certainly prove daunting.

The only possibility remaining for control of the Internet was outlined in a BBC interview with a Singapore official: 'After making very eloquently the point that the model of "gate keeping" is failing every day, he explained that the function of censorship is to provide a SYMBOL. In other words to dress up society in the strait-jacket of self-denial, self-limitation and self-censorship.'[35]

Filtering/Blocking Software

Confronted with the failure of 'gatekeeping' by governments and the courts or through direct legislation such as the CDA in the United States, politicians have now turned to a second method of regulation of Net content: the use in the private and/or public sector of filtering/blocking software produced by commercial software or shareware designers, which permits parents, employers, ISPs, and public institutions to block the flow of specifically designated content. The unequivocal decision by the U.S. Supreme Court concerning the CDA had also recognized the future possibilities for filtering/blocking software as a less limiting alternative. Immediately following that court decision in June 1997, President Clinton pledged his government's determination to have successful filterware developed and made available to parents wishing to protect their children against illegal and offensive material on the Internet.

In Canada, IHAC had already supported the need for a technology to filter or block offensive material. Its report had called particular attention to the possibility of using some Internet-adapted version of the V-Chip, which was then being developed in the engineering faculty at Simon Fraser University to permit the blocking of violence on TV. Probably, if IHAC had been fully aware of the difficulties and complexities of using such a chip on the Internet, it would have opted instead for the development of specially designed blocking/filtering software.

At first, the use of filtering/blocking software may seem like a simple, reasonable solution, free from any threat to the freedom of expression of adults. Yet, on further examination, serious problems arise when filtering/blocking software providers select the sites and program the categories to be blocked. An alternative solution is to have the filtering/blocking software block sites on the basis of self-classification – what the industry has dubbed self-labelling – by individuals who operate a website, bulletin board, or newsgroup. The difficulties inherent in this scheme are succinctly summarized by the Singapore official quoted above, since it 'dress[es] up society in the strait-jacket of self-denial, self-limitation and self-censorship.'

The filtering/blocking software currently in use, in which the software companies have pre-selected the sites to be blocked, raises questions concerning what might or might not be specifically blocked, by whom, for whom, and in whose interests. The use of such software has not been free from controversy. First of all, while these software packages are essentially designed to permit parents to protect children from accessing certain sites, there have been frequent demands that such software be installed on the computers of public institutions such as libraries. It is also being used by some employers, including some branches of government. Second, though such software allows the parent, institution or employer to select what *categories* of material are or are not blocked, the makers do not usually provide any detailed information concerning precisely which sites they have selected for blocking. For example, a category chosen for blocking by the manufacturer might be described as sexual explicitness. But such a category, in addition to blocking sites that might be considered by most users as sexually explicit, might also block sites providing information about sexual disease, birth control, abortion, or AIDS, without the users' knowledge. Third, since the manufacturers do not reveal the specific sites that are being blocked, pleading that a list of specific sites is a commercial secret and that releasing it would provide a guide to indecent and patently offensive material which impressionable children or teenagers might access, it is possible for the designers of the software to implement hidden agendas by blocking sites with whose views they do not agree. Fourth, filtering/blocking software can also be used by nations with repressive political administrations to block speech and other expression that they deem to be unsuitable. Fifth, since the manufacturers of such software make the ultimate decision of what to block or not to block without any public accountability, this certainly constitutes a type of public censorship by private-sector businesses which is in conflict with section 2 of Canada's Charter of Rights.

Self-Labelling: Self-Censorship

An alternative, favoured by many, including the White House, parents groups, and industry, is to develop a system in which owners of various sites on the Internet (webpages, newsgroups, chat rooms, and so on), or some neutral third party, rate and label the potential degree or level of indecency or patent offence which appears at the site.[36] Since it would be both highly problematic and prohibitively expensive to develop a third-party monitoring organization which could visit and evaluate the content on all sites, the only practical solution appears to be to require individual owners to self-label their sites. To support the use of such self-labelling software, SurfSafe, one of the two producers of rating systems that might be used, argues that legislation must be put in place similar to its proposal for an 'Online Cooperative Publishing Act,' designed to provide a 'Safe Internet Without Censorship.' SafeSurf points out that there would have to be a civil and/or criminal recourse against those who 'mislabel' their sites, which ought to involve penalties on non-compliance ranging from initial fines of up to $5000 (US) to larger fines and incarceration for repeat offences. SafeSurf also provides a document explaining its rating system entitled 'The SafeSurf Internet Rating Standard,' which proposes categories or types of different sites for which filtering would be provided and which, therefore, should be labelled for blocking. These nine categories, SafeSurf notes, which were 'designed with input from thousands of parents and Net Citizens,' are then subdivided into nine caution levels by age. These caution levels are then applied to specific categories. This complex classification system goes far beyond indecent and patently offensive material, including categories such as intolerance of another person's racial, religious, or gender background; glorifying drug use; other adult themes; and gambling. The application of the 'caution levels' clearly indicates the highly subjective, emotive, and somewhat ambivalent language that is involved.[37]

Since public non-profit organizations such as SurfWatch have already recommended that filtering software also be used by libraries and other institutions to which children have access, there is no doubt that such filterware as they propose would be directed to a market which includes schools, libraries, businesses, and institutions. Perhaps with the category of 'late teen,' there would also be some pressure for the use of filtering software in colleges and universities. In 1997 Boston where in 1997 the city government required all public institutions to use filtering software on their computers (including the public library); the city libraries in Austin, Texas used 'censorware'; and the state of Texas introduced a labelling law. By the summer of that year, it seemed apparent that governments would attempt to legislate the use of a labelling system and that many constituencies would require these to be used in colleges, universities, libraries, and possibly other public institutions.

With an awareness of the growing enthusiasm for blocking/filtering software and self-labelling, the American Library Association through its intellectual-freedom committee released in July 1997 a 'Statement on Library Use of Filtering Software' to supplement its 'Library Bill of Rights.'[38] The statement asserts: 'The use in libraries of software filters which block constitutionally protected speech is inconsistent with the United States Constitution and federal law and may lead to legal exposure for the library and its governing authorities. The American Library Association affirms that the use of filtering software abridges the Library Bill of Rights.'[39]

Citing examples of the inevitable blocking of legal and useful materials, the ALA reasserts that 'libraries are places of inclusion rather than exclusion,' and that as publicly supported governmental institutions they are subject to the First Amendment, just as in Canada libraries in particular must certainly be subject to section 2 of the Charter.

Self-labelling must necessarily be a form of 'self-denial, self-limitation and self-censorship.' Under current conceptions of freedom of expression, linking it with specific criminal or civil sanctions imposes a prior restraint on speech, expression, and communication. Courts both in Canada and in the United States admit that there is no clear, demonstrable evidence to sustain allegations that there are inherent dangers in indecent, patently offensive, pornographic, (including child pornography) or obscene material. Yet 'popular wisdom' sees such dangers as clear and present.

The Canadian-based Nizkor Web Page, which posts all material pro and con concerning the Holocaust and which has been universally praised, has illustrated a much better way of handling adult debate. Parents and teachers must assume their responsibility to supervise and monitor their children's use of the Internet, discussing the matter with the children themselves and using filtering software if this is deemed appropriate. The complexity of the new medley of technologies requires such an approach, which combines parental responsibility with the inculcation of responsibility in children. The cost of not placing primary responsibility on the parents, complemented by instruction in schools, to foster responsible use of the Net, rather than depending on censorship and state control, will be to reduce the global discourse among adults to what is acceptable to young children or to the most narrow community standards.

The Intellectual and Artistic Communities

The concern expressed after 1994 by the Canadian (particularly the Ontario) arts communities about the censorship exercised through legislation and judicial opinions (such as *Butler* v. *Regina*) was sparked by, but by no means limited to, the Eli Langer case.[40] Their critiques dramatically illustrate the dilemma of artists or writers, critics, publishers, gallery owners, or curators being confronted with an imposed necessity to self-censor. Most artists cannot afford or risk the possibility of their work falling victim to a criminal charge or even a civil action. Since the Net is being used internationally by artists and writers to exchange ideas and even exhibit and distribute their works or replicas and/or photographs of their works, self-censorship through ratings would seriously inhibit their creativity and impose limitations not experienced by their peers in other parts of the world. Similar problems would affect scholars and digital libraries. For example, the rating of a site reproducing electronic versions of *Catcher in the Rye*, *Ulysses*, or *The Stone Angel* would run into the problem of how to rate their appropriateness to a specific age group. If eighteen and over was the classification decided upon, would a seventeen-year-old, first-year university student be banned from reading the novels online while an eighteen-year-old in the same class could not? Or would the eighteen-year-old have to forego the experience since it would not be suitable to her classmates under eighteen? Would a scholar posting an electronic edition of D.H. Lawrence's

Lady Chatterley's Lover be guilty of an offence if in labelling it he chose to say that it was not restricted to adults only? While it might be suggested that first-class speech such as that of either D.H. Lawrence or Margaret Laurence could hardly be in danger of censorship, it is important to remember that there have been attempts to censor these two writers in public libraries. The issue here is not banning but a law that would criminally penalize misclassification. That would certainly provide a strong disincentive for an owner of a webpage to decide that *Catcher in the Rye* was appropriate reading for a teenager, since he might discover that a court had deemed such a classification erroneous. The obvious solution, therefore, is to classify the book as available only 'as adult supervised' or 'adults.' In any case, would it be promoting maturity to deny a high school student access to such a book without parental permission? When the problem is laid out in this manner, the threat posed to the rights of maturing young women and men becomes clear. In a society where *The Tin Drum* is awarded an Oscar in one community, and condemned in another as child por-nography (this film was originally censored in Ontario), a self-classification system is going to have a chilling effect — and an even more chilling one when we move from first-class to second-class speech. If the U.S. Supreme Court thought that the CDA would endanger free speech on the Internet, surely rating and classification would absolutely annihilate it.

The Internet, Moral Panic, and History

Why does the emergence of the Net as the maturing and merging of a series of different technologies raise such great concern about media censorship? In light of the history of communication technologies, the answer is obvious, since suc-cessive waves of censorship – often through severe repression of speech and expression – have accompanied the beginnings of all major technologies for the production, reproduction, or dissemination of communication. Let us select just a few examples. The early days of printing saw the rise of the Roman Catholic Index of Prohibited Books and the Inquisition; the beginnings of mass printing saw the campaigns of censorship in the late seventeenth and eighteenth centu-ries and the appearance of laws such as those governing criminal libel which extended beyond books and newspapers to the theatre. The twentieth century has witnessed waves of censorship sparked by advances in publishing, in radio, in film, and in television successively. While there is no simplistic relation between cause and effect, technological change has frequently played a major role in generating attempts to control speech and expression in all media. For example, the shift from *morality* to *harm* in legislating and adjudicating forbid-den speech and expression, which has been given vast impetus in recent years by activists, began in the 1960s as a concern about the supposed effects of TV violence – a question that is still being heatedly debated. Certainly, it is not surprising that the Internet as a new phenomenon, barely understood, has given a new energy and sense of urgency to those who regard the media as *harmful*. But, as Ithiel de Sola Pool points out, the history of communication technologies, of censorship, and of misunderstanding media should rather lead to caution in curtailing the technologies of freedom.

The Internet presents a fundamental challenge to society, for the issue now involves the tremendous potential for enriching human learning and interchange that this new medley of technologies offers. Since it is ultimately not possible to control the Net effectively, short of dismantling it or at the very least rendering it substantially less effectual, this fact alone dramatically demonstrates the dangers in the very idea of censorship or in any control of content on the Internet – except that promoting criminal acts. As far as Canada is concerned, then, the government and the Supreme Court must reassess the Charter so that restrictions on the 'freedom of communication and expression' offered by the Internet – in order to protect the interests of specific groups, even children – are not deemed '*reasonable* limits prescribed by law as can be *demonstrably justified* in a free and democratic society.'

NOTES

1 The research of this paper has profited greatly from online conversations on the Internet and and discussion groups maintained by Electronic Freedom Canada and by Fight-Censorship in the United States. On Fight-Censorship, the contributions of Declan McCullough, Jonathan Wallace, Jim Tyre, and Professors Peter Junger of Western Case University and Seth Feldman of MIT have been particularly helpful, but all participants have assisted my thinking. Jonathan Wallace's book *Sex, Law and Cyberspace* was extremely useful in understanding current issues in the United States. Dov Wiseboard of LOGIC (Canada) was encouraging and his papers on the LOGIC website were particularly helpful. Talks over the years with my colleague John Fekete have complemented my interest in censorship.

2 Bertrand Marotte, 'Censorship hot topic at conference,' Southam News Background in Depth, 13 February 1996. Available at http://www.southam.com/mmc/waves/depth/tech/censor0213.html

3 Hon. John Sopinka, 'Freedom of Speech and Privacy in the Information Age,' address to Symposium on Free Speech and Privacy in the Information Age, University of Waterloo, 26 November 1994.

4 For a short history of the Internet, see Bruce Sterling, 'Science Column #5: Inter-

net,' *The Magazine of Fantasy and Science Fiction*, February 1993. Available as 'A Short History of the Internet' at: http://www.magnet.gr/internet/guides/bruce.html

5 For an interesting Canadian study on these issues, see Dov Wisebrod, *Controlling the Uncontrollable: Regulating the Internet* (1995) 4M.C.L.R.331 (updated) at http://www.Catal.aw.com/dov/docs/dw-inet.htm

6 It should be of some interest that David Johnston, who later became chair of the Information Highway Advisory Council appointed by the Canadian government, was principal of McGill at the time of the ban in the Homolka case.

7 See Marotte, 'Censorship hot topic.'

8 [1990] 3 S.C.R. 229; (1990), 76 D.L.R. (4th) 545.

9 At least according to President Clinton, for in remarks he made in the East Room on 2 July 1997 about 'The Framework for Global Electronic Commerce,' he observed that Al Gore had coined the term 'Information Highway' seventeen years earlier.

10 Vancouver *Regional Freenet Assn.* v. *Minister of National Revenue*, 8 July 1996, 137 D.L.R. (4th), 206.

11 Ibid., 215.

12 Malcolm Lowry to Johnathan Cape, 2 January 1946, in *Sursum Corda! The Collected Letters of Malcolm Lowry*, ed. Sherill Grace (London: Jonathan Cape 1995). vol. 1: 506.

13 For a discussion of the phenomenon of moving beyond media, see Donald Theall, *Beyond the Word: Reconstructing Sense in the Joyce Era of Technology, Culture and Communication* (Toronto: University of Toronto Press 1995), 91–109.

14 Ithiel de Sola Pool, *Technologies of Freedom* (Cambridge, Mass.: Harvard University Press 1983), 7.

15 Ibid., 7–8.

16 Theall, *Beyond the Word*, and 'Beyond the Orality/Literary Dichotomy: James Joyce and the Pre-History of Cyberspace,' *Post Modern Culture* 23 (May 1992), an electronic journal available at http://muse.jhu.edu/journals/postmodern_culture/v002/23theall.html

17 Ibid., see especially the discussion on censorship in the conclusion of *Beyond the Word*.

18 The two statutory provisions of the CDA germane to the ALA-ACLUs challenge involve provisions in section 223 (a) (1) (B) and section 223 (d) (15).

19 For a full list of participants associated with the ACLU and the ALA, see *American Civil Liberties Union et al.* v. *Janet Reno*, United States District Court, Ed. Pennsylvania, 11 June 1996, 929 *West's Federal Supplement* (1996), 'Notes to panel 2 and 3. It should be noted that the decisions of the Federal District Court and the Supreme Court did not make any decision respecting the Fifth amendment.

20 *ACLU* v. *Reno*, 824–84, Finding of Fact #74.

21 In Marshall McLuhan's *Letters*, ed. Matie Malinaro, Corinne McLuhan and William Toye (Toronto: Oxford University Press 1987), 78, we discover that he favoured this conception over 'global village.'

22 (1962) Ltd., [1963] 2 C.C.C. 103 (Man. C.A.) at 116–17.

23 Dickson C.J. in *Towne Cinema Theatres Ltd.* v. *The Queen* [1985] 1 S.C.R. 494, 508–9.

24 Justice Sopinka's remarks at the University of Waterloo clearly indicate the tendency of university administrations, their boards, and their senates to act precipitously in the regulation of speech.

25 J. Shallitt, 'The Real Meaning of Free Speech in Cyberspace.' An invited talk for the conference 'The Internet: Beyond the Year 2000,' University of Toronto, 1 May 1996. Available at http://insight.mcmaster.ca/org/efc/pages/doc/b2000.html

26 Gareth Samson, 'Illegal and Offensive Content on the Information Highway: A Background Paper,' produced by Industry Canada, 19 June 1995. Available at http://insight.mcmaster.ca/org/efc/pages/doc/offensive.html

27 *Connection, Community, Content. The Challenge of the Information Highway. Final Report of the Information Highway Advisory Council* (Ministry of Supply and Services, Canada 1995), ch. 4, 'Illegal and Offensive Content.'

28 Dov Wisebrod, 'Controlling the Uncontrollable: Regulating the Internet,' sections 1b and 4 respectively. Available at: http://www.catalaw.com/dov/docs/dw-inet.htm

29 Available at http://strategis.ic.gc.ca/SSG/it03117e.html.

30 *The Cyberspace Is Not a 'No Law Land': A Study of the Issues of Liability for Content Circulating on the Internet* (Industry Canada 1997).

31 Ibid.

32 Ibid., 23.

33 For a discussion of this problem see Michael S. Koch, "Square Pegs and Round Holes: CRTC Regulation of the Internet," 1996, posted at the Smith & Lyons web site: http://www.smithlyons.ca/it/crtc/what_is.htm.

34 It should be noted that for a brief period after *Satanic Verses* was published Canada Customs banned this book.

35 Example provided by George Koulikis <georgek@ndirect.co.uk>

36 The descriptive notes from the appendix of the ACLU's white paper on rating and blocking, 'Fahrenheit 451.2: Is Cyberspace Burning?' (14 October 1997), available at http://www.infowar.com/class_1/class1_080897a.html-ssi, provide elementary descriptions of the components involved in a self-rating or a third-party rating scheme.

37 Available at http://www.safesurf.com/online.htm

38 Available at http://www.ala.org/alaorg/oif/filt_stm.html

39 The formal resolution of the Council of the ALA was adopted on 2 July 1997. Available at http://www.ala.org/alaorg/oif/filt_stm.html
40 For a series of representative articles and further bibliography, see Lorraine Johnson, ed., *Suggestive Poses: Artists and Critics Respond to Censorship* (Toronto: Toronto Photographers Workshop and the Riverbank Press 1997).

13

The Social Psychology of Censorship[1]

JAMES M. OLSON and VICTORIA M. ESSES

In this chapter we present a social-psychological perspective on censorship. Social psychologists study 'how the thought, feeling, and behaviour of individuals are influenced by the actual, imagined, or implied presence of others.'[2] Thus, social psychologists study *social* settings, where one person is influenced by another. The discipline of social psychology encompasses both the causes and the consequences of social behaviour.

We define censorship in a manner analogous to Klaus Petersen's recommendation in the opening chapter of this volume. Specifically, censorship is *a value-based attempt to control or interfere with the production and/or dissemination of verbal or pictorial information*. Given that censorship involves the attempts of one person or group to interfere with the information available to another person or group, censorship falls squarely into social psychology's domain of interpersonal influence.

We address three fundamental issues in this chapter. First, we consider the determinants of censorship. That is, we identify some of the variables that predict either when censorship will occur or whether people will support censorship. Second, we discuss possible justifications for censorship. That is, we review psychological research that has examined possible deleterious effects of certain kinds of information. Finally, we address the consequences of censorship. That is, we discuss the effects of censorship on people's thoughts, feelings, and behaviour. Throughout the chapter, when possible, we describe empirical research that has provided evidence to document a particular aspect of censorship.

Determinants of Censorship

Social psychologists have identified some of the psychological characteristics that lead to attempted censorship or to support for censorship. In this section, we describe two categories of these factors – individual differences and group factors.

A variety of individual differences have been shown to predict support for restrictive laws. Probably the most-studied characteristic has been *authoritarianism*,[3] which refers to a dogmatic and rigid adherence to and support of standards established by authorities. Social psychologist Robert Altemeyer[4] developed a measure of right-wing authoritarianism that assesses three principal attitudinal clusters: *authoritarian submission*, which refers to a high degree of submission to authorities who are perceived to be legitimate; *authoritarian aggression*, which refers to aggressiveness against people or groups who are perceived to threaten established authority; and *conventionalism*, which refers to adherence to established social conventions and values. Clearly, these components imply an unwillingness to tolerate unconventional views and ideas.

Right-wing authoritarianism has been shown to predict prejudice against groups to which the perceiver does not belong,[5] with high authoritarians expressing more negative attitudes than low authoritarians towards religious and ethnic minority groups, immigrants, homosexuals, and other groups that are perceived to be 'deviant' in some fashion. Authoritarianism has also been shown to be associated with several attitudes that directly support censorship. For example, high authoritarians stress the importance of conformity with social customs and of maintaining established traditions, which leads them to see minority groups as posing a threat to mainstream values. Thus, for example, high authoritarians support restrictive immigration laws. High authoritarians also agree with the idea that their country has 'too much freedom'; consequently, they are more likely to think that the Charter of Rights and Freedoms (in Canada) or the Bill of Rights (in the United States) should be repealed.[6]

Why do high authoritarians support censorship? Altemeyer[7] suggests that an important component in their responses is fear – fear of the unknown, fear of change. Thus, high authoritarians want restrictions on any information that challenges their own conventional values or established authorities. They worry that minority groups represent new practices and values that will be dramatically different from the current norms. High authoritarians also tend to be self-righteous, which, when combined with their fear of change, produces a willingness to impose their own standards on others (for example, censorship of deviant views).

Another individual-difference variable that predicts support for censorship is religiosity. Whether religiosity is defined as positive attitudes towards religion, attendance at church, or orthodoxy of religious beliefs, it has consistently been shown to be associated with prejudice towards and intolerance of 'outgroups.'[8] For example, highly religious individuals endorse more punitive treatment of criminals, delinquents, prostitutes, mental patients, and other social 'misfits' than do the unreligious.[9] Religious people also are intolerant of minority ideologies, such as communism and socialism, and express support for constraints on the expression of these deviant views.[10] These associations between religiosity and censorship are particularly strong for fundamentalist religions and for what has been called 'extrinsic' religiosity, which refers to religiosity that is a means to other ends, such as social status or security, rather than an end in itself.[11]

Perhaps not surprisingly, authoritarianism and religious fundamentalism are correlated, such that high authoritarians tend to be more religiously fundamentalist. Religious beliefs can contribute to the previously mentioned self-righteousness of high authoritarians, giving them a sense of superiority that justifies the imposition of their views on others.

Censorship is, by definition, a group phenomenon. That is, the values or ideas of some members of a group are silenced or restricted by other members via the control of information production and/or dissemination. Sometimes the values or ideas of the censors are shared by most members of the group (as in censorship of child pornography in our society) and sometimes they are held by few members (as in Nazi control of information in countries captured during the Second World War). Because censorship is a group phenomenon, group factors influence the likelihood of censorship being imposed and the likelihood of it being successful. In this section, we discuss four such factors: leader power, social norms, group cohesiveness, and external threat.

The more powerful a leader's position, the more likely he or she is to attempt to impose censorship and to be successful when such attempts are made. Leader power depends on both structural aspects of the group and personal characteristics of the leader. First, some leadership roles are structured to give the leader considerable decision-making and resource-distribution power.[12] For example, leaders of autocratic governments typically have the authority to make unilateral decisions about a wide range of important matters, which gives them great power over their citizens, whereas leaders of democratic governments typically have much less unilateral power. Other structural features that increase leader power include centralized communication networks and a diversity of resources available to the leader for distribution.

Second, personal characteristics of the leader interact with structural features to influence total power. For example, the leader's knowledge or expertise can give him or her power to influence decisions. Also, some leaders are more willing than others to *use* the power that is available to them; relevant personality factors include self-confidence or self-esteem, ambitiousness, and leadership 'style.'[13] With respect to this last concept, research has shown that some leaders adopt a style that is primarily 'task-oriented'(focusing on achievement of group goals), whereas other leaders adopt a style that is primarily 'socio-emotionally oriented' (focusing on morale and relationships within the group); task-oriented leaders are more likely to utilize rewards and coercion to achieve their goals than are socio-emotional leaders.[14]

Whether power accrues from structural aspects of the position or personal characteristics of the leader, powerful leaders are more likely than weak leaders to impose their ideas and their goals on others in the group. Indeed, 'the more power a person has the greater the probability that he or she will use it.'[15] Thus, the availability of power leads to its utilization (as implied in the cliché, 'power corrupts'). Consequently, censorship, among other things, is more likely when leaders are powerful. In addition, of course, since powerful leaders have the means to influence group members in important ways, censorship is more likely to be successful for powerful than for weak leaders (which may be, at least in part, why powerful leaders are more likely than weak leaders to attempt censorship in the first place). This conclusion is compatible with the observation that the most blatant exercises of censorship in history have typically been led by strong, autocratic, and authoritarian leaders who have had the power to enforce their constraints with significant rewards and, perhaps especially, costly punishments.

Social norms also influence whether censorship will occur in a group. Groups that have a tradition of less censorship and more open and honest exchange of ideas are more likely to continue to follow such practices than are groups with a history of tighter control of information and less democratic decision making. This influence of norms can be seen in groups as small as the family and as large as cultures or societies. Parents who set strict rules for television viewing, for example, are more likely to attempt also to control their children's reading material and friendship networks than are more laissez-faire parents.[16] Societies that have endured authoritarian governments for many years often seem to have difficulty adjusting to democracy; it is as if members of the society are willing to revert to autocratic decision making at the first sign of trouble. One reason for this willingness is that greater degrees of censorship and state control have been the 'norm' to which group members have become accustomed.

A third group factor that can motivate censorship is group cohesiveness. Group cohesiveness has two components: a high degree of attraction to the group and a strong sense of identity or 'we-ness.'[17] In highly cohesive groups, members want very much to remain part of the group, because their identity is tied to it. Examples of highly cohesive groups include some sports teams and some high-level decision-making groups in government (for example, the inner cabinet of the prime minister or of the president). High group cohesiveness might be expected to produce less censorship of ideas. After all, members know one another well and should feel comfortable exchanging divergent views on an issue. In fact, however, evidence suggests that members of highly cohesive groups are motivated to seek agreement or concurrence, as reflected in a unanimous decision. As a result of this concurrence-seeking, members of highly cohesive groups are actually *more* likely to censor information than are members of less cohesive groups. Such censorship includes both 'protecting' the group from external information that is inconsistent with the group's dominant view and *self*-censorship during group discussions (refraining from expressing thoughts or ideas that are inconsistent with the majority opinion). The strong desire to remain in the group makes members hesitant to express divergent opinions for fear of being ostracized, and the sense of 'we-ness' leads members to identify with others in the group and to conform to their opinions. Indeed, psychologist Irving Janis[18] has identified a phenomenon that he labelled 'groupthink,' which occurs almost exclusively in highly cohesive groups. Groupthink occurs when group members are so highly motivated to obtain consensus that they suppress dissent and avoid careful appraisal of alternative options. Janis identified numerous events in recent history that he considered to be examples of groupthink, where high-level decision-making groups made disastrous and, in retrospect, obviously poor decisions because they did not deliberate in an open and frank manner (for example, the decision by President John Kennedy and his cabinet in 1961 to invade Cuba at the Bay of Pigs). These groups ignored negative evidence and suppressed personal doubts. Often, the leader of the group took a strong, directive role, expressing his or her opinion at the beginning of the deliberations and stating the importance of coming to a unanimous decision. Under such pressure from the leader, members often censored others and themselves. Thus, perhaps paradoxically, group cohesiveness serves to increase the probability of self-censorship. Janis recommended that, to avoid groupthink, leaders of highly cohesive groups should adopt a non-directive role, including not stating their opinion at the beginning, and should explicitly encourage the expression of divergent views by members.

Finally, the presence of an external threat to a group increases the probability that censorship will be both imposed and tolerated. When a group is threatened by outside forces, at least two things occur that make censorship more likely. First, groups become more secretive; leaders and members are concerned that important information might leak to the source of the threat.[19] Second, people are more willing to accept simple, black-and-white solutions to problems. Threat induces anxiety, which is aversive. Because of a desire to reduce the anxiety, people want quick 'answers,' despite the fact that the threat is often complex and requires complex solutions.[20] Because of the desire for a quick fix when threatened, people are more willing to tolerate, among other things, restrictions to their own freedom. For example, when the War Measures Act was invoked by Prime Minister Pierre Trudeau in 1970 to impose significant restrictions on Canadians' individual freedoms, there was little immediate complaint, because most Canadians felt very threatened by the extremist Front de libération du Québec (FLQ), which had kidnapped two political figures. Subsequently, however, after the immediate threat (and associated anxiety) had eased, many Canadians concluded that the government's behaviour had been heavy-handed and undemocratic. Of course, political leaders know that people are more tolerant of personal restrictions during periods of threat; it has not been uncommon for leaders who are trying to maintain their power to 'create' a bogus crisis (for instance, to claim that a neighbouring country is planning to attack) before imposing restrictive laws or military control.

Possible Justifications for Censorship?

Those who support censorship often justify it on the ground that it is being used to protect individuals in society from harm. That is, they suggest that the type of materials and information that are being censored can produce harmful effects. But is there any evidence to support this assertion? In this section, we describe psychological research examining the potential harmful effects of two primary targets of censorship in Canada today: language (ethnic slurs and derogatory humour) and media presentations (television violence and pornography).

Derogatory labels and slurs directed at minority groups in society are today considered socially unacceptable and may be subjected to public censorship. Is there evidence that this language has harmful effects? A series of studies has been conducted to examine the effects of derogatory ethnic labels on perceptions of individuals and groups. The first such study[21] looked at the effect of overhearing a derogatory ethnic slur on listeners' evaluations of the person to whom the slur was applied. In a laboratory setting, a debate was staged between a black and a white individual, in which the black debater performed poorly or well. Participants in the audience were asked to observe the debate and rate the performance of the debaters. To examine the effect of a derogatory ethnic label, an assistant of the experimenter (posing as a participant) behaved in one of two ways prior to the rating of the debaters: did nothing (control condition), or whispered a comment to another assistant at a volume loud enough to be heard by all other participants. The comment either involved an ethnic slur, 'There's no way that nigger won the debate,' or was non-racist, 'There's no way the pro debater won the debate.' Results demonstrated that when the black debater performed poorly, the racist comment led to especially negative evaluations of that debater's performance. This result can be interpreted as indicating that when an individual hears an ethnic slur, any negative beliefs and feelings associated with the ethnic group that exist within the individual will be brought to mind and applied, if appropriate (for example, when the black debater performed poorly).

A second study[22] examined whether this effect would extend beyond the specific target of the derogation. Participants, seated in a room together, were asked to read a trial transcript and rate a black defence attorney and his white defendant, and provide a verdict regarding the guilt of the defendant. Again, a confederate of the experimenter either said nothing or made one of two comments to another confederate in a voice loud enough to be heard by all participants: 'God, Mike, I don't believe this. That nigger defence lawyer doesn't know shit' (derogatory ethnic label), or 'God, Mike, I don't believe this. That shyster defence lawyer doesn't know shit' (no ethnic slur). Results revealed that the derogatory ethnic label led to more negative ratings of the black defence attorney, more negative ratings of the white defendant, and higher certainty that the defendant was guilty. Thus, derogatory ethnic labels seem to have reliable deleterious effects on evaluations of both targeted individuals and others associated with them.

In order to explore more fully the mechanism responsible for these effects, an experiment was conducted to determine whether pre-existing attitudes towards the targeted group would influence the strength of the effect of derogatory ethnic labels.[23] Results revealed that the negative effects of an ethnic slur were especially strong when the person hearing the comment initially held a relatively unfavourable attitude towards the targeted group. This supports the contention that ethnic slurs may cue pre-existing negative beliefs and feelings for the target group, which are applied to individual group members (and their associates) when relevant.

Does disparaging humour directed at social groups have similar negative effects? A recent series of three studies[24] failed to find any such effects. In these studies, participants were exposed to disparaging humour about men or lawyers or were not exposed to such humour, and they were then asked to complete a number of measures regarding their perceptions of the relevant group. Across the three studies, exposure to the disparaging humour had no demonstrable effects. It should be noted, however, that the targeted groups in these studies were advantaged rather than disadvantaged groups. Thus, we cannot be certain that this failure to obtain detrimental effects of exposure to derogatory humour would extend to humour targeted at disadvantaged groups in society.

In contrast to these null effects, there is some evidence that derogatory humour about a disadvantaged group can have an effect on the *communicator* of the humour. In one study, participants[25] were asked to recite either jokes that disparaged Newfoundlanders or non-disparaging jokes into a tape recorder. Results revealed that telling disparaging humour about Newfoundlanders led to the subsequent expression of more negative stereotypes of the group. Thus, there is evidence that disparaging jokes can affect the beliefs of people who tell them.

It has been suggested that public censorship should be applied not only to slurs directed at minority groups but also to group labels that, although not explicitly derogatory, might carry with them negative perceptions or misperceptions of a group. Thus, for example, the term 'Native Indian' should no longer be used; instead, terms such as 'First Nations,' 'Native Peoples,' or 'Native Canadians' should be utilized.[26]

In response to this assertion, a recent study[27] tested whether the label used to identify native peoples would influence perceptions of the group. University participants were asked to complete a questionnaire assessing attitudes towards natives, who were identified with one of five labels: 'Aboriginal Peoples,' 'First Nations People,' 'Native Canadians,' 'Native Indians,' or 'Native Peoples.' In addition to indicating their overall attitudes towards the group, participants were asked to indicate their thoughts and feelings about the group. Results revealed that attitudes towards natives were indeed influenced by the label used to identify the group. Surprisingly, however, attitudes towards natives were least favourable when the labels 'First Nations' and 'Native Canadians' were utilized. This effect was at least partially mediated by the thoughts that came to mind in response to these labels. For example, when the label 'Native Canadians' was utilized, respondents were more likely to think that native peoples threatened both the work ethic and national unity.

These findings indicate that the label used to identify a group may indeed make a difference in determining attitudes towards the group. Thus, language that is not explicitly derogatory can affect perceptions of a group, though not necessarily in the direction suggested by groups concerned about equity. In fact, the research indicates that two of the labels for native peoples specifically recommended by equity groups, 'First Nations' and 'Native Canadians,' can have deleterious effects in terms of both attitudes and more specific thoughts about the group.

There has been considerable debate as to whether children's viewing of television violence leads to an increase in their aggressive behaviour in both the short and the long run.[28] The substantial body of evidence on this issue collected to date suggests that, indeed, there is a relation between the viewing of television violence and aggression, though the causal nature of this relation may be questionable.

The psychological theory most often used to explain this potential relation is social learning theory.[29] According to social learning theory, children learn to perform behaviour to some extent by observing the behaviour of others and the situations in which they occur. Thus, children may learn not only particular aggressive acts from television, but they may also learn that aggression is appropriate in many different social settings.[30]

Three methodological approaches have been used to examine this issue: correlational studies, laboratory experiments, and field experiments. In correlational studies, measures are taken of amount and type of television viewing and of aggressive behaviour. The relations between these measures are then examined. Across a number of studies, results consistently demonstrate that children who watch a greater amount of television violence are significantly more likely to behave aggressively.[31] This finding alone does not demonstrate that television violence *causes* aggression, however, because the direction of effect is not evident. For example, an equally plausible conclusion from this finding would be that aggressive children are more likely to choose to watch violent television.

To determine the causal direction of effects, controlled experiments must be performed in which the amount of television violence to which children are exposed is manipulated and the effect on aggressive behaviour subsequently assessed. Laboratory experiments conducted in this context have typically brought participants into the laboratory to view a violent or non-violent television clip and then provided a situation in which they might choose to behave aggressively.[32] Results of these experiments have generally demonstrated greater aggression in the violent television condition than in the non-violent television condition.[33] One might conclude from these findings that television violence does cause aggression in the real world. However, these studies have been criticized on the grounds that they are highly artificial in both the presented opportunity to observe television violence and in the opportunity to behave aggressively, and that the assessment of effects occurs immediately following the manipulation of television viewing.[34] Thus, one may question whether effects obtained in the laboratory actually can occur in real-world settings and over the long term.

To address this concern, field experiments have been conducted in which the content of children's television viewing is controlled for a set period of time, and aggressive behaviour in more naturalistic settings is observed. The results of these experiments have been mixed, with some showing increases in aggression following the viewing of television violence and others showing weak or no effects.[35]

In sum, although the correlational research and laboratory experiments suggest that television violence can cause increases in aggressive behaviour in children, the field experiments have provided less definitive evidence. Further research on this issue is clearly needed, but, in the meantime, we should at least be concerned about the possible impact on children of excessive viewing of television violence.

A rather similar question has been raised as to whether exposure to pornography leads to increased aggression against women. In this case, it is first necessary to clarify how pornography is defined. In particular, the effects of exposure to sexually explicit materials may differ depending on the content of the materials. Thus, it is necessary to differentiate between sexually violent pornography, degrading but non-violent pornography, and non-violent and non-degrading sexual materials.[36]

The research evidence to date suggests that it is sexually violent pornography, rather than the other two categories of pornographic material, that is most likely to have detrimental effects.[37] In the typical laboratory study addressing this issue, male participants are brought into the laboratory and asked to watch a film. Next, they may be provided with an opportunity to behave aggressively towards a female confederate or be asked to complete some sort of self-report measure of their attitudes and behavioural tendencies. A number of such laboratory experiments have demonstrated that exposure to sexually violent pornography leads to increased levels of aggression against women and to greater acceptance of rape myths (for example, 'women enjoy rape') and of violence against women.[38]

The interpretation of these findings is complex for at least two reasons. First, because the pairing of sex and violence is most likely to cause harmful effects, it is unclear whether these effects are caused by the violence in the depictions, the sexually explicit nature of the materials, or both.[39] In fact, there is some evidence to suggest that materials depicting violence against women without sexual explicitness may produce similar harmful effects.[40] These materials would not be defined as pornography.

A second concern in interpreting this research is whether we can apply the results of laboratory experiments to aggression outside the laboratory. As with the research on television violence, the laboratory experiments may be criticized as being highly artificial in both the presented opportunity to observe pornography and the measures of aggressive behaviour.[41]

Field studies conducted to address this concern about external validity have looked at the reactions of actual sexual offenders to pornography.[42] These studies have not supported the hypothesized relationship between pornography and aggression against women. First, sexual offenders do not report greater amounts or frequency of experience with pornography (including violent pornography) than do non-offenders. In addition, more controlled research has shown that for rapists, arousal to depictions of forced sex is significantly lower than arousal to depictions of consenting sex. Thus, rapists do not seem to be especially susceptible to violent pornography.

Field studies have also analysed crime statistics in countries where the availability of pornography (including violent pornography) has increased over time.[43] In general, these studies have found no evidence that the incidence of rape and other forms of sexual violence increased during the years when pornography became widely available.

Thus, the issue of whether pornography, and in particular sexually violent pornography, leads to increased aggression against women in society has yet to be definitively resolved. The findings of laboratory studies have not been paralleled in field research. To date, the evidence is certainly not strong enough to warrant a call for censorship on the ground of harm-based control.

Consequences of Censorship

Censorship involves a restriction of people's production of, expression of, or access to verbal or pictorial information. How do people react to such restrictions? Do they willingly accept them, grudgingly acquiesce in them, or fight against them? Of course, all of these reactions are possible; thus, the question becomes *when* or *why* do these various reactions ensue? Several lines of research in social psychology provide some clues about the conditions that elicit various reactions to censorship.

Reactance theory[44] is based on the idea that people are motivated to protect their freedom to think, feel, and behave however they wish. More precisely, people are assumed to be motivated to protect those freedoms to which they have become accustomed or to which they feel entitled. Attempts by others (including authorities) to impose new restrictions on thoughts or behaviour are postulated to result in the arousal of *psychological reactance* – a motivation to restore the threatened freedom. For example, a parent's decision that his or her child cannot watch a popular television program because it is too violent will produce psychological reactance in the child. One nearly inevitable initial consequence of psychological reactance is that the threatened freedom becomes more attractive (the child wants to watch the banned television program even more). A second possible consequence is that the child might attempt to restore his or her freedom directly by performing the threatened act (ignoring the parent's order and watching the television program at a friend's house). A third possibility, less likely than the first two, is aggression against the agent who is restricting the freedom (shouting at the parent).

By definition, censorship involves a restriction of freedom, namely, free access to information or free expression of ideas. Therefore, reactance theory predicts that censorship will produce psychological reactance so long as it restricts access to information that individuals are accustomed to having or to which they feel entitled. If censorship arouses psychological reactance, access to the restricted information will become more attractive to individuals, which might motivate them to resist censorship and seek out the information. Also, reactance might motivate individuals to change their attitude towards the topic of the information. For example, angered by censorship, individuals might become more favourable to positions advocated in banned information, as a way of showing their resistance to the restrictions (for example, adopting anti-Semitic attitudes in reaction to the censorship of information claiming that the Holocaust was a hoax).

In one of the first psychological experiments investigating censorship per se,[45] university students who arrived at a laboratory were told that they were supposed to hear a speech taking the position that police either should or should not be allowed on college campuses. They were also told, however, that the dean of their university had censored the speech, so they would not be allowed to hear it. Subsequently, participants' attitudes towards allowing police on campus were measured. Compared to subjects in a control group who simply expressed their attitudes without any mention of a speech or censorship, students who were censored (not allowed to hear a speech) changed their attitudes in the alleged direction of the censored speech. That is, if students were told that the prohibited speech took the position that police should be allowed on campus, they reported more positive attitudes towards allowing police on campus. If, on the other hand, students were told that the prohibited speech took the position that police should not be allowed on campus, they reported more negative attitudes towards allowing police on campus. The researchers suggested that the prohibition of the speech aroused psychological reactance in the students, who felt that their freedom to hold the position advocated in the communication had been threatened. Thus, the students re-established their freedom by adopting attitudes consistent with the proscribed position.

Several experiments were subsequently conducted to replicate and extend this initial investigation of censorship. The principal goal in the follow-up studies was to test whether the effects of censorship on attitudes depend on the attractiveness or expertise of the censor. In the earlier study,[46] it is possible that the students initially evaluated the dean who censored the message negatively, which led them to embrace whatever position he attempted to censor. In some circumstances, however, censors are likeable and/or expert. Will censorship by such individuals also create psychological reactance?

In one follow-up study,[47] university students who arrived at a laboratory were told that the experimenter had planned to play a taped message that took the position, 'police should never be allowed on college campuses.' Participants were told that, unfortunately, they would not be able to hear the communication because a campus group had learned of the topic and asked that the speech not be used in the study. Some participants were told that the censoring group was the YM-YWCA (which was a positively rated group), whereas others were told that the censoring group was the John Birch Society (which was a negatively evaluated group). Participants subsequently expressed their attitudes towards allowing police on campus. Compared to those in a control group who simply expressed their attitudes without any mention of a speech or censorship, participants in *both* censored groups expressed attitudes that were more consistent with the alleged position in the censored message (namely, they expressed more opposition to allowing police on campus). Thus, the attractiveness of the censor did not affect the consequences of censorship. Reactance seemed to be aroused in both conditions, thereby producing the 'boomerang' effect against the censorship (that is, agreement with the proscribed position).

In a subsequent study,[48] university students were again told that they would not be able to hear a taped message because a campus group had complained. As in the previous study, the campus group was either attractive or unattractive. Also, the campus group was either well informed and expert on the issue or was not well informed. The banned message allegedly took a position with which the participant either agreed or disagreed. Compared to participants in a control group who simply expressed their attitudes without mention of a speech or censorship, participants in every condition but one expressed attitudes that were more consistent with the alleged position in the censored message. *Only* when an attractive and expert censor prohibited a position with which participants initially disagreed did participants *not* alter their attitudes towards the prohibited position. Thus, psychological reactance (and attitude change towards the banned message) was the most common response to censorship. Only under conditions where individuals would be extremely sympathetic to censorship (censorship of a position with which they disagreed by an attractive and expert censor) did the reactance effect disappear.

In a more recent experiment,[49] again with university students, the 'boomerang' effect of censorship on desire to see information and on attitudes was shown to be more likely when people had previously been given the explicit freedom to hear a message (but were then denied it) or when people learned that other individuals had already heard the message. Thus, psychological reactance in response to censorship was more likely when hearing the prohibited message was something to which participants felt entitled, based either on previous promises or on the opportunities of others. This finding supports the assumption in reactance theory that threats to freedoms are particularly likely to produce reactance when they are directed against behaviour that people consider to be part of their available repertoire, that is, when they restrict behaviour that people expected to be able to perform.

In general, then, research on reactance theory has identified a potential paradoxical effect of censorship, in which restricted access to information generates greater interest in the information and even attitude change in the direction of the information. As we will see in the next section, this effect may not be inevitable or long-lasting, but it is a definite possibility, at least in the short term. An example of this process would be the banning of an issue of a sexually oriented magazine, which ironically can produce media attention, public interest, and increased sales (at least in locations where the magazine remains available). 'Boomerang' effects provide a sobering thought for parents and authorities who want to censor information for the good of others; if the target feels entitled to having the information, censorship can backfire and produce exactly the kind of prurient (or other) interest that was feared in the first place.

History teaches us that censorship often 'works.' That is, censors often restrict people's access to or dissemination of information without producing strong protest or complaint from those affected. Indeed, the public often supports censorship wholeheartedly, agreeing that the prohibited information should not be easily available. For example, Canadian laws against tobacco advertising, distributing pornography, and inciting racial hatred are widely supported. If the only psychological process relevant to censorship was reactance, it would be difficult to understand such passivity and support. Two other social psychological theories, however, provide insight into why censorship may be endured and even internalized.

Dissonance theory[50] proposes that people see themselves as generally intelligent, rational, and principled individuals. For example, people want and try to behave in ways that are consistent with their knowledge, attitudes, and values. Becoming aware of personal behaviour that was illogical or inconsistent with one's values is presumed to be distressing, and people are motivated to convince themselves that their behaviour *was* sensible or worthy. Sometimes, this attempt to 'rationalize' behaviour results in changes to attitudes and beliefs. For example, researchers have shown that people who have invested a lot of time, effort, or money in a project come to believe that their investment was worthwhile, even when objective criteria suggest otherwise.[51] Similarly, people tend to justify decisions they have made by increasing the perceived attractiveness of the chosen alternative and decreasing the perceived attractiveness of rejected alternatives.[52] Finally, people who are induced to behave in a fashion that contradicts their own attitudes often change those attitudes to be more consistent with their behaviour. For example, university students who agree to write an essay arguing in favour of a tuition increase (an idea to which most students are opposed) come to express more support for such an increase.[53]

Dissonance researchers explain these findings in terms of people's motivation to view themselves as rational beings who act in logical ways. One important prerequisite for dissonance effects is that the behaviour being rationalized must have been freely performed, that is, under volitional control.[54] If people think that their action was controlled by strong external forces (such as threat of punishment or offer of reward), they will feel little pressure to 'rationalize' it, because the external forces already provide sufficient justification.

How is dissonance theory relevant to censorship? If people believe that their compliance with censorship guidelines is voluntary, they might justify their compliance by coming to agree with the prohibitions. An analogue of this situation was created in an interesting study[55] where five-year-old children were told by an adult that they should *not* play with a very attractive toy while the adult was out of the room. Some children were warned that severe consequences could result from disobedience, whereas other children were given only a mild warning. The adult then left the room for several minutes, during which time no child in either threat condition played with the forbidden toy. When the adult returned, the child rated the attractiveness of the toy. Children in the mild-threat condition (who had less reason to avoid the toy) rated it less positively than children in the severe-threat condition (who had good reasons to avoid the toy). It appears that children in the mild-threat condition interpreted their avoidance of the toy as having been voluntary, at least in part, and rationalized their behaviour by deciding that they did not really like the toy after all. Returning to censorship, compliance with rules governing access to or dissemination of information might produce attitude change in favour of the censorship when individuals view their behaviour as volitional.

Of course, censorship is often prescribed by laws or other constraints that actually carry considerable force. To the extent that individuals recognize the strength of these constraints, they should not view their compliance as voluntary and should not feel that they need to rationalize their compliance. Thus, agreement with the censorship may not occur. But the salience of laws as causes of behaviour probably fades over time, in which case dissonance effects may eventually appear. This possibility is rendered even more plausible by evidence that, in general, people *over*estimate their freedom to act as they wish, *under*estimate the power of external forces on their behaviour, and take *more* personal responsibility for their actions than is probably warranted.[56] Thus, it seems reasonable to expect that many individuals will interpret their compliance with censorship laws to be voluntary, which should motivate them to rationalize their compliance by deciding that they are not really interested in the prohibited information.

Dissonance theory assumes that people rationalize their behaviour because it is *distressing* to think that one has behaved illogically; that is, dissonance theory is a *motivational* model. A simpler, *non*-motivational model that makes many of the same predictions as dissonance theory is self-perception theory.[57] Self-perception theorists propose that people believe that they behave in accordance with their attitudes and beliefs (which, of course, is often true). Therefore, people think that it is possible to use their own actions to *infer* their attitudes: 'If I did X, then I must believe X.' In other words, self-perception theorists postulate that perceivers sometimes use their own overt actions as a means of judging their own attitudes and beliefs (just as perceivers use other people's actions to infer others' attitudes and beliefs). These inferences are *not* assumed to be rationalizations of behaviour motivated by dissonance, but rather they are simply logical conclusions that follow from the assumption that there is a connection between attitudes and behaviour. Thus, self-perception theory challenges the usual assumption that people 'know' their attitudes directly; rather, self-perception theorists postulate that people sometimes *infer* their own attitudes based, at least in part, on an analysis of their own behaviour.

Like dissonance theory, self-perception theory predicts that individuals' compliance with censorship can lead them to infer attitudes that are consistent with the prohibitions. For example, someone who does not view pornography might infer, 'I don't view pornography, so I must not like it.' Again, it is necessary that people must perceive their compliance as voluntary before self-perception effects can occur (otherwise, compliance would not necessarily reflect personal attitudes). Given that people overestimate their behavioural freedom, however, inferences of attitudes consistent with censorship (for example, not liking pornography) seem possible.

As the preceding sections indicate, reactance theory makes a dramatically different prediction about the effects of censorship than do dissonance and self-perception theories. Can these apparently opposing theoretical views be reconciled? We suggest that a longitudinal perspective is helpful in this regard.

Reactance theory applies when people perceive strong, external forces restricting their freedom. Such perceptions may be especially likely when censorship is initially imposed. When people first learn that they are being denied access to information (or the ability to disseminate information), the external constraints on them will be salient. Under these conditions, the restricted information will become more attractive and people may actively resist the attempted control.

In contrast, dissonance and self-perception theories apply when people see their compliance with restrictions as voluntary, at least in part. Such perceptions seem more likely when the external restrictions have been in force for an extended duration. Over time, people are likely to underestimate the impact of those guidelines and overestimate the impact of their own preferences on their behaviour. Consequently, both dissonance (motivated rationalization) and self-perception (rational inferences) will serve to create attitudes that are consistent with the censorship.

Thus, reactance followed by dissonance/self-perception may represent a common temporal sequence that occurs after the imposition of censorship. Initially, opposition might occur, with people expressing heightened interest in the prohibited information and challenging the restrictions. Over time, however, if the censor can weather the initial resistance, people may come to accept the restrictions as natural and even conclude that they are not interested in the prohibited information.

Conclusion

Censorship is a broad and complex phenomenon – a point illustrated dramatically by the diversity of perspectives on censorship taken in this volume. We have reviewed some of the work in social psychology that relates to censorship. The principal feature of a social-psychological approach is the assumption that censorship can be understood only by taking the perspectives of those who initiate, support, oppose, or are affected by it.

Social-psychological theories help us to understand the determinants of censorship and support for censorship. For example, authoritarianism and religious fundamentalism predict support for censorship, and group processes like leader power, social norms, and group cohesiveness influence the likelihood of censorship. Social-psychological research also assists in the assessment of possible justifications for censorship. For example, at the current time, we would argue that the weight of the evidence suggests that viewing violent television increases children's aggressiveness, whereas viewing pornography per se has not been shown convincingly to cause aggression against women. Finally, social-psychological theories contribute to our understanding of the consequences of censorship. One possible consequence is resistance, typically accompanied by an increase in the attractiveness of the censored information. A second possible consequence is acquiescence, which may be followed by attitudes that support the restrictions. We suspect that resistance may be a common initial response to censorship, whereas acquiescence may often occur later in the temporal sequence.

NOTES

1 This chapter was prepared while both authors were supported by research grants from the Social Sciences and Humanities Research Council of Canada.

2 G. Allport, 'The Historical Background of Social Psychology,' in G. Lindzey and
E. Aronson, eds., *Handbook of Social Psychology*, 3rd ed., vol. 1 (New York: Random House 1985), 1–46.

3 T.W. Adorno, E. Frenkel-Brunswick, D.J. Levinson, and R.N. Sanford, *The Authoritarian Personality* (New York: Harper 1950).

4 B. Altemeyer, *Right-Wing Authoritarianism* (Winnipeg: University of Manitoba
Press 1981); B. Altemeyer, *Enemies of Freedom: Understanding Right-Wing
Authoritarianism* (San Francisco: Jossey-Bass 1988); Altemeyer, 'Reducing Prejudice in Right-Wing Authoritarians,' in M.P. Zanna and J.M. Olson, eds., *The Psychology of Prejudice: The Ontario Symposium*, vol. 7 (Hillsdale N.J.: Erlbaum
1994), 131–47.

5 V.M. Esses, G. Haddock, and M.P. Zanna, 'Values, Stereotypes, and Emotions as
Determinants of Intergroup Attitudes,' in D.M. Mackie and D.L. Hamilton, eds.,
Affect, Cognition, and Stereotyping: Interactive Processes in Group Perception
(New York: Academic Press 1993), 137–66; M.J. Rohan and M.P. Zanna, 'Value
Transmission in Families,' in C. Seligman, J.M. Olson, and M.P. Zanna, eds., *The
Psychology of Values: The Ontario Symposium* vol. 8 (Hillsdale N.J.: Erlbaum
1996), 253–76.

6 Altemeyer, *Enemies of Freedom*.

7 Ibid.

8 Ibid.

9 C. Kirkpatrick, 'Religion and Humanitarianism: A Study of Institutional Implications,' *Psychological Monographs*, 63, no. 304.

10 S.A. Stouffer, *Communism, Conformity, and Civil Liberties* (New York: Doubleday
1955).

11 C.D. Batson and C.T. Burris, 'Personal Religion: Depressant or Stimulant of Prejudice and Discrimination?,' in Zanna and Olson, eds., *The Psychology of Prejudice:
The Ontario Symposium*, vol. 7: 149–69.

12 F.E. Fiedler, 'A Contingency Model of Leadership Effectiveness,' in L. Berkowitz,
ed., *Advances in Experimental Social Psychology*, vol. 1 (New York: Academic
Press 1964), 149–90; M.E. Shaw, *Group Dynamics: The Psychology of Small
Group Behavior* (New York: McGraw Hill 1976).

13 E. Hollander, 'Leadership and Power,' in G. Lindzey and E. Aronson, eds., *Handbook of Social Psychology*, 3rd ed., vol. 2 (New York: Random House 1985),
485–537.

14 R.F. Bales, *Interaction Process Analysis: A Method for the Study of Small
Groups* (Cambridge, Mass.: Addison-Wesley 1950); Fiedler, 'A Contingency
Model.'

15 Shaw, *Group Dynamics*, 269.

16 Altemeyer, *Enemies of Freedom*; M.K. Jennings and R.G. Niemi, 'The Transmis-

sion of Political Values From Parent to Child,' *American Political Science Review*, 62 (1968), 169–84.

17 Shaw, *Group Dynamics*.

18 I.L. Janis, *Victims of Groupthink* (Boston: Houghton Mifflin 1972).

19 Ibid.

20 R.W. Rogers, 'Cognitive and Physiological Processes in Fear Appeals and Attitude Change: A Revised Theory of Protection Motivation,' in J.T. Cacioppo and R.E. Petty, eds., *Social Psychophysiology* (New York: Guilford 1983), 153–76.

21 J. Greenberg and T. Pyszczynski, 'The Effect of an Overheard Slur on Evaluations of the Target: How to Spread a Social Disease,' *Journal of Experimental Social Psychology*, 21 (1985), 61–72.

22 S.L. Kirkland, J. Greenberg, and T. Pyszczynski, 'Further Evidence of the Deleterious Effects of Overheard Ethnic Slurs: Derogation Beyond the Target,' *Personality and Social Psychology Bulletin*, 13 (1987), 216–27.

23 L. Simon and J. Greenberg, 'Further Progress in Understanding the Effects of Derogatory Ethnic Labels: The Role of Preexisting Attitudes Toward the Targeted Group,' *Personality and Social Psychology Bulletin*, 22 (1996), 1195–1204.

24 J.M. Olson, G.R. Maio, and K.L. Hobden, 'The (Null) Effects of Exposure to Disparagement Humor on Stereotypes and Attitudes,' *Humor: International Journal of Humor Research* (1999).

25 G.R. Maio, J.M. Olson, and J. Bush, 'Telling Jokes That Disparage Social Groups: Effects on the Joke Teller's Stereotypes,' *Journal of Applied Social Psychology*, 27, no. 22 (1997), 1986–2000.

26 President's Standing Committee for Employment Equity of the University of Western Ontario, draft of 'Equity in Communication Policy' (London, Ont.: University of Western Ontario 1992).

27 D.W. Donakowski and V.M. Esses, 'Native Canadians, First Nations, or Aboriginals: The Effect of Labels on Attitudes toward Native Peoples,' *Canadian Journal of Behavioural Science*, 28 (1996), 86–91.

28 S. Feshbach, 'Television Research and Social Policy: Some Perspectives,' in S. Oskamp, ed., *Television as a Social Issue* (Newbury Park, Calif.: Sage 1988), 198–213; J.L. Freedman, 'Television Violence and Aggression: What Psychologists Should Tell the Public,' in P. Suedfeld and P.E. Tetlock, eds., *Psychology and Social Policy* (New York: Hemisphere 1992), 179–89; L.R. Huesmann, L.D. Eron, L. Berkowitz, and S. Chaffee, 'The Effects of Television Violence on Aggression: A Reply to a Skeptic,' in Suedfeld and Tetlock, eds., *Psychology and Social Policy*, 191–200.

29 A. Bandura, *Aggression: A Social Learning Analysis* (New York: Holt, Rinehart and Winston 1973); A. Bandura and R.H. Walters, *Social Learning and Personality Development* (New York: Holt, Rinehard and Winston 1963).

30 L.R. Huesmann, 'Psychological Processes Promoting the Relation Between Expo-
    sure to Media Violence and Aggressive Behavior in the Viewer,' *Journal of Social
    Issues*, 42, no. 3 (1986), 125–39.
31 L.R. Huesmann, 'Television Violence and Aggressive Behavior,' in D. Pearl, L.
    Bouthilet, and J. Lazar, eds., *Television and Behavior: Ten Years of Scientific
    Progress and Implications for the Eighties*, vol. 2, *Technical Reviews* (Washington,
    D.C.: U.S. Government Printing Office 1982), 126–37; L.R. Huesmann and L.D.
    Eron, *Television and the Aggressive Child: A Cross-National Comparison* (Hills-
    dale, N.J.: Erlbaum 1986); J.L. Singer and D.G. Singer, 'Some Hazards of Grow-
    ing Up in a Television Environment: Children's Aggression and Restlessness,' in S.
    Oskamp, ed., *Television as a Social Issue*, 171–88; C.W. Turner, B.W. Hesse, and
    S. Peterson-Lewis, 'Naturalistic Studies of the Long-Term Effects of Television
    Violence,' *Journal of Social Issues*, 42, no. 3 (1986), 51–73.
32 R.M. Liebert, J.N. Sprafkin, and E.S. Davidson, *The Early Window: Effects of Tele-
    vision on Children and Youth* (New York: Pergamon 1989).
33 J. Condry, *The Psychology of Television* (Hillsdale, N.J.: Erlbaum 1989); R.G.
    Geen, *Human Aggression* (Pacific Grove, Calif.: Brooks Cole 1990).
34 Freedman, 'Television Violence and Aggression.'
35 Condry, *The Psychology of Television*; L. Friedrich-Cofer and A.C. Huston, 'Tele-
    vision Violence and Aggression: The Debate Continues,' *Psychological Bulletin*,
    100 (1986), 364–71; Singer and Singer, 'Some Hazards of Growing Up in a Tele-
    vision Environment'; W. Wood, F. Wong, and J. Chachere, 'Effects of Media Vio-
    lence on Viewers' Aggression in Unconstrained Social Interaction,' *Psychological
    Bulletin*, 109 (1991), 371–83.
36 W.A. Fisher and A. Barak, 'Pornography, Erotica, and Behavior: More Ques-
    tions Than Answers,' *International Journal of Law and Psychiatry*, 14 (1991),
    65–83.
37 Ibid.; D. Linz, N.M. Malamuth, and K. Beckett, 'Civil Liberties and Research on
    the Effects of Pornography,' in Suedfeld and Tetlock, eds., *Psychology and Social
    Policy*, 149–64.
38 E. Donnerstein, D. Linz, and S. Penrod, *The Question of Pornography* (New York:
    Free Press 1987).
39 Linz, Malamuth, and Beckett, 'Civil Liberties and Research on the Effects of Por-
    nography.'
40 E. Donnerstein and D. Linz, 'Sexual Violence in the Mass Media,' in M. Con-
    stanzo and S. Oskamp, eds., *Violence and the Law* (Thousand Oaks, Calif.: Sage
    1994), 9–36.
41 A. Brannigan and S. Goldenberg, 'The Study of Aggressive Pornography: The
    Vicissitudes of Relevance,' *Critical Studies in Mass Communication*, 4 (1987),
    262–83.

42 B. Kutchinsky, 'Pornography and Rape: Theory and Practice?' *International Journal of Law and Psychiatry*, 14 (1991), 47–64.
43 V. Esses, 'Field Data on Availability of Pornography and Incidence of Sex Crime in Denmark: Fuel for a Heated Debate,' *Canadian Criminology Forum* 7 (1985), 83–91; Kutchinsky, 'Pornography and Rape.'
44 J.W. Brehm, *A Theory of Psychological Reactance* (New York: Academic Press 1962); J.W. Brehm, *Responses to Loss of Freedom: A Theory of Psychological Reactance* (Morristown, N.J.: General Learning Press 1972).
45 R.D. Ashmore, V. Ramchandra, and R.A. Jones, 'Censorship as an Attitude Change Induction,' paper presented at the Eastern Psychological Association Convention (April 1971).
46 Ibid.
47 S. Worchel and S.E. Arnold, 'The Effects of Censorship and Attractiveness of the Censor on Attitude Change,' *Journal of Experimental Social Psychology*, 9 (1973), 365–77.
48 S. Worchel, S. Arnold, and M. Baker, 'The Effects of Censorship on Attitude Change: The Influence of Censor and Communication Characteristics,' *Journal of Applied Social Psychology*, 5 (1975), 227–39.
49 S. Worchel, 'Beyond a Commodity Theory Analysis of Censorship: When Abundance and Personalism Enhance Scarcity Effects,' *Basic and Applied Social Psychology*, 13 (1992), 79–92.
50 L. Festinger, *A Theory of Cognitive Dissonance* (Evanston, Ill.: Row, Peterseon 1957); L. Festinger, *Conflict, Decision, and Dissonance* (Stanford, Calif.: Stanford University Press 1964).
51 J. Cooper and D. Axsom, 'Effort Justification in Psychotherapy,' in G. Weary and H. Mirels, eds., *Integrations of Clinical and Social Psychology* (New York: Oxford University Press 1982), 214–30.
52 J.M. Olson and M.P. Zanna, 'Repression-Sensitization Differences in Responses to a Decision,' *Journal of Personality*, 50 (1982), 46–57.
53 C.M. Steele, L.L. Southwick, and B. Critchlow, 'Dissonance and Alcohol: Drinking Your Troubles Away,' *Journal of Personality and Social Psychology*, 41 (1981), 831–46.
54 J. Cooper and R.H. Fazio, 'A New Look at Dissonance Theory,' in L. Berkowitz, ed., *Advances in Experimental Social Psychology*, vol. 17 (New York: Academic Press 1984), 229–62.
55 E. Aronson and J.M. Carlsmith, 'Effect of the Severity of Threat on the Devaluation of Forbidden Behavior,' *Journal of Abnormal and Social Psychology* 66 (1963), 584–8.
56 L. Ross and R.E. Nisbett, *The Person and the Situation: Perspectives of Social Psychology* (New York: McGraw Hill 1991); S.E. Taylor and J.D. Brown, 'Illusion and

Well-Being: A Social Psychological Perspective on Mental Health,' *Psychological Bulletin*, 103 (1988), 193–210.

57 D.J. Bem, 'Self-Perception: An Alternative Interpretation of Cognitive Dissonance Phenomena,' *Psychological Review*, 74 (1967), 183–200; D.J. Bem, 'Self-Perception Theory,' in L. Berkowitz, ed., *Advances in Experimental Social Psychology*, vol. 6 (New York: Academic Press 1972), 1–62.

14

The Muted Bugle: Self-Censorship and the Press

RANDAL MARLIN

'Some censorship is hard to fight because it is in our own souls.'

Robert Fisk

'Self-censorship silences as effectively as a government decree, and we have seen it far more often.'

Tom Wicker

There is a story about the training of elephants: they are initially bound by chains of a certain length. Once they become accustomed to these chains, the chains can be removed. The elephants will not stray, because invisible bonds exist in their memories. Something similar occurs in the newsroom. After seeing words taken out, texts altered or spiked, a reporter learns to think and write in the approved manner. The external corrections are no longer needed. The same is sometimes true of official censorship. A few brushes with the official censor suffice, following which the censor is no longer necessary. Charles Lynch, a celebrated war correspondent in the Second World War, described the situation well: 'We were a propaganda arm of our governments. At the start the censors enforced that, but by the end we were our own censors. We were cheerleaders.'[1] Writers who value getting their material published will have an incentive to adapt what they say to conform with whatever powers control access to print or broadcasting. This is where a serious problem arises for a democracy which values freedom of expression. Official censorship operates more or less as a known quantity. But individual self-censorship commonly is known only to the person involved. Any discussion of censorship that fails to consider self-censorship is likely to miss a large part hidden from view.

My aim in this chapter is first to draw attention to the importance of the sensitive topic of self-censorship. Many people faced with the dilemmas posed by self-censorship would prefer to ignore open discussion of the question, for reasons that are easy to find. It takes some courage – some might say, foolhardiness – to admit that there is a serious problem. Who wants to confess to having withheld important news because of the fear of displeasing an important news source, advertiser, publisher, or other powerful body? Such an admission might well affect one's credibility, and hence one's livelihood. Only those who are secure in their profession, or perhaps people who have retired, could afford to make this kind of admission. A French television program recently focused on the question of political and economic constraints on journalists, pointing out that non-conforming writers were subject to the sanctions of non-publication or even dismissal. Significantly, *Le Monde* noted that in the ensuing debate this topic was treated evasively, the invited participants preferring to deal only with generalities.[2]

My purpose in this chapter is threefold: to give an idea of the scope and importance of self-censorship; to focus, though not exclusively so, on the Canadian experience; and to comment on ethical dimensions of the subject, as well as suggesting, where possible, kinds of remedial action that might be taken to defend democracy and expressive freedom against threats posed by self-censorship. The nature of the subject is such as to require an unusual amount of reliance on anecdotal evidence, and I make use of clippings and correspondence accumulated over a period of some twenty-five years. Evidence is necessarily hard to come by: to ask journalists who are actively pursuing their careers to talk frankly about self-censorship in their own case is to invite the thought that you are insulting simultaneously both their integrity and their intelligence. Nevertheless, there exists important research and documentation on the subject.[3] Some of the examples I offer should be considered as supplementary to the existing body of evidence.

Definition

Not everyone is comfortable using the term 'self-censorship,' and it is sometimes used only in scare-quotes, as if there were no respectable definition of the term. Difficulties enough exist with the definition of 'censorship' and these are compounded in the case of 'self-censorship.' Ordinary censorship typically provides us with a duality: a censoring authority and the censored communicator. How then, where censor and censored are one and the same person, does the notion of censorship get a foothold? We must suppose a duality within that person. One impulse or desire moves the person in the direction of expressing something, but some other impulse or desire checks the first. Now, people check themselves from saying offensive, stupid, or incoherent things all the time. The same is true of writing and editing. If we are led to call this self-censorship the term would have a very broad meaning, perhaps one without a significant role to play in discussions relating to freedom, democracy, and the media. Can the term 'self-censorship' be defined so as to play an especially useful role?

Two elements have so far been indicated in connection with 'self-censorship.' These are the communicator, presented as a duality, and the omission, alteration, and so on of a text. I propose to add a third element, namely, that the motive for making a given change or omission be something *extraneous* to the literary, journalistic, and other defensible moral standards that ordinarily are expected to govern our communication. So, for example, if a writer or editor has decided that a story is worthy of publication on the basis that it serves the public interest and satisfies all the other usual criteria, but retracts it on the basis that it might conflict with the private interests of the publisher, there would be a case of self-censorship.

The concept I am proposing should be recognized from the start as a 'defeasible' one. To preserve the duality implicit in describing an individual as a 'self-censor,' we must assume that some sort of conflict exists within that person. If, in cases where a normal individual *would* experience a conflict but an unusual individual does not (say, because he or she lacks developed moral sensibilities), then in the interests of clarity we ought to allow that the term 'self-censorship,' though presumptively applicable, is not applicable to that individual once the absence of conflict has been demonstrated. The liability of the term 'self-censorship' to be defeated in this way does not lessen its usefulness in moral evaluation, however. One who pleads absence of relevant moral standards to escape the charge of self-censorship risks self-incrimination of a more serious offence or defect.[4] We should also note that an individual writer or editor might be in a state of mental conflict without being fully conscious of so being. A writer or editor in a state of self-deception might deny the existence of conflict, but the term 'self-censorship' might still fit that person's action of altering or omitting parts of a text. In this way the existence of the 'invisible chains,' to revert to the elephant analogy, might coherently be dealt with under the rubric of self-censorship.

We can usefully extend the concept of self-censorship to cover cases where an actual text does not exist but is only contemplated. Self-censorship would then be, not just excision, or straightforward omission to publish some material, but also the failure to engage in investigative journalism for reasons unrelated to journalistic principles. Let us say that complaints from readers suggest to an editor the desirability of investigating car dealerships. The idea is dismissed solely because of fear that important advertising would be withdrawn. That would be self-censorship, even though no story has been written.

Reference was made earlier to journalistic and moral standards. This immediately raises questions of relativity. Whose standards? Whose morals? Journalistic standards or principles are subject to change over time, along with moral values generally. But in spite of this there is a measure of agreement on the matter, embodied in the 'Statement of Principles' of the Canadian Newspaper Association.[5] For example, the statement affirms the existence of a 'community responsibility,' a need for 'accuracy and fairness,' 'courtesy and fairness,' and 'independence.' 'Conflicts of interest, real or apparent, should be declared,' it states (a pre-1995 version used the expression 'must be avoided' instead of 'should be declared'). There is enough material here to give scope to the definition I have proposed, even if editors or publishers should later modify or even retract some of the principles.

Problems of moral relativism remain, especially in the light of expressions such as 'the public good,' 'common sense,' and 'decency' to be found in the 'Statement of Principles.' But these questions are best raised following an exploration of the topic, not before.

Classification

Frank Giles has confirmed what many others have observed, that self-censorship is harder to document than 'formal, open censorship or direct state control of the media,'[6] and there is difficulty in classifying the subject. One reason is that 'there are numerous cases of editors treating with caution, discretion or sometimes ignoring altogether certain types of news ... in the interest of social, racial or international harmony.'[7] He seems reluctant to call this kind of thing 'self-censorship.' The definition I have proposed gives a reason for this reluctance. The question for my definition would be: 'Is the editing done in the light of journalistic and defensible, commonly accepted moral values, or is there some extraneous, usually self-serving, motive?'

Self-censorship can be classified in different ways. First, there are the different *motives*. One common motive is economic, which could vary from survival of a newspaper or magazine to simply fattening an already healthy revenue. Other motives might be political, or they might involve the desire to preserve one's life, health, or job. The motive could involve friendship, prestige, patriotism, or simply preserving credibility. A pervasive motive is the desire to gain and maintain readers. Another important motive is the desire to avoid time-consuming hassles or lawsuits. Insiders have also noted that sometimes a paper will not touch a story, not because it is not newsworthy, but because the competition got there first. Sometimes proprietary concerns affect what is left out.[8]

Second, there are different *levels* at which censorship takes place. Some cases are purely *personal,* known only to the self-censor. Others are *institutional,* where, say, a higher authority within a newspaper rules against publication approved at a lower level. The author of the copy is not self-censoring, but the institution is. Somewhat problematically, in the light of the definition I have offered, we might also contemplate possible cases pertaining to a whole *industry.* There are voluntary agreements, by members of the advertising industry, to subscribe to the Code of Ethics governing advertising. This code is upheld by Advertising Standards Canada (formerly the Canadian Advertising Foundation; in Quebec, Les normes canadiennes de la publicité). Likewise, as already mentioned, there is the 'Statement of Principles' of the Canadian Newspaper Association and the norms built up by decisions of press councils, such as the Ontario Press Council. The problem with regarding application of these norms as a form of self-censorship is that these have already been presented as the kinds of norms to be expected in ordinary editorial decision making, which we have argued should be kept distinct from cases of self-censorship. It might seem that in this supposed industry 'self-censorship' is therefore inappropriately so-described. However, if any one of the norms passed by the industry should deviate in any way from defensible norms, then there would be a basis for speaking of self-censorship. For example, should excessive deference to automobile manufacturers result in a general and absolute prohibition against naming makes of cars involved in accidents, there would be space for application of the term. But there are also other reasons for wanting to allow the term 'self-censorship' to have industry-wide application, not the least of which is that the definition I have offered is not meant to capture all the ways in which people may reasonably speak of 'self-censorship.'

Third, self-censorship might be thought of in terms of the *form* it takes. For example, it can take the form of euphemistic or pejorative language. To accommodate a publisher's known bias, a reporter might use words such as 'regime' instead of 'government' against his or her better journalistic judgment.[9] Similarly, a reporter for a conservative newspaper might reluctantly use the word 'henchmen' in reference to aides of a labour leader.[10] Robert Fisk has remarked on a double standard in the use of the word 'terrorist' and on the reluctance to call a dictator a dictator when he is on 'our' side, in which case he is a 'strongman.'[11] Martin Bell, reporting for the BBC in Belfast in August 1969, was told that he could not describe victims of burned-out homes in the Shankill and Falls Road areas as 'Catholics' even though it was clear that that was what they were. He would have to describe them instead as 'refugees.'[12]

Another form of self-censorship involves omitting key details of a story which would help readers form a truthful, but unwanted (by the publisher, editor, reporter, and so on), conclusion. Sometimes material is printed as a news story which does not merit the space by ordinary journalistic standards. It is done, say, to repay a favour from an important news or advertising source. The self-censorship would then exist wherever silence about the motivation for printing the story would materially affect the reader's grasp of its significance.

Fourth, self-censorship might be distinguished in the light of the different sorts of *pressures* that make it likely. One large category would be all cases where formal censorship exists, because self-censorship tends to be a kind of penumbra extending beyond the official boundaries of prohibited expression. There is always some uncertainty as to how a censorship rule will be applied, and those who do not wish the publicity or other effects of direct censorship are likely to show restraint in excess of the minimum required to avoid contravening the law. Outside formal censorship, there are many kinds of forces at work encouraging the use of self-censorship. Edward S. Herman and Noam Chomsky list five different kinds of 'filter' operating on the mass media of today. These pertain to:

- structure and business orientation of the mass media, that is, their ownership and profit orientation (in Canada we can point to the statement of mission in the 1995 annual report of the Thomson Corporation, which encompasses Thomson newspapers, publishers of the *Globe and Mail*: 'Our mission is equally clear – it is to increase shareholder value substantially on a continuing basis');
- advertising, on which the mass media depend for the most part;
- reliance on information provided by government and business, and 'experts' funded and approved by the same;
- 'flak' (strong criticism from people whose opinions are considered important) as a means of disciplining the media; and
- 'anticommunism,' as something akin to a national religion and acting as a control mechanism.[13]

In contemporary Canada ownership is of particular significance, with the majority of daily newspapers owned by one individual, Conrad Black, and most of the remaining circulation concentrated in the hands of very few individuals with multiple publishing, broadcasting, cable, or other business interests. Black's power extends into Canadian Press, because of the combined voting power of his newspapers, and consequently into broadcast news. He also controls the monthly magazine *Saturday Night* and the British *Telegraph* newspapers, copy from which has recently made a sharply increased appearance in some Southam newspapers. It might seem obvious that an ambitious journalist would be attuned to the different powers controlling the media. One would expect, for example, that a journalist seeking to advance far in the Conrad Black empire would not emulate the reporting practices of, say, Linda McQuaig, a distinguished reporter who has incurred his publicly expressed dislike.[14]

The fourth classification, according to pressures, provides a useful jump-off point for drawing attention to the main concerns regarding press self-censorship in Canada today. What follows is a survey of pressures to self-censor under different headings, not necessarily in order of importance and not claiming to be complete.

Government

As earlier indicated, self-censorship hovers on the fringes of official censorship, so an understanding of the scope of the former will involve some acquaintance with the latter.[15] Among the many different forms of what amounts to censorship by government are laws against publication of official secrets, hate propaganda, obscenity, criminal libel, and the reporting of names or proceedings in certain court cases. Blasphemy and sedition are nominally prohibited, but their status under the Canadian Charter of Rights and Freedoms remains uncertain.

The amount of legislation affecting what gets published is rather larger than most people would suspect. The Canadian Code of Advertising Standards (issued by Advertising Standards Canada) lists no less than eleven different federal acts and a total of about forty-two provincial acts, codes, or regulations, in addition to the Criminal Code.

The legitimacy of censorship initiatives is often in doubt. But not every publisher is willing to go to the legal expense of pursuing court challenges. Both in Canada and the United States, fears have been expressed that sections of the media have become increasingly preoccupied with profits rather than good journalism. Such a mentality is conducive to greater self-censorship, to avoid legal expenses.

Earlier this century, Quebec Premier Maurice Duplessis intimidated the press by a wide variety of means, including jeopardizing their newsprint supply. Alberta Premier William Aberhart also tried to restrict press freedom by imposing on newspapers the duty to print a reply whenever the government felt that had been attacked. It is not surprising, then, that the press in Canada today is vigilant concerning government initiatives involving control over the media. The press reacted with the utmost hostility to a proposal, in 1982, of a Canadian newspaper act. The act was partly aimed at stopping increased concentration in the media, but it also sought to give the public a forum for complaints by establishing a Canadian advisory council on newspapers.[16] Pressure from the media, and the increasing unpopularity of the Pierre Trudeau government, led to the government jettisoning this plan in 1983. Whether in response to the threat, or because it saw a new light, the newspaper industry has taken steps since then to protect its public image by joining press councils in droves. Currently every daily newspaper in Ontario is a member of the Ontario Press Council, despite earlier resistance to the idea.[17]

Governments have other powers, one to be discussed under the heading 'sources' below, for disciplining or intimidating the media. Canadian law, under the Broadcasting Act, lays down general criteria that licensees are to meet under pain of having their licence revoked. It also provides for an administrative body, the Canadian Radio-television and Telecommunications Commission (CRTC), which lays down regulations binding licensees. Questions about conformity with the regulations are frequently resolved through consultations between broadcasters and regulators. There is a source of possible industry self-censorship in the form of the Broadcast Standards Council, which rules on complaints against TV and radio broadcasters, using guidelines developed by the Canadian Association of Broadcasters.

Canada experienced severe publication restrictions during the October crisis of 1970, with the invocation of the War Measures Act, but these were relatively short-lived. There is also an Official Secrets Act and parliamentary privilege, each of which, in Peter Desbarats's words, enables parliamentarians to 'examine and punish offensive journalists,'[18] though neither appears to have been used in such a way as to create sustained and major apprehension about threats to freedom from that source. In 1983 Robert McConnell, publisher of the *Montreal Gazette*, defended before a House of Commons committee 'not merely the right but the obligation' to print a story that referred to Liberal MP Bryce Mackasey as a 'paid lobbyist.'[19] The committee did not censure the *Gazette*, as Mackasey had asked, though it said that the privileges of the House were violated by the *Gazette's* articles. Members of the press stated at the time that the prospect of having to spend a few days testifying before the committee could inhibit smaller newspapers from publishing a damaging investigative story.[20]

Other kinds of government-related inducements to self-censorship stem from fear of removal of government subsidies or tax benefits.[21] A charitable organization must not engage in political lobbying, but determining what is political and what not involves some discretion. It seems clear that government subsidies and threats can provide inducements to self-censorship, but there are also examples of subsidized alternative newspapers which have attacked government policies, the Toronto paper *Guerrilla* being one such paper I remember from the early 1970s.

Another form of government influence on self-censorship is a direct appeal to a publisher. Quebec Premier Maurice Duplessis once warned a *Montreal Star* reporter, 'If you write once more that [Quebec Liberal leader Georges-Émile] Lapalme has made a fine speech, I'll have to phone my friend [*Montreal Star* publisher J.W.] McConnell.'[22] Another case of this kind of institutional self-censorship came to light only many years after the event. The story, as reported in the *Ottawa Citizen* on 18 February 1986, involved a call from then-Prime Minister John Diefenbaker, four days into the 1962 election campaign. He wanted John Bassett, publisher of the now-defunct *Toronto Telegram*, to discontinue publication of Douglas Fisher's weekly column in that paper. Both Fisher and Bassett were candidates for office, for the New Democratic Party and the Progressive Conservatives respectively. Bassett obliged and the column was discontinued for the duration of the campaign. The whole incident came to light only because Bassett was speaking on a mobile telephone in his car, making possible the taping of the call by a third party (the Royal Canadian Mounted Police being suspected of having done this). The transcript makes for humorous reading. In a concluding remark, Bassett reassures Diefenbaker about the latter's concern for secrecy: 'Nobody knows you objected. Nobody knows you called me, except you and me.'[23]

While some of the cruder forms of political influence seem to have abated, the above examples give some indication of the enormous range of government power to intimidate the press into self-censorship. Should the threats become overpowering, it may be questioned whether 'self-censorship,' as distinct from ordinary censorship, is involved. Kin-ming Liu, vice-chair of the Hong Kong Journalists Association, has argued that Hong Kong editors currently are so subservient to Beijing's will that the word 'censorship' rather than 'self-censorship' should be applied.[24]

Ownership

One form of institutional self-censorship occurs when the aim is to protect a perceived interest of the owner of a given publication. In Canada, as in the United States, the practice appears to have been more common, or at least more explicit, earlier this century than today. John DeMott writes about newspapers under K.C. Irving in New Brunswick that 'the newspaper executives didn't have to be told what K.C. wanted; they just instinctively understood. They kept vigilant watch over the shoulders of the reporters, rewrite men and editorial writers to ensure that nothing that they thought would disturb their owner darkened the pages of their papers' and 'when Tom Drummie was at the helm of the Saint John dailies, the fact that the Irving interests ranked over everyone else's was baldly stated in the newsroom.'[25] Supposedly things have changed since then, but at the time of the Royal Commission on Newspapers hearings in 1981, Commissioner Borden Spears noted an incident where an Irving paper relegated news, adverse to Irving interests, to the obscurity of the obituary pages.[26]

According to Richard (later Senator) Doyle, long-time editor of the *Globe and Mail*, Canadian newspapers underwent a change in character around the time of the Second World War. Prior to that, he said, newspapers were the instrument of an owner and his publisher. Usually a town would have two newspapers, one of which was Conservative, the other Liberal. The *Globe* had been Reform in its politics and Presbyterian in its religion. In those days there was nothing dishonourable about 'hiding all your warts,' as he said in response to my request for examples of self-censorship.[27] But by the 1960s there were attempts by newspapers to appeal to audiences across the board. In particular, Senator Doyle said, Oakley Dalgleish, publisher of the *Globe*, made it clear that while he, Dalgleish, would be involved in politicking, he did not want his editor to do any politicking for him. This background is helpful for understanding Senator Doyle's reference, in his book, *Hurly-Burly*, to the treatment accorded a self-censoring initiative on the paper: 'A *Globe* reporter once held back on reporting a scandal of which he was aware because the story might offend a close friend of the publisher. He was moved to a job where he could no longer make foolish judgments.'[28] The reason the reporter was 'foolish' was that the paper had to fight the general assumption among the public that the newspaper was an instrument of the publisher.[29] Other media observers have noted the phenomenon of reporters being 'more royalist that the king,' in other words, sensing more in the way of policy demands than publishers actually intended.[30]

Conrad Black has revealed, in his autobiography, important instances where he deliberately used his publishing acquisitions for political ends. For example: 'I reasoned *Saturday Night* could be transformed into a somewhat authoritative publication, should that be our wish, but that it would be useful at the least in neutralising or rallying opinion in the rather conformist Canlit fraternity. I had in the back of my thoughts a possible bid for Southams and, in that event, would not have wished English Canada's entire published intelligentsia becoming too vocally hostile.'[31] That Black should change the political orientation of the magazine does not, in itself, bespeak self-censorship. But it is hard to reconcile earlier publication of a rigged poll in one of his newspapers, and silence about its non-scientific character, with sound journalistic principles. His failure to reveal the character of his 'poll' would constitute prima facie grounds for the existence of self-censorship.[32] More important, journalists looking for long tenure in his enterprises would surely have a motive for soft-pedalling views he is known to dislike, a situation ripe for self-censorship.

Another example of apparent publisher influence on self-censorship involved the downplaying, in the *Toronto Star* on 28 February 1981, of an acquisition by Torstar Corporation's (owner of the *Star*) Metrospan of a rival chain of weekly newspapers called Inland.[33] Sometimes the evidence for self-censorship is only circumstantial. Significant issues of monopoly control were arguably underplayed in the *Globe and Mail*'s coverage, on 24 February 1981, of Thomson Newspapers' bid for an important interest in the paper manufacturer Abitibi-Price.[34]

Some publishers are of the 'hands on' variety and others are not. Charles King, for many years associate editor of the *Ottawa Citizen*, speaks highly of his freedom under Southam and their defence of him against what he believes were the entreaties of Prime Minister John Diefenbaker to have him fired, although he believes that at least a couple of his editors were 'beholden' to Mr. Diefenbaker.[35] King told me: 'The one and only time when I had a column killed was when I chose to make fun of our opposition, the *Ottawa Journal*, which I used to label "Brand X." Bob Southam asked me – asked, I emphasize – to kill the column because he didn't like to admit the *Journal's* existence, and didn't want to get into a war of words with an opponent whose existence he refused to recognize.'[36]

The feeling of freedom, expressed by King, may be due in no small part to a sharing of ideological outlook with publishers and editors. Boyce Richardson, a left-wing film-maker and author and a long-time foreign correspondent for the *Montreal Star*, tells a different story. He recalls that writers were instructed around the 1950s not to use the term 'Sugar' in the name 'Sugar Ray Robinson,' apparently because it was thought to cause image problems for the sugar refinery owned by the newspaper's publisher.[37] On another occasion, Richardson was assigned a story about a man who lived to be 101. He found out that the man never ate meat and drew attention to this in the lead paragraph. The city editor at the time asked him if he might rewrite the lead paragraph. 'We've had trouble with Canada Packers before,' he said.[38] Even when there is no overt pressure, with self-censorship we deal with perceptions and impressions, as noted earlier. Subtle considerations, such as the possibility of getting facts wrong, may lead a wary reporter or newspaper to avoid tackling a risky subject.

Faced with trying to have material published by conservative editors and publishers of the *Montreal Star* around the 1950s, Richardson explains how he developed his own particular method for reaching readers with his more left-wing message:

One of my techniques of avoidance was that over those many years I became rather skilled in the arts of ambiguity, writing in such a way as to suggest things that the paper would not knowingly print, but that the thicker brains handling the copy might not catch. The apex of my slyness came when I reported one day on the bizarre visit to Montreal of Fidel Castro a few months after he took office. One of my bosses congratulated me. 'I see you don't think much of our friend Castro,' he said approvingly, greatly to my surprise, for I had really admired the man. On the same evening, a couple of more perspicacious readers who had picked up what I was really trying to say phoned me to ask how the devil I had ever got such a story into that conservative newspaper.[39]

Richardson says that he felt no satisfaction in having learned to master the special mode of writing that would enable him to be published: 'I have to say that this mastery of ambiguity is a self-destructive art that I wish I had never learned. Following the death of my career as a staff journalist it took me years to discover how to say again what I really mean.'[40] His experience bears comparison with that of Mark Twain, and the genesis of Twain's ironic style, as described by Shelley Fisher Fishkin.[41]

When publishers claim that they give their editors a free hand, the record sometimes indicates otherwise. Rupert Murdoch took control of *The Times* and the *Sunday Times* of London at the start of 1981 amid much fanfare about editorial independence. Readers of the *New Statesman* of 30 January 1981 read, however, that the very editorials proclaiming this editorial freedom had been vetted by Murdoch himself.

A significant case of at least potential publisher influence over newspapers was that of the sustained advertising campaign, conducted by Ontario members of the Canadian Daily Newspaper Association and the Ontario Community Newspaper Association, against the pro-labour amendment to the Ontario Labour Relations Act, Bill 40, in the fall of 1992. It would be a bold editor or reporter who would write favourably of Bill 40 following such a vehemently expressed collective opinion by newspaper publishers. Admittedly, Jim Coyle, then Queen's Park correspondent for the *Ottawa Citizen*, did question the advertisements ('Labour Act reform: Have media compromised credibility with ads?' 22 September 1992). But a lengthy content analysis by Edward Silva makes a case for the existence of bias against Bill 40 in Toronto newspapers.[42]

Clear examples of self-censorship are to be prized, just because of the general difficulty of detecting them. The general problem is likely to be much greater than can be documented.

Defamation

If there is one area in which the press admit, more or less freely, to self-censorship, it is that of libel. Even giant corporations south of the border, such as the

American Broadcasting Company and the Columbia Broadcasting System, have backed down in the face of huge actual or anticipated legal actions by tobacco companies.[43] Thus, there was some consternation in the Canadian media when the Church of Scientology of Toronto lost its case before the Supreme Court of Canada in a decision on 20 July 1995. The court upheld a $1.6-million judgment against the Church of Scientology, including $500,000 in aggravated damages and $800,000 in punitive damages. A Media Coalition had argued in favour of capping the amount of the damages, on the ground that without a cap, 'libel chill' would inhibit freedom of expression in the press. It is not difficult to see why. Defending such a case is already expensive. If added to this is a potentially huge payment on losing, few would want to take the risk even with a high probability of winning. Under such circumstances the maxim, 'when in doubt, leave it out,' tends to come into play. The Coalition would have liked a cap on punitive damages, such as the United States Supreme Court affirmed in 1996.[44]

In the Scientology case, the court took account instead of what seems to me a sound argument that if there were a cap, anyone with sufficiently deep pockets could libel another with relative impunity. As I read the case, the malice and conscious disregard of truth was so blatant that any journalist concerned only to make the truth known should have no disincentive from that particular court ruling. But, of course, if publishers, editors, and writers look only at the amount of money and not at the details of the case they could easily be intimidated.

It is worth noting that, in presenting its case, the Media Coalition did not feel it necessary to provide evidence of libel chill. It acknowledged that the evidence would be anecdotal, since statistics are not available in the nature of things, but argued that 'evidence is not needed to show the deterrent effect of libel law on the publication of stories critical of individuals and corporations. The deterrent effect is a necessary and intended result of the law.'[45] The admission is useful. It tells us that large financial implications have an impact on what and how things are reported. If that is so, we have a basis for supposing that large financial implications of other kinds than libel might have a similar impact.

The kind of experience *Toronto Life* went through, following a suit by the Reichmann brothers over an article about the family by Elain Dewar in 1988, would likely discourage anyone contemplating further exposés on the rich and powerful. The suit was for $102 million and has been described as 'one of the most notorious and certainly one of the most costly libel cases in Canadian history ... The settlement ... forced the publishers to apologise and donate a substantial sum of money to charity.'[46]

Senator Doyle acknowledges that libel considerations led him to kill a story concerning payola, illegal gambling, and babies for sale that an investigative reporter for the *Globe and Mail*, Harold Greer, had spent six months preparing. The story made allegations of scandal involving the Ontario Provincial Police and the attorney general, and the *Globe*'s lawyer advised that the paper could be sued for all it was worth. Senator Doyle says that Greer, who may have thought the publisher was trying to protect Premier Leslie Frost, resigned and went to work for John Wintermeyer, Ontario Liberal leader, in 1962, with the end result that a Royal Commission on Crime under Justice W.D. Roach was launched.[47]

Senator Doyle believes that newspapers tend to cave in too much on smaller matters, including the *Globe*'s revelation of Carswell Printing Company's slip-shod placement of sensitive unshredded budgetary documents in a garbage bag in early May 1983. The *Globe* settled a libel suit out of court for $10,000 plus $485. Doyle expressed anger at this kind of settlement. He thinks that, if the paper is wrong, it should pay money and apologize, but not otherwise. To do so breeds 'unhealthy habits.' 'It's much worse now than it was,' he said. 'The *Globe* makes money and can afford to fight battles [such as the garbage-picking one].'[48] He did not spell out the nature of the 'unhealthy habits,' but it is reasonable to assume that increased self-censorship would be among them. If journalistic principles take second place to financial considerations where libel settlements, after publication, are involved, why not also *before* potentially libellous statements are printed?

It is important to recall that, in the definition I have been using, it is not self-censorship simply to be conscientious and cautious about printing potentially defamatory material. It becomes self-censorship only when caution is taken to excess in the light of an extraneous motive, such as the desire to avoid the expense and bother of an unmeritorious lawsuit.

Advertising

Journalistic history has some alarming examples of the powers of advertisers. Zechariah Chafee, Jr has written about the fate of the *Cleveland Press* after it supported Robert La Follette's presidential campaign as a Progressive candidate in 1924. 'On the day after election, the owners purged the staff, discharging 85 men out of 103; only a few underlings were left, and a new crowd was then brought in. This was in response to a widespread withdrawal of advertising by large Cleveland stores.'[49]

Such an extreme case is unlikely today. But there is plenty of evidence that advertising influences self-censorship in magazines. A study reported in the January/February 1978 *Columbia Journalism Review* showed a wide difference in coverage of tobacco's threat to health in magazines depending on whether the publications did or did not accept tobacco advertising.[50] Over a seven-year period the author of the study, R.C. Smith, was 'unable to find a single article ... that would have given readers any clear notion of the nature and extent of the medical and social havoc being wreaked by the cigarette-smoking habit.'[51] *Reader's Digest*, which did not carry cigarette advertising, provided 'the most thorough and aggressive coverage of the links between cigarettes and disease. By contrast the 'records of national magazines that accept cigarette advertising can only be called dismal.'[52] Included in this category were *Time, Newsweek, Ladies' Home Journal, U.S. News and World Report, Penthouse*, and *Playboy*. In case there were any doubts about the matter, the article quotes an editor at *Ms.* who 'quite frankly linked *Ms.*'s failure to publish anything about cigarettes and health to the fact that the magazine is "heavily dependent on cigarette advertising."'[53]

Many journalists believe that the public has an exaggerated view about the influence of advertisers on what is written and published. The point they make is this: to sell newspapers, the readers' interests must be served, and they will not be served by distorting news in favour of commercial interests. When interviewing senior *Ottawa Citizen* editors in the summer of 1996, I was told that the newspaper declined to publish a story on the opening of a new franchise of a fast-food chain, despite being reminded by an executive of the firm that it advertised in the paper.[54] The reason the editors gave was that the story would fail to interest readers, and without readers the advertisers themselves would not be interested.

The view of Borden Spears, expressed in the 1970 report of the special Senate committee on mass media, accords with the *Citizen* editors' position.[55] He noted, however, that drug manufacturers in 1962 protested against a series of articles on over-medication in *Maclean's* magazine by Sidney Katz, one company cancelling $80,000 worth of scheduled advertising. Also, when Maclean-Hunter's *Financial Post*, shortly thereafter, commented adversely on a takeover of Canadian Oil by Shell, the president of Shell pulled *all* his company's advertising out of *all* Maclean-Hunter's publications. In both cases, Spears noted, Maclean-Hunter management stood up to the pressure. 'A struggling publisher, or one who puts profit before editorial liberty, might hesitate to risk the alienation of a major revenue source,' he said.[56] But he added that such overt interference is seldom attempted.

When newspapers are deluged with advertising, such as Bell Canada's sponsorship of an issue of the *Financial Post* in August 1996, it is difficult to believe that the editorial content will be completely unaffected. Marina Strauss remarked in a *Globe and Mail* article: 'The *Post* edition raises thorny questions about the potential of advertisers to erode journalistic integrity – and independence – if the very existence of the editorial product becomes so dependent on one company.'[57] The *Ottawa Citizen* carried over five full pages of Bell Canada advertising the same day, 19 August 1996, which coincided with the beginning of hearings before the CRTC on matters affecting Bell's ability to compete with cable and other telecommunications systems. The *Ottawa Sun* the same day had a four-page insert with its own logo on the front and the headline 'Telecommunications.' It looked like a *Sun* news story or editorial, but a call to the newspaper revealed that the material had been supplied by Bell Canada. This seemed to me in violation of the Canadian Code of Advertising Standards, in particular clause 2: 'No advertisement shall be presented in a format or style which conceals its commercial intent.' I lodged a complaint with the Canadian Advertising Foundation and my complaint was upheld.

The rise of so-called 'advertorials,' advertising supplements that mimic news content, pits journalistic integrity against the profit-maximizing forces in a newspaper. This situation would seem to be ripe for encouraging self-censorship. Special care is also needed in the case of tobacco interests. Imperial Tobacco may not be allowed to engage in lifestyle advertising, but its controlling company, Imasco, also owns Shoppers Drug Mart/Pharmaprix and Canada Trustco, both of which are regular newspaper advertisers. Kraft and General Foods with their subsidiaries are other major advertisers under the control of Philip Morris, the U.S. tobacco manufacturer. When Ontario sought to ban tobacco sales from drug stores, a Shoppers Drug Mart official was quoted in some newspapers as opposing the law, without the tobacco connection in the ownership structure being identified.[58] The question is left open whether this was simple oversight or the kind of oversight which lucrative advertising helps to foster. There are other cases of this kind. *Saturday Night* carried tobacco-sponsorship advertising prior to the October 1997 issue, with an occasional tobacco-sympathetic article. Similarly, when I did a critique of what I argued was a misleading series of three tobacco-industry advocacy advertisements (against Bill C-71, later enacted as the Tobacco Act of 1997) each taking up over half a page in major newspapers across Canada, only the *Montreal Gazette*, among eight papers, chose to publish it.[59]

A highly revealing episode in the history of tobacco influence on publishing is recounted in the March/April 1996 of *Mother Jones*. Not long after the founding of this left-wing publication the editorial board had to decide whether to accept tobacco advertising, and it voted 3-2 to do so on the ground that it did not want to act as censors to free expression. To show they were not going to be influenced, however, the board members commissioned a powerful exposé on the deadly effects of smoking, stressing the addictive effect of nicotine ('Why Dick Can't Stop Smoking,' January 1979). As is customary, the magazine gave the tobacco industry advanced warning, so it could pull their ads for that issue.

(This practice, of course, provides a clear disincentive for magazines to run such articles.) But the response was more extreme than anticipated. 'Philip Morris, Brown & Williamson, and others responded by cancelling their entire commitment: several years' worth of cigarette ads. In a show of corporate solidarity, many liquor companies followed suit.'[60]

A blatant attempt at influencing newspaper coverage through advertising occurred in 1986 when the federal Energy Department offered newspapers across the country a lucrative advertising deal if they would agree to publish a number of government articles. If the aim was to obtain a more general compliance, it clearly failed in at least a number of instances.[61]

My impression is that advertiser-friendly copy has been on the increase in Canada in recent years, with an upsurge in special advertising supplements. The danger is that the normal editorial process will be undermined. As Ronald Collins has written, 'advertiser-friendly stories require, by definition, the suppression of any unfriendly information, however correct or consequential.'[62]

Sources and Publicists

Another important motive, beside the economic one, for engaging in self-censorship relates to maintaining good relations with significant news sources. Dramatic examples of this kind of self-censorship are apparent in the United States, notably the Pentagon in time of war. Robert Fisk claims that reporters who refused to join the American 'pool' of reporters during the Gulf War 'often sent dispatches back to their newspapers which were both more graphic – and more truthful – than television reports emerging from the "pool."' U.S. television networks conformed to the pool restrictions, he thinks, because of their need for good pictures. 'Pictures were the only and all-immediate commodity, more important than the moral issue of refusing to be censored.'[63] The reporting had to be safe and patriotic to maintain the supply of such pictures.

In some cases, the motive for self-censorship can be a simple quid pro quo. Senator Richard Doyle describes how a British official, Lord Moran, reacted to a *Globe and Mail* request for an interview with Margaret Thatcher. The interview would be possible, the *Globe* was told, but only if it gave more favourable coverage than it had been doing. The demand sought in effect a kind of self-censorship, but it was resisted.[64] The story is revealing, however, about the kind of pressures that can exist. Barbara Rogers, in a study by the United Nations Educational, Scientific and Cultural Organization (UNESCO), gives an indication of a similar general policy in operation at the British Foreign and Commonwealth Office via daily press conferences. As she explains, 'although access to these press conferences is fairly easy, it is a privilege which could be withdrawn if the correspondent published something which seriously embarrassed the government.'[65] Peter Stoler is one among many White House observers who have noted that a reporter deviates from the official line at his or her peril.[66]

Sources may also be incompletely identified with a view to obscuring facts that would undermine the credibility of a story. Dalton Camp, a writer and prominent Progressive Conservative Party theorist, once brought such an incident to light in a column for the *Toronto Sun*, on 1 November 1984. He took the *Globe and Mail* to task for its choice of experts advising what should be done following the alleged discovery of marijuana in Premier Richard Hatfield's valise. The *Globe* had quoted Professor Dan Hurley of the University of New Brunswick Law School as saying that there was no doubt Premier Hatfield had received special treatment from the RCMP, that the RCMP should press charges, and that the premier should resign. Camp's point was that the *Globe* should have pointed out that 'Prof. Hurley has twice run as a provincial Liberal candidate and also lost. He is a past president of the York County Liberal Association.'

Sources may be incompletely identified for political reasons, or for reasons of journalistic prestige. Prestige can be at stake where leaks are concerned. If a newspaper gets a hot story handed to it on a platter in an anonymous brown envelope, it may prefer not to mention this fact. To reveal that sensational materials were unsolicited might detract from the impression of careful sleuthing by intrepid reporting staff. The late Sydney Freifeld, both a Canadian ambassador and a talented media analyst, has argued that a newspaper should reveal as much about the circumstances of a leak as it can without violating a commitment to the author of the leak.[67] Thus, if anonymity were guaranteed to the source, the publisher should provide as much information as would be possible without giving away the identity of the source. The reason has to do with a commitment to properly informing readers. The more circumstances are revealed, the better position the reader will be in to judge the motivation for the leak, and therefore to weigh its overall veracity. The leak is a common tool of media manipulation by government or business.

When the price of access is the sharing of confidential information, the opportunity arises for news manipulation on a large scale. The independent journalist I.F. Stone deliberately avoided using highly placed sources who would give not-for-publication backgrounders, because he saw this as corrupting of the journalistic mission. The journalist would be made to feel important, a kind of statesman, wining and dining with the history makers. But the result would often be self-censorship and a belief that the public ought not to know certain things about the workings of government policy.[68] Bob Woodward, of Watergate fame, confirms this practice in an offhand way in *Veil: The Secret*

Wars of the CIA 1981–1987, referring to Admiral Bobby Ray Inman: 'He was one of the few intelligence officials who would talk to reporters and get them to hold off on stories that compromised intelligence.'[69] James Reston is an example of a top-level Washington correspondent, for the *New York Times*, who was taken into confidence, withholding news about U2 flights and about the impending Bay of Pigs invasion in 1961. Reston believed, however, that he was right in suppressing the information, and there is a basis for robust debate about whether his action did or did not constitute 'self-censorship' as I have defined the term.[70] (The question would hinge on whether sound journalistic and moral principles could justify the action, as distinct from an appeal to prudential but extraneous considerations such as maintaining good relations with his news sources. 'Self-censorship' would be appropriate to the latter, but not the former situation, in the definition I have proposed.)

In Japan, reporters are said to have close ties with politicians and business people through special clubs. *The Times* of London reports: 'The 12,000 members of the 400 such clubs can be relied upon not to break any news that might embarrass their principal news source; to do so would be to ensure that they were henceforth barred from the club and any other they might try to join.'[71]

Lower on the scale of importance, but not negligible, are inducements in the form of 'freebies,' free meals, drinks, gifts, or the like. Influence from sources can come from the threat of being cut off from the list of recipients. Some light was thrown on Canadian practice in the 1978 Ontario Press Council study, 'Press Ethics and Freebies.' John McCallum, a Ryerson journalism teacher, revealed some of the kinds of inducements offered to reporters while he was practising journalism. These included the annual Sportsman's Show in Toronto and a ferry ride with drink provided by Metro Toronto and Ontario Hydro, which, 'with the biggest public relations organisation in the country, puts on a big freeload' at the annual Canadian National Exhibition. 'I have benefited,' McCallum said, 'but I think they are wrong. We all know we are expected to say things *and not to say things* because we get these benefits.'[72] A more recent example, involving expenses-paid offers to journalists, is described in a *New York Times* article on Walt Disney World in 1986.[73]

Readers and Organized Groups

Newspapers can afford to stand up to unreasonable demands of individual advertisers, but an organized boycott is something different. 'Cancel my subscription' is an idle threat from a few individuals, but not when it approaches a tidal wave. Readers and advertisers will tolerate, indeed welcome, the occasional gadfly article. But a sustained assault on the deeply held and cherished beliefs and values of its readers or advertisers is likely to be suicidal. Community newspapers sometimes rely on the good will of volunteer deliverers. Causing offence to a large section of volunteers could result in the demise of a publication. Editors and publishers know this, and they realize that there is a limit to how far and soon they can promote ideas which they believe are right but which are likely to cause offence to their audience. Long-established principles of rhetoric dictate a measure of caution in trying to persuade an audience of views contrary to those they hold. 'Editorial discretion' or 'accommodating speech'[74] are phrases that come to mind more readily than 'self-censorship,' in such cases, and such a way of speaking seems to me compatible with the definition I have proposed. Those less sensitive to rhetorical needs, who feel that the unvarnished truth should be stated boldly, whatever the audience reaction, are entitled to argue that 'accommodating speech' is indeed self-censorship. It seems to me a merit of the definition I have presented, and not a defect, that it can provide a focal point for such debate.

It has been observed[75] that Mark Twain's ironic style frequently involved writing from the standpoint of a person sharing the prejudices of the reader. He would take the prejudices to a ridiculous extreme in such a way that all but the most obtuse or hard-hearted readers would feel a tug towards decency. To some, this guarded form of expression might seem to involve a lack of candour and hence be a form of 'self-censorship.' The better opinion seems to me to view Twain's approach as accommodating truth, or what one believes to be such, to a readership so as to communicate it in a way most likely to succeed. But, as Boyce Richardson indicates, the sustained practice of truth 'accommodation' can also be demoralizing.

Should a newspaper or other publication show an inconsistency in its approach to two different situations, where the underlying principles governing them would seem to be the same but where public opinion is greatly at variance, we have reason to suspect self-censorship. A case to bear in mind in this context is the Toronto *Globe and Mail*'s reaction, or rather non-reaction, to the refusal by the Toronto Transit Commission (TTC) to carry an advertisement for the Toronto Right to Life Association in 1981. The advertisement showed a toy soldier with a tear falling down its cheek. The caption stated: 'Some toys will have less children to play with this year – some 65,000 aborted children less.' The advertisement was originally accepted by the TTC Board, and a $3,780-cheque for the advertising space was cashed, before the decision was reversed.[76] The reversal followed presentations by the Canadian Abortion Rights Action League and others, and a strong editorial in the Toronto *Sunday Star* ('Withdraw offensive TTC ad') on 8 November 1981.

One point at issue in this case is whether the desire not to cause offence should outweigh the need to present, with emotional force, what one body of opinion sees as something wrong in society that needs to be corrected. It is important that a criterion, such as bad taste, for withholding publication (viewing the advertisement as a 'publication' in this context) not be used as a pretext for refusing material should the real objection be fear of public reaction to an unpopular message.

Transferring the argument to a different set of cases, we may note that Robert Fisk has argued against the sanitizing of news from war zones, and in favour of showing pictures that relay the horror involved, as a way of mobilizing public opinion to counter the causes of such strife. Such pictures may offend people, but offence is preferable to ignorance in these matters, he says.[77]

Clearly the abortion case differs from the case discussed by Fisk, in that abortion is a matter about which opinion, in Canada at least, is profoundly divided. But the war example should serve to show that the issues are deep and far-reaching, and that perceived offensiveness ought not always to be the finally determining factor.

The same point can be made in relation to a *Globe and Mail* advertisement showing what appeared to be a cancer patient screaming in agony, 'Please help! I beg you!' and stating, 'What a tragedy every Canadian can't hear the screams and feel the pain of terminal cancer patients' (Dead patients can't smell roses, 10 June 1988). The advertisement, by the W. Gifford-Jones Foundation, was aimed at supporting portable pumps delivering programmed doses of narcotics. This advertisement also might be viewed as causing anguish to people newly diagnosed as with cancer, to people in remission, and to relatives of cancer patients.[78]

A newspaper that is willing to publish such advertisements would owe its readers an explanation were it to support the TTC ban on the Toy Soldier advertisement referred to above. At the time, however, the *Globe and Mail* was editorially silent about the TTC decision. This omission was all the more striking in that the newspaper, earlier in 1981, had thundered against pressure groups, such as the Coalition for Better Television, causing Procter and Gamble to withdraw support for a number of television offerings. The editorial proclaimed, 'There is only one value being espoused by these groups, and it is censorship. And that, coalitions and leagues of decency notwithstanding, is ugly and immoral.'[79] My point in all this is not to take a position for or against the TTC decision, the showing of gory war pictures, or the depiction of screaming cancer patients. My point is simply to draw attention, first, to the interconnectedness of the issues, and second, to the way in which the *Globe*'s position illustrates the possibility of a certain kind self-censorship, even though there might be facts counting against inferring its existence in the present case. The *Globe* might have had acceptable reasons for remaining silent, though when I raised the issue at the time my letter went unpublished and unanswered.

Ethics and Public Policy

Even if we think of self-censorship in a negative sense, the questions of ethics are not foreclosed. The verb 'to lie' and cognates, for example, also have a negative connotation, but only a few ethicists would maintain that lying is never justifiable morally.

Where self-censorship is wrong, the wrongness stems from avoidance of a journalist's duty, in a democracy, to report, for example, socially relevant wrongdoing wherever there is appropriate evidence of its existence; or, since wrongness is not always obvious, to report on significant facts which will enable a reader to make his or her own informed judgment about possible wrongdoing. Self-censorship may be done through cowardice, venality, or some other unworthy motive. The disgraceful soft-pedalling of the deadliness and addictiveness of cigarettes is a case in point. Or it may be done through an elitist sense that the people really are not able to judge facts properly and should not be told certain things because it might affect their judgment adversely. There are sometimes laudable motives, such as the desire to reduce ethnic violence, which lead journalists and their editors to withhold reports that might further inflame a violent mood among the public.

Even so, there are strong arguments in favour of going ahead with such reports. A set of guidelines for journalists covering ethnic conflicts was issued recently, and it was excerpted in *Nieman Reports* in the spring of 1994. The guidelines were a result of a cooperative project between member countries of the former Soviet Union and the United States. One of the questions asked by the group was, 'Can self-censorship or government censorship of potentially explosive news ever be justified?'[80] Their answer tends towards the negative, based on empirical realities. They acknowledge that media coverage 'often has an effect upon the level of conflict,' but they are against the idea that 'removing the media reports will reduce the level of conflict.'[81] Their point is that censoring will have worse effects. Journalists, to have any effect, need first of all to have the trust of their audience, and if they lose this through suppressing facts their efforts will have been 'misplaced and counterproductive.'[82] There is evidence that, where established news disseminators are not believed, people will turn to alternate, and sometimes unscrupulous, alternative sources, including 'propagandists and traditional rumour networks.' There is also the point that with modern alternative means of communication – faxes and the Internet come to mind as obvious examples – self-censorship as well as the more common kind are not likely to work. The group accepts the position taken by John Stuart Mill, namely, that when an angry mob is gathered outside a grain dealer's house, it would be wrong to proclaim that he is a starver of children since this would be likely to incite a riot. But, equally, they note that the application of this principle by Oliver Wendell Holmes, Jr of the U.S. Supreme Court resulted in criminalizing the speech of draft-resisters in the First World War.[83] The upshot is that well-motivated assaults on free speech need to be treated with more diffidence in the light of their practical applications. And ostensibly sound motivations may serve as a camouflage for cowardice or lazy neglect of establishing the true situation. Martin Bell's observations about the loss of influence by the BBC as a result of failing to report relevant details ('the whole truth') are pertinent. 'If you shade the truth, as I had done, there will be nobody out there watching.'[84]

But what constitutes 'shading the truth'? Is there to be no thought given to the possible social consequences of publishing gruesome and inflammatory materials? Or to the violation of the dignity of individuals who become, at a time of catastrophe, a subject for public attention? A reflex policy of ignoring such questions, on the ground that they will involve the news industry in making moral judgments and thus becoming elitist, does not seem right either. What needs careful watching is whether the criteria for self-censorship are applied in an even-handed way, and not selectively invoked to the detriment of a particular disfavoured group or groups.

One example where 'shading the truth' seems desirable is where the public has stereotyped views on certain minority groups in society. An effort to combat false stereotypes may be desirable – not to the point of falsifying reality, but at least of not highlighting facts that will only encourage a distortion which already exists. The motive of social responsibility can be perverted, of course, into priggery, and self-serving motives can come with a gloss of social responsibility which is deceiving. What is important is for the journalist, editor, and publisher to be alive to the variegated pressures to depart from their central mission, and to do an honest job of informing the public notwithstanding those pressures. That different individuals will come to different conclusions about what constitutes an 'honest job' will come as no surprise. But everyone can recognize certain principles of fairness, and the need for insulation from inducements by special interests to depart from them.

Of the various public-policy measures that have been suggested[85] to reduce the conditions that give rise to self-censorship, the following seem to have merit. First, there should be a concerted effort to reverse the path where ownership of the media has come to be dominated by a few individuals. Second, the problem of self-censorship needs to be more widely publicized. Third, a body should exist to keep track of instances of self-censorship, noting the extraneous inducements involved. A documentation centre is needed. Fourth, advertising in any form should be clearly identifiable as such. More problematic are suggestions for a whistle-blower law, to prevent adverse treatment of an employee who reveals a hidden conflict of interest in a media outlet. How can such a law be drafted that is both effective and yet does not lend itself to misuse by someone seeking job security? I do not agree with the suggestion that withdrawal of advertising, as a way of protesting against media content, should be made illegal. If I do not like the views of Howard Stern, I do not see why I should be compelled to continue advertising in a radio station that carries him.

More important than any specific legislative measure, which may have unwanted ramifications, is for the public to appreciate the existence and nature of the problem. The path of self-censorship is a slippery slope described by Václav Havel, the president of the Czech Republic. He described the effect of years of living under totalitarian rule: 'The worst thing is that we live in a contaminated moral environment. We fell morally ill because we became used to saying something different from what we thought. The danger is self-censorship growing by degrees, changing the spirit of journalism and education from that of challenge and enlightenment to one of conformity with power.'[86] He was talking about life under socialism, but corporate, capitalist society has its own norms. Societal pressures towards conformity in thought and expression are not limited to any given creed.

NOTES

1 Quoted in Phillip Knightley, *The First Casualty* (London: Deutsch 1975), 333.
2 Florence Hartmann, 'Les maux de l'information,' *Le Monde*, 9 April 1997.
3 For example, James Winter, *Democracy's Oxygen* (Montreal: Black Rose Books 1997); Warren Breed, *The Newspaperman, News and Society* (New York: Arno Press 1980); and Ronald K.L. Collins, *Dictating Content: How Advertising Pressure Can Corrupt a Free Press* (Washington: Center for the Study of Commercialism 1992), 41.
4 I owe this point to Wendy Donner. Thanks also to Robert Stainton for the next point.
5 The 'Statement of Principles' can be obtained from the Canadian Newspaper Association, 890 Yonge St., Suite 1100, Toronto, Ont. M5W 3P4.
6 Frank Giles, 'Obstructions to the Free Flow of Information,' United Nations Educational, Scientific and Cultural Organization (UNESCO), International Commission for the Study of Communication Problems (Paris), *Study* 52 (1978), 10.

7 Ibid., 11.
8 I owe this point to Senator Richard Doyle.
9 H.G. Classen, *The Time Is Never Ripe* (Ottawa: Centaur Press 1972), 184.
10 An example taken from Breed *The Newspaperman*, 128.
11 Robert Fisk, from a public lecture given at Carleton University, 18 April 1997.
12 Martin Bell, *In Harm's Way* (London: Hamish Hamilton 1995), 205–6.
13 Edward S. Herman and Noam Chomsky, *Manufacturing Consent: The Political Economy of the Mass Media* (New York: Pantheon Books 1988), 2. For a fuller account of the different pressures within the newsroom situation, see Breed, *The Newspaperman*.
14 See Conrad Black, *A Life in Progress* (Toronto: Key Porter Books 1995), 303.
15 The specific topic of official censorship is dealt with elsewhere in this volume.
16 The statement of the proposals is contained in the document 'Government Proposals on Freedom of the Press in Relation to the Canadian Daily Newspaper Industry,' by James Fleming, minister of state, 25 May 1982.
17 For an indication of the threat, and publishers' reactions, see Ian Mulgrew, 'Accept Ottawa's press plan or face law, publishers told,' *Globe and Mail*, 23 September 1982. As an example of earlier resistance to press councils, see the editorial, 'No unanimity on a bad idea,' *Globe and Mail*, 25 April 1972.
18 See Peter Desbarats, *Guide to Canadian News Media* (Toronto: Harcourt Brace Jovanovich 1990), 155.
19 James Rusk, 'Ex-publisher defends stories on Mackasey,' *Globe and Mail*, 21 October 1983.
20 Robert Winters, 'Press "shouldn't be intimidated" by report on Mackasey,' *Ottawa Citizen*, 2 December 1983, 14.
21 Brian Maracle, 'Erola assails newsletter art,' *Globe and Mail*, 23 September 1983, 421.
22 Pierre Laporte, *The True Face of Duplessis*, (Montreal: Harvest House 1960), 131.
23 *Ottawa Citizen*, 18 February 1986.
24 Kin-ming Liu, 'Hong Kong's "self-censorship" myth,' *Ottawa Citizen*, 29 September 1997, A13.
25 John DeMont, *Citizens Irving* (Toronto: Doubleday 1992).
26 Royal Commission on Newspapers, transcripts, 7356.
27 Private interview with Senator Richard Doyle, Ottawa, 20 June 1996.
28 Richard Doyle, *Hurly-Burly: A Time at the Globe* (Toronto: Macmillan 1990), 318.
29 Doyle interview, 20 June 1996.
30 Breed, *The Newspaperman*. 168.
31 Conrad Black, *A Life in Progress*, 385. See also 125, 324, 365, 374, 383, 393, 422, 425–7, 431, 433, 467.
32 Ibid., 125.

33 Royal Commission on Newspapers, *Report* (Ottawa: Ministry of Supply and Services 1981), 224. See also the transcripts of commission's hearings for a more complete examination of the issues at stake in Metrospan's take-over of Inland; the testimony of Beland Honderich, chairman of Torstar, is at 6009–50.

34 See my '"Freedom of press" can have its blind spots,' *Ottawa Citizen*, 5 March 1981.

35 Charles King, private communication to the author, 28 June 1996.

36 Ibid.

37 Interview with Boyce Richardson, Ottawa, 26 February 1997.

38 Ibid.

39 Boyce Richardson, 'Oh, sure, editorial writers are free ... Aren't They?' submitted to the *Ottawa Citizen*, 6 January 1991, but rejected.

40 Ibid.

41 Shelley Fisher Fishkin, 'Twain in '85,' *New York Times*, 18 February 1985.

42 See Edward Silva, *More Perishable Than Lettuce or Tomatoes: Labour Law Reform and Toronto's Newspapers* (Halifax: Fernwood Publishers 1995).

43 See the editorial 'Self-Censorship at CBS,' *New York Times*, 12 November 1995; also, Gloria Cooper, 'Briefings,' *Columbia Journalism Review*, March/April, 1986. Lawrence K. Grossman's 'CBS, 60 Minutes and the Unseen Interview,' in the *Columbia Journalism Review* (January/February 1996), spells out threats of a somewhat different kind.

44 'U.S. court puts limit on punitive damages,' *Globe and Mail*, 21 May 1996.

45 Factum of the Media Coalition, in the Supreme Court of Canada, Court File no. 24216, 8.

46 Stevie Cameron, 'Defenders of the Pen,' *National* (publication of the Canadian Bar Association), Ottawa, May 1993, 14–17.

47 See Doyle, *Hurly-Burly*, 138–9. Other material is from the interview conducted with Senator Doyle on 20 June 1996.

48 Ibid., Doyle interview.

49 Zechariah Chafee, Jr, *Government and Mass Communications*, a report from the Commission on Freedom of the Press, vol. 2 (Chicago: University of Chicago Press 1947), 520–1.

50 R.C. Smith, 'The magazines' smoking habit,' *Columbia Journalism Review* (January/February 1978), 29–31. The *Review* states that it itself accepts cigarette advertising, giving free-speech reasons similar to those of *Mother Jones*. See n.60 below.

51 Ibid., 29–30.

52 Ibid. 30.

53 Ibid. See also Ronald Collins, *Dictating Content*. For recent examples of advertising pressure on magazines, and the response of the industry, see 'Magazine publishers circling wagons against advertisers,' *New York Times*, 29 September 1997, D1.

54 Interviews with Charles Lewis, Peter Calamai, Graham Parley, and James Travers, *Ottawa Citizen,* summer 1996. (Peter Calamai, editorial-page editor, and James Travers, editor, have since left the paper.)

55 Report of the Special Senate Committee on Mass Media, *Good, Bad, or Simply Inevitable*, Vol. 3 (Ottawa: Queen's Printer 1970), 199.

56 Ibid., 200.

57 Marina Strauss, 'When one sponsor "buys" a newspaper,' *Globe and Mail*, 15 August 1996, B9.

58 See, for example, Elizabeth Payne, 'Proposed tobacco bill going up in smoke,' *Ottawa Citizen*, 22 September 1993, A3.

59 Randal Marlin, 'Industry ads misrepresent anti-tobacco bill,' *Montreal Gazette*, 3 March 1997. The same piece was faxed to the *Globe and Mail,* the *Toronto Star,* the *Ottawa Citizen*, and the *Vancouver Sun.* A translation was sent to *Le Droit, Le Devoir*, and *La Presse.*

60 Eric Bates, 'Smoked Out,' *Mother Jones*, (March/April 1996), 27.

61 See 'Ottawa offers ads to newspapers if they print government articles,' *Globe and Mail*, 19 May 1986.

62 Robert Collins, *Dictating Content*, 32.

63 Robert Fisk, 'Threats, Lies and Videotape: Reporting the Middle East,' public lecture delivered at Carleton University, 19 April 1997. See also 'Spin Control Through Censorship: The Pentagon Manages the News,' *Extra*, published by FAIR (Fairness and Accuracy in Reporting, 175 Fifth Avenue, New York), May 1991, 14.

64 Doyle interview, 20 June 1996. This account should be compared with Doyle, *Hurly-Burly*, 465–7.

65 Barbara Rogers, "The Image Reflected by Mass Media: Manipulations,' UNESCO, International Commission for the Study of Communication Problems, *Study 58* (1979), 9.

66 Peter Stoler, *The War Against the Press* (New York: Dodd, Mead 1986), 131.

67 Freifeld expounded his theory as a guest lecturer in my course, 'Truth and Propaganda,' at Carleton University during the 1980s.

68 These ideas are expounded in the film 'I.F.Stone's Weekly,' made in New York, Philadelphia, and Amherst, Mass., 1970–3 by Jerry Bruck.

69 Bob Woodward, *Veil: The Secret Wars of the CIA 1981–87* (New York: Simon and Schuster 1987). See also, 'Reader, Beware of Press Self-Censorship,' letter, *New York Times*, 18 March 1985.

70 James Reston, *The Artillery of the Press* (New York: Harper and Row 1967), 20–1. See also Tom Wicker, *On Press* (New York: Viking 1978), 261.

71 David Watts, 'No club, no comment,' *The Times* (London), 13 January 1988, 30.

72 John McCallum, testimony in *Press Ethics and Freebies: Should Newspapers or Their Employees Accept Free Services and Gifts?* (Ottawa: Ontario Press Council

October 1978), 28. Emphasis added. See also Michael Clow with Susan Machum, *Stifling Debate: Canadian Newspapers and Nuclear Power* (Halifax: Fernwood Publishers 1993).

73 Alex S. Jones, 'Many journalists accepting "no strings" offer by Disney,' *New York Times*, 16 September 1986.

74 There is an interesting paper on this subject, 'Double Truth,' presented in 1878 to the Metaphysical Society, London, by the rector of Lincoln College, Oxford, Mark Pattison, and held in the British Museum Library.

75 By Shelley Fisher Fishkin; see 'Twain in '85.'

76 See the *Catholic Register*, 28 November 1981 ('Toronto transit rejects poster after women's groups protest,' by Mark Terry), 3.

77 Robert Fisk, 'Threats, Lies and Videotape.'

78 See Richard B. Stern, M.D., 'Agonizing ad,' letter, *Globe and Mail*, 30 June 1988.

79 Editorial, 'Sponsor to censor,' *Globe and Mail*, 22 June 1981; and Randal Marlin, 'Not all censorship immoral, says Ottawa reader,' *Globe and Mail*, 24 June 1981.

80 Bruce J. Allyn, et al., 'Proposed Guidelines for Journalists Covering Ethnic Conflicts,' *Nieman Reports* (spring 1994), 79.

81 Ibid., 80.

82 Ibid.

83 Ibid.

84 Bell, *In Harm's Way*, 207.

85 What follows are some of the suggestions found in Ronald Collins's *Dictating Content*, 57–60.

86 Václav Havel, 'New Year's Address,' 1990, in *Open Letters, Selected Prose* (London: Faber and Faber 1991), 391.

15

Censorship by Inadvertence?
Selectivity in the Production of TV News

LYDIA MILJAN AND BARRY COOPER

Several years ago the sociologist Herbert Gans observed that journalists 'almost always have more available information than they can use.'[1] What they use, therefore, is selected. News production is essentially, not accidentally, a matter of selection. Selection, in turn, is constrained, which immediately introduces the question of criteria: on what grounds is information selected and used? This question brings us to the heart of any TV news show, the producer.

As the title indicates, his or her job is to *produce* the news. During the early days of British Broadcasting Corporation (BBC) television, the story goes, one news-reader ended the news hour after forty minutes with the announcement, 'There is no further news today.' The remaining twenty minutes featured light music to accompany the BBC test pattern. If such a thing happened today, the producer would be fired for non-performance of duty.

To say news is produced is to say that events and information are not news. The legendary BBC announcer was claiming that he had no further information to convey about significant events; more boldly, he was claiming that the shortened newscast accounted for all events of significance. However strange it may seem today when news has become a post-industrial commodity, the BBC announcer did draw attention to an important point: news is *of* events. The preposition indicates an action by a reporter or producer of selection and transformation.

The title of this chapter refers first of all, then, to the selection process. We do not wish to imply that specific producers and reporters never have political agendas or that they never choose their angles or hooks or storylines in order to advance those agendas. On occasion, there is no doubt that reporters do have an explicit political message, and that they try to convey it. In his long and detailed study of the American media during the 1960s and 1970s, for example, David Halberstam wrote: 'Once, during the mid-sixties, Perry Walff, a producer on sabbatical, called his friend Marya McLaughlin. "What are you doing today?"

he asked. "Trying to decide whether or not to cover a demonstration which wouldn't be taking place if we didn't cover it," she answered.'[2]

Such decisions may even occur on a regular basis. They are not evidence of censorship in the classic sense of government action, but they are deliberate, not inadvertent, decisions. Moreover, they will have the same consequences as deliberate censorship by the state insofar as such decisions may prevent the diffusion of information to citizens or other interested parties.[3] Interest groups, for example, often monitor each other's media coverage to assure that their demonstrations are given the same or equal attention as those of their opponents. *B.C. Report*, known for its small-c conservative views and Christian beliefs, often criticizes the mainstream media for not providing pro-life demonstrations with the same attention as pro-choice demonstrations. In making its claim, the magazine often points to news decisions that were based on an inverse relationship between the number of protesters and the newsworthiness of the demonstration. That is, when smaller pro-choice demonstrations are given more, and more prominent, attention than larger pro-life demonstrations, *B.C. Report* argues that the media is biased against the pro-life movement. Similarly, Robert Hackett of Simon Fraser University[4] often uses the number of people at peace protests as a benchmark for newsworthiness, arguing that large demonstrations against military operations such as the Gulf War are routinely ignored and censored by the media. Such charges of bias are nothing if not charges that information is being suppressed or censored. Such a position implies that omitting information, whether of statistics or events, and for whatever reason, amounts to censorship of that position and enhancement of the opposing position.

Inadvertent decisions, which are the subject-matter of this chapter, may also prevent information from being diffused. In these instances, producers need have no explicit political and social agenda in mind. For our purposes it is enough to assume only that they want to produce technically good TV news. When they do, their decisions and actions have consistent effects: some kinds of things typically are emphasized, others are ignored, and the pattern of coverage produces consequences that can be described more or less accurately. This is not an argument in favour of a doctrine of technological determinism: TV technologies do not make choices for producers yet, as with any activity, the production of TV news is conditioned by its environment. That is, the actual means by which TV news is created and broadcast conditions the result. By considering the result, moreover, one may draw inferences about what went into the decisions that produced it, and one may speculate on the consequences for the wider political world.

Television news, Edward Jay Epstein has said, is 'news from nowhere,' by which he means, among other things, that the news, the product, happens nowhere on earth except through the mediation or intervention of a specific technology of selection, transmission, and diffusion.[5] TV technology makes it possible to move information and imagery from one context (for example, the Somalia bush or a village in Bosnia) into another (for example, a bar in Prince George or a living room in Mississauga). Television, one may say, creates the form within which the 'news of the day' exists.[6] The formal characteristics of TV news production intimately influence the content and the effects of diffusing news in a mass public.

The most pervasive formal characteristic of TV is that it mediates events or information in such a way that one's experience is always of television and not of events or realities transcendent to it. Conceptually, one might say that the medium is opaque with respect to the reality – namely, information and events – that transcends it. In other words, television can be a universal mediator of the world, which is to say, of events or reality, to itself. In common-sense language, it is both part of our way of experiencing reality and part of the reality that we experience. This is why it is so much easier to discuss what is *on* television than to discuss the formal impact of television as such. More simply still, we are so well adjusted to TV that it is sometimes difficult to know what it is that we are adjusted to.

One indication of the difficulty can be extracted from the arresting observation of Neil Postman: 'The phrase "serious television" is a contradiction in terms [because] television speaks only in one persistent voice – the voice of entertainment.'[7] As an example, Postman reported that he watched forty-two hours of tele-evangelical shows before writing the chapter in his book dealing with religion on TV. Five hours, he said, would have been sufficient to draw two important and general conclusions. First, religion on television is as entertaining as a game show, hockey, or cartoons. 'Everything that makes religion an historic, profound, and sacred human activity is stripped away; there is no ritual, no dogma, no tradition, no theology and, above all, no sense of spiritual transcendence.' Second, what makes religion so entertaining is not the intentions or the motives of the preachers, which doubtless are varied, but the transformative effects of the medium. When practised in churches or in daily life, which is to say, in reality, Christianity (for example) is an experientially demanding and serious experience, not Sunday entertainment. The threat posed by television to religious practice, therefore, 'is not that religion has become the content of television shows but that television shows may become the content of religion.'[8] If TV can so transfigure religious experience, which does, after all, invite human beings to orient their lives towards a world-transcendent reality, one should not be surprised to learn that it can similarly transform the merely world-immanent realities of daily life produced as news.

The univocal description of TV as a medium of entertainment only is supported by Walter J. Ong's notion of 'secondary orality.'[9] By applying this term to television, Ong indicates that TV and, more broadly, electronic media, share certain characteristics with orally based thought. These characteristics appear to literates as surprising, and often as defects. Literate discourse, for example, relies on grammatical structures of subordination, whereas oral discourse is additive and relies on gestures and intonation to convey meaning. Oral style is aggregative, redundant and formular rather than analytic, linear, and discrete. Oral knowledge is conservative or traditional and innovation appears on the occasion of the performance of the story, not on the basis of new information or as speculation. The secondary orality of television shares these characteristics in a slightly transformed mode: gestures and intonation convey information, but often the speech of an anchor or correspondent has previously been written out; The formulas tend to be visual or musical rather than verbal, for example, an aerial shot of the House of Commons, a visual or musical theme that introduces a program, a warship or tank, a cheering crowd. Moreover, visuals are redundant in the sense that they have been chosen to reinforce the voice of the anchor or correspondent.[10] Similarly, the introduction and the wrap-up by an anchor are often redundant as well because they may simply restate the main theme of the story presented by the correspondent.

TV deals in time, not space. Newspapers and magazines sell space, advertising space. Both advertising space and the 'news hole,' which is also a spatial metaphor, can be expanded with relatively little effort or trouble. TV sells time, commercial time, and it can neither be expanded nor condensed because TV is perceived in *real* time. What comes between commercial time is program-time, for example, news-time, and, like all time, it is continuous. The translation of time into images, which we perceive as speed, also limits what can be conveyed as information. Speed is, however, an index of drama, of excitement, of news.

To summarize all these familiar attributes, television is theatre. The events of the world are not accompanied by music but the events of the operatic stage and the evening news are. News music introduces a world of the dramatic and the symbolic; there is tension in the air; sometimes news workers are shown scurrying around the news set, contributing their mobile sense of urgency as well. And at the centre, in command of the frenetic staff and the late-breaking news, sits the calm anchor, the anchor in a storm, the host of chaos, who converts it into cosmos, order – or at least into news. The orderliness of the anchor surrounded by untidiness makes him or her much more than the old BBC news-reader. An anchor welcomes the audience into the theatrical space of the newscast and then guides them to the various locales where filmed sequences and correspondents show them around the local sites. The anchor then welcomes the audience back when the correspondent is finished.

Credibility is central to all television shows, just as it is central to the familiar oral cultures of childhood fairy tales and the remote oral cultures of antiquity. The reason is obvious enough: since it is harder to fake an expression than to make up 'facts,' the inherent appeal of television is that it be believed. Truth, for TV, is therefore indistinguishable from belief. Credibility depends upon consistency both for news shows and for more obvious entertainment shows. If Bart Simpson turned into a sweet young man or if Homer Simpson developed a brain, the premise of *The Simpsons* would be destroyed. The same is true for debate shows such as *Crossfire* in the United States or *Faceoff* in Canada: one host will always take the liberal side on the issue of the day, the other the conservative one. The notion that the two hosts could switch sides, take the same side, or, as happens in real life, ever persuade the other to modify his or her opinion, is rigidly excluded.

Consistency is believed to be central to the credibility of the news as well, notwithstanding the experience of daily life that the world is full of the most interesting inconsistencies. For TV news, once a storyline or angle is established it is difficult to change. The reason is not because new information is unavailable, but because changes in perspective that new information might provide, like changes in Homer Simpson's IQ, are believed by producers to reduce credibility. One study found, for example, that about 90 per cent of sources offered no evidence to support their assertions or claims, which means that, for TV news, credibility is all.[11] In this context, however, credibility does not refer to the track record of a storyteller whose statements have been tested against the hard facts of reality. More generally, trustworthiness is important in oral and secondary oral cultures as an index of the validity of the information transmitted. This is one reason why television news is presented without ambiguity or uncertainty. As P.H. Weaver has argued, 'there is hardly an aspect of the scripting, casting, and staging of a television news program that is not designed to convey an impression of authority and omniscience.'[12] The mantle of authority is worn most conspicuously by the anchor, which is why one never sees his or her knees, knees being a symbol of vulnerability at least since the days of Homer.[13] Likewise, reporters adopt an authoritative tone: the meaning of events is clear, as are peoples' motives and intentions; trends are obvious, problems and solutions perfectly understood. Anything that challenges this pose, such as altering the perspective on a story, is bound to be resisted.

Most Canadians are incapable of challenging this authoritative pretence. This is one reason why so many people persistently indicate that television is their main source of news despite the fact that all the words uttered in an hour of TV news would not fill the front page of a newspaper. It also accounts for the widespread belief that TV provides the most complete, intelligent, and objective news.[14] The style of presentation is deliberate, but even if it were not, the structure or the grammar of TV as secondary orality would ensure the production of 'authorized knowers.'[15]

Other characteristics shared by oral cultures and television are more obvious. Both conceptualize and verbalize all their knowledge in terms of what is already familiar and concrete: neither oral cultures nor television have much use for abstractions such as statistics or for complex logical discussion. Conflict and struggle are central to both because they can provide a meaningful and dramatic context. The name-calling of children's oral communication is recapitulated in the television sound-bite. The description of physical violence is enthusiastic in oral poetry and is achieved on television by the equally enthusiastic use of visuals, 'good pictures.' Knowledge for both television and oral culture is intimate and participatory, not objective or separated. Just as oral societies live in the present and quickly forget irrelevant memories, so too, nothing is as stale as yesterday's news. There are dictionaries neither for television nor for oral cultures, so that words acquire much of their meaning from the repertoire of human expressiveness. In short, the televised word is a performance.

But it is just here that we must notice the importance of the adjective in Ong's concept. Television is an instance of *secondary* orality. Unlike oral cultures, televised orality is in no way spontaneous. With the exception of live sports, where the requirements of orality are still obvious (in the performance of colour commentators such as Don Cherry, for instance), television production may go through several 'drafts.' The correspondent's submission may be cut, spliced, and edited; the anchor's words are scripted; several takes or 'fakes' of visuals can be made; file visuals may be used along with sound tracks and special effects in order to produce a deliberate and contrived word-mosaic, where each piece has been carefully shaped to fit the overall picture.

The voice of entertainment is amplified because television is a money-making enterprise in North America. Commercials are on TV because TV is commercial. TV as a whole is not simply a public service and neither is TV news. Occasionally, the example of CBC TV news is invoked in order to qualify the generalization that TV news is not commercial.[16] It is true, of course that until 1996 CBC TV news was partially shielded from the impact of commercials. News anchor Peter Mansbridge has voiced his objections to the new regime: 'I never thought I would ever see the day when we had them [commercials] in *The National* ... The thing is that this was sacred ground – it was never was supposed to be like this.'[17] To which a not entirely philistine query might be: Why not?

The answer that is given, or rather, the assumption that appears to be self-evident to Mansbridge, is that being commercial-free means a 'better' news show. As proof, he might point to the fact that CBC regularly captures the lion's share of awards for 'excellence.' Leaving aside the delicate question of whether the universal and involuntary support by Canadian taxpayers amounts to a kind of public-sector commercial, one must still consider Postman's thesis regarding the single voice of TV. If 'good TV' is measured in terms of audience appeal, not a shelf full of Geminis or Nellies, then CTV produces a 'better' TV news show because more people regularly watch it. The difference between the 'commercial' and the 'public' TV broadcasters, in other words, is not that one is better than the other but that CBC TV news appeals to an audience whose taste in entertainment approaches the taste of those who offer awards for 'excellence.'[18] In our view it would be more accurate to say that audiences' taste in the entertainment package provided by CBC and CTV differs, rather than make large claims for the superiority of 'commercial-free' television news.

Whether supported by commercial advertising, corporate sponsors, voluntary audience contributions, or involuntary tax dollars, TV shows are expensive to produce. In 1992 it cost around a million dollars to produce an hour-long sitcom for American television. It cost about half that to produce an hour-long news or 'public affairs' show. Assuming that the ratio, if not the dollar figure, is about the same in Canada,[19] it follows that news programs can be significant profit-centres. Moreover, the demographics of news audiences are highly appealing to advertisers: they are attentive, educated, and have more disposable income than other audiences. Accordingly, if a news show attracts anything over half the audience of a sitcom, and if it can be supported by the same number of commercials, it will contribute relatively more to the bottom line than the 'pure' entertainment of a sitcom.

Epstein has summarized the foregoing observations by arguing that political, economic, and organizational imperatives establish the 'operating rules' of news production. Such 'rules' do not predetermine any particular story but rather define the formal characteristics of all stories: time, ease of transmission, the 'on-the-one-hand/on-the-other-hand' or point/counterpoint format, definitions of context by trends and not individual reportorial choices or 'events,' all give consistency and drama to television news.[20] The several attributes are internally connected and mutually reinforcing. The point/counterpoint format, for instance, is usually invoked as evidence of the importance of 'balance' or 'objectivity.' One study found virtual unanimity (98 per cent agreement) regarding the proposition that 'the norm of objectivity forms the core of the defining logic and mission of news creation.'[21] At the same time, however, the emphasis on 'objectivity' places a premium on 'hard news,' which is to say, coverage of specific events and episodes accompanied by 'good pictures.'[22] Episodic coverage and good pictures are bound to provide entertaining news if presented with a modest degree of technical competence.

In a similar fashion, James Fallows has summarized the conventions that govern the production of local news: the broadcast usually starts with crimes, fires, or auto wrecks, on the principle of 'if it bleeds, it leads.' Then there is political news, almost always in the context of horse-race politics – the mayor is criticizing his opponents, the city council is arguing with the mayor. There are teases for the weather forecast – 'We'll hear what kind of a weekend Bob has in store for us' – and for the latest sports results, details of which will come only near the end of the show. Even more than broadcast coverage of national or world events, local TV news suggests an environment of generalized menace which cannot really be understood but from which viewers should try to insulate themselves. If destructive events are placed in any perspective at all it is usually the perspective of raw politics – for instance, whether a shooting at a high school means that the superintendent of schools must step down.[23]

In their study of CBC Toronto and of the *Globe and Mail*, Richard Ericson and his colleagues have given conceptual precision to Fallows's additive 'conventions' and Epstein's mutually reinforcing 'operating rule.' What, they ask, is the *method* of contemporary journalism? The authors' answer is that 'visualization – making something visible to the mind even if it is not visible to the eye – is the essence of journalism as method.'[24] Like any method, visualization can be applied to any subject-matter whatsoever. In putting it into practice, they argue, a journalist offers an account of reality that allows, enables, or prompts the audience to visualize adequately the intended meaning of events. More particularly, as the title of their book indicates, the media, and especially TV, visualize *deviance*, which is 'the defining characteristic of what journalists regard as newsworthy.'[25] By the term deviance, the authors mean non-normal behaviour. The range of non-normal behaviour can extend from serious criminality to trivial violations of common opinions and expected order. The social and often the political response to deviance is control; journalism, therefore, contributes to social consensus and thereby to social order by highlighting what is odd. Whatever else it may be, news of deviance, of the failures of social control, is usually highly entertaining.

On its own terms, visualizations of deviance are also visualizations of correction or reform. More broadly, the experience of failure, even in the virtual form of TV images, is essential to the creation of visions of what might be improved, or to progress. Put more emphatically, since there can be no vision of progress without a vision of failure, news that emphasizes failure (because it is dramatic and entertaining, that is, because it makes for good TV) reinforces success and so fosters the imaginative purposes of 'progress.' In short, good TV necessarily enhances the commitment of persons in mass technological societies to a belief in 'progress,' especially when the news reports deviance.

The argument of Ericson et al. is intended to describe the self-understanding of TV news producers. Dramatic entertainment expressed as visualized deviance is concisely captured in the principle mentioned earlier by Fallows: 'if it bleeds, it leads.'[26] Because even small and peaceful communities may on occasion suffer bloody mishaps in their midst, there is an endless supply of imagery 'that life has turned into a *Blade-Runner*-ish hell.'[27]

Journalists, however, see things differently. Armed with the lance of objectivity and shielded by the conventions of balance, 'the news media has a generally positive view of itself in the watchdog role.'[28] What counts, therefore, is not factual accuracy but a meaningful story. In order to 'tell' a good story journalists regularly use 'fakes' (unrelated visuals) and 'staging' (the use of actors, rehearsed interviews, and so on). A good journalist, therefore, is a good storyteller, a good interpreter or visualizer of news, and not necessarily a good reporter of events. One result is that, by incorporating important and emotionally engaging natural, social, and political dramas, the news helps 'to create their communities within the mythical configurations employed by authorized knowers. The myths become deeply embedded in consciousness so that they do indeed direct our ways of knowing, as well as our knowledge of the world.'[29] The myths, in turn, can lead to their own interpretations. On the one hand, for example, it has been argued that reporting deviance encourages deviance;[30] on the other hand, it is argued that reporting deviance turns it into an element of social ritual, the chief effect of which is to reinforce consensus.[31] In our view, such interpretations simply use a more complex, obscure language to articulate Postman's thesis: TV news is essentially entertainment.

Most of the criticism directed at the production of TV news focuses on political coverage rather than on coverage of religion or sports. Two classes of criticism bear on our topic.

The first is concerned with the visualization of politics as a game for professionals (who include elected officials, bureaucrats, and members of the media) rather than an important concern of citizens. As Fallows has said:

When ordinary citizens have a chance to pose questions to political leaders, they rarely ask about the game of politics. They mainly want to know how the reality of politics will affect them – through taxes, programs, scholarship funds, wars. Journalists justify their intrusiveness and excesses by claiming that they are the public's representatives, asking the questions their fellow citizens would ask if they had the privilege of meeting with presidents and senators. In fact they ask questions no one but their fellow political professionals cares about. And they often do so with a discourtesy and rancor, as at the typical White House news conference, that represents the public's views much less than it reflects the modern journalist's belief that being independent boils down to acting hostile.[32]

Fallows's point is not so much that the pros are wrong and the civilians right but that there is a major gulf between the two.

When politics is visualized as a game, the essential feature is competition and controlled conflict. Electoral politics in particular lends itself to the imagery of the horse race: someone will win, others will lose; someone is ahead for the moment, but she may fade in the stretch. Emphasis on the race itself rather than what the race is about amounts to 'a powerful disincentive for candidates to take national issues seriously.[33] The fact is, however, that 'issues' – policy options and alternatives – constitute the substance of politics. In short, politics is not just a game. When, for example, Don Cherry entertains the nation between periods on Hockey Night in Canada with his excesses and eccentricities, the actual game still exists independent of what this hockey pundit and buffoon says. It is, after all, *between* periods. Politics, however, is less independent of the words of political pundits and buffoons because what these people say may influence the perception of citizens. Self-government, like politics generally, involves conflict. But it also involves conciliation, compromise, and agreement. So far as TV news is concerned, the chief difference between the two is that conflict is entertaining and for that reason deserves air-time, and compromise is not and so is hardly ever shown.

What counts in electoral politics is which low-information[34] messages are presented to the public and how those messages dictate how candidates are to be judged. Consider, for example, the 1996 British Columbia election campaign, where NDP leader Glen Clark was portrayed as the best leader but his party was given the lowest approval ratings on its ability to handle economic issues.[35] In contrast to Clark, the leader of the Liberal Party was described by one television reporters as 'an albatros around the Liberals' neck'[36] but at the same time the party had an economic platform that was most in keeping with popular support. The public, through television news, was encouraged to judge the campaign through the low-information of leadership and ignore the high-information details of economic policy. In other words, by focusing on leadership, crucial information about the economy and who best could deal with it was sidetracked and did not become the main focus for making electoral decisions.

At the same time that low-information cues were highlighted at the expense of high-information cues, those same low-information cues were selected and some were suppressed. The NDP government prior to the election campaign was rocked by financial scandal. The low-information cue of scandal, which normally tends to be emphasized by television news because of its deviance, went ignored in television's coverage of the election campaign, with only twenty-nine CBC and eighteen BCTV newscasts mentioning the issue during the four-week campaign. This contrasts sharply to the previous British Columbia election, when the incumbent Social Credit Party received 463 CBC and 399 BCTV mentions of the scandal surrounding its previous leader.

The point here is not to argue whether the B.C. television media are left or right-leaning, although a case might be made of bias, but that they chose both the issues and, more important, which low-information cues would resonate with the electorate. In short, they influenced the basis for electoral judgment. In their defence, the media claimed that *they* did not emphasize the NDP scandals because the Liberals did not emphasize them. This defence ignores two facts: first, the 'if it bleeds it leads' addage dictates that, for better entertainment and hence better ratings, the television stations would always choose scandal over policy or positive news; and second, because the media had already branded the Liberal leader as sleazy, he could not be the one to be seen as attacking the NDP for sleaze. Had the Liberal leader attacked the NDP on this front, the media, and not the NDP, would have claimed a credibility gap on the Liberal leader's part. Censorship, then, can occur on the basis of newsroom rituals and decisions, but more pervasively it can occur because of strategic decisions on the part of parties and candidates to avoid negative coverage or unflattering news frames.

Other inaccuracies in the TV visualization of politics have been summarized by Iyengar as 'episodic framing.' A 'frame' is his word for a format. Frames are either episodic or thematic: the episodic frame focuses on specific and particular events, whereas the thematic frame places events and issues in a more general context. Episodic framing has the result that the interconnections among issues are ignored and the ability of audiences to cumulate information into patterns that lead to 'logical' consequences is thereby inhibited.[37] Iyengar is of the view that 'domain specific' political thinking is inferior to ideologically coherent political thinking because it leads to 'individualistic rather than societal attributions of responsibility,' which is, in his view, wrong.[38] His language is, perhaps, not the best, but it does indicate a genuine problem: citizens know that issues do run together, 'but by journalistic convention these are treated as separate 'items' on a political or legislative agenda.'[39] The problem with producing 'in-depth' analyses of interconnected political problems, the problem, in Iyengar's language, of using a thematic frame, is not just that it results in TV shows that are not particularly entertaining, but that 'interpretive, "subsurface" reporting is much more vulnerable to charges of bias and editorialising.'[40] On the other hand, Fallows has argued that 'public journalism' or 'journalism in the public spirit' can be successful in presenting 'non-objective' and in-depth or thematic stories.[41] Nearly all his examples, however come from print, not TV journalism. And, of course, *journalisme engagé* has its own problems.

For critics, these inaccuracies and distortions are typical and have identifiable consequences, which leads them to make a second general point. Karl Kraus once said that perversion is fun for a while, but then it gets boring. Likewise a cycle of bad-news sensationalism eventually 'deadens' an audience: they become oblivious to the difference between truth and fiction; they dismiss all visualizations as demeaning not specific groups but the whole of society. A steady diet of deviance visualized as dramatically as possible is profoundly demoralizing. The consequence is that TV news contributes to public 'cynicism.'[42]

The way modern journalists *choose* to present the news increases the chance that citizens will feel unhappy, powerless, betrayed by, and angry about their political system. And because the most powerful journalistic organs are unwilling to admit that they have made this choice, it is almost impossible for them to change.[43] And yet critics want TV news to change. In Postman's view, they want to break the self-contradiction of the notion of 'serious television.'

According to Fallows, for example, today's journalists can choose:

Do they want merely to entertain the public or to engage it? If they want to entertain, they will keep doing what they have done for the last generation. Concentrating on conflict and spectacle, building up celebrities and tearing them down, presenting a crisis or issue with the volume turned all the way up, only to drop that issue and turn to the next emergency. They will make themselves the center of attention, as they exchange one-liners as if public life were a parlor game and make fun of the gaffes and imperfections of anyone in public life. They will view their berths as opportunities for personal aggrandizement and enrichment, trading on the power of their celebrity. And while they do these things, they will be constantly more hated and constantly less useful to the public whose attention they are trying to attract. In the long run, real celebrities – singers, quarterbacks, movie stars – will crowd them off the stage. Public life will become more sour and embittered, and American [or Canadian] democracy will be even less successful in addressing the nation's economic, social, and moral concerns.[44]

For Fallows, despite all the evidence that he has accumulated, there is still a real or true purpose for the media, including TV, that is other than entertainment. 'Part of the press's job,' he said, 'is to keep things in proportion. TV's natural tendency is to see the world in shards.' But seeing the world in 'shards' is just what makes good TV. 'Journalism is not mere entertainment,' said Fallows, 'it is the main tool we have for keeping the world's events in perspective. It is the main source of agreed-upon facts we can use in public decisions.'[45]

Who is right, Fallows or Postman? Can TV in particular speak with any voice but entertainment? We have argued that the *formal* attribute of television, which following Ong we have called secondary orality, means that any other voice will be silenced. When Marshall McLuhan announced, a generation ago, that 'the medium is the message,' he drew attention to the overriding importance of form as compared to content. In our view Postman is right. It is no accident, therefore, that the 'civic journalism' that Fallows praises is overwhelmingly practised by newspapers. The form of a newspaper permits and even encourages a plurality of voices. Good TV, however, means entertaining TV. People watch TV not because it is 'good for them' but because they like to. Accordingly, the inadvertent censorship that is required to produce entertaining news shows, news shows that people like to watch, seems inevitable.

NOTES

1 Herbert Gans, *Deciding What's News* (New York: Vintage 1979), 81.
2 David Halberstam, *The Powers That Be* (New York: Knopf 1979), 407.
3 For a preliminary consideration of this problem, see Barry Cooper, *Sins of Omission: Shaping the News at CBC TV* (Toronto: University of Toronto Press 1994).
4 Robert Hackett, *Engulfed: Peace Protest and America's Press during the Gulf War: An Occasional Paper* (New York: New York Center for War, Peace and the News Media 1993).
5 Jay Epstein, *News from Nowhere* (New York: Vintage 1974).
6 This has been argued in different ways by Neil Postman, *Amusing Ourselves to Death* (New York: Penguin 1985), chs. 1–2; Philip Schlesinger, *Putting 'Reality' Together: BBC News*, 2nd ed. (London: Methuen 1987); Richard V. Ericson, Patricia M. Baranek, and Janet B.L. Chan, *Representing Order: Crime, Law and Justice in the News Media* (Toronto: University of Toronto Press 1991), 345–6.
7 Postman, *Amusing Ourselves*, 24.
8 Ibid., 116–17, 124.
9 Ong developed his concept as a revision of some of the theories of Marshall McLuhan. See Walter Ong, *Orality and Literacy: The Technologizing of the Word* (London: Methuen 1982).
10 Experimental evidence indicates that there is no significant difference in the way audiences understand audio only as compared with audio plus video. See Richard A. Pride and Gary L. Wamsly, 'Symbol Analysis of Network Coverage of the Laos Incursion,' *Journalism Quarterly*, 49 (1972), 635–40.
11 Richard V. Ericson, Patricia M. Baranek, and Janet B.L. Chan, *Representing Order*, 351.
12 P.H. Weaver, 'Newspaper News and Television News,' in D. Cater and R. Adler, eds., *Television as Social Force: New Approaches to TV Criticism* (New York: Praeger 1975), 84.
13 See R.B. Onians, *The Origins of European Thought about the Body, the Mind, the*

Soul, the World, Time and Fate (Cambridge, U.K.: Cambridge University Press [1951] 1989), ch. 4. Halberstam made a similar observation regarding an unusual event at CBS News. 'At one point Walter Cronkite came out of his chair to do some graphics, and the audience immediately knew it was important, *Walter would not have come out of his chair for just anything*, and yes, there he was showing his legs, which of itself was unique. Walter did not show his legs lightly. Proof that it was not your average story.' Halberstam, *The Powers That Be*, 653.

14 R.T. Bower, *The Changing Television Audience in America* (New York: Columbia University Press 1985). This finding is echoed, as one might expect, by Canadian studies. In 1980, 73 per cent of respondents to a large survey conducted by Goldfarb Consultants indicated that they regularly used television as a news source: Canada, Department of External Affairs, *Perspectives on World Affairs and Foreign Policy Issues: A Research Report for External Affairs Canada* (Ottawa: Minister of Supply and Services 1980), 10. Likewise, over fifteen years ago, the Kent commission reported that 52 per cent of Canadians believed that television kept them most up-to-date: Canada, Royal Commission on Newspapers, *Report* (Ottawa: Minister of Supply and Services 1981), 254.

15 The term 'authorized knower' is borrowed from Gaye Tuchman, *Making News: A Study in the Construction of Reality* (New York: Free Press 1978).

16 Americans on occasion make the same claims regarding PBS.

17 *Globe and Mail* 15 February 1997, C2.

18 Likewise, regarding PBS, its claim to provide 'better' TV news because it is partially shielded from commercial pressure must be balanced by considerations of audience size, to say nothing of the question of equivalence between corporate donors to PBS and corporate sponsors of 'commercial' TV news.

19 The figures are taken from Neil Postman and from Steve Powers, *How to Watch TV News* (New York: Penguin 1992), ch. 1.

20 Jay Epstein, *News from Nowhere*, 42–3; see also Gans, *Deciding What's News*, 82–3; 279–81.

21 B. Phillips, 'Approaches to Objectivity: Journalistic versus Social Science Perspectives,' in P. Hirsch, P. Miller, and F. Kline, eds., *Strategies for Communications Research* (Beverly Hills, Calif.: Sage 1977), 65.

22 Shanto Iyengar, *Is Anyone Responsible? How Television Frames Political Issues* (Chicago: University of Chicago Press 1991), 138.

23 James Fallows, *Breaking the News* (New York: Vintage 1996), 200.

24 Richard V. Ericson, Patricia M. Baranek, and Janet B.L. Chan, *Visualizing Deviance: A Study of News Organization* (Toronto: University of Toronto Press 1987), 4.

25 Ibid. For a more elaborate but by no means contradictory account of what counts as news, see Johan Galtang and Mari Ruge, 'Structuring and Selecting News,' in

Stanley Cohen and Jock Young, eds., *The Manufacturing of News: Deviance, Social Problems and the Mass Media* (London: Constable 1973), 62–73; and John Hartley, *Understanding News* (London: Methuen 1982), ch. 5.

26 This was also the title of Doug Saunders's piece in the *Globe and Mail* mentioned earlier. In it he compared the CBC lead story with the CTV one. His lead paragraph was the CBC lead: 'The convulsing bodies spewed surprising volumes of dark gooey blood as they were dragged across the snow. Big eyes wide with mindless agony, the seals flapped at the end of grappling hooks and left long, ketchupy trails before they were skinned alive.' CTV, in contrast, led with a less gory but equally entertaining story, the denouement of the O.J. Simpson saga: the assessment of punitive damages for causing wrongful death.

27 Fallows, *Breaking the News*, 142.

28 Ibid., 202.

29 Richard Ericson et al. *Negotiating Control: A Study of News Sources*, 398.

30 See G. Pearson, *Hooligan: A History of Respectable Fears* (London: Macmillan 1983).

31 See, for instance, S. Hall, 'The Rediscovery of Ideology: The Return of the Repressed in Media Studies,' in M. Gurevitch, et al., eds., *Culture, Society and Media* (London: Methuen 1982), 56–90.

32 Fallows, *Breaking the News*, 24.

33 Iyengar, *Is Anyone Responsible?*, 142. In addition, Iyengar observes that 'horserace coverage modifies perception of electoral viability and thereby indirectly alters voting preferences, providing a strong favourable impetus toward the candidate whose prospects appear brightest' (134).

34 Samuel Popkin, in *The Reasoning Voter: Communication and Persuasion in Presidential Campaigns* (Chicago: University of Chicago Press 1994), argues that low-information is the information that voters use about basic policy directions offered by opposing candidates. Using Anthony Downs's perceptions that voters use shortcuts, he argues that the seemingly trivial information about leaders and campaigns is important to the decision-making process. Low-information rationality or 'gut' reaction is the 'kind of practical thinking about government and politics in which people actually engage. It is a method of combining, in an economical way, learning and information from past experiences, daily life, the media and political campaigns' (7).

35 Information from the 1996 British Columbia election campaign was obtained from the National Media Archive publication 'The Test of Incumbency: Comparing the 1991 and 1996 B.C. Election Campaigns,' *On Balance*, 9, no. 7 (1996).

36 3 May 1996, BCTV News.

37 Iyengar, *Is Anyone Responsible?* 5, 133–6, 143.

38 Ibid., 16, 127, 143.

39 Fallows, *Breaking the News*, 245.
40 Iyengar, *Is Anyone Responsible?* 138.
41 Fallows, *Breaking the News*, ch. 6 and epilogue.
42 Ibid., 155, 202–3.
43 Ibid., 262. Iynegar's version is expressed in a more technical vocabulary: 'The "accessibility bias" of TV leads to particular effects – the agenda-setting effect, the priming effect, the bandwagon effect and the framing effect – all of which have mutually reinforcing consequences for audiences, namely the trivialization of politics and the erosion of electoral accountability.'
44 Fallows, *Breaking the News*, 267.
45 Ibid., 53, 128.

16

Selective Marginalization of Aboriginal Voices: Censorship in Public Performance

ALLAN K. McDOUGALL and
LISA PHILIPS VALENTINE

If one acknowledges that censorship is a device to control the breadth of communication in the name of realizing some value espoused by those in authority, then its analysis as a tool can be extended to the dynamics of marginalization. If this is done, the definition of the scope of censorship in law is crucial as one struggles with the role of the state in a liberal democracy. Although censorship does not always present itself in this way, what should or should not be available through communication or text reflects our institutionalized certification of tolerance or intolerance. Much legal debate and political struggle rests appropriately in this domain. This chapter focuses on censorship as it applies to the struggle of the Stoney Point community to regain control of its land and to acquire band status within the First Nations of Canada. The case will define censorship as the refusal of entitlement – the denial of the right to a voice to speak and to be heard – both in the arenas of public power and in the organizational structure of the First Nations themselves.

When looking at this case we must distinguish between the denial of entitlement, which silences a voice, and the rejection of an argument which conflicts, or is not compatible, with the priorities of the organization concerned. In this distinction, the importance of politics emerges. In the public sphere, a demand, once made, may be ignored or accepted, or even massaged into some altered form as an aspect of governance. For politicians, the day of reckoning comes with the next election. The denial of voice, or refusal of entitlement, on the other hand, leaves the advocate silenced unless that voice is asserted in other arenas and gains enough attention to be heard by the public.[1] The case of Stoney Point illustrates this dynamic and the relationship between the openness of communication and the form of public performance.

At a second level, this case illustrates the construction of that performance in the media. In a liberal, pluralistic society the media reports on events to most of the population. Few will have independent means to discover the details. Thus, the Stoney Point issue as reported by the media is also constructed by it. That construction tailors public perception and, at the same time, offers us a window into the media's own construction of stereotypes and value hierarchies as the reader absorbs the reports.[2] The analysis of the construction of the Stoney Point issue will be examined through reports in the major regional newspaper, the *London Free Press*. That data in turn will offer a diachronic view of the construction of the Stoney Point issue by the media. Throughout, the reported facts will offer insight into the public construction of events, the relationship between spokespersons and the community, and the significance of a 'fractionalized' state structure.[3]

The importance of the peaceful solution of cross-cultural tensions has been addressed eloquently by a number of Canadian authors. Their primary concern has been national unity and chronic cross-cultural cleavages in Quebec and Canada. Two of these authors, Charles Taylor and Simone Chambers, offer a contextual ground from which the analysis of censorship in the Stoney Point case can proceed.

In *Multiculturalism and 'the Politics of Recognition'* (1992), Taylor argues for the need to recognize people in their diversity while maintaining that fundamental rights should be universal. According to Taylor, the struggle between demands for 'diversity,' or distinctiveness, and equality can be mediated through dialogue. But that dialogue has to be substantial, not condescending, equal, and rooted in standards acceptable to the parties. As Taylor argues:

Equal recognition is not just the appropriate mode for a healthy democratic society. Its refusal can inflict damage on those who are denied it. The projection of an inferior or demeaning image on another can actually distort and oppress, to the extent that the image is internalized. Not only contemporary feminism but also race relations and discussions of multiculturalism are undergirded by the premise that the withholding of recognition can be a form of oppression.

If the dialogue is between established communities with a significant history, protracted discussion may result in a new awareness of the others' perceptions and eventually the emergence of an overarching vision which recognizes the perspectives of the various participants. The result is a new awareness which can recognize the diversity of the positions and, at the same time, a common net of values linked to human recognition and dignity.[4]

Taylor's analysis raises a major contextual factor in relations between the hegemonic state dominated by European culture, on the one hand, and First Nations' communities on the other. The relationship since the conclusion of treaty negotiations has not been one of equals. The state and dominant society have treated First Nations communities as marginal, inferior entities. Children were forced from their homes into residential schools at which they were punished if they spoke their ancestral language. Reserves were treated as economic hinterlands and 'Indians' were subjected to discriminate application of criminal laws. The implementation of treaty rights was left to a department of government that itself was on the margin of the governmental priority list. Assimilation was, and is, a recurrent theme when solutions to the 'Indian problem' emerge on the government's agenda.[5]

To realize Taylor's standards of a dialogue between equals, significant change is required in relations between state structures and the First Nations. Since 1982 some progress has been made but the voices of the First Nations are not yet treated as equal to those of the hegemonic state nor are community members recognized for their status and distinctiveness in the Canadian milieu. The Stoney Point First Nation's case illustrates this discrepancy through its media construction. Simultaneously, it reveals the emerging potential for negotiations when issues erupt of such significance that recognition of common humanity transcends habitually constructed cultural presuppositions.

Simone Chambers in *Reasonable Democracy* (1996) accentuates the importance of perpetual negotiation to resolve fundamental differences across the cultural divide in Quebec. She offers additional analytic potential by exploring the dialogue from the perspective of the participants, grounding her analysis in the contest of the participants.[6] Given the grievances and arrogance in state/First Nations relations over the last century, the inclusion of the history of those relations and the need to transform the assumptions upon which the dialogue rested become readily apparent.

As with Taylor, agreement for Chambers will reflect an adjustment in understanding or the reconstruction of the views of the participants. In an idealized homogeneous, stable community, such mediation might rest on many shared values, understandings, or experiences. As society becomes more specialized, or 'decentred,' the reasoning that legitimatizes different types of decisions will differ. Those differences in rationales reduce the coherence of the hegemonic state, social life, and monolithic culture as the framework for ordering human life. The diversity of 'reasons why' opens the potential for individual rationalization and/or debate within and between cultural entities. Areas of overlap in the definition of what is appropriate between participants in discourse determine the potential for agreement. That agreement will be constructed from shared understandings and alternate interpretations. Thus, it is not a linear process which focuses on maximizing some good. Instead, as Chambers notes, the route to a consensus rests in extended, substantial dialogue. In the process, it involves a shifting of understanding and a probing for shared grounds of what is appropriate. This adjustment of priorities and understandings resembles Taylor's conclusion that an overarching cross-cultural vision with new boundaries must transcend, but may also coexist with, the earlier cultural visions of the participants.

The significance of communication emerges at a number of levels. The dialogue must be substantial and equal. The participants must be engaged and reflexive (that is, with a critical eye directed inwardly). That reflexivity must be aimed at understanding the broader potential of the issues. And the process itself must be self-conscious. As Chambers argues: 'A rational reflection on the genealogy of my own beliefs can be empowering, but it is very difficult to achieve alone. Clarification of what I believe and why I believe it often requires the critical distance that only a dialogue partner can offer. And here it is very important that my dialogue partner be not the voice of Big Brother but the voice of an equal.'[7] Censorship, or the silencing of voice, in this context precludes the balance needed to transcend cross-cultural issues, and it denies equality should a diversion offered by one party open new avenues for dialogue in a decentred society.

Attention to discourse analysis provides dynamic insights into the performance of public power in multiple arenas. By tracing its form and substance, discourse can define issues, the framing of those issues by the participants, and the techniques used to rationalize their positions. It can also uncover techniques used by hegemonic actors to give the impression of 'attending to marginalized voices' while simultaneously stripping those voices of power. As the Stoney Point issues travel across a number of discourse domains they illustrate clearly the import of decentred society and its relationship to censorship in specific venues. At the procedural level, discourse analysis offers insights not only into power relations and the construction of political spectacles but also into emerging areas of potential consensus across the cultural boundary.

We begin with an examination of the concept 'entitlement,' which is defined by Amy Shuman as follows: 'If a speaker's right to be sole talker is a claim to a turn to talk, entitlement concerns the right to make that claim. Challenges to entitlement raise questions about the ownership of talk as well as, by implication, the ownership of experience. Any claim to the authority to report on experience, to disclose, withhold, or conceal information, to be an author of events, and to repeat an other's remarks is an entitlement claim.'[8] These claims, when granted, open situated knowledge to the audience or other participants. If those claims have their origins in established communities, which do not share a common culture and relate to affairs of mutual concern, they fall within the criteria set by Taylor and Chambers.

The concept of entitlement thus opens an analysis of different and situated knowledges. On a broader scale, such divergence is especially symptomatic of a technologically based, individualistic society. In Shuman's analysis, each person has a perspective. To assert entitlement is to speak to that perspective along with the referential content of that statement. Its impact is linked, on the other hand, to shared knowledge. In liberal-democratic theory, one solution to this multiplicity of voices is to argue that everybody should be allowed to speak. However, that does not solve the problem, because even when everyone is given the opportunity to speak, there remains the problem of the power differential between voices.

Issues of entitlement and its use in censoring social groups are exquisitely illustrated in reports from the *London Free Press*. The articles examined below encapsulate ways in which government has directly undercut the discourse of First Nations people to deny entitlement both explicitly and implicitly. Prior to offering a close analysis of the multiple levels of denials of entitlement apparent in these data, we will provide a contextual overview of the events that frame the current discourse.

The relationship between the First Nations and the various governments in Canada has not been mutually supportive. The federal government actively discouraged regional or national political organizations sponsored by the First Nations until the 1940s. After the Second World War, respect for the native communities increased in recognition of their considerable contribution to the war effort. Legal restrictions imposed on the community were reduced in 1951 and again in 1957. Government-sponsored studies documented the plight of First Nations communities in the late 1950s and throughout the 1960s. During this period, a National Indian Brotherhood was formed to present the interests of the native communities to government.

The period from 1969 to 1975 marks a transition in native/government relations in Canada. In 1969 the Trudeau government introduced a white paper which extended the post–Second World War pattern of reducing restraints on native communities by suggesting that they should be extended the rights of Canadian citizens. It proposed to remove guarantees provided by the Indian Act and to return the management of land to local native communities. The proposal ignored the fact that members of the First Nations had special rights rooted in their treaties with the Canadian state and in their status as the original inhabitants of the area. Reactions from spokespersons for the native communities against the Trudeau initiative were rapid and articulate and generated extensive support from the media and the general public.

In June 1970, 200 Indian leaders met the federal cabinet in Ottawa to express their displeasure over the white paper. The government, now on the defensive, asked the National Indian Brotherhood and the regional associations present to submit proposals for dealing with treaty and aboriginal rights and for the settlement of land claims. These associations were then offered funding to conduct the research necessary to document their positions. They also were asked to assume responsibility for some social services previously provided by the federal government. By 1972 the offer had transformed the associations. For example, the Western Indian Association's budget grew from $69,000 in 1969 to $1.5 million in 1972.[9] At the same time the federal government offered the bands funds to research their land claims. The industry that emerged as a consequence led to a massive review of aboriginal rights. By 1975 the native associations and the federal government had agreed that the basic issues surrounding claims would be presented to cabinet ministers through the appropriate provincial or territorial association before they would be submitted to detailed negotiation. Federal political and financial support thus combined to create a hierarchy of associations, with the Assembly of First Nations at its apex.

By the mid-1970s, band politics in southwestern Ontario were bounded by the reification of a native associational hierarchy which complemented the state structures. Combined, they defined 'legitimacy' for local assertions of identity. Bands had to be listed in the governmental rolls to be recognized as legitimate. Inclusion on the list required the approval of the regional association. The impact of the events from 1969 to 1975 thus provided First Nations with the financial capacity to research and present arguments that could be heard by the state system in the legal discourse of that system. It made them responsible for the delivery of an increasing range of social services. It changed the status and capacity of the associations, and it increased their budgets in a manner that transformed their function from advocacy to that of an intermediary between local communities and the state.

In our examination of systemic constraints on the entitlement of 'non-entities' in the eyes of this extended association/government system, we found that the non-entity is neglected ('invisible') until a non-systemic incident occurs, at which point marginalization moves towards overt censorship through the denial of voice to that 'non-entity'.[10] The Stoney Point claims to the military Camp Ipperwash and the adjacent Ipperwash Provincial Park is a case in point. In 1942, under the War Measures Act, the government of Canada declared the area later known as Camp Ipperwash necessary for the training of military recruits. Its offer to purchase Stoney Point was rejected by the band by an overwhelming vote. The government responded under the War Measures Act by promulgating an order-in-council expropriating the land and removing the people from their homes. When it was enforced, the Stoney Point people living on the land were given a week's notice to move to the Kettle Point Reserve. Members of the Stoney Point band who did not move within this period found their houses razed and their belongings destroyed. Ironically, there were several residents of Stoney Point who could not respond since they were soldiers fighting in the Canadian armed forces in Europe. After the war, the land was not returned and the Stoney Point people remained with the Kettle Point band. With the increased significance of band lists after 1970, the Stoney Point people had a problem for they were then formally inscribed as a part of the 'Kettle and Stony[11] Point band.' In 1993 'Stoney Pointers' began acting outside the system. A few of them moved onto the military base in May 1993, camping out in rudimentary dwellings. Military personnel also moved onto the base to 'secure military assets and try to keep a non-confrontational state in place,' as the *London Free Press* reported on 31 July 1995 (A1). In 1994 the federal government agreed in principle to the return of the land. Extended negotiations followed. On 29 July 1995, as a protest against the slow progress in these negotiations, a contingent of about 100 Stoney Pointers returned 'home' by occupying the military base. Then, on 4 September at the end of the camping season, the Stoney Pointers took possession of the adjacent Ipperwash Provincial Park. The incidents received broad media coverage, and their construction will be the focus of what follows.[12]

The style of the relationship as reported by the press was one of mediation. The First Nations group was seen as asserting traditional land rights and the federal government was seen as willing to negotiate the transfer of the land. The pace of negotiations and their impact on established economic activity in the surrounding community, on the other hand, were quickly defined as areas of tension by the press. Throughout, the Stoney Pointers remained a non-entity because the federal government assumed the legitimacy of the band lists.

On 1 May 1995 the *Free Press* gave considerable space to the negotiating parties in its front-page report: '"The defence department will continue to negotiate the return of the land with the chief of the Kettle and Stoney [sic] Point First Nation," McGuire said. The government still doesn't acknowledge the existence of the Stoney Point First Nation, regardless of that group's occupation of the military camp, he added. "We are in contact with Chief [Tom] Bressette. It's his call if he wants to include those people in negotiations."'

Within two weeks of the July 1995 occupation, problems of names and the band list were so significant that the *Free Press* outlined nuances of the band designations as follows: 'Stony, as in the Kettle and Stony Point First Nation, refers to the band recognized by the federal government. Stoney refers to a group not recognized by the federal government who say they are a separate band. The Stoney group has taken over Camp Ipperwash' (12 August 1995, A7).

Thus, in the early stages of federal negotiations, entitlement was given to a single Kettle and Stony Point 'band' as defined by the band list held by the federal government. Until the removal in 1942, the two bands had lived on separate land bases, although there had been considerable interaction between the two. The problem of designation had begun, however, as a means of minimizing the cost of Indian agents in the nineteenth century. At that time the Kettle Point and Stoney Point bands had been treated on paper as if they were a single entity, continuing an earlier practice of treating the Chippewas of Sarnia, Kettle Point, and Stoney Point as a single band for administrative purposes (and prior to that, these three bands had been lumped in with the Walpole Island band). The competent band according to the federal government was thus that named on the band list. Entitlement did not reside in what was considered a subgroup, either under the structure of the native associations or within the framework of the federal government.

In September 1995 the incident entered a new phase when Stoney Pointers occupying the old military base moved onto the adjacent Ipperwash Provincial Park. In so doing, they challenged the provincial government and its Ministry of Natural Resources which was responsible for the administration of provincial parks. The provincial response differed from the federal one in that it immediately defined the Stoney Pointers' action as criminal.

The provincial government avoided offering entitlement to Stoney Point voices by invoking organizational nuances within the state structure. The slippage between federal and provincial jurisdictions as defined in sections 91 and 92 of the Constitution Act of 1982 was central. Specifically First Nations' issues fall under federal jurisdiction (91[24]), while the provincial park lies within provincial jurisdiction. In addition to the nuances of the federal-provincial division of powers, a second division of powers (that between the provincial politicians and the administration of justice, including the provincial police) was invoked to cloud responsibility and thus the capacity of Stoney Point advocates to address the state. The obfuscation denied entitlement to the natives. This denial of entitlement by the provincial government is illustrated in a number of ways in the following observations of the *Free Press* on 13 September 1995 (B1):

In Toronto, Premier Mike Harris met with Assembly of First Nations Grand Chief Ovide Mercredi and other native representatives, then issued a statement saying the government will not discuss the occupation of the provincial park. Harris has maintained the stand-off will be handled by provincial police, not the government. He had resisted meeting with Mercredi, and kept the native leader waiting two hours. The premier, who refused to answer questions after the 30-minute meeting, said in his statement that he had agreed to meet as a courtesy. 'I personally delivered the government's message that we will not discuss the illegal occupation of Ipperwash,' Harris said.

Harris's response as constructed in the media reflects Taylor's concern that meaningful dialogue will require the participants to go beyond their assumed understandings of their world. A further step in denying Stoney Pointers entitlement was the government's consistent use of the name Ipperwash to refer to the Stoney Point land. As discussed below, the Stoney Pointers countered by calling for a public inquiry into the circumstances surrounding the death of one of their people, Dudley George. Such an inquiry would give the Stoney Pointers a voice.

The construction of the occupation as an illegal or criminal act by Harris defined the issue as falling under the jurisdiction of the police and courts. This construction was extended through reports of law-enforcement activity 'on the ground.' Interestingly, events in the legal realm eventually were to assert further pressure on Premier Harris and to clarify the impact of the early denial of voice to the Stoney Point community. We shall trace this construction to show how a decentred state can result in complex patterns of communication which in turn yield significant intra- and extra-systemic political consequences.

The shooting death by the Ontario Provincial Police of Dudley George, a Stoney Point member, on 6 September 1995, as he and a group of protesters attempted to cross police lines, was one of the biggest issues to arise in the occupation of Ipperwash/Stoney Point by Stoney Point people. Here the jurisdictional separation between government and the police was, and continues to be, used by the Harris government to its advantage. On 19 April 1996 the *Free Press* commented on its front page:

OPP Chief [Superintendent Chris] Coles said the decision to confront the protesters was made by police, independent of Queen's Park, but [regional chief of the First Nations of Ontario Gord] Peters says that some natives received calls from contacts at Queen's Park before the confrontation telling them a cabinet meeting had been held to discuss the protest at Ipperwash Provincial Park and the decision to send in police had been made. 'We were told it came from the top,' said Peters. He nodded when asked if he believes the order came from Premier Mike Harris's office. Harris's press secretary Bob Reid said it was 'absolutely false' to suggest the premier ordered police to confront the natives. 'The premier was never directly involved in any formal meetings on Ipperwash,' Reid said.

Aside from the importance of the historical content in the excerpt above, we also find interesting displays of entitlement given to two native leaders: MLA Elijah Harper from Manitoba and Gord Peters, a regional chief representing the First Nations of Ontario. Both these men held established roles in the Canadian governmental context, but neither came from the band(s) involved. The issue of representation is one of the systemic assumptions of state and becomes a key means of denying entitlement to such 'non-entities' as the people of Stoney Point. This is illustrated in the front-page comment of the *Free Press* on 19 April 1996: 'It's not clear how the Stoney Pointers believe the park will be returned to them because no single person speaks for the natives at the camp ... Kettle and Stony Point First Nation Chief Tom Bressette could not be reached for comment. Stoney Pointers are named as members on the Kettle and Stony Point band list, but they say they are a separate group. The federal government does not recognize them as a separate group.' Note that the newspaper coverage is consistent with governmental practices of looking for a 'representative' to speak for the group. Failing the discovery of one at the site, the media designated their representative as the elected chief of the federally recognized band, Kettle and Stony Point.

Another thread in denying entitlement and voice is to evoke the spectre of 'legality' and 'the court system' as extending the only 'legitimate' site in which one can assert a claim to voice. Following is an example from the same issue of the *Free Press*:

The Victoria-Haliburton MPP also said he's heard 'rumours' the Ipperwash protest could spill over somehow to nearby Pinery Provincial Park, adding any disputes should be solved legally ... [Natural Resources Minister Chris] Hodgson said he's aware a native land claim on Ipperwash is in the offing, and said he wrote the chief of the Kettle and Stony Point band earlier this week offering provincial assistance to help speed the process. He said the province remains convinced it owns the park, and a land claim shouldn't prevent Ipperwash from reopening ... 'You don't get ownership until you've proven the validity of the claim,' he said.

The legitimacy of (systemic) legal discourse is echoed below in the response from two local band chiefs and the national chief to 'a local man's effort to claim Pinery Provincial Park' (*Free Press*, 24 April 1996, section B). Note, too, that the person whose claims are being denied also accepts the legal framework. The construction of law as the medium for dispute resolution thus seems universal:

Kettle and Stony Point Chief Tom Bressette, Chippewas of Sarnia Chief Phil Maness and Walpole Island Chief Joe Gilbert met with National Chief Ovide Mercredi and 'unanimously condemned this individual, Maynard T. George.' ... 'Many claims in the area are the common concern of all three First Nations and no one individual has the right to advance treaty claims based on their personal interpretations of historic fact,' a news release from the chiefs' said ... George has said he will continue his claim through 'legal channels' ... Bressette said George's actions have 'started a lot of trouble' for area native bands. 'We want public support. We don't want the public to think we're all running off to claim land ... there's a process for these things.' (24 April 1996, section B)

By that fall, a second construction had become dominant in the media, that of the native people as 'militants,' 'criminals' and 'zealots':

The militant Indians behind the barricades and elsewhere tend to look on their elected leaders as pawns of a white people's government. Indian Affairs Minister Ron Irwin has said that those behind the barricades are the greatest possible hindrance to the aboriginal cause and are nothing more than zealots. He is by no means alone in the criticism. At a stand-off at Gustafsen Lake in British Columbia, where there have been shootings and woundings, an RCMP officer spent part of Wednesday reading out the numerous criminal records of Indians who have taken a stand there in a dispute over land. He said this was not a matter of Indian rights but simply a 'criminal agenda.' (*Free Press* 16 September 1995, section C)

Here we return to the earlier theme of entitlement under 'appropriate' representation and to the conflict between legal and community prescriptions. Any group that did not accept 'elected leaders' as legitimate was considered 'militant,' and this construction allows for a denial of entitlement for persons who might disagree with current governmental systems, unless the disagreement is addressed within governmentally approved channels or is framed in appropriate statist discourse.

This device also is invoked within the structures of state itself, where voice rests with MPPs, because they have a place in the system, but not with 'non-entities' as defined by their lack of position within structures recognized by the state. This is illustrated in an article in the *Free Press* (14 May 1997, A1) which describes an MPP demanding a public inquiry and members of the community (merely) 'echoing' that voice: 'Phillips among other opposition MPP's wants a public inquiry held to clear lingering and disturbing questions about the shooting. Their call has been echoed by members of George's family.'

Premier Harris has maintained his position of sidelining the broad issue to the justice system and thus has continued to deny a forum for the voice of the community outside the constraints of the legal system. The *Free Press* reported:

Allegations of government cover-up at Ipperwash continue to confront Harris who denies any involvement. He continued to refute allegations Monday and he accused Phillips of distorting the truth. 'In opposition you can be irresponsible, quote rumours,' said Harris. Phillips, among other opposition MPPs, wants a public inquiry ... Harris will not rule out an inquiry but says he wants to wait until all legal issues, including Deane's appeal are exhausted. A wrongful death civil suit filed by George's family must also be dealt with, he said. (14 May 1997, A4)

In such cases, when governmental representatives deny entitlement by defining the issue as legal or criminal in contrast to political, the voice of the community is silenced. In all cases, entitlement falls to entities recognized by office and thus with significance in the system. Their status and potential change dramatically as one selects the 'appropriate' forum for discussion. Both practices can silence the voice of non-entities. On the other hand, when the non-entity's claim is voiced by an officeholder in the system, that voice is heard, but it is once removed from that non-entity. It, too, can be denied or discredited by invoking nuances of system to maintain the power of the hegemon.

The 'Ipperwash incidents' had a significant impact on the local residents in the surrounding area. Established economic patterns and assumptions about land tenure were challenged. A local group of property holders in the region demanded to be heard – that is, they demanded a voice – first through their local government and then though petitions to both the provincial and federal governments.[13] Their claims, when reported, constructed a contra-voice in the media which inflamed political polarization around the issue, and this in turn played a significant role in the emerging political struggle over the demand for a public inquiry into the events leading up to the death of Dudley George. A public inquiry was the remedy sought by the Stoney Pointers denied a voice by the Harris government. In a letter to the editor in response to a *Free Press* article of 22 February 1996, a member from the surrounding community wrote: 'The information is reversed probably because of the source. From the original illegal take-over of the military camp and then the occupation of the park grounds, the news media, for the most part, talked only to native people and presented their side. The media ignored the problems and effect this situation was having on permanent residents. Our government also ignored these people and showed a lack of care for their safety or protection of their homes.'

An incident in July 1996 became the symbol for the coalescence of grievances of this emerging group. On 21 July 1996 a cabin cruiser was beached by high waves at Indian-occupied Ipperwash Provincial Park. The owner was quoted by the *Free Press* as follows:

'Then the Indians discovered it and started to strip it.' ... E. said he called Grand Bend OPP 'where everybody was fully aware of what was going on. They said it was out of their jurisdiction.' However the OPP brought in a negotiator ... who obtained agreement from the Indians to allow Burnette to recover the boat. 'I felt relieved, but within half an hour five pickup trucks pulled up at my boat and they just started stripping it ... The OPP advised me to stay the heck away.' E. said he has had no direct contact with the Indians. 'I'm being backed 100 per cent by people who live along the shoreline. They said I'm a godsend, that they have been harassed for years by Indians who claim the beach,' E. said: 'I'm calling my attorney and anybody else I can get involved. Certainly, the Canadian government doesn't care,' he said. (22 July 1996, B1)

The next day, a rebuttal appeared under the headline, 'OPP defend actions during boat's looting.' (*Free Press*, 23 July 1996, A1). The OPP were reported as arguing: 'No, we're not going to go storming down the beach and take back the boat. You know the history of this area. We negotiated so there were no problems. This was resolved and he got his boat back.' That same day an editorial argued:

Ontarians can't be blamed for wondering exactly what is going on at Ipperwash. The occupation is a year old, yet both levels of government seem caught in a state of paralysis. There's lots of rhetoric but no one seems intent on trying to settle the land claim dispute. The police, while admitting they should have acted immediately, are facing their own credibility problems. The result: Ipperwash shows signs of spiralling into anarchy. Patience is diminishing on all sides ... The senior governments should ... show some leadership.

The call for action reflected concern for the growing polarization in the region between the 'natives' and 'local residents.' Issues of law enforcement and order maintenance were quickly grafted onto the provincial government/Stoney Point issue. On 24 July 1996, the *Free Press* carried two front-page stories on Ipperwash. The lead headline read: 'OPP officer charged in native's death,' with the subheading, 'But members of ... George's family say [the officer] is a scapegoat and they want others charged.' The article reiterated the Stoney Pointers' demand for a full public inquiry. In the second front-page article, headed 'Locals call it "lawless land,"' local residents demanded more police protection. The following day, 25 July, another article focused on the law enforcement, or the lack of it, in the area. This article contrasted the police position of maintaining order and protecting life with residents' claims of 'harassment, vandalism and theft' by local aboriginal people, (*Free Press*, 25 July 1996, B1).

Between 21 and 25 July 1996, a complex construction of politics revolved around the Ipperwash incident. A landowners group was attacking Stoney

Pointers over issues of property values, safety, and public order. The Stoney Pointers were partially vindicated when a police officer was charged for Dudley George's death. At the same time, his family persisted in their demand for a public inquiry. The OPP, on the other hand, were attacked by the group of local landowners for not being more aggressive in their dealings with the Stoney Pointers. The police responded moderately, placing the value of life above property. Both the landowners and the Stoney Pointers built their alliances at the local, national, and international levels. A film-maker was reported as planning to make a film presenting the Stoney Pointer's position. By the fall, the *Free Press* was reporting on police efforts to mediate the dispute.

This configuration of voices remained relatively stable until April 1997 when the police officer charged with George's death was found guilty. The verdict received province-wide headlines. In the *Toronto Star*, Ian Urquhart argued:

The conviction yesterday ... is far from the end of this story. Rather, it is just the beginning. For the real story here is not who pulled the trigger that killed George, but the circumstances that led up to the shooting – the first by police of an Indian in a land dispute this century. The government has done its best to cover the trail, but some footprints have been uncovered. The government ought to drop the excuses and launch a full inquiry. Failure to do so will justify the view that it has something to hide. (29 April 1997, A1)

The next day, the *Free Press*, in its report on the issue as it was debated in question period in the Ontario legislature, also focused on alleged links between the Harris government's refusal to negotiate and the killing of Dudley George. On 30 April the *Globe and Mail* stated: 'Opposition MPP's call for Ipperwash inquiry.' It reported on the civil suit which the George family was launching for 'wrongful death' and that they would consider 'dropping their civil suit if they were satisfied that an inquiry would get to the root of the events in the park' (30 April 1997, A19).

These constructions of the Ipperwash story focusing on the questionable role of the state were complemented by coverage of the main community voice, ONFIRE,[14] which supported the police and defined the Stoney Pointers as a threat. The result was the construction of a polarized community.

When the Stoney Pointers acted to recover their land, they were outside both the native and state hierarchies. The community was invisible to the system and the system reacted by denying it entitlement, explicitly and implicitly. The premier of Ontario defined the natives as criminals and refused to talk to them: the government was willing to play 'musical offices' when Stoney Point demanded a voice. With respect to the federal negotiations, the media and native system deferred to the entitlement given through the official band-list system to the Kettle and Stoney Point band. As the federal and provincial issues unfolded, residents in nearby communities felt ignored. Again, voice was demanded. Again, the legal milieu was inappropriate since they had no 'standing,' although the claims commission did grant public hearings. The result was a new media actor opposing the voice of the Stoney Pointers. Its presence constructed regional polarization.

The Ipperwash story offers a set of contrasting insights into entitlement, the place of voice, the construction of the other, and the challenges of governance. The peaceful occupation of the military base contrasts with the confrontation surrounding the occupation of the provincial park. In the former case, entitlement to voice was contested within the First Nations communities. The negotiations still proceed slowly, and the tensions among the federal government, Stoney Pointers, and the 'Kettle and Stony Point Band' are not resolved. The dialogue, however, is evolving according to the tortuous path predicted by Taylor and Chambers.

The Ipperwash Provincial Park story differs since the provincial government denied a voice to the community, instead labelling the incident as 'criminal.' The definition precluded a negotiated settlement of contextual grievances and led to an extensive struggle for voice and hence entitlement. The Stoney Pointers have persisted, but state response has forced the dialogue into the realm of law enforcement. The senseless killing of Dudley George contrasts with the moderation later shown by the OPP in protecting life and in respecting the normal law-enforcement responsibilities of the First Nations. The contrast reflects the significance of the systemic definition of issues by those in power.

To silence a voice that speaks for an established cultural identity differs according to Taylor's test from those making singular, ad hoc assertions. Sensitivity to that distinction seems absent if one evaluates the actions of the Ontario government. That insensitivity has led to the construction of a confrontational politics at the local level and an increasing crescendo for openness at the provincial level. That construction has helped polarize residents in the region. In both cases, the denial of voice, or censorship, has had its human price. The 'nuances' surrounding voice thus become a major concern as one studies censorship in its social, rather than in its narrower legal, garb.

NOTES

1 See Rosemary Coombe, 'Identifying and Engendering the Forms of Emergent Civil Societies: New Directions in Political Anthropology,' *PoLAR*, 20, no. 1 (1997), 1–2. For an interesting analysis of these dynamics, see also J.M. Edelman's *Constructing the Political Spectacle* (Chicago: University of Chicago Press 1988), especially

ch. 6; and for some historical context, see W. Lippmann, *The Phantom Public* (New York: Harcourt, Brace 1925).

2 For more on the constructions of publics, see Edelman, *Constructing the Political Spectacle*; and for the construction of value hierarchies, see L.P. Valentine, 'Creating Enemies: Value Hierarchy and Presentation of First Nations Issues in a Mainstream Canadian Press,' *Proceedings of the 28th Algonquian Conference* (Winnipeg: University of Manitoba Press 1998).

3 The term 'fractionalized state' refers to the 'decentered' character of the modern liberal-democratic state. It parallels, at the institutional level, what Jurgen Habermas noted at the level of explanation and meaning in increasingly differentiated spheres; see S. Chambers, *Reasonable Democracy* (Ithaca: Cornell University Press 1996), 128–9; and Edelman, *Constructing the Political State*, chs. 1–2.

4 C. Taylor, *Multiculturalism and 'The Politics of Recognition'* (Princeton, N.J.: Princeton University Press 1992), 36.

5 An introduction to this topic includes: Michael Asch, ed., *Aboriginal and Treaty Rights in Canada: Essays on Law, Equality, and Respect for Difference* (Vancouver: University of British Columbia Press 1997); Michael Asch, *Home and Native Land: Aboriginal Rights and the Canadian Constitution* (Toronto: Methuen 1984); Noel Dyck, ed., *Indigenous Peoples and the Native State: Fourth World Politics in Canada, Australia and Norway* (St John's: Institute of Social and Economic Research, Memorial University 1985); Noel Dyck and J.B. Waldram, eds., *Anthropology, Public Policy and Native Peoples in Canada* (Montreal: McGill-Queen's University Press 1993); J.S. Frideres, *Native People in Canada: Contemporary Conflicts* (Toronto: Prentice Hall 1983); A. Grant, *No End of Grief: Indian Residential Schools in Canada* (Winnipeg: American Publishers 1996); K.M. Hazelhurst, ed., *Legal Pluralism and the Colonial Legacy* (Avebury 1995); and A. Turner, ed., *The Politics of Indianness* (St John's: Institute of Social and Economic Research, Memorial University 1983).

6 Chambers, *Reasonable Democracy*, 126–7. Habermas's rich phrase 'life-worlds' is the metaphor used in Chambers's analysis.

7 Ibid., 232.

8 In Amy Schuman, 'Get Out of My Face: Entitlement and Authoritative Discourse,' in J. Hill and J. Irvine, eds., *Responsibility and Evidence in Oral Discourse* (Cambridge, U.K.: Cambridge University Press 1992), 135.

9 See Frideres, *Native People in Canada*, ch. 4.

10 One of the many issues central to the discussion of the Stoney Point claims is that of 'representation,' a theme that is implicit through much of the discourse. We could easily substitute the term 'entitlement' for most uses of this word in the texts. In these texts, multiple levels of government systems are invoked which constrain entitlement.

11 The difference in spelling is significant and not an error. The Stoney Point First
   Nation peoples usually use an 'e' in the spelling of the separate band.

12 Ipperwash Provincial Park forms part of the original Stoney Point reserve. In October 1927 the land was acquired by two local land developers, White and Crawford,
   under disputed conditions. The portion that now forms the park was subsequently
   sold to the province of Ontario and in 1938, by an order-in-council, was made a
   provincial park. For details of the original land surrender, see Indian Claims Commission, Chippewas of Kettle and Stoney Point First Nation: *Report On: 1927 Surrender Inquiry* (March 1997).

13 The residents were granted public hearings by the federal Native Lands Commission. Members from the community formed an association, drafted a petition can-
   vassing for funds to defend against a court challenge to native control of the
   disputed lands, and became active locally and through the media.

14 The *London Free Press* on 31 August 1996 (A12) describes the community as follows: 'Ontario Foundation for Individual Rights and Equalities (ONFIRE) formed
   in October 1995 of about 1,400 non-natives alarmed over native unrest, plummet-
   ing property values and what they say is lawlessness on the former army camp.' It
   is worth noting the values underlying the organization as constructed by the report.

17

The Ironies of Academic Freedom

PAUL AXELROD

Historians in Canada and the United States have demonstrated that the road to academic freedom is paved with the courage and periodic martyrdom of nonconformist professors. From the mid-nineteenth century to the early 1960s, a coterie of freethinking secularists, socialists, civil libertarians, and administration critics elicited the wrath, and sometimes the strong arms, of university presidents and powerful politicians. Hostility to political radicalism exposed left-leaning academics to censorious treatment during the 1930s; so did the Cold War 'witch-hunts' of the 1950s, particularly in the United States. For criticizing the principal of Winnipeg's United College in a private letter to a colleague, Harry Crowe was dismissed from his teaching position in 1958, an event that inspired the formal constitution of the Canadian Association of University Teachers. For refusing in 1954 to cooperate both with the House Un-American Activities Committee, headed by Joseph McCarthy, and with an internal university panel probing his political convictions, University of Michigan professor Chandler Davis was fired and eventually jailed for a six-month term.[1]

These important cases, and numerous less notorious ones, point to the dangers of administrative and political coercion in the governing of universities. As citadels of intellectual vitality, universities now elicit vigilant opposition if they censure or discipline dissident professors. The convention of academic freedom and the institution of tenure are intended to enhance the autonomy of scholars by protecting them from authoritarian and arbitrary treatment. Universities have been tested anew by recent conflicts over 'inclusive' institutional policies governing the subjects of gender and race. Academics are deeply divided on these matters, and their right to challenge university policy (from whatever perspective) without fear of sanction or dismissal remains essential. Ensuring the integrity of academic life thus requires protecting professors from the unwarranted intervention of external authorities, be they university administrations, governments, business lobbyists, or citizen pressure groups.

Most professors would likely agree with this received academic wisdom, but I believe that the approach that informs it insufficiently grapples with the subject of academic freedom. As Klaus Petersen observes in his introduction to this book, public discourse is regulated by both direct and indirect means. This chapter argues that academic life is constrained by forces that arise, not only from the abuse of administrative authority and political interference, but also from the culture and institutions that professors themselves largely control. I examine the ways in which tenure, peer review, and academic entrepreneurialism impose conditions and qualifications on the autonomy and freedom of academics. Even in the absence of managerial coercion and censorship, the professoriate has always regulated academic culture. It has not always acknowledged the complexity and irony of its own conduct.

Tenure has a long and complex history, reaching back to the Middle Ages, when universities, and by implication the 'masters' within them, were granted by European sovereigns immunity from 'both ecclesiastical and temporal authorities and the right to make rules and regulations affecting the conduct of their own affairs.'[2] The modern concepts of both academic freedom and tenure arose from the nineteenth-century German practice of 'Lehrfreiheit,' which gave academics 'lifetime' appointments to pursue teaching and research as long as they forswore 'religious heterodoxy' and political 'subversion.'[3] Under this system, scholars thus secured considerable autonomy, but surviving as they did at 'the pleasure of the state,' their freedom was clearly conditional.

Throughout the twentieth century, North American professors and the associations representing them – gradually, and not always in unison – sought to strengthen the principle of academic autonomy, while removing the externally imposed qualifications attached to its preservation. By the mid-1960s, tenure codes gave greater protection to professors holding unorthodox political views, and incorporated the judicial principle of 'due process' into dismissal and other disciplinary procedures. Today, those obtaining tenure hold permanent academic positions which can be abrogated for cause, normally including professional misconduct, incompetence, and refusal to carry out assigned duties.[4] Tenure is granted, at least ideally, to scholars and teachers deemed by their peers to be capable of making a significant contribution to their academic discipline, to the institution, and to the profession as a whole. How these criteria are precisely defined, and how the tenure process is structured, differ from place to place. As a major American study of the subject observed: 'On every aspect of tenure ... criteria [and procedure] for appointment, reappointment, and award of tenure; length of probationary period; categories of personnel eligible for tenure; ... procedures for appeal from adverse decisions; methods of evaluating teaching, scholarship, and public service; ... the range of variation among the 2600 institutions of higher education [and sometimes even within institutions – from division to division or even department to department] is enormous.'[5]

The variability of standards and procedures for the achievement of tenure exposes candidates to a peer-review process that is simultaneously demanding and uncertain. Unmistakably superior applicants would likely be tenured at any university, while the converse is true of those who are palpably inferior. However, since most candidates fall between these two extremes, institutional, and even departmental, particularities matter enormously. Herein lies one of tenure's ironies. Designed to protect academics from the tyranny of unwarranted external pressures, it makes them vulnerable to internal procedures that can be surprisingly capricious.

One informative handbook advises applicants to 'view tenure as a political process' with respect to both the academic and the non-academic criteria which govern outcomes.[6] Candidates should be aware of these and prepare for them. Given such factors as changing market conditions, the priorities of a university, or simply the make-up of a tenure committee, academic 'excellence becomes whatever a majority of voting tenured faculty members in a particular department at a particular time say it is.'[7] Thus, what is the candidate's expected publication output? What journals are considered by senior colleagues to be prestigious or 'second rate?' Is one in a department that rewards a close adherence to dominant intellectual paradigms, or alternative ones?

It is even suggested, without evident cynicism, that in some departments, candidates who are too prolific may be putting themselves at risk:

Productive tenure candidates may actually be penalized for being too good and thus being 'rate busters.' Low-producing, already tenured department members may be threatened by the implied rising expectations for research and publication if frequently publishing junior colleagues are tenured. Tenuring high producers changes the dynamics for distributing salary increases within the department by increasing the level of competition and expectations for doing well. Low producers used to coasting while collecting regular salary increases may fear that they will no longer be competitive for the highest raises. If you publish much more than your colleagues, you are advised to downplay the difference, at least until you are tenured. 'When possible, choose a job where your colleagues' expectations match your abilities.[8]

Henry Rosovsky, economist and former dean of arts and science at Harvard, points to another problem in the evaluation process – the tendency for aging professors to lose touch with newer academic currents outside their own defined fields of study: 'When subjects change rapidly and new techniques emerge, it grows harder for older professors to judge the young. For example, my own background, training and competence does not allow me to read current mathematical economics. In making choices in that field, I have to take what my colleagues say on faith. Generalists are an endangered species in modern universities; nearly all of us are highly and narrowly specialized.'[9] Thus, not only might the interdisciplinary generalist face special obstacles in obtaining a position, or in achieving tenure, but candidates cannot be confident that the decision makers themselves are especially well informed.

The latter problem is generally addressed by seeking the input of external referees, most of whom are expected to have an 'arm's-length' distance from the candidate. Departmental and upper-level tenure and promotion committees are thus aided in their evaluations by scholars considered to be experts in a candidate's field. Critical assessments will almost certainly damage a candidate's prospects. If the list of referees is assembled in a judicious, widely consultative manner, and if the referees themselves are comprehensive in their consideration and fair in their judgments, the process should work reasonably well. But there are potential difficulties. Some fields are so small that assessors are bound to know the candidates, and their views could be affected, positively or negatively, by personal factors. Candidates who establish personal and academic networks beyond their institutions before being considered for tenure are probably better positioned than those who do not.[10] Where renowned scholars are asked to assess the work of junior academics, influential verdicts may be supported by exceedingly superficial evaluations. (Renowned scholars, writing evaluative reports, do not always feel the need to justify their opinions.) A candidate who has critically cited the work of a referee or, perhaps worse, not cited him/her at all, may elicit negative assessments. In the end, one can never know the real basis of a referee's judgment. Ideological disagreements, personal relations, self-interest, sensitive egos, or sheer laziness are unlikely to be the dominant factors behind most assessors' letters. But, if even a single candidate has been the victim of such non-scholarly considerations, his or her academic freedom and future have been compromised, and in ways that are unlikely to be detected, given the confidentiality of the assessment process.

Assessments of scholarship and teaching are the most important bases for tenure decisions, but in most institutions one's service to the university or the community are also taken into account. Some departments specify service requirements, but most do not, leaving candidates the political challenge of 'managing their service appearance'[11] in ways that enhance rather than harm their prospects. Too little service might raise questions about one's commitment to the department, while too much may be considered an inappropriate allocation of one's time.[12] Furthermore, service activities are particularly vulnerable to subjective assessments. Evaluators, usually drawn from the ranks of one's colleagues, could well differ in their perceptions of important departmental tasks. Candidates who do other's bidding and who 'toe the departmental line' may elicit more favourable assessments than those who question conventional departmental practices.

The assessment of one's 'collegiality,' therefore, also plays a role, at least informally, in tenure considerations. In the view of Marcia Lynn Whicker et al., it may be used to weed out candidates who do not 'fit' or who are not good department citizens. 'Before tenure you will be able to get away with alienating one or even two powerful department members who already hold tenure, depending on the size of the department. But alienating most of the tenured members is almost always fatal. [If you make your colleagues] ... anxious, nervous, threatened, irritated or angry ... you will probably be rejected.'[13]

A study of American university journalism programs, in which a small minority of women are employed, found a perceived pattern of 'non-intentional discrimination' in the recruitment and promotion of females. Burdened with domestic responsibilities while lacking female mentors and role models, women faculty had not 'the time, the experience, the financial and emotional support, the networks and the coalitions often necessary to conduct many activities that they [were] convinced would help pave the way toward advancement within the Department.'[14]

Strong departmental chairs, who counsel tenure candidates effectively, protect them from the snare of political conflict, and ensure that their teaching and service loads are reasonable and balanced, can smooth the applicant's career development. However, opportunistic or ambitious chairs in a polarized department might themselves enlist the loyalty of new appointees, assign them to inappropriate tasks, and leave them politically exposed at the moment they come forward for tenure. Because the peer-review and tenure processes are decentralized in most institutions, 'your chair may not be able to protect you even if he or she wants to.' Thus, candidates are advised to establish 'cordial relations with all of your departmental colleagues.'[15]

If factors other than pure academic merit can affect the academic life and prospects of non-tenured faculty, thereby imposing conditions on the academic freedom they enjoy, this applies especially to contractually limited and part-time faculty who lie outside the 'tenure stream' and who comprise a growing proportion of university teachers across North America. In 1991–2, some 25,000 Canadian and 300,000 American faculty were categorized as part-time, temporary, or non-tenure track.[16] Normally, universities do not even offer the contractual language of academic freedom to such faculty, and by any realistic measure, their autonomy is seriously constrained. They generally work under conditions that offer them no security and little incentive or reward to pursue scholarly research, and their numbers include a far higher concentration of women than do full-time faculty ranks. Being reappointed to a part-time teaching position may well require – at least in the eyes of the instructor – excessive deference to departmental authority, willingness to teach in unfavourable conditions, and undue political quiescence. Canadian and American faculty associations tend – correctly – to blame university-administration hiring strategies or government-funding policies for this situation, but full-time, tenured faculty have scarcely made the plight of their part-time colleagues a major political or academic priority.[17] While sharing academic space and professional responsibilities, the two groups lead a separate and unequal existence. Indeed, as Edward Monahan and Henry Rosovsky both note, the system of tenure often 'protects the academic freedom of those who need it the least, the more senior faculty, while it ignores the problems of those who need that protection, young untenured faculty.'[18]

It might be alleged, with some justification, that the previous discussion is very pessimistic and highlights worst-case scenarios in the tenure process. (The same, of course, could be said of the famous censorship/academic freedom cases, such as those referred to earlier.) Further, it is unrealistic to expect organizational tensions, professional competition, economic exigency, or human relations to play no role in the life of the university, including in the tenure process. In fact, there are checks and balances that help make the system fairer, less arbitrary, and more workable than it otherwise might be. Because single faculty or administrators seldom control the tenuring process, which normally draws upon the input of many individuals and several committees, then personal conflicts, abuses, and unfair assessments may well be identified and prevented from influencing final outcomes. Appeal processes provide additional protection to candidates. Nevertheless, the system is far from pristine, and improper and unjust decisions have unquestionably been made.[19] Conditioned to be highly sensitive to the actions of censorious non-academic authorities, professors should be no less vigilant in protecting their own colleagues from the mistreatment and manoeuvrings of their own colleagues.

If tenure is the ticket to academic security, scholarly publication is the supreme currency of the academic marketplace. One's productivity, academic rank, professional reputation, access to research grants, and income are all conditioned by the quantity and perceived quality of articles and manuscripts in 'refereed' or 'peer-reviewed' publications.[20] One recent survey, echoing previous studies, found that publication by professors in prestigious, refereed journals ranks 'highest among all activities listed' in tenure and promotion criteria.[21] The ability of tenured and non-tenured academics alike to exercise meaningfully their academic freedom, to find an outlet for their scholarship and voice, is, to a large degree, dependent on positive peer reviews of their submitted work.

It is difficult to imagine an alternative to peer review, unless one takes the position that all research is of equal merit and that everything written should be published. But, as with the system of tenure, there are imperfections in the peer-review process which merit critical scrutiny.

How does a journal or book publisher achieve superior ranking within an academic discipline? It must be 'refereed,' but since almost all academic journals employ some version of this, other criteria matter. If it publishes the work of senior scholars, if its editors are themselves prominent academics, if it has a high 'rejection rate,' or more important, and mysterious, if it is simply recognized through formal and informal surveys as a 'leading' publisher ... then it is.

Researchers studying this system confirm that senior academics do rank scholarly journals, and that they judge the value of their colleagues' work on the basis of such assessments. But also important is this finding: the same academics may be unaware of the existence or content of large numbers of journals within their own fields. In one Canadian study, 139 senior academics in education were asked to rank 40 journals, 20 of which were refereed and 20 of which were not, and to rate only those journals with which they were familiar. 'The average respondent rated less than three quarters of the serials ... [which] raises a disturbing question, namely how can administrators make sound tenure and promotion decisions if they themselves do not know their own serials?'[22] Given such knowledge gaps, profound work in a relatively unknown journal might well be downgraded, or even dismissed, thus damaging a young scholar's professional reputation.

Scholarly innovation and critical analysis might also be impeded by the ranking system. Prestigious journals often, though by no means inevitably, reflect established values and paradigms within their respective disciplines. Having gained 'professional' legitimacy, particular research conventions and methodologies will receive more favourable treatment than unconventional work which 'falls outside the cognitive boundaries created by the social limits of the [dominant] group.'[23]

A detailed study of the manuscript assessment process used by *Angewandte Chemie*, one of the world's leading chemistry journals, found many of the criticisms of peer review to be overstated. Still, the *A.G.*'s publications showed a distinct bias in favour of submissions by senior professors over more junior scholars whose 'highest academic degree was a doctorate.'[24] The national origin of aspiring contributors also affected publication prospects. Scholars from Germany had a higher rate of success in the journal than other nationals, and those from developing countries were clearly the least successful, reflecting an international tendency – and bias – in scholarly publishing.

While evidence of discrimination against women by assessors and editors is mixed,[25] it is certainly the case that the subject of gender studies has only recently achieved scholarly legitimacy in the social sciences. Women's studies journals provide new outlets for such work, but these publications still run the risk of lower professional ranking when questions of tenure, merit, and promotions arise.[26] Similar challenges face scholars working in other emerging fields, especially if they are critical of traditional approaches. Whicker et al. advise young scholars who are uncertain about particular disciplinary or institutional standards to 'cover' themselves by 'publishing at least some traditional pieces.'[27]

Anonymous assessors engaged by publishers and editors thus have considerable influence on the professional lives of fellow academics. While expressing overall confidence in the system and gratitude for the uncompensated labours of their reviewers, editors themselves have identified problems with the process. A former editor of the sociological journal *Social Problems* received a submission critical of the work of a senior scholar. The initial reviews were contradictory – some favourable and some not – and following an entire year, in which a total of ten reviews were solicited, the piece was rejected. The editor was particularly concerned about the possible impact of such a controversial piece on the reputation of his journal. In retrospect, he remained uncertain about the correctness and ethics of his decision.[28]

Another editor pointed to the different strategies used in soliciting assessment. In the interests of obtaining the fullest criticism, some editors avoid choosing reviewers who could be expected to be sympathetic to a writer's approach, while others take the reverse tact, believing that those who share the author's conceptual perspective are better equipped to assess its empirical rendering. Clearly there are risks in both approaches: the former may provide an overly critical assessment, the latter an overly gentle one.[29] That authors have no way of knowing which strategy a particular journal will use can make the submission and evaluation process somewhat serendipitous. Publication may well depend on the 'luck of the draw.' Blind reviewing – the concealing of the author's identity from the assessor – is one procedure employed by many journals to protect the integrity of the evaluation process. However, a survey of reviewers for the *American Journal of Public Health* found that, when given the opportunity, the majority of assessors were able to identify the authors of the articles under review.[30]

Whatever assessment method an editor chooses, a common problem is the shallowness and personal nature of many reviews. A number of editors participating in a study attempting to measure 'bias' and 'emotionalism' in the assessment process expressed concerns about 'the declining reliability and quality of reviewers, having received too many reviews which could be classified as praised but not read, or vehemently opposed with no reason.'[31] As one observer noted: 'Bland opinion expressing nothing that can be challenged may be offered as verdict.'[32] Anonymity certainly invites referees to be frank in their assessments; at the same time it offers them a cover to conduct political or personal battles with colleagues whom they dislike without the need for accountability. According to psychologist Seymour Epstein, 'one can assume that those [reviewers] who are threatened by the findings reported in an article will be less sanguine about its publication than those with a vested interest in its publication.'[33] Indeed, a study of the 'evaluative' criteria used by scientists to assess the work of their peers found a bias against manuscripts reporting negative and mixed results and a bias in favour of those reporting positive results. This demonstrated the presence of 'confirmatory bias,' or 'the tendency to evaluate positively those results that are consistent with one's own beliefs and to evaluate negatively those that are inconsistent with them.'[34] A stark indication of the system's potential weakness was a study carried out by two psychologists who 'submitted re-titled published papers to the same journals which had already published them, [and] found that eight out of nine were rejected the second time.'[35] Nor has peer review prevented the publication of work later found to be fraudulent, as evidenced recently by a number of sensational cases, particularly in the field of science and medicine.[36]

That the careers of academics and the legitimization of scholarship are affected by published work in peer-reviewed journals is indisputable. That the system is imperfect and currently in flux is also evident. The creation of new academic specialties and the voluminous growth of journals in recent years has led to a high turnover of editors who work part-time and depend, increasingly, on ad hoc evaluations. 'Referees may be chosen with few grounds for assessing their competence as reviewers and with no mechanism for monitoring their performance.'[37] The changing technology and economics of the publication industry may also have diminished the quality of peer review. It is now easier to publish journals quickly, so that the system is far more competitive. According to one observer, the increased 'need for copy' and 'the parallel fractionalisation of audiences has reduced the concern among scholars for large questions and tended to a certain insular back-scratching among specialists – so that ... tough minded peer review has become less frequent.'[38] Some journals, anxious to meet publication deadlines, by-pass the peer-review process altogether, though they would be loathe to acknowledge this practice for fear of diminishing their reputations. The publication protocol and methods for assessing the academic status of online journals appearing on the Internet are still uncertain.[39] What is clear is that peer review continues to play a central role in the conduct of academic life and in the allocation of its material (and symbolic) rewards, and scholars everywhere ought to pay more attention to the system's numerous shortcomings.

Market forces and academic entrepreneurialism also affect the culture of the contemporary university in ways that can constrain the academic voice. This assertion might seem counter-intuitive. Should not the 'marketplace of ideas' open the university, more than ever, to intellectual diversity? Given recent economic pressures, exactly the opposite may well occur.

Universities in Europe, North America, and the developing world have endured severe funding restraints particularly over the past decade and have been driven into the marketplace in search of alternative sources of income.[40] The most successful among them have secured contracts and partnerships with private corporations, especially in the areas of biotechnology, information services, and micro-electronics. Many academics, largely in the fields of science and technology, have themselves become entrepreneurs by forming private companies or by independently undertaking contract research in exchange for private-sector grants which help sustain their universities in these challenging times. Governments generally favour these arrangements because they can help offset the decline in public funding, and because they link universities more directly to the mission of promoting economic growth.

But the consequences of these strategies for an academic culture that is based on independent scholarship, 'pure' research, the free flow of information, and the centrality of the liberal arts are potentially profound. In a competitive environment, graduate students and young faculty could frame their research not around an issue that truly interests them but towards a project designed to draw research funds from a self-interested patron. Or, in the interests of career advancement, they may be pressured to participate in contract research secured by senior professors, including their academic supervisors.[41] According to Amy Guttman, 'the ... problem lies not in the influence that a particular consulting contract has on the integrity of one scholar's work, but in the way in which the widespread acceptance of consulting contracts can skew the types of problems that scholars pursue – drawing them away from serious problems that have fewer immediate pay-offs or away from equally serious problems that afflict people who cannot afford to hire consultants.'[42]

Research contracts with private corporations commonly require academics to withhold publication of their completed work for a specified period in order to keep it out of the hands of the sponsor's industrial competitors. According to Derek Bok, former president of Harvard, this process can sully the academic environment: 'Because the financial stakes are high, investigators may not merely withhold ideas from publication; they become closemouthed and refrain from the free, informal discussions with colleagues that are essential to the process of discovery.'[43] Despite his general support for closer ties between business and universities, Bok issues this warning:

It is one thing to consult for a few hundred dollars a day or to write a textbook in the hope of receiving a few thousand dollars a year. It is quite another matter to think of becoming a millionaire by exploiting a commercially attractive discovery. With stakes of this size, the nature and direction of academic research could be transmuted into something unlike the disinterested search for knowledge that has long been thought to animate university professors. In short, the newfound concern with technology transfer is disturbing not only because it could alter the practice of science in the university but also because it threatens the central values and ideals of academic research.[44]

While hardly typical, the tragic events at Montreal's Concordia University in 1992 led to an investigation and exposure of problems arising from that institution's entrepreneurial culture. Claiming that his career advancement had been unjustifiably blocked, and that his scholarship had been appropriated by others, Valery Fabrikant, a member of the Department of Mechanical Engineering, killed four of his colleagues, wounded one secretary, and was subsequently sentenced to life imprisonment for murder. Invited to investigate the standards of 'academic and scientific' integrity at Concordia, a commission headed by Harry A. Arthurs (a legal scholar and former president of York University) found that at least some of Fabrikant's charges were legitimate. Decision making in the Faculty of Engineering and Computer Science was 'arbitrary, patronage-based, and worse, [its] collegial structures were weak; authority was exercised by the Dean personally or through subordinates; a small group of faculty members enjoyed favorable arrangements while others were routinely denied support; and the favored few, in turn, were allowed to pursue their own priorities with relative impunity, essentially free from accountability requirements.'[45] Senior academics had indeed attached their names to publications that had essentially been produced by more junior scholars. And faculty with 'copious academic credits and large contracts generally enjoyed financial support for their research, prestige and influence. This privileged access to resources in turn allowed them to continue publishing while others were denied the means of becoming more productive.'[46]

Nor were these competitive, restrictive and unhealthy circumstances necessarily unique to Concordia. According to the Arthurs report, the culture that had developed over the previous twenty-five years in Canada was based on a 'political economy' that emphasized a 'production system of research' in which publications served as the 'unit of currency.' In this atmosphere, there were hazards: 'the risks of undermining primary responsibilities for teaching and academic research, the risk of succumbing to the temptation to engage in undesirable procedures, to falsify results, even to engage in fraud.'[47] These were not the inevitable consequences of the emerging relationship between the university and the marketplace. But, as the Concordia case demonstrated, only the naive would deny the potential for financial exigencies and self-interest to warp the academic culture and to favour some professorial voices over others.

Despite its unusually critical tone, this chapter is not intended as a argument against tenure, peer review, or contract research, all of which can serve the academy well if they are based on sound principles, are effectively regulated, and are carefully monitored. But, as I have attempted to argue, there are pitfalls in each of these processes which can lead to the stifling of academic speech. The threat to expression in the university comes not only from the arbitrary use of administrative authority but also – and less overtly – from within the academic culture itself. When they assess tenure files, review manuscripts, or consider forging commercial relationships, academics ought to be self-reflective. They are likely to discover that academic freedom, like freedom itself, is far from absolute.

NOTES

1 Donald Savage, 'The CAUT, the Crowe Case, and the Development of the Idea of Academic Freedom in Canada,' *CAUT Bulletin*, 14, no. 3 (December 1975), 22–37. The decision to fire Crowe was later rescinded, but he resigned from the college. See also Michiel Horn, ed., *Academic Freedom: Proceedings of the Harry Crowe Memorial Lectures* (Toronto 1987); Michiel Horn, 'Professors in the Public Eye: Canadian Universities, Academic Freedom, and the League for Social Reconstruction,' *History of Education Quarterly* (winter 1980), 425–47. On the United States, see Ellen W. Schrecker, *No Ivory Tower: McCarthyism and the Universities* (New York: Oxford University Press 1986), 3–4, 219–33.

2 Edward Monahan, 'Tenure and Academic Freedom in Canadian Universities,' in Ian Winchester, ed., *The Independence of the University and the Funding of the State: Essays on Academic Freedom in Canada* (Toronto: OISE Press 1984), 96.

3 Ibid.

4 Ibid., 101.

5 William R. Keast et al., *Faculty Tenure: A Report and Recommendations by the Commission on Academic Tenure in Higher Education* (San Francisco: Jossey-Bacs Publisher 1973), 3. See also William G. Tierney and Estela Mara Bensimon, *Promotion and Tenure: Community and Socialization in Academe* (Albany, N.Y.: University of New York Press 1996), 27–36.

6 Marcia Lynn Whicker, Jennie Jacobs Kronenfeld, and Ruth Ann Strickland, *Getting Tenure* (Newbury Park, Calif.: Sage Publications 1993), 139.

7 Whicker et al., *Getting Tenure*, 26.

8 Ibid., 27–8.

9 Henry Rosovsky, *The University: An Owner's Manual* (New York: W.W. Norton 1990), 194.

10 Whicker et al., *Getting Tenure*, 61.

11 Ibid., 111.

12 Tierney and Bensimon, *Promotion and Tenure*, 68–70.

13 Whicker et al., *Getting Tenure*, 13.

14 Larissa A. Grunig, 'Sex Discrimination in Promotion and Tenure in Journalism,' *Journalism Quarterly*, 65, no. 1 (spring 1989), 99.

15 Whicker et al., *Getting There*, 24.

16 Kevin Banks, 'The Misuse and Abuse of Sessional Appointments,' *CAUT Bulletin* (May 1995), 3. The increasing use of contract faculty in Britain is discussed in Tom Schuller, 'The Exploding Community? The University Idea and the Smashing of the Academic Atom,' *Oxford Review of Education*, 16, no. 1 (1990), 3–14.

17 American studies of this phenomenon include J.M. Gappa, *Part-time Faculty: Higher Education at a Crossroads* (Washington: ASHE–ERIC Higher Education Research Report, no. 3, 1984). For Canada, see I. Rajagopal and W.D. Farr, 'Hidden Academics: The Part-Time Faculty in Canada,' *Higher Education*, 24 (1992), 317–31.

18 1918. Rosovsky asks, 'Do not young non-tenured teachers need protection just as much or even more [than tenured faculty]? It is sometimes suggested that a corps of senior (tenured) unafraid colleagues serves as guarantors of liberty for all. This is not convincing. During the early 1950s a number of Harvard instructors and assistant professors became victims of McCarthy-style political pressures. Some term appointments were prematurely rescinded; a few left 'voluntarily' rather than facing investigation of their political opinions or affiliations. The same was true

everywhere else, and I do not recall that their elders organized an effective defense anywhere.' See *The University*, 180–1; also, Paul Blumberg, 'Lockouts, Layoffs, and the New Academic Proletariat,' in Arthur S. Wilke and B. Eugene Griessman, *The Hidden Professoriate: Credentialism, Professionalism, and the Tenure Crisis* (Westport, Conn.: Greenwood Press 1979), 33–58.

19 For extended discussions of a number of such cases in the United States – admittedly recounted from the 'victims' perspectives – see Wilke and Griessman, *The Hidden Professoriate*.

20 See James M. Banner Jr, 'Preserving the Integrity of Peer Review,' *Scholarly Publishing*, 19, no. 2 (January 1988), 109–15.

21 G. Patrick O'Neill and Paul N. Sachis, 'The Importance of Refereed Publications in Tenure and Promotion Decisions: A Canadian Study,' *Higher Education*, 28 (1996), 428.

22 Ibid., 432. See also T.M. Nelson, A.R. Buss, and M. Katzko, 'Rating of Scholarly Journals by Chairpersons in the Social Sciences,' *Research in Higher Education*, 10, no. 4 (1983), 469–97, which found an even higher rate of unfamiliarity.

23 Anthony M. Orum, 'Sociology's Self-Imposed Moral Dilemma,' *American Sociologist*, 21, no. 1 (spring 1990), 73. See also Jon Huer, *Tenure for Socrates: A Study in the Betrayal of the American Professor* (New York: Bergin and Garvey 1991), 155–68.

24 H.-D. Daniel, *Guardians of Science: Fairness and Reliability of Peer Review* (New York: UCH 1993), 73. The author examined the 449 submissions to the journal in 1984.

25 Ibid., 4–5.

26 Paula Caplan, *Lifting a Ton of Feathers: A Woman's Guide to Surviving in the Academic World* (Toronto: University of Toronto Press 1994), 41.

27 Whicker et al., *Getting Tenured*, 83. See also E. Rae Harcum and Ellen F. Rosen, *The Gatekeepers of Psychology: Evaluation of Peer Review by Case History* (Westport, Conn.: Praeger 1993).

28 Joseph W. Schneider, 'The Case of the "Unfair" Review: Ethical Issues from an Editor's File,' *American Sociologist*, 21, no. 1 (spring 1990), 89–95.

29 Sheldon Stryker, 'Ethical Issues in Editing Scholarly Journals,' *American Sociologist* 21, no. 1 (Spring 1990), 84–7.

30 Alfred Yankauer, 'How Blind is the Blind Review?' *American Journal of Public Health*, 81, no. 7 (July 1991), 843–5.

31 N.J. Spencer, Jack Harnett, and John Mahoney, 'Problems with Reviews in the Standard Editorial Practice,' *Journal of Social Behaviour and Personality*, 1, no. 1 (January 1985), 29.

32 Malcolm Atkinson, 'Regulation of Science by "Peer Review,"' *Studies in History and Philosophy of Science*, 25, no. 2 (April 1994), 149.

33 Seymour Epstein, 'What Can be Done to Improve the Journal Review Process,' *American Psychologist*, 50, no. 10 (October 1995), 884.

34 Domenic V. Cicchetti, 'The Reliability of Peer Review for Manuscript and Grant Submissions: A Cross-Disciplinary Investigation,' *Behavioral and Brain Sciences*, 14 (1991), 129. The original study was M.J. Mahoney, 'Publication Prejudices: An Experimental Study of Confirmatory Bias in the Peer Review System,' *Cognitive Theory Research*, 1 (1977), 161–75.

35 Benjamin D. Singer, 'The Criterial Crisis of the Academic World,' *Sociological Inquiry*, 59, no. 2 (May 1989), 133. For the original study, see Douglas P. Peters and Stephen J. Ceci, 'Peer Review Practices of Psychological Journals: The Fate of Published Articles Submitted Again,' *Behavioral and Brain Sciences*, 5 (1982), 187–96.

36 Several of these are described in Singer, 'The Criterial Crisis,' 127–8. See also Beth Savan, *Science under Siege: The Myth of Objectivity in Scientific Research* (Montreal: CBC Enterprises 1988), especially ch. 5.

37 Mary Frank Fox, 'Scientific Misconduct and Editorial and Peer Review Processes,' *Journal of Higher Education*, 65, no. 3 (May/June 1994), 300.

38 James M. Banner Jr, 'Preserving the Integrity of Peer Review,' *Scholarly Publishing*, 19, no. 2 (January 1988), 109. See also Larry Z. Leslie, 'Peer Review Practices of Mass Communication Scholarly Journals,' *Evaluation Review*, 14, no. 2 (April 1990), 151–65.

39 'Plan Outlined to Change Peer Review with Electronic Publishing,' *The Chronicle of Higher Education* (28 February 1997), A28.

40 See several articles in Sheldon Rothblatt and Björn Witrock, eds., *The European and American University since 1800: Historical and Sociological Essays* (Cambridge 1993); Raj Pannu, Daniel Schugurensky, and Donovan Plumb, 'From the Autonomous to the Reactive University: Global Restructuring and the Re-forming of Higher Education,' in Lorna Erwin and David MacLennan, eds., *Sociology of Education in Canada: Critical Perspectives on Theory, Research and Practice* (Toronto: Copp Clark Longman 1994), 499–526; and Janice Newson and Howard Buchbinder, *The University Means Business: Universities, Corporations and Academic Work* (Toronto: Garamond Press 1988).

41 Canadian Broadcasting Corporation, Ideas Series Transcript, *The Academic Industrial Complex* (Toronto: Canadian Broadcasting Corporation 1982), comments of Stanford immunologist Leon Woofsy, 3.

42 Amy Guttman, *Democratic Education* (Princeton, N.J.: Princeton University Press 1987), 198–9, cited in Schuller, 'The Exploding Community?' 6. For a critique of university-industry collaborations, see Beth Savan, *Science under Siege*, ch. 4.

43 Derek C. Bok, *Beyond the Ivory Tower: Social Responsibilities of the Modern University* (Cambridge, Mass.: Harvard University Press 1982), 150.

44 Bok, *Beyond the Ivory Tower*, 142.
45 H.W. Arthurs, Roger A. Blais, and Jon Thompson, *Integrity in Scholarship: A Report to Concordia University* (Montreal: Concordia University 1984).
46 Ibid., 12.
47 Edward J. Monahan, 'The Fabrikant Case at Concordia University: Some Lessons for the Better Management of Universities and Improved Academic Ethics,' *Minerva*, 33 (1995), 146.

18

The Market and Professional Censorship of Canadian School Textbooks

ROWLAND LORIMER

This chapter looks at two intertwined examples of what some might call censorship and what others might call control, ideological dominance, or even discrimination. My main point is that market organization, and more particularly the organization of investment in textbook development, favours certain ideas and, in excluding others, acts as a censor. My subsidiary point deals with the initial difficulties I had during the late 1970s and early 1980s in making the case with government officials, publishers, and academic colleagues that a certain limited set of ideas did indeed prevail in school-learning materials.

In making these points, rather than move towards condemnation as the reader might normally expect, I pose a seemingly more subtle question: What principles should be used, and articulated by whom, to guide change? And, coincidentally, by labelling something censorship, do we, at least in some instances, foreclose on understanding the dynamics of preservation of societal values, consideration of new ideas, and social change? The sense I have is that censorship is a social practice deeply embedded in the organization of society and is resistant to change. Inevitably, it would seem, there must be a struggle for significant change to come about, and while censorship acts to preserve what already exists and must eventually be overcome, it can also represent a holding action in which the ramifications of change emerge.

The Nature of Censorship

For me, censorship has a broad meaning. It is a boundary-maintaining or -servicing activity involving the adjudication of the interests or ideas of one group or individual and the differing interests of another group or individual.[1] Most often, in censorship issues, one side is seen as representing the broad interests of community, and the other side is seen to speak for the interests of a subgroup within that community, a subgroup that believes in something more strongly than is allowed for in the current organization of the community of which it is a part.

Most often, censorship is named and receives public attention when the issue involved touches a nerve in society. Thus, because sexuality touches many biological and social nerves in any society, there will always be censorship struggles with roots in human sexuality. Similarly, because child-rearing is so central to our biological and cultural continuity, censorship struggles with roots in how children should be raised will always be with us.

Censorship tends to become named and a matter for public debate when the matter at hand is seen to be profoundly and genuinely threatening to society, or a segment thereof. Take discussions of homosexuality, for example. For some, homosexuality is a private matter of personal sexual preference. For others, it must necessarily be part of public discourse because, if a person-to-person bond is taken to be the foundation of marriage and the family unit, laws that do not recognize homosexual unions as equivalent to heterosexual unions are discriminatory and wrong. Removing that discrimination on matters such as pension and health benefits is one matter. Making homosexual couples equal in other ways, for example, equally eligible to adopt children, deals not just with the rights of adults but with the raising of children. Here we run into a second set of principles surrounding child-rearing. There are those who fear exposure of children to discussions and examples of homosexuality, rather like the fear many have of excessive exposure to television violence or sex education. The possible portrayal of two, well-meaning, economically comfortable, homosexual adults in a story meant to be read by children is bad enough. The possibility of portraying more than two homosexual adults operating as a family unit positively sends shivers down certain spines.

For some, these matters are simple matters of principle. In child-rearing, they believe, what is necessary for (biologically natural) procreation should be the foundation of social law, custom, and literature, especially when that literature and behaviour is made public by such socialization institutions as schools. For others, the appeal to principle is equally simple but opposite: those for whom a political framework is dominant may claim that equal individual rights for everyone no matter what their sexual preference should be the foundation of social law, custom, and 'official' literature.

Principled position statements are one thing. Understanding these matters is not quite so simple, essentially because the boundary between biology and society is unclear, variable, and rendered further complex by gender-adjustive medical technology. Is exposure to homosexual parents or portrayals of homosexual parents more likely to produce homosexual children? If so, is a higher incidence of homosexuality, as a result of exposure, a bad thing? Who is to say? Is homosexuality something society should discourage? If so, why? If homosexuality has genetic roots, does homophobia? Should both be respected? Equally?

Censorship tends to become a public issue when societies line up behind one position or another and with a certain level of commitment. Conflict and tension escalate when societies or groups within them rally, quickly and emotionally, to protect what they see as an attack on their foundations. At the extreme is the incensed mob. Words may inflame as well as suppress emotions. Some can do both, simultaneously. Words such as 'white trash' or the more polite 'gone Indian' are terms of ostracism that seem to allow the preservation of racism. They also may be a call *not* to take up arms while maintaining classism.

Considering the Content of Canadian Schoolbooks

In the mid 1970s, encouraged by the existence and activities of a new wave of Canadian book publishers, some students and I began examining elementary school textbooks for the ideas they introduced to school children. We concentrated on language arts and on the themes of the stories, the central ideas the stories conveyed to children about the world.

We found the following. First, the stories were strongly anthropomorphic. Perhaps not surprisingly, although in children's literature it is often different, the central characters were people. When animals were presented, or any story element with volition, they were anthropomophized – made to act as if they were human beings. The presentation of community was also distinctive. Only 3 per cent of stories had a community-participation theme, in contrast to 12 to 15 per cent where community figures were involved in acting out their official roles, for example, mayors judging contests. The remaining 85 per cent portrayed no community at all. Instead there were stories of families, kids playing, and so forth. With regard to gender, we examined male-female ratios (about 2/1); roles in which women and men were portrayed (a mere 3 per cent of women were in non-domestic roles); and breadth of character traits (restricted for women, elaborated for men). We also discovered that interactions between characters were presented within a unidimensional hierarchy. Men, especially men with position, were consistently in authority, and boys, girls, women, and pets lined up behind them in that order. (Little action took place without reference to this pecking order.) As a consequence, in virtually every episode, characters interacted as adversaries rather than in cooperation with or in celebration of one another. We also noted that, while the stories could easily be identified as rural (45 per cent) and urban or suburban (7 per cent), in the 287 stories examined there were only 10 specific references to Canada, one being Paul Bunyan digging out the St Lawrence River with his ox, Blue. (The Canadianness of Paul Bunyan is, of course, questionable.) We also found a parallel presentation of the world in other curriculum materials, including dictionaries, where boys were featured in illustrations over girls by a factor of nine to one.[2]

Based on our research, we concluded that there were four critical elements of language arts 'textbook realities.' They were as follows:

- presentation of social relations as a unidimensional competitive hierarchy;
- unequal gender presentations, in terms not just of number of occurrences or lesser numbers of women doctors and lawyers but of restricted roles and restricted sets of personality portrayals, especially of women – and to a lesser extent, girls;
- lack of Canadian content, and its complement; and
- presentation of a generic geographic, social, and cultural world devoid of specificity.

Because impending change was easy to see in gender presentations as a result of the efforts of both women teachers and academics, an interesting phenomenon in itself, and because there were plenty of others lined up to fight that battle, for the most part I set gender bias aside in favour of attending to the other three themes – the predominance of a unidimensional social hierarchy, the lack of Canadian content and the ubiquity of generic content, and the nature of the control system which determined content.

It was difficult to make any headway arguing against the social world being presented as a unidimensional social hierarchy. The fact that such a perspective plays a foundational role both in the capitalist marketplace and in intellectual circles probably explains a fair amount.

On the one hand, there are many in the intellectual and educational establishment who believe in a unidimensional hierarchy. Having achieved their positions by dint of genetic inheritance and intellectual effort, to say nothing of social class, they are inclined to believe in a performance meritocracy. In the marketplace, competition among products for market share is an article of faith for determining which products and companies will survive. Presumably because this sense of the world is so well entrenched, few were willing to accept that the stories did indeed present a unidimensional hierarchy. The major form of denial was to argue that the presentation of ideas in literary form allows for many layers and possibilities of interpretation. Of course, the ultimate conclusion of this stance is that literary presentations of ideas cannot be said to mean anything.

In one piece of research, reported in part by myself and Margaret Long,[3] the contrast between a unidimensional hierarchy and a more exploratory and artistic rendering of the world was vivid. The exploratory view was contained in one series of grades four to six readers published by Nelson.[4] The general ideology put forward was characterized by a community-building orientation, a respect for plurality, and a specific cultural articulation, along with an idealism and a sense of the boundedness of community.[5]

For the other reading series, published by Ginn,[6] the unidimensional world found there was marked by a focus on individualism with several associated characteristics: worldwide cultural homogeneity, common rules of accepted behaviour across all situations, and a view of the social world as arbitrary and demanding of individual initiative or capitulation.[7]

Such differentiations notwithstanding, recognition of the prevalence of a unidimensional social hierarchy in school readers was not forthcoming. It was not that anyone disputed our research findings; rather, they were simply unwilling to accept that the consistent presentation of characters and character interactions in terms of a rather strict pecking order was problematic.

The inability even to raise a debate on the nature and value of the world view presented was disappointing. It was not that this world view was unnoticed by others. In particular, a study of the Canadian curriculum by the Organization for Economic Cooperation and Development (OECD) noted that Canadians spend considerable amounts of money on education even though education in Canada has no articulated national or cultural purpose.[8]

The lack of Canadian content was an easier finding to gain acceptance. Articles on Canadian content were relatively easily placed, and within them the generic world of most learning materials was described as the contrast to ways of life in Canada.[9] Once anyone went looking, counting specific references to Canada was a simple matter. There were few such references throughout the curriculum, including in social studies in grades one through six.[10]

By 1979 it was clear that there was a significant story to tell about the control system which determined the content of school-learning materials. Through interviews and other background research I identified the major players: educational publishers, curriculum departments of provincial educational ministries, curriculum-review and materials-adoption committees, teachers, teacher associations, education professors, textbook authors, and politicians.

By 1981 I had produced a book-length manuscript examining curriculum-development, curriculum- and learning-materials reviews and the development of new curricula, the development, procurement, and marketing of learning materials as well as their market-servicing functions, teacher training, the orientations and professional activities of education professors, and so forth. In the latter half of my sabbatical in 1982 I spent time at the Canadian Learning Materials Development Centre housed at Dalhousie University in Halifax, reworking the manuscript with the help of various academics and staff.

Our conclusions were as follows. Throughout the grades, in the study of language arts and literature, there was, and to some extent there still is, a distinct lack of Canadian content. At the level of the textbook materials themselves, the lack of Canadian content derived from the presentation of generalities rather than specifics. Families go on holidays to a lake. The family, the lake, the environment, the holiday are not outlined in any specific detail. The event could happen to any North American at the very least anywhere. Similarly, social hierarchies and situational psychology were a central story dynamic which prevailed over specific cultural practice. Literature studies focused on 'world class' literature understandable by school students, that is, the U.S. and U.K. literary canon embodying the central themes of Western civilization, for example, *Lord of the Flies*, *Animal Farm*, and *To Kill a Mockingbird*. Only occasionally did Canadian writings with Canadian settings find their way into the classrooms, for instance, the books of Farley Mowat. In some cases, when the materials were adapted from U.S. editions, in addition to generic content, there were numerous references to American realities some of which were removed rather crudely and replaced with Canadian content that was inexact and relatively trivial when compared to the U.S. version.[11]

In social studies, content was determined by a number of factors. The first was an 'expanding horizons' orientation, from the local (the individual, the family, the neighbourhood) to the global (world communities) and historical (ancient civilizations). There was also an emphasis on engagement of the interest of students and this was done by focusing on the values inherent in such social organizations. Inherent in this latter perspective was crude socialization in which foreign realities were evaluated for their affirmation of Western ideals.

In many cases, while there were occasional forays into Canadian specificity and a plurality emphasizing native communities alongside foreign specificity (the central core of Paris, a sheep station in New Zealand, a small town in Manitoba, an Inuit village), a systematic expansion of horizons in concrete terms gave way to a worldwide scope. In one notable example, McGraw-Hill's *Social and Environmental Studies*,[12] only in one grade in the six-grade series was any Canadian content to be found.

At the junior high school level, rather than studying Canada and the world community from a Canadian perspective, Canadian history and geography were often isolated from world history and geography. At this level, the values orientation was most objectionable, with questions suggested in teachers' guides such as 'Should individual worth be maximized in Afro-Asian society?'[13] At the senior high school level, while in some provinces pan-Canadian studies of history and geography were common (with little emphasis on the students' home provinces), in other provinces (for example, Alberta) there was a branching out into a study of social-science disciplines rather than deeper understandings of the communities and regions that make up the Canadian plurality.

Teacher training turned out to be organized in psychological and universal terms. Teachers took three types of courses, methodological or pedagogical courses (how to teach), teaching-subject courses (for example, math, history, literature), and foundations courses. In the teaching-subject courses, prospective teachers were not encouraged to focus on Canadian history, geography, or literature; the subject study itself was regarded as sufficient. Thus, in one instance, an immigrant from the Indian subcontinent with a BA in history (including no Canadian content) found herself in Newfoundland teaching Canadian history. In the foundations courses the opportunity for discussion of the social and cultural realities as an educational foundation was severely restricted. Courses with a psychological base outnumbered courses with a Canadian content base (for example, the constitutional legal, policy, and social foundations of education in Canada) by eleven to one (and no mandatory requirements counteracted this course availability). School boards across Canada were questioned on their hiring practices to determine if they attempted in any way to assess the relevance of teacher training for particular communities. The vast majority (about 75 to 80 per cent) did not.

Our research into the professional qualifications and activities of education professors determined that, while many education professors may have been born in Canada, few took Canadian advanced degrees and, once launched in careers, they spent far more time at U.S. rather than Canadian professional conferences presenting and listening to research papers.

The study paid particular attention to the development, review, and adoption of the curriculum and, following that, learning materials. It found that, in general, curriculum was developed by provincial bureaucrats, usually with advanced education degrees, working in conjunction with outstanding teachers on a province-by-province basis. Their view of the child was as a 'learner' with certain 'cognitive capabilities,' a view reflective of their psychologically based training. No real attempt was made to coordinate curriculum across provinces and develop market bargaining power through increased coordinated buying. (Fiscal constraint has forced this to change somewhat.) It was only when politicians intervened (as Alberta did with $8.3 million) that the curriculum-development process turned strongly towards Canadian realities.

This curriculum development process was complemented by the activities of large (multinational or transnational) educational publishers who maintained close contact with curriculum-development divisions of education ministries in order to find out the membership of curriculum committees, to know which teachers were regarded as outstanding and likely to be interested in trying their hand at the development of learning materials, and to foster friendly relations with schools which might test materials that were likely to be competing for a provincial 'buy.' So cosy was this relationship in the early 1980s that ministries made it a practice to send calls for learning materials only to a select few publishers. In the mid-1980s this public-procurement process was opened up to all publishers who expressed an interest.

The study described the materials review-and-adoption process in some detail, noting how, from a financial perspective, it was really only open to large publishers with considerable capital and favoured those operating in the entire North American market. Such publishers were in a position to maintain a presence in the marketplace promoting their materials. They could finance the development of integrated series, some requiring about $15 million. They could afford to lose an adoption in one province (amounting to millions in revenue) because they could amortize costs over other markets. They could develop mock-ups to open the bidding on new series at a cost of $250,000 to $500,000. And they could afford to offer outstanding educators lucrative opportunities to participate in editorial projects.

Perhaps the most significant finding of this research was how over-determined the lack of Canadian content was. Essentially, at every point of influence – curriculum development, teacher training, teacher hiring, learning-materials development, financial organization of markets, and the training and activities of education professors – Canadian content was not in the cards. This was true whether that content was in the stories in language arts, the discussion of communities in social studies, or, as we found in later research never formally published, the principles emphasized in the teaching of science.

By the time the study was completed, I had come to the conclusion that, in the same way that medical doctors and drug companies are interlinked, the interests of the education profession and multinational textbook publishers had become wedded to each other, ignoring the obvious value of learning materials that speak to children on a foundation of their own social, cultural, and national realities. In *The Nation in the Schools*,[14] I saw the multinational publishers as the primary agents with the greatest control, much as some see the drug companies manipulating health professionals, especially doctors. The multinational publishers had managed to gain control over the market and had had their priorities written into the curriculum. Thus, generic content made it possible for these companies to present essentially the same materials to a wide variety of jurisdictions. (The same materials with slight adaptations were being used in Britain, the United States, Canada, and Australia.) Outstanding and ambitious educators were captured by the rewards such publishers were able to offer if educators would help them develop products to their specifications. The publishers were the only players who, as a group, had a vested interest in the prevailing content and ideology which resulted in cross-market learning materials. (A certain number of ambitious and mobile education professionals shared that interest.)

In sum, this overall curriculum-development and learning-materials procurement process excluded not only small Canadian-owned, culturally oriented publishers but also content that was specific to geographic or culturally constructed communities. So was this censorship? ideological capture? the fallout of a well-organized imperial propaganda campaign? The naming process is difficult.

It was certainly true that the multinational publishers continuously pressed their advantage. However, even as an argument for their pressing their advantage could be made, I was aware that their advantage-pressing was in collusion with the education profession. To understand this convergence of interests I drew on my own training in educational psychology (with some dollops of educational philosophy) and came across Hilda Neatby's *So Little for the Mind*,[15] an interesting educational spin-off of the Massey Commission on Arts, Letters and Sciences and a best-selling conservative work along the lines of George Grant's *Lament for a Nation*.[16] The implications of the arguments put forward by Neatby and Grant are that the denial of legitimacy, of geographically local and national as well as culturally heterogeneous references, can be found in American liberalism and the pragmatism of John Dewey. After some intensive rereading of Dewey, Patrick Keeney and I published a paper drawing the connections between what I had observed and its connection to Deweyan philosophy.[17] In summary we argued that Dewey's conception of the child as a bio-social creature neglected the child's cultural context entirely. Not only did Dewey's theorem present U.S. democratic, melting-pot individualism as a universal ideal, banishing plurality, culture, and the history of civilization before it, but they also provided an unshakeable foundation for the provision of universally appropriate learning materials produced for world markets from a central source. While Dewey's universal humanism has more to recommend it than I was prepared to grant at the time of writing, there is no denying that it excludes cultural heterogeneity. In short, the learning materials used in Canadian schools cut children off from their immediate community and culture by categorically excluding the cultural and national level of personal identity.

At the foundation of Deweyan ideology is a conception of the child as a bio-social entity equipped with curiosity, a trait that could be tapped to assist the child to discover not only the universal laws of physics but also the universal

laws of society. On this foundation was built in the 1970s and 1980s the teachings and organization of faculties of education. Within such faculties the professoriate dealt in such universal values as humanitarianism, justice, and
individualism, even cooperation; universal role models such as high achievers,
self-sacrificing individuals, and respectful if not obedient children; universally
desirable communities that protect individuals and are tolerant; universally
desirable nations that respect individual freedoms such as freedom of religion,
speech, and assembly; and a universally desired civilization (no 's') which
embodies all these universal ideals.

This set of assumptions was made manifest in the school system by means of
a working practice ideally suited to multinational publishers – engaging materials with high-production values capable of being used with only minor adjustments in a wide variety of markets.

An Academic Side-Show

Lucky, you might think, that we have academe, and that I was able and perhaps
even encouraged to pursue this research. Yet the academic side of this story did
not unfold in quite that manner. In a sense, a case for attempts at censorship
were more clearly visible in my efforts to pursue and publish the very research I
have just reported. I will provide a short account of those events. In so doing, of
course, I now slip into autobiography and its attendant unreliability. All I can
offer you as a reader is the assurance that sufficient time has passed, and my old
grudges have sufficiently faded, that I believe I can provide, if not a wholly
accurate, then at least a useful account of the dynamics of academe in this case
and its openness to ideas.

Looking at these findings in 1997 does not invoke surprise, nor, I would
think, would they now induce defensiveness among educators or publishers. We
have learned over the last twenty years, if we did not know it already, that mainstream media are often, at best, conservative in their portrayal of various groups
and individuals within society. We also know that producers protect their markets, and economic theory is based on such 'rational' behaviour. Yet between
1977 and 1984, reception of the examples I offered of this phenomenon was, to
say the least, problematic.

In putting my ideas forward, at first in essay form, that is, a qualitative analysis of the themes, plots, and characters, I encountered not interest but resistance,
not so much among teachers, who knew full well what the realities were, but in
the academic world. Effectively I, the young, but thankfully tenured, academic
was told: there are many ways to interpret literature (even stories in elementary
school books). Yours is just one. Your findings could probably not be repli-

cated. This is not legitimate research but polemics. It is hard to ignore systematic under-representation in terms of access to a wide range of roles, character traits, and simple numerical occurrence, but, rest assured, the data I presented and my interpretation of it were characterized repeatedly as 'not objective' and therefore invalid.

In fact, it was this resistance that produced the numbers quoted in this essay. Essentially, I was forced into a reductionist stance. Unaware of the then-forming British cultural studies, which would have offered a legitimizing framework for my work, I turned to the analytical technique of content analysis. Thus, I compared the portrayal of men to women, boys to girls, U.S. photos to Canadian photos, and so forth. This merely occasioned a more determined resistance but, in true academic style, it was waged in terms of methodological sophistication. One particularly memorable tack taken by my critics (on my promotion and tenure committee) was to note my failure to use inferential statistical tests, tests designed to define the parameters of the real world to which the sample being studied applies. When I countered that I was not dealing with a sample but the entire content of the books which approximately 80 per cent of grade one through three British Columbia students were using to learn to read, the response of my critics was not acceptance, nor admission of incorrectness, but a demand that I write and have published a methodological paper to determine the acceptability of my methodological stance. Writing such a paper was one thing (I did write the paper). Publishing it was another, essentially because the paper argued an elementary statistical point and had the limited goal of proving that my methodology was something worth discussing. (The paper was never published. I believe I never submitted it.)

It seems to me reasonable to conclude that the resistance to this research amounted to censorship by the academy. You, the reader, cannot know. The papers written might simply have been inadequate. My only comment can be that my findings were eventually published and, while expressed slightly differently in later papers, I was essentially saying the same thing.

What the censorship was aimed at and why it emerged is more difficult to explain. My best guess is that it represented a resistance to using research to challenge generally accepted institutions and ideology. My suspicion is that had those leading the resistance been brought before a blue-ribbon committee and asked if they rejected the findings of the research, their answers would have been negative. The problem seemed more to be a resistance to using research as a tool for social change. (It was not insignificant that those leading the resistance were U.S.-trained male academics.) The only other reason I can think of for my colleagues' behaviour was that they simply wanted to get rid of me. This is possible. I had been 'unproductive' in terms of publishing research for several years, and I was, fairly clearly, a nationalist. In any case, having my research published seemed only to draw fire rather than diminish hostilities. Who is to know?

Fortunately, as these events were unfolding, a close colleague who had been a fellow student, Jack Quarter, took over the editorship of a Canadian educational policy journal, *Interchange*, and my work began to be published.[18] In one small way this represented a capture of the tools both of legitimacy and of the dissemination of ideas by a peer who shared roughly the same view of the role of research as did I.

However, even with publication, my work and career continued to be attacked by my departmental colleagues for lacking methodological rigour and my promotion was denied twice. Ironically, the first time around, the promotion was rejected by a departmental tenure committee and supported by a dean. The second time around, the majority on the departmental tenure committee voted in favour, the chair of the department voted against, and the same dean switched sides and voted against (in spite of my having published additional work). That second time, the university committee also voted against promotion and it took a presidential intervention for my promotion to associate-professor status to be granted. The intervention came on the ground that I may not have been receiving a fair hearing. This promotion removed the threat to my academic career. The grounds of the presidential reversal were that four independent academic assessors, all of whom were chosen with the knowledge that I was challenging some quite basic and widely held educational assumptions, judged that I qualified for promotion at their institution.

These decisions, both negative and positive, were made in the context of my publications in *Interchange* and the obvious interest in my research demonstrated by numerous teacher magazines and magazines of social commentary (see the articles cited above plus others.)[19] These days such articles are highly valued as transfer of knowledge. At the time they were regarded as largely irrelevant to evaluating my contribution as an academic, that is, not refereed and thus irrelevant.

The struggle to get the book manuscript published was also not easy. It was really only through Jack Quarter, based at the Ontario Institute for Studies in Education (OISE), that OISE Press was persuaded to consider the manuscript. In 1984 *The Nation in the Schools: Wanted, a Canadian Education* was published.[20]

What can one say? I can only point to the continued reference to and use of *The Nation in the Schools* and related research, now out-of-print but tracked by Cancopy. And my reasonably successful subsequent career suggests that this early work has some validity. But enough autobiography.

Reflections and Conclusions

While in the instances reported in this essay the market acted to forbid entry to a thorough infusion of Canadian realities and participation of small, undercapitalized, Canadian-owned cultural publishers who were in the best position to provide such content, the market was effective in playing this resistive role only as a result of publishers working their complementary interests alongside the strongly believed-in and applied ideology of the education profession.

The obvious question is: Is this censorship? The difficulty with using the term censorship is that it is simultaneously conceptually reductionist and emotionally inflationary. It forecloses on an examination of the subtleties of the principles involved, the wisdom of constraint in this instance, and encourages the perception of a set of (unthinking) protective manoeuvres. It intimates close-minded determined opposition. It suggests a response to threat. And it implies, in a liberal society, condemnation.

To my knowledge, no groups of individuals were convening meetings to exclude Canadian content, nor a balanced treatment of the sexes, nor a cooperative ethic, nor a multidimensional plurality. Nevertheless, these perspectives were excluded in the content examined. Moreover, in spite of the findings being generally known throughout Canada (virtually every provincial curriculum department knew of my research), very little happened. My naive expectation, to be blunt, was that, once revealed, Canadian educators would realize the shortcomings of the system, recognize the value of cultural specificity (in simple form, Canadian content), make alliance with Canadian-owned publishers who were anxious to bring Canadian content forward, and get on with the job of Canadianizing and building Canadian culture into the curriculum. It didn't happen.

Was there an open-minded consideration of the ideas put forward? At some level there was. Notably, groups of teachers were enthusiastic and even anxious to affirm Canadian content, to teach kids about their own community and culture. Yet, at other levels, there was a determined and seemingly unconsidered resistance and a feeling of threat. In numerous interviews, a simple question about Canadian content to a provincial education official would elicit a staunch defence of the status quo. Education bureaucrats would defend the foundations of curriculum development, the 'sophistication' of educational publishers, the vested (and non-educational) interests of Canadian-owned publishers, and the inappropriateness of Ontario-developed materials for the rest of Canada. Notable resistance also occurred among the education professoriate. Being concerned with more abstract conceptualizations, they treated the local, the specific, the national as beneath them. For them (within their philosophical or psychological framework),

ethnic or other community attitudes were elements of a reality demanding understanding and compensation through the adjustment of teaching methods. Not for
them was the celebration of ethnic diversity as contributory to positive community dynamics and worth teaching about.

These responses of professionals did seem to be determined opposition to a
perceived threat. With publishers, parallel determined opposition most often
took the form of denial and a refusal to be engaged. The denial amounted to an
insistence that, because the content was edited by Canadian educators, it was
suitably Canadian. The refusal to be engaged took the form of a complete lack
of public response to defend identified shortcomings, even at professional-
development seminars and education conferences. In fact, the only defence I
ever encountered from an industry person was put forward by a U.S. employee
of Ginn, USA at an education conference in New Orleans.

So at some level it seemed as if censorship was taking place not by such marketplace forces as predatory pricing or forced acquisition of competitors but
rather by the erection and defence of barriers to the entry of other producers.
This erection and defence of barriers was not an industrial action but a profes-
sional/industry partnership that would not have been effective if either group
had acted alone.

And so we move to the matter of condemnation and it is here that I have benefited greatly from reading Joy Gugeler's recent essay.[21] Gugeler's essay
allowed me to see that those of us involved in attempting to institute change had
been unsuccessful mainly because we were unable to organize sufficient
momentum. Had we been able to do so, my sense is that change would have
been forthcoming. Because we were unable to do so, change has come in small
increments.

For instance, a major inquiry parallel to that undertaken into book publishing
itself[22] was never successfully launched. What was done was the following. At
the level of school boards, certain people got elected and undertook research to
demonstrate the lack of Canadian content and cultural realities. More appropriate materials were developed, for example, the *Where We Live* reading series,
and adopted in multicultural classrooms as supplementary materials.[23] Lobbying was carried out, especially with the Ontario Ministry of Education, and a
Canadian learning-materials development fund was established alongside a federal equivalent through the Canadian Studies directorate of the Secretary of
State's office. These funds allowed for the development of materials in specialized areas such as multicultural and remedial learning materials. The process of
approving materials for use in Ontario schools was made more open, and, in
addition to already operating Canadian manufacturing rules, enforcement of
Canadian content regulations for Ontario learning materials was strengthened.

In other provinces, as mentioned, calls went out for submissions of Canadian-content texts and supplementary materials. The library profession was lobbied and, through the work of many librarians, especially Francess Halpenny,[24] the legitimacy of buying Canadian-authored and -published books was established. The legitimacy of Canadian studies within universities was established through the reports of Robin Mathews, James Steele,[25] and Thomas Symons.[26] This meant that a greater number of Canadian teachers at least had an opportunity to be exposed to Canadian literature, geography, history, sociology, and so on. In certain provinces, including British Columbia and Ontario, Canadian studies became a legitimate teaching subject. A Canadian Learning Materials Development Centre was established (as mentioned, in Halifax) but it was overseen by young, keen, committed academics and not, for example, by a blue-ribbon committee of eminent and established Canadian historians, politicians, and other assorted elders.

In short, while the issue was fought in the trenches, a battle was never declared because neither the Canadian public nor politicians could be persuaded that the established order of developing and acquiring learning materials demanded their attention. While the challenge was issued, the requisite structures were not put in place to determine whether the prevailing educational philosophy in Canada was or is appropriate to our time and place. Beyond a few young voices, no body was commissioned to study the operation of the markets and the materials. The inability to mobilize societal resources to address these questions stymied quick and decisive social change.

Could it have been otherwise? With education being a provincial responsibility, national action was and is all but impossible, even if it were restricted to the English-speaking provinces. Very likely, such efforts might have been derailed or ignored, just as the strongly questioning 1975 OECD report on Canadian education was. So bereft is Canada of a national platform from which to consider education that the OECD report had to be published by the Canadian Association of Adult Education and the Students' Administrative Council of the University of Toronto. Even the expression of many of the same ideas in the report of the Task Force on Canadian Unity had little effect.[27]

My sense is that, while incremental change along the lines we were calling for has occurred and is still occurring, the orientation of Canadian education has never become a national concern for three reasons beyond the playing out of the vested interests of education professionals and the educational publishing industry. The first is the fact that, as noted, our constitution places education in the hands of eleven different jurisdictions (now expanding for the north). The second is, like it or not, the content of the textbooks I studied reflects an ideology deeply embedded in Canadian society and it is this ideology that is manifest in subject content, market dynamics, and professional outlook and practice. That ideology contains, among other things, a muted nationalism alongside an abundant awareness of other-than-Canadian realities. And while this muted nationalism has its pitfalls, for instance, a lack of a strongly held allegiance to Canada itself, it also has certain positive attributes such as the acknowledgment of the plurality of cultures and communities which make up the world and a tolerance and even celebration of other cultures and societies.

The third reason is the natural conservatism of any society, and this takes us back to a consideration of the principles that are basic to all censorship struggles and to the question posed at the opening of this chapter. Having determined that there was a lack of specificity in learning materials which resulted in a lack of Canadian content, a prevalence of psychological over cultural dynamics, a unidimensional social hierarchy, and a gender-based bias, we can ask the question: What principles should be used, articulated by whom, to guide change?

During the 1980s I became aware of a fairly concerted effort by the political right in the United States to criticize the content of U.S. textbooks for their inclusion of such radical theories as evolution. Later, as interest-group politics strengthened in Canada, I also became aware of the fragmenting forces acting on the education system and the difficulty the education system has experienced in articulating a set of core experiences to which all Canadian school students should be exposed.

As of this writing, I find myself opting for supporting the education system itself, insisting that it keep itself open both to the plurality of the realities and values that constitute Canada and to the other-than-psychological conceptions of humanity. The situation is now much different from what it was in the 1970s and early 1980s. If gender bias, a unidimensional social hierarchy, and the lack of Canadian content were a threat to some of the education bureaucrats, professors, and industry members I encountered, I doubt that these people would react the same way today. Furthermore, teachers themselves were open to our findings when we made them known. Since then, the education system has broadened its conception of the child, even if the thoughts of John Dewey still have a commanding presence. I saw my colleagues grow to accept that the research I had conducted was indeed legitimate and reflective of a set of emerging values. I also have had more experience with classroom teachers. And, while they are buffeted around by provincial directives, educational theories, and oftentimes inadequate learning materials, they have a profound concern for the best interests of students, something not found at any other level of the education system. To that extent, the 'education system' is, to a degree, self-correcting. When one part of it gets too far off track, other parts of it refuse to move. Intellectual analysis, while useful, cannot replace that profound, intergenerational concern.

With regard to Canadian content itself, little by little, in parallel with an increasing self-awareness in Canadian society brought about by Canadian film, sound recording, trade-book publishing, television production, and magazines, Canadian-owned publishers are coming to see more of their materials used in Canadian classrooms. Yet there is still a long distance to go.

In the end, I see the research I undertook, the resistance it met, and the resulting changes as part and parcel of the larger cultural task of continuously creating Canadian society, encouraging it fully to embrace its changing peoples and evolving social values. Necessarily, society must be conservative. And while there are issues that cry out for immediate justice, specifically Native issues, the framework I have come to see as apt is one that embraces both the fundamentals of what now exist and the ideals of what we might like our society to become.

Three questions have been asked of me by the editors of this volume. Would I censor religious views on evolution? Do I see my view of the curriculum as 'truer' than the one I was arguing against? And how might I respond to charges that I am promoting censorship/propaganda?

To answer the first two questions I would point to the social fabric. Were I a teacher, I would try to explain to my students why religion is important, why evolution constitutes a threat to certain focused religious-belief systems, and how spirituality is a realm of human existence just as is materiality.

Is my curriculum 'truer'? Well, that depends on the social and political priorities of Canadians. My main objective in the 1970s and 1980s was to articulate what was excluded both inadvertently and systematically and how entrenched that exclusion was in education and educational publishing. Having found a narrow view of social affairs and a lack of Canadian information and ideas, I argued that they should be included. Should they have been? That all depends on social priorities. And I am glad that the curriculum has moved in the direction I was arguing for.

Am I promoting censorship and/or propaganda? On this issue, I am drawn to the writings of Charles Taylor.[28] While liberal individualism has much to say for it, there must be a way for community interests to be recognized and affirmed over and above the passage of laws. Choices must be made and they must be made on the basis of the ever-changing values and make-up of society.

To return to the beginning, censorship is a boundary-maintaining and -servicing activity. In being challenged, society may censor but it may also adjust, though perhaps not immediately. As such challenges take on a broader coherence and come to be recognized by both claimants and defenders of the status quo as legitimate, they become foundations for evolution. True, this does not happen in every instance and there are times when those pressing for change must use every force they can muster. Censorship should surely not be encouraged but it may, in dealing with expression of ideas, act as a buffer against a call to arms, giving the various players time to sort out exactly the nature of the challenge and how to rise to, rather than against, that challenge.

NOTES

1 Rohan Samarajiva, 'Privacy in Electronic Public Space: Emerging Issues,' *Canadian Journal of Communication*, 19 (1994), 87–100.

2 Rowland Lorimer, Margaret Hill, Margaret Long, and Barbar MacLellan, 'Consider Content: An Analysis of Two "Canadian" Primary Language Arts Reading Series,' *Interchange*, 8, no. 4 (1977), 64–77; and R. Lorimer and Margaret Long, 'Sex-role Stereotyping in Elementary Readers,' *Interchange*, 10, no. 2 (1979), 25–45.

3 Ibid.

4 John McInnes and Emily Hearn, eds., *The Nelson Language Development Reading Program* (Toronto: Nelson Canada 1971).

5 Lorimer and Long, 'Sex-role Stereotyping.' 40.

6 Bill Moore and Heather Hooper, eds., *Starting Points in Reading* (Toronto: Ginn 1973).

7 Lorimer and Long, 'Sex-role Stereotyping,' 40.

8 Organization for Economic Cooperation and Development, *External Examiners' Report on Educational Policy in Canada* (Toronto: Canadian Association for Adult Education and the University of Toronto Students' Administrative Council 1975).

9 Rowland Lorimer, 'Your Canadian Reader,' *Lighthouse*, 2, no. 3 (1978), 6–16; idem., 'Publishing and the Canadian Content of Readers,' *Orbit*, 10, no. 4 (1979), 24–6; idem., 'Publishing and the Canadian content of readers,' in Paul Robinson, *Publishing for Canadian Classrooms* (Halifax: Canadian Learning Materials Centre 1980); idem., 'A Canadian Social Studies for Canada,' *The History Teacher* 16, no. 4 (1982), 45–55.

10 Benjamin Vass, ed., *Social and Environmental Studies*, (Toronto: McGraw-Hill 1974).

11 Rowland Lorimer, 'Your Canadian Reader,' with reference to Theodor Clymer, et al., ed. *Reading 360* (Toronto: Ginn 1972).

12 Vass, *Social and Environmental Studies*.

13 David Close and Douglas Bartels, 'The Socializing Effect of Regime Supportive Textbooks: First Results and Second Thoughts,' *Socialist Studies*, 1 (1979), 81–97.

14 Rowland Lorimer, *The Nation in the Schools: Wanted, A Canadian Education* (Toronto: OISE Press 1984).

15 Hilda Neatby, *So Little for the Mind: An Indictment of Canadian Education* (Toronto: Clarke, Irwin 1953).

16 George Grant, *Lament for a Nation* (Toronto: McClelland and Stewart 1965).

17 Rowland Lorimer and Patrick Keeney, 'Defining the Curriculum: The role of the Multinational Textbook in Canada,' ch. 13 in Suzanne De Castell, Allan Luke, and Carmen Luke, eds., *Language, Authority and Criticism: Readings on the School Textbook* (London: Fulmer Press 1989), 171–83.

18 Lorimer, Hill, Long, and MacLellan, 'Consider content'; Lorimer and Margaret Long, 'Sex-role Stereotyping.'

19 Rowland Lorimer, 'Reading Lots but Reading Little,' *Prime Areas*, 19, no. 2 (1977), 34–9; idem., 'Take Me to Your Reader,' *This Magazine*, 11, no. 4 (1977) 14–16; idem., 'What's Being Taught Besides Reading When Reading Is Being Taught?' *This Magazine*, 11, no. 2 (1977), 15–18; idem., 'Reading Lots but Reading Little,' *Alberta English*, 16, no. 3 (1978), 41–6; idem., 'The Story about the Circular 14 Story,' *Orbit*, 10, no. 5 (1979), 26.

20 Lorimer, *The Nation in the Schools.*

21 Joy Gugeler, 'So Little for the Nation: A Canadian Education Policy Manqué' (unpublished paper, 1997).

22 Ontario Royal Commission on Book Publishing, *Canadian Publishers and Canadian Publishing* (Toronto: Queen's Printer and Publishers 1972).

23 George Martell, Linda Sheppard, and Linda Wile, eds., *Where We Live: About Nellie and Me* (Toronto: James Lorimer 1978).

24 Francess G. Halpenny, *Canadian Collections in Public Libraries* (Toronto: Book and Periodical Development Council 1985).

25 Robin Mathews and James Steele, *The Struggle for Canadian Universities: A Dossier* (Toronto: New Press 1969).

26 Thomas H.B. Symons, *To Know Ourselves* (Toronto: Book and Periodical Development Council 1978).

27 Joy Gugeler, 'So Little for the Nation.'

28 Charles Taylor, *Reconciling the Solitudes: Essays on Canadian Federalism and Nationalism* (Montreal: McGill-Queen's University Press 1993).

Sense and Censorship: Towards a Different Account of Expressive Freedom

ALLAN C. HUTCHINSON

One thing that should be clear from all the essays in this collection is that the whole way in which censorship is thought about is more than ready for serious reappraisal. There is an urgent need to rethink and develop a fresh account of the theory and practice of censorship that is better suited to the conditions of late-twentieth-century Canada. This involves a wide slate of issues, but it particularly necessitates examining the circumstances in which information and opinion are constructed and disseminated. In doing this, traditional approaches are as much part of the problem as the solution. Any fresh account must emphasize the productive as well as the repressive aspects of the social economy – without some of the forces that are decried as 'repressive' (that is, the media), there would be no outlets or, at least, severely reduced means of dissemination. Moreover, even if the censorial instinct is dulled, this will not mean that a thriving and varied practice of public debate will spring forth in its place. As a number of contributors to this volume emphasize, the problem is as much about knowledge-production as it is about speech-repression; the so-called 'free flow of ideas' is not enough. Censorship is about the quality of public discourse – who participates, how they participate why they participate, and who gets to decide. As such, it is not only a technical issue or a constitutional conundrum: it is a political challenge of the most compelling kind. The discourse on censorship is as much affected by current conditions as the incidence and response to censorship itself. Consequently, I maintain that it is impossible to understand and deal with censorship without a more sustaining and sophisticated account of what counts as expressive freedom; freedom and constraint are intimately connected and mutually reinforcing.

Accordingly, in this concluding chapter, I want to begin the important task of suggesting the shape that such a theory of censorship and expressive freedom might take and the kind of practical orientation that it might recommend. In particular, I will concentrate on how best to retheorize censorship so that it is possible to glimpse a different vision of expressive freedom that owes more to democratic dialogue than to individual rights. In the first part of the chapter, I sketch the theoretical and practical challenge that has to be faced: I illustrate the practical inadequacy of present thinking and highlight its debilitating effects in dealing with censorship and expressive freedom. The second part digs a little deeper into the soil of existing theoretical frameworks in order to get at the roots of their problems; I concentrate on the impoverished notions of language and individuals, and the crucial interaction between the two. In the third part, I propose the outline of a more substantive account of censorship and expressive freedom that is better equipped to capture and respond to the complex challenges of contemporary society. Throughout, I will be guided by the coordinates of power and value: the need to ensure that everyone can participate as equals in the constitutive dialogue of democratic politics, and an accompanying concern with the substantive worth of the ensuing debate. In short, insofar as Canada prides itself on being a democratic and pluralistic society, it ought to aspire to a democratic and pluralistic understanding of censorship.

Choice and Control

At the heart of the censorship debate is a conundrum that is typical and pervasive in liberal societies – how is it possible to enhance one person's freedom without restricting that of another? This challenge is graphically illustrated time and again in the efforts to come to grips with what are and are not appropriate restrictions on people's freedom of expression. Few people suggest that there should be no restrictions on people's rights to express themselves. Indeed, if 'expression' is understood broadly, such a position is almost absurd; violence and threats are regularly and universally condemned as illegitimate expressions of personal freedom. Consequently, all agree that some restrictions are necessary, but there is huge disagreement over the nature and extent of those restrictions. In demonstrating the contradictory nature of freedom, three sets of circumstances referred to in this book make the point neatly:

- A prominent and politically active entrepreneur gains control of a large number of media outlets. He installs his own editors who share his general political orientation and signs up those leading columnists with views similar to his own. As a consequence, the newspapers and TV stations take a clear stance on most controversial issues and there is little news or favourable editorial commentary about other political views. Is this censorship? What is the importance of editorial freedom? Why should the owner be prevented from indulging his political fancies? Why would it not be censorship if we tell him otherwise? And whose political views will prevail if the owner's do not?

- As part of its general public-relations policy, a large bank agrees to sponsor a contemporary art exhibition of local artists at a public gallery. The organizers put together a wide range of different styles and include some controversial canvases about the Catholic Church. A heated debate takes place in the media about the artistic merit of these paintings and the appropriateness of display-ing them publicly. A significant group of citizens boycott the exhibition and mount protests against the exhibition. As a result, the bank withdraws its sponsorship and the exhibition is forced to close. Is this censorship by the bank? Are the citizen protests an act of censorship? Why should the bank be obliged to refrain from having an influence over the choice of the art to be exhibited? Does the creator of the controversial canvases have any entitle-ment to be exhibited?

- A local school board decides to introduce an anti-homophobic standard in the use of teaching materials in grade schools. As well as banning any books or resources that contain homophobic views, the policy requires the inclusion of books and materials that actually have positive images of gay and lesbian people. While there is much support for this initiative, a vocal group of par-ents object to the policy and insist that their children must not be taught that homosexuality is morally or socially acceptable. As a result the school board revokes its policy and simply encourages teachers not to use teaching materi-als that are homophobic. Is this censorship? Why should the views of one group of parents prevail over another? Who decides on what is to be taught? Why are anti-homophobic views more acceptable than homophobic ones? Is it censorship to ban homophobic teaching materials or teachers?

In each of these situations, a simplistic resort to traditional accounts of cen-sorship does little to resolve the difficulties entailed in regulation and decision making or to capture the troubling consequences of crude regulation. To be blunt, one person's censorship is another person's propaganda: whereas censor-ship prevents people from speaking, propaganda requires people to speak or at least listen. Moreover, it should be clear that censorship cannot be sensibly extended to any decision not to publish or approve certain information or ideas; editorial control, policy making, or self-control are not only and always acts of censorship. In particular, the traditional way of thinking about censorship slips too easily into two general errors. First, it assumes that, once all restraints are removed, there will be a free flow of ideas and views. This is mistaken in that there is never a situation of 'no choice' in which the free flow of ideas can assert itself unhindered when impending restrictions are removed. Without the contextual constraints of particular situations, people would find it difficult to cultivate any views at all: the creation and maintenance of people's views are socially influenced in the sense that people adopt the views that they have because of the social milieu in which they function. This assumption also leads to the dubious conclusion that personal choice is valid only if one speaks one's mind rather than holds back. Second, the traditional way of thinking about censorship focuses too narrowly on whether decisions of selection are made. Such an approach is unhelpful when it is absolutely clear that they are. Indeed, it would be difficult to imagine how it would be possible to dispense with such decisions. Consequently, the key questions need to be about how, why, and by whom those decisions are made; the creation as well as the censorship of views and ideas are dependent on such decisions.

While the spectre of censorship hovers over many such decisions, it does not contaminate or settle on them all. The consequences of 'private choice' may be as significant as public censure, but this is not enough to condemn those consequences as illegitimate or invalid. As the three incidents set out above make plain, there is a very fine line between censorship, propaganda, and choice. While that line always exists, it is constantly on the move: the debate about what constitutes censorship and, therefore, free expression generally is a political one.[1] Any theory of censorship must ensure that it is neither too broad nor too narrow. It will be too broad if it manages to embrace, but only to trivialize, obvious acts of repressive conduct and if it is blind to its own repressive effects; it will be too narrow if it fails to encompass obvious acts of repressive conduct and if it validates too much questionable expression. An adequate account of censorship must have a more sustaining theory of expressive freedom. This will require a recognition that information and ideas are not self-generated but are rather closely connected to the social environment in which they arise and take root; there is an intimate relation between the structure and substance of social conditions and the particular views that are disseminated and maintained. Consequently, any sophisticated understanding of censorship must pay as much attention to the circumstances and forces that produce knowledge as to those that suppress existing views. In short, the practice of censorship can be identified and remedied only if there is first a clearer sense of what would constitute expressive freedom and what a society that took it seriously might look like.

The villain of the piece is not so much a lack of enthusiasm or will to confront acts of censorship, but the inadequacy of the informing intellectual apparatus within which censorship and the conditions for expressive freedom are identified and understood. Traditionally, censorship has been considered to be the official control of people's freedom of expression and their access to information. While they disagree over the important details, all societies agree that some control is acceptable and perhaps necessary – wartime communication, defamation, criminal threats, and so on. While this remains an important concern, it is now widely acknowledged that it is mistaken to imagine that, in technologically sophisticated and commercially saturated societies (like Canada), the state is the only threat to freedom of expression; private centres of powers can have equally repressive effects on people's lives. However, this recognition exposes the inadequacy of the traditional approach to censorship. Once the simple and monochromatic vision of an oppressive state and empowered individuals is abandoned, and the complex and technicolour reality of multiple actors and institutions in the social power-play is glimpsed, the available modes of understanding and critique are seen to be anachronistic and unhelpful. In particular, the negative view of freedom that underpins the censorship debate – that, once restrictions are lifted, a natural free flow of expression will assert itself – is shown to be severely wanting: expressive freedom is as much about flow-management in which freedom is not the absence of constraints but a particular mix of constraints that protects individuals and enables substantive choices. Accordingly, if there is to be an informed and effective practice of anti-censorship, there must first be developed a theory of expressive freedom that is better attuned to the actual circumstances of modern society.

Only if there is a fundamental shift in our way of thinking about and responding to the institutional maldistribution of speech power can the existing order be seriously threatened. The days of the street-corner orator are gone: we live in a high-tech society in which large corporations have the power to regulate the information pulse of modern political life. The real impediment to free expression comes as much, if not more, from the private sector as from the state: those who can exert control over the image in a world which is dominated by the mass communication of images are well on their way to controlling that world. A.J. Liebling's quip would be amusing if it were not so tellingly true: the only person with freedom of the press is a person who can afford to own one. The extent of media concentration, its tendency to commodify news, and its need to placate advertisers all combine to underline the power of the media and its structural alignment to established interests.[2] Moreover, the courts' almost pathological insistence on treating huge private bureaucracies as though they were individuals and bestowing constitutional rights on them is a large step in the wrong direction. In societies, like Canada, that subscribe to representative democracy and vilify totalitarian practices, the major vehicle of popular control is not violence and coercion but a more subtle process of establishing 'the framework for thinkable thought ... [propaganda] is to democracy what violence is to totalitarianism.'[3] Accordingly, expression is a source not only of knowledge and enlightenment but also of fabrication and indoctrination. Without succumbing to a debilitating paranoia, talk of free expression against such a social backdrop as currently exists is fanciful.

One particular failing of current ideas is the theoretical insistence that there is a single and uniform response to problems of expression and censorship. There seems to be no possibility to recognize the importance of context in determining what is censorship and what is not. For instance, the teaching of certain materials raises different concerns depending upon whether it involves grade 4 children or university students. Whatever the need to ensure robust exchange and the inclusion of all different views, no matter how unpalatable, in university seminars, it seems entirely another matter to permit or encourage certain views to be taught to eight-year-olds. Similarly, while it might be thought appropriate to ration access to the media on the basis of advertisers' ability to pay, it seems entirely another matter to allow money to dominate election campaigns. Also, the way certain views are presented and framed can be crucial; deciding whether to broadcast scenes of torture might well be treated differently depending on whether such scenes are part of a documentary decrying torture or of an entertainment segment for psychopaths. Any theory of censorship and, therefore, free expression must be able to address and accommodate such nuances if it is to be of value in responding to practices of censorship and free expression.

As all this suggests, politics and political theorizing are inescapable dimensions of any informed debate about censorship and expressive freedom: it is a highly charged terrain of political contestation, not a haven from such ideological engagement. A good example of how some critics seek to claim a political neutrality for their defence of free speech is the debate over *political correctness*. For instance, the late Mr Justice John Sopinka (of the Supreme Court of Canada) cast himself as a friend of free speech and chastised those who want to appropriate it for their own political agenda. For him, freedom of expression is above partisan politics and must be kept that way: 'We must still rely on the common sense of public opinion to stand up for the right to say things no matter how unpalatable they may seem.'[4] Yet, like most critics of political correctness, Justice Sopinka constructs an argument that is as transparent as it is disingenuous. If politics is the crime, then he is as guilty as those he so earnestly accuses. By labelling certain views as *politically correct*, Justice Sopinka and others attempt to impugn the ideological motives of their free-speech opponents and, at the same time, insulate their own views from the charge of political affiliation. However, contrary to such 'apolitical' moves, the opponents of political correctness are committed to a distinct, if very different, political agenda as the politically correct. Because almost all conduct qualifies as expression, it is necessary to identify what expression is to be granted constitutional protection. Murder, rape, and violence generally are the most expressive and, as Justice

Sopinka puts it, 'unpalatable' of human acts, but they do not qualify for protection. Moreover, like lunches, speech is never free. It can only be had at the price of other competing values, like equality and dignity.

Consequently, the real debate is not over who is in favour of free speech but what are to be the limits of free speech and how it is to be balanced against other values. And that is a political debate. Whereas those labelled as *politically correct* tend to stress a more social and egalitarian vision of justice, Justice Sopinka relies on a more individual and libertarian ideology. At least the politically correct are candid about their political commitments. To suggest, as Sopinka does, that professors' rights to offend always ought to take precedence over students' rights to be treated equally and with respect is a political and obviously controversial stance. It has to be defended as such and cannot be simply paraded under the dubious rubric of 'common sense,' which is notoriously not always sensible and even less often common. Of course, I do not intend to defend any particular views that are held by those described as *politically correct*; that would be to miss the political point of my intervention. Both sides are political and neither has the lock on truth, justice, or anything else. It is as problematic to see racism, sexism, and homophobia in everything as it is to treat them as secondary to incursions on people's primary freedom to express themselves. It is no better   to accuse a black writer of being elitist because she fails to communicate with those who cannot read than it is to leap to the defence of the white supremacist. Nor is condemning *Romeo and Juliet* as homophobic because it deals only with heterosexual relations any better than championing the dissemination of gay-bashing material. If censorship is the fear, then it is already here. Although his intention was different, Justice Sopinka is right to conclude that 'the greatest threat to free speech does not come from actions of the state but from ourselves.' What gets expressed and what does not is determined by those who control the means of communication. This is truly a 'marketplace of ideas' in that the haves speak and the have-nots listen. The problem is not who favours freedom of expression but who benefits most from elevating it above other values. To put it crudely, those who have the power speak, those without it do not. Established interests – corporate, white, male, straight, moneyed, and so on – have more to gain from favouring free speech over equality: it serves to preserve the status quo rather than to change it.

Accordingly, it is no longer viable or wise to persist in discussing censorship within the confines of present theories about free expression; it is time to leave the dominant liberal theory of free speech behind and work towards a more satisfying account of expression and control. While concern with state efforts at control will remain a significant aspect of such an account, it will be vital to appreciate the positive role that a democratic state can play in enhancing the quality of public discourse. However, before intimating the direction that a constructive account of censorship and expressive freedom might take, it is advisable to dig a little deeper into the soil of existing theoretical frameworks in order to get at the roots of the problems.

Uprooting Expression

In all its different threads and strands,[5] the contemporary tapestry of free speech draws on an inadequate set of premises and assumptions; it has an impoverished view of human personality, language, and the crucial relation between the two. As part of the more general liberal theory of freedom, the approach to free speech is premised on a social world compromising an aggregation of distinct individuals with a set of pre-social preferences and values. Social interaction provides opportunities to satisfy better their given preferences and to achieve a desirable level of self-fulfilment: shared values are a possible product of a just society but not a condition for its existence. Within liberal society, language is understood as a neutral medium that is available to all and that stands independent of the ideas and world it is intended to convey or depict; it is the letter-carrier delivering a letter or the librarian handing out a book.[6] In its various renderings, the liberal objective is to facilitate this intellectual economy of exchange and to enhance individual choice and self-determination. Consequently, the pillars of liberal free speech are the private individual with 'different and indeed incommensurable and irreconcilable conceptions of the good'[7] and the transparency of language as a public medium through which to communicate them.

Apart from the naive failure of most scholars to recognize its scope for domination, the liberal view fails to take language seriously and presents a falsely dichotomous view of the world. For the modern liberal, the challenge is to steer a middle course between the extreme images of an heroic Rodinesque individual and an overbearing Stalinesque state; people must stand free and alone or else risk being enslaved to a hostile community. Emancipation is suspended in the space between a public instrumentalism and an esoteric privatism. Of course, liberal theory ceaselessly vacillates in this posture and is forever seeking to mediate the competing influences of the government as a threat to and guarantor of individual freedom. Unfortunately, while discursive socialization or indoctrination is almost inevitable, it is not uniquely attributable to the actions of the government. Power is not the sole preserve of the government but is distributed among an elite corporate sector. To check the abuse of dialogic power, there must be a critical shift of analysis from its sources and quantity to its consequences and quality. For instance, liberals seem to adopt simultaneously the contradictory positions that language can be a neutral conduit in which speakers can fully and freely express themselves and that language can be a potent vehicle for the indoctrination of some speakers by others. Yet the particular stance adopted will usually depend upon the identity of the speaker. When spoken by self-possessed individuals, language will be considered a transparent medium; when uttered by government, it will more often be treated as a suspect tool.

Today's Canadian reality is more nuanced and less polarized. Whereas government is occasionally the voice of the muted many against the voluble few, moneyed voices often speak in the language of dissemblance. In its own lumbering fashion, of course, liberalism is struggling to come to terms with the non-essential nature of language and its potential for both education and obfuscation. But, by adopting its particular stance, liberals are unable to grasp the dialectical and dialogic nature of individual identity and social action. Social reality, language, and intentionality converge and conflict in mutually sustaining and transforming patterns. Language is not a transparency through which the world is observed nor a catalogue of labels to be attached Velcro-like to the appropriate contents of the world. There is no form of pure communication that merely represents instead of creating. The world is within the language and the language within the world. Language is a social medium. It shapes society and its individuals as they work to reshape it. No one is free to describe the world as they wish; they are always and already constrained by the prevailing ways of speaking. As such, discourse is as much constitutive of reality, both personal and collective, as it is constituted by that society. It is a cultural and political artefact of the first order 'in the sense that it serves to constitute an authority structure.'[8] The world cannot speak for itself; it must be spoken for. Social reality is constantly being negotiated and constructed, renegotiated and reconstructed. Language is not a system of static symbols but a form of social action and history making. To acquire and exercise a language is to engage in the most profound of political acts.

Modern scholars are belatedly becoming aware of the shortcomings of liberal theorizing. In particular, they have found it hard to ignore the all-too-cozy relation between politics and economics; franchise and finance are seen to be increasingly mutually dependent and reinforcing. The libertarian tradition was developed to act as a citizen's shield against the slings and arrows of state censorship, especially those that were targeted at the content of certain speech. Yet, in a modern hi-tech world in which the paradigmatic speaker is CTV rather than the street-corner orator, any continued reliance on that outmoded tradition will not only fail to protect democratic politics but runs the considerable risk of impairing it. Each citizen's medieval shield offers little defence against the expensive and communicative subtleties of technological weaponry: the journey from the soapbox to the VCR has altered much on the socio-cultural landscape. In today's social world, it is the commercial dilution of public discourse to a distracting and anodyne patter that is as much a threat as Big Brother. Citizens are choking on a commercial glut of inconsequential information rather than starving on a constrained diet of official misinformation. It is necessary to ration the supply of ideas and facts only when people still retain the crucial capacity to be selective and care enough to exercise it. However, what is ignored by many is that the most effective censorship occurs through the dulling or trivialization of that cognitive process of discrimination.[9]

A rich source to illustrate the challenge and failure of present thinking is legal doctrine. While it can be an arcane and privileged arena, the courts' stylized discourse offers a sustained practice of the never-ending and never-endable controversies about the proper forms of social life and, in particular, the tension between censorship and free expression. The American and Canadian constitutional doctrines seem to consist of an endless process of making, refining, reworking, collapsing, and rejecting doctrinal categories and distinctions. By the time one has gained a rudimentary understanding of the difference between speech and non-speech, protected and unprotected speech, political and commercial speech, private and public forums, and the like, the courts have already modified the distinctions and their protean doctrinal infrastructure. Two themes or principles run through Supreme Court decisions. There is a dominant commitment to a formal neutrality which rests on a notion of negative liberty: individuals and private institutions must be free from governmental intrusion in their efforts to have others hear their views and the law should be deployed as their protective shield. But this dominant tradition has had to graft on limitations that derive their force from a more positive notion of liberty which looks towards collective self-determination: individuals must have more genuine opportunities to engage in public debate which is uninhibited, robust, and wide open and in which the law is wielded as their affirmative sword.[10] As is true of open political debate about censorship and free expression, legal doctrine is characterized by its ambivalence and confusion over how to understand and respond to the complex practices and ambitions of contemporary society. While there is much talk about objective justification and political neutrality, the fact is that there are only contingent accommodations which draw on the competing social visions that inspire and animate the collective struggle towards the good life.

No amount of tinkering with the liberal project will suffice in completing this substantive undertaking: it is the very liberal structure of social practice and organization that prevents a successful resolution of the free-speech problem. While these questions do not lend themselves to easy answers under any theory or practice of social justice, liberalism provides no theoretical framework for even understanding, let alone resolving, distributional issues of this kind. It requires the very conception of substantive good that it so proudly eschews, but so badly needs. Consequently, in order to offer a viable alternative to a liberal approach to censorship and expressive freedom, it will be necessary to vacate the liberal territory and rethink the problem from the ground up: the nature of 'freedom' and 'expression' must be constructed afresh. In short, if there were a different and better understanding of the mutually constituting dialectic between people and discourse, there would be a different and better understanding of censorship and the conditions for its control.

Democratic Dialogue

The world, and people's ideas about it, take on meaning within historically specific modes of communication. Language is not an echo of being or the trace of a universal metaphysic. A society's resources for conversation determine not only the knowledge at its disposal but also its very ways of knowing. Consequently, the need to understand dialogue – the discursive interactions between individuals – as the crucible of social action in which individuals mutually constitute and reconstitute themselves and others is paramount. By accepting that dialogue is both the producer and the product of interacting individuals, it becomes apparent that the challenge is twofold: to ensure that the quality of that dialogue is sufficiently open and fluid so that people might confront each other in the routine practices of daily life as equal participants, and, also, that it is sufficiently shared and certain to protect people from its unscrupulous manipulation. It is only by establishing such conditions of face-to-face intimacy and engaging in such dialogic encounters that we will reach and share satisfactory knowledge and truths. Moreover, in striving to establish a dialogic community, the prevailing circumstances of social power will have to be recognized and rectified; conversation is inimical to hierarchy. Accordingly, a cogent account of censorship and expressive freedom must take seriously the idea that both practices are about the conditions, distribution, and operation of power.

Insofar as we live by a *telos*, it will not be found in History, The Human Condition, or Rights-Talk, but will be created and criticized in our shared efforts at mutual understanding and debate. Meaning and normative standards will be available and real but will hold no claim to universal validity. A society constitutes its own conception of rational argument rather than uncovers an independent criterion of rationality. Appropriately, conversation offers no objective foundations. Instead, each participant is bound by their acceptance of the contingent, yet real, status of their own conversation and their shared commitment to respect its dynamic. Criticism can be intelligible, engaged, constructive, and authoritative. People define and transform others as they themselves are reciprocally defined and transformed by others. There is a profound connection between conversation and who people, as participants in that conversation, are and can be. Indeed, by its very nature, true dialogue is always critical and challenging. The vision of a dialogic community – 'mutual understanding, respect, a willingness to listen and to risk one's opinions and prejudices, a mutual seeking of the correctness of what is said'[11] – is not abstract or disembodied but can give concrete guidance to our practical lives. By adopting such a dialectical view of the relations between language, social action, and individual intentionality, attention shifts from individuals to the circumstances of their dialogic and constitutive interactions. Conversation and connection become important and valuable in themselves and not simply as a means to the personal end of self-expression: they are the pith and substance of social life.

An alternative concern with the establishment of a dialogic community focuses as much on the interactive conditions of human development as on the interacting individuals. This permits the individualistic notion of free speech to be replaced by a more 'solidaristic' understanding of expressive freedom in which freedom becomes a facilitation and mediation of engaged conversations. By viewing the individual self as constituted in and through its intersubjective connections, the notions of autonomy and solidarity can be better and differently understood: criticism and commitment, innovation and connection can be mutually supported. At the heart of this enterprize is the understanding that self-definition is a function of intersubjective experience; it is the relation and not the relating entities that should be protected and nurtured. Within such an understanding of dialogic democracy, people are recognized as being socially situated, but not socially saturated. Freedom is no longer associated with a lack of constraint. There is never a situation of 'no constraints', but only an historical dialectic of openings and closings: the issue is which constraints, not whether some or none. The individual does not precede social encounters, but takes on substance within them. Freedom does not stand in opposition to community, but exists only within communities. Social worth and self-esteem are embedded in and nourished by affective affiliations. To live in a community is not to experience life as a forced march in strict formation; that is one conception of community, but it is not the only or best one. In place of order, rank, and stability, there must be a fluid, participatory, and egalitarian vision of community in which conflict and disagreement are facilitative of its enduring value. Such a vision will embrace difference as a celebration of individuality and avoid a stultifying levelling that legislates an homogeneous 'other' against which people are encouraged to define and measure themselves.

Of course, in the same way that it must not be over-valued, the liberal campaign for free speech ought not to be under-valued; its solicitude for the interests of individual speakers against unwarranted state interference is of great significance. There will remain the very real need to be vigilant against the possibilities for abusive bureaucratic control of expressive freedom. However, a continued resort to the precepts and foundational premises of liberal theory can have only reactionary effects and results; it misses more than it captures and manages to deflect attention away from more insidious sources and styles of censorship. The history and terrain of censorship in contemporary Canadian society is much too varied, too dynamic, and too complex to fit into a single empirical pattern or theoretical framework. What is needed is a less reductionist theory of politics which understands the distribution and exercise of power in a much more multifaceted, heterogeneous, and ubiquitous way. It will be one in which the state is not so much always the problem as occasionally part of the solution; not so much a source of social relations as an expression of their contingent organization; not so much a unified set of social arrangements as a site for a struggle over them; and not so much a solid and centralized phenomenon as a fluid and diffuse network of confrontations. Such a theory will not only facilitate a more cogent and instructive critique of prevailing circumstances, but will recommend a more suitable and effective set of concrete proposals for changing society in a way that best avoids the possibility of reproducing today's deep and problematic structural faults.

For example, a vision of dialogic community will help to break the theoretical impasse in dealing with the issue of censorship and expressive freedom as it relates to the media. As things currently stand, the historical promise of mass media to extend democratic dialogue and collective consciousness has been partly fulfilled and partly reneged on. Dominated by the oligarchic operations of huge corporations, the media has reached the point where its primary *raison d'être* is not disseminating news or providing entertainment but the making of money and the accumulation of capital. Even the state-owned CBC has in effect to function as a commercial undertaking. Moreover, not only are media corporations considered to be beyond the scope of legitimate government regulation, but they are accorded special constitutional privileges.[12] The modern hi-tech world has meant that control over the channels of mass communication is the basis for broader control; politics has become more a visual spectacle than a substantive debate. In such circumstances, the abdication of such power to private interest is folly. If information is the lifeblood of contemporary society, large corporations are allowed to regulate the pulse of the body politic in accordance with the dictates of economic logic. It is naive to think that in any society, no matter how democratic, the media will cease to wield huge power.

However, the challenge is not to dissipate that power but to place it in the service of democratic politics and under popular control. In effecting a democratic reform, no particular weight might be placed on the distinction between private and public bodies; the CBC, the *Globe and Mail*, and the *Midland Times* would be regulated by the reference to the substantive impact of their actions on public debate and the extent to which they were already democratically controlled.

In this way, it becomes possible to get beyond the straitjacket of traditional thinking and to appreciate censorship and expressive freedom in more nuanced and positive terms. A concern for dialogic authenticity cuts across present preoccupations with speaker autonomy and state suppression. While both concerns are important and must be respected by any progressive proposal for change, a reliance on either as the exclusive regulative ideal is ultimately self-defeating. Dialogue turns us away from liberal notions of individual freedom, whether singly or aggregately expressed, and points us towards the democratic activities of associational individuals. By abandoning the stale ethical vocabulary of means and ends, the formal conditions for conversational encounters embody and inculcate a substantive relationship between interlocutors that is important in and for itself. Within such a dialogic community, freedom would be understood not as a splendid but desolate isolation in which a right to soliloquize might be the extent of freedom, nor as a state-enforced conformity in which the right to hear another's monologue might exhaust freedom. In contrast, the regulative ideal of dialogue incorporates a right to hear, to be heard, and to be answered. It establishes and maintains the social conditions for open-ended, continuing, and meaningful conversations in which people engage as equals. In place of the traditional reliance on individual rights to free speech, there might exist a set of social processes to facilitate open discourse in which the censorial threats and ennobling opportunities of collective action are debated and determined.

A commitment to 'democratic conversation' requires a changing and changeable mix of interventions and abstentions. It eschews sweeping statements about, for instance, whether any collectively sanctioned interference in media activities is desirable. While a mandated entitlement of public access to large-scale media outlets might be necessary, the universal availability of access to fringe publications would be self-defeating. Access by the powerful to the small presses of the relatively powerless threatens to replicate the existing imbalance and to stymie the development of a diversely democratic culture. Moreover, a concern for dialogue obliges us to reconsider the meaning and operation of censorship in such circumstances. It forces an acknowledgement that harm results not simply from the silencing of certain voices but also from allowing certain voices to dominate social exchange and operate a virtual monologue: the response that 'the answer to bad speech is more speech' is limited and simplis-

tic. A fully developed dialogic entitlement might combine active steps to bring
in previously stilled and marginalized voices with positive moves to shut down
stentorian and partial voices. Democratic dialogue demands not just the existence of speech somewhere by someone but a realistic opportunity to have that
speech heard and, preferably, responded to by others. With an informed appreciation of the dialogic forum being limited and finite in its economic and discursive dimensions, such collective efforts might concentrate less on the content of
expression and more on the control of the means of expression; it is the concentration of economic power and its expressive capacity that is at the core of the
media problem.

Furthermore, democratic conversation requires an abandonment of the public-
private distinction. This does not mean that everything becomes public and individuals lose all sense of privacy or personal autonomy; media moguls have as
much (but no more) of a claim to privacy and autonomy as anyone else. The abuse
of power that the distinction is intended to address should remain central to any
serious account of the theory and practice of censorship. Consequently, what an
abandonment of the public-private distinction does mean is that people will have
to decide democratically on those moments and activities when society-at-large
should devolve full power and authority to individuals and establish a space in
which they are immune from collective interference. This will not be a collective
abdication of responsibility for the fate of others, but it will represent a constructive affirmation of the need for everyone to be involved in providing a positive
and empowering expressive freedom for each citizen. Nor will this devolution be
a once-and-for-all reckoning; rather, it will be a continuing and evolving responsibility to rework and realign these publicly created and sustained occasions of
privacy. It is as much a problem to obliterate the distinction as it is to reify it. The
challenge is to demystify the distinction and recognize its artefactual character
and emancipatory potential; society ought to put it in service to democratic ideals
rather than make these ideals serve its counterfeit authority.

Within such a refreshed account of censorship and expressive freedom, the
debate around pornography presents itself in a different and more instructive
light. Instead of it being cast as a battle between the authority of state-backed
prudes (or progressives) and the liberty of individual perverts (or bohemians), it
can be grasped as a contested and contextual practice that is neither always
good nor always bad but another organic site for continued political struggle
and future revalorization. Of course, in saying this, I am not arguing that all sexually explicit representations are good or that they are all bad; that would be to
take the same essentialist position as many current contributors on the political
right and left. To be anti-censorship is not to be pro-pornography: this is a ludi-
crous drawing of ideological lines that distorts and disables any political posi-

tion. As with all disputed social practices, there is no safe or secure political ground on which to stand or from which to intervene in the pornography debate. As a political engagement, it is always an unstable and shifting medium. Whichever way one turns, there will be trade-offs to be made. To defend sexually explicit representations against legislative prohibition is to be on the side of the pornography industry and its commercialization of all sex. On the other hand, to oppose sexually explicit representations is to be on the side of the Moral Majority and its related campaign against abortion, gays, lesbians, and so on. Accordingly, the struggle over pornography is not usefully or effectively carried out by prohibiting it entirely. It is surely better effected by appropriating and revamping the discourse of pornography so that it can be turned into a democratic discourse of political dissent and sexual diversity over 'what makes sex a good and positive dimension to our humanity.'[13]

Conclusion

My aim has been to suggest a richer and more subtle approach to censorship that better captures and responds to the conditions of *fin de siècle* Canada. And my hope is that this will help to energize the continuing battle against censorial practices. This includes not only the more traditional forms of repression but also the proliferating and more subtle modes of communication and constraint that threaten to saturate modern society. Most important, I have tried to suggest that any effective approach to censorship will have to pay greater attention to expressive freedom and the social conditions that will be needed to nurture and protect its practice. In meeting this challenge, the only process and standard to which resort can be had is a substantively democratic one. Of course, what democracy demands at any particular time and on any particular occasion will itself always be open to debate and disagreement. And this is how it should be. The most potent threat to social justice is the dulling of the appetite for dialogue and the neglect of the capacity for critical engagement. Since it is necessary to ration the supply of ideas and facts only when people still retain a critical intelligence and care enough to exercise it, censorship is most effective when it masquerades as choice. Current theorizing facilitates that possibility; a different account, along the lines that I have sketched, might not.

NOTES

1 See Stanley Fish, *There's No Such Thing as Free Speech, And It's a Good Thing Too* (New York: Oxford University Press 1994).

2 See Harry Glasbeek, 'Entrenchment of Freedom of Speech for the Press – Fetter-
   ing of Freedom of Speech of the People,' in Philip Anisman and Allan M. Linden,
   eds., *The Media, the Courts and the Charter* (Toronto: Carswell 1986), 101; and
   Michael Parenti, *Inventing Reality: The Politics of News Media* (New York: St Martin's Press 1993).

3 Noam Chomsky, 'The Manufacture of Consent,' *Our Generation*, 17, no. 83
   (1985), 100, 106.

4 John Sopinka, 'Freedom of Speech under Attack,' *University Affairs*, 34 (April
   1994), 13.

5 See E.M. Barendt, *Freedom of Speech* (Oxford: Clarendon Press 1985), 8–23.

6 See Thomas Hobbes, *Leviathan*, ed. C.B. Macpherson (New York: Viking Penguin
   1982); and John Locke, *An Essay Concerning Human Understanding*, Bk. 3, ch. 2,
   ed. A. Pringle-Pattison (1924).

7 John Rawls, 'The Basic Liberties and Their Priority,' in *Liberty, Equality and Law:
   Selected Tanner Lectures on Moral Philosophy* (Salt Lake City: University of Utah
   Press 1987), 17.

8 J.G.A. Pocock, *Politics, Language and Time: Essays on Political Thought and History* (Chicago: University of Chicago Press 1989), 15. See also Gary Peller, 'The
   Metaphysics of American Law,' *California Law Review*, 73 (1985), 1181. This
   insight is not new, but the older view did not pursue the political implications of
   social construction through discourse. See Benjamin Lee Whorf, *Language,
   Thought and Reality: Selected Writings*, ed. John B. Caroll (Cambridge: MIT
   Technology Press 1956).

9 See Neil Postman, *Amusing Ourselves to Death: Public Discourse in the Age of
   Show Business* (New York: Viking 1985), 138–41 and 155–63.

10 See Allan Hutchinson, *Waiting for Coraf: A Critique of Law and Rights* (Toronto:
   University of Toronto Press 1995), 187–97; and Joel Bakan, *Just Words: Constitutional Rights and Social Wrongs* (Toronto: University of Toronto Press 1997).

11 R. Bernstein, *Beyond Objectivism and Relativism* (Philadelphia: University of
   Pennsylvania Press 1983), 163. See also Frank I. Michelman, 'Foreword: Traces of
   Self-Government,' *Harvard Law Review*, 100, no. 4 (1986), 33.

12 See *Hunter* v. *Southam Newspapers*, [1984] 2 S.C.R. 145.

13 Brenda Cossman et al., *Bad Attitude/s on Trial: Pornography, Feminism, and the
   Butler Decision* (Toronto: University of Toronto Press 1997).

Film Censorship

Because of their wide appeal to mass audiences, motion pictures have always been more severely censored than any other media. Fear of their potentially immoral or subversive effect on society was (and is) too strong to allow them freedom from restrictions. In Canada, film is the only form of expression subjected to prior censorship; film material must be submitted to a film-censor board for approval and classification before it may be publicly screened. Since their inception in the years before the First World War, provincial censor boards have been busy banning, cutting, and classifying films, many of which – if produced abroad – had been already cut in their country of origin.

Malcolm Dean's *Censored! Only in Canada* (1981) gives a fully documented account of both Canada's film-control legislation and the activities of the provincial censors to 1980. Dean analyses the powers of the boards, the bureaucratic processes, the values underlying board decisions, and the effect of bans and cuts on the film industry. The treatment of classics like *All Quiet on the Western Front*, *Last Tango in Paris*, and *The Tin Drum* are discussed in detail.

The prior censorship of films as practised by the Ontario Film Censor Board was successfully challenged as unconstitutional once the Canadian Charter of Rights and Freedoms had been introduced in 1982. In its decision of 25 March 1983, the Ontario High Court of Justice held that the Ontario Censor Board's 'Standards for Classification and/or Censorship' were in violation of the Charter because they were too vague and did not qualify as law. The court affirmed the government's right to censor or prohibit the exhibition of film but found that limits to the freedom of expression could not be left to the whim of an official. This decision put the onus on the provincial governments to overhaul their film-control legislation, and until that happens film censorship in Canada is bound to remain more lenient.

As it stands, the 1983 decision of the Ontario High Court of Justice constitutes a turning point in the history of Canadian film censorship. We include an excerpt from the decision in order to update the information provided in Malcolm Dean's book and to offer the reader an insight into another important area of censorious activity in our country.

[HIGH COURT OF JUSTICE]
DIVISIONAL COURT

Re Ontario Film and Video Appreciation Society and
Ontario Board of Censors

J. HOLLAND, BOLAND   25TH MARCH 1983.
AND LINDEN JJ.

Constitutional law – Charter of Rights – Freedom of expression – Censorship – Provincial legislation authorizing board to censor films – Whether limitation on freedom of expression – Theatres Act, R.S.O. 1980, c. 498, ss. 3(2)(a), (b), 35, 38 – Canadian Charter of Rights and Freedoms, 9. 2(b).

[...]

This application raises the question of the constitutional validity of the censorship (prior restraint) provisions of the Theatres Act, R.S.O. 1980, c. 498, and the standards and procedures of the Ontario Board of Censors pursuant to which the board has carried out its statutory mandate relating to films to be shown to the public or for gain. The application was precipitated by the enactment of the Constitution Act, 1982, and in particular by the guarantee of the right to freedom of expression as contained in s. 2(b) of the Canadian Charter of Rights and Freedom which provides:

2. Everyone has the following fundamental freedoms:
   (b) freedom of thought, belief, opinion and expression ...

Any limitation upon this guaranteed freedom must meet the tests set out in s. 1 of the Charter, which reads as follows:

1. The Canadian Charter of Rights and Freedoms guarantees the rights and freedoms set out in it subject only to such reasonable limits prescribed by law as can be demonstrably justified in a free and democratic society.

Section 52 provides for primacy in the following way:

52(1) The Constitution of Canada is the supreme law of Canada, and any law that is inconsistent with the provisions of the Constitution is, to the extent of the inconsistency, of no force or effect.

We are asked to find that the censorship (prior restraint) provisions of the Theatres Act and/or the standards and procedures of the board do limit the freedom of expression so guaranteed and do not successfully meet the tests set out in s. 1 and accordingly must be constitutionally invalid.

Before setting out the particular sections of the Theatres Act which are impugned, we should record that the right of the province to enact such legislation is not in issue: see *Nova Scotia Board of Censors et al.* v. *McNeil*, (1978] 2 S.C.R. 662, 84 D.L.R. (3d) 1, 44 C.C.C. (2d) 316. Further, there has been no challenge to the system of film classification in operation in Ontario for some time, nor of the general regulation of theatres and projectionists and other matters dealt with in the statute. Nor has there been any assault upon the provisions of the Criminal Code of Canada which continue to proscribe forms of expression which unduly exploit sex and violence.

What is impugned in this proceeding is the power granted to the Ontario Board of Censors to 'censor any film' (s. 3(2)(a)), to 'prohibit ... the exhibition of any film in Ontario' (s. 3(2)(b)), as well as the requirement that 'all film' be 'submitted to the Board for approval' (s. 35) and the prohibition against exhibiting 'any film that has not been approved by the Board' (s. 38). It is vigorously contended by the applicants and the intervenors that this system of censorship is a prior restraint of expression, which cannot continue in this province in the face of the new Charter. The Crown has defended, no less strenuously, the constitutionality of the present censorship scheme.

In April of 1982, immediately following the proclamation of the new Charter, the applicant submitted four films to the board of censors, seeking approval for public showings. The 'Art of Worldly Wisdom' and 'Rameau's Nephew' were both approved for exhibition, but only at one time and at one place. 'Not A Love Story' was rejected on the ground that the National Film Board, the owners of the film, had not released it for public exhibition by the applicant on a commercial basis. The fourth film, 'Amerika,' was rejected by the board of censors, which gave reasons having to do with the explicit portrayal of certain sexual activity. The members of this court have not viewed the films in question, because this was not felt to be necessary in disposing of the application. (There are several administrative law issues arising from the facts, which will be dealt with later.)

The provisions of the Theatres Act which are relevant include s. 3, which reads:

3(1) The board known as the Board of Censors is continued and shall consist of the Director who shall be chairman of the Board and the Assistant Director who shall be vice-chairman of the Board and such other persons as the Lieutenant Governor in Council may appoint.

(2) The Board has power,

(a) to censor any film and, when authorized by the person who submits film to the Board for approval, remove by cutting or otherwise from the film any portion thereof that it does not approve of for exhibition in Ontario;

(b) subject to the regulations, to approve, prohibit or regulate the exhibition of any film in Ontario;

(c) to censor any advertising matter in connection with any film or the exhibition thereof;

(d) subject to the regulations, to approve, prohibit or regulate advertising in Ontario in connection with any film or the exhibition thereof;

(e) to classify any film as adult entertainment;

(f) to classify any film as restricted entertainment; and

(g) to carry out its duties under this Act and the regulations.

Section 35 stipulates as follows:

35. All film before being exhibited in Ontario shall be submitted to the Board for approval, accompanied by the prescribed fee.

Section 38 states:

38. No person shall exhibit or cause to be exhibited in Ontario any film that has not been approved by the Board.

The word 'exhibit' is defined by s. 1(c) as follows:
In this Act,

(c) 'exhibit,' when used in respect of film or moving pictures, means to show film for viewing for direct or indirect gain or for viewing by the public and 'exhibition' has a corresponding meaning ...

It should also be noted that s. 63(1), para. 9 of the Theatres Act authorizes the making of regulations 'prohibiting and regulating the use and exhibition of film or any type or class thereof' but none have been prepared. Section 63(1), para. 14 authorizes the making of regulations 'prescribing the terms and conditions under which film or any type or class thereof may be sold, rented, leased, exhibited or distributed,' but none have been issued.

The relevant provisions of the Theatres Act have been in place in this province since 1911 and we are advised that the present application is the first court challenge to be made upon these provisions or upon the board's operation thereunder. This must speak well of the conduct of the board members in carrying out the board's legislated duty, which undoubtedly involves difficult and controversial matters. We should point out that the application before us did not involve criticism of the board except to the extent that it is said the statutory provisions and the standards and procedures of the board were inconsistent with the guaranteed freedom of expression and did not meet the test set out in s. 1. The issue is essentially legal and not factual.

Over the years the board has issued several versions of a document entitled 'Standards for Classification and/or Censorship of Films' to which it purports to adhere in exercising its authority. These standards set out descriptions of the type of material that would be classified as 'general,' 'adult entertainment' or 'restricted' as well as the type of material that it would recommend to be eliminated. It is explained that a film might be rejected altogether, something it says is 'very rare,' if the required eliminations were 'so extensive as to ruin the continuity of the film.' Most of the offensive types of material deal with sexual explicitness, violence or the exploitation of children, but 'blasphemous' and 'sacrilegious' matter is also mentioned. It has also circulated to the public and any interested persons several versions of a pamphlet entitled 'Film Classification and Censorship,' which sets out much of the same material contained in the standards. All of these publications, however, are conceded by the Crown to have no legal status; they are distributed merely for the assistance of the public in order to indicate the general approach of the board. It is clear that the standards are not legally binding on the board, although it is asserted that they are generally used by the board as guide-lines.

When Her Majesty proclaimed into force the new Charter of Rights and Freedoms, all Canadians were guaranteed certain fundamental freedoms set out in s. 2, such as 'freedom of ... expression, including freedom of the press and other media of communication.' This section is mainly declaratory of the freedoms which have long existed in Canada (see *Nova Scotia Board of Censors et al.* v. *McNeil, supra, A.-G. Can. et al.* v. *Dupond et al.*, [1978] 2 S.C.R. 770, 84 D.L.R. (3d) 420, 19 N.R. 478 sub nom. *Dupond* v. *City of Montreal*, and *A.-G. Can. et al.* v. *Law Society of British Columbia et al.*; *Jabour* v. *Law Society of British Columbia et al.* (1982), 137 D.L.R. (3d) 1, 66 C.P.R. (2d) 1, 43 N.R. 451 (S.C.C.)), for we Canadians have always enjoyed a full measure of freedom of expression, as well as the other freedoms. Nevertheless, our political leaders concluded that these freedoms should be entrenched in a Charter in order to guarantee these rights for all Canadians, including future generations, and, possibly, to permit expansion over the years ahead.

These fundamental freedoms guaranteed in the Charter are not absolute. The Charter recognizes that it is sometimes necessary to restrict freedom of expression to an extent to protect the interest of society. Consequently, it is possible for our governments to circumscribe the freedoms enunciated in s. 2. They may do so by invoking the notwithstanding clause (s. 33). Alternatively, they may do so by observing the provisions of s. 1 of the Charter, which indicates that the rights and freedoms set out in it are 'subject only to such reasonable limits prescribed by law as can be demonstrably justified in a free and democratic society.'

It is not in dispute that in the event that legislation is enacted which limits any of these freedoms, the government bears the onus of demonstrating that the limit comes within the language of s. 1. The presumption of constitutional validity, which generally applies in cases of ordinary legislation, is not available once it is shown that there has been an interference with one of the fundamental freedoms: see *Quebec Ass'n of Protestant School Boards et al.* v. *A.-G. Quebec et al.,* (No. 2), 140 D.L.R. (3d) 33 (September 8, 1982); *Federal Republic of Germany* v. *Rauca* (1982), 38 O.R. (2d) 705, 141 D.L.R. (3d) 412, 70 C.C.C. (2d) 416; Tarnopolsky & Beaudoin, *The Canadian Charter of Rights and Freedoms: Commentary* (1982), at p. 70.

We are all of the view that ss. 3(2)(a) and (b), 35 and 38 impose a limitation on the freedom of expression of the applicant as guaranteed by s. 2(b) of the Charter. It is clear to us that all forms of expression, whether they be oral, written, pictorial, sculpture, music, dance or film, are equally protected by the Charter. The burden, therefore, falls upon the Attorney-General to satisfy us on the balance of probabilities that the requirements of s. 1 of the Charter have been met, and 'the standard of persuasion to be applied by the court is a high one if the limitation in issue is to be upheld as valid': see Evans C.J.H.C. in *Rauca,* supra (at p. 716 O.R., p. 423 D.L.R.I. By placing such an onus on governments, the Charter inhibits the courts from permitting the dilution of the guaranteed fundamental freedoms. Hence, any limit placed on these freedoms must be shown to be demonstrably justifiable in a free and democratic society; it must be a reasonable limit; and it must be a limit that is 'prescribed by law.' Let us examine each of these three items in turn.

Demonstrably Justifiable in a Free and Democratic Society

As for being demonstrably justifiable in a free and democratic society, it has been held that there must be a reasonable ground upon which a limitation can be based for it to be 'justifiable': see Chief Justice Evans, *Rauca,* supra. Chief Justice Deschênes has suggested that we must focus on the 'validity' of the 'objective' of the legislation: *Quebec Ass'n of Protestant School Boards* case, supra. It is obvious that the Theatres Act (and its predecessors back to 1911) primarily seeks, among other things, to prevent socially offensive films from being publicly shown in Ontario. Eight other provinces and many other free and democratic countries have similar legislation: see *Report of the Committee on Obscenity and Film Censorship*, U.K. Cmnd. 7772 (1979). Moreover, the federal criminal prohibition against obscenity is evidence that there is and has been sufficient concern in this country about this problem to enact legislation to combat it. We are satisfied, therefore, that some prior censorship of film is demonstrably justifiable in a free and democratic society. (No one questioned that Canada and each of its constituent provinces and territories are free and democratic.)

Reasonable Limits

The next issue to consider is whether the limits placed on the freedom of expression by the Theatres Act are reasonable ones. Counsel for the Crown argued that the limits are reasonable since they curtail only the freedom of those who wish to exhibit films to the public or for gain. He points out that any one can make films, show them privately, rent them and sell them. Hence, it is said the freedom of expression is only curtailed to the extent that a person wishes to exhibit film to the public or for profit. It would be fair to assume that the prime purpose of making films is to exhibit them to the public. If a film-maker cannot show his film to the public there is little point in making it. Moreover, the profit motive cannot be a valid reason to prevent a film-maker from showing his work, for one who shows film for profit can have no less freedom of expression than one who does so not for profit. The extent of freedom of expression cannot depend on that, for there is nothing wrong with making a profit from one's art or one's ideas. In addition freedom of expression extends to those who wish to express someone else's ideas or show someone else's film. It also extends to the listener and to the viewer, whose freedom to receive communication is included in the guaranteed right.

Another argument advanced by the Crown is that a prohibition can be reasonable if it applies only to film-makers, not to authors of books, publishers of papers, performers on the stage, TV producers, etc. We cannot agree. The Charter, in allowing reasonable limits, does not countenance the total eradication of freedom of expression for those who use a particular form of expression such as film. If film is the medium in which an individual works, he could thereby be denied completely his only means of self-expression. To say that other media are available to him is no comfort at all. This argument really involves the question of fair treatment between various forms of communication. Hence, although one particular form of expression may not be prevented completely, a legislative body, acting within its jurisdiction, may place limits only upon one type of expression and not on others provided that such limits meet the test set out in s. 1.

As to whether the standards issued by the board of censors would be considered to be reasonable limits, we express no views. They may or may not be acceptable, but in the light of the position we take on the next issue, it is not necessary for us to express a view. One thing is sure, however, our courts will exercise considerable restraint in declaring legislative enactments, whether they be statutory or regulatory, to be unreasonable.

Prescribed by Law

The next issue is whether the limits placed on the applicant's freedom of expression by the board of censors were 'prescribed by law.' It is clear that statutory law, regulations and even common law limitations may be permitted. But the limit, to be acceptable, must have legal force. This is to ensure that it has been established democratically through the legislative process or judicially through the operation of precedent over the years. This requirement underscores the seriousness with which courts will view any interference with the fundamental freedoms.

The Crown has argued that the board's authority to curtail freedom of expression is prescribed by law in the Theatres Act, ss. 3, 35 and 38. In our view, although there has certainly been a legislative grant of power to the board to censor and prohibit certain films, the reasonable limits placed upon that freedom of expression of film-makers have not been legislatively authorized. The Charter requires reasonable limits that are prescribed by law; it is not enough to authorize a board to censor or prohibit the exhibition of any film of which it disapproves. That kind of authority is not legal for it depends on the discretion of an administrative tribunal. However dedicated, competent and well meaning the board may be, that kind of regulation cannot be considered as 'law.' It is accepted that law cannot be vague, undefined, and totally discretionary; it must be ascertainable and understandable. Any limits placed on the freedom of expression cannot be left to the whim of an official; such limits must be articulated with some precision or they cannot be considered to be law.

There are no reasonable limits contained in the statute or the regulations. The standards and the pamphlets utilized by the Ontario Board of Censors do contain certain information upon which a film-maker may get some indication of how his film will be judged. However, the board is not bound by these standards. They have no legislative or legal force of any kind. Hence, since they do not qualify as law, they cannot be employed so as to justify any limitation on expression, pursuant to s. 1 of the Charter. We draw comfort in this conclusion from the views of Professor Beckton, in *The Canadian Charter of Rights and Freedoms: Commentary* (1982), p. 107 (Tarnopolsky & Beaudoin, editors), where she wrote:

Clearly statutes which create censorship boards without specific criteria would be contrary to the guarantees of free expression, since no line is drawn between objectionable and non-objectionable forms of expression. Now standards will have to be created to measure the limits to which obscene expressions may be regulated.

This does not mean that the censorship scheme set out in the Theatres Act is invalid. Clearly the classification scheme by itself does not offend the Charter. Nor do we find that ss. 3, 35 and 38 are invalid, but the problem is that standing alone they cannot be used to censor or prohibit the exhibition of films because they are so general, and because the detailed criteria employed in the process are not prescribed by law. These sections, in so far as they purport to prohibit or to allow censorship of films, may be said to be 'of no force or effect,' but they may be rendered operable by the passage of regulations pursuant to the legislative authority or by the enactment of statutory amendments, imposing reasonable limits and standards.

We turn now to the several other constitutional and administrative law issues to be addressed relating to the specific request made to the board. The decision of the board that the two films could be shown at one time and one place is a valid exercise of the board's power to 'regulate' pursuant to s. 3(2)(b).

The decision concerning 'Not A Love Story' is defensible as a refusal by the board to engage in an academic exercise. The applicants were seeking permission to show a film they did not own and which they had no right to exhibit. The board does not have to spend its time engaging in theoretical activity. Although no copy of the film was submitted to the board as required by the Act, this ground was not relied upon by the board. While it is said that the reason the board gave, that the National Film Board had not released the film for public commercial showing, was an improper interference with freedom of expression because there is no specific legislative authority for doing so, in view of the above, we need not decide this issue.

The decision to prohibit the public exhibition of 'Amerika' must be quashed because it was an interference with the freedom of expression of the applicant that was not based on a legally binding standard.

As for the denial of natural justice, procedural fairness, and the need for a hearing pursuant to the Statutory Powers Procedure Act, R.S.O. 1980, c. 484, this much can be said. It is not clear on the evidence before us that there was any infringement of the right to be heard. The Standard Procedures for Classification and Censorship of Film distributed by the board provides for a written report by the board without a hearing. However, if there is an objection, the distributor may, within 15 days, make submissions in writing, which the board will consider. The board may request a meeting with the distributor to discuss the submission. After that another report will be made by the board. In this case, following the reports of the board on the four films, the applicant did not object in writing or request a hearing, but commenced legal proceedings immediately. We are of the view that the applicant has not exhausted its remedies and hence we decline to exercise our discretion to invoke any prerogative remedy that may be available.

The decision of the board of censors concerning *Amerika*, therefore, is quashed. The application in all other respects is dismissed.

Counsel have agreed that there should be a stay of execution of this decision pending the time limited for appeal and we so direct. In the event that no appeal is to be taken, we may be spoken to, before the time for appeal lapses, about a further stay of execution.

We make no order as to costs to any party.

Application granted in part.

Select Bibliography

Alexander, Michael. 'Censorship and the Limits of Liberalism.' *University of Toronto Faculty of Law Review*, 47, no. 1 (1988), 58–100.

Bakan, Joel. *Just Words: Constitutional Rights and Social Wrongs*. Toronto: University of Toronto Press 1997.

Beckton, Clare F. *The Law and the Media in Canada*. Toronto: Carswell 1982.

Bewley, Lois. 'Censorship and Librarians.' *Canadian Library Journal*, 40 (1983), 353–7.

Book and Periodical Development Council. *Books Challenged or Banned in the Last Eleven Years, 1974 to 1985*. Toronto: Book and Periodical Development Council 1985.

Booth, David. *Censorship Goes to School*. Toronto: Pembroke Publishers 1992.

Botting, Gary. *Fundamental Freedoms and Jehovah's Witnesses*. Calgary: University of Calgary Press 1993.

Boyd, Neil. 'Censorship and Obscenity: Jurisdiction and the Boundaries of Free Expression.' *Osgoode Hall Law Journal*, 23, no. 1 (1985), 37–66.

– *Sexuality and Violence, Imagery and Reality: Censorship and the Criminal Control of Obscenity*. Working Papers on Pornography and Prostitution, report no. 16. Ottawa: Canadian Department of Justice, Research and Statistics Section 1984.

Braun, Stefan. 'Freedom of Expression v. Obscenity Censorship: The Developing Canadian Jurisprudence.' *Saskatchewan Law Review*, 50, no. 1 (1985–6), 37–66.

Burress, Lee. *Battle of the Books: Literary Censorship in the Public Schools, 1950–1985*. Metuchen, N.J.: Scarecrow Press 1989.

Burstyn, Varda, ed. *Women Against Censorship*. Vancouver: Douglas and McIntyre 1977.

Campbell, Robert M. and Leslie A. Pal, eds. *The Real Worlds of Canadian Politics: Cases in Process and Policy*. Peterborough, Ont.: Broadview Press 1989.

Carmichael, Don J.C., Thomas C. Pocklington, and Gregory Pyrcz. *Democracy and Rights in Canada*. Toronto: Harcourt Brace Javanovich 1991.

Connolly, Edward Anthony. 'Censorship, Canon Reformation and Text Selection: Curriculum Concerns for English Studies in Canadian Secondary School Systems.' Ph.D. diss., Memorial University of Newfoundland 1992.

Conolly, Leonard W. 'Religion, Politics and Morality: Theatre Censorship in Canada,' in Richard Sherwin et al., ed., *At the Edge: Canadian Literature and Culture at Century's End* (Jerusalem: Magnes Press 1995), 18–27.

Cossman, Brenda. *Censorship and the Arts: Law, Controversy, Debate, Facts.* Toronto: Ontario Association of Art Galleries 1995.

Cossman, Brenda et al. *Bad Attitude/s on Trial.* Toronto: University of Toronto Press 1997.

Curry, Ann. *The Limits of Tolerance: Censorship and Intellectual Freedom in Public Libraries.* Lanham, Md.: Scarecrow Press 1997.

Daily, Jay E. 'Censorship, Contemporary and Controversial Aspects of,' in *Encyclopedia of Library and Information Science*, vol. 4 (1970), 338–81.

Dean, Malcolm. *Censored! Only in Canada: The History of Film Censorship – The Scandal Behind off the Screen.* Toronto: Virgo Press 1981.

De Montigny, Yves. 'The Difficult Relationship Between Freedom of Expression and Its Reasonable Limits.' *Law And Contemporary Problems*, 55, no. 1 (1992), 35–52.

Dick, Judith. *Not in Our Schools?!!! School Book Censorship in Canada: A Discussion Guide.* Ottawa: Canadian Library Association 1982.

Downs, Robert B. and Ralph E. McCoy, eds. *The First Freedom Today: Critical Issues Relating to Censorship and to Intellectual Freedom.* Chicago: American Library Association 1984.

Eisenstat, Lorraine Weinrib. 'Hate Promotion in a Free and Democratic Society: R. v. Keegstra.' *McGill Law Journal*, 36 (1991), 1416–49.

Fish, Stanley. *There's No Such Thing as Free Speech, and It's a Good Thing, Too.* New York: Oxford University Press 1994.

Fraser, Paul. *Pornography and Prostitution in Canada.* Report of the Special Committee on Pornography and Prostitution, Summary. Ottawa: Special Committee on Pornography and Prostitution 1985.

Freedom of Expression Committee. *Freedom to Read Week, February 16–23, 1990* [kit].Toronto: Book and Periodical Development Council 1989.

Fuller, Janine and Stuart Blackley. *Restricted Entry: Censorship on Trial.* Vancouver: Press Gang Publishers 1995.

Green, Jonathon. *The Encyclopedia of Censorship.* New York: Facts on File 1990.

Hoffmann, Frank. *Intellectual Freedom and Censorship. An Annotated Bibliography.* New York, London: Scarecrow, Metuchen 1989.

Hurwitz, Leon. *Historical Dictionary of Censorship in the United States.* Westport, Conn.: Greenwood Press 1985.

Hutchinson, Allan. *Waiting for Coraf: A Critique of Law and Rights.* Toronto: University of Toronto Press 1995.

Index on Censorship. London: Writers and Scholars International 1972 –

Information Freedom and Censorship. World Report 1991. Chicago: American Library Association 1991.

Intellectual Freedom Handbook, Nicholas Barakett and Diane Granfield, eds. Toronto: Ontario Library Association 1990.

Jansen, Sue Curry. *Censorship: The Knot That Binds Power and Knowledge.* New York: Oxford University Press 1988.

– 'Non-Government Censorship,' in: *International Encyclopedia of Communications*, vol. 1 (1989), 249.

Johnston, Jude et al., eds. *Issues of Censorship*, Toronto: A Space 1982.

Lacombe, Dany. *Blue Politics: Pornography and the Law in the Age of Feminism.* Toronto: University of Toronto Press 1994.

– *Ideology and Public Policy: The Case Against Pornography.* Toronto: Garamond Press 1988.

LaSelva, Samuel V. 'Controlling Obscenity: What Difference Does the Charter of Rights Make?' CPSA PAPERS, 1986, section B, paper 5, fiche 6. Published by the Canadian Political Science Association 1986.

Law Reform Commission of Canada. *Working Paper 50: Hate Propaganda.* Ottawa 1986.

MacDonald, Michael. 'Obscenity, Censorship, and Freedom of Expression: Does the Charter Protect Pornography?' *University of Toronto Faculty Law Review*, 43, no. 2 (1985), 130–52.

Macintosh, Kathryn Laurie. 'The High-school Literature Program: Book Selection, Censorship and Dissenting Values.' Ph.D. diss. University of Toronto 1992.

MacKinnon, Catharine A. *Only Words.* Cambridge, Mass.: Harvard University Press 1993.

Mahoney, Kathleen E. 'The Canadian Constitutional Approach to Freedom of Expression in Hate Propaganda and Pornography.' *Law and Contemporary Problems*, 55, no. 1 (1992), 77–105.

McCormack, Thelma. 'Censorship and "Community Standards" in Canada,' in Benjamin D. Singer, ed., *Communications in Canadian Society.* Don Mills, Ont.: Addison-Wesley Publishers 1983.

Mertl, Steve. *Keegstra: The Trial, the Issues, the Consequences.* Saskatoon: Western Producer Prairie Books 1985.

Moffett, James. 'Censorship and Spiritual Education.' *English Education*, 21 (1989), 70–87.

Moon, R. 'Drawing Lines in a Culture of Prejudice: R. v. Keegstra and the Restriction of Hate Propaganda.' *University of British Columbia Law Review*, 26 (1992), 99–143.

Neill, S.D. 'Censorship – a Clash of Values.' *Canadian Library Journal*, 45 (1988), 35–9.

Office for Intellectual Freedom of the American Library Association. *Intellectual Freedom Manual*. Chicago: American Library Association 1989.

Patterson, Annabel. 'Censorship and Interpretation.' *University of Toronto Quarterly*, 56 (1987), 456–60.

Peleg, Ilan, ed. *Patterns of Censorship around the World*. Boulder, Colo.: Westview Press 1993.

Regal, Alan R. 'Hate Propaganda: A Reason to Limit Free Speech.' *Saskatchewan Law Review*, 49 (1985), 303–18.

Schneiderman, David, ed. *Freedom of Expression and the Charter*. Calgary: Thomson Professional Publishing 1991.

Schrader, Alvin M. 'A Study of Community Censorship Pressures on Canadian Public Libraries.' *Canadian Library Journal* 49, no. 2 (1992), 29–38.

Schrader, Alvin M. and Keith Walker. 'Censorship Iceberg: Results of an Alberta Public Library Survey.' *Canadian Library Journal*, 43, no. 2 (1986), 91–5.

Toronto Arts Group for Human Rights, eds. *The Writer and Human Rights*. Toronto: Lester and Orpen Dennys 1983.

Tribe, David. *Questions of Censorship*. London: Allen and Unwin 1993.

Valois, M. 'Hate Propaganda, Section 2(b) and Section 1 of the Charter: A Canadian Constitutional Dilemma.' *Revue Juridique Themis*, 26 (1992), 373–431.

Weiler, Joseph M. and Robin M. Elliot, eds. *Litigating the Values of a Nation: The Canadian Charter of Rights and Freedoms*. Toronto: Carswell 1986 Writers' Union of Canada, ed. *C*ns*rsh*p: Stopping the Book Banners*. Toronto: The Freedom of Expression Task Force of the Book and Periodical Development Council 1978.

Writers' Union of Canada, ed. *C*ns*rsh*p: Stopping the Book Banners*. Toronto: The Freedom of Expression Task Force of the Book and Periodical Development Council 1978.

Contributors

Paul Axelrod is a professor in the Division of Social Science at York University. He has written widely on the political, economic, and social history of higher education in Canada. His most recent book is *The Promise of Schooling: Education in Canada, 1800-1914* (1997).

Joel Bakan is a professor at the Faculty of Law, University of British Columbia. He studied law at Oxford (as a Rhodes Scholar) and Dalhousie universities and did graduate work in law at Harvard University. Prior to coming to UBC, he worked as a law clerk to Chief Justice Brian Dickson of the Supreme Court of Canada, articled in Toronto, and taught at Osgoode Hall Law School, York University. He specializes in constitutional law and theory and recently published *Just Words: Constitutional Rights and Social Wrongs* (1997).

Barry Cooper, currently professor of political science at the University of Calgary, has published widely in the areas of political philosophy and Canadian public policy. He is a Fellow of the Royal Society of Canada.

Ann Curry, an associate professor at the School of Library, Archival, and Information Studies at the University of British Columbia, worked as a library manager in academic, special, and public libraries for twenty years before joining the UBC faculty. She is active in professional library associations at both the provincial and the national level and teaches in the areas of collection management, public libraries, and information access.

Victoria Esses is associate professor of psychology at the University of Western Ontario. She has published a number of scholarly articles and book chapters on intergroup relations, focusing on ethnic relations, attitudes towards immigrants and immigration, and the causes and consequences of prejudice and discrimination. She is currently on the editorial board of the *Canadian Journal of Behavioural Science*, the *Journal of Personality and Social Psychology*, and the *Personality and Social Psychology Bulletin*.

Allan C. Hutchinson is a professor at Osgoode Hall Law School, York University, Toronto. He has published widely in academic and popular forums. His most recent books include *Waiting for Coraf: A Critique of Law and Rights* (1995) and *It's All in the Game: A Non-Foundational Account of Law, Politics and Adjudication* (1999).

Samuel V. LaSelva is associate professor in the Department of Political Science at the University of British Columbia. His research interests focus on political theory and the Canadian constitution. His publications include *The Moral Foundations of Canadian Federalism* (1996), which was awarded the Smiley Prize by the Canadian Political Science Association.

William Leiss is a fellow and president-elect (1998–9) of the Royal Society of Canada. He is currently professor of policy studies and holds the Eco-Research Chair in Environmental Policy at Queen's University, Kingston, Ontario. Starting in 1999, he will be professor in the Faculty of Management, University of Calgary, where he will hold the NSERC/SSHRC Industry Research Chair in Risk Communication and Public Policy. He has held previous academic appointments in political science, sociology, environmental studies, and communication and is author, collaborator, or editor of ten books and numerous articles.

Rowland Lorimer is professor of communication and director of the Canadian Centre for Studies in Publishing at Simon Fraser University. He is editor of the *Canadian Journal of Communication* and the author of several books including *Mass Communication in Canada* (with Jean McNulty, 3rd edition 1996), *Mass Communication: A Comparative Introduction*, (with Paddy Scannell, 1994), and *The Nation in the Schools* (1984). He has served on a Canada Council advisory committee, on the National Library Advisory Board, and as president of the Association for Canadian Studies. Currently he is the president of the Canadian Association of Learned Journals.

Allan McDougall, associate professor of political science at the University of Western Ontario, specializes in public-policy processes, Canadian politics, and language and politics. He is the biographer of Ontario premier John P. Robarts and has published in the areas of Ontario politics and policing.

Michael Manley-Casimir, dean of education at Brock University, specializes in various aspects of the socio-legal context of educational policy and practice. He is a founding director of the Center for Education, Law and Society at Simon Fraser University and his most recent publication is an exploration of the normative character of teaching as an occupation, *Teachers in Trouble* (with Stuart Piddocke and Romulo Magsino, 1997).

Randal Marlin teaches in the Department of Philosophy at Carleton University, Ottawa. His main published writings are in the areas of morality and the criminal law, propaganda, free-speech policy, and the ethics of communication. In 1993 he edited the issue 'Propaganda and the Ethics of Rhetoric' for the *Canadian Journal of Rhetorical Studies*. He is a frequent contributor of articles to newspapers and is currently vice-president of the Civil Liberties Association, National Capital Region.

Lydia Miljan, an H.B. Earhart Fellow, is doing her doctoral work on politics and the media at the University of Calgary. She is also the director of the National Media Archive, a division of the Fraser Institute, where she has designed and initiated over eighty content analyses of media during the past ten years.

James Olson, professor of psychology at the University of Western Ontario, is a social psychologist interested in attitudes and persuasion. He is currently an associate editor of the *Journal of Personality and Social Psychology* and has published more than seventy articles, chapters, and books.

Klaus Petersen, professor of German at the University of British Columbia, teaches German literature and cultural history. He has written in the areas of Expressionism, the Weimar Republic, and censorship in Germany.

Bruce Ryder, associate professor at Osgoode Hall Law School, York University, has published extensively on issues such as racism and the constitution, obscenity, freedom-of-expression guarantees, equality rights, and sexual orientation. In October 1994 he was a witness before the British Columbia Supreme Court in the Little Sisters Book and Art Emporium's constitutional challenge to the censorship powers of Canada Customs.

Shaheen Shariff recently completed her MA (Ed.) degree at the Center of Education, Law and Society at Simon Fraser University. Her program of study involves the intersection of law and education, with particular focus on constitutional issues and the impact of the Charter of Rights and Freedoms on educational administration and policy. She has worked at various prestigious law firms including Bull, Houser & Tupper and Campney & Murphy. As well, she has served in an advisory capacity on committees of her local school board in Coquitlam, British Columbia, regarding educational programs for children with special needs.

Donald F. Theall was Molson Professor at McGill University before becoming president and vice-chancellor of Trent University (1980-7), where he is now university professor emeritus. His books include *The Medium Is the Rear View Mirror: Understanding McLuhan* (1971); *Studies in Canadian Communications*, with G.J. Robinson (1975); *Beyond the Word: Reconstructing Sense in the Joyce Era of Technology, Culture, and Communication* (1995); and *James Joyce's Techno-Poetics* (1997).

Lisa Philips Valentine, associate professor of anthropology at the University of Western Ontario, teaches in the area of language and culture, discourse analysis, and language and politics. She has published widely on First Nations communicative practices in both English and aboriginal languages.

Mariana Valverde works at the Centre of Criminology, University of Toronto. Her main research interest is moral regulation. Her publications include *Sex, Power, and Pleasure* (1985), *The Age of Light, Soap and Water: Moral Reform in English Canada 1880s-1920s* (1991), and *Diseases of the Will: Alcohol and the Dilemmas of Freedom* (1998).

Scott Watson is associate professor of fine arts and director of the Morris and Helen Belkin Art Gallery at the University of British Columbia. He has published widely on the subject of contemporary art and received the Hubert Evans Prize for Non-fiction for his book *Jack Shadbolt* (1990).

Lorraine Weir is professor of English at the University of British Columbia. Her research interests include deconstruction and semiotics, feminist and queer theory, and twentieth-century literature ranging from James Joyce to Nicole Brossard. She served as a witness in the Little Sister's case before the British Columbia Supreme Court in October 1994. Her publications include *Writing Joyce – A Semiotics of the Joyce System* (1989), *Jay Macpherson* (1989), and numerous articles on Canadian women's writing.

Reg Whitaker is professor of political science at York University in Toronto. He has published extensively on Canadian politics, his books including *A Sovereign Idea: Essays on Canada as a Democratic Community* (1992), *Cold War Canada: The Making of a National Insecurity State* (with Gary Marcuse, 1994), and most recently *The End of Privacy: How Total Surveillance Is Becoming a Reality* (1999).

Index

tabloids, 140, 141

talk: ownership of, 337

Tariff Board, 133, 134

Task Force on Canadian Unity, 381

Taylor, Charles, 8, 325, 383

Telecommunications Act of 1996 (U.S.), 250

television: as a medium of entertainment, 320, 321, 329; as 'secondary orality,' 321, 323, 329; tele-evangelical programs, 320; technology of selection, 320; transformative effects, 320, 321, 323; as a universal mediator of the world, 320

television advertising directed at children, 104

television news: and accuracy, 326; agendas, 318; the anchor's role, 321, 322; charges of bias, 319; and commercial advertising, 323, 324; and consensus, 326; and credibility, 321, 322; and electoral decisions, 327, 328; 'episodic framing,' 328; inadvertent censorship, 330; inadvertent decisions over content, 319; and interest groups, 319; omiting information, 319; operating rules, 324; as post-industrial commodity, 318; as profit centres, 324; producer, 318; production of, 318; selection process, 318–33; as theatre, 321; truth and belief, 322; visualization of deviance, 325, 326

Thatcher, Margaret, 306

Theatres Act, 404, 405, 406, 409, 411

Theory of Justice, by John Rawls, 43

Tin Flute, The, by Gabrielle Roy, 208

Tobacco Act (1997), 101, 102, 107, 108, 112, 115, 122, 305

tobacco advertising and self-censorship in the press, 304, 305

tobacco influence on publishing, 305

'Tobacco, Nicotine and Addiction' (report of the Royal Society of Canada), 114

tobacco product advertising, 101–28; the federal government's policy on restricting it, 121, 123; social interest in controlling it, 109, 115, 121, 122

Tobacco Products Control Act [TPCA], 101, 104–9, 112, 113, 121

tolerance, 71; benefits of, 49; and censorship, 49; limits of liberal tolerance, 48, 49, 52; the paradox of, 49;

Tom of Finland Foundation, 230

Toronto Arts Group for Human Rights, x

Toronto Life, 302

Toronto Right to Life Association, 309

Toronto Star, 300

Toronto Sun, 307

Toronto Transit Commission, 309

Towne Cinema Theatres Ltd. v. *The Queen* (1985), 62, 63, 65, 66, 67, 68, 69, 70, 74, 252, 253

Tropic of Cancer, by Henry Miller, 147

Tropic of Capricorn, by Henry Miller, 147

Trudeau, Pierre, 46, 296

Trudeau government, 338

truth production, 204, 205, 207, 213

TV violence, 264

Ulysses, by James Joyce, 132

United States Bill of Rights, 42

United States Supreme Court, 41

universities, 32; academic autonomy, 351; academic entrepreneuralism, 360; administrative authority, 352, 362; administrative coercion, 351; assessment of scholarship, 354, 358, 359; contract research, 360, 361; economic pressures, 360; established values and